POLITICS

POLITICS *an introduction*

Second Edition

George A. MacLean
Duncan R. Wood

OXFORD
UNIVERSITY PRESS

OXFORD
UNIVERSITY PRESS

Oxford University Press is a department of the University of Oxford.
It furthers the University's objective of excellence in research, scholarship,
and education by publishing worldwide. Oxford is a registered trade mark of
Oxford University Press in the UK and in certain other countries.

Published in Canada by
Oxford University Press
8 Sampson Mews, Suite 204,
Don Mills, Ontario M3C 0H5 Canada

www.oupcanada.com

Library and Archives Canada Cataloguing in Publication
MacLean, George A. (George Andrew), 1967–
Politics : an introduction / George MacLean, Duncan Wood.
— 2nd ed.

Includes bibliographical references and index.
ISBN 978-0-19-544894-8

1. Political science—Textbooks.   I. Wood, Duncan R. (Duncan
Robert), 1968–   II. Title.

JA66.M25 2013   320   C2013-901106-4

Cover images: Iraqi woman voter: photo by Majid Saeed/Getty Images; flags:
iStockphoto/Thinkstock; protest in Egypt: iStockPhoto.com/MOHPhoto;
inside Parliament of Canada building: Songquan Deng/Shutterstock;

Printed and bound in Canada

3 4 5 — 18 17 16

Brief Contents

Contents

1 STUDYING POLITICS 2

2 FINDING A COMMON VOCABULARY: POLITICAL CONCEPTS 26

3 POLITICAL THOUGHT, PHILOSOPHY, AND IDEOLOGY 52

4 THE ROLE OF GOVERNMENT 90

5 BRANCHES OF GOVERNMENT 122

6　POLITICAL SYSTEMS　150

7 POLITICAL PARTICIPATION: ELECTIONS AND PARTIES 178

8 POLITICAL SOCIALIZATION AND CULTURE 200

9   POLITICS IN DEVELOPED STATES   226

10   POLITICS IN DEVELOPING STATES   264

11 INTERNATIONAL POLITICS AND FOREIGN POLICY 304

12 INTERNATIONAL SECURITY 338

13   INTERNATIONAL POLITICAL ECONOMY   364

14 CONCLUSION   394

Preface

One of the most difficult tasks involved in introducing students to the study of politics is choosing an appropriate textbook. Every instructor has his or her own preferences about the material, concepts, themes, and pedagogy contained in a first-year political studies text; therefore, no book could possibly meet every requirement and partiality. Putting together an introductory text, then, is a delicate endeavour. How might one assemble a coherent preparatory volume that both addresses disparate views on what is to be presented and poses some fresh and innovative ideas?

This book is an attempt to answer that very question. Fundamentally, its intent is to provide first-year post-secondary students with a comprehensive introduction to the study of politics. This text incorporates some essential questions regarding politics: Who has power in society, and why? How might groups participate in political activity? How can we distinguish among so many types of political systems? Why is conflict so prevalent in the world today? How is wealth distributed, and why does such inequity exist? In our design of this book, we considered a wide variety of theoretical and analytical ways to answer these questions. We decided that the best method was to lead you through different approaches and topics. The "answers," of course, will vary depending on your perspective and experience. This text presents you with a challenge: you may or may not already have views on the nature of politics, but by the time you finish this book and course, you will likely have more questions than before. You might also think differently about what you assume you already know! If that's the case, this book will have done its job.

Organization

This book is organized to introduce you to the study of politics in a comprehensive and constructive manner. Chapter 1 presents the fundamental nature of politics and the field of political studies. We explore some major approaches, concepts, and themes in the study of politics in this chapter, as well as how politics affects so many aspects of our daily lives. We also discuss the nature of citizenship and what it means in the specific context of being Canadian. The substance of this chapter lays the foundations for the rest of the text.

Chapters 2 and 3 examine some of the major terms and areas of political thought in greater detail. Chapter 2 begins with an exploration of some important political concepts, including power, government, the state, legitimacy, equality and justice, and sovereignty. It also addresses identity and how we connect with others in society. Chapter 3 follows with an overview of political philosophy and the major schools of thought used in political studies, such as liberalism, socialism and communism, conservatism, environmentalism, feminism, nationalism, and fascism. It looks at both dominant and critical political ideologies and the ideas that have driven the study of politics. This chapter also refers to ideologies and political philosophy in Canada and provides an overview of other approaches, such as Confucianism and political Islam.

Chapters 4, 5, and 6 look at the importance of government. In Chapter 4, we examine the main forms of government throughout history and into the present day. The chapter deals with systems of government, the nature of government, objectives and activities of different governments, and points of view regarding the fundamental role that government ought to play. In this chapter, we explain the distinctions among liberal democracies, authoritarian governments, and totalitarian systems. Government in Canada is given special attention here. Chapter 5 covers primary structures and roles of government agencies and institutions. It delves into the important levels of government activity, including the executive, legislative, judicial, and bureaucratic divisions. The two main types of government systems in the world today, parliamentary and presidential, are also compared and contrasted. Finally, Chapter 6 considers how different political systems are organized in terms of their responsibilities and decision-making systems. Unitary, federal, confederal, and devolved political systems are all examined, with special attention to the history and development of power-sharing in Canada.

Chapters 7 and 8 are concerned with the roles played by individuals and groups in society. Chapter 7 considers decision-making and electoral systems, campaign contributions, elections and referenda, and political parties. Chapter 8 picks up the theme and looks at the social and political process of participation. Education, opinion polls, socialization, interest groups, media, and culture all have abundant effects on how our political systems are run and the role we play in them. Together, these two chapters trace the formulation of ideas and information that influence citizens and the way in which these ideas are played out on the political stage.

The next section of the book is dedicated to country case studies. This two-part examination of politics is undertaken in a comparative context, considering development and underdevelopment in today's world. We begin in Chapter 9 with a consideration of politics in many developed countries, including Canada, the United States, Japan, and members of the European Union. These cases offer distinctive examples of how political and economic spheres influence governance. Chapter 10 carries this discussion to the developing world, contemplating some of the significant approaches and perspectives regarding development in the so-called Third World and, in particular, how the development process is as varied as the countries involved. By way of example, the chapter surveys the development experiences in Mexico, China, India, and Mali, presenting a diverse stance on the myriad of issues facing countries in the developing world.

The final chapters take on the study of politics on the world stage, using some of the primary concepts and themes discussed earlier in the book. Chapter 11 examines the state and sovereignty in a modern world, as well as the nature of and approaches to the international system. This chapter scrutinizes some current themes and issues in global politics, including globalization, foreign policy-making, geography and population, diplomacy, nationalism, and different actors (e.g. states, non-state actors, individuals, and multinational corporations). Chapter 12 is dedicated to the complicated issue of global insecurity: war, terrorism, peacekeeping, intervention, and conflict management. Here we also look at Canada's changing military role. Chapter 13 turns its attention to the important dynamic of the international political economy and its impact on domestic politics. This chapter illustrates the importance of international trade, production, and finance, as well as current themes such as world debt, leadership, and economic regionalism.

Finally, Chapter 14 provides some concluding thoughts by focusing on the important question, Where do we go from here? Future studies, careers in political studies, and the ways we can apply what we've learned are all given some thought in this chapter.

Key Features

PEDAGOGICAL FEATURES

Political studies, like any other academic discipline, has its own vocabulary and terminology. Marginal definitions, provided in each chapter, emphasize key terms and concepts, and a full glossary is included at the end of the book. Every chapter contains self-assessment questions, a list of further readings, and suggested websites. Throughout the chapters, boxes provide specific examples of important themes, events, and actors. Images, tables, graphs, and figures illustrate important points without interfering with the text itself. Finally, an index of all important terms, concepts, themes, events, and individuals is included at the end of the book.

THEORETICAL FRAMEWORK

Most introductory textbooks begin with a survey of significant concepts (e.g. the state, power, government, legitimacy, etc.) and a review of the philosophical tradition of political analysis (Plato's *Republic*, Aristotle's *Politics*, Hobbes's *Leviathan*, and so on). Taking a comparative theoretical approach (meaning that no specific theory is used as a core focus), this text shows how the development of theory in political studies flavours the manner in which we must consider a contemporary and changing political climate, both domestic and international. The methodology of this text is not intended to be heavy-handed or overly theoretical; theory is central to the purpose of the book, but its principal goal is to demonstrate the sensitive and changing nature of philosophical thought in politics.

Acknowledgements

Like any book project, this text is the product of various contributions from many people. In the very early stages, Oxford University Press sales and editorial representative Alan Mulder and acquisitions editor Katherine Skene were largely responsible for urging us to move ahead with a prospectus for a new introductory textbook in political studies. We are grateful to them for their vision and support.

A number of developmental editors were involved with the production of this book, but Peter Chambers deserves special recognition for his unflagging support. His good humour, professionalism, and encouragement made our work on this second edition a true pleasure. Janna Green is one of the best content editors we have worked with, and we are grateful for her excellent comments and suggestions.

This book has also benefitted from the many useful comments made by several colleagues who took on the task of reviewing it in its many stages. We are indebted to them for their time and suggestions, which have contributed to this final work. We join the publisher in thanking the following reviewers, along with those who wish to remain anonymous, whose thoughtful remarks have helped to shape this text as well: Todd Alway, McMaster University; Mona Brash, Camosun College; Terry L. Chapman, Medicine Hat College; Noemi Gal-Or, Kwantlen Polytechnic University; Logan Masilamani, Simon Fraser University; Marda Schindeler, Lethbridge College; Bruce Smardon, York University; John Soroski, Grant MacEwan University; and Yasmine Shamsie, Wilfrid Laurier University.

We would be remiss in not thanking our students, who have inspired us to always question what we think we know and to be open to new perspectives. The improvements in this second edition are in many ways due to them and their aspirations for excellence.

Some of our associates and research assistants were fundamental in the completion of parts of this book. We would like to thank Rashide Assad at the Instituto Tecnológico Autónomo de México (ITAM) for her extremely important help on this project. We also thank the University of Manitoba, ITAM, and the Asociacion Mexicana de Cultura for their support during the writing of both editions of this book.

We have discovered that writing a book such as this one takes more than simple authoring. It is the result of efforts both small and large by numerous people, some close friends and associates, and some colleagues we have not met. The final product is our own, however, and we alone take responsibility for any errors that it may contain.

George MacLean and Duncan Wood
May 2013

Features

Thorough Analysis

The text presents a survey of political concepts and ideologies before examining topics such as the importance of government; political systems, participation, and culture; developed and developing countries; global security; and the international political economy. This new edition also includes expanded coverage of power, the environment, the EU, and Mexico.

Personal influence, leadership, economic, military, and public protest are just a few of the various forms of power.

Dalai Lama, Bono, Harper, Obama: GP8 NSEA/iStockphoto; currency, soldiers: Thinkstock; protest: Ryan Rodrick Beiler/iStockphoto

to cynicism. Rather, we view political studies as optimistic, a field that tries to build on success and correct failures, with the ultimate goal of creating a better political world that represents the many interests within it.

In this opening chapter, we will try to answer what may be the most important question you have going into the course: Why study politics? It is a basic question but one that affects everything we will touch on in the textbook. As well, this chapter will briefly introduce the chapters that follow; however, nothing here or anywhere in this book is the final word. (Politics is nothing if it's not about constant debate!) Each point outlined in the chapter's learning objectives will also be examined in greater detail in other parts of the book, but this first chapter will serve as a general overview.

Power and Politics

To begin, we will look at one of the most important political ideas: power. How do you define power? As leadership? Certainly, the two terms seem to relate naturally to one another. Think about Canada's Prime Minister Stephen Harper or US President Barack Obama. Is there a more powerful individual in either country? Power can come from wealth too—whether it's in our local communities or in the global system, economic wealth buys (literally and figuratively)

power
ability to achieve goals in a political system and to have others do as you wish them to

---

© Timothy Marcus / Minneapolis / Alamy

The London Underground and transit buses were targeted in a coordinated attack on 7 July 2005.

geopolitics
association between a state's political relationships and its geographical location

Security and Insecurity

Security exists when there is a relatively low probabi[lity] of threat or damage to citizens, government, territ[ory,] resources, wealth, and even values such as cultur[e and] identity.[3] As discussed previously, conflict comes ab[out] when there are disputes concerning these areas, parti[cu]larly when groups of people are involved. And war [may] take place when these groups resort to the use of arm[ed] hostilities. Security can never be completely assured [for] any state in the world, even the most powerful (co[n]sider, for example, the insecurity felt in the Uni[ted] States after 9/11, in London after the bombings o[f 7] July 2005, or in Boston after the April 15, 2013 bom[b]ings). Individuals and even states can feel insecure [due] to real threats and violence or an imagined threat [from] in the international system. Whether a nation is un[der] direct attack from another or merely feels that its val[ues] and culture are threatened by the influence of anoth[er,] insecurity may indeed be present.

A state's security was once almost completely ba[sed] on its location and its proximity to potential allies [and] enemies. States in Western Europe, for instance, we[re] constantly balancing the power of other alliances in an effort to keep one side from becoming strong enough to threaten another with force. This relationship between political interactions and a state's geographical location is known as geopolitics. Access to resources, beneficial or detrimental relations with neighbours, physical strength, population, and natural attributes all fall into the considerations of geopolitics. Although security is thought of differently today, geopolitics is still relevant. Think of the geographical position that Canada occupies in the world. It is close to the United States, a superpower and Canada's closest ally, is separated physically from some of the most dangerous regions in the world by oceans and the Arctic, and benefits from one of the best standards of living thanks to its peaceful system of politics, large resource base, and educated citizens. If Canada were in the Asian subcontinent or the Middle East, its relative security would undoubtedly be challenged by unstable regional politics, concerns over access to resources, and uncertainty about potential threats from neighbours. It would certainly be a very different environment for Canadians.

Geopolitics is also important because it allows states to achieve certain goals without necessarily having to possess the features required for those objectives. Some states, such as Japan, are unable to produce or obtain what is required for their very existence. However, in the modern world, such states only have to have access to them. This access is possible through trade and alliances with other states.

8.2 QUEBEC'S STUDENT PROTESTS

As you are probably all too aware, the cost of university tuition has been rising across Canada in recent years, resulting in complaints from students and parents alike that higher education may be moving beyond their means. Tuition rates are not the same across the country; therefore, increases have affected some provinces more than others. Quebec presents an intriguing case. Historically, the province has had the lowest tuition in Canada. Tuition fees were frozen at $540 per student per year between 1968 and 1990, a direct result of social protests in the late sixties. In 1994, Quebec fees rose to $1668 but were again frozen until 2007. By comparison, tuition in Nova Scotia was $1941 in 1990 and rose to $6571 by 2007, becoming the third highest in the country (after Ontario and New Brunswick).

In November 2011, the Quebec government responded to rising costs and budget shortfalls by announcing that tuition fees would increase by $254 annually for seven years. After years of resisting large tuition fee increases, Quebec's student movement organized a walkout in February 2012. Over the next few months the "strike" gathered strength and numbers, with sit-ins and violent protests taking place on university campuses and on the streets of Quebec cities and preventing a large number of students from attending classes. The protests split public opinion between those who advocated open access to higher education and those who felt that, because the fees were still lower than those in other provinces, Quebec students had little to complain about.

In May 2012, the National Assembly of Quebec passed emergency legislation, commonly known as Bill 78, that suspended the academic year and placed severe restrictions on student protests. A particularly controversial provision of the law states that police have to be given eight hours' notice before large demonstrations may proceed. Commonly seen as restricting political rights, Bill 78 helped to galvanize public support for the student movement.

Demonstrators march through Ottawa in support of the Quebec student protests.

This issue presents us with a classic dilemma for governments. University education is expensive and, even with the higher fees, Quebec's students would pay only a fraction of what their classes cost the Quebec and Canadian taxpayer (Quebec is a net recipient of transfer payments). At the same time, having a well-educated population is important in the maintenance of a growing and competitive economy. What's more, universities provide a nurturing environment for young people before they enter the workforce (which they would otherwise enter at a much younger age) and serve as the centres of much innovation and research. How much should the taxpayer be willing to subsidize this education in order to receive the social and economic benefits of university education? What should governments do to streamline their finances, improve fiscal responsibility, and make education more efficient? On a different level, how tolerant should we be of social protest, even if it severely disrupts social or educational services and infringes on the rights of others?

The importance of socioeconomic status must also be taken into account. A person's belief system and values will be fundamentally influenced by the economic and social opportunities available to him or her. To give a simplistic example, someone in a high tax bracket is less likely to be in favour of a progressive taxation system that requires the rich to pay more income tax than people who make less money.

4.7 DEMOCRACY TOPPLES AUTHORITARIANISM?

The Republic of the Union of Myanmar, commonly referred to as Myanmar or Burma, is a heavily populated and geographically large country in Southeast Asia that has been part of several political empires in its history, including the Mongol empire. After being colonized by Britain in the 1860s, Burma finally achieved independence in 1948, only to see its fledgling democracy threatened by civil conflict. Eventually, a military junta took over in 1962 and ruled the country until 2010. Burma suffered drastically during this period, as many countries in the world (including Canada) imposed economic sanctions against a government they felt was illegitimate. The 1980s witnessed a popular movement for democracy in Burma, leading to calls for elections. In 1990, a vote led to the election of Aung San Suu Kyi, whose parents were instrumental in the early days of political independence, and her National League for Democracy (NLD) party, which received over 80 per cent of the popular vote.

Suu Kyi espoused the values of Mahatma Gandhi, who urged non-violent means for political change. The military government refused to step down, however, and placed her under house arrest. During her captivity, she received several awards for her peaceful demands, including the Nobel Peace Prize in 1991. (She is also an honorary citizen of Canada, one of only five people to receive the title.) International pressure for democracy and Suu Kyi's release continued, and despite the junta's crackdowns, domestic protests made it

Political leader Aung San Suu Kyi addresses a crowd of supporters in Yangon, Myanmar (Burma) in 2010.

impossible for the government to maintain power without the risk of a complete civil war. In 2010 Suu Kyi was released and democratic elections were permitted; the military junta dissolved formally the next year. However, the military-backed Union Solidarity and Development Party won the election, under disputed results. Suu Kyi is now an opposition leader in a new political order that shows both the promise of democratic reform and the legacy of an authoritarian past.

Although authoritarian states are prone to control as much of the state and society as possible, there are often areas of private life that remain free. Citizens may, for example, hold views that differ from an authoritarian government or even support challengers to the rulers. However, this is done at much greater risk than in liberal democracies, where opposition is fostered and considered a healthy part of a diverse political system. There is no guarantee that these limited rights may be upheld, and authoritarian states differ widely on the degree to which debate and resistance may be permitted.

totalitarianism authoritarian political system that not only controls most social interaction but is also marked by a government's desire to force its objectives and values on citizens in an unlimited manner

Totalitarianism

Often used as an equivalent of authoritarianism, totalitarianism is in fact a variant of authoritarian rule. But what distinguishes the two is the emphasis

National and International Coverage

While emphasizing Canadian politics, the text maintains an international perspective. Boxes and case studies provide detailed examples of significant events, major issues, and influential figures—both past and present—from Canada and around the world.

Currency

The text's focus on the latest political developments illustrates the dynamic nature of the political landscape. Topics new to this edition include Scottish independence, the recent financial crisis, and the Arab Spring.

International Politics, International Relations, Foreign Policy, and the State

Just as politics affects our everyday lives, sometimes in ways that we do not necessarily notice, international politics influences many of our daily activities. Topics trending on Twitter, blogs, news feeds, and newscasts let us see, often in immediate and vivid detail, the surprising closeness of our global community. Election and war coverage, sporting events, entertainment, and even local weather broadcasts are available to us on demand. Streaming information over the Internet—from around the block or from the other side of the world—is made instantaneously available to us.

11.2 THE TWITTER EFFECT: ELECTIONS IN IRAN

Iran has a very young demographic, with over half of its population between the ages of 14 and 30. Its political leaders, however, tend to be much older. A major study by the RAND Corporation in 2008 accurately concluded that ... would lead to political, ethnic, religious, and ...herabilities and inevitable "popular dissatisfac... current system."[1] The 2009 election was seen ... Iranians as an opportunity to change the ...gence of President Mahmoud Ahmadinejad's ...Ahmadinejad is a polarizing figure whose rhet... the destruction of Israel and the "deviant" ...hristianity and Judaism, along with charges of ...al behaviour, contribute to the global condem...ian domestic and foreign policy. The country's ...citly develop nuclear weapons added to inter...ism, not to mention anxiety over its objectives. ...voting in this election was regarded as being ...ed, with charges of manipulation and voter ...ranians, who are used to election fraud, were ...the level of deception. Despite a huge voter ...s were announced just two hours after the polls ...al impossibility. Ahmadinejad was declared the ...izens took to the streets in protest. ...news coverage of these demonstrations was ...o a government crackdown, individuals began ...events via social network updates, blogs, and ...weets. Many major news outlets also used this

Thousands of Iranians gather in Tehran in 2009 to protest the election results.

information as a major source for their stories. As a result of this reliance on social media, the protests were termed the Twitter Revolution. Similar protests during the Arab Spring were also detailed in tweets. While the "revolution" may not have brought about a change in government in Iran, it certainly made clear the growing role for social media in news-gathering and reporting.

Note

1. Keith Crane, Rollie Lal, and Jeffrey Martini, *Iran's Political, Demographic, and Economic Vulnerabilities* (Santa Monica, CA: RAND Corporation, 2008), xvii.

In the two decades following the 1992 elections, Mali was hailed internationally as a model for African democracies, with peaceful transitions between parties. Economically, however, not much changed. The Malian people still experienced extreme levels of poverty, high fertility and infant mortality rates, and a fragile relationship with representative government and peace.

THE PEOPLE OF MALI

Mali is a good example of a multi-ethnic state, being comprised of diverse linguistic and cultural groups. The Bambara is by far the largest group in the country and the Bambara language is spoken by approximately half of the population, but eight other major ethnic groups (Soninké, Khassonké, Malinké,

10.11 CANADA AND MALI

For over 50 years, Canada has been actively engaged in aid activities in Mali, financing poverty reduction projects, health programs, and public policy support through the Canadian International Development Agency (CIDA, which is now part of the newly restructured Department of Foreign Affairs, Trade and Development). In 2009, CIDA had identified 20 "countries of focus"—including Mali—to which 80 per cent of the agency's resources would be devoted. Although the Canadian government suspended its aid payments to Mali after the coup d'etat in 2012, it continued to deliver development assistance through NGOs and multilateral channels.

When the international intervention in Mali (known as Operation Serval) began in January 2013, the French government requested that Canada provide heavy lift capacity for transporting troops, equipment, and military transports. In response, the Canadian government committed a transport plane (a Royal Canadian Air Force CC-177 Globemaster III, sometimes called the C-17) and 40 Royal Canadian Air Force personnel. In the first month of the operation, the Canadian plane conducted 27 flights, moving more than 765,000 kilograms of personnel and equipment around the African country.

The Harper government had earlier announced that it would not undertake any direct military mission in Mali. Furthermore, it has not committed to playing a direct role in any future peacekeeping mission, which the Canadian press saw as further evidence of the decline in Canada's

An official guides a C-17 Globemaster III into position. Canada contributed one of its large C-17 military cargo planes to deliver supplies to Bamako after a request from France.

capacity and willingness to engage in international military operations. Despite Canada's proud history of participating in peacekeeping missions, by January of 2013 the country ranked 56th out of 114 countries in terms of contributions to peacekeeping operations.[1]

Note

1. Lee Berthiaume, "Canada Can Help Bring Stability to Mali, UN Official Says," 18 March 2013, http://o.canada.com/2013/03/18/canada-can-help-bring-peace-and-stability-to-mali-un-official-says/.

Extensive Pedagogy

Chapter learning objectives, key terms, self-assessment questions, weblinks, and further readings enhance student understanding and promote active learning.

Full Ancillary Package

Supplemental material includes the following components:

- an instructor's manual
- PowerPoint slides
- a student study guide
- a text bank/test generator
- podcasts
- news clips

Chapter 1 | Studying Politics 25

Self-Assessment Questions

1. How might we distinguish among the different types of power in politics?
2. Why did Hobbes think that life would be "solitary, poor, nasty, brutish, and short" without government?
3. How does political studies fit with the other social sciences?
4. Why and how is politics such a central component of society? Can we become truly apolitical? Why or why not?
5. How are the forces of division and connection entwined in a globalized world?
6. How does immigration contribute to the multinational character of Canadian society?

Weblinks

Canadian Citizenship Test
www.cic.gc.ca/english/citizenship/cit-test.asp

Canadian Political Science Association
www.cpsa-acsp.ca

Careers for Political Scientists
www.cpsa-acsp.ca/guides.shtml

Freedom House
www.freedomhouse.org

Further Reading

Almond, Gabriel A. *A Discipline Divided: Schools and Sects in Political Science.* Newbury Park, CA: Sage, 1990.
——, G. Bingham Powell, Jr, Russell J. Dalton, and Kaare Strøm. *Comparative Politics Today: A World View.* 9th edn. Toronto: Longman, 2008.
Aristotle. *Politics.* Translated by T.A. Sinclair. Harmondsworth, UK: Penguin, 1986.
Asimov, Isaac. *Asimov on Science Fiction.* New York: Doubleday, 1981.
Easton, David. *The Political System.* 2nd edn. Chicago: University of Chicago Press, 1981.
Hobbes, Thomas. *Leviathan, Or, the Matter, Forme and Power of a Commonwealth Ecclesiasticall and Civil.* Edited by Michael Oakeshott. New York: Collier Books, 1962.
Laozi. *Tao Te Ching.* Harmondsworth, UK: Penguin, 1963/1976.
Lasswell, Harold. *Politics: Who Gets What, When, How.* New York: Meridian Books, 1958.
Przeworski, Adam, and Henry Teune. *The Logic of Comparative Social Inquiry.* New York: Wiley, 1970.
Seymour, Michel, ed. *The Fate of the Nation-State.* Montreal and Kingston: McGill-Queen's University Press, 2004.

News Clips

Visit the companion website for *Politics: An Introduction*, 2nd edn, to access news clips related to the content of this chapter.

COMPANION WEBSITE

George A. MacLean and Duncan R. Wood

Politics: An Introduction 2e
ISBN 13: 9780195448948

About the Book

Guiding students through the basics of political ideologies and institutions before moving on to more complex concepts, this text is a comprehensive yet accessible introduction to political studies. Emphasizing Canadian content while maintaining a global perspective throughout, the text ties theory to practice using case studies and current examples from Canada and around the world.

Inspection copy request

Ordering information

Contact & Comments

Sample Material

Get Adobe PDF reader [US | UK]

Instructor Resources

You need a password to access these resources. Please contact your local Sales and Editorial Representative for more information.

Student Resources

List of Boxes

1

Studying Politics

◀ A young man uses a laptop in Cairo's Tahrir Square on 25 January 2013, exactly two years after the overthrow of former president Hosni Mubarak. Social media played a pivotal role in the revolution, making possible a completely new politics and mode of political organization.

Photo: Ed Giles/Getty Images

After reading this chapter, you will be able to

- distinguish the various approaches used in political studies;
- understand how politics affects our daily lives;
- consider the coexisting pressures of division and connection in a changing world;
- examine politics at the international and the domestic levels; and
- consider what it means to be a citizen in Canada.

Introduction

Welcome to this textbook and to the study of politics. We hope that this book not only broadens your understanding of the field but also stirs some interest in the political world that surrounds you. Although this may be your first formal introduction to political studies, you probably think about its subject matter more than you realize. Indeed, politics is one of those areas in life that we cannot avoid. Even if we try our best to steer clear of it, we are affected by it in some way. The good news is that the more we get involved and become aware of the complexities of politics, the more we see how important our role is in our political world. Being involved means being better informed.

People are often cynical about politics. Perhaps they are convinced that their elected officials will never live up to their promises or that their own role in the political process is so insignificant that their contribution will never be felt. In reality, our input is much greater than we think and our involvement is crucial to the process. After all, if we cut ourselves off from the process entirely, how would we ever hold those elected officials to their promises? Healthy skepticism is a good thing—it keeps us informed and focused on improving our system. But cynicism without reflection really won't get us anywhere. It's better to be involved, and even critical, than to simply dismiss the entire process.

This book takes a critical look at politics. It questions our assumptions about politics, the approaches we take to study it, and how effective it is. Such study, we believe, is part of a healthy examination. But we don't stoop

Dalai Lama, Bono, Harper, Obama: GYI NSEA/iStockphoto; currency, soldiers: Thinkstock; protest: Ryan Rodrick Beiler/iStockphto

Personal influence, leadership, economic, military, and public protest are just a few of the various forms of power.

to cynicism. Rather, we view political studies as optimistic, a field that tries to build on success and correct failures, with the ultimate goal of creating a better political world that represents the many interests within it.

In this opening chapter, we will try to answer what may be the most important question you have going into the course: Why study politics? It is a basic question but one that affects everything we will touch on in the textbook. As well, this chapter will briefly introduce the chapters that follow; however, nothing here or anywhere in this book is the final word. (Politics is nothing if it's not about constant debate!) Each point outlined in the chapter's learning objectives will also be examined in greater detail in other parts of the book, but this first chapter will serve as a general overview.

Power and Politics

To begin, we will look at one of the most important political ideas: **power**. How do you define power? As leadership? Certainly, the two terms seem to relate naturally to one another. Think about Canada's Prime Minister Stephen Harper or US President Barack Obama. Is there a more powerful individual in either country? Power can come from wealth too—whether it's in our local communities or in the global system, economic wealth buys (literally and figuratively)

power
ability to achieve goals in a political system and to have others do as you wish them to

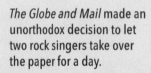

The Globe and Mail made an unorthodox decision to let two rock singers take over the paper for a day.

Brian Gable/*The Globe and Mail*/CP

influence
the ability to change behaviour in others without exerting direct power over them

power and authority. Or perhaps you think of power as the strength that comes along with weapons and armies. Human history shows the massive effect of military might in society.

There are other ways of seeing power. Consider the Dalai Lama. He controls no military, has little wealth, and "led" a country (he handed his political power over to the Central Tibetan Administration in 2011) that many feel isn't even independent; however, he has tremendous **influence** and attracts followers all over the world. Likewise, U2's Bono also has political influence. He uses his celebrity on a world crusade for human rights, fair development, and ecological balance. As a nod to this power, *The Globe and Mail* handed over editorial duties to Bono and fellow musician/activist Bob Geldof on 10 May 2010. In a well-regarded edition,[1] the duo brought attention to the plight of Africa and the future of global organization.

Regardless of their personal fame and influence, people can be powerful, especially when they form groups. Political protests, marches, and sit-ins—all examples of "people power"—can create change. Often this political organization becomes more formalized into, for example, interest groups or action bodies, showing how power can be formed and utilized in still different ways.

The forms of power discussed here don't represent an exhaustive list. But they do illustrate the point that there are many ways to think of power. The same can be said for the terms *freedom*, *justice*, and *development*. You can likely think of various interpretations of these concepts. Simply put, no single explanation is the only "correct" definition or indicative of all points of view.

As we'll see in this book and in this course, power is inexorably tied to politics. That's one good reason why we started with a discussion of power, but it also helps us understand from the very beginning that we should prepare ourselves for many challenging views of what we think we already know.

Why Study Politics?

Political studies is just one of several disciplines presented to you as you begin your post-secondary studies.[2] So why choose it? What can this course, and this text, tell you about your daily life and the world around you? What can you do with your studies once you graduate?

Since you are reading this text and taking this course, it is already clear that the field of political studies holds some interest for you. And it should: studying

political studies
formal study of politics within and among nations

1.1   CAREER PATHS FOR POLITICAL STUDIES GRADUATES

You likely won't be surprised to learn that there are no postings for political scientists on most employment websites. Then again, this is the case for most university fields. Political studies, like most other disciplines in the social sciences and humanities, does not train its students for specific careers; because there are so many different directions that graduates may take, it would be impossible to identify a particular training area.

Political studies students become good writers and develop skills at public presentation, research, and problem-solving. They also learn to be critical and analytical thinkers. Critical thinking is not just about debating or finding fault. It is a response to arguments, positions, evidence, experience, and observations with considered opinions about a proper course of action. Analytical thinkers take complex ideas and issues and break them apart to get at more deep-seated questions, such as why events take place, how situations can be improved, and how we come to know what we do.

The opportunities for students of politics are as wide as one's imagination. Some pursue graduate education at the master's and doctoral level to carry out research and teaching in political science. Others use their degrees to follow additional professional accreditation, such as the law,

"Well, you ought to at least *minor* in political science."

Some careers are a natural fit for political studies.

journalism, or commerce. Politics can be useful for many political careers, including positions in public service, public administration, or policy-making, as government liaison workers, or even as politicians.

Some people can find "politics" in anything!

politics helps us understand more of our immediate surroundings, from what we see on the Internet or on TV to our direct involvement in the political process. You might think that you aren't involved, but you'll come to see that you are already politically engaged.

Studying politics helps us understand how events and decisions that seem far removed from our lives actually affect us, our families, and our communities in ways that we have not even thought about. Consider, for instance, these questions: What do people want out of life? What do countries try to provide for their citizens? How do we as individuals—and countries in the world arena—deal with others in our systems? Your activities and circumstances invariably affect your view of the political world.

Political studies also demonstrates how we organize ourselves in a social environment. It teaches us how some individuals and groups benefit from society while others do not. Since politics is an essential part of our daily lives, it is important that we try to understand how humans organize themselves into communities and the effects that these communities have on society as a whole. After all, politics allows for our collective survival. Without a formal organizing structure, we would be left to fend for ourselves and be pitted against each other. Some of you may be skeptical of this idea and may feel that we'd be better off on our own rather than under the auspices of **government**. There is even a whole ideology—anarchism—that fits with this opinion. However, even anarchism represents some form of political order or organization, which serves our more general point: politics seeks order.

Though debate and conflict over power and authority are inevitable in human communities, so too are attempts to resolve differences. Although politics is about both **conflict** and **conflict resolution**, humans are by nature competitive creatures who rely—for better or worse—on their political communities to ensure their personal survival.

What Is Politics?

As much as politics seeks order, modern political life often results in conditions that are anything but equal or fair. Indeed, politics in contemporary life is often marked by discord and controversy. This has been the case since individuals first began organizing themselves into political units. Nevertheless, one of the fundamental goals of politics is fairness in society. However elusive this goal may be, politics has always involved controversy as well as co-operation, debate as well as accord.

government
the institutions and people responsible for carrying out the affairs and administration of a political system

conflict
differences in preferred outcomes among social groups

conflict resolution
process in domestic or international affairs that attempts to reconcile antagonism (either existing or potential) through the use of mediation and negotiation

socialization
process whereby individuals act in a social manner; creation of social and political authority and rules to regulate behaviour and thus permit operation of social units

Lindsay Foyle/CartoonStock

In the seventeenth century, the English philosopher Thomas Hobbes argued that, without society and the political authority that accompanied it, humans would suffer in what he termed a "state of nature," or a situation marked by an "everyone for themselves" frame of mind. Life would be, in Hobbes's view, "solitary, poor, nasty, brutish, and short."[3] He suggested that shaping human society—the process of **socialization**—is essential for the security of life itself. Politics, then, is a response to the natural tendency among human beings to come together and create larger organized groups. An integral part of that tendency is to seek a way to allocate the benefits and responsibilities that accompany the creation of a social unit. Politics and the sharing of benefits are also essential for the preservation of life.

One way to see how the "political" exists in society is to consider how important decisions that affect a political community are made. Individual citizens who vote in an election or attend town hall meetings are part of a broader process that leads to **decision-making** by political authorities. Indeed, lack of participation is also significant because it can be viewed as tacit agreement with the status quo.

These actions, of course, are just one part of the decision-making process, which results in policies, laws, rules, and regulations that guide and shape society. This process is critical to the survival of a political community because it provides a framework that enables all members of the society to decide what acceptable conduct is.

Harold Lasswell neatly described the fundamental question of politics with the title of his book *Politics: Who Gets What, When, How.*[4] Lasswell was one of the so-called Chicago School of political scientists, a group that approached political studies from the viewpoint of a scientific endeavour. Many have come to define political studies in terms of Lasswell's title because it alludes to the notion of power in the political sphere and, more to the point, who holds it. The book examines how the essential **public goods** that result from political life are allocated to members of society. In every civilization (historical or present), political power has been used to gain control over wealth and resources.

Understanding public goods is essential to the study of politics. Public goods are the various benefits that a government provides to all its citizens: social welfare, economic efficiency, security from external attack, public safety, political freedoms and opportunity, etc. Not surprisingly, the type of

To create the famous cover image for his book *Leviathan*, Thomas Hobbes worked with the artist Abraham Bosse. Note how the giant is made up of bodies, signifying how politics is formed of the people.

Library of Congress: www.loc.gov/exhibits/world/images/s37.jpg

decision-making
mechanism or pattern of relations involving different levels of government in which determinations and judgments regarding the governance of the political system are made (sometimes referred to as the black box)

public goods
resources that are present in a political system whose use by one individual should not affect use by others

liberal democracy
political system based on freedom and the principle that governance requires the assent of all citizens through participation in the electoral process, articulation of views, and direct or indirect representation in governing institutions

authoritarianism
political system requiring absolute obedience to a constituted authority

non-governmental organization (NGO)
non-profit group organized on a local, national, or international level

government that holds authority will in many ways dictate the relative access to these public goods. For instance, political freedom is more widespread in **liberal democracies** than in **authoritarian** regimes (other important distinctions between these two systems are discussed in Chapter 4). Politically speaking, the term *freedom* can be broadly categorized and applied to political systems around the world. Different studies of political freedom, democracy, human rights, and openness in societies have been undertaken, but one of the most comprehensive is conducted by the international **non-governmental organization (NGO)** Freedom House, which identifies states as "free," "partly free," or "not free." Some have found fault with this approach, but few such organizations have been involved in this work for so long.

It is useful to consider political life as a competition for scarce resources. Whether they are immediate and tangible goods such as money, food, or minerals or more intangible goods such as power and influence, these resources are available to a political community. However, they are limited and (in most political systems) the method of distributing them results in inevitable divisions between and within different social strata in society: rich and poor, powerful and weak. Politics also leads to competition for other non-material objectives. For instance, not everyone shares the same values or recognition; some will have more of a participatory role in their political system and see their particular values upheld over others, while some may feel marginalized.

Although resources are limited and competition for them is great, the role of political authority is to allocate them to members of society. Allocation takes place through a system of decision-making. Political actors, faced with the need to provide their citizens with public goods (or to protect those goods), consider the best avenues through which their political and economic system can generate and distribute public goods. Numerous specific goals are available to actors in a political system; decisions, therefore, are an indispensable component of political life. As members of society, we often spend our time concentrating on the outcomes of decisions at the expense of understanding the process that facilitated them. But to truly understand the full extent of the determining factors that lead to such results, we must analyze the process of decision-making.

Once decisions have been made, they are restricted or enforced by the rule of law. While relationships and choice in society may be considered natural consequences of human interaction, specialized agencies such as government are not; they are the product of human invention. Specialized agencies such as bureaucracies and armed forces are necessary to provide a means of regulating and maintaining society. In their own way, governments make decisions that govern societal relationships.

Politics is often regarded in a pejorative way. We often hear of how things reflect "politics as usual" or the "politics of the situation" to describe events that have a negative impact on individuals and groups. But while politics has its negative aspects, political studies considers much more than that. It looks at competition, conflict resolution, resources and justice allocation, the exercise of power and choice, and means of understanding. Political studies is, and has

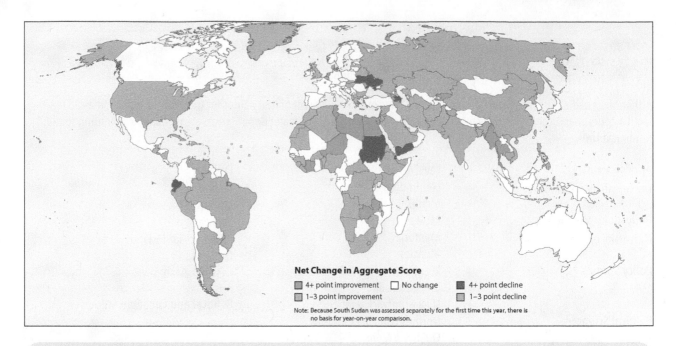

Figure 1.1 Freedom in the World 2011-12

For over 70 years, Freedom House has rated countries for their openness and freedom. This map shows changes (positive and negative) across the world.

Freedom House, *Freedom in the World 2012: The Arab Uprisings and Their Global Repercussions* (Washington, DC: Freedom House, 2012), 33. http://www.freedomhouse.org/report/freedom-world/freedom-world-2012

to be, a deliberately complex subject, given the wide array of issues to which it must attend.

Approaches Used in the Study of Politics

The study of politics is about the description and explanation of events, as well as a consideration of how things ought to be (on this last point we can see again the "progressive" nature of politics, which seeks to improve how we do things). In this way, political studies strives to contribute to a better environment for citizens and political units. Political studies is a systematic examination of events in society. As a discipline, there is no consensus on how this analysis should be accomplished, resulting in a rather fragmented but vibrant and challenging field of study with several important subfields of interest.

Political studies has a rich history, stemming from the roots of the early philosophies of Aristotle and Plato. Aristotle, in fact, thought that politics was inherently human: "That man is more of a political animal than bees or any other gregarious animals is evident."[5] He meant that, while other creatures on

1.2 NAMES OF POLITICS DEPARTMENTS IN CANADA

Although Canadian university and college departments may use different official names for the study of politics, they all teach similar courses and conduct research in the same fields. Here is a list of major departments across Canada, according to their nomenclature:

Applied Politics
Université de Sherbrooke

Philosophy and Politics
University of the Fraser Valley

Policy Studies
Mount Royal

Political Science
Acadia
Alberta
Athabasca
British Columbia
Brock
Calgary
Cape Breton
Carleton
Concordia
Dalhousie
Guelph
Huron (Western)
King's (Western)
Lakehead
Laurentian

Laval
Lethbridge
McGill
McMaster
Memorial
Moncton
Montreal
Mount Allison
New Brunswick (Fredericton)
Northern British Columbia
Québec à Montréal
Regina
St. Francis Xavier
St. Mary's
St. Thomas
Simon Fraser
Toronto
Toronto at Mississauga
Victoria
Waterloo
Western
Wilfrid Laurier
Windsor
Winnipeg
York

Political Studies
Bishop's
Manitoba
Ottawa
Prince Edward Island
Queen's
Saskatchewan

Political and Canadian Studies
Mount St. Vincent

Politics
New Brunswick (Saint John)
Trent

Politics and Economics
Royal Military College

Politics and Public Administration
École nationale d'administration
    publique
Ryerson

The University of Manitoba, part of which is pictured here, is just one university that offers a program in political studies.

Arpad Benedek/iStockphoto

earth may live in groups, only humans possess *logos*, the Greek word for both "language" and "reason." Therefore, we humans can consider both "just" and "unjust" actions and ultimately strive to make our political systems serve us better. We are, then, political animals by nature.

The first university departments of political studies (also called government, politics, or political science) appeared in the late 1800s, primarily in the United States and United Kingdom. These departments reflected a need to understand more rigorously the nature of political philosophy and governance. Political studies is one discipline in the **social sciences**; others include economics, education, sociology, law, psychology, anthropology, social geography, and linguistics. Each of these disciplines has its own areas of interest and its own theories, concepts, and frameworks. Furthermore, each of these disciplines informs us about important aspects of our lives as social beings. Political studies is concerned with the governance of social units, the allocation of power and responsibility, and the relationship among political actors in society.

Politics can be studied from the vantage point of political institutions, human sociability, or ideologies. As the relatively new discipline of political studies developed and matured during the twentieth century, several competing approaches (or frameworks of analysis) were developed and fostered by political scientists. These and other methods suggest ways to view the world, as well as the specific field of analysis that attempts to appreciate and comprehend politics in a way that is both meaningful and useful.

social sciences
scientific study of human society and social relationships

© ClassicStock / Alamy

The destruction caused by World War II–such as that shown here in Cologne, Germany–led political scientists to consider ways that politics could contribute to the cause of peace. Throughout this book, we'll consider the massive effect this war had on politics.

analytical approach
perspective that views politics as an empirical discipline rather than a science; argues that politics cannot be broken down into parts but must be seen comprehensively

empirical
analysis based not on concepts and theory but on what can be observed or experimented upon

traditional approach
method in politics drawing heavily on fields of law, philosophy, and history and relying on subjective evaluation of the observer; also called the analytical approach

behaviouralism
perspective that concentrates on the "tangible" aspects of political life rather than values; objective was to establish a discipline that was "scientific" and objective

subjective reality
perspective of reality that is influenced by our personal experiences and bias

post-behaviouralism
approach that attempted to reconcile the problems of behaviouralism by allowing for values and ideology in its analysis

structural-functionalism
approach that focuses on the role of political structures and their functions in society

The oldest and most common method is called the **analytical approach**. This perspective views political studies as an **empirical** discipline rather than a science and as a comprehensive field rather than one that can be broken down into parts. Sometimes called the **traditional approach**, this method argues that facts cannot be separated from values. In this theory, human values and convictions are just another part of political life that cannot be fragmented from the field. The implication here is that any observer of political activity will have his or her own view and bias, which will implicate and affect his or her analysis. In other words, it is impossible to observe events in an objective manner; therefore, political studies can never be a scientific discipline.

The analytical approach had its challengers. In an effort to make the field more precise, the **behaviouralists** emerged in the 1950s and 1960s, particularly in American political studies departments. They focused on the "tangible" aspects of political life rather than on the value-laden perspective of the analytical approach. The objective of the behaviouralists was to establish a discipline that was "scientific" and objective: political "science." They argued that human behaviour was at the heart of all political activity; hence, humans should be the centre of research. Behaviouralists concentrated on the scientific method, using variables, theories, axioms, and hypotheses in their research.

The behaviouralist "school," however, was criticized for its attention to the scientific method, which many thought came at the expense of other important issues, such as values or ethics. Many political scientists argued that, in its attempt to be truly scientific, political studies had come to neglect the fact that values were an intrinsic element of political life (i.e. the very focus of the behaviouralist approach—the human being—is steeped in values, opinions, beliefs, and views of the world). After all, we are all affected by what we think, so our "reality" is influenced by our own views or bias and creates a sort of **subjective reality**. Furthermore, the behaviouralist approach had trouble accounting for so-called irrational actions. Scientific rigour, then, could only go so far in interpreting politics. A new approach, **post-behaviouralism**, was a reaction to the negative aspects of behaviouralism. Post-behaviouralists tried to reconcile the problems encountered by behaviouralism by allowing for values and ideology in their analysis. People were once more the focus of attention, and sentiment and views were again added to the mix of analysis.

Nevertheless, there were still others who continued to disagree with the scientific method of both the behaviouralists and the post-behaviouralists and who also rejected the analytical approach as too broad. Such theorists looked at specific aspects of politics. The **structural-functionalists**, for one, concentrated on the role of political structures and their functions in society. What, for example, is the effect and role of the legislature? How does the bureaucracy affect politics? Is the judiciary an important actor in a particular system? Structural-functionalists represent a group within a larger classification of researchers called systems theorists. These analysts view politics as a system of interaction, binding political structures such as government to individual

1.3   BEHAVIOURALISM AFTER WORLD WAR II

The Soviet Union's successful launch of Sputnik 1 not only heated up the space race with the United States but also inadvertently changed the study of politics. The space race caused governments and universities to put more money into science than they had in the past, leaving fields like political studies to question their future. In fact, the term *political science* came under some scrutiny for its lack of a scientific basis. The behaviouralist approach to politics emerged at this time, promising an objective method of predicting and explaining behaviour. It utilized the scientific method of observing, testing, and measuring events in an effort to establish hypotheses and conclusions about political events.

Criticisms of political science and behaviouralism continued, however, as it became increasingly clear how difficult it is to quantify human behaviour. The approach fell into some disrepute, leading many to abandon the goals of prediction and universal assessment. The methods used in behaviouralism, however, remained in several streams of political science research: testing, hypothesis, conceptual development, comparison, and falsification. Political science

David A. Hardy/Science Photo Library

Sputnik 1, the first artificial satellite, was launched in 1957. It transmitted data to earth for 22 days, and circled the planet for three months before burning up on re-entry.

will never be like the natural sciences because humans act in variable and sometimes infinite ways; however, the methods shared among the fields continue to be useful.

action. **Systems theory** argues that politics is a dynamic process of information flows and responses that encompasses political institutions, groups, and individuals. Systems theorists try to understand this process of decision and reaction among various types of political actors.

For political economists, another group of political scientists, the major drawback to all these approaches is that they do not focus on the relationship between power and wealth, or politics and economics. According to **political economy**, an approach that views "interests" as paramount, political studies is the relationship among people, government, and the economy. How those interests are identified and pursued shows the fundamental power and influence in a political system, particularly because those interests tend to be focused on resources that are quite scarce. Political economy is an inherently "critical" approach to the study of politics; in many ways, it brings us back to what Lasswell had to say about "who gets what, when, how" in politics. Because governments affect many of the economic particulars of our lives, and of those around us, political economists explore the role that governments have in both

systems theory
approach that views politics as a system of interaction, binding political structures such as government to individual action; argues that politics is a dynamic process of information flows and responses that encompasses political institutions, groups, and individuals

political economy
approach that views political and economic spheres as harmonious and mutually dependent perceptions of the world; relationship between people, government, and the economy

the political and economic spheres of the environment around us. Political economists also pay close attention to other non-governmental institutions, such as banks and corporations, which are important economic actors.

Chapters 2 and 3 of this book will delve into political concepts, philosophies, and approaches in much greater detail. But, simply put, all forms of political studies are concerned with five pervasive and related questions:

1. What is the political issue at hand?
2. Who is involved?
3. How did the events unfold?
4. Why did the events take place?
5. How was society affected by these events?

As you can now see, there are various ways to try to answer these fairly basic questions. A change in government, for example, might be explained in terms of different parties, methods, or ideologies; institutional transformation; individual personalities; or the result of the political system itself. For instance, the Canadian general election of 2011 resulted in a majority government for the Conservatives. As a result, the government's structure, functions, and decision-making took on a new approach. (We'll look closely at majority and minority governments in Chapter 7.) Even with this change, political scientists still asked these questions in their analysis of Canadian politics. This book will introduce you to a wide variety of approaches, but we'll see that there is at least some agreement on the fundamental questions posed.

Despite the fact that we'll be discussing many different political approaches, this book does have a central methodology. Using these five questions as a baseline, this book uses three main forms of analysis. First, it explores how politics is integral to modern life; we cannot separate ourselves from the political in our society. Political decisions and events have a direct implication on our livelihoods and relationships in our communities. After all, a primary motivating factor for forming groups is to improve and preserve the conditions of what might be termed "the good life"—security, prosperity, and fairness. We've introduced this idea already, but we'll come back to it throughout the text.

comparative approach
method of political analysis that compares different systems of political authority based on system type, time period, or form of leadership

Second, this book takes a **comparative approach**, a wide-ranging method that looks at many aspects of political systems and processes, including government structures, political culture, socialization, interests in society, political parties, and policy.[6] Though it is directed toward a Canadian audience, this book's focus is not exclusively Canadian or even North American. Instead, we use examples and case studies from around the world, from Latin America to Europe, Africa, and Asia. This gives us a cross-section of different political systems and viewpoints that can be placed in the context of the Canadian experience. This approach is part of a whole field of political studies called (not surprisingly) comparative politics, or the comparative method. Simply put, it's one thing to understand a political system or a country on its own, in absolute terms. It's another entirely, however, to see that system or country in relative terms. We learn so much more about how political systems are used by comparing them with others or over time. Furthermore, if we want to understand our own political environment and avoid **ethnocentrism**, we must look at other examples.

There are various comparative methods, including comparing more than one country at a given time period, comparing different systems over time, and comparing individual systems as they change over time. In terms of the last method, think about how Canadian political parties have changed over the last century.

Different types of comparative analysis include **most similar systems** and **most different systems**. The former involves systems that appear to be the same but have variables that can be identified as differences. An example is Canada and Australia, which share many analogous features. But Australia's elected Senate may cause different outcomes for electoral politics or legislation than Canada's appointed Senate does. Most different systems analysis looks at systems that lack similar features in an effort to explain why shared political outcomes occur. Canada and China have very different political systems, but researchers would be interested in how a shared result—say, growth in international investment—came about in each country. Both methods produce important conclusions.[7]

The third and final methodology of this text involves attention to several levels of political life. Various **levels of analysis** include the individual, groups, the state, and the international system. Our assumption here is that we get a better view of a problem or phenomenon if we try to consider several perspectives. Think about how limited our view of a painting would be if we looked at only one corner of the image or how little we would understand about how an airplane works if we examined only the flaps. However important that perspective or information may be, it is not comprehensive. Using levels of analysis, we recognize the complexity of political studies. Of course, we can never fully understand every element in a political event; there is just too much at play. Yet our decision to focus on an aspect of a political event acknowledges that our analysis will be only part of a greater whole. Our focus on several levels shows the comparative nature of this textbook and provides a more rounded introduction to the complex and ever-changing field of political studies.

Political Studies and Our Daily Lives

We often do not consider the political aspect of our daily lives unless we are faced with a situation that brings us directly into the political process, such as voting, filing an income tax return, or taking part in political protests. Yet politics surrounds us, even if we are unaware of it or feel that we don't know anything about it.

When we think about it, politics really is part of our daily lives since it involves organizing ideas, influence, wealth, or power over others. We frequently

ethnocentrism
belief that one's culture or group is superior to others or that other cultures or groups must be examined in relation to one's own

most similar systems
method of comparative analysis that examines political systems that have many common features in an effort to identify different variables.

most different systems
method of comparative analysis that examines political systems that share no (or few) common features yet have a similar outcome or phenomena

levels of analysis
approach to political studies that suggests that accurate analysis must be inclusive of international, domestic, and individual arenas of interaction

hear of the "politics" of the family, organized religion, business, sport, or the entertainment industry. Indeed, all aspects of our common experiences seem to be influenced in some form by politics or political conflict, even in the case of people who think they know nothing about politics. The political nature of the family unit, religion, business, sport, or entertainment involves how these elements of our society are organized, who controls them, and how we may all benefit from (or perhaps miss out on) their collective gains. Politics also affects almost every part of our lives, from health and social care to laws that regulate our behaviour and to the provision of goods and services. As a result, it influences our activities within society in a very direct manner.

Division and Connection in a Changing World

Isaac Asimov, the American biochemist and science fiction writer, wrote: "The only constant is change, continuing change, inevitable change. No sensible decision can be made any longer without taking into account not only the world as it is, but the world as it will be."[8] Politicians would do well to heed Asimov's advice and plan for both the present and the future. Political change is certainly a constant force in our era. Extraordinary changes in our political environment include shifting global security threats, new political forces at home and abroad, a better understanding of shared issues such as those facing the global environment and poverty, and a greater degree of interconnectivity. These changes have presented new challenges as well as opportunities as we begin to understand the nature of this new milieu of domestic and international political affairs.

globalization
intensification of economic, political, social, and cultural relations across borders

Increasingly, individuals, groups, and states are intricately connected to one another through political, economic, strategic, and cultural links. The **globalization** of the current era, where information about other systems and cultures is readily available to us from media sources, our educational system, and the Internet, affects both how we get information and how we use it. Yet at the same time, growing divisions are indicative of a complex and competitive environment for political and economic relations. **Ethnic and religious conflict**, the growing gap between rich and poor, economic **protectionism**, and political isolationism all reflect aspects of modern political life that are divisive and contrary. Often these problems are deeply rooted in efforts by political leaders to provide goods and services to their citizens, efforts that inevitably result in some inequity. Change is indeed constant, but it is also constantly affected by the forces of connection and division.

ethnic and religious conflict
war or opposition among different racial, linguistic, or religious groups

protectionism
tendency of countries to safeguard their own economic sectors or industries through tariffs, quotas, or other forms of trade and investment legislation

An example of these forces working simultaneously occurred in Moscow in January 1990. Over 30,000 Muscovites lined up in Pushkin Square for a meal that cost approximately half an average worker's daily wage but was hardly haute cuisine. Instead, it was a Big Mac combo, available for the first time in the (then) Soviet Union. This event still holds the record for the most meals served

© Reuters/Corbis

"Do you want картофель-фри with that?" Thousands queue in the Moscow cold for American-style fast food.

at a McDonald's franchise in one day. Although it might not seem remarkable now, selling American-style fast food in a communist country was a big story at the time. The arrival of McDonald's in Russia brought two very divided political and economic systems together. Oddly, it represented a good example of globalization as well. **Multinational corporations (MNCs)** and a market-driven commodity met the closed order of Soviet-style politics. And there was clearly an "appetite" for it: 30,000 people don't wait for hours for something they don't want!

Division and connection illustrate a basic paradox in current political life: we may think that we're more linked with others in the world, but often our "understanding" leads to greater confusion and enmity. After all, just knowing someone doesn't mean we will get along with them, and (notwithstanding the enormous success of fast food in communist countries) being exposed to new ideas won't necessarily mean we will accept them. As the Chinese Taoist text *Tao Te Ching* reminds us, "[T]he more you know, the less you understand."[9] This isn't to suggest that we should just give up and not try to expand our knowledge of the world; it's simply a reminder that exposure does not ensure wisdom, understanding, or peace. In fact, looking at the world today, one is struck by the number of groups that seek to create their own nation-states—a goal that is inherently about division—in an era of unprecedented information and access to others. In short, division and connection are coexistent forces, and they remind us of the need to look both outward and inward.

multinational corporations (MNCs) corporate bodies that operate in more than one country

1.4　INVOLVEMENT: APATHY TO ACTION

Successive generations have been criticized for their lack of interest in political affairs. This criticism is usually made by the preceding generation and is often based on a false nostalgia for the way things used to be. To label an entire generation as apathetic is both simplistic and unfair. Indeed, any generation has its share of those who get involved and those who do not. On the other hand, it is fair to say that political involvement today is different than it was in the past, specifically prior to the 1960s. During that decade, a unique change took place for a specific generation. As the baby boomers (those born between 1946 and 1964) became young adults, they reacted viscerally and harshly to the expectation that they would emulate their parents and grandparents. In short, their coming of age in the postwar period instilled in them a need to change the way we see politics. Deference to authority, an aggressive military stance, societal norms such as marriage and jobs at a certain age were questioned and even rejected as people became involved in peace movements, social justice, and global order.

Clearly, a quick scan of today's world situation reveals that the 1960s didn't alter everything. But much did change, such as matters regarding civil and women's rights, government transparency, and a greater expectation that politics should serve the people rather than the other way around. Today's

This kind of attitude didn't push the civil rights movement!

younger generation is no less involved, from volunteer work to active engagement in the political process. The sheer quantity of information available to us now makes the 1960s demand for immediate change seem unachievable or even naïve, but we should remember that any change takes time and that meaningful change probably requires action by groups of individuals who seek it. If we aspire to real progress, everyone must commit to political action rather than succumb to apathy.

Domestic and International Politics

Politics doesn't limit itself to borders, and political studies isn't restricted to the study of our own nation-states. A truly comprehensive view of the world of political studies takes into account the domestic and the international. One of the important lessons we learn in political studies is that the borders that exist among states don't necessarily divide them; countries can be intricately connected to one another in ways that seem to transcend nationality and national frontiers. In fact, it might be argued that certain parts of Canada are more connected to the United States than they are to each other. Political studies, then, recognizes the inherent relationship between domestic and international subject areas.

Domestic politics is a subfield of political studies that concerns itself with the politics, governance, and political administration of national governments and individual countries. Depending on where you take your classes in political studies, the options available to you regarding domestic politics can take you far from your home country. In Canada, most departments of political studies have a concentration on Canadian politics; however, it's not unheard of to find courses on the politics of countries such as Cambodia, Switzerland, or Niger as well. Although these and other countries may not have full courses prescribed to them in Canadian universities, they likely are dealt with in courses that cover Asian, European, or African politics. But were we to look at university course offerings in Phnom Penh, Bern, or Niamey, their countries would undoubtedly be the focus. Whether Canada would be listed among courses in those institutions is another question.

The point here is that where you are will reflect highly on the areas that you are expected to study. We may be in Canada, but we are expected to know a little bit about European politics, a lot about American politics, and some more about other places too. Domestic politics restrains our focus to the country in question—its governing institutions, laws, economy, and relations with the outside world.

That outside world is the realm of **international politics**. Often called international relations or world politics, this subfield takes a wider view of politics. Political relations among and between countries are as much an influence on our domestic frame of reference as what takes place "at home." International politics is concerned with the social, environmental, economic, military, and cultural relations across the globe, whether they are across one border between two countries, within a geopolitical region, or widely dispersed around the globe. Specifically, this subfield examines the political aspects of these interactions.

international politics
the study of foreign policy and relations among states and other actors at the international level; also called international relations

© Francis Vachon / Alamy

In some Canadian and American towns, residents can literally step "abroad" by crossing the street. How might we gauge "citizenship" in these cases?

Although most of the material in this text could be used by those interested in either domestic or international politics, there aren't any artificial lines drawn to distinguish the subfields. Some sections of the text deal with government institutions and decision-making; others deal with international security and economics. But as we move through the subject matter, we will come to see the natural relationship between the two areas.

Citizens and Canada

When did the United Empire Loyalists come to Canada? Which four provinces first formed Confederation? Which province is the only officially bilingual one? Don't despair if you can't answer these questions off the top of your head; most of us can't. But these are the types of questions that new Canadians have to answer before they are granted **citizenship**. New immigrants to Canada must successfully pass a quiz on topics related to Canadian history, politics, economics, geography, and the privileges of citizenship. Although a passing "grade" is just 60 per cent, the questions aren't easy. Many citizens by birth would likely have trouble successfully completing the test. (If you want to check your citizenship suitability, here are the correct answers: 1775 to 1783; Ontario, Quebec, New Brunswick, and Nova Scotia; New Brunswick.)

What does citizenship actually mean? Are there things that are specific to Canadian citizenship? These aren't questions that we would commonly think about since they seem to be just part of being Canadian. Yet being Canadian means not being something—or someone—else. Aside from dual citizens, Canadians aren't American, British, or French. Generally, citizenship is specific, and people are entwined with their birth nation or country of adoption.

Citizenship denotes membership in a political system, complete with the rights and responsibilities of that membership. Usually citizenship is related to nationality or the national identity to which we assign ourselves. That said, some people relate themselves to a "nation" even if they are citizens of another country. Scots, Hausa-Fulani, or Cree people, for instance, may all be Canadian but still maintain their distinctive nationalities. We'll return to the issue of nationality and nationalism later in this text. In any case, citizenship brings with it the protection of the state as well as a legal relationship with a country.

Once people become citizens, they can receive a wide array of benefits. In Canada, for instance, this means a number of rights and freedoms (including legal rights, equality rights, mobility rights, Aboriginal peoples' rights, the right to peaceful assembly, freedom of thought, freedom of speech, and freedom of religion). With rights come responsibilities, and for Canadians that includes respecting others' rights and freedoms, obeying the law, and preserving Canada's heritage and environment. In short, citizenship is not a blank slate—it's a relationship between the state and the citizen to work together to protect and develop Canada.

citizenship
status granted to people that comes with responsibilities and duties as well as rights

1.5 CITIZENSHIP QUIZ

Questions on the Canadian Citizenship Test change frequently. Here is a sample provided by the public library in Richmond, BC, based on multiple choice questions found in *A Look at Canada 2011*. Even if some of the questions may be out of date by the time you read this book, trying the test will give you a sense of what new immigrants face. Answers are given at the end of the box.

1. Who are the Métis?
   a. The distinct Aboriginal people of Atlantic Canada.
   b. A people of mixed Inuit/First Nations ancestry most of whom live on the Prairies.
   c. First Nations people speaking the Michif dialect.
   d. A distinct people of mixed Aboriginal and European ancestry.

2. When did the Canadian Charter of Rights and Freedoms become part of the Canadian constitution?
   a. 1867.
   b. 1905.
   c. 1982.
   d. 1878.

3. Who was the first prime minister of Canada?
   a. Louis Riel.
   b. Sir John A. Macdonald.
   c. Lester B. Pearson.
   d. Abraham Lincoln.

4. What will you promise when you take the Oath of Citizenship?
   a. Pledge allegiance to the queen, observe the laws of Canada and fulfill the duties of a Canadian.
   b. Pledge to be faithful to the queen.
   c. Promise to observe the laws of Canada.
   d. Fulfill duties as a Canadian citizen.

5. What are the territories of Northern Canada and their capital cities?
   a. Alaska (Juneau) and Yukon Territory (Whitehorse).
   b. Northwest Territories (Yellowknife) and Alaska (Juneau).
   c. Northwest Territories (Yellowknife).
   d. Yukon Territory (Whitehorse), Northwest Territories (Yellowknife), and Nunavut (Iqaluit).

6. Which region covers more than one-third of Canada?
   a. Central Canada.
   b. Prairies.
   c. Atlantic Canada.
   d. Northern Canada.

7. One-third of all Canadians live in which province?
   a. Quebec.
   b. Ontario.
   c. Northwest Territories.
   d. Manitoba.

8. What is a major river in Quebec?
   a. Fraser River.
   b. St. Lawrence River.
   c. Niagara.
   d. Hudson Bay.

9. What are the three parts of Parliament?
   a. The queen, governor general, and prime minister.
   b. The House of Commons, the Legislative Assembly, and the Senate.
   c. The queen, the Legislative Assembly, and the Senate.
   d. The queen, the House of Commons, and the Senate.

10. What do you call the Sovereign's representative in the provinces?
    a. Premier.
    b. Member of the Legislative Assembly
    c. Lieutenant-Governor.
    d. Senator.

Answers
1. b 2. c 3. b 4. a 5. d 6. d 7. b 8. b 9. d 10. c

multiculturalism
peaceful coexistence of several racial, cultural, or ethnic identities in one nation

In addition to new Canadians by birth, approximately 160,000 people (or three-quarters of 1 per cent of the country's population) become Canadian citizens in any given year. This number changes based on the priorities and preferences expressed by the federal government; however, it's a substantial number. Immigration is not a minor affair in Canada. Time spent in any major city or town shows the pluralistic and **multicultural** nature of Canadian society. Canadian society has been described as a mosaic, an image only truly recognized with all its pieces in place. Others, like York University political scientist Kenneth McRoberts, have called Canada "multinational," marked most notably by its French and Aboriginal "internal nations."[10]

The nature of the course material means that we will spend a considerable amount of time examining what it means to be a citizen of Canada. Yet as this chapter has suggested, knowing what it means to be Canadian—or a citizen of any other country, for that matter—means knowing a bit about the rest of the world as well. Therefore, one goal of this text is to integrate our introduction to political studies so that we reflect both our national and international perspectives.

Conclusion

This chapter has introduced you to the discipline of political studies and acquainted you with the broad nature of political inquiry, our relationship to the political "world," and our undeniable connection with the global framework of political relations. Political studies is about decisions and process, how decisions are made and in whose benefit. It is also as much about the resolution of conflict as it is about conflict itself.

The following chapters explore some of these themes. Chapter 2 provides a more detailed account of the major concepts in political studies. Related closely to Chapter 2, Chapter 3 explores the main political philosophies and ideologies that form the basis of modern political studies. Chapter 4 introduces the role that government plays in our lives, including its different forms, schools of thought, and shared activities at all levels. Chapter 5 builds on the previous chapter, breaking government down into its specific parts and institutions. Chapter 6 examines the variety of political systems that exist in the world today. Chapters 7 and 8 consider the ways that we participate in our political system, from election votes to the impact of global media. Chapters 9 and 10 explore the distinctions between the developed and developing worlds, including some case studies of important examples from around the globe. Chapters 11, 12, and 13 look at the international nature of political studies, including foreign policy, international relations, security and strategic studies, and the international political economy. Finally, Chapter 14 provides a conclusion to the course and the text.

Self-Assessment Questions

1. How might we distinguish among the different types of power in politics?
2. Why did Hobbes think that life would be "solitary, poor, nasty, brutish, and short" without government?
3. How does political studies fit with the other social sciences?
4. Why and how is politics such a central component of society? Can we become truly apolitical? Why or why not?
5. How are the forces of division and connection entwined in a globalized world?
6. How does immigration contribute to the multinational character of Canadian society?

Weblinks

Canadian Citizenship Test
www.cic.gc.ca/english/citizenship/cit-test.asp

Canadian Political Science Association
www.cpsa-acsp.ca

Careers for Political Scientists
www.cpsa-acsp.ca/guides.shtml

Freedom House
www.freedomhouse.org

Further Reading

Almond, Gabriel A. *A Discipline Divided: Schools and Sects in Political Science*. Newbury Park, CA: Sage, 1990.
——, G. Bingham Powell, Jr, Russell J. Dalton, and Kaare Strøm. *Comparative Politics Today: A World View*. 9th edn. Toronto: Longman, 2008.
Aristotle. *Politics*. Translated by T.A. Sinclair. Harmondsworth, UK: Penguin, 1986.
Asimov, Isaac. *Asimov on Science Fiction*. New York: Doubleday, 1981.
Easton, David. *The Political System*. 2nd edn. Chicago: University of Chicago Press, 1981.
Hobbes, Thomas. *Leviathan, Or, the Matter, Forme and Power of a Commonwealth Ecclesiasticall and Civil*. Edited by Michael Oakeshott. New York: Collier Books, 1962.
Laozi. *Tao Te Ching*. Harmondsworth, UK: Penguin, 1963/1976.
Lasswell, Harold. *Politics: Who Gets What, When, How*. New York: Meridian Books, 1958.
Przeworski, Adam, and Henry Teune. *The Logic of Comparative Social Inquiry*. New York: Wiley, 1970.
Seymour, Michel, ed. *The Fate of the Nation-State*. Montreal and Kingston: McGill-Queen's University Press, 2004.

News Clips

Visit the companion website for *Politics: An Introduction*, 2nd edn, to access news clips related to the content of this chapter.

2

Finding a Common Vocabulary: Political Concepts

◄ Political vocabulary is expressed on a wall in Cochabamba, Bolivia. This graffiti was especially relevant during the country's vote of confidence referendum in August 2008. With over two-thirds of the vote, President Evo Morales remained in power.

Photo: AP Photo/Dado Galdier/CP

LEARNING OBJECTIVES

After reading this chapter, you will be able to

● define and explain concepts relating to political organization, action, and values;

● understand and use key terms in the vocabulary of political studies;

● identify the connections between the state and society;

● understand the difference and links between agency and structure; and

● give examples of the significance and real-world applicability of these concepts.

Introduction

As you have probably already noticed, post-secondary education comes with new challenges, responsibilities, opportunities, freedoms, and expectations. It also comes with a new vocabulary containing the specialized terms that we use in our classes and studies. Like all disciplines, political studies has its own language that distinguishes it from other fields of study. This vocabulary is important because it allows us to avoid unnecessary misunderstandings and engage in meaningful and effective discussions. Furthermore, it helps to shape our identities as scholars of politics and to create a mental picture of some of the more significant ideas utilized in political analysis.

concept
general idea emerging from events or instances

Concepts are general notions or abstract ideas that are encapsulated in a specialized vocabulary.[1] The fact that this language is specialized is crucial, for political studies often devises distinctive interpretations of terms that might otherwise be understood in a different sense. For instance, as explained later in this chapter, the manner in which we consider the concept of nation in politics and the way we think about the term in everyday life are somewhat different.[2] Just as importantly, the ability to distinguish one kind of right (say, human) from another (civil) becomes important in both theory and practice.

This is not to say that all concepts are universally regarded or agreed upon. In fact, unlike the so-called hard sciences (such as physics and chemistry), which generally accept some basic ideas, "laws" or theories in political studies are hotly contested. For instance, in politics there is no corresponding political theory to that of the theory of relativity, which is accepted as fundamental in the hard sciences. Politics, like many of the social sciences, is marked by an ongoing debate about the utility of certain theories and concepts, as well as their interpretation.[3] Despite this substantial disagreement, many of our important ideas can be defined in a manner that allows us to use them in a fairly recognized manner. This is part of what gives political studies its richness and diversity as an area of study and produces lively and entertaining debates between scholars.

This chapter will introduce you to key concepts used in the field and explain their significance in both theory and practice. Specific examples (often contained in the text boxes) will demonstrate the relevance of these theories in the real world. We will cover concepts related to both the organization and practice of politics, as well as the ideas and values that lie behind them.

Political Organization

In many ways, politics concerns the organization of life and relationships in a society. For this reason, the way we define and think about the organizational aspects of politics is vital.[4] In this section, we will examine some of the key terms and concepts relating to political organization.

As a form of social interaction, politics encompasses the way human beings govern themselves. But governance may take place only with the existence of certain specialized agencies. Governing also requires a polity, which is the form or process of organized government. It can mean a state, or it can refer more generally to a collection of individuals in a community that have a political relationship with one another. This form of political grouping, commonly called a **body politic**, is a set of individuals tied together in a political connection.

We classify the body politic in a number of ways. Groups of people form political relationships with each other for many reasons, creating different types and forms of identity. In some cases, this identity is geographical. Here, the political relationship is rather self-evident, as groups of people that share a common territory will often create political units as a means of protecting that place or of regulating behaviour within it. Over time, the affiliations and relationships among people living in the territory will become based on more than just feelings toward land or where they live. Values, belief systems, attitudes, and images of one's world are deeply shaped by the socialization people receive in their political communities, creating a system where identity may be based on a multitude of reasons and rationales.[5] How we conceptualize political communities, and the labels we place on them, are essential elements for our political analysis.

Order is essentially the condition in which both actors and interaction within a political system are marked by regularity and stability with the imposition of accepted and enforced rules, structures, and practices.[6] Indeed, one of the basic preconditions for civilization is order, so as to provide a degree of customary activities and predictability within society. However, order is often difficult to establish without sacrificing other desired conditions, such

body politic
entirety of a political community

order
condition in which both units and interaction within a political system are marked by regularity and stability with the imposition of accepted and enforced rules, structures, and practices

democracy
political system based on the principle that governance requires the assent of all citizens through participation in the electoral process, articulation of views, and direct or indirect representation in governing institutions

monarchy
form of government by a single ruler who holds at least nominally absolute power

tyranny
government by a single ruler who often exercises arbitrary power for his or her own benefit rather than that of the community

system
group of individual entities or actors that interact with each other to form an integrated whole

international system
system of two or more actors that interact regularly in the global arena, using established processes in given issue areas

organizations
structured relations existing within a political community that are established to distribute both the responsibilities and the privileges that arise from formal association with others

institutions
groupings that have developed to attend to particular societal needs

as freedom. Order is not only a condition but also, as we will see later in this chapter, a value to which many individuals and groups in society may aspire.

A political order, then, is the collection of rules, laws, norms, customs, and conventions that delimit and maintain a society. Different kinds of political order include **democracy**, **monarchy**, and **tyranny**, terms that were first used by ancient Greek philosophers such as Socrates, Plato, and Aristotle (see Chapter 3). Democracy is a particular kind of political order in which the people choose leaders; in fact, the word comes from an ancient Greek term meaning "rule of the people." Democracy can take many different forms and expressions depending on time and place, but in the Canadian context we most commonly think of a democracy as a **system** in which there are free and fair elections and minority rights are respected and protected. A monarchy is a system in which an individual holds power as the ultimate authority in the land (the term comes from the ancient Greek meaning "one ruler"). Of course, in the modern world most monarchs have found their powers limited by other political institutions—Canada is a clear example of this—although "absolute monarchs" continue to exercise power in some parts of the world. Lastly, the term *tyranny* refers to a political system in which an individual or group of individuals seizes power and exploits it for their own benefit with little regard for the welfare of the population.

In the language of political science, a system is closely linked to the idea of a political order and refers to a connected and organized body that represents a coherent whole. A political system, for example, is a conglomerate of numerous political structures that work together to drive the political aspects of social interaction. Since the parts of the coherent whole are so interrelated, change in one part usually means a change in all, such as the way in which changes in party leadership affect the politics of a state's entire political system. Equally, an alteration in the rules concerning voting will have a far-reaching impact, not just on political parties and elections but also on the balance of political power in the country. At the global level, the international political system embodies the individual units—the states—as well as the functional non-state actors (such as non-governmental organizations and multinational corporations) that comprise and affect the world arena. When there is a change in the distribution of power in the **international system** (such as the rapid and dramatic rise of China in recent years), it has an impact on all the actors involved.

Within any particular system, the term **organizations** refers to structured relations existing within a political community that are established to distribute both the responsibilities and the privileges that arise from formal association with others.[7] Organizations may range from political parties and interest groups to private groups that allocate resources on a different level. It is important to recognize that these organizations can be local, national, or international; public or private; and based on economic, political, information, cultural, ethnic, racial, or religious ties.

Directly related to organizations are **institutions**, arrangements that have developed and are mandated to attend to particular needs for society.[8] Not just simply a grouping of individuals, institutions have strict definitions

2.1 INSTITUTIONS AND DEVELOPMENT

The successful political and economic development of a state is dependent on the construction and maintenance of strong institutions within it. These institutions include the organs of government (executive, legislative, and judicial branches and bureaucracy), the institutions related to public security (policing and the courts), economic management (central bank, monopolies commission, stock markets, banking system), and information flows and transparency (a free media, access to government records). In almost all developing countries, at least some of these institutions are weak, and strengthening them is seen as a necessary precursor to advancing development.

It is important to recognize that institutions can be public or private, formal or informal, and are not limited exclusively to organizations but incorporate rules and conventions. In the case of Latin America, for example, scholars such as Guillermo O'Donnell and Douglass North have argued that the weaknesses of institutions such as electoral commissions, the rule of law, and organs guaranteeing accountability have played a role in underdeveloping the countries of the region. Of course, the most important institution that we deal with in political studies is the state.[1]

Note

1. Joel S. Migdal, *State in Society: Studying How States and Societies Transform and Constitute One Another* (Cambridge: Cambridge University Press, 2001), 6.

regarding their structure and functions and set out distinct roles for their members. Institutions may or may not be organizations; similarly, not all organizations are necessarily institutions. Institutions may exist at the national or international level. Courts, the free media, and political assemblies such as parliaments are national institutions; the United Nations (UN) is an international one. Institutions, and their strengths and weaknesses, have become one of the most important areas of political analysis in our discipline. Institutions are held to be strong when they are autonomous, transparent, accountable, and durable. Strong institutions are generally perceived to be an essential element of building a stable political and economic system in a country. Weak institutions, on the other hand, are often cited as a contributing factor to political instability, corruption, underdevelopment, and undemocratic practices.

The highest form of political organization within individual countries can be found in the extremely specialized entity of the **state**, the collection of public institutions that regulates a country's political and, to a greater or lesser extent, economic life. States are the highest representation of authority within a given territory and carry with them a wide range of both privileges and responsibilities. As such, states are the only actors that exercise what is known as **sovereignty**, the capability and legal status to hold absolute control over a defined geographical area. The Canadian state exercises sovereign control over the geographical territory known as Canada. Within those borders, no other entity—not even the UN—can legally tell the Canadian state what to do. The sociologist and political economist Max Weber famously noted that sovereign states maintain a monopoly over the legitimate use of violence in their territories, a facet that gives them enormous power and authority.[9]

state
recognized political unit, considered to be sovereign, with a defined territory and people and a central government responsible for administration

sovereignty
recognition by other political authorities that a government is legitimate and rightful for a political community

2.2 THE CONCEPT OF NATION AND SOVEREIGNTY IN CANADA

Although this book tries to give you a clear definition of the terms we use in political studies, meanings can be blurred, contested, and often cause protracted political conflict in the world. In Canada we use the term *nation* to refer to the country's people. But the word is also used in Quebec to refer to the Quebec people as a nation within the Canadian nation. For many years, this situation has caused confusion and dispute within political circles and has exacerbated Québécois calls for an altered relationship with the rest of Canada.

The issue was finally addressed at the federal level in November 2006, when the House of Commons passed a motion stating "That this House recognize that the Québécois form a nation within a united Canada." The Conservative government's motion was introduced in response to one from the Bloc Québécois that stated that the Québécois formed a nation without any reference to Canada. Prime Minister Stephen Harper explained afterward that the term *nation* was used in a socio-cultural rather than a legal sense. In other words, the acknowledgement of Quebec as a nation does not imply independence or any sort of sovereignty outside of Canada. The debate regarding Quebec's status, however, is far from over.

Sovereignty includes both internal and external dimensions. For the state to be sovereign, it must exert internal control over its territory and people; externally, it must be recognized by other states in the international system as being the sovereign power. The sovereign state, however, also bears a responsibility to its citizens: it must provide them with security from threats and with the conditions for order, stability, and prosperity. A state that fails to do these things will, sooner or later, be punished by its citizens through revolution or democratic change.

In everyday life, the term **nation** is also often used to refer to a country. But *state* and *nation* actually have quite different meanings. As we have just seen, states are legalistic entities with sovereign authority over defined people, resources, and territory. A nation is a group of persons who share an identity that is based on, but not limited to, common ethnic, religious, cultural, or linguistic qualities. These persons are part of a largely unacquainted group since it is virtually impossible for them to know everyone who shares their sense of identity. The term **nation-state** refers to those sovereign states that are constructed along a shared national identity; true nation-states, therefore, are actually quite rare. Although these three terms refer to very distinctive relationships, they are sometimes used interchangeably in political discourse, such as references to Canada as a nation, the member states of the UN, or nation-states in the international system.[10] It is important to be aware of the different meanings of these terms and to the contested nature of their usage.

The institution that controls the state at any given time is referred to as the government. This part of the political system may take many different forms, including those defined on page 30. The government is distinguished from the state by its more temporary nature: whereas the state and its institutions remain more or less constant, governments will change. For example, although

nation
group of persons who share an identity that is based on, but not limited to, shared ethnic, religious, cultural, or linguistic qualities

nation-state
autonomous political unit of people who share a predominant common culture, language, ethnicity, or history

the party of government in Canada may change, the foundations of the country endure.

Above the state, we find the international system. This term refers to the organization of states among themselves and the interactions they undertake. At this level, all states share the same legal status; in this sense they are equal. Nonetheless, they are differentiated from one another by their size, internal structures, natural resources, ideologies, wealth, and capabilities. Thus we can distinguish between the rich (developed) and the poor (developing) states, between capitalist and communist states, or between democratic and authoritarian states. But in the international system they will organize themselves into alliances and groupings according to their interests and preferences. They will interact with each other through diplomacy, trade, investment, cultural exchanges, and war. The international system may be said to be more or less stable depending on the frequency of armed conflict and the sustainability of economic growth that it experiences.

war
use of armed forces in conflict with an enemy

Political Action

In addition to understanding the role played by institutions, government, and the state, we must leave room in political studies for political action by individuals and groups of individuals. It is here that the concept of **agency** becomes important and useful. Agency is a term borrowed from sociology that signifies the capacity of people to exercise their free will and to act independently. In other words, it is the ability that each of us has to exert our autonomy and make an impact on our environment. Agency is commonly contrasted with structure, which refers to enduring restrictions on the freedom of human action, including social, political, and economic institutions and culture and natural forces.

agency
individual or group action in a social context

The relationship between these two factors is not merely one-way or deterministic in the sense that structure limits agency. Human agency in turn shapes structures, which allows for change in the world. As agents and actors express their preferences, the potential exists for new patterns of interaction, cultures, and institutions to emerge. The agency-and-structure question is fundamental to understanding the role of individuals and groups and that of institutions in politics. It helps us to understand the limitations as well as the incentives for political action and shows how the struggle to control those institutions becomes a source of power for individuals.

As you will recall, this book began with an overview of power in its many facets. We started with this idea because it is central to the study of politics. Indeed, many of the most important concepts in political analysis have to do with relationships of control. Much of political life centres on how power is distributed, whether it is among persons and groups in society or among all the states in the international system. What differentiates these concepts from those dealing with the relational and more active nature of power is the way that power is sought and maintained.

Power is often referred to as the principal concept in political studies because it attends to both the dynamic and static nature of political life.[11] That is, power may be pursued or sustained in an active (dynamic) manner through, for instance, the exercise of force, repression of opponents, war, or use of spending power to achieve goals. Power may also be thought of as a measurement of politics (static), since we may compare actors in political life based on their access to and control of power sources such as economic resources (e.g. campaign financing), natural attributes (oil and arable land), or influence (diplomatic expertise and respect). Power is an operative concept in that it represents the capacity to do what we want or act how we like. Furthermore, it allows us the opportunity to create a hierarchy of actors and interests in political systems. The exercise of power involves the limiting or impairing of the recipient's choice: to exercise power over someone involves controlling his or her freedom of action to some extent.

It is important for us to distinguish between different forms and manifestations of power. The kind of power wielded by the police or the military is clearly very different from that exercised by big corporations or wealthy individuals. Even when we are talking about the same actor, there will be different power resources available. In a famous treatment of governmental power, Steven Lukes argued that there are "three faces" of power: decision-making, non-decision-making, and ideological power. The first concerns the most obvious and well-known form of governmental power, the kind seen through policy-making, legislation, and its implementation. The second form is the ability to set the agenda for discussion and debate, determining what issues receive priority in the policy process. The third is the ability to influence people and mould the way they think.[12]

separation of powers
division of powers among several government institutions (e.g. legislature, executive) to avoid concentration of authority

2.3 THE ABUSE OF POWER

The media often refer to an abuse of power in politics. Whether this term involves corruption to gain access to limited resources or the use of political influence to escape from prosecution or to change the rules of government for the benefit of political elites, the abuse of power has a long history. In *The Spirit of the Laws* (1748), French social commentator Montesquieu argued that the **separation of powers**–the division of the executive, legislative, and judicial branches of government–was the only certain defence against the abuse of power stemming from the concentrated control of a small group of actors. But even with the separation of powers, people can abuse their privileged status. There are countless examples of political appointees who received their post in exchange for supporting the governing party or making significant financial contributions to electoral campaigns.

Since it was passed in October 2001, the Patriot Act has been the basis of countless accusations of power abuse in the United States. A reaction to the 9/11 attacks, the Act gives the US government far-reaching powers in the areas of border security, surveillance of private citizens, and the tracking down and apprehension of suspected terrorists. Of particular concern is the legislation's provision that allows the government to tap phones, access voice mail, and detain foreigners entering the country if it suspects intent to commit a terrorist act.

Just from Lukes's brief treatment of power, we can see how diverse, multi-dimensional, and complex the term can be. Power can be derived from military, economic, ideological, knowledge-based, social, and patronage sources. A wide range of political, economic, religious, and social actors can exercise power. But if we want to define power at its most basic level, we can say that it is the ability of an actor to achieve the goals that he or she sets for himself or herself. The actor does this by controlling either the environment in which he or she operates, other individuals, or both in such a way as to facilitate the achievement of his or her goals. Regarding international relations, Susan Strange usefully distinguished relational power (that is, the ability of actor A to get actor B to do something that actor B would not otherwise do) from structural power (the ability to change and modify the political, social, and legal environment within which other actors have to operate).[13] Similarly, some political scientists, such as rational choice theorists (who look at how people make choices that can maximize their gains), have argued that power can be examined in two dimensions: the ability to achieve outcomes and the ability to change incentives and costs for other actors to achieve those same outcomes.

We must also distinguish between hard power and soft power.[14] Hard power refers to the ability to provide incentives and punishments (carrots and sticks, respectively) to others in order to achieve the desired outcomes, whereas soft power relies on less tangible factors such as ideology, ideas, culture, and media. In international relations this distinction has become especially important when referring to the power resources of middle powers (neither the most powerful nor the weakest countries in the system). These countries, of which Canada is one, have limited hard power resources (e.g. military or economic power) but enjoy prestige and high standing in the global community due to their status as ethical states that contribute to peacekeeping, human rights, and multilateral institutions.

Whether at the level of the individual, group, state, or international system, the pursuit of power is a fundamental facet of politics. It is also considered to be a rational form of behaviour, as it enables the aforementioned actors to achieve the political, economic, and social goals they set for themselves.

Influence is closely related to the concept of power.[15] Like power, influence is also an operative concept because it represents the capability of actors to persuade others to do their will. Power and influence are often referred to in tandem by virtue of their logical connection: influence is most often used to procure power, and power is often an essential requirement for influence. Influence and persuasion are more difficult to quantify than most forms of power, but this does not mean that they are less significant. Think of how important influence can be or has been in your own life: the influence of other individuals, groups, or even ideas can change behaviour. In politics, influence matters because of the way that it can serve as a substitute or complement to power. It also gives us pause to remember that actors who seem to lack power resources can still play a role and are worth studying as their ideas, knowledge, or culture may help to decide outcomes.

2.4   THE CULT OF PERSONALITY

In many authoritarian or totalitarian regimes (for a full explanation of these terms, see Chapter 4), legitimacy in the domestic political arena is increased by using propaganda and the mass media to develop a cult that venerates and worships the leader. In countries as diverse as Argentina, Zimbabwe, Italy, North Korea, Cambodia, and China, governments have encouraged the bolstering of myths surrounding the personality of political leaders. As leader of the Soviet Union from 1924 to 1953, Joseph Stalin used all means available to him to establish himself as an unchallengeable authority in the Soviet political system. His happiness and well-being were equated with those of the country as a whole, and he was credited with being the father of the nation, an unusually talented strategist, and ultimately infallible.

Stalin's example has been echoed in more recent times by North Korea's Kim Jong-il and Venezuela's Hugo Chavez. Kim Jong-il led North Korea from 1994 to 2011. Known to his people as the "Dear Leader," he is credited not only with being the supreme leader of the nation but also as the source of all happiness and good things. Chavez, a former army colonel, ruled Venezuela from February 1999 until his death in March 2013. He won the presidency of Venezuela democratically and was re-elected by large majorities. Chavez became

Mary Evans Picture Library/ALEXA/CP

Joseph Stalin cemented his control over the Soviet state by using a propaganda machine to build up his cult of personality.

adept at using the media to build a personal connection with the Venezuelan electorate, including his own weekly television show, *Aló, Presidente*, in which he answered phone calls from citizens and responded to their requests for governmental assistance. (For more on this program, see Box 8.5, p. 212.) This type of populism was effective in getting his message across to voters and in generating support for his policies.

authority
power or right to force obedience

rights
socially acceptable, morally correct, and just privileges granted to members of a political community

Authority is essential in understanding the use of power in a political system. This concept basically refers to the right of an individual or group of persons to exercise procedures that are required to regulate the community.[16] Authority involves the granting of **rights** and responsibilities to particular individuals and groups that undertake to govern the political unit. Because it would be impossible for members of a political system to govern themselves directly and still maintain social order, individuals and groups are chosen to represent the interests of the broader community in order to administer the system's activities. Max Weber's classic typology of authority identified three different forms: traditional, rational-legal, and charismatic. Traditional authority refers to the authority of actors whose validity derives from the fact that their power is passed down from one generation to the next, either within a family or a larger social group. Rational-legal authority is most common in modern states and societies and derives from the existence of and respect for a set of accepted laws, norms, and rules. In charismatic authority, the recognition of the right to rule derives from specific qualities of the person concerned. In some cases, a mixture of two or maybe even all three of these types of authority may be present in a leader.[17]

Leadership is a concept that plays an important everyday role in politics.[18] Despite the existence of well-formed, solid institutions, and though a political system may be highly democratic, strong or weak leadership on the part of individuals or groups may determine the capacity of the system and society to advance, resolve pressing problems, and overcome political stalemate. Leadership may or may not be associated with power, as it is possible to be a leader without exercising power. In fact, just as with power and influence, we can point to diverse forms of leadership. Knowledge-based leadership, for example, refers to a situation in which possession of a specialized form of knowledge confers a leadership role upon an individual or group. Closely related to this understanding is the concept of leadership as problem-solving, in which an individual or group provides a way out of a tricky situation or dilemma. We can also think of leadership in the sense of "being first" in achieving a goal, or in the sense of leading by example. Influence often plays a crucial role in deciding leadership and is one of the factors that help to make the latter difficult to quantify.

Legitimacy is integral to the notion of authority.[19] Legitimacy refers to a political community's belief that those who are in authority are there for justifiable and worthy reasons. Certification of a rightful mode of governance, then, is transferred from the constituency to political authorities through the granting of the right to rule. For instance, in most democratic states (including Canada), the legitimacy to rule is granted when individuals elect politicians to act on their behalf in the greater interest of the political unit. But, as we previously noted, legitimacy can derive from other, less rational factors. For many centuries, the legitimacy of the kings and queens of European states derived from their bloodline or their family ties. Even today in Canada, we have a monarch who claims legitimate rule over the country because of her connection to a line of monarchs in the British Isles. It is important to remember that legitimacy can be gained but must be maintained. It can also be lost and very difficult to regain.

In the modern world, political (as opposed to religious or moral) legitimacy depends upon a number of factors, including the capacity to deliver public goods and guarantee basic safety, freedoms, and standards of living to the majority in society. Any political authority that fails to do so will lose legitimacy and risks being turned out of office. The connection between this kind of failure and legitimacy is fundamental to understanding both democratic changes of government and revolutions (violent or otherwise). We should also emphasize that success in delivering public goods to society will often help non-democratic forms of government maintain their legitimacy in the absence of elections. The link connecting power, authority, and legitimacy is an intriguing one and has been a subject of theoretical and philosophical inquiry for centuries. For political authority must exercise power in order to establish its

leadership
group of individuals that lead society

legitimacy
what is lawful, proper, and conforms to the standards of a political system

2.5   CHARISMATIC LEADERSHIP

We have already discussed the phenomenon of the cult of personality in politics. Closely connected with that is the notion of charisma and the highly particular way in which some leaders are able to gain the support of others and exercise influence by means of their personality. Identified by Weber as one of the three forms of authority, charismatic leadership is exhibited by those individuals who display extraordinary and exceptional qualities. Sometimes this charm has to do with intelligence; in other cases it concerns a more complex mix of physical attractiveness, wit, and achievement. An example is former US president Bill Clinton, widely recognized as one of the most charismatic leaders in American history.

But there are other examples that are more puzzling. Adolf Hitler, for example, was responsible for some of the most heinous crimes against humanity and is almost universally recognized as evil. Nonetheless, he was considered a very charismatic personality by most of the German people in the 1930s and 1940s. His passion, his oratory, and his background as a proto-revolutionary gave him a standing with the masses that helped him to win and maintain power.

© David Turnley/Corbis

Former US president Bill Clinton is renowned for his charm and charisma and for using them to achieve political goals.

primacy and to rule, but it must exercise that power in an acceptable way to maintain its legitimacy. If the authority loses legitimacy, it risks losing power, unless it rules through coercion and imposition in an authoritarian fashion. We might therefore posit that, to maintain its legitimacy, political authority must focus not only on the exercise of power but also on the legitimate use of power to maintain social support.

laws
rules imposed on society by the governing authority

Laws are rules that are customarily enacted in societies to prohibit or promote certain activities. Furthermore, these rules are enforced with the imposition or threat of punishment by organized authorities in society. Put another way, laws are a regulatory mechanism within political systems that not only prescribe punishment but also provide incentives and encourage certain types of behaviour. Norms, beliefs, customs, and ideas also shape behaviour within political units but lack a punitive dimension.

legislation
laws enacted by a governing authority

A special kind of law is known as **legislation**. Also called statutory law, this type of law is passed by the legislative branch of government, or in Canada's case, by Parliament. Legislation is one of the most obvious manifestations of governmental power and activity and occupies much of the government's time and efforts. In Canada, legislation that is enacted by the legislative branch is known as an Act of Parliament. To be effective, the executive branch of government must implement legislation, and this is where government bureaucracy becomes crucial.

Connected to legislation is the concept of **policy**. Public authorities, private corporations, social groups, or even individuals can make policy. In this book, we will refer primarily to government policy, but in everyday discourse you will hear diverse actors talking about their "policy." A policy is simply a coordinated plan of action designed to achieve a predetermined set of goals. Its link to legislation is that governments will probably seek to enact legislation as part of their policy but will use a whole range of other political actions as well, including special appointments, media campaigns, and even diplomacy. Policy, therefore, is an integral aspect of government activity, and its direction, strength, and success can be used to judge governments.

As with laws, legislation and policy also provide incentives and deterrents for certain kinds of social, economic, and political behaviour. In this way, laws, legal systems, legislation, and policy form an important component of the political structure of society, a structure that, through their agency, actors will try to change to further their interests. The use of power, influence, and leadership (in their many diverse forms) will be fundamental to ensuring success in this regard.

There remains one fundamental set of concepts that drives and underlies the concepts discussed in this section. **Values** are the ideas that we hold most dear in our political, social, and personal lives, and the hierarchy of these values in society will be crucial in explaining why one particular political reality dominates over other possibilities.

policy
law or principle of performance adopted by a government

values
principles, standards; what an individual or community esteems as meaningful

Values

As a method of establishing the relationship among members of a social unit, political analysis is very much concerned with quality of life.[20] We know that we need one another to live and prosper, but we do not always find our current human situation entirely satisfactory. In response to the desire to achieve a better life, questions arise about how political authorities maintain and oversee the distribution of public benefits, as well as opportunities. The preference given to certain values over others, therefore, is a basic subject in political studies.

Values are important to us as students of politics because their hierarchy in a society and a political system will vary across time and space. For example, importance of gender equality (and equal opportunities in general) in Canada today is much greater than it was 50 years ago. Similarly, there is a big difference between the importance given to that value in Canada and in Saudi Arabia. Alternatively, values such as justice have always been a priority in political affairs. The meaning of that term, however, varies widely from place to place and generation to generation.

equality
parity in a political system

One of the most commonly discussed values in politics is that of **equality**. Though it is customary to refer to the equality of humans, our notion of this value would be challenged if we were to carefully study the differences among individuals, as well as the level of opportunities and benefits available to them. In the real world, all persons have different qualities and strengths, which translate into different levels of benefits based along distinctive areas of interest. We should be careful, then, to distinguish between different kinds of equality. Political equality, for instance, refers to the right to participate in the political activities of one's society and to be treated evenly by it. Social equality indicates the equal status given to everyone's basic characteristics and needs as part of a larger social conglomerate. Economic equality refers to the approximate equivalent distribution of benefits accrued from the exchange of goods and services.[21] It is important to bear in mind that, in all these forms, equality designates an attempt to provide parity of opportunity to all these public goods. Furthermore, equality is directly related to freedom since individuals and groups must be allowed to seek out social benefits for true equality to exist.

The concept of equality has been fundamental to the development of political ideas in the Western world since the work of the modern political philosophers, including Thomas Hobbes and John Locke. The ancient Greek theorists, such as Plato and Aristotle, refused to accept the equality of human individuals, seeing the differences between them as more important. Considering humans as equal in terms of their physical and mental capacities is just one perspective. Hobbes and Locke changed our understanding of the word so that it came to be seen in terms of deserving equal consideration or treatment. This is political equality. The justifications for this kind of equality are varied. Hobbes claimed that no individual was so far superior to others in terms of capacities as to be invulnerable to them or able to subdue them permanently. Locke, on the other hand, argued that human equality stemmed from the fact that all humans were equal inheritors of the earth.

It is important to note here that Locke based his understanding of equality on the idea that human beings inherited the earth from God and that our equal rights can therefore be traced back to a fundamentally religious origin. For those people who do not believe in the existence of a divine supreme being, we need to devise another justification for our belief in human equality. Should we return to Hobbes's ideas that equality stems from the essential vulnerability of all humans? Or should we look instead to philosophers such as John Rawls, who argued in *A Theory of Justice* (1971) that all rational humans would choose an initial preference for equality if they were unsure of the opportunities that would be extended to them in life?

By the second half of the twentieth century, it had become a standard idea in Western political philosophy that individuals should be treated equally, regardless of their physical strength, wealth, race, or beliefs. This does not, of course, translate into equality of wealth, political influence, or opportunity. Most philosophers and political thinkers have developed theories in which high degrees of economic and political inequality are justified. Locke allowed for an economic system of unequal appropriation despite his insistence on individuals' fundamental equality, and Adam Smith relied on a premise of equality to justify the free market system, insisting that such economic relations would help to reinforce equality. And leaders in all political systems are chosen to exercise authority over the vast majority of society despite the fact that those same systems explicitly recognize the inherent equality of all. Karl Marx, on the other hand, pointed to the essential equality of human individuals as a justification for a more equal distribution of goods and power within society.

The basic concept of equality illustrates many important consequences for the real world of politics. Racial equality stresses the equal treatment of individuals from all racial backgrounds. Gender equality, referred to earlier, emphasizes the equal treatment of males and females. Though political philosophers in the past wrote of the equality of all humans, they generally referred to men only. With the suffragette movement of the early 1900s and the rise of feminism as a political and social movement in the 1960s demanding gender equality in terms of pay and opportunities, this irrational imbalance has been redressed in political philosophy.[22] The rise of feminism, as well as demands for equal treatment of racial minorities, shows the continuing importance of the value of equality for both political theory and political practice.

Social order is one of the values in political philosophy that is both necessary to secure other values and may contradict those values.[23] We can understand order as the absence of chaos and the presence of a recognized structure of power, responsibility, and liberty. Although this value may be taken for granted by Canadian students of politics in the twenty-first century, such is not the case for many people in the world today and certainly not for the political philosophers of earlier times. Much political philosophy was written at times of upheaval or turmoil in human society. While many welcomed the change, others felt that it threatened to replace established political, social, and economic structures with little more than chaotic anarchy. To Hobbes, this was the fundamental issue in political philosophy. He sought to establish the conditions by which human individuals would be protected from the ravages of civil war. Only with assured order would there be the possibility of human development in other areas such as industry, agriculture, or the arts.

social order
recognized structure of power, responsibility, and liberty

As the examination of political ideologies in Chapter 3 will show, order is a value of primary importance for the ideologies of conservatism and fascism,[24] but it can also be seen as a crucial prerequisite for more liberal theories. An emphasis on the value of order can change across time and space. In a post-conflict society, order will be a primary goal, but less attention will be given to it as the society stabilizes.

Security may also be a primary value for individuals and groups in society, depending on the political, economic, and social climate.[25] Closely related to order, security is a value that we tend to take for granted until we lose it or find it threatened. Prior to the terrorist attacks of 9/11, security was not an issue that gave the majority of Americans pause. Afterward, security rose to the top of the political agenda and was recognized by most people as a priority for

security
freedom from danger or injury

2.6   RISING VIOLENT CRIME AND THE CRISIS OF STATE LEGITIMACY IN CENTRAL AMERICA

Since the 1980s, when Central American states faced the turmoil of civil war, insurgency, guerrilla movements, and repressive regimes, the region has slowly been recovering and moving toward stable democratic government. However, beginning in the early twenty-first century, organized crime and violent gangs began to play an increasing role in the destabilization of these countries. By the late 2000s, the *maras* (gangs) in countries such as Guatemala posed a serious threat to the state's ability to govern its territory effectively and to maintain security and public order. Meanwhile, Mexico began a war on drug cartels operating in its territory. These cartels moved some of their operations into the relative havens offered by Central America's weak security institutions, thereby exacerbating the region's problem. Working with the *maras* and employing far more force and firepower than the local governments, the cartels have come to challenge the state as the dominant military force in several countries in the region. This challenge to the state's capacity to provide security for its citizens has in turn led to a crisis of legitimacy and growing doubts about the benefits of democratic elections in this part of the world.

© Roberto Carlos/Reuters/Corbis

Honduran special police stand over Mara Salvatrucha gang members in Tegucigalpa.

government. As time has passed and other priorities for the United States have arisen (such as the financial crisis of 2008–09 and the subsequent economic recession), the American political system has become more preoccupied with generating economic growth and prosperity and less concerned with security. In comparison, in many parts of Latin America (including Mexico and the countries of Central America), the question of personal security has dominated political debates in recent years as levels of violence and kidnapping have soared with the onset of drug-related violence and insurgency.

progress
advancement in society toward a better and improved state of affairs; an integral element of liberal political theory

Progress is spurred by the belief that a better society is possible through the nurturing and development of a state of affairs in order to improve conditions and advantages.[26] The belief aspect of progress is significant because at the core is the confidence that the goal of a better life is obtainable. Belief in progress is essentially optimistic, suggesting that betterment comes through the passage of time and is buffered by scientific knowledge, which allows us increased control over our destiny and an improved understanding of the human condition. Inherent in progress is a recognizably elevated outlook on the world. This is in the tradition of liberal humanism, which regards all reform and social movement as part of the effort to release humans from the oppressive nature of superstition and seeks to create an environment of controlled improvement.

We have to be careful, though, when we talk about progress. What some see as a step forward may be viewed with suspicion and fear by others. For example, in the nineteenth century, European cultures firmly believed that they were bringing progress and enlightenment to Africa through colonization; we can now appreciate the costs of that idea. In the contemporary world, the replacement of traditional social and cultural arrangements by more "modern" systems, an integral part of globalization, may be seen as progress but is not without its negative aspects. Although we would not necessarily want to live in those more traditional societies, their disappearance often means the loss of cultures, languages, and social diversity that may have direct costs for the individuals in those societies and unforeseen long-term costs for us all.

What's more, the link between progress, technology, and control over our destiny has become all the more complicated in recent decades with the rise of genetic engineering and biotechnology, which adds to the debate about what kind of progress we want. In some parts of the world, such as China, political elites resist pressure from Western governments who seek to promote human rights and democracy (concepts that we would identify as being closely related to progress) by arguing that such values are essentially Western, and that "Asian values" should be protected in Asian societies. This cultural relativism is an aspect of international relations and comparative politics that is important for us to remember as we study other political systems and societies.

Justice is an intractable issue in political life, since the many will always be governed by the few. The result is concern about the possibility of abuse in the political system. A just system, then, is one where activities are sought in the interest of the community as a whole, not simply the limited interests of the political governors. Justice ought not to be in the interest of those in political power alone; it embodies the exercise of legal authority in the interests of the political community—the pursuit of the equitable and legitimate aspirations of the ruled.

justice
state of affairs involving the maintenance of what is right and fair within a society

However, we must recognize how the understanding of justice varies across time and space. Justice acquires a different meaning depending on the society, its prevailing preferences, and the particular political order that governs it. Justice can be understood variously as equivalent to equal treatment, the maintenance of order and stability, or the provision of a minimum level of economic opportunity for individuals.

There are three senses of justice that require discussion here. First, the concept of justice is most commonly associated with legal affairs. We say that a legal outcome is just if we believe that fairness has prevailed, all relevant evidence has been taken into consideration, and the individuals or groups concerned have received what they deserve. A modern Western legal system is considered just if every individual receives equal treatment in the eyes of the law, regardless of race, wealth, religion, or social position. In that sense, legal justice is closely associated with the value of equality.

social justice
equitable distribution
of goods and values
in society

duties
related to rights;
responsibilities to
protect rights

economic justice
redistribution of economic
resources from certain
groups in society to others

liberty
freedom from despotic
control

freedom
ability to act without
constraint

negative liberty
areas of activity in which
governments do not
interfere and an individual
is free to choose

The second meaning of justice in its political and social sense is something quite different. It has its roots in the political philosophy of the ancient Greeks and concerns not the legal relationships within society but the structure of society itself. When we talk of **social justice** in contemporary political discourse, we refer to the same issue: Upon which principles do we structure our society?

The most famous discussion of justice in this sense was written by Plato, who lived in Athens from 427–347 BCE. Although his ideas on the division of responsibilities and **duties** in society seem alien to modern Western readers, Plato nonetheless put forward a convincing case as to why his model was just. He claimed that it was appropriate for each individual to carry out the role in society to which he or she was best suited by his or her nature. By doing so, he argued, individuals would be able to develop their best capacities and society as a whole would benefit from the appropriate application of their talents. Later philosophers, while developing markedly different models of justice, have continued to structure these models based on their understandings of what human nature is. Some, such as Hobbes and Locke, have chosen the concept of fundamental human equality, while others, such as Marx, have built on their understanding of humans as creative beings.

The third type of justice is **economic justice**, which refers to the economic system in a country, region, or the entire world. Again, economic justice can take on various meanings, based on efficiency, equality, or equity, that is, the hierarchy of values chosen by the political authorities concerned. The notion of redistribution (taking economic resources from certain groups in society and redistributing them to others) is commonly associated with economic justice. Most often this concept involves redistributing wealth from the rich to the poor, but it is possible for the opposite to happen. Over the past 50 years, there has been an ongoing redistribution of wealth from society to the ruling classes in many developing countries, often through corruption and exploitation. Marx held that capitalism was responsible for a redistribution of wealth that led to the increasing impoverishment of the masses and growing wealth for the capitalist classes.

Such debates about economic systems and the idea of economic justice have been among the most important political issues of the second half of the twentieth century, both nationally and globally. Even within the countries of the developed world, we see a rising discontent with the growing gap between the ultra rich and the rest of society. The Occupy Wall Street (OWS) movement in 2011 attracted support and copycat movements across the world as disadvantaged groups expressed their outrage at the massive salaries and bonuses that continue to be paid to financial executives despite the fact that their actions led to the worldwide financial crisis of 2008–09.

Liberty is one of the most important values in political studies and is often used interchangeably with the word **freedom**. In everyday usage we talk about the liberty to be able to do certain things not prohibited by law. But liberty is a more complex concept in political studies. The philosopher Isaiah Berlin identified two forms of liberty, one negative and the other positive. He talks of **negative liberty** as being central to the philosophies of Anglo-Saxon political

2.7 ECONOMIC JUSTICE AND THE WELFARE STATE

The notion that a minimum standard of living should be provided for all citizens, regardless of their income, is well established in political theory. But it didn't become a reality in most developed countries until the second half of the twentieth century and still has not been achieved in any developing state. Although examples of state-run pension plans occur throughout history, the origins of the modern welfare state lie in the United Kingdom's 1942 Beveridge Report, in which Sir William Beveridge outlined the need for a comprehensive state program to address the terrible problems facing the poor. By providing adequate income, a national health service, a comprehensive education system, subsidized housing, and full employment, the state could overcome these problems. Beveridge's ideas resulted in the creation of the welfare state in the UK, a model that was copied in many other countries around the world.

During the economic crises of 2008–09, the welfare state came to be seen as crucial to protecting ordinary citizens from financial collapse. Unemployment benefits, public health care, and social security acted as a safety net for those individuals who could no longer support themselves. However, as governments around the world continue to struggle with the lasting effects of the crises, the social contract of the welfare state itself has increasingly come under threat. Governments facing budget deficits and rapidly rising national debts are now trying to reduce expenditures and

Popperfoto/Getty Images

Sir William Beveridge was the founder of the modern welfare state in the UK, arguing that it was necessary to fight the "five giants": want, disease, ignorance, squalor, and idleness.

thus ensure the long-term financial health of their countries. In many cases, this means cutting back on social services, government payrolls, and expensive public health programs. The future of the welfare state remains to be seen.

thinkers and the kind of liberty that we refer to most often. The negative part of this term means the areas of activity in which governments do not interfere, where an individual is free to choose. An example of a negative liberty is the freedom to choose one's lifestyle. It is obvious that this notion of liberty is closely associated with the idea of rights.

Positive liberty, on the other hand, is understood as the freedom to achieve one's full potential.[27] This is the kind of liberty included in the political philosophy of Jean-Jacques Rousseau. It involves being free from human desires and the destructive or divisive emotions that prevent human individuals and human society from reaching their true ability. Freedom from desires could take the form of developing beyond greed, racism, or laziness, or it could involve being provided with the economic means, education, and guidance to be able

positive liberty
freedom to achieve one's full potential

to escape such feelings. Positive liberty reserves a significant area of activity for the state to restrain, re-educate, or engage in programs of redistribution so that individuals can be free from their own harmful impulses or have the economic means to be able to fulfill their potential.

These two forms of liberty seem to be diametrically opposed: it would be impossible to maximize positive liberty while maximizing negative liberty. However, it is possible for them to coexist and it is not difficult to find many examples of both types in contemporary Western society. For example, many societies hold the freedom of expression (a negative liberty) as sacred while promoting programs of positive discrimination (positive liberty) in the workplace. Governments defend the right to privacy while using progressive taxation systems to fund health care and **welfare** systems. In fact, economic redistribution and the welfare state are the clearest examples we have of positive liberty.

One last point needs to be made about liberty. Modern political philosophers such as Locke made a distinction between liberty and **licence**.[28] The former concerns personal freedom but is limited, whereas the latter suggests unlimited freedom to do as one pleases. To exercise liberty, an individual must not compromise the liberty or rights of others. In this way, liberty carries with it responsibilities and, some have argued, duties (see below).[29] The concept of rights, as mentioned earlier in this chapter, is intimately linked to the concept of liberty. Moreover, it is a concept that is commonly used in everyday political, legal, social, and economic discourse.[30] We hear criminal suspects on television shows claiming that they "know their rights" and that they have a "right to a fair trial." All adults over the age of 18 in Canada claim the right to vote. American citizens claim a right to free speech. But what are rights? How do we know that they exist?

Rights can take different forms. There are civil rights as well as human rights. Civil rights are defined particularly, depending on the political and legal system concerned. Human rights, on the other hand, are commonly considered to be universal, inalienable (that is, they cannot be given up or transferred) and are generally held to be the most precious and basic of human assets. Nonetheless, it would be difficult to say that any rights are absolute or predetermined. Even human rights are defined differently in different times and places. They are essentially creations of a particular political system and age. The universal right to be free from slavery, for example, took shape over the course of the nineteenth century and was finally enshrined in 1948 in the United Nations Universal Declaration of Human Rights. Women's right to vote was not universal in Western political systems until the twentieth century. Women in Canada were first given the right to vote in Manitoba in 1916, and the Canadian Parliament passed a limited franchise act for women the next year, expanding rights in 1919. Most provinces followed suit, but Quebec did not grant women voting rights until 1940. The United States passed the 19th Amendment in 1919 (ratified in 1920), allowing women the vote. In Switzerland, women were not permitted to vote until 1971.

Thus, rights are intimately linked to political and social development. This realization brought the nineteenth-century English philosopher Jeremy Bentham to claim that rights were "nonsense on stilts," that is, a meaningless

welfare
legislation or social action taken to provide citizens with physical, financial, health, or other assistance

licence
unlimited freedom to do as one pleases

idea elevated so that it appears much more important than it really is. It would be difficult to publicly defend such a position today, but it shows that, no matter how universal we consider rights to be, they are nonetheless temporal. It is only if we believe that rights are given by a deity or nature that they take on a universal and eternal character.

Philosophies that focus on individual rights have been criticized as being atomistic, based on selfishness, and destructive of the idea of community. A focus on the individual, it has been stated, ignores another more important aspect of human life, namely that we are social animals. One response to this criticism is that rights are but one side of a delicate balance in political life. Along with the possession of rights goes the need for duties. It can be said that duties are the corollary of rights. Whenever an individual or group holds a right to a particular freedom or resource, there exists a concomitant duty on the part of someone else to provide or protect that right. But the relationship between rights and duties is more complex than this simple equation. It has been argued that possessing rights in society carries with it a duty to respect those of others and to contribute to society as a whole in some form (e.g. economic, cultural, or functional). By stressing that individual duties are inextricably linked to individual rights, it is possible to maintain a healthy respect for the individual, as well as an emphasis on human community.

Duties in the contemporary world range from tax payment to respect for the law and compliance with the military draft in times of war. Therefore, duties are an integral element in society and, just as our rights depend on others' respect of our freedoms, so we must show the same respect to them. As a *quid pro quo* (an equal exchange), our failure to respect the rights of others may result in the loss of our own rights. This kind of social contract between the members of society is enforced by the state, which plays a key role in implementing laws, particularly to defend those who cannot defend themselves.

As noted earlier in this chapter, many political philosophers have focused not on the importance of the individual but on the social nature of human beings. To philosophers such as Plato and Rousseau, the individual was less than human when separated from a society and community. Such philosophers believed that a political system should be structured so as to preserve, protect, and nourish the needs of the community ahead of those of the individual. To put it in Rousseau's terms, the general will must come before any particular or private desire. We will learn more about these philosophers and their ideas in the next chapter.

Related to these philosophers' theory is the concept of **community**.[31] Community consists of the social, political, cultural, and economic ties that bind individuals to one another. To some extent, tradition plays an important role, though community can be preserved or even extended by changing established practices. Community is a context, an environment in which human individuals develop their particular talents, capabilities, and (perhaps most importantly) their identities. Without that environment, human beings cannot develop their true potential, or even their very humanity. In those philosophies that emphasize the value of community, duties and positive liberty play a central role.

community
social, political, cultural, and economic ties that bind individuals to one another

2.8 COMMUNITY AND THE INDIVIDUAL

One of the most important political questions in today's world is the relationship between the individual and the community. As you will see in Chapter 4, liberal approaches to politics hold the individual as sacred and work toward expanding the area of individual freedom. This perspective impacts directly on our conceptions of society and community. What responsibilities does the individual human being have to the society in which he or she lives? To what extent does that individual depend upon society and community for his or her well-being? What, ultimately, is the link between rights and duties?

As noted elsewhere in this chapter, many believe that humans cannot be separated from the societies in which they exist, that being human depends upon the families, groups, and nations in which we live. Certainly it is difficult to imagine life without the company of others. But where does our responsibility to the group as a whole begin and end? Should we be willing to sacrifice personal freedoms so that the lives of others are improved? Or should personal freedoms be held as sacred?

In Britain in the late 1990s, a debate about anti-social behaviour arose. The government of Tony Blair responded by creating a new form of legal provision whereby people engaging in public drunkenness, lewd acts in public spaces, vandalism, or begging could be brought before a magistrate and prohibited from performing such acts in the future by threat of fines or imprisonment. These anti-social behaviour orders (ASBOs), primarily directed toward youth, generated enormous social and political controversy and are currently under review by the present government. However, ASBOs received significant support from the segments of British society who look back to a more peaceful and supposedly harmonious past in which young people "knew their place" and "respected their elders."

Community is an important concept in politics for other reasons. Through a community we gain both rights and responsibilities, as already discussed. But we also find ourselves becoming part of a whole that is bigger than the sum of its parts. This means that we take on a commitment to a set of values that will define and limit our behaviour as individuals within the community. Think of the values that new immigrants to Canada pledge to respect and it becomes clear that the concept of community is central to understanding politics.

identity
a person's understanding and expression of their individuality or group membership

Through these values, it can be said that a community has a certain **identity**, something that helps to define it and sets it apart from other communities. As part of the community, we take on that identity for ourselves. Just as being part of the community in your hometown forms part of your identity, being part of your university community gives it a new element. Identity is, as we will see in the next section, an important factor.

Identity

In an earlier section of this chapter, we talked about national and regional identities. But identity has recently become an increasingly important concept in political studies in many ways. Ask yourself the question, What is my identity? You will find that it has multiple dimensions: you may be a woman, daughter, sister, student, Liberal, Canadian, environmentalist, and feminist or a man, son, brother, father, Italian-Canadian, athlete, hockey fan, and vegan. Identity not only involves the understanding that each of us has our individuality and group membership, but it also includes the ways in which we express those elements in society.

Individual identity is what marks each of us as unique, whereas group identity is what ties us to others. Cultural or ethnic identity, for example, is important because it makes us part of a broader social group. What is important to note here, however, is that both individual and group identities are defined in relation to the society in which we live and operate. Our understanding of what it means to be a man or a woman, masculine or feminine, or French or English Canadian are all concepts that most of us define within parameters set by our society. In this way, we can say that identity is "socially constructed." This does not mean that individuals play no role in defining their own identity but that they do so within an existing social, cultural, political, and economic structure that, to a greater or lesser extent, shapes their ideas.

Clearly, our identity is partly constructed by our interactions with society, but we also have the right and ability to define ourselves in the terms we see fit. Thus, how one person defines himself or herself as a liberal may be very different from how another liberal individual sees himself or herself. The same could apply to many different identities, which gets us into the debate between essentialism and non-essentialism. These theories ask whether there are absolute, fundamental traits that define us (as men, women, Canadians, liberals, conservatives) or whether the reality is much more diverse.

In contemporary Canada, identity politics are perhaps more important than ever before. The concept of identity is no longer restricted to questions of party affiliation, ethnic background, religion, or geographical location (as it was, say, in the 1950s) but now embraces questions of gender, sexual orientation, diet, art and the media, and the environment. A prime example of identity politics in modern societies exists in the lesbian, gay, bisexual, and transgender (LGBT) movement. Embracing a wide range of advocacy issues, including same-sex marriage, the age of consent for same-sex activity, adoption laws, and military services, the LGBT movement has become an influential transnational social campaign and a powerful voice in political and social debate across North America, Europe, and in parts of Asia and Latin America.

Conclusion

The purpose of this chapter was to acquaint you with some of the most important terms and concepts in political studies and to demonstrate their significance and relevance in the real world of politics. This approach initiates you into the specialized language of political studies and creates a common language among you as a group of students, allowing you to enter into more fruitful debates and discussions. These concepts will be essential tools for you throughout this course and your continuing research in political studies, but they are also relevant outside of this setting. These terms will appear to you continuously in everyday life, in the press, on television, and above all in parliamentary debates and political disputes. As we progress through this textbook and this course, you will find yourself using these terms more frequently, but it will be important for you to refer back to this chapter to check the meaning of and connections between them. You should discuss them with your classmates to fully appreciate the diversity and culturally specific understandings that they possess. As with everything in our field of study, these concepts are constant sources of controversy and debate.

Self-Assessment Questions

1. What is the difference between the state and the nation? How does this difference apply to Canada?
2. In what ways can you exercise your powers of agency in the political sphere?
3. What should the limits of state power be? Do you think that the Canadian state has too much power, too little, or just the right amount? How has the Canadian government abused its power?
4. When does the legitimacy of the state come into question? Does democracy automatically confer legitimacy on the state? Why or why not?
5. Research a particular government policy and find out what pieces of legislation have come out of it. Who proposed the policy and who did the legislation benefit?
6. Should society give more emphasis to freedom, equality, security, or some other value? How should these various values be balanced? Are there some values that should always take priority, or does this depend upon time, place, and current events? Give examples to support your answer.
7. How can we balance the rights of individuals with the welfare of the community?
8. What is the relationship between rights and duties in your daily life? How does this relationship apply in the world of politics?
9. What identities do you possess? To what extent were these identities given to you and to what extent have you defined them yourself?

Weblinks

Amnesty International
www.amnesty.org

Democracy Online Game
www.positech.co.uk/democracy/democracy1.html

Democracy Watch
www.dwatch.ca

Department of Justice Canada
www.justice.gc.ca

Human Rights Watch
www.hrw.org

Universal Declaration of Human Rights
www.un.org/en/documents/udhr

Further Reading

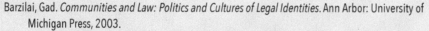

Barzilai, Gad. *Communities and Law: Politics and Cultures of Legal Identities*. Ann Arbor: University of
    Michigan Press, 2003.
Berlin, Isaiah. *Four Essays on Liberty*. New York: Oxford University Press, 1990.
Calhoun, Craig. "Social Theory and the Politics of Identity." In *Social Theory and Identity Politics*, edited by
    Craig Calhoun, 9–36. Oxford: Blackwell, 1994.
Gaus, Gerald F. *Political Concepts and Political Theories*. Boulder, CO: Westview Press, 2000.
Gunther, Richard, José Ramón Montero, and Juan J. Linz, eds. *Political Parties: Old Concepts and New
    Challenges*. Oxford: Oxford University Press, 2002.
Heywood, Andrew. *Political Ideas and Concepts: An Introduction*. New York: St. Martin's Press, 1994.
Huntington, Samuel P. *Political Order in Changing Societies*. New Haven, CT: Yale University Press, 1968.
Inglehart, Ronald. *Human Values and Social Change: Findings from the Values Surveys*. Leiden, The
    Netherlands, and Boston: Brill, 2003.
Kenny, Michael. *The Politics of Identity: Liberal Political Theory and the Dilemmas of Difference*. Cambridge:
    Polity Press, 2004.
Keohane, Robert O., and Joseph S. Nye. *Power and Interdependence: World Politics in Transition*. 2nd edn.
    Cambridge: HarperCollins, 1989.
Lukes, Steven. *Power: A Radical View*. 2nd edn. Houndmills, UK: Palgrave Macmillan, in association with the
    British Sociological Association, 2005.
Migdal, Joel S. *State in Society: Studying How States and Societies Transform and Constitute One Another*.
    Cambridge: Cambridge University Press, 2001.
Miller, David. *Liberty*. New York: Oxford University Press, 1991.
Mingst, Karen A. *Essentials of International Relations*. 3rd edn. New York: W.W. Norton, 2004.
Putnam, Robert. *Bowling Alone: The Collapse and Revival of American Community*. New York: Simon &
    Schuster, 2000.
Richter, Melvin. *The History of Political and Social Concepts: A Critical Introduction*. Oxford: Oxford University
    Press, 1995.
Weber, Max. *Weber: Political Writings*. Edited and translated by Peter Lassman and Ronald Speirs.
    Cambridge: Cambridge University Press, 1895/1994.

News Clips

Visit the companion website for *Politics: An Introduction*, 2nd edn, to access news clips related to the
content of this chapter.

3 Political Thought, Philosophy, and Ideology

◀ In *The Social Contract*, political philosopher Jean-Jacques Rousseau—immortalized in this statue in Geneva—sought to establish his concept of the general will as the basis for legitimate government.

Photo: Fabrice Coffrini/AFP/Getty Images

LEARNING OBJECTIVES

After reading this chapter, you will be able to

- appreciate the importance and place of political philosophy and ideology in the study of politics;

- explain the relationship between theory and reality in political studies;

- understand political philosophy as an ongoing dialogue of ideas across the centuries;

- identify the major political ideologies and differentiate between them; and

- recognize many of the most important political philosophers of the past two and a half millennia.

Introduction

In this chapter, we will discuss the importance of abstract political thinking and why it matters for our understanding of political life and activity in the real world. In doing so, we will cover the most important philosophies, ideologies, and thinkers of the last 2500 years, which may seem a daunting prospect. But we should view the history of political philosophy as a vibrant and exciting area of study in which we can participate in debates and dialogues that have fascinated human beings for millennia. The systems of thought described in the pages that follow have had a huge impact on the development of political activity throughout history, and many are still relevant in both policy and academic circles in the twenty-first century.

Although the scope of the area means that we cannot go into great detail about these philosophical figures and their ideas, this chapter will serve as an introduction to the subfield of political philosophy and will hopefully inspire you to engage in further research. The chapter begins with a discussion of what political philosophies and ideologies are, so that you will be able to determine the significance of the ideas discussed. There then follows a survey of the most important ideologies that a political studies student will encounter, focusing on both their political and economic aspects. Lastly, the chapter explores the relevance of ideas, philosophies, and ideologies for the everyday business of politics. Throughout the chapter, several boxes are dedicated to individual political philosophers and thinkers to give you an idea of their lives, contributions, and impact.

What Is Political Philosophy?

Before addressing this fundamental issue, we must ask another question: What is **philosophy**? The word comes from the ancient Greek word φιλοσοφία (*philosophia*), meaning "love of knowledge." Philosophy concerned investigations into the nature of life and its constituent elements. The early philosophers of the Western world, such as Heraclitus and Pythagoras, conducted theoretical investigations into the essence of Nature itself. In that sense, they conducted an early form of natural science but one that relied less on practical tests than on the forming of ideas and connections between them. Philosophy is thus a search for understanding.

Political philosophy can be said to follow a similar logic. It is an investigation into the nature of politics, one that seeks understanding of things political. It is an endeavour to understand the nature of political life, not just at a given time or place but also across the spectrum of human experience. In other words, it attempts to be ageless. That said, political philosophy is not so much a form of inquiry that tries to understand the mechanics of politics and political systems as it is one that represents a creative process of analyzing what happens in the world of politics and attempts to construct modes of improving that world. In this way, political philosophy seeks to understand more than just the nature of politics. Political philosophers also attempt to explain the significance of political phenomena in order to improve our understanding of politics and to better design solutions for the problems that mark human life and society. It is therefore both descriptive and prescriptive.

This explanation implies, quite correctly, that there is a definite and inescapable link between political philosophy and the real world of politics. This connection is two-dimensional. Political thinkers have always held that their philosophy must have some root in the realities of politics, social interaction, human nature, and ultimately Nature itself. If this link is somehow lost, the work of philosophers would be useless, for their ideas would be too far removed from the real world and would probably be meaningless as well. Thomas Hobbes, for example, whose ideas are examined later in this chapter, related his political philosophy to his understanding of human nature in both its physical and psychological meanings. He saw humans as selfish, aggressive, and often violent individuals. Jean-Jacques Rousseau, on the other hand, held a very different conception of human nature, one that viewed humans as being essentially peaceful, empathetic creatures; he therefore produced a body of theory that stands in stark contrast to Hobbes's work. What's more, political philosophies are shaped by the times in which they are created. Plato's concerns for a declining Athenian city-state, Hobbes's desire to see an end to the social and political chaos of the English Civil War, and Karl Marx's reaction to the horrors of **capitalism** in nineteenth-century England each shaped the analysis of the nature of politics and of human society.

Yet political philosophy is much more than an exercise in studying political and social realities. It is linked to the real world in another, more creative and timeless fashion. For political philosophy not only tells us *what is*, but also *what*

philosophy
study of questions about existence, knowledge, ethics, justice, and morality based on logical reasoning rather than empirical methods

capitalism
economic system in which production and distribution of goods rely on private capital and investment

Utopian
idealized place or system, an ideally perfect society; individual or approach aspiring to impractical perfection

ought to be. This is not merely a **Utopian** enterprise that seeks to create a perfect world.[1] Because of its basis in the perceived realities of human nature and society, political philosophy seeks to define the political conditions that will create the best possible society. There are many examples of this kind of endeavour in the history of political philosophy, from Plato's *Republic* to John Rawls's *A Theory of Justice*. Each examines the basic conditions surrounding human life and seeks to correct the failings of the real world by designing specific political structures. An excellent example is the political and economic theory of Marx. He based his ideas for the improvement of society directly on his observations and analysis of the social, political, and economic conditions that prevailed in nineteenth-century capitalist societies. Without this information, Marx's ideas

3.1 PLATO (427–347 BCE)

The city-state of ancient Athens was a highly developed society that generated great advances not only in the areas of the arts and sciences but also in political and social thought. Plato, a teacher in the city's academy, was the first thinker to write down his thoughts on politics and philosophy in a comprehensive fashion. He wrote his most famous work, *The Republic*, as a narrative between his teacher, Socrates, and other prominent Athenians. This format means that we are do not know whether the ideas conveyed in this book are those of Plato or his master. Either way, *The Republic* exists as both a work of philosophy and a record of the debates about the political future of ancient Athens. However, as some have put it, *The Republic* is a "city in speech" and serves as an ideal type that can be juxtaposed with reality. It is also a work of political philosophy that transcends the particular circumstances of time and place.

The Republic is a book about justice in its broadest, most philosophical sense of "what is right." Plato proposes social and political justice through a state organized according to individuals' capabilities and personalities. Those who are naturally equipped to be strong and courageous should engage in militaristic functions; those who excel at an art or craft should devote themselves to such activities. Most important, however, those individuals who are best equipped to be philosophical should become the rulers of the state, for they best understand the idea of justice. The image of Plato's republic is of a rather repressive, controlling state, one that does not allow for much personal freedom

Plato's ideas about the role of government and the good society are still debated today.

and is unappealing to contemporary students of politics. Yet it would be wrong to judge it by today's standards. Plato was attempting to find permanent solutions to the problem of political order, and his proposal is an ideal, probably unachievable, form of political organization. In outlining such an ideal, Plato gives us the first offering in a debate about the just or good state that continues to the present day.

on the need for revolution and the creation of a more just society would have been baseless.[2]

The History of Political Thought

As we have already noted, it is important that we recognize that the history of political philosophy goes back several thousand years. In this sense, political philosophy can be seen as a debate across the ages and across cultures and geographic space. This view reinforces the idea that political philosophy is really about timeless questions concerning political life. Such political inquiry took place across the world. Chinese, Japanese, and Islamic branches of political philosophy are fascinating comparisons to the Western spheres, and other traditions such as Aboriginal and Meso-American thought present compelling alternatives. This chapter focuses mainly on the history of Western philosophy, due to the influence that it has had on Western political systems and movements. That history begins with the classical philosophers of ancient Greece, such as Plato and Aristotle. Their work (and that of their fellow philosophers) in investigating the nature of politics, political life, and good government created the bases for future inquiry and set the tone for the kind of questioning that

3.2   ARISTOTLE (384–322 BCE)

Aristotle was the intellectual inheritor of Plato's philosophy, yet his work is quite different. A student of Plato, Aristotle was concerned less with proposing an ideal state than with the practical application of philosophy to the problems of everyday politics. In this way, we can say that Aristotle was a philosopher who believed in the politics of the possible. In addition, Aristotle can be seen as the founder of the scientific study of politics, for a large part of his work is concerned with classifying and rating different political systems in an attempt to determine the best possible organization of the state.

Although Aristotle's approach to political philosophy is very practical and scientific, it also seeks to establish a link between ethics and politics, to seek the "good." Aristotle's two most famous works, *The Nicomachean Ethics* and *The Politics*, examine the two areas separately, but there is little doubt that he sees an inescapable connection between them. Indeed, the only difference between ethics and politics for Aristotle is that ethics concerns what is right and good for the individual, whereas politics concerns what is right and good for the community. Aristotle had a clear idea that the needs of the community came before those of the individual, and for him the height of rational behaviour was public action, or participation in the running of the city-state. What is more, a good individual can prosper only in a good community; therefore, politics is fundamental to ethics and vice versa. Although Aristotle favoured aristocracy—a city-state ruled by a select group of men who dedicate themselves to the good life both for themselves and the city—he argued that it would face problems in the real world; he supported a system of mixed government, combining elements of aristocracy, monarchy, and democracy.

Aristotle also explicitly recognized the importance of economics in the organization of political systems. A "good" economic system must allow individuals to acquire wealth, for this is a natural inclination in humans. People seek wealth because it allows them, in turn, to acquire goods that satisfy their natural needs and desires.

would mark Western political philosophy for the next two millennia or more. Essentially, the Greeks asked simple questions about politics that have produced incredibly complex and diverse answers. Questions about justice, stability, and the relationship between individuals and the state have always featured strongly.

After the classical period, we move on to the medieval political philosophers. During this time, political inquiry in the Western world was driven by questions concerning the relationship between political life and Christianity. Best exemplified by the thought of Thomas Aquinas, medieval political philosophy placed the requirements of theology above the requirements of human needs. Aquinas made two major contributions. He introduced the medieval Christian world to Aristotle's theories (which had for a long time been preserved only in the Muslim world), and he sought to bring Christianity and politics into harmony. His "scholastic" method, using deductive reasoning, was copied by political philosophers for centuries after.

"Modern" political philosophy can be said to begin with the work of the Renaissance thinkers, such as Niccolò Machiavelli, who applied a purely secular, non-religious approach to politics. By examining the nature and use of political

3.3   DEDUCTIVE AND INDUCTIVE METHODS

The medieval philosopher and theologian St. Thomas Aquinas used the deductive method of analysis. In very simple terms, this method starts with a hypothesis, or proposed explanation. Based on predictions of the outcome, observations are then made to support the hypothesis. This practice differs from the inductive approach, which begins with the observations or experiments, leads to generalizations, and, finally, a hypothesis or theory.

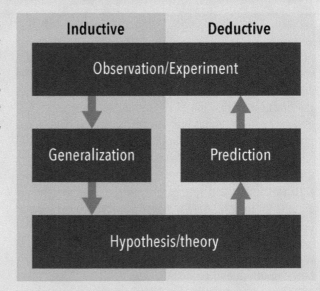

Figure 3.1   Deductive and Inductive Methods

3.4 NICCOLÒ MACHIAVELLI (1469–1527)

From Aristotle through to St. Augustine and the Christian political philosophers, there was a perennial commitment to combining ethics and morality with politics. The work of Niccolò Machiavelli marks a dramatic break from that tradition. Machiavelli, who was intimately involved in the politics of the Italian city-states of the late fifteenth and early sixteenth centuries, put forward a new political philosophy based on political expediency, where ethics and ideals played a secondary role to the pursuit of power and control. This philosophy, known as **political realism**, has been one of the most important theoretical and analytical approaches in the study of politics ever since.

It should not be thought that politics had never before been based on these principles—we know that governments have behaved in such a way since the time of the ancient Greeks and probably earlier. However, Machiavelli was the first philosopher to defend them explicitly as a basis for sound government. As with most philosophers, Machiavelli's work can be understood and interpreted on two levels: as an attempt to find solutions to the most important political problems of his time (in this case, the internal divisions of the Italian city-states) and as a prescription for political action that would provide for sound government regardless of time and place.

Machiavelli argued that there should be a definite separation of ideals and morality from politics. Politics should instead be guided by an examination of human behaviour. If governors, or (as he prefers) princes, understand human nature and behaviour, they will be better able to formulate policies to rule effectively and consolidate their power. He proposed that it is better for a prince to be feared than loved by his people, though this must be achieved without inspiring popular hatred of the government. Machiavelli's approach to the study of politics can be seen as the beginning of modern political philosophy.

power, Machiavelli opened the way for other thinkers, such as Hobbes, to examine the basis of power and its use in creating a stable form of government. A number of philosophers who focused on the question of rights and liberty and founded the liberal branch of political theory followed. The influence of thinkers such as John Locke and Jean-Jacques Rousseau is remarkable: their ideas are still quoted in political debates today.

The modern era is said to continue until the early twentieth century and to incorporate the ideas of Adam Smith, John Stuart Mill, and Karl Marx. These thinkers show the variety and diversity of political philosophy in the modern period by defending and critiquing capitalism, arguing for liberty and tolerance, and proposing alternative modes of production and government, respectively.

In the twentieth century, the contemporary period of political philosophy began. Again we see huge diversity. The work of thinkers such as John Rawls and Robert Nozick reflected many of the classic questions of political philosophy concerning good government and the community, whereas the postmodern movement in political thought has focused on a more critical approach to philosophy, questioning the origins of our ideas and beliefs and arguing for a more social constructivist understanding of politics. **Social constructivism** argues that values and beliefs are the result of particular social relations, processes, and realities and that it is therefore difficult, if not impossible, to establish any objective concept of what is good or just. In short, how have we arrived at what

political realism
approach to politics that emphasizes power and interests over ideas or social constructions

social constructivism
sociological and political meta-theory that explains the interactions between individual agents, their social groupings, and their environment

we "know"? Constructivism presents a critical perspective on knowledge and "truth." It is both a philosophical approach and a way of understanding political life that has acquired great importance in recent years in many branches of social and political studies.

How does political philosophy proceed or, to put it another way, how is it done? Essentially, political philosophy concerns the asking of questions and the proposing of answers to those questions. The questions are perennial: Are humans naturally good or bad? Should the community come before the individual? What should the extent of my liberty as an individual in human society be? When is a government action legitimate? What would life be like in the absence of government? How should wealth be divided among society's members? The answers to these questions, however, are particular to each philosopher. For example, Rousseau's response to the importance of the individual vis-à-vis the political community emphasizes the latter as an organic body that takes precedence over the former. Locke's answer focuses on the importance of individual liberty.

It is frequently stated that political philosophy constitutes a quest for the good life, the good society, and, of particular importance, the *just* society. Social justice is an ever-recurring theme throughout the history of political philosophy, but its meaning and form change from philosopher to philosopher. As the studies included in this chapter show, the Platonic or Socratic conception of justice is difficult to relate to the formulation of the same concept in Rousseau, just as Marx's conception of justice is wildly different from Locke's. This tells us that, to a large degree, these conceptions of justice depend upon the social, economic, and political conditions of their time and thus can be seen as socially constructed. It is important for us to remember that what is considered just and fair today may not be seen the same way in the future.

Norms established by political philosophers depend upon their own knowledge, personal experiences, and their individual societies, so the idea of "what is just" varies from century to century and from philosopher to philosopher. Understanding justice remains a goal of political philosophy up to the present time. As previously noted, political philosophy is not merely a descriptive exercise but an attempt to establish rules or ideals for political behaviour and political reality. Examining different philosophers' preferred definition of the just society is an intriguing exercise that can also help us to put our own conceptions in a broader context. One reason for the (often wide) variations in the conception of the just society is that philosophers have placed different emphases on various moral and political values. To some, such as Hobbes, the idea of social order is paramount. To others, such as Locke, the concept of liberty (formulated as freedom from interference by authority) receives the most attention, though not to the neglect of equality. For Rousseau, liberty is again fundamental, yet he defines the term less as freedom from interference and more as freedom from human passions and desires. For some philosophers, individualism and preserving individual liberties is central. Others believe that humans are incomprehensible apart from their social setting, and this

3.5 THOMAS HOBBES (1588-1679)

Whereas Machiavelli brought to the study of politics a determination to see things as they really are, Thomas Hobbes developed both a scientific approach that was unrivalled in his time and a body of philosophy that addressed the most basic of political questions, namely, how to avoid civil strife and the breakdown of society. His most important work, *Leviathan*, remains an essential text for contemporary students of political philosophy.

Hobbes's overriding focus in his writings was to establish the theoretical foundations for strong and enduring government. This concern arose from his having lived during the English Civil War and believing that this conflict resulted from a crisis of authority in the English political system. He compared the chaos of this period to an imaginary one in history before the creation of governments. He called this period the state of nature and insisted that it would be wholly unsuitable for human life. In essence, it is a state of war of all against all, where there is no room for industry, agriculture, or the arts and every human is at the mercy of others. Hobbes held firmly to the idea of the essential equality of human beings, in that none was so strong or clever that another could not kill him or her. The only way out of this terrible situation is the creation of a government, led by a sovereign, which would have almost unlimited power over its subjects. According to Hobbes, this would be the only way that peace would endure.

Though Hobbes granted his sovereign extreme rights, he also gave the office duties toward its subjects. The sovereign must provide peace and a system of law and order to maintain that peace if individuals are to give up the freedom they possess in the state of nature and subject themselves to an overarching power. It is important to note that, for

Hobbes's idea of the state was one of a supreme authority that could protect and control all members of society.

Hobbes, human beings are fundamentally rational in their behaviour. However, Hobbes goes further, stating that the sovereign must also provide for the basic necessities of the people. He is quite specific that, if the sovereign does not guarantee a basic standard of living, he or she will be unable to rule. Hobbes is quite practical about this point—unless the office of the sovereign takes care of its subjects, they are sure to rebel and return to the state of war. Hobbes's legacy was to show the importance of order before freedom as the prerequisite for all other goods in society.

understanding of humans as social animals guides them toward philosophies that emphasize the general over the particular or private good. Most influential political philosophers have recognized the importance of more than one value; what is key in determining the political systems they outline is the priority that each gives to a series of values. Is equality the most important value to be respected by society? Or should order be ranked higher than equality?

The differences between value hierarchies, and thus between political philosophies, have created a philosophical debate that stretches across not only geographical space but also time. Though it should not be thought that Hobbes was directly responding to Plato's ideas when he wrote *Leviathan*, he was joining in a dialogue about political ideas in which Plato had participated. The existence of these contrasting and sometimes conflicting philosophies creates the possibility for comparison and cross-fertilization of ideas for the student of political studies. It is this discourse that makes the study of political philosophies so challenging and at the same time rewarding: to view the collected wisdom of history's most eminent political thinkers and to evaluate their ideas on the basis of social and political conditions, both when these ideas were transcribed and in the present day. Just as important, this discourse makes political philosophy a living and vital part of political studies. The discussion that continues across the centuries ensures that politics is an ever-changing, always fascinating area of study, and you are encouraged to join in this intergenerational, inter-societal conversation.

Ideology

The words *ideology, ideological,* and *ideologue* have acquired a distinctly negative connotation in recent years. Seen as removed from the real world and considerations of practicality, the terms are used as insults in contemporary political discourse. But this use ignores a long history during which ideologies defined political reality and were a major influence on national and international history.

ideology
set or system of ideas that form the basis of a political or economic system and provide guidance and direction for political leadership

What constitutes an **ideology**? Essentially, it is a set of related, generally consistent ideas and beliefs that provides a basis for political action. Ideologies contain both descriptive and normative elements; that is, they contain interpretations of the world and statements of how it should be. They reflect particular hierarchies of values and help to shape people's perceptions and images of reality. One ideology might focus on the value of order over liberty while another might emphasize the value of efficiency over justice. By examining the hierarchies of values embodied in ideologies, we can identify the differences between them and also understand the impact they have on the world of politics.

Political (and economic) ideologies bear some resemblance to religions: they are more or less coherent belief systems (based on assumptions and preconceptions), can be proved neither wrong nor right (yet often contain normative judgments and assumptions), and provide a basis for human action. Religious inquiry was a common concern for the political thinkers of Greece, Rome, and medieval Europe, and it still finds some representation in political thought in contemporary Anglo-Saxon political systems. Ideologies, however, generally focus on the material and physical aspects of life, rather than the spiritual. Although politicians claim that they are focused on the challenges of the real world rather than belief systems, ideologies remain a fundamental aspect of political life because they frame the debates that dominate political

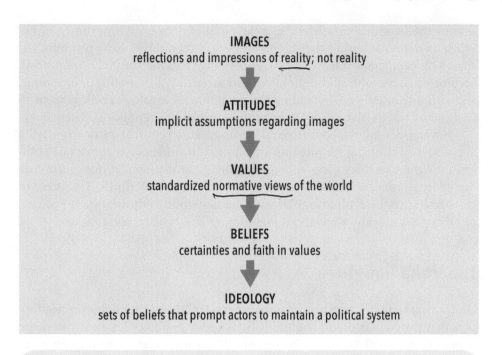

IMAGES
reflections and impressions of reality; not reality

⬇

ATTITUDES
implicit assumptions regarding images

⬇

VALUES
standardized normative views of the world

⬇

BELIEFS
certainties and faith in values

⬇

IDEOLOGY
sets of beliefs that prompt actors to maintain a political system

Figure 3.2   What Makes Ideologies?

and economic systems and guide political action, which in turn helps determine both political and economic reality (see the section on the relevance of ideas on p. 86). Most important, ideologies often drive political action and can bring conflict, progress, repression, or transformation. This is what really distinguishes an ideology from political theory: though its major ideas may come from a particular branch of political theory, an ideology is a call for action in the real world rather than merely an inquiry into the way things are.

Because ideologies are sometimes based on the philosophy of groups of thinkers, they can be said to follow schools of thought. Ideologies are by their nature divisive phenomena, in large part because different ideologies contain markedly different ideas, perceptions of reality, and prescriptions for the just or best political system. It is common, therefore, for ideological conflict to cause, or at the very least *colour*, many political debates. Ideologies, however, are not necessarily mutually exclusive. An individual, group, political party, or society can be both liberal and nationalist, as was the case of the United States during the **Cold War**. Similarly, a political grouping can combine nationalist economic policies with a socialist political plan of action. Ideologies are flexible and often blended with ideas taken from other schools of thought.

Furthermore, there is surprising variation to be found within ideologies; there may be individuals or groups within one school of thought who appear to be diametrically opposed. Indeed, the conflicts that develop between groups

Cold War
period of rhetorical, non-violent hostility; most often used as a reference to the period of 1945–91 and the relationship between the United States and the Soviet Union

sharing the same or similar ideologies can be among the most bitter and divisive. When two groups within the same school find themselves in opposition, the charge of "ideological heresy" becomes common and the conflict is intensified. Ideologies also evolve and both affect and are affected by political, economic, and social realities. Understanding the evolution of ideologies will help us to understand progressive as well as revolutionary change in political systems.

Having distinguished between ideology and political philosophy, the remainder of this chapter presents a treatment of different categories of political thought. The discussion is by no means exhaustive, but it does introduce the most significant political belief systems of modern times. Take care to cross-reference these philosophies with the descriptions of important political philosophers to learn more about their origins and broader implications.

Liberal Thought

Underlying both political and economic forms of liberal thought is an assumption that progress is possible and likely in human affairs.[3] Progress can mean many things to different people, but for liberals it implies an improvement of the human condition in terms of material possessions, intellect, or freedom. Thus it would be tempting to say that liberal thought is an optimistic system of political thought, one that expects progress and provides a political and economic program that should generate progress. However, it rests on an essentially negative perception of human nature, namely, that human beings are selfish and need laws and rights to live together in harmony. Liberal thought is also generally a diverse, often divergent, philosophy containing many different strands. As a result, it is quite possible for two liberals to be opposed over seemingly fundamental issues. In the past hundred years or so, some of the most complex and divisive ideological and political debates have occurred within the school of **liberalism**.

Liberal political thought finds its roots in the philosophy of Locke but has evolved since the seventeenth century into a diverse branch of philosophy incorporating the ideas of many political thinkers. It is founded on the notion that the individual is the basic unit of human society and must be held sacred. The human individual is believed to be a rational, self-interested creature whose desires and interests are of paramount importance. Individuals are to be held responsible for their own actions and credited for their own achievements. Society takes its nature from the way in which it protects and nurtures the individuals within.

Because of this focus on the individual, the values of liberty and rights—the means of protecting the individual from the state and other individuals—are central to liberal thought. **Self-determination**, the ability to decide one's own fate, is therefore vital. State laws should be directed toward maximizing the self-determination of each individual, the only limit being that such self-determination does not inhibit that of others.[4] Equality is also fundamental to liberalism but only in terms of liberty and rights, not of wealth or social status.

liberalism
view of politics that favours liberty, free trade, and moderate social and political change

self-determination
ability to act in free choice without external compulsion

3.6 JOHN LOCKE (1632–1704)

Just as Hobbes viewed the experience of the English Civil War as a crisis of authority, John Locke saw the same event as stemming from a lack of legitimacy on the part of the English monarchy. This perspective coloured Locke's approach to political philosophy, and we have come to associate him with a school of thought that demands legitimacy from government. In Locke lie the roots of modern liberalism, in which the concept of consent is central.

In his most famous work, *Two Treatises of Government*, Locke's understanding of the state of nature was markedly different from that of Hobbes. Locke saw it as being more peaceful but still inconvenient and certainly unproductive. His idea of human equality was also different from Hobbes's, for he held it to be equality of right, not mere equality of vulnerability. How did human beings come to leave this state of equality and create civil societies? Locke's answer exists in the notion of consent; he argued that, for a political system to be legitimate, the consent of the governed must have been obtained and be maintained.

Locke also used consent as a key concept in explaining economic systems. He argued that all humans were equal inheritors of the earth and therefore deserved equal access to its fruits and riches. How, then, did we reach a system of unequal acquisition and such great inequalities of wealth? He proposed that the original condition of equality was fundamentally inefficient; as time went on and populations expanded, it made more sense to combine individual landholdings so that more efficient agricultural methods and economies of scale might be employed. However, in order for people to legitimately transfer their equal rights to access to the land, Locke supposed that they gave their consent.

© North Wind Picture Archives / Alamy

Many consider John Locke the father of liberalism. A philosopher and physician, Locke presented many of the fundamentals of liberal thought.

Being rational individuals, the only way in which they would agree would be if their condition were equal to or better after the transfer than before. For Locke, then, unequal acquisition is legitimate only if the poor are better off than they would be if the transfer of their equal right to the earth had never occurred. The protection of their property, the rule of law, and good government are the focus of Locke's emphasis on what we would call negative liberty.

In this regard, equality also concerns equality of the opportunity to exercise preferences but not equality of outcomes. This type of equality is of particular importance with regard to economic liberalism.

It is important to identify two strands of liberalism that are directly connected with the two meanings of liberty. Lockean, or classical, liberalism is based on Locke's political philosophy and emphasizes the idea of negative liberty. This strand has developed in Anglo-Saxon societies and is deeply concerned

3.7 JEAN-JACQUES ROUSSEAU (1712-78)

Jean-Jacques Rousseau remains one of the most eccentric, unique figures in the history of political philosophy, and his work is markedly different from that of the English philosophers of the seventeenth and eighteenth centuries. Though Rousseau also used the notion of the state of nature as a beginning for his philosophy, his understanding is different from that of both Hobbes and Locke. In *The Second Discourse* (also known as *The Discourse on Inequality*) he described the state of nature as one of perfection in which humankind lived in harmony and peace with itself and nature. What ended that paradise, according to Rousseau, was the institution of private property, which brought with it inequality, conflict, and all the evils now known to humans. For with property came power, and humans began to dominate and subjugate one another.

Rousseau's description of the corruption of humankind is chilling, and we are tempted to think that he advocates a return to the idyllic state that preceded civilization. However, Rousseau believed that such a return was impossible; instead, he proposed a new political system that establishes a contract between government and subjects. He outlined this system in *The Social Contract*, a work that sought to establish the basis for legitimate government, that is, one that does not contradict the will of its subjects. To achieve such harmony, Rousseau invented the concept of the **general will**. When humans create a civil society and establish a sovereign to rule over them, they must also establish laws that reflect the general will, that is, the will of the community as a whole. This idea should not be misinterpreted as an extreme form of democracy. In fact, Rousseau meant for the general will to reflect not just the will of the people but also their true interests, or what is good for them.

This approach leaves the door open for authoritarianism in Rousseau's political thought. Should an individual's **particular will** not synchronize with the general will, the government would have the right to try to reform that person's will so that it came into line with the general. The greatest evil for Rousseau was when a government refused to follow the general will or when particular wills came to dominate the general. To prevent the latter from happening, Rousseau proposed that individuals be educated to overcome their selfish desires, to free themselves from their passions. This notion of being free from our baser instincts is now known as positive liberty.

general will
will of the community as a whole

particular will
will of the individual, as expressed by Rousseau

with political rights. Reform liberalism carries with it the idea of positive liberty and an expanded role for state action. This branch of liberal thought developed much more strongly in continental Europe and finds its roots in the philosophy of Jean-Jacques Rousseau.[5]

The individual is sacred in both strands of liberalism; therefore, the idea of consent plays a very important role. Government is seen as being legitimate only if it carries out its functions with the consent of the governed. If a government has the consent of those it rules, the actions it takes will not violate their individual rights. If a government lacks the consent of the people, however, the actions it takes will be imposed and the principle of individual self-determination will have been contradicted. This situation establishes the idea of the contract in liberalism, the notion that an implicit deal exists between individuals in society and between them and the government. If either side violates that contract, rights and privileges can be revoked. Throughout the history of liberal thought, contracts have held an almost hallowed status, and a breach of the arrangement signifies a breakdown in social harmony.

It would be an ideal (and perhaps disturbing) world, though, if there were unanimous consent for every government policy or course of action. Under liberal thought, governments act on principles of majority consent, in varying forms. This practice suggests that a minority of subjects in the political system will be unable to exercise their right to self-determination fully. How does liberalism deal with this problem? First, it can be argued that, as long as everyone has had the chance to express his or her preferences, justice has been served under the principle of equal opportunity (not equality of outcomes). Second, liberalism carries with it a commitment to the principle of tolerance. In liberal systems, minorities are respected, protected, and even encouraged. John Stuart Mill, for example, argued that the existence of minorities and diversity in human society was something that benefited everyone in that society.

The need for self-determination, consent, and tolerance has linked modern liberalism closely with democracy, although it is important to remember that the classical liberals were far from being democrats in either theory or practice. Liberals such as Locke distrusted democracy and remained highly elitist. It was only in the nineteenth century that liberalism and democracy became connected. The form of democracy is crucial—pure democracy threatens to bring about the tyranny of the masses and the stifling of minorities.[6] What is needed is a form of democratic government in which minorities are allowed to flourish. Democracy is important for modern liberals because it is the process by which each individual exercises the right to self-determination, gives or denies consent to government, and allows for the representation of minority views. It is here that voting, which is essentially where the contract between government and society is made explicit, becomes a fundamental issue for liberals.

The economic form of liberalism stems from the political and also relies on the value of liberty. What's more, there is a strong sense of crossover between liberal political and economic theories. Locke used his political theory as a defence of unequal or capitalist acquisition. Adam Smith argued that market relations between individuals would serve to reinforce notions of equality and liberty. Beginning with Smith, liberal economic thought has been committed to free markets. Because of this adherence to market economy, the economic form of liberalism is often referred to as capitalism, a system that rewards competitiveness and efficiency.[7] The market mechanism is held to be the most efficient way of organizing an economic system and of maximizing individual, as well as societal, welfare. As with liberalism's political form, human individuals are represented as self-interested creatures who seek personal gain. In addition, humans are seen to be by their nature economic and as having a natural tendency toward trade and exchange. Markets are thus seen as occurring naturally wherever human communities exist.

Like the classical and reform strands, economic liberalism holds the individual as the crucial and most important unit. Individual property rights are seen as one of the most basic, and liberals have argued that property is an extension of the self. Individuals are rational utility maximizers, which means that they seek to maximize their preferences. They will continue to do so until the cost of pursuing those preferences outweighs the benefit to be had from them. This highly rational conception of human beings is often seen as a weakness of liberal thought.

The existence of selfish individuals acting rationally in their own interests serves to benefit not just themselves but also society as a whole. This principle of the harmony of interests is well established in liberal theory. Bernard de Mandeville first explicitly made references to it in his 1705 work, *The Fable of the Bees, or Private Vices, Publick Benefits*. He argued that humans acting in their own interests are like bees gathering nectar. Each bee does so because it enjoys nectar, yet it also benefits the hive in general by bringing nectar back for the production of honey. If the bees become committed to the virtues of honesty and selfless behaviour, the hive will simply cease to function. Mandeville claimed that, in the same way, civilization advances through individuals' selfish behaviour. As each person seeks his or her own benefit, wealth is accumulated, property is constructed, and nations are built. Smith adapted this principle and called it the **invisible hand**.[8] Under market economics, self-interested individuals will maximize efficiency and economic growth over time as they engage in competition against each other, thereby benefiting society as a whole. However, these advantages will not be distributed equally, nor is it guaranteed that all individuals will benefit.

invisible hand
Adam Smith's notion that economic forces left on their own would lead to maximum efficiency and economic growth over time as they engage in competition against each other; benefits to society as a whole exist without political interference

3.8   ADAM SMITH (1723–90)

In the mid-eighteenth century, Scotland produced several important political and economic thinkers in a movement known as the Scottish Enlightenment. Adam Smith emerged as the most famous of the group and it is his influence, perhaps more than any other philosopher of his period, that is still keenly felt in contemporary political economy. Smith incorporated a distinct economic thought into the liberalism of Locke and introduced the doctrine of the free market into political economy.

Like the political philosophers who came before him, Smith had his own political program—he was determined to provide an ideological opposition to the doctrine of economic nationalism and particularly mercantilism, which he saw as both inefficient and conflict causing. In *The Wealth of Nations*, he saw market relations as working to the benefit of all people because everyone would benefit from more efficient modes of production. He introduced the concept of the invisible hand, a force inherent in economic liberalism that would ensure progress for all without any conscious direction from government.

Yet Smith wrote not only of the economic advantages of market-based economics but also of their political consequences. He argued that economic relationships based on contracts and bargains required that individuals see each other as essentially equal. Indeed, he credited market relations with ending the oppression of feudalism.

Smith believed strongly in the liberation of the economy from government interference. Furthermore, he argued for free competition between firms and the free movement of goods in and out of countries, workers, and capital. This freedom would lead to progress, which Smith defined as rising real per capita income. Smith fundamentally altered the way we look at economics, and it is in his work that all liberal economists find their ideological roots.

In the social sphere, liberalism is marked by a tolerance for different lifestyles, ethnic and racial diversity, and equal treatment for all. These characteristics reflect the ideas of Mill, who established the notion that diversity in society, the existence of eccentrics, and non-interference from others in private lives was not only desirable but also beneficial for human society. In some otherwise ostensibly liberal countries, this approach to social values is highly controversial. For example, despite the existence of liberal economic and political systems in the United States, conservatism (see pp. 75–77) is common in the social sphere. Equally, we can find people who are socially liberal but believe that the state should play a more interventionist role in economics.

utilitarianism
branch of political thought that states that the worth of a particular action is determined by its contribution to overall utility, meaning the balance of happiness and unhappiness in society

toleration
acceptance or protection of individuals, groups, and types of behaviour that may be disapproved of by the majority in society

3.9 JOHN STUART MILL (1806–73)

One of the most important liberal thinkers of the nineteenth century, John Stuart Mill strongly influenced modern economics, politics, and philosophy. Mill was the son of James Mill (1773–1836), who with Jeremy Bentham (1748–1832) had founded **utilitarianism**, a philosophy that seeks to maximize the pleasure, or utility, of individuals in society. J.S. Mill took the precepts of utilitarianism and adapted them to what he saw as the main challenges of nineteenth-century British society. Of particular importance for this chapter and this book, Mill saw himself as a political economist and sought to combine the lessons of both politics and economics to produce a version of social science that could be applied to policy at the local and national levels. He argued that the lessons of political economy should be used to improve society and the lives of individuals. His thought was deeply influenced by his wife, Harriet Taylor, and it is seen as a more humanitarian doctrine than that of his father and Bentham. He was sympathetic to the ideals of socialism and was one of the first male proponents of women's rights. Among his works, *On Liberty* is his best-known book, but *Principles of Political Economy* and *Utilitarianism* marked him as a great political philosopher and political economist.

John Stuart Mill was both an economist and philosopher whose ideas blended the two fields.

One of Mill's central preoccupations was with individuality. This focus led him to advocate **toleration** of eccentricities and unusual behaviour and practices, as long as such things did not interfere with the freedom or well-being of others. He saw that democracy was in danger of suppressing individuality as the masses dominated minorities and that conformity would bring about a mediocre society. This attitude toward the individual informed Mill's opinions on political economy. Though agreeing with many of the principles of socialism, he argued that the state should limit its economic role to the distribution, not the production, of goods.

Socialism

The roots of socialism as a political and economic system of thought are not quite as long as those of liberalism.[9] Socialism emerged in France and Britain in the 1820s as a term favoured by the political movements of the Owenites in Britain and the Saint-Simonians and Fourierists in France.[10] Although the term **communism**, which has close links to socialism, appeared earlier (in the late eighteenth century), it is appropriate to view communism as one form of socialism.[11] The same is true of Marxism, the subset of socialism that has been dominant in its history.

Socialism has provided the most important philosophical, political, and economic challenge to liberalism over the past 160 years, and its principles are generally opposed, in both political and economic realms, to the liberal tradition. Although the great socialist experiments in the Soviet Union and other parts of the world failed, socialism as a system of political thought has evolved into an important mainstream perspective. Indeed, the sheer ideological diversity of socialism is impressive. Utopian socialism, revolutionary socialism, reformist state socialism, ethical socialism, pluralist socialism, and market socialism are all important subsets of socialist thought. This section provides a description of the most significant political and economic elements that can be said to constitute the heart of socialist thought.

Each branch of socialism shares with the others a concern for human community and society and for order over concerns about the individual and his or her rights. This can be seen in the origins of the word *socialism*. The Latin roots of the term suggest community and companionship between human individuals. Humans can be understood only as part of society, for without that common tie individuals are held to be less than human. Human nature for socialists is inseparable from society and social life. The emphasis on the group above the individual is seen clearly in Marxist analysis, which focuses on the role of social classes in human history. Humans are identified as belonging to one class or other, and their identity and interests are defined with reference to those classes. However, socialist thought dictates that humans are rational and capable of self-development and progress, elements shared with liberalism.

Though some socialist philosophers can be critical of egalitarianism except as a final goal, socialism is fundamentally an egalitarian belief system, teaching that all human individuals, men and women of any race and creed, are deserving of equal treatment.[12] Socialism does not teach that all humans are equal in terms of their capabilities or faculties; it recognizes the many differences found among individuals. Nonetheless, it argues that these differences are less important than the underlying similarities shared among them. This position does not seem much different from liberalism, yet the consequences for socialist ideology are radically different. Essentially, as we will see in reference to the economic elements, it implies a doctrine of redistribution based upon the principle of "from each according to their capabilities, to each according to

communism
political theory, based on writings of Marx and Engels, that espouses class conflict to form a system where all property is publicly owned and each citizen works to his or her own best ability and is compensated equitably

materialist
in Marxism, understanding the physical and economic basis for society

dialectics
in Marxism, points where ideas and processes throughout history come up against each other and form a new reality

3.10 KARL MARX (1818–83)

Karl Marx is probably the most important political philosopher of the nineteenth century, and his ideological legacy dramatically altered the course of history. Marx's system of thought was deeply affected by his own personal experiences. Living in London, he observed with horror capitalist industry's treatment of the working classes. The working conditions and pay levels of labourers in England (and across Europe) at that time were desperately low and things seemed to be getting worse. These observations were confirmed by his friend and lifelong colleague and supporter, Friedrich Engels, who had been studying the living and working conditions of the working class in Manchester.

Marx's approach to political thought had two major dimensions. It was **materialist**, meaning that it took as its starting point an understanding of the physical and economic basis for society. For Marx, the system of production is the basis on which any social and political system is founded. By examining the distribution of economic power and, most important, by determining which social groups control the means of production, Marx argued that one could then explain the nature and shape of a society's political system.

The second key concept in Marxist thought is that it uses **dialectics**. Throughout history, ideas and processes clash, creating a new reality. For Marx, the whole of human history could be explained by materialism and dialectics. As economic change took place, so would social and political change.

Applying his own approach, Marx saw the history of humankind as the history of conflict between the social classes. As the economy changed from agricultural to capitalist, society was transformed from feudal to capitalistic and the political order became dominated by the bourgeoisie, or middle classes, in the place of the aristocracy. This change, however, was merely a forerunner to the eventual transformation of society that would occur when capitalism inevitably reached its own crises of overproduction and

© GL Archive / Alamy

The horrific conditions in many Victorian factories inspired Karl Marx to launch his attack on capitalism.

underconsumption. At this point, the working classes would overthrow the bourgeoisie in a socialist revolution.

Though these predictions about capitalism have yet to come to fruition, it is Marx's analytical approach that makes his system of thought so important to the study of politics and political economy. The way in which Marxian thought studies the interaction of politics and economics is a fine example for modern students, no matter what is thought of Marxism as an ideology.

their needs." Further, socialism is committed to equal access to health care and education so that equality extends beyond the purely economic domain. In this sense, socialism attempts to satisfy human needs rather than merely provide the opportunity for individuals to do so themselves.

Socialism is generally seen as defending the state and its role in human society and the economy. For many socialists, however, the state has been seen as the enemy, a system of repression that represents the interests of one class over others. Marx, in particular, argued that the state was controlled by the **bourgeois**, those who own the "means of production" and would therefore need to be overthrown so that the working classes could claim the political and economic power that was rightly theirs.[13] Most modern socialists call for an expanded role for the state in fulfilling the economic, social, and political needs of the people, once the revolution has occurred and popular control of the political process has been established. The state should represent the will of the people, a will that is assumed to be egalitarian in nature.

The economic side of socialist thought has already been touched upon, in the sense that socialists generally hold to the principle of economic redistribution to satisfy the needs of all individuals in human society. This theory implies an expanded role for the state in the economy, and many socialists argue for a command economy, run in its entirety by the state. Those socialists who do not go quite as far still prefer that the state play an active role in the economy, one that works to even out the inequalities caused by capitalism. Public ownership of industry is a common theme, as is progressive taxation. The economy is to be harnessed by the socialist state so that it adequately serves the needs of human society.

For socialists, the economy and politics are inextricably linked. In fact, it is impossible to understand Marxist thought without understanding this association. Marxists argue that political relations and processes stem from and are shaped by economic relations and processes.[14] Socialism is highly critical of capitalism as it is destructive of the very values that socialists seek to promote, such as community and fellowship. Further, unequal or capitalist acquisition creates severe material inequalities in society, which the socialist state will then have to rectify.

It is also important to point out that Marx believed that human nature itself was inherently linked to labour and production. Human beings, he argued, were best able to express themselves through creative means, by mixing their labour with raw materials through the means of production. According to Marx, the capitalist economic system of the nineteenth century was harmful to the worker's nature because it involved the alienation, or separation, of a worker from his or her labour and its products. This concern brings Marx to insist upon equal access to the means of production for all humans so that they may exercise their human nature. The importance of labour as the source of value in an economy is an element held in common with liberal thought, though with radically different outcomes.

At the beginning of the twentieth century, socialism underwent a crisis from which two main streams emerged. The first, revolutionary socialism, was

bourgeois
according to socialists such as Marx, the property-owning class that exploits the working class (proletariat)

championed by Rosa Luxemburg and argued that the only way for capitalism to be overthrown was through violent revolution. The second variation, led by Eduard Bernstein, looked to the possibility of reform rather than revolution. Bernstein's ideas, known as evolutionary socialism, or reformism, were important because they led to the formation of political parties that represented the "acceptable face" of socialism and evolved into the social democratic movement. The Social Democratic Party (SPD) in Germany, the Labour Party in Britain, the New Democratic Party (NDP) in Canada, and left-wing democratic parties across the world find their intellectual heritage in Bernstein's ideas. The creation of the modern welfare state and the mixed economy, whereby government and private business work alongside each other in the productive process, were made possible by the ideological framework of social democracy.[15]

Nationalism

Nationalism arose as a political phenomenon in the late eighteenth century, with the onset of the French Revolution and then the Napoleonic Wars. This ideology spread throughout Europe during the nineteenth century and was harnessed by governments as a way to increase their political power. It featured as a central political movement in both world wars and in the interwar period. In the postwar period, nationalist approaches continued to be important during the Cold War and in the process of decolonization as new developing countries entered the international system and their governments tried to strengthen their control over society.

In recent years, nationalism has once again emerged as an important ideology in the world, acting as a central element in the outbreak of ethnic violence in areas such as the Balkans. In Russia, Vladimir Putin's efforts to re-establish his country's dominion over neighbouring states have been heavily coloured with nationalistic rhetoric. The economic manifestations of nationalism have also been increasingly evident, as many countries have reacted negatively to the dramatic rise of China and also as the financial crisis of 2008–09 began to take hold. Most intriguing is that nationalism has experienced a recent rebirth in Canada, with the Stephen Harper government emphasizing Canadian values, the role of a strong military in national and international affairs, and a stronger independent agenda regarding trade and commercial relations.

Nationalism has been one of the most powerful ideological tools employed by politicians throughout the years. It represents an appeal to human individuals to unite with other members of their nation, to recognize the ties that simultaneously bind them and set them apart from people of a different nationality, and to create, promote, or protect political institutions designed around the national identity. It is the political form of a fundamental impulse in human nature, the need to belong. By marking ourselves as part of a heritage common to those we see as similar to us, which is at the same time different from the heritage held by other groups in human society, we create a distinction that is an extension of the human family or tribe. In this sense, nationalism creates a juxtaposition of "us" and "them," a pride in the national character, and (in many cases) a fear or mistrust of the "other."

What, though, is a nation? As we noted in Chapter 2, writers on nationalism have pointed to several features that a group of people must share to be called a nation:

- language
- territory
- traditions, culture, and history
- race or ethnicity
- religion

Though some nationalities do not hold the elements of race or religion in common, each has played an important part in forming nations and in marking them off from other social groupings throughout history.[16] In the sixteenth century, for example, Henry VIII used religion (the Anglican Church) to unite the English people against both the Scots and the Catholic peoples of continental Europe. Race was a central element in Nazi nationalist ideology, which asserted the superiority of the Aryan people over all others.

But what is nationalism? Essentially, it is an ideology that not only seeks the separation of one nation from others but also strives to create and protect the political institutions and mechanisms needed to ensure the prosperity of that nation, its values, traditions, and culture.[17] Its most prominent form is seen in the demands of certain groups for independence or sovereignty. For instance, such demands are frequently heard from Irish nationalists, Scottish nationalists, and Quebec nationalists. We might therefore say that, just as individual self-determination is important for liberals, national self-determination is fundamental for nationalists.

Because national self-determination is seen as a supremely important goal, violence is not unusual in the political programs of nationalist movements. Yet the political form of nationalism is not only seen in social movements demanding independence. It is also apparent in the actions of governments that discriminate against and persecute what they consider to be alien elements in their societies. Throughout history, Jewish people have been used as a target for nationalist governments trying to unite their populations. In more recent memory, immigrants have become a target in many European and North American countries as an identifiably separate and, certain political parties claim, threatening element in society. Xenophobia, or fear of foreigners, is sometimes a consequence of extreme forms of nationalism.

Nationalism once again signifies the superiority of the group over the individual. It has been commonly used to suppress individual rights and freedoms in order to boost the strength and solidify the identity of the nation. Throughout history, nationalist forces have been responsible for much of the violence, persecution, and bigotry that have plagued human affairs. There is clearly a very close link between nationalism and war. In the eighteenth, nineteenth, and twentieth centuries, governments considered nationalism a useful ideological instrument in times of war, and war itself is a powerful driving force behind nationalist sentiment. Indeed, the identification of a foreign or even domestic enemy is a commonly employed argument for promoting nationalism. However, nationalism has also been a positive tool that has united sometimes-disparate peoples and has led to the creation of political and economic institutions that have proved to be more efficient than their predecessors. It has also led to revolts by anti-colonial movements, freeing peoples from external control. The rise of nationalism marked a significant phase in political development and contributed greatly to the political landscape that persists with us today.

Just as the focus of political nationalism is the creation and preservation of the institutions of statehood, economic nationalism sets the strengthening of the nation-state through economic means as its goal. Economic nationalism grants the state an expanded role in the economy, not just through economic policy but also often through actual ownership of certain sectors. Economic nationalism can and does occur equally in democratic and authoritarian societies, though there are deep philosophical tensions in the case of the former.

Other Systems of Thought

CONSERVATISM

When we say that someone is conservative, we generally mean that they are cautious, in favour of established methods and lifestyles, and resistant to change. As a political ideology and perspective, conservatism shares many of these features. It seeks to protect the best of what has come before for future generations and is concerned with maintaining political and social traditions and customs, which are seen as being an integral part of human life. The origins of conservatism exist in the work of Edmund Burke, a British political writer and activist in the eighteenth century. He argued that, far from improving peoples' lives, the dramatic developments and turbulence of the French Revolution had in fact degraded the human condition and endangered social stability.[18] This attitude toward rapid change remains a marked feature of conservatism. It would be wrong, however, to say that conservatives are opposed to all change; they are instead concerned with its pace and extent.

Conservatives view society as being organic and essential for human development. This outlook is a crucial difference to liberalism. For conservatives, the individual can be understood only in relation to the greater whole of society and his or her place in it. On the other hand, the smooth and effective functioning of society depends on people fulfilling their own individual functions. Due to this division of labour, society is not only organic but also hierarchical in nature. Conservatives believe that some perform functions in society that are more important than others and that they should receive greater

The French Revolution led conservatives such as Edmund Burke to recommend some sharing of economic benefits to avoid similar social strife. This painting shows the storming of the Bastille prison, the symbol of the French royal rule, on 14 July 1789, an event that galvanized the revolutionary forces. The date is now a public holiday in France.

© The Gallery Collection/Corbis

rewards and be more influential than those who perform less crucial functions. In addition, conservatives traditionally believe that history has defined certain societal groups to be more important than others and has suited them for that role. It is from this claim that the notion of social classes is legitimated in conservative thought.

As intimated earlier in this chapter, history plays a central role in conservative thought in defining both the shape of society and the nature of its government and constitution. The state is seen as having evolved throughout history and not as being created from nothing, as the liberal contract theorists would argue. Traditions and customs play a key role in government, and for conservatives the constitution is not merely a collection of written statements but also the conventions that have developed around them. This makes conservatism less legalistic but, at the same time, more human and easier to relate to than a lot of liberal theory.

This element of evolution in the nature of government is mirrored by conservatives' changing views toward democracy. Early conservatives were highly skeptical of giving the choice of leadership over to the masses, but latter-day conservatives in Canada, the United States, and Britain, for example, have become firm defenders of the principles of **representative democracy**. Nonetheless, there remains a strong sense of paternalism in conservative thought. What's more, leaders are not only there to exercise power but also to protect the interests of those whom they lead, and such interests may be defined by the leaders

representative democracy
political system in which voters elect others to act on their behalf; also called indirect democracy

just as legitimately as those they govern. One of the key priorities that persists among conservatives is that of law and order, which for many is given preference over concepts such as equality and freedom. Furthermore, there is often a heavy tendency toward nationalism among political conservatives.

That said, it would be wrong to paint a picture of conservatives as favouring the state over individual rights. Conservatives have been fervent defenders of rights and equality throughout history. For example, John Adams, the second president of the United States and generally considered the father of American conservatism, argued for **republicanism**. Although he believed firmly in the idea of social classes, he also argued for the inclusion of all men in the political process, regardless of their social status (though he did believe that owning property should be a prerequisite in this regard).

It is important to point out that there are significant variations in conservative doctrine across countries. One such difference is concern about the role of religion and morality in society. Since its origins, conservatism has been concerned with social ethics, norms, and morality because they are seen as being amongst the most important traditions that bind society together. In modern times, conservatives in Canada and the UK have been more willing to adopt a more liberal approach to such issues. In 1942, Canada's Conservative Party was officially renamed the Progressive Conservative Party, the result of a deal with the former leader of the defunct Progressive Party. Although the name sounds like an oxymoron, "progressive conservative" hinted at the more socially liberal dimensions of conservatism in twentieth-century Canada. In 2003, the party merged with the Canadian Alliance (a right-wing political party based in Western Canada) and the name reverted to the Conservative Party of Canada. Some pundits have suggested that this move has led to a more nationalistic political agenda and more traditional social policies. Meanwhile, conservatives in the United States have been much more emphatic about the central role to be played by Christian morals in defining the "good society."

republicanism
political idea that gives supreme power to the people or elected representatives of the people

FEMINISM

The ideals of feminism began with a very simple maxim: equal rights for women. This early feminist demand may seem unremarkable to many today, yet it was a truly revolutionary slogan in the late nineteenth and early twentieth centuries.[19] To understand this, we only have to recognize the inordinately unequal treatment of women throughout history. Women have been placed at the mercy of the male gender in almost every aspect of their lives and, with few exceptions, have led an existence that can at best be described as highly restricted. Feminism is a system of thought that has grown from the mere recognition of this historical reality into a set of demands concerning the status of women in every part of life. Like all philosophies, there is a great variance among thinkers and writers within the feminist school. As with all ideologies, there are moderates and extremists, and such labels shift over time.

Mary Wollstonecraft (1759–97) was a writer who championed women's rights and argued that men and women are fundamentally equal. Her ideas inspired the women's protest movement in nineteenth-century Britain.

suffrage
granting of the right to vote

The goal of equal treatment for women is an inherently liberal one because liberalism calls for equal rights and freedoms for all human individuals regardless of gender. Yet none of the classical liberal philosophers sought to apply their principles to the matter of gender, and it was only Mill who addressed the issue directly (in *The Subjection of Women*, 1869). Previously, however, Mary Wollstonecraft had launched an early philosophical defence of the rights of women in her 1792 work, *A Vindication of the Rights of Women*. It was left to female political activists of the late 1800s and early 1900s to demand the rights for women many of us now take for granted. In the mid- to late eighteenth century, Susan B. Anthony, an American, became the most heralded feminist activist as she campaigned for the right to vote (**suffrage**). Though the struggle was not won in her lifetime, women in the United States eventually received the right to vote in 1920. Limited franchise, meaning that only those who were over the age of 30 and who rented or owned property could vote, was granted to women in England in 1918, followed by full voting rights in 1928. The Canadian provinces granted women voting rights at various times between 1916 and 1940.

These gains, however, did not signal the end of the feminist struggle but instead marked the beginning of a long fight to change the lives of women around the world. As the movement has developed, so has the ideology behind it. Feminism has changed from a simple claim for equality to a complex and varied grouping of political, social, and economic thought.

The two main thrusts of modern feminism are concerned with justice and gender roles. The former relates to the issue of equal treatment for women in the workplace and society. Issues such as equal pay, the "glass ceiling" (whereby women are prevented from rising to senior managerial and executive positions), affirmative action, maternity (or parental) leave, and sexual harassment are some of the higher profile and indeed most important issues for the feminist movement.

These are, however, only the most obvious of feminism's aims. Just as important are its concerns with the broader issue of gender, including the roles of men and women in society, language, and even gender-specific patterns of thought. *Gender* is different from the word *sex* because it refers to the socially constructed roles and images we have of men and women, not to the biological nature of a person (male or female). Women's roles in society are about more than just the right to work or to hold positions of influence. Feminism questions traditional roles for women as wife, mother, or caregiver. The institution of marriage has been questioned because of its use over the centuries to subjugate women and to treat them as property. In terms of the family, the issues of choice, timing, and who should be the primary caregiver are greatly debated in modern society, largely due to the work of feminists.

One of the highest profile issues of the feminist movement has been the area of reproduction, particularly the right to abortion. This debate has remained a hotly contested one for many years in many countries, especially the United States. While there have been significant advances for those arguing for women's freedom to choose, it is far from being a decided issue. Neither should it be thought that all feminists agree on abortion rights; as with so many other issues and ideologies, diversity of opinion marks contemporary feminism.

In the past 20 years, a "third wave" of feminist thought and action has emerged. This approach takes issue with earlier waves' basic, "essentialist" idea that all women share a common nature or identity and with the dominance of middle-class, predominantly white female conceptions of what women want and need. The third wave argues that women should be encouraged to define their own identities and their own conception of feminism. Authors and thinkers such as Rebecca Walker and Amy Richards have emphasized this more pluralistic, diverse interpretation of feminist thought.

Feminist discussions about and arguments in favour of gender and sexual freedom have proven inspirational for the **lesbian, gay, bisexual, and transgender (LGBT) movement.** Like the third wave of feminism, the LGBT movement advocates the recognition of diversity in sexual and gender identities and calls for equal treatment for all, regardless of sexual orientation.

lesbian, gay, bisexual, and transgender movement (LGBT) movement recognizing diversity in sexual and gender identities

An interesting phenomenon to observe within feminism is how seemingly radical issues have crossed over to become mainstream in their nature. The right to vote was considered a radical and revolutionary issue when it first emerged; the same could be said for women in Parliament, equal pay for women, or even the exclusionary nature of words such as *chairman* or *mankind*. In political studies, gender analysis was seen as a marginal and unusual subfield for a long time—it is currently viewed as an established, mainstream dimension of the discipline.

ENVIRONMENTALISM

The "green movement" that arose in the 1980s in Europe and North America and forced changes in government policy regarding the environment marked the birth of a new approach oriented toward the protection of the earth's natural resources and the promotion of simpler lifestyles. Environmentalism is truly both a political and an economic ideology because it identifies modern economic systems as the scourge of nature. It also shares certain ideas with anarchism (discussed later in this chapter) because it sees modern industrialism as a hierarchical system that restricts human freedom.[20]

The ideological roots of environmentalism are several, existing not only in anarchism but also in romanticism, pacifism, and socialism. The anti-nuclear

3.11   ENERGY EFFICIENCY

In recent years, governments have responded to years of research and advocacy on environmental efficiency. New policies and programs have rewarded homeowners and businesses for "going green." The Canadian government implemented widespread programs, such as the ecoENERGY initiative, to persuade Canadians to upgrade their houses and modes of travel to more environmentally friendly options. NGOs such as Alliance to Save Energy, Greenpeace, and the Consortium for Energy Efficiency have been presenting arguments in favour of long-term energy-saving plans for years. One NGO, the American Council for an Energy-Efficient Economy (ACEEE), publishes dozens of reports every year detailing ways that public policy could support energy efficiency. One yearly report (found at http://greenercars.org) ranks all motor vehicles based on their emissions, fuel economy, and production costs. The worst offender? Surprisingly, it's not a large SUV but the Lamborghini Murcielago, a recently discontinued Italian supercar that burns a whopping 29.4 litres of fuel for every 100 kilometres driven. At this rate, filling the vehicle's 98-litre tank would yield only 334 kilometres of driving. By comparison, a Honda Prius uses only 4.61 litres/100 kilometres, meaning that it could reach 2124

The Lamborghini Murcielago (2001–10) produced the worst fuel economy of any production vehicle.

kilometres on the same size tank before running out of fuel. It is fair to say, however, that these two cars attract very different buyers. Lamborghini's replacement to the Murcielago, the Aventador, has better fuel economy: 21.4 litres/100 kilometres, which ranks third worst in the world.

movement of the 1970s and 1980s produced significant political momentum that, combined with the work of NGOs such as Greenpeace and Friends of the Earth, helped to change public opinion and raise consciousness about the problems facing the global and local environments.

Within environmentalism is a belief that the destruction of the biosphere, the finely balanced system that sustains life on this planet, is imminent unless radical changes are made. Science has played a key role in the ascendance of this ideological approach. As more and more scientific evidence concerning climate change, ozone depletion, and ground, air, and water pollution—along with their harmful effects on human health—has emerged, more and more people have become aware of the need for more environmentally friendly approaches to economic development. There is a current focus on re-educating public opinion so that people call for governmental change with regard to pollution and the use (and overuse) of non-renewable natural resources. The main targets for environmentalists are heavy industry and petroleum companies, and the ideology promotes alternative sources of energy (such as solar power, wind energy, or biofuels) and lifestyles that consume less.

The economic implications of environmentalism are closely connected to this overall vision. This school of thought seeks to persuade individuals to seek natural rather than consumer pleasures and to reduce the amount of energy and goods that people consume. This goal is a direct challenge to contemporary Western lifestyles and an indirect one to the Western economic system. Environmentalism attacks this system more directly by focusing on **sustainable development** rather than economic growth. Sustainable development is a concept that embraces not only the provision of basic needs and the expansion of economic activity but also health, individual freedoms, education, and human longevity of this and future generations.

Environmentalism has enjoyed many successes at the practical level. Without the efforts of this movement, we would not have seen new national policies on recycling and pollution control. At the international level, the notion of sustainable development has become a maxim for international aid agencies and development organizations. The reality of climate change has made almost everyone aware of the need for more ecologically sound policies and practices, and environmentalism has moved firmly into the mainstream.

sustainable development
model of economic growth that seeks to use renewable resources so as not to destroy the environment in which human beings have to live

FASCISM

Fascist is one of those words that has passed from politics into everyday use in English. We use it to indicate that someone or something is dictatorial and intolerant. However, the true meaning of the term lies in the ideology of fascism and its close cousin, National Socialism. These ideologies, close enough to be examined as one, call to mind the atrocities of World War II and modern brown-shirted skinheads threatening racial violence. But they must also be examined at the level of their underlying philosophical ideas.[21]

Fascism's perception of human psychology is fundamentally different from many mainstream ideologies because it rejects the laws of human reason that are fundamental to liberalism and socialism. It sees human individuals as influenced more by myths and romanticism than by logic and appeals to them in this way. One of the most important myths for fascism and National Socialism is the myth of blood, race, or *volk*. Such nationalism is central for fascism because it promotes the group (in this case, the folk or nation) over the individual, an essential element of fascist thought. The individual takes his or her identity only from within the nation and must direct all efforts toward helping that group. Indeed, the origins of the word *fascism* come from the Italian *fasces*, which were bundles of sticks or rods that were bound together as a symbol of authority for Roman magistrates and were used for corporal punishment. The significance of these bundles of sticks is that an individual piece can easily be broken, but several tied together create a strong and intimidating unit.

For fascists, property is privately held but must be used to strengthen the nation as a whole, not for personal gain. The *volk* is to be protected from all other nations or races, and racial superiority is commonly a part of National Socialist political **propaganda**. This element of racism in fascist thought was manifested

propaganda
spreading of information, true or otherwise, for the purpose of aiding a cause or making an audience react in a certain way

in Nazi Germany in the form of anti-Semitism, but it also took the form of anti-Asian and anti-African ideas, stressing the natural superiority of the white race.

According to fascist thought, the nation should be organized within, by the state, with a national leader (*führer* in German) at its head. This leader is an unquestioned authority who determines the interests of the nation and directs not only state policy but also individual morality. The leader represents, indeed embodies, the will of the people and is seen as the only person capable of interpreting that will. The structure of the state is hierarchical, with a clear chain of command from the leader down. In practical terms, this system means extreme authoritarianism and the will to use force, indeed violence, to ensure order and compliance. Violence and militarism are also celebrated by fascism as forces that unite society.

ANARCHISM

libertarianism
ideology based on a limited government role and freedom of speech, action, and thought

The word *anarchist* makes most people think of an individual, probably young, who is committed to the violent overthrow of government and society. The thought system of anarchism, however, is much more complex than (and not nearly as extremist as) the popular image suggests. Anarchism is actually concerned with the primacy of the individual, in which outside interference into the people's lives (especially that of government and the state) is minimized. It is a form of **libertarianism** that stresses the sanctity of the human individual and seeks to promote the moral autonomy of the same.[22]

3.12 JOHN RAWLS (1921–2002)

In the 1970s, John Rawls took an idea from the political philosophy of Hobbes, Locke, and Rousseau and started a debate that helped to shape political philosophy at the end of the twentieth century. In *A Theory of Justice*, Rawls took the concept of the state of nature and renamed it the original position.

Instead of a mythical state in which humans are removed from society and subjected to the will of others and to the wilds of nature, Rawls formulated a hypothetical situation in which each individual is ignorant of everything about himself or herself, including the proclivity for risk-taking. By asking what the human individual in this situation would choose in creating a political and economic system, Rawls hoped to find the basis for a just society. His answer was that each individual would likely opt for a political and economic system that is democratic and that guarantees a minimum level of material welfare.

Shortly after Rawls published *A Theory of Justice*, Robert Nozick wrote *Anarchy, State, and Utopia*. In this rebuttal to Rawls, Nozick argued that, rather than providing the ethical and philosophical basis for the welfare state, the original position (as formulated by Nozick) would promote the choice of libertarian society in which the role of the state is severely restricted and the individual is held sacred. The debate between Rawls and Nozick became one of the most important of the twentieth century, and it brings to mind the contrast between the philosophies of Hobbes and Locke.

Anarchism has a long history that extends back to early Christian thought and beyond. The word simply means the opposite of hierarchy and therefore absence of government. It is important to remember that anarchy is not the same thing as chaos or the absence of peace and order. Most anarchists believe firmly that human life would be more peaceful and human needs more completely managed in the state's absence. Anarchism as an approach seeks change not through politics but through society or the overthrow of government. However, some anarchists have pointed out that revolution generally leads to the installation of a new government and thus a new authority structure to struggle against. Nonetheless, throughout the late nineteenth and twentieth centuries, the most obvious form of anarchist activity has been to strike against the representatives of authority. Anarchism has at times been a potent ideological force that has inspired direct political action, often in the form of violent attacks upon the organs of government but also in the form of peaceful protest and propaganda.[23]

Anarchist thought has a rather unique perspective on the economy and, in particular, on modern industrial economic development. It blames the process of industrialization for much of the oppression of the modern individual because industrial organization requires a passive, compliant, and ordered populace for its workers. According to the ideas of anarchism, government and industry work alongside one another to suppress individual freedoms and impose a set order upon society. Further, anarchists argue for a simple lifestyle in which needs are taken care of, yet excess is not known. This marks anarchism as a deeply anti-consumerist ideology. Pierre-Joseph Proudhon, possibly the most famous anarchist writer, stated that "property is theft," though not all anarchists go to such extremes.

Anarchist thinkers do not believe that all forms of economic and social organization will be absent in the world they envision. Instead of governments forcing citizens to comply with rules, laws, and modes of interaction, society would organize itself with an emphasis on community management and the mutual solution of common problems. Michel Albert's ideas on providing alternatives to capitalist globalization and his emphasis on community-based organization are clear examples of this kind of thinking.[24] Although some may criticize this concept for its essentially idealistic nature, a number of anarchist experiments in small communities around the world have been successful over time.

Pierre-Joseph Proudhon (1809–65) felt that society would be better off without possessions, money, and the state.

© The Print Collector / Alamy

POLITICAL ISLAM

Islamic philosophy has an even longer history than its European Christian counterpart. It was Islamic culture that preserved the ideas of Aristotle, which were then reintroduced into European thought by Thomas Aquinas. Islamic political inquiry showed a level of sophistication and realism that surprised contemporary European thinkers. Medieval Islamic thought in particular highlights the link between politics and Islam, as well as the connection between political philosophy and the realities of power. The strongest example can be found in the idea of the *khilafat* or *caliphate*, a government inspired by Islam that rules over its subjects using Islamic law. In fact, the caliphate of Sunni Islam at its high point in the eighth century extended over an area from North Africa to the Middle East, Eastern Europe, and Spain.

Also of importance is the concept of *ummah*, which emphasizes the global community of Muslim peoples. It is a key idea in Islam that stresses not only internationalism but also the superiority of Islam over other religions and cultures. Other central components of early Islamic thought are the link between science and religion, the methodological search for the truth, and the importance of studying nature.

The best known Islamic philosopher, one whose ideas are still cited as relevant and insightful, was Ibn Khaldun. Writing in the fourteenth century, he was a scholar whose interests included history, economics, law, military strategy, and astronomy. Khaldun's work on the nature of the state and its rights

caliphate
government inspired by Islam that rules over its subjects using Islamic law

Ibn Khaldun (1332–1406) and Sayyid Qutb (1906–66) are considered two dominant Islamic philosophers. Qutb's writings influenced radical groups such as al-Qaeda. Qutb is shown here in an Egyptian prison.

Ibn Khaldun: © Art Directors & TRIP / Alamy

and duties is surprisingly modern in its understanding of the way in which the state often abuses power. He wrote about concepts such as the importance of social or tribal cohesion and the role of religion in generating such unity, and he understood the historical tendency for empires to decay rapidly.

Modern Islamic political thought reflects some of these established tendencies, but it has also moved into a more radical phase. Sayyid Qutb, in particular, wrote extensively on the immoral nature of American society and argued for a revival of traditional Islamic values. He proposed the use of Islamic law, or **sharia**, and the use of **jihad** in both defensive and offensive ways against the West.

Qutb's ideas were inspirational and helped lead to the rise of **Islamic fundamentalism**. These movements were seen most dramatically in the Iranian Revolution in 1979 and in the ongoing struggle of organizations such as al-Qaeda, the group behind the 9/11 (and many other) terrorist attacks (see Chapter 12). The spread of these ideas across the globe is one of the most important influences on political stability in the developing world and on relations between Islam and the West.

We should not assume that all Islamic political thought can be tied to fundamentalism, jihad, or al-Qaeda. Contemporary political Islam should be seen as a vibrant force with moderate elements that are opposed to the strict imposition of sharia. However, many dominant trends in today's Islamic thought are more traditional and fundamentalist.

CONFUCIAN POLITICAL THOUGHT

Though Confucius is most commonly thought of as a moral or religious philosopher, his particular branch of political philosophy is crucial to our understanding of some of the bases of East Asian political culture. Born into the upper levels of Chinese society, Confucius was a justice minister in the Han dynasty's royal court. His system of thought centred on the classic philosophical questions of personal morality, social relationships, and justice. He emphasized the need for sincerity, honesty, respect, and virtue in human behaviour. **Confucianism** has been the most important and influential branch of Asian philosophy over the past 2000 years.

With regard to political affairs, Confucius again stressed the importance of individuals willingly behaving in accordance with their "natural morality" rather than being forced to do so by laws and coercion. Virtue, duty, and a sense of shame are not only a guide for how citizens should behave but also, and just as important, for the actions of rulers. Confucius favoured a unified monarchy in which the emperor

sharia law
sacred law of Islam

jihad
moral struggle or struggle for righteousness; form of holy war

Islamic fundamentalism
religious movements advocating a return to the fundamentals of Islamic religious texts

Confucianism
philosophy and political thought of Confucius that stresses social harmony, obedience, and morality

Confucius (551–479 BCE) was a Chinese philosopher whose teachings formed the basis of Confucianism.

© Ivy Close Images / Alamy

and the governing class would be chosen according to their morality and would therefore serve as an example to society. In return, his inferiors should show respect and obedience to the emperor and his government.

In Confucian political thought, therefore, the principles of social harmony, obedience, and moral behaviour play a primary role. This helps us to understand, at least in part, the greater acceptance of authoritarian regimes in East Asian societies in the modern period. It also helps us gain an insight into the very different relationship that exists between government and society in those countries.

The Relevance of Ideas

Throughout history, the evolution of ideas has had a dramatic impact on the real world of politics and the economy. For example, we can look to Marx's ideas as the basis for a transformation of political–economic systems at both national and international levels in the nineteenth century and—more so—the twentieth. In this case, a new way of understanding politics and economics inspired organized social unrest, new government approaches to social and economic programs, and ultimately revolution. But we could also mention the importance of nationalism and liberalism in motivating governments and groups within society to organize themselves and prepare for both conflict and competition.

The interaction between philosophy and government policy was never more clear than in Western governments' adoption of Keynesian economic and social policies in the 1940s and 1950s (see Chapter 4). By seeking to smooth capitalism's highs and lows and thus reduce its negative effects on the population, Keynesian economic policy became the norm for most of the postwar period, and the consensus only broke down in the 1970s during a prolonged period of economic stagnation. At that time, the ideological approach known as neo-liberalism appeared, which in turn influenced government policies throughout the world. With the economic and financial crisis at the end of the first decade of the twenty-first century, a neo-Keynesian approach to economic policy-making seems likely to emerge.[25]

It is in such transitions that we see the other side of the interaction between political thinking and political practice. The movement of history and developments in the world of politics and the economy bring reform, revolution, and the creation of new ideas in the world of political and economic thought. Unless philosophical inquiry reflects the realities of the human world, it will remain separate and disconnected from it. Philosophy, remember, should help us to understand our political and economic systems before it shows us ways to change them. Marx's ideas were shaped by his experiences of the Industrial Revolution and the terrible working conditions of British manufacturing labourers. He explained the causes for these conditions before arguing that revolution was the only way to improve the workers' lot.

Today we benefit from the normative discussions contained in classical and modern philosophy when we contemplate the relationship between the state and individuals and society, particularly in debates over rights. Think, for example, of current debates in the United States over the rights of undocumented migrants. Are these immigrants equally deserving of access to education, health care, and social security as American citizens are, even though they entered the country illegally? How should we define citizenship? Luckily, we have thousands of years of relevant arguments and ideas stored in the annals of political philosophy that serve us well in such situations.

Political ideas and philosophy, then, are essential, living, and evolving elements of political studies. It is all too easy to dismiss the importance of ideas, to classify them as mere castles in the air. Future trends in politics, at both national and international levels, will be shaped equally by developments in the practical and theoretical worlds. It is our job as political scientists to understand the major strands of political philosophy and their impact on debates in the real world and to participate in the intergenerational debate over their validity.

Conclusion

This chapter has looked at the central place occupied by ideas, philosophies, and ideologies in the world of politics. As you have seen, these ideas constitute a huge spectrum of thought that extends not just from left to right, as we have traditionally perceived politics, but also in many other directions and dimensions. The debates and compromises that take place between ideological and philosophical positions remain one of the most vibrant and important areas of political studies.

The ideas put forward by the most important thinkers throughout history have become a basis for political debate, social movements, political change, and (at times) revolution. Just as important, though in a less dramatic manner, political thought has influenced the structures of governance, specifically their shape and level of public inclusiveness. Ideological and philosophical perspectives underlie all such structures in the real world, and it is to these that we now turn.

Self-Assessment Questions

1. In what way is political philosophy a timeless exercise?
2. Give examples of philosophical debates that spread across generations.
3. On what basis should we view all humans as equal? Give reasons to support your answer.
4. How can Western liberal ideas and the tenets of political Islam and/or Confucianism be seen as compatible?
5. Which school of thought covered in this chapter is closest to your personal political concerns? Why do you support this one above the others?

Weblinks

American Council for an Energy-Efficient Economy (ACEEE)
www.aceee.org/consumer

Feminist Theory Website
www.cddc.vt.edu/feminism

Greenpeace
www.greenpeace.org

Liberal International
www.liberal-international.org

Socialist Worker
http://socialistworker.org

UN Women: Gender Issues
www.unifem.org/gender_issues

Utilitarianism Resources
www.utilitarianism.com

Further Reading

Alvarez, Sonia E., Evelina Dagnino, and Arturo Escobar, eds. *Cultures of Politics/Politics of Cultures: Re-visioning Latin American Social Movements*. Boulder, CO: Westview Press, 1998.

Balaam, David N., and Michael Veseth. *Introduction to International Political Economy*. 4th edn. Upper Saddle River, NJ: Prentice Hall, 2008.

Beramendi, Pablo, and Christopher J. Anderson. *Democracy, Inequality, and Representation: A Comparative Perspective*. New York: Russell Sage Foundation, 2008.

Cohn, Theodore H. *Global Political Economy: Theory and Practice*. 5th edn. New York: Pearson Longman, 2010.

Giddens, Anthony. *The Global Third Way Debate*. Cambridge: Polity Press, 2001.

Heywood, Andrew. *Political Ideas and Concepts: An Introduction*. New York: St. Martin's Press, 1994.

Kriesi, Hanspeter. "The Organizational Structure of New Social Movements in a Political Context." In *Comparative Perspectives on Social Movements: Political Opportunities, Mobilizing Structures, and Cultural Framings*, 3rd edn., edited by Doug McAdam, John D. McCarthy, and Mayer N. Zald, 152–84. Cambridge: Cambridge University Press, 1996.

McCaffrey, Stephen C. *Understanding International Law*. Newark: LexisNexis, 2006.

Migdal, Joel S. *State in Society: Studying How States and Societies Transform and Constitute One Another*. Cambridge: Cambridge University Press, 2001.

Norris, Pippa. *Electoral Engineering: Voting Rules and Political Behavior*. Cambridge: Cambridge University Press, 2004.

Olson, Mancur. *The Logic of Collective Action: Public Goods and the Theory of Groups*. Cambridge, MA: Harvard University Press, 1971.

Shklar, Judith N. *Political Thought and Political Thinkers*. Edited by Stanley Hoffmann. Chicago: University of Chicago Press, 1998.

News Clips

Visit the companion website for *Politics: An Introduction*, 2nd edn, to access news clips related to the content of this chapter.

4

The Role of Government

◄ Parliament is the seat of Canada's federal legislative government and hence of national governmental roles and responsibilities. Parliament Hill, pictured here, is located in Ottawa.

Photo: Danielle Donders–Mothership Photography/Getty Images

LEARNING OBJECTIVES

After reading this chapter, you will be able to

- contrast various points of view regarding the role of government;
- identify the main objectives of a government system;
- compare the primary forms of government systems and their features;
- recognize how governments may change their role in society; and
- understand the government system used in Canada.

Introduction

Starting in December 2010, a wave of protest movements swept through many countries in the Arab world, a region that includes Northern Africa and the Middle East and extends into Western Asia. These protests were primarily about people's lack of voice in those countries and were a call for change in the nature of government–citizen relations. The movement was termed the Arab Spring, not just because of the time of year (the protests began to take effect in the spring of 2011) but also because it symbolized a wellspring of action in countries across the region. The Arab Spring had real influence: governments collapsed in Tunisia, Egypt, and (as a result of a civil conflict) Libya. In many other countries, calls for change led to reforms, additional protests, and demands for revolution. The challenge to the old order extended beyond the Arab world as well. For example, protests against the concentration of power in Russia led thousands to take to the streets in late 2011 and early 2012 to demand real democratic change.

Thanks to the Arab Spring, many governments that had been authoritarian for years changed in a short period of time. The movement ushered in a new role for governments in the region and a new **balance of power**. It also continues a long lineage of change in government functions and compositions. For instance, the period after World War II saw the rise of a new brand of capitalist economies, which was integrated into and co-operated with the collective development and restructuring of a global order. Things changed in the 1970s

balance of power
situation in international politics in which states strive to achieve equilibrium of power in the world in order to prevent any other country or coalition of countries from dominating the system

Egyptians gather in Tahrir Square in January 2011 to call for President Hosni Mubarak to step down. Mubarak eventually did resign in February and was later tried for crimes of corruption and abuse of power.

© EPA European Pressphoto Agency b.v. / Alamy

and again in the 1980s, with different interpretations of the role of government. The 1990s witnessed the collapse of the Communist bloc, including the Soviet Union and its allies, resulting in a new movement for democracy and market economies (one that endures two decades later in Russia and elsewhere).

This chapter will introduce you to the numerous forms of government that currently exist, as well as the ideologies and roles played in the relationship between government actors and citizens. You will find that the types of governments operating in today's international system are affected by the principles outlined in Chapter 3. All governments are rooted in some type of ideology, and there certainly are different views on what the relationship between governments and citizens should be.

We continue the theme of change in politics by closely examining the nature of variation in government systems and how dominant approaches, such as market economies and democracy, form the basis of how we view government roles over time. We begin with an overview of what governments do, regardless of their ideology. Here we will look briefly at different political systems and the various schools of thought regarding the role of government. Our focus then shifts to government composition, particularly the distinctions between federal and unitary systems. This is followed by an account of some of the major forms of government today, that is, liberal democracy, authoritarian, and totalitarian. Then, we will examine the process of change in government roles. The philosophers and thinkers discussed in Chapters 2 and 3 couldn't possibly have imagined a political world like the one we live in today, but their ideas persist in a different form. Revolutions in thought and action result in new roles for governments and new ways of thinking about state–society relations. Finally, we evaluate the unique role that government plays in Canada and the country's parliamentary system, which is the consequence of its distinctive history and links to the Westminster form of government established in the United Kingdom.

The different ways that we think about government are important because our attitudes shape its role in our society. Citizens in a liberal democracy such as Canada will have a very different perspective about the tasks and responsibilities of government than those in an authoritarian system. In fact, Canadians probably have different perspectives than citizens who also live in a liberal democracy. For example, Canadian views about government are quite different from those of American citizens. Overall, a better understanding of the ideologies that underlie various governments helps us grasp the functions that institutions and branches of government have. We will return to these topics in Chapter 5, which also explores the forms and activities of government and the methods that different systems use to carry out their duties. As you read both chapters, look for the overlap between them.

What Do Governments Do?

member of Parliament (MP)
representative of voters in a parliamentary system

Depending on the types and needs of particular societies, governments can be structured in distinctive ways and look very different from each other. Some emphasize the role of the legislature. Canada is an example—here, cabinet ministers and even the prime minister must also be **members of Parliament**. (Cabinet ministers can have a seat in the Senate rather than the House of Commons, but this option is rarely exercised.) Others, however, focus on separating the powers of the legislature from those of the executive level of government. As we will see in the following chapter, American politics has always been based on this balance of power between its Congress and the presidency (in this system, a person cannot be a member of both the executive and the legislature). Nevertheless, in all cases, government provides a means to regulate societal activities and to enforce the rules and regulations necessary for social interaction to work.

Various theories have been offered to explain the tendency of humans to organize themselves and make rules for their community. Some have suggested that political communities are created in response to the human fear of isolation. This idea reflects what Hobbes said about the "state of nature" and its consequences. That is to say, individual freedoms, though desirable in some respects, also bring about demands from people that often conflict with those of others. Individual freedoms can also lead to the fear of being conquered by another. Political organization and the creation of political units result in a form of "security in numbers" because individuals no longer fear isolation. Politics, after all, is about how we form political communities, and there is always a delicate balance between freedoms and security. Most political systems, at least liberal democracies, seek ways to best achieve this equilibrium. In addition, political communities produce accumulated benefits, such as

4.1 SOMALIA: STATE OF NATURE?

In his most famous work, *Leviathan*, Thomas Hobbes described the unnatural tendency we have to form governments given that the "natural" state for humans was complete independence, with no overarching authority. The problem, however, was that this natural state would be unlivable because everyone would do whatever it took to survive, leaving us in a situation without law or order.

Somalia, a state located in the Horn of Africa, has been without a functioning government since 1991. Faced with continued civil conflict and **insecurity**, Somalis have endured famine, economic underdevelopment, an almost total lack of services, and violent conflict. It is estimated that over 300,000 Somalis have died in the decades since the civil war began, and the country is now considered a "failed state" with no legitimate government and one of the lowest rankings of human development in the world. A quasi-sovereign state exists in the northwest (Somaliland), and the northeast region of Puntland sees itself as autonomous. But there is no central authority; forms of law and politics are disputed; and the economy is best described as "informal." None of this presents a positive situation for the future.

Although it might not represent a complete case of Hobbes's "state of nature," Somalia shows the serious problems that emerge when there is no legitimate authority. To their credit, Somalia's leaders have been attempting to put together a coalition system of government since 2008, and some progress has been made. But with different factions vying for control and a country under duress, the road to recovery will undoubtedly be a long one.

---

the distribution of responsibilities and access to greater wealth, justice, and social guardianship.

In very basic terms, governments exist to accomplish two goals. The first is to provide the necessary security assurances for its citizenry by maintaining and protecting territorial integrity, national resources, and the population from outside attack or exploitation. The second goal concerns the welfare goals of its citizens and involves providing adequate social conditions, opportunities, and benefits for its people. As you can see, there is a very important relationship between security and welfare. Security must be in place before welfare can be provided to citizens. But if citizens feel that their standard of living could be improved or, worse, that government has impeded their ability to gain or maintain access to the basics of life, they may rise up. Citizens might simply challenge their government by electing other politicians who promise to provide benefits. But they could rebel against their government if they felt that their standard of living was threatened by their rulers. A citizenry that accepts and supports its governing structure is therefore also a requirement for a secure and stable political system.

Government, then, is an agency to regulate behaviour in society. It represents a process through which society is protected and sustained. But it is also a set of administrative, legalistic, and political structures that carry out the process of governance. The judicial structure of government, for instance, is responsible for interpreting, applying, and upholding the laws of the land. Similarly, legislative structures establish a forum for interaction among political actors (usually

insecurity
threat of danger or injury

elected officials). There are generally many levels of structures within a political unit, as well as numerous significant political representatives (i.e. politicians) who all compete and work within government. We will consider these structures in greater detail in Chapter 5.

Not surprisingly, political analysts are particularly interested in both the process and structure of political interaction. They think about the way politics plays out and the political arrangement or composition of government that is in place. Indeed, these two dynamics are central for political inquiry because they inform us about the primary actors in a political unit and the environment in which they act.

Political scientists who study Canadian politics (often called Canadianists) look at how politics functions in Canada, as well as the decisions and policies that are put in place. Think about the federal budget, for example. Every year the Canadian government must declare how it intends to spend taxpayers' money. Defence, social programs, new roads, and equalization payments to provinces (which we will examine later in this chapter) are all accounted for. The budget process, however, is about more than just dollars and cents. It involves a number of stages, starting with priority-setting in the cabinet and ruling political party, consultations with experts and other levels of government, and financial accounting, right up to the presentation of the budget to Parliament and votes in both the House of Commons and the Senate. To understand the budget properly, we need to consider both the structures that guide it (cabinet, bills in Parliament, powers of the government and the two houses) as well as the process of decision-making (how a government establishes priorities, who has authority, and how those decisions are made). Taken together, the process and structure of politics tell us much more about why and how decisions and policies are made.

Studies of political anthropology show us that society comes before government in the natural and evolutionary phase of human organization. After all, a society must be in place in order to govern it. But government is essential to create a political unit. Even before states as we know them today existed, there was always some type of political authority in place. Tribes, villages, city-states, and even families have some hierarchy. We may not call them all government, but they contain much of the same process: in each grouping, we have to think about security, economic welfare, decision-making, authority, and justice.

It is important to recognize that the role of government in society and the economy is far from static. Political systems around the world have seen shifts in the extent of government intervention in social, political, and economic issues across time and space. Totalitarian governments throughout history have attempted to exert control over extensive aspects of public and private life. However, in many ways the resources available to governments determine how much control they can exercise over society and the economy. These resources can be military, propaganda-based, ideological, economic, regulatory or, most importantly, financial. As financial resources have increased, government's reach has extended. Perhaps the biggest change in this regard occurred between the end of the nineteenth century and the end of World War II. During the 1930s and 1940s, Western governments saw a massive increase in their responsibilities as they built up the welfare state, adopted new economic functions by nationalizing industries, and strengthened their defence capabilities. This increase was matched by a dramatic surge in government spending and, of course, taxing and borrowing. Figure 4.1 highlights the increase in US government spending between 1903 and 2010. The new resources available to governments enabled them to carry out their functions and to exert a hitherto unknown influence over society and the economy. But resources are not the only elements that determine the size and role of government. The ideology of government also matters, as we will see in the section on schools of thought.

Governments and politics are closely related because, in order to move beyond a loose hierarchy toward something more established and permanent, people need to agree on how society will be run. Rules need to be in place, and some authority must enforce them. For instance, consider the differences between the game of football and the jungle chase between hunter and prey. Simply put, both are competitive environments, with the benefits of one (a football team or the hunter or prey) eliminating those of the other. After all, only one team can actually win a football game, and either the hunter or the prey will prevail in the jungle. Which environment, then, is closer to that of politics? The answer to this question lies in the *nature* of the competitive environment. Although there are similarities between the football and the jungle examples,

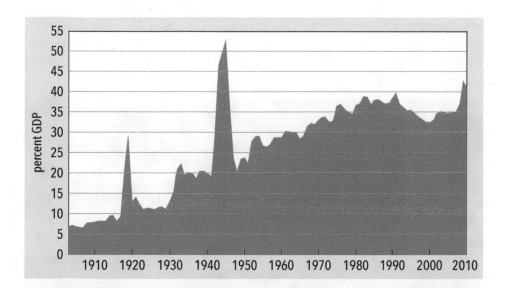

Figure 4.1   US Government Spending as Per Cent of Gross Domestic Product (GDP) US from fiscal year 1903 to FY 2010

Source: www.usgovernmentspending.com/spending_chart_1903_2010USp_13s1li011lcn_F0t_US_Government_Spending_As_Percent_Of_GDP

there is one very important distinction: the football game involves rules and referees. In a football game with no officials, the rules could not be imposed, and disagreement and disorder would prevail. But not every environment includes an authority. There are, of course, no "referees" judging the conduct or outcome of the jungle hunt, and the participants are left to their own devices regarding the outcome.

Government acts as the authority in political systems. In one sense, governments are rather like referees: they exist to create and pattern the basic rules of the system so that order may prevail, both domestically and internationally. However, not all governments have the same rules. The Canadian budget example mentioned earlier involves a different process and set of political structures than we would see in, say, the United States. It is also possible, of course, for governments to break rules. We see this repeatedly throughout history: governments contravene or circumvent the rules that they have agreed to protect. But in general we would like to think that governments enforce rules.

Because governments are given the right to exercise the legal use of force, they are able to enforce the rules and laws of a political unit. Yet to maintain this control and power, a government must have the support of its people. Although some governments may secure this backing through fear (for example, through authoritarian rule that leaves no other options), they are most successful by meeting the community's security and welfare goals.

Governments may be considered a political outcome because organizing social units inevitably leads to the creation of governing bodies. Governments are considered the representatives of sovereignty, and have the legitimate authority to make and administer rules and regulations on behalf of the community. However, it is always important to remember that their authority and

We may argue with referees' calls, but the game would be bedlam without them.

© Richard Wareham Fotografie (Nieuws) / Alamy

legitimacy derive from the consent of the people they govern, which can be lost or removed if they damage the interests of society or major groups within it.

Some Shared Objectives of Government

The primary objective of every government is to provide for the independence, stability, and economic and social well-being of all its citizens. Some are far more effective at meeting these goals, and others are obviously less concerned about their citizens. However, the type of government is crucial because some, such as authoritarian systems, consider the well-being of their citizens in markedly different ways than liberal democracies do. This isn't that surprising because authoritarian governments do not have to rely on the electoral support of their people.

genocide
deliberate and systematic killing of a group based on their ethnicity, nationality, culture, or race

---

4.2 THE PROBLEM WITH SOVEREIGNTY

Prior to the Peace of Westphalia, sovereignty had various interpretations, depending on the type of political system in question. Sovereignty was even applied to individual rulers in some cases, meaning that sovereign authority literally moved with the individuals granted the powers. The Peace of Westphalia ended a lot of this confusion by connecting sovereign authority to governments and introducing the idea of non-interference, which meant that other governments would not have the right to meddle in the affairs of others. Today, there are problems with sovereignty. One is that there are no formal rules for granting it. For instance, the People's Republic of China (PRC) considers Taiwan a breakaway part of the territory under its sovereign rule. In deference to the PRC, Canada does not recognize the sovereignty of Taiwan, even though we happily trade with and travel to that country all the time. It is up to individual countries, then, to decide whether to grant sovereignty to other governments and to live with the consequences.

Another problem with sovereignty is the doctrine of non-interference. Does this mean, for example, that we have to ignore cases of **genocide** (when groups are deliberately being targeted, often by their own government)? As we will see later in this text, the concept of sovereignty has come under increasing pressure in the twenty-first century.

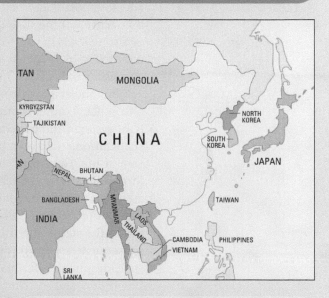

Figure 4.2 China (People's Republic of China) and Taiwan (Republic of China) both lay claim to the name "China"

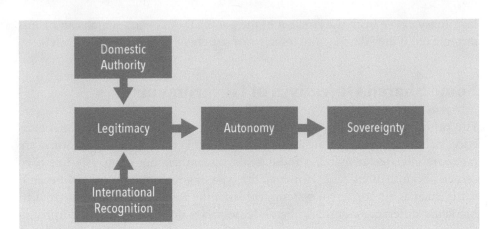

Figure 4.3   The Path to Sovereignty

Despite their differences, every country in the international system is first and foremost concerned with maintaining its national survival. This is part of the security of the state that we discussed previously. The continued endurance of a state leads in part to its legitimacy being recognized by the rest of the international system. When other states acknowledge the legitimate authority and autonomy of a state, it may be considered sovereign.

But sovereignty depends on both domestic legitimacy and external recognition. Governments must preserve national peace through the maintenance of legal systems and policing. Furthermore, they maintain their legitimacy—especially among their own people—by creating the conditions that lead to a better way of life. Governments may improve the individual welfare of their citizens through access to education, social benefits, health care, attempts to eliminate poverty, technological advances, and infrastructure enhancements. Part of external recognition relies on the stability of the country. In turn, this stability lies in the state's governing authorities being able to transfer political power to subsequent leaders through an established manner. This process preserves the state, despite significant changes to its core.

Some Activities of Government

The role of government was once fairly simple. At the time of the Peace of Westphalia (1648), which ended the Thirty Years' War in the Holy Roman Empire and the Spanish–Dutch Eighty Years' War, governments were largely responsible for, and concerned about, protecting themselves from attack from without or within. The Peace of Westphalia instituted our modern sovereign recognition of states and led to new ways of thinking about the responsibility of governments, but many still thought that the perfect role for the state would be as minimal as possible.

Minarchists believe that the powers of the state ought to be limited to providing citizens with basic security. Popularized in the 1800s, the idea of a "night watchman state" was one example of the minarchist ideology. In theory, the state's only role would be to ensure law and order, while other aspects of politics would be left to citizens. For those who see freedom in every aspect as the state's goal, minarchism makes a lot of sense. Ultimately, however, the call for these night watchman states dissipated as citizens became more democratically involved and groups within society more organized. Labour unions, for instance, grew in strength and number during this time, as greater attention was paid to the worker's plight. More emphasis was given to social democracy because minarchism could not provide the resources or welfare benefits that groups demanded. The sovereign authority granted to states by the Peace of Westphalia, coupled with later demands for welfare benefits, changed the nature of government action. Still, some people feel that government intervenes too much in society. Libertarians, for instance, share the minarchist idea about a significantly reduced role for government.

Until the mid-twentieth century, and even with calls for more welfare benefits, governments were primarily affected by the need to preserve and maintain their own security, as well as that of the nation. Since then, however, governments have grown much larger and the emphasis on citizens' needs has occupied an increasingly important role. Deepening democratization is one reason that the role for the state has increased. As people became more engaged in their political systems, the call for greater distribution of public goods also grew. Governments came to see the challenge posed by ideological newcomers, such as communist parties. As we will see later in this book, governments adapted by including elements of socialist ideology in a new form of democratic socialism that stressed the importance of redistribution and equality even more strongly. With this shift came the growth of the modern welfare state.

Even with this change, security from attack and war remains a great concern for governments. In Canada, the military and defence budget is about 8 per cent of the total yearly budget (not including debt and deficit financing), or about 1.5 per cent of its **gross domestic product** (GDP).[1] Other countries spend much more. In the United States, for instance, defence accounts for 19 per cent of the whole budget, or about 4.7 per cent of American GDP.[2] The US budget is more than three times larger than Canada's, but it is the percentage of defence spending that highlights the importance of the issue. Nonetheless, population growth, economic challenges, competition for scarce international resources, the increased complexity of decision-making, the nature of bureaucracy, and rising (and decidedly different) demands of citizens have led to sustained growth in governments' size and power. A fundamental challenge to this growth in mandate and demands is the way in which governments may carry out these new and wider responsibilities. Citizens increasingly insist that governments give them increased services for the same

gross domestic product (GDP)
total value of goods and services produced in a country in one year

amount of taxes paid, and calls for reduced taxation are a perennial feature in many countries.

In broad terms, government activities fall under four main categories: economic management, government aid and **subsidies**, institutional and bureaucratic regulation, and program development and administration. Each of these functions is fundamental to the effective governing of society and to the provision of public goods. Economic management occurs when governments pass resources from one revenue source to other bodies without setting designated requirements as to their use. Think, for instance, of the diverse levels of economic strength in Canada, where whole sets of provinces are referred to as "haves" or "have-nots" based on their economy relative to the other provinces. The problem that arises with such widespread and disparate levels of economic activity concerns the ability of governments to provide services at an equal level. If Canada were simply one province or territory, the level of services such as welfare, health care, and education would be based on the strength of one economy and therefore one source of tax revenue. However, with 13 different economies, the ability to provide basic services in Prince Edward Island is quite different than in Ontario. The result is equalization, or transfer, payments, which redistribute revenue from wealthier provinces to the poorer ones in order to align services available to all Canadians.

Government aid and subsidies represent a more active form of intervention, in which monies are provided to some individuals and groups but usually with requirements regulating their use. An excellent example of this occurred in 2009, when the governments of Ontario and Canada subsidized General Motors and Chrysler with over $10 billion to keep their Canadian plants open. Alternatively, governments may wish to encourage exploration of new resources or research

subsidies

payments made by governments to compensate businesses for inefficiencies and lack of competitiveness

4.3 EQUALIZATION IN CANADA

Equalization payments are a portion of revenue (taxes) collected by the federal government that is divided among provinces and territories (the three territories are given funds through a separate federal program called Territorial Formula Financing). The federal government assesses per capita revenue in each province based on taxes (personal, property, business, and consumption), as well as income from natural resources. That figure is then compared to the national average per capita to determine which provinces are "haves" and which are "have-nots." The latter receive equalization payments to spend as they deem necessary.[1] Other federal payments include the Canada Social Transfer and Canada

Health Transfer, which are meant to fund social and health programs in each province to ensure equal services across the country. Equalization has existed in one form or another since Confederation, but the plan was formalized in 1957 when Louis St Laurent was prime minister. Equalization payments today cost the Canadian government almost $14 billion per year (the total federal budget in 2013 was $282.6 billion).

Note

1. "Have-Not Is No More: N.L. Off Equalization," *CBC News*, last updated 3 Nov. 2008, www.cbc.ca/news/canada/newfoundland-labrador/story/2008/11/03/have-not.html.

In 2009 the Canadian government took the controversial decision to aid the flailing auto industry in Ontario. Not surprisingly, many felt that the manufacturers had inflated the costs (which were far higher than this cartoon suggests).

and development in a particular sector that holds the promise of future employment and revenue, such as oil exploration or the microchip industry.

Regulation refers to the rules of conduct imposed by government on its individual and corporate citizens' affairs. Although traditional areas of regulation include a nation's criminal code, governments may also use this activity as a policy instrument for a number of purposes. More so than any other role, the regulatory responsibilities of government have a significant effect on our daily lives. From regulating the macro economy (monetary and fiscal policy) and the micro economy (labour, industry, pricing, markets, subsidies, etc.) to social policy, political processes, and even morality (setting age admissions for films, laws on alcohol consumption, or age limits for sexual activity), governments perform important regulatory functions on an ongoing basis.

Program development and administration allows governments to move beyond merely supervising how other people conduct their affairs and creates opportunities for governments to complete tasks on their own. For instance, a government may seek a free trade arrangement with another country or increase social welfare. Two examples include a government's role in its national defence and diplomacy, where government actually exercises a monopoly over these tasks. An example of how difficult program development can be concerns health care in the United States. In the early 1990s, First Lady Hillary Clinton addressed the topic. Her proposals for universal health care were criticized for their cost and government involvement and were eventually defeated.[3] The

Obama administration returned to the thorny issue of providing universal health care for Americans, finding it just as controversial. After much haggling between Congress and the White House, the Patient Protection and Affordable Care Act (PPACA, or Obamacare) was passed in 2010. A watered-down version of Obama's initial proposal, the Act was to be phased in over four years and permitted private health care in America to co-exist with the new public plan.[4]

Schools of Thought Regarding the Role of Government

Government is involved in society in many ways: militarily, culturally, economically, and ideologically. Opinion varies widely, however, as to how governments can best advance the economic and social well-being of their citizens. Recall, for example, our earlier mention of minarchism, libertarianism, and social democracy. One of the best ways to see the distinction among such views is in a government's approach to and control of economic issues in society. Indeed, the three most dominant schools of thought regarding the role of government—the liberal approach, socialism, and mixed economy—have their roots in how they perceive economic benefits for the public. We will examine each of these in turn, looking at their general perspective for government and the specific attention paid to the government's role in the economy.

The liberal approach is customarily associated with the writings of Adam Smith. Smith was the best-known proponent of **laissez-faire** ("let be") economics and argued that government is an opponent of human liberty and should therefore be severely curtailed in economic activities.[5] The laissez-faire approach holds that governments should not act as a regulatory agency within the economy, thereby allowing a free market. In this system, citizens could strive for their own pursuits, allowing competition and self-interest to produce the conditions for every community member to work to his or her own best advantage to create a society where everyone benefits from such actions. Working to each individual's personal maximum potential is referred to as comparative advantage, where individuals' sacrifices and deeds serve the interests of the larger society. Free markets and laissez-faire policies constitute what we commonly think of as a capitalist system.

Socialism argues the opposite of the liberal approach. Socialist theorists claim that the possibility that every member will work to his or her own greatest potential in the interests of serving the common good is offset by the more probable reality that a few overly self-interested persons will do particularly well in a political-economic system and the majority of the population will do poorly. Socialism holds that government, not individuals, ought to maintain ownership and control of the modes of production and instruments of the economy to regulate a system that will truly serve the interests of society at large. We can see here how socialism is a criticism of capitalism: whereas

laissez-faire
"to let be"; economic theory that suggests that a reduction in political control will benefit the economic system

capitalism suggests that individuals should be left free to decide how economic benefits will be distributed in the system, socialism holds that such distribution should be overseen by the government. Rather than yielding to a competitive environment where social welfare relies on the community concerns of individuals, socialism assumes that individuals must suppress their own interests in order to serve the greater good of the community.

The final approach is something of a mix of the first two and best represents the type of political systems that exist in most advanced democracies today. The mixed-economy approach essentially allows for a system that is governed by a laissez-faire style but also gives governments the authority to restrict any abuses of the system. A welfare state that provides the means for individual protection and quality of life, such as health care, employment insurance, pensions, and social programs for the elderly, children, and unemployed is created. Simultaneously, private interests and not the government largely run the economy. The welfare state is exemplified in Canada, the United States, and Scandinavian countries such as Sweden.

Of course, these are general approaches that do not represent complete versions of government "types" in any system. Instead, individual systems will take on aspects of different approaches. It is also true that government types will change over time. We can look at our own government systems for examples.

Starting in the years following World War II, the Keynesian state model gained strength. John Maynard Keynes, argued that failures of the private sector in the economy would need to be addressed by the public sector (i.e. government). Keynesian economics sees a cycle of gains and drops in the economy. A cycle might be good for the economy in the long term, if we assume that relative strengths will eventually emerge. But in the short term, such fluctuations can be catastrophic. Keynesianism sees a mix of private and public activity in the

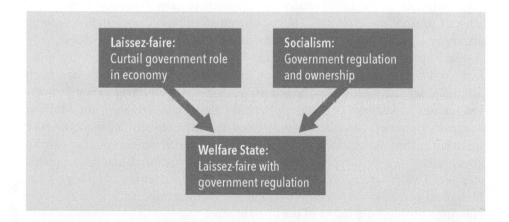

Figure 4.4   The Welfare State

4.4 THE WELFARE STATE

The welfare state assumes that government has a responsibility to provide the conditions for well-being and happiness to all its citizens. A relatively new phenomenon in government, this idea has roots throughout history. The ancient Greeks considered this role for government in their discussions of justice and the proper relationship between government and the governed. Welfare state policies include providing health care, employment benefits, care for the aged, and the infrastructure needed for citizens to achieve their highest potential.

The welfare state has an interesting relationship with capitalism, which sees wealth and production as the responsibility of private interests. The benefits of capitalism brought greater opportunities for governments to assist their citizens, largely through more taxation revenue. Meanwhile, the welfare state allowed twentieth-century capitalist economies to blunt the socialist criticism that capitalism was fundamentally inequitable and biased against the poor. As more and more capitalist states adopted welfare state policies in the twentieth century, the role for government increased and the power of capitalism grew. Keynesianism, neo-liberalism, and the Third Way all shared–to varying degrees–an emphasis on providing welfare benefits to citizens.

economy, with a crucial role for government: when the economy drops, governments should step in and provide stimulation to boost economic strength. Stimulation could involve reducing interest rates (to spur more borrowing and purchasing) and launching infrastructure projects (to invest money directly into the economy and increase employment).

Keynesianism was credited for avoiding another major economic depression. However, the other half of Keynesian thought—government needs to step back after its stimulus is done—wasn't successfully implemented. Governments continued to stay involved in the economy through the 1960s and 1970s, and things began to go awry. Inflation, high unemployment, rising oil costs, and declining trade balances in the 1970s caused governments to take desperate measures to attempt to right the economy. But out-of-control inflation rates and continuing economic troubles led to a widespread dismissal of Keynesian economics.

In its place came a new approach to liberal ideas of competition, free markets, and the removal of government interference. Neo-liberalism had been around since the 1930s, but the economic disasters of the late Keynesian period revived it. Led by US President Ronald Reagan and British Prime Minister Margaret Thatcher, neo-liberalism reversed the decades-old approach to state interventionism. Economic markets were reformed with a much smaller part for government. The principal idea was **deregulation**, meaning that governments stepped back from their prior, more prominent, role in the economy. Neo-liberalism spread in the Western world as more economies became increasingly entwined through the forces of the open market.

This change also led to ebbs and flows in national economies and to major governments considering alternatives by the early 1990s. US President Bill Clinton and British Prime Minister Tony Blair, along with other leaders such as Germany's Chancellor Gerhard Schröder, Brazil's President Henrique Cardoso,

deregulation
removal of government controls in an economic sector

and Canada's Prime Minister Jean Chrétien, adopted the so-called Third Way, which melded ideas that centred on either the public or private sector. Based on the theories of British sociologist Anthony Giddens,[6] this approach rejected the extreme positions of both Keynesians and neo-liberals and sought greater equality and benefits through better distribution of wealth, equal opportunity, balanced budgets, reduced government control, and improved government–private sector co-operation. To a large extent, elements of the Third Way are prevalent in most Western political systems and emerging economies.

These three examples show us how ideologies and approaches actually get implemented. The period covered by Keynesianism, neo-liberalism, and the Third Way was punctuated by serious economic challenges. Not surprisingly, the response of governments involved various competing notions of how the economy might be managed.

Other political perspectives are less economically based. As we've already discussed, libertarianism reflects the minarchist model in that both envision a greatly reduced role for the state. Some go so far as to compare libertarians with anarchists (who feel that government should be eradicated entirely), but the former see a limited role for government, constitutionally bound and restricted. Citizens are seen as responsible to themselves. The authority of government is based on a sense of mutual agreement between the governed and the governors, used mainly to protect citizens from harm or injustice caused by others. The individual freedoms of citizens, both political and economic, are to be ensured at all costs, and governments are never to wield the power of the law over their citizens without justification.

There are many other types of government that may or may not share similar frames of reference for the role for government. Monarchies (mentioned in Chapter 2) are those with supreme power in an individual, **theocracies** are ruled by religious leaders, **aristocracies** have hierarchical elites, **despots** have absolute power, and **juntas** are military governments, usually dictatorships.

Objectives of Political Systems

In some respects this chapter provides a connection between the more detailed explanation of political ideologies in Chapter 3 and the overview of government institutions in Chapter 5. It is important that we see the interaction among political structures, as well as the environment in which they interact, in order to fully comprehend the implications of ideology and political thought for government. To get there, we must first take a closer look at the ideologies that frame political systems.

From a strictly functional perspective, just about anything a government does (or does not do, for that matter) stems from one of four main objectives:

1. Maintaining the political system: Unless a system has a capacity for persisting over time, it will disappear or be overtaken by a more powerful

theocracy
political system ruled by religious leaders

aristocracy
political system ruled by a hierarchical elite

despot
political leader who rules with absolute power and authority

junta
military government, usually a dictatorship

form of governance. System maintenance involves providing political and economic goods to the community at large with the broader goals of preserving the government. Examples include national parks, border security, economic development initiatives and cultural programs that the central government will provide country-wide. Though it may seem a little severe, it is nonetheless possible that the Canadian federation could break apart—or at least be challenged greatly from within and cause social cohesion to suffer greatly—were there to be serious differences in what citizens were able to enjoy in one part of the country or another.

terrorism
strategy of violence designed to bring about political change by instilling fear in the public at large

2. Adapting the political system: Governments must adapt to a variety of changes, including population, distribution of wealth, technological advances, and challenges from within (e.g. revolution or **terrorism**) and without (war). Some of these changes are radical; civil war, for instance, could lead to the breakdown of the government or even the creation of a new political system. But most adaptation is more evolutionary, as governments respond to challenges such as an economic upheaval or a crisis in resource availability. One perennial concern in Canada is the matter of housing in the north, particularly in Aboriginal communities. Isolation, transportation challenges, and the higher cost of goods and services in the north means that comparable housing in these areas is at a much lower standard than in other areas of the country. In fact, most Canadians find the conditions deplorable for an economically well-off country that is committed to equality. Successive governments have increased funding for Aboriginal housing—the figure is currently over $250 million per year—but the crisis has not been solved. The issue points to the real challenges that countries such as Canada face in adapting the system to meet all citizens' needs.

3. Integrating interests and needs: A political system has to work continuously at making a whole out of parts. To do so, a system must have the political, cultural, and economic tools necessary. For instance, Canada has to contend with provincialism and regionalism and uses policies of power-sharing, Canadian culture promotion, and economic distribution to maintain its federal structure. Equalization is an example of such a policy. Canada's government distributes funds throughout the country to ensure that interests in one part do not come at the expense of those in another. Canada has also embraced multiculturalism as an approach to ethnic diversity in the country, encouraging respect and peaceful coexistence between multiple ethnic groups. It's not a perfect system, and one shouldn't assume that there is complete ethnic harmony in Canada, but diversity has been a long-standing principle of Canadian governments and has been enshrined in legislation such as the Canadian Charter of Rights and Freedoms (the Charter).

4. Goal-setting: Every political system must set its objectives. Individual governments do this all the time; for instance, the Speech from the Throne opens a new session of Parliament (or provincial legislatures)

in Canada. Governments use the speech to outline the direction and goals for the coming session and to remind citizens of their intentions. A properly functioning and integrated government will continually reference its objectives—for example, job creation, national security, or tax reduction—in statements and speeches in an effort to establish priorities and an agenda. The continued viability of a system is in large part contingent on the attainability of these goals.

It should be kept in mind that these four functions of political systems are mutually dependent. That is, success in one role usually depends on success within another. And, despite widespread differences among political systems, each basically pursues these similar goals.

Political observers have long noted the distinctive ways that governments achieve their goals. In *The Republic*, Plato considered how the conduct of rulers and their institutions affect the relationship between state and society. He offered a typology (a method of classification and interpretation of concepts) of government, distinguishing among the different types of governance that existed during the Greek era.[7]

Interestingly, most of the types outlined by Plato are still exemplified in current forms of government or strongly resemble contemporary systems. In *Politics*, Aristotle (one of Plato's students) examined the "natural" relationship between the rulers and the ruled, one that he described as a partnership. This Platonic/Aristotelian model distinguished forms of governments, classifying them according to the manner and conduct of rule and those charged with governing the political community. But in every case, a special responsibility lay with government in its partnership with the community.[8]

However, Plato felt that other forms of rule, such as monarchy and aristocracy, were superior to democracy. He considered politics a vocation requiring expertise; hence, opening up the process to all meant that politics could—and likely would—be overrun by those who made decisions on their passions or instinct rather than their knowledge and intellect. He feared that democracy would lead to mob rule, with no checks over authority and an inequitable allocation of public goods. Plato suggested that "rule by the many" required a legal framework to manage the relationship between rulers and the ruled and to avoid the potentially adverse effects of majority rule (particularly the submission of minority interests to majority rule). Plato's answer to the question of how to link government with citizens was the polity, or constitutional democracy. Understanding modern democracies, then, requires some thought about laws and constitutions.

Constitutions: The "Basic Law"

A constitution refers to a basic element of an object or principle, an essential component. For political studies, **constitutions** are a part of a broader legal and

constitution
the basic law of a country, upon which all other laws are based

statutory environment that serves to structure the activities permitted within a political unit. Though we often consider constitutions to be the domain of democracies, it is important to note that many other types of political systems have adopted constitutions as a central institution for government rule and political relationships.

The relationship between government and citizens in contemporary society is a complex one. In an age of mobility, transparency, and broad freedoms, there nonetheless needs to be a clear set of parameters regarding what is permissible in society. Sovereignty, then, is still essential. We grant sovereignty to governments not to limit the freedoms of individual citizens but to provide a system within which those freedoms can best be secured. For a variety of reasons, it is fairly evident that we require a legalistic framework such as a constitution as a necessary component of a modern political system.

First, constitutions formalize the principal institutions of government and their interrelationship. The constitution is the best place to start when you want to know what the various branches of your government are supposed to do (we will deal with this topic in more detail in Chapter 5). Second, constitutions provide the framework within which ordinary laws are made. In fact, the German constitution is called the *Grundgesetz*, which literally translates to "basic law." Most other laws are extensions of the core principles of a constitution. Criminal codes and the laws of the land must be "constitutional" in order to be effective. Third, a constitution may define the relationship between government(s) and individual citizens, prescribing what a government can and cannot do to its citizenry. Finally, constitutions are more than just legalistic documents. They also represent a symbol of the nation. Constitutions provide a portrayal of a country's character, its core ideology, and belief system. In the case of the United States, for example, the American constitutional goals, and indeed the intent of the nation, can be summarized in its preamble:

> We the people of the United States, in order to form a more perfect
> union, establish justice, insure domestic tranquility, provide for
> the common defence, promote the general welfare, and secure the
> Blessings of Liberty to ourselves and our posterity, do ordain and
> establish this Constitution for the United States of America.

In Canada, "peace, order and good government" (POGG)—which is really a constitutional "residual" clause stipulating that powers not allocated explicitly in the Canadian constitution would go to the federal government—has come to represent a larger sense of purpose for Canadian society. POGG is often used by the Canadian government to describe its interests at home and abroad.

Constitutions may be "written," in which one may refer to a single basic law, or "unwritten," in which a collection of documents and laws are used for consulting and interpreting legislation and legal behaviour in a country. The United States and Canada have written constitutions, while the United Kingdom's is unwritten. Both types are referred to as living documents because they are

4.5 UNWRITTEN CONSTITUTIONS

It would be reasonable to assume that the basic law for any country would be written down in a single document. The US constitution, for instance, can be seen at the National Archives in Washington, DC. But some countries do not have a written constitution. One might conclude that an unwritten constitution has no enforcement value because it is not compiled in one document. Making matters more perplexing is the idea of codification, which means to collect jurisdictional laws in a legal code. However, in constitutional circles, a codified constitution is considered one passed into law as a single legal instrument.

Most states, including Japan and the United States, have codified constitutions. Other countries, such as Canada, have more than one constitutional document. The constitution of Canada is made up of the Constitution Act of 1867 and the Constitution Act of 1982 (the Canada Act). There are also unwritten constitutional elements in the Canadian constitution and amendments. Yet these uncodified constitutions (that is, not in a single source) are still binding and, in the Canadian case, are "written." Written and unwritten constitutions are not necessarily codified and uncodified, respectively. In the UK, the constitution is unwritten (it is made up of written judgments, treaties, and statutes, as well as unwritten royal privileges and prerogatives and political conventions) and uncodified, but it is nonetheless legal.

amended or changed often. The American constitution has been amended 27 times; the Canadian, 10. New understandings of constitutions, however, may appear without an amendment. Different legal interpretations over time may mandate new understandings. For instance, the courts constantly interpret and apply the constitution in legal determination, resulting in different meanings of the basic law in a different time or place. The original drafters of the Canadian constitution would not likely have foreseen challenges to Canadian law on issues such as same-sex marriage or shopping on Sundays. This is the very reason why constitutions must be allowed to change: values and preferences vary over time, and so do factors such as economic conditions or political relations.

The Canadian constitution is an excellent example of a living document. Like other constitutions, it sets out the basic law for the country, outlines the mechanism of government, and lists the rights of Canadian citizens. Most Canadians know that there were two major constitutional Acts that created our current constitution. The British North America Act of 1867 gave legislative authority to the new "dominion" of Canada, and all other constitutional powers were granted to Canada in 1982, when the British Parliament passed the Canada Act. The first "constitution of Canada," however, was the Constitutional Act of 1791; this Act was preceded by the 1763 Royal Proclamation, which set out the constitutional rules for the province until it was replaced by the Quebec Act of 1774. Real independence from the UK came with the Statute of Westminster in 1931, when Canada received legislative authority equal to the UK. Still, the British Parliament had to assent to any Canadian constitutional amendment—though this was largely a formality—until 1982. In any case, the 1867 and 1982 Acts comprise the core of the Canadian constitution. The latter

4.6 THE CONSTITUTION ACT, 1982

With political independence from the UK and autonomy in policy-making, Canada was considered sovereign before 1982. However, it still required approval by the British Parliament before it could change any basic law. The Constitution Act, 1982–introduced by the government of Pierre Trudeau–would make Canada legally responsible for its own affairs (including legislation) and fully sovereign.

The lead-up to the signing of the Act was not without its controversies. The Trudeau government had to work with the provinces to form clauses on issues such as Aboriginal rights, equalization, an amendment formula, the notwithstanding clause (which gives provinces limited rights to override the constitution), and the inclusion of the Canadian Charter of Rights and Freedoms. The 7/50 formula, which requires approval from 7 out of 10 provinces with at least half of the country's population and is currently used to make constitutional changes in Canada, did not exist. As a result, the Act passed without Quebec–which wanted a constitutional veto–supporting it. The province has never signed and two attempts to further amend the constitution to include it–the

The Canadian Press/Stf-Ron Poling

Queen Elizabeth II officially signs the Constitution Act, 1982. The Act brought amendments to the constitution and introduced the Canadian Charter of Rights and Freedoms.

Meech Lake Accord (1987) and the Charlottetown Accord (1992)–have failed. However, as the basic law of Canada, the constitution still applies in Quebec.

also includes the Charter of Rights and Freedoms, which presents the constitutionally bound individual and collective rights of citizens. Constitutional challenges—same-sex rights, freedom of religion, and the like—are based on the rights provided in the Charter.

Now that we understand the activities, objectives, opinions, roles, and constitutions of government, we will turn our attention to three variants of political systems: liberal democracy, authoritarianism, and totalitarianism.

Liberal Democracy

Democracy owes its roots to several strains of political thought. However, its most influential foundation may be found in the tradition of liberalism. In fact, the two terms are often used interchangeably, though they ought not to be, given their strict definition. *Democracy* has become one of the most common terms in political analysis today, to the point that it might be considered one of the most overused concepts available to political scientists and observers. Consequently, it has as many implications and meanings as there are employers of the term.

Given the Platonic roots of democratic thinking, it is not surprising to learn that the term *democracy* is taken from the Greek *demos*, meaning "the people," and *kratos*, which means "authority." Far from the simple conclusions about mob rule, democracy takes into account the need for **checks and balances** over political authority (in order to avoid the appropriation of interests by the few, for example) and the fact that many interests exist within a political community. In short, democracy recognizes that rule by all is simply impossible but that **pluralism**—the idea that power in a political system is distributed among many different groups—is essential for security and equity.

The compromise between what the ancient Greeks saw as the potential failure for democracy (the "tyranny" of the majority) and the need to allow for public participation came in the form of the previously mentioned polity, with a central role for constitutionalism and the rule of law. Essentially, this arrangement required even the majority to accept the rule of law and limit its behaviour. The central components of liberal democracy include the following:

- Equality of political rights: This type of equality allows every member of the society to participate in activities of the political unit—voting, running for office, protesting, and the like. Of course, certain restrictions exist, such as the legal age of majority, which must be met in order to be considered a legal adult. In Canada, people must reach the age of 18 before they can vote in elections. No particular political rights are held for a select group of people; for instance, though parliamentarians in Canada alone are permitted to vote in the House of Commons or Senate, almost everyone has the right to seek such offices (see Chapter 7).
- Political participation: Related to the equality of political rights, this factor refers to distributing political responsibilities among the ruled and the rulers. This may involve direct participation of individuals, such as in a referendum, or indirect participation, where political authority is transferred to individuals elected by the masses to represent their views. Interest groups, or pressure groups, are another example of how citizens become involved in the policy-making process through lobbying politicians (discussed in Chapter 8).
- Majority rule: In majority rule, all votes are held equally so that the majority of votes govern; however, the rights of the minority need to be protected.
- Political freedom: A citizen's right to participate freely in the political process is limited only by the laws of the community. Participation and representation can be considered legitimate only if individuals are encouraged and allowed to share in the political process in a free environment.

Liberal democracy in Canada is based fundamentally on classical liberal ideas. Individual rights, free economic markets, and the responsibility of

checks and balances
system of inspection and evaluation of different levels and branches of governments by others

pluralism
society in which several disparate groups (minority and majority) maintain their interests and a number of concerns and traditions persist

government to its citizens are all hallmarks of both traditional classical liberal democracy and Canada's version. In many ways similar to liberal democracy in the United States—at least with regard to the points listed above—Canada's model adopted an allegiance to the British monarch rather than the republicanism inherent in American liberal democracy. The hereditary nature of monarchism has led some critics to suggest that Canada's political system is actually aristocratic or monarchical at the top, but in reality the monarch's legal and actual role in Canada is largely symbolic and without real political effect.

In addition to the classical liberal aspects of Canadian liberal democracy, we must also consider the social elements of Canada's case. Social progressivism and internationalism, coupled with a redistributive state (see commentary elsewhere in this chapter regarding equalization, for instance), are representative of the other half of Canada's liberal democracy. Minority rights, freedom from religious prosecution, and equality of the sexes are just a few of the examples we might use to describe the social liberal nature of Canada's liberal democracy. This is an important point because, while liberalism tends to be related most closely to politics and the economy, liberal democracy in Canada demonstrates an important social liberalism as well. We'll return to this difference in Chapter 9.

Authoritarianism

In our everyday lives, most of the states that we hear about are liberal democracies. In many ways, this is a function of where we live, our domestic political environment, and the culture in which we have been socialized. It is also a result of the interaction of our political community with others: generally, the lion's share of Canada's international activities is with other liberal democratic countries. But if we define the term *liberal democracy* as more than just voting by citizens, most studies (including those of non-aligned private institutes such as Freedom House) conclude that most current political systems are not of this type. Instead, they might best be described as authoritarian systems, requiring a high degree of obedience to a constituted authority and a severe lack of freedoms.

In short, authoritarian systems are the antithesis of liberal democracies. At their root, they require their citizens to submit to the will of government institutions. Authoritarian states are coercive in that they may rely on the use— or threat—of force to gain acceptance of the ruled and to suppress dissent. Authoritarian regimes (as such concentrations of absolute power in government are often disparagingly called) are governed by a powerful, often wealthy, minority, and all political (and often social, economic, and cultural) activities are strictly overseen by state authorities. Although authoritarian systems may use ideology as a tool of control, they are not ideologically bound; they may be left-wing, right-wing, religious, military, civilian, capitalist, or communist. They also tend to be highly concentrated and insular, which provides greater control and authority over individuals and groups.

4.7 DEMOCRACY TOPPLES AUTHORITARIANISM?

The Republic of the Union of Myanmar, commonly referred to as Myanmar or Burma, is a heavily populated and geographically large country in Southeast Asia that has been part of several political empires in its history, including the Mongol empire. After being colonized by Britain in the 1860s, Burma finally achieved independence in 1948, only to see its fledgling democracy threatened by civil conflict. Eventually, a military junta took over in 1962 and ruled the country until 2010. Burma suffered drastically during this period, as many countries in the world (including Canada) imposed economic sanctions against a government they felt was illegitimate. The 1980s witnessed a popular movement for democracy in Burma, leading to calls for elections. In 1990, a vote led to the election of Aung San Suu Kyi, whose parents were instrumental in the early days of political independence, and her National League for Democracy (NLD) party, which received over 80 per cent of the popular vote.

Suu Kyi espoused the values of Mahatma Gandhi, who urged non-violent means for political change. The military government refused to step down, however, and placed her under house arrest. During her captivity, she received several awards for her peaceful demands, including the Nobel Peace Prize in 1991. (She is also an honorary citizen of Canada, one of only five people to receive the title.) International pressure for democracy and Suu Kyi's release continued, and despite the junta's crackdowns, domestic protests made it

Political leader Aung San Suu Kyi addresses a crowd of supporters in Yangon, Myanmar (Burma) in 2010.

impossible for the government to maintain power without the risk of a complete civil war. In 2010 Suu Kyi was released and democratic elections were permitted; the military junta dissolved formally the next year. However, the military-backed Union Solidarity and Development Party won the election, under disputed results. Suu Kyi is now an opposition leader in a new political order that shows both the promise of democratic reform and the legacy of an authoritarian past.

Although authoritarian states are prone to control as much of the state and society as possible, there are often areas of private life that remain free. Citizens may, for example, hold views that differ from an authoritarian government or even support challengers to the rulers. However, this is done at much greater risk than in liberal democracies, where opposition is fostered and considered a healthy part of a diverse political system. There is no guarantee that these limited rights may be upheld, and authoritarian states differ widely on the degree to which debate and resistance may be permitted.

Totalitarianism

Often used as an equivalent of authoritarianism, **totalitarianism** is in fact a variant of authoritarian rule. But what distinguishes the two is the emphasis

totalitarianism
authoritarian political system that not only controls most social interaction but is also marked by a government's desire to force its objectives and values on citizens in an unlimited manner

on ideological control. That is, totalitarian political systems not only control most social interaction but are also marked by the government's desire to force its objectives and values on citizens in an unlimited manner. Totalitarianism has the dubious record of being behind many of the most dictatorial and treacherous governments of the modern age, including those of the current North Korean regime, the Taliban rule in Afghanistan, the Soviet Union, East Germany, and fascist Italy.

Governance in a totalitarian regime is best described as tyrannical (the harsh and arbitrary exercise of authority). Freedoms are greatly restricted, opposition—in party or any other form—is usually denied, and ideological control is evident in the government's methods of monitoring or managing every aspect of life. Since there are usually no rules protecting citizens, majority participation is replaced by the interest of the dominant political authority, and the use of strength and fear is often used to maintain supremacy. One aspect of totalitarian rule is its emphasis on ideologically redeveloping society from the top down, including fundamental belief systems and values. This results in the further consolidation of the leader's power. Totalitarian leaders tend to form an elite, as government control is concentrated in a few individuals and often involves a single leader with inordinate power. Despite all this, totalitarian regimes will often attempt to maintain the semblance of democratic institutions, such as holding elections that are manipulated to meet the requirements and wishes of the government. However, dissent is suppressed (often forcibly), so forming an alternative option to totalitarian rule is practically impossible.

Another way to maintain the appearance of a democracy is to establish a constitution. It was often said during the Cold War (1945–91) that the Soviet Union had the most democratic constitution in the world. Rights and freedoms were ensured in Soviet basic law, but in real life they were only words on paper. Totalitarian regimes will control information as well. The less information getting in from the outside world, the lower the probability of dissent. State-controlled media in China stringently limit free access to outside voices of opposition. During the Beijing Olympics in 2008, Chinese authorities were criticized for banning open access to online information about political protests in Tibet.

A final tactic of totalitarian governments concerns their use of fear to achieve political goals. For example, citizens in Cold War Hungary lived in dread that the secret police (the ÁVH) would take them away to be tortured or executed (the police headquarters on Budapest's Andrássy Avenue is now a museum depicting those dark days under communist and fascist rule). Children were encouraged to report teachers or even family members whom they suspected of plotting against the government. Those of us who were raised in a liberal and free political environment can only imagine how terrible such a state would be.

Although there are numerous variants of governments (such as **transitional governments**), liberal democracies and authoritarian and totalitarian regimes represent the basis for most political communities. Right-wing or left-wing, secular or religious, elitist or pluralist, multicultural or ethnically restricted, all political systems roughly fit into one of these broad classifications.

transitional government
political system in which the move from authoritarianism to liberal democracy results in elements of both, with a gradual change to democracy

The composition of government, on the other hand, is another way of arranging political systems. Once we understand the basic ideological underpinnings of a system, it is equally important to consider the manner in which political authority and decision-making are appropriated. We will examine these topics in greater detail in the following chapter.

Government and Canada

Like any other country, Canada shares characteristics with others but also has its own unique features. It is an example of a liberal democracy, something it has in common with many of its closest allies, including the United States, the United Kingdom, France, and Germany. Canada's government is a constitutional monarchy, meaning that its constitution grants ultimate authority to its head of state, the British monarch. The prime minister is the head of government in Canada; he or she controls the direction that policy-making

4.8   ARE GOVERNORS GENERAL JUST CEREMONIAL?

There are times when the governor general of Canada makes decisions that are quite significant. In 1926 Governor General Lord Byng refused Prime Minister Mackenzie King's request to dissolve Parliament (usually a ritual performed without question) and invited the opposition to form a government. That government, led by Arthur Meighen, failed to gain the support of Parliament, and Mackenzie King won the next election. The "King–Byng" affair was quite controversial because, even though Byng acted within his constitutional rights, he was criticized for getting involved in electoral politics.

Governors general occasionally have no choice but to make decisions that have real political implications. In 2008, then governor general Michaëlle Jean allowed Parliament to prorogue (discontinue for a period of time). In this case, Prime Minister Stephen Harper requested the suspension to avoid a vote of non-confidence by the other parties in the House of Commons, which would have permitted them to join forces and form a coalition government or have led to another election. This situation was controversial because the governor general, who is not elected, made a choice that significantly affected the Canadian Parliament and allowed the Conservatives to stay in power.

The Canadian Press/Fred Chartrand

Governors general are often considered simply ceremonial, but at times their duties can have a serious impact on Canadian politics.

takes. The head of state is a largely ceremonial figure and is represented by the governor general. (Other countries, such as the United States, combine the powers of head of state and head of government.) In turn, the governor general (on the advice of the prime minister) appoints a lieutenant governor in each province to be his or her representative. This position does not exist in the three territories, which have no independent jurisdictional powers but derive their authority from what the federal government grants them. Therefore, they have a commissioner who represents the federal government rather than the monarchy. Although the governor general has the highest level of political responsibility as far as the Canadian constitution allows (for instance, he or she must provide royal assent to federal statutes before they become law; lieutenant governors do the same for provincial laws), his or her role is largely symbolic.

Canada is also a parliamentary democracy, which means that its legislature—the federal parliament—has elected members. The House of Commons is made up of elected members based on constituencies in all provinces and territories. However, the other part of Parliament, the Senate, is not an elected body. Here, the governor general appoints members on the advice of the prime minister. In this respect, not all of Parliament is "democratic," but the part that has the most responsibility (the House of Commons) is composed of elected representatives. With two houses, the Canadian Parliament is **bicameral**; however, the provinces and territories are **unicameral**.

Further authority and powers are given to the provinces, territories, municipalities, and Aboriginal communities. But the ultimate authority resides in the central government (Canada is not a federal state in the strictest sense of the word but is more of a "quasi-federal" system; we discuss this in Chapters 5 and 6). Recall that the POGG clause of the constitution assigns any residual powers to the federal government.

With such a large country to govern (geographically the second largest in the world, after Russia), combined with its difficult geography and distinctly regional economic advantages (e.g. oil and gas, fisheries, and manufacturing), Canada has unique challenges regarding economic management, equal provision of services, and program development. More than 90 per cent of the Canadian population lives within 160 kilometres of the US border. As we will consider in Chapter 9, this means that the highly interdependent economic relationship between the two countries tends to frame much of Canada's commercial activities. And, as Canada is a trading state out of necessity, the US market is more than just essential for the standard of living Canadians have come to expect.

Yet Canadians live all over the country, and the government is responsible for administering its programs everywhere. We have already touched on the role of equalization payments in balancing access to such services. Canada is a welfare state, meaning that it provides certain resources to citizens, such as health care, employment insurance, and old age benefits based on need. This is

bicameral
legislative or parliamentary body with two assemblies

unicameral
legislative or parliamentary body with one assembly

another example of the redistributive aspect of Canadian politics and economics, which we will return to from time to time in this text.

Canada is also a regulatory state. The economy in Canada can be defined as capitalist, albeit one with a large degree of government involvement. Government not only regulates the macro economy, setting interest rates, taxes, and monetary policy, but it also has a large role in the micro economy, with important regulations for industry and maintenance of the economic infrastructure. This degree of involvement is necessary given the sheer size of the Canadian economy (the tenth largest in the world) and its heavy dependence on international relations.

At various points in this text, we will take a closer look at other aspects of Canada's government. In Chapter 5, for instance, we will examine the institutions and branches of the Canadian government, picking up on some of the points we have looked at here. Throughout the remaining chapters, we look more directly at Canadian federalism, elections, and interest groups, economic relations abroad, and foreign policy.

Conclusion

No two governments are the same. While certain characteristics may be shared, such as a type of economy or political system, each one has its specific aspects. In Chapters 9 and 10 we look at some individual cases to see just how diverse countries in the world are today. But part of what we do as political scientists is draw comparisons and distinctions among political systems. This comparative method of analysis has been part of our field for as long as people have looked at their own governments and thought of ways to improve them.

In this chapter we have looked at the three main categories of governments—liberal democratic, authoritarian, and totalitarian systems. We have examined the main goals of countries, namely to provide security and stability for citizens and, at least in liberal democracies, to protect freedoms and wealth. Governments manage economies, offer aid and subsidies to maintain a degree of equal distribution of goods and services, regulate the bureaucratic and administrative elements of the political system, and extend welfare benefits to the general public. With this in mind, we will turn our attention to the branches of government in the following chapter.

Self-Assessment Questions

1. How are sovereignty and legitimacy interconnected?
2. How are minarchism and libertarianism similar?
3. What are the four objectives of political systems?
4. How does Keynesianism respond to economic cycles?
5. What are the central components of liberal democracy?
6. What is the difference between authoritarianism and totalitarianism?

Weblinks

Canadian Constitution
http://laws.justice.gc.ca/en/const/index.html

Canadian Government
http://canada.gc.ca/home.html

Hungary's House of Terror
www.terrorhaza.hu/en/museum/first_page.html

Peace of Westphalia
www.historylearningsite.co.uk/peace_of_westphalia.htm

US Constitution
www.archives.gov/exhibits/charters/constitution.html

US Government
www.usa.gov

US President's Office
www.whitehouse.gov

Westminster Parliament
www.parliament.uk

Further Reading

Acemoglu, Daron, and James A. Robinson. *Economic Origins of Dictatorship and Democracy: Economic and Political Origins*. Cambridge: Cambridge University Press, 2006.

Almond, Gabriel A. *A Discipline Divided: Schools and Sects in Political Science*. Newbury Park, CA: Sage Publications, 1990.

Brooks, Stephen. *Canadian Democracy: An Introduction*. 7th edn. Toronto: Oxford University Press, 2012.

Clarke, Paul A.B., and Joe Foweraker. *Encyclopedia of Democratic Thought*. London: Taylor & Francis, 2001.

Deakin, Nicholas, and Margery Garrett Spring Rice. *Origins of the Welfare State*. London: Routledge, 2000.

Easton, David. *The Political System: An Inquiry into the State of Political Science*. 2nd edn. Chicago: University of Chicago Press, 1981.

Hobbes, Thomas. *Leviathan, Or, the Matter, Forme and Power of a Commonwealth Ecclesiasticall and Civil.* Edited by Michael Oakeshott. New York: Collier Books, 1962.

Howlett, Michael, Alex Netherton, and M. Ramesh. *The Political Economy of Canada: An Introduction.* Toronto: Oxford University Press, 1999.

Jackson, Robert. *Sovereignty: Evolution of an Idea.* Cambridge: Polity Press, 2007.

Lasswell, Harold. *Politics: Who Gets What, When, How.* New York: Meridian Books, 1958.

Linz, Juan José. *Totalitarian and Authoritarian Regimes.* Boulder, CO: Lynne Rienner Publishers, 2000.

News Clips

Visit the companion website for *Politics: An Introduction*, 2nd edn, to access news clips related to the content of this chapter.

5 Branches of Government

◀ The legislative and judicial branches of Canada's government appear together as members of the Supreme Court leave the Senate Chamber following the 2009 Speech from the Throne.

Photo: *Toronto Star* via Getty Images

After reading this chapter, you will be able to

● identify the four main branches of government;

● understand and explain the distinctive roles that each branch plays in democratic systems of government;

● compare and contrast the American (presidential) and Canadian (parliamentary) systems of government; and

● discuss the form and composition of the Canadian government.

Marty Bucella/CartoonStock

"You can't take the Ethics course-you're a Political Science major."

Though the common view may be that *political* is separate from *ethical*, the two are entwined.

Introduction

Do all politicians have the same role to play? What does it mean to be "in cabinet"? Should judges be elected? What do bureaucrats really do, aside from apparently making the political process unnecessarily complicated? These are just a few of the many questions that are frequently asked regarding our political structures and the people who work in them. Often we simply decide that the whole thing is too complex—or frustrating—to figure out, and we throw up our hands and declare, "It's all so political." Well, it *is* political; that's the point!

But as we're discovering in this book, the word *political* doesn't have to mean impenetrable. In fact, a little knowledge about our political system goes a long way toward a better understanding of why things are so complicated. A country such as Canada is a huge entity and not just in geographical terms: to understand life in our country, we must consider politics, economics, culture, and all the other parts of our society. Governments must be large organizations because there's so much involved in even the everyday activities of government, not to mention the more immediate and sometimes emergency measures that political actors must occasionally take.

Institutions of Government

To answer questions like the ones posed in the introduction, we need to know a little bit about the mechanics of government, the institutions, or branches, that work together in the interests of citizens (at least in theory). The political structures in our country represent the largest organization in our entire society. Various levels of authority, huge numbers of government workers, and a vast and integrated system of departments and agencies deal with every aspect of our political organization, from law-making to law enforcement, culture and the arts, security and defence, and the economy. It's actually hard to imagine that politics could ever be simple. Let's take the time, then, to think about how the whole structure fits together. This will go a long way to stem the "it's all so political" attitude that we might otherwise fall back on. We'll begin by answering the questions that began this chapter.

Not all politicians have the same job. Some are part of the government, which has the power to make and enforce the laws and regulations of the land. The governing authority in a political system is made up of many different actors with varying levels of power. Some have far more responsibility and more latitude or influence in government decisions and initiatives. A newly elected member of Parliament (MP) in Canada, for example, won't have nearly the same influence in real decision-making as one who has been chosen to be part of cabinet. And a cabinet minister will have substantially less latitude than the prime minister. (We will return to the role of cabinet later in this chapter.) As in any other organization, there is a hierarchy in government. Many politicians have relatively little real power in setting a government's agenda; opposition party members, for instance, have minimal say in what governments set out to do. But even the **opposition** has a crucial role to play in the performance of government. It cajoles and questions, criticizes, and even occasionally works with the government to make policies and laws. A proper look at the branches of government, then, must take into account all the various political roles played by elected politicians.

Not all actors in the political process are elected. For example, judges are appointed in Canada. Some Canadians argue that appointed judges may become out of touch with citizens or may be chosen for political reasons or even **cronyism** or **nepotism**. These critics of the Canadian system feel that citizens must choose the people who will oversee the job of the courts. But the opposing point of view is compelling as well. Courts and judges are supposed to be independent and non-political. While judges might reflect the desires of those making their appointments, they are usually chosen for their expertise,

opposition
one or more parties that are not part of government but form a check on the ruling power of the elected party

cronyism
in politics, the practice of choosing or preferring friends or associates for positions of authority

nepotism
in politics, the practice of choosing or preferring relatives for positions of authority

5.1 GUN LAWS AND LEVELS OF GOVERNMENT

Owning guns in Canada has always been more complicated than in other countries, such as the United States. Since the 1930s, handguns have required registration in Canada, and certain weapons (e.g. fully automatic firearms) are prohibited. The restrictions on guns were made more stringent by the Liberal government of Jean Chrétien in 1995, when Bill C-68 (the Firearms Act) was passed, requiring all gun owners to register weapons that were not already subject to registration. The government felt that it was responding to demands that weapons be curtailed, especially following such horrible events as the 1989 Montreal Massacre, when Marc Lépine murdered female engineering students at École Polytechnique. However, the costs and controversy over the registry grew, and the Conservative Party under Stephen Harper declared that it would end the law. After several failed attempts, the Conservative majority government introduced Bill C-19 (Ending the Long-Gun Registry Act) in 2011. It came into effect in April 2012.

The Canadian gun registry shows the interplay of the different levels of government. First, the executive level played a crucial role in introducing and ending the bill. The legislature was important because it debated the relevant bills and was largely the voice of MPs who moved both governments to propose their legislations. The courts were used to interpret the laws, and the bureaucracy played a role as well. Notably, the Department of Justice and the Auditor-General's Office were responsible for implementing the law and

The Canadian Press/Ryan Remiorz

The killing of 14 women at Montreal's École Polytechnique on 6 December 1989 forced a stunned nation to consider new laws on gun ownership. This plaque was unveiled in Montreal on the twenty-second anniversary of the massacre.

reporting on its costs and management, respectively. With every form of political action, all levels of government have their role to play, and it is rare that any are removed from the process.

electorate
people in a political system with the right to vote in elections; enfranchised citizens

experience, and ability to provide a balanced interpretation of the law. Were they elected, we could similarly be suspicious of political interests coming into play; after all, they'd have to win the support of the **electorate**. How would they do this without showing some preferences?

As we'll see later in this chapter and in Chapter 9, judges in Canada are chosen on the basis of judicial independence, a concept that is integral to the notion of freedom of decision-making. But in certain countries, such as the United States, some judges are elected, which is a nod to the argument that they should reflect the will of the people. In fact, both of these points of view can be seen as democratic, since democracy is about the involvement of the people and the preservation of their independent will.

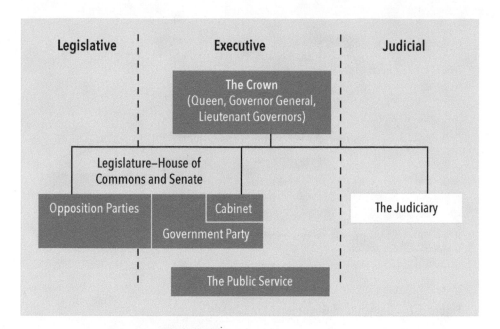

Figure 5.1   Three Branches of Government

The role of civil servants, or bureaucrats, in the political system is perhaps the most misunderstood and therefore most unpopular and maligned among Canadians. However, bureaucrats are indispensable to the execution of a government's agenda. Governments initiate legislation (but they need the legislature to get the laws in place), opposition parties criticize and look for changes, judges interpret and advise, and bureaucrats implement. That, as we will see later in this chapter, is an oversimplification of the process; however, it's fair to say that governments would be completely ineffective without the bureaucracy.

This chapter and the next build on Chapter 4's discussion of the various types of government, their activities, and their objectives by providing more detail about branches and systems of government. Here we examine the key political structures and actors that shape government action in liberal democratic systems. Three represent the common divisions of power in these systems (**executive**, **legislative**, and **judiciary**), and the other is the **bureaucracy**, the largest and in some ways the most active (though perhaps also the most ignored) wing of government. The bureaucracy isn't an autonomous branch of government, however, because it is responsible for implementing the policies and actions of the executive. These four branches of government comprise the basic parts of the government machinery. Take away one, and a vital part of what we need government to do will disappear. Working together, they complement each other's roles in an effort to provide citizens with the wide range of services they expect.

executive
usually the top level of government or the leader; maintains leadership of the entire political system and often reflects the leadership and preoccupations of the dominant political party

legislative
referring to the body of a political system with the responsibility to make laws; known as the legislature

judiciary
judicial (courts) level of governance

bureaucracy
division of government responsible for carrying out public policy and staffed by public employees

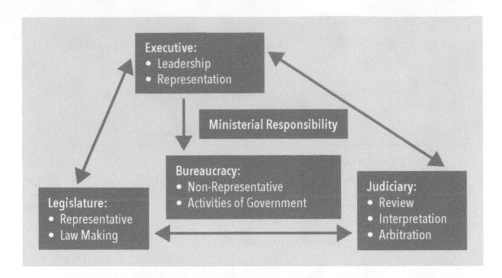

Figure 5.2   Branches of Government in Canada

In many respects, however, the way that political offices are chosen, the relationships they have with the other branches of government, and their ultimate jurisdiction over their respective countries could not be more different. Even in cases where the countries seem to have so much in common, a close examination of their political systems reveals such disparity that one might think they are based on completely different principles. For example, Canada and the United States are both democratic states and share many values and objectives. However, the image of Canadians and Americans being somehow the same (at least politically) doesn't hold up to inspection. History, tradition, law, custom, and ideology have resulted in two quite different systems that provide a perfect case study for how governments are distinct. We will take a close look at the presidential and parliamentary systems of government in this chapter to see how the application of government roles can evolve into unique examples. Later, in Chapter 9, we'll examine the United States and Canada in a broader context.

The Executive

The executive branch in government is the "top level" of administration and authority. Regardless of the various strains of political systems (presidential, parliamentary, democratic, etc.), those who hold office at the executive level are responsible for carrying out the business of government and representing the country. In modern political systems there are basically three types of executives. Their differences are mostly based on their degree of separation from the legislative branch.

The first instance involves an executive that is part of the legislative body. The parliamentary system used in the UK and Canada is an example of this type (sometimes referred to as the Westminster model, after the home of the British Parliament). Here the executive is merged with the legislative branch and is directly responsible to the legislature through such practices as **question period**, where the government must answer the queries and criticisms of opposition MPs.

The second executive type is characteristic of the presidential system of government, which formally separates the executive (the president and cabinet) from the legislature. The United States is perhaps the best example of this model. Put simply, if a member of the US Congress (which includes the House of Representatives and the Senate) is named to the president's cabinet, he or she must resign his or her congressional seat. There is also no comparable practice of question period in the United States.

Finally, the third type of executive also involves a formal separation of powers between the legislature and the executive. However, the real power of the regime is usually centred in the party executive of the governing elites. Such is the case in authoritarian systems, where elected politicians may exist but do not have actual power. The legislature in these systems has far less influence and authority than in other forms of government. The governing systems of the former communist states of Eastern Europe and the current government in Cuba illustrate this model.

question period
time allotted in the House of Commons for MPs to ask questions of the prime minister or cabinet ministers

5.2 VP OR SENATOR? JOE LIEBERMAN AND THE 2000 US ELECTION

Former vice-president Al Gore and senator Joe Lieberman appear before delegates at the 2000 Democratic Convention at the Staples Center in Los Angeles.

© Visions of America, LLC / Alamy

The 2000 election in the United States is primarily remembered for the controversy regarding the votes in Florida. But another story emerges from this event: Joe Lieberman, a senator from Connecticut, effectively ran for two positions at the same time.

Lieberman ran for the vice-presidency on the Al Gore ticket and allowed his name to stand for re-election for senator. Of course, the separation of powers in the United States would preclude him from keeping both positions. The Gore-Lieberman team lost the election to George W. Bush and Dick Cheney, but Lieberman won the Connecticut senatorial race. He returned to the Senate, where he sat as an independent Democrat, given his tendency to vote with Republicans on issues such as foreign and defence policy.

5.3   QUESTION PERIOD OR SHOUTING MATCH?

Canadians who have seen clips of parliamentary sessions will be aware of the seeming rancour that occurs in the House of Commons. For the uninitiated—and indeed for many familiar with the system—question period seems to be more of a free-for-all than a formal role for the Parliament. Nonetheless, it is an essential part of Canada's political system, one with a long history.

The first question period took place in 1867, just after Confederation, as an opportunity for the opposition members to hold the government to account. Today, question period is held either in the morning or afternoon, Monday through Thursday while Parliament is in session, and lasts for 45 minutes. Questions may be asked of the prime minister or members of the cabinet and are overseen by the Speaker of the House, who is elected by the MPs. The Speaker's job is to maintain decorum, which has become all the more difficult with the advent of television coverage, as politicians have been known to "play to the camera." Though it may seem otherwise, question period is bound by many rules, including who may ask questions of whom, when, and for

The Canadian Press/Sean Kilpatrick

Saskatchewan MP Andrew Scheer was elected Speaker of the House of Commons in 2011. At 32, he is the youngest Speaker in Canadian history.

how long. Members must ask questions indirectly, speaking through the Speaker. Hence the refrain "Mr (or Madam) Speaker" precedes each question.

Executive bodies perform many different functions in society, government, and the party elected to rule. Some are constitutionally laid out, and others are more a matter of practice. In most states, the executive, particularly the leader, provides leadership for the whole political system. As we saw in Chapter 4, this role is filled in Canada by the prime minister, who has more substantive political power than the country's head of state (the British monarch) and his or her representative (the governor general). In the United States, the president is head of both the state and the government.

The executive in many systems (including Canada's) provides partisan leadership to the party that is in power. The Canadian prime minister is also the leader of the party that forms a government, so this level of the Canadian political system also represents a particular political party and its associated ideologies and platforms. In fact, the prime minister is first selected to lead the party and becomes the prime minister only as a result of electoral victory. In those systems that link the executive to the legislature, the former provides leadership within the latter.

Perhaps most importantly, at least on a day-to-day basis of governing the country, the executive provides leadership and supervision for the whole

5.4   WHEN PARTIES MUST CO-OPERATE: COALITION GOVERNMENTS

Sometimes parliamentary government isn't so simple. While governments are ordinarily formed on the basis of a ruling party–the one that receives the most votes in a federal election–there are times when there is no single party in power. Coalition governments are formed when two or more parties create a unified executive branch. Usually, this is because none of the parties received the majority of votes; however, minority governments (formed by the party that received the most votes) are quite common too. Though they are often difficult to manage, coalition governments offer an alternative to the uncertainty of minority governments and the possibility of calling elections in quick succession. Countries that have a tradition of many strong party options, such as Italy or Israel, are examples of coalition governments. Other countries have only two major parties; the United States is an example where the two main parties receive most of the vote and one is therefore given a majority.

In Canada, there has been a long tradition of third-party influence with the New Democratic Party (NDP). In 2011, the NDP stepped out from its long-standing role as the "third party" in national politics when it won enough seats in the federal election to receive status as the official opposition party. More recently, there has been a growth in popular support for several different parties, including the Green Party, which won its first seat in Parliament in 2011. This change has resulted in more talk of coalition governments in Canada because the prospects for majorities seem less likely than in the past.

bureaucracy. In a legal–constitutional sense, the bureaucracy has no independent life of its own but is supposed to be the technical arm of the cabinet. In Canada, this relationship is well illustrated by the doctrine of **ministerial responsibility**.

Ministerial responsibility can be seen in all instances of the Westminster parliamentary model. Stemming from a tradition established in the UK, ministers in this system are responsible for the actions of all agencies and civil servants under their jurisdiction. This is an important concept because it means that ministers cannot simply call on the collective decision-making of cabinet or even a party **caucus** but must explain (and sometimes defend) their department's activities to Parliament. It is also an important example of democratic principles: bureaucrats are not elected, remember, so they must be accountable somehow. This task falls to the minister.

Cabinet ministers are chosen from the party caucus, a group of elected officials, usually based on party lines. When we speak of the New Democratic Party (NDP) caucus, we mean all the parliamentarians (both in the House of Commons and Senate) who are elected or appointed under the NDP banner. However, caucuses can also be made of other groupings, such as ideologies, regions, or gender. The European Union's Parliament has a wide variety of caucuses, ranging from political philosophy to gender issues and specific policy matters such as the environment and arms control. Members of different parties may even be part of these different caucuses.

In modern politics, two views regarding the relationship between the executive and the legislature have become widespread. The first claims that legislative

ministerial responsibility
principle in parliamentary systems that requires members of the political executive, both individually and as a group, to remain accountable to the legislature

caucus
group of elected representatives, usually based on party membership but which may also be grouped by race, gender, geographic representation, etc.

bodies are simply "rubber stamps" for executive decisions. This idea would suggest that the real authority in politics lies at the top and that the elected legislatures, which are ultimately directly responsible to the people, have far less influence. According to this view, democratic principles are replaced by executive rule with little (if any) accountability to the parliament. Perhaps in response to such concerns, ministerial responsibility is considered vital in the parliamentary tradition. Political scientists speak of **legitimation** in this context, referring to how political institutions grant legitimacy to politicians' actions through a formal and legalized process.[1]

The second view goes even further, arguing that the bureaucracy governs most political systems, thereby increasing the distance between the people and decision-makers. After all, members of the bureaucracies are anonymous, frequently protected by their terms of office, and free from scrutiny by the electorate. We'll return to the bureaucracy presently, but it is important to recognize that bureaucracies are the administrative arm of government; whereas real decisions and direction come from the executive and legislative branches of government, the bureaucracy is responsible for implementing those decisions.

The Legislature

Historically, legislative bodies developed as a means of reducing the absolute power of the monarch or absolute ruler. Even today, the US Congress or Canadian Parliament represents an institutional check on the otherwise unbridled power of the executive (think, for instance, about the rules for declaring war, explained in Box 5.5). Legislatures present a voice for citizens in the form of representation, a formal law-making entity, and a chamber for debate and discussion.

From a legal point of view, there are three main types of legislatures. The first one operates within the doctrine of legislative sovereignty, or supremacy. Britain's Westminster parliamentary model is a prime example of this type, which rests on a number of principles. For example, the legislative branch of government is the highest authority. This means that a government (presidential or parliamentary) requires the assent of the legislature before decisions can be carried out. In these systems, the legislature is beyond interference by either the courts or the executive. There will always be an exchange of information and ideas among the levels, but the legislature remains independent and ultimately autonomous.

In this model, legislatures have no limits to the extent of their jurisdiction, although there are reasonable boundaries to what they will undertake. In practice (and in law) the absolute power of the legislature is limited by the rule of law, constitutional conventions, and other customs and practices entrenched in the legal and political culture of the country. But legislatures cannot establish rules or laws that would bind future legislatures; a law created today cannot be expected to last forever. Legislatures must always be permitted to re-examine

legitimation
providing legitimacy, or legal force or status, to political decisions; in accordance with established or accepted patterns and standards

5.5 THE ULTIMATE POWER? THE RIGHT TO DECLARE WAR

The US presidency is often referred to as the most powerful position in the world. There are many good arguments that support this idea. But the president, like any other head of government, must work with the legislature. The independent powers of the presidency, such as appointments, clemency, some emergency powers, and certain foreign policy roles are limited, and the most important decisions, such as those involving the lives of US soldiers, are made by Congress. As a result, the president cannot independently declare war. A majority in both houses of Congress must vote in favour of taking such action.

In Canada, declaring war is a prerogative power, meaning that it is made by the sovereign–that is, the governor general as the representative of the British monarch. When a declaration of war is made, it is effective immediately, but a motion of confirmation is made before both the House of Commons and the Senate. However, according to the Emergencies Act (1985), Parliament has the right to revoke a declaration. Interestingly, Canada has declared war only once, against Germany in 1939. It waited a week after the British declaration as a demonstration of its independence.

In both the American and Canadian traditions, we see the importance of the legislature. In the US case, Congress holds the ultimate power of declaring war; in Canada, Parliament has the role of confirming declarations.

laws for another time and place. Imagine, for instance, if the laws that prevented women from voting were to last forever. It would be ridiculous to think that we should live by an unchangeable code implemented in the past. Of course, some past laws are perfectly acceptable today. We just do not know which ones will fall out of favour in the future. That said, new governments cannot simply come to power and change what they disagree with. They must follow the established process of changing legislation.

The second type of parliamentary institution operates in a constitutionally prescribed context. It usually divides governance between the legislative branch and the executive and is usually subject to judicial scrutiny through the process of **judicial review**. This model is followed in the United States, where certain powers are reserved for the presidency and others are granted to the Congress. Foreign trading relations, declaring war, creating militia, and establishing post offices are some of the many powers given to Congress in the US Constitution.

The third category, of which Canada is a good example, is a "mixed" system. In such systems, the legislature is viewed as a supreme authority but subject to several limitations. Thus, the Canadian Parliament shares its supremacy with the provincial legislatures. Certain rights and roles, such as education policy, are given to the provincial legislatures rather than the federal parliament. Another good example is health care policy. The current health care agreement between the provinces and the federal government, reached in 2004, is set to expire in 2014. Efforts to restructure the accord before the deadline began in earnest in 2011, with divergent views about how policies should be applied. Different provinces hold varying opinions on such matters as maintaining public funds, accessing primary care, enticing new health care professionals, and providing pharmaceutical care.

judicial review
power of a country's courts to interpret its constitution, varying from the ability to resolve disputes between levels of government in federal systems to the ability to annul legislative and executive actions outright

5.6 CONSTITUTIONALITY AND SAME-SEX MARRIAGE

The struggle to recognize same-sex unions has been ongoing for some time in Canada. In 1999, the Supreme Court ruled that same-sex couples were entitled to the same financial and legal benefits as other couples. This decision started a process of judicial review of marriage definitions and the extension of rights. Ultimately, legalizing same-sex marriage was a result of a judicial review concerning the constitutionality of banning it. Interestingly, although provinces and territories had bans on same-sex marriage, constitutional reviews of the laws revealed that only the federal government has the right to define marriage, and it had not, to that point, either included or excluded same-sex couples. The unconstitutional positions of the provinces and territories led the federal government to investigate inclusion.

In 2003, the Canadian Alliance introduced a motion in the House of Commons to uphold a heterosexual interpretation of marriage. The motion was defeated, and the Liberal government requested that the Supreme Court examine the constitutionality of same-sex marriages. This assessment led to the 2005 legislation of Paul Martin's Liberals to expand the legal definition of marriage to include same-sex couples. Parliament's decision to change the laws regarding marriage is a good example of how social mores and prevailing attitudes change over time, demonstrating the importance of the legislature's ability to make different decisions at various times.

constitutionality
being in accordance with a constitution

Parliament's role in the courts is also restricted. The Charter of Rights and Freedoms gives the Canadian courts greater scope for judicial review than it previously had. Consequently, the courts are often asked to rule on the **constitutionality** of certain issues, illustrating the limits of any "supreme authority" that might be granted to Parliament in Canada.

LEGISLATIVE STRUCTURES

Not all legislatures have the same powers, and not all legislatures look the same. Chapter 4 indicated that the division of the Canadian Parliament into the lower House of Commons and the upper house of the Senate makes it a bicameral legislature. Many other legislatures use two chambers. The United States, Mexico, Italy, the UK, Russia, India, and Brazil are all bicameral. In some systems (e.g. the United States), both chambers are of roughly equal status and power, though responsibilities may differ. In others, the second, or upper house, is largely symbolic and frequently appointed or based on hereditary membership (for instance, the Senate in Canada and the House of Lords in the UK).

Having two chambers provides greater oversight and checks regarding the activities of others. For instance, though the Canadian Senate is often criticized for having appointed members, it has an important function. It reviews legislation coming from the House of Commons and offers amendments or suggestions; this process has been known historically in Canada as a "sober second thought." It may seem quaint to have such a role in modern government, but the Senate does present another opportunity for review, or even introduction, of potential legislation.

There are also unicameral (single house) legislative bodies. These types are usually found in smaller political systems or in those that have a very strong unitary form of government (see the following chapter for more details about unitary governments). Provinces and territories in Canada, for instance, are unicameral. National governments in Israel, Hungary, Finland, and Turkey, among others, all use this structure. Although bicameral systems are touted as having built-in oversight and checks, advocates of unicameral models see the second house as redundant.

Legislative structures, unlike bureaucracies or courts, operate for an arranged period of time. However, the term of a legislature may be concluded early by a call for an election. In Canada, the maximum period for parliament to sit is five years. Furthermore, the manner in which legislative bodies operate (regardless of the type) is constrained by a multitude of written and customary rules that, to a considerable extent, dictate outcomes. Legislatures also operate with a variety of committees and legislative subgroups.

LEGISLATIVE FUNCTIONS

Although the word *parliament* has its origins in the French verb *parler* ("to speak"), the law-making function is always mentioned as the first and foremost occupation of any legislative body. We previously mentioned question period as an important tradition of demanding accountability from the executive, but the ultimate objective is to set out laws. Another function of legislatures is the control, scrutiny, and audit of the executive and bureaucracies. Legislatures do this in a number of ways. First, legislative proposals have to be introduced in Parliament. The Canadian cabinet may have an initiative it wishes to pursue, but it cannot be legal until Parliament passes it. Second, when governments propose initiatives that involve spending taxpayers' money, they must have the Parliament's authority for these expenditures. Government budgets, for instance, must be passed by the legislature. The performance of government in the area of fiscal management, as well as the meeting of policy objectives and the activities of the executive and the civil service, are subject to parliamentary critique (see our discussion of question period).

Yet perhaps the greatest function that legislatures perform is **representation**. Given the connection between politicians and their constituencies, the former view themselves as representatives of, and are expected to represent, the latter. This role is performed in several ways. Political representatives bring the general policy expectations and evaluations of their constituents to the attention of the executive and the legislature. They are expected to secure some benefits (such as jobs, government contracts, infrastructure spending, and industrial development) for their local constituency. They also assist individuals (or groups) who face bureaucratic "red tape" or have grievances against the government. Through politicians' representation, debates, and voting, legislatures ensure the accountability of the executive. Legislatures are also agents of political socialization, since we frequently become aware of certain issues as a result of parliamentary debate.

representation
the act of standing for the views of others; election of a representative to symbolize the collective view of all constituents

5.7 CAN GOVERNMENT "STOP"? LESSONS FROM THE CLINTON ERA AND TODAY

Imagine a scenario where a government proposes a budget and a hostile legislature refuses to pass it. What happens? In the Canadian case, there would be a vote of non-confidence, followed by an election. (This situation occurred in 1979, when Joe Clark's Progressive Conservative government was brought down and Pierre Trudeau's Liberals were elected.) In the United States, on the other hand, it could lead to a stalemate. In 1995, the Clinton administration proposed a budget to Congress that the Republican-dominated legislature refused to pass. The Republicans, led by Speaker of the House of Representatives Newt Gingrich, thought that this refusal would show the weakness of Bill Clinton's presidency, then in the middle of its first term. Clinton refused to budge, hedging his bets that the US public would support him. The impasse led to an effective shutdown of the US government, as it no longer had a budget mandate to pay for its operations. Over US$800 million in wages and salaries were held up, and the American people came to see the matter largely as a dispute between Gingrich and Clinton. Gingrich unadvisedly made comments that Clinton was not giving him proper respect. In *No Retreat, No Surrender: One American's Fight* (2007), former Republican House leader Tom DeLay wrote that Gingrich said he forced the shutdown because Clinton made him sit in the back of Air Force One on the return flight from Israeli Prime Minister Yitzhak Rabin's funeral.

Political and public support swung heavily to the Clinton side of the debate. The budget eventually passed, and Gingrich lost a great deal of political support from his own party and from the electorate. In the congressional election the following year, the Democrats gained seats at the expense of the Republicans and won back control of the House. Interestingly, a shutdown almost happened again years later, when President Barack Obama's budget proposal failed to receive support from Congress by the deadline of 30 September 2010. Seven budget extensions over seven months led to a confrontation in April 2011. Faced with a final deadline that would result in another government closure, a compromise was negotiated with just hours remaining.

© Allstar Picture Library / Alamy

President Bill Clinton and Speaker of the House Newt Gingrich share a rare light moment at the White House in March 1995 during highly partisan negotiations surrounding the federal budget impasse.

At the end of 2012, the US Congress was once again embroiled in a debate over whether to increase the limit on government spending and/or raise taxes. This situation led commentators to speculate that the government was about to fall off a "fiscal cliff," meaning that it would run out of money and be unable to perform many of its basic functions. Tax cuts created under the Bush presidency and then extended in 2010 under President Obama were due to expire; meanwhile, the government faced mandatory cuts in spending due to the Budget Control Act of 2011. The negotiations between the two parties, and between the Congress and the presidency, went on until a compromise was eventually reached on 1 January 2013. This compromise, signed into law as the American Taxpayer Relief Act of 2012, raised new tax revenue for the government but failed to resolve the question of mandatory spending cuts. In March 2013, some of these cuts came into force through a process known as sequestration, resulting in compulsory unpaid leave for some government workers and a cutback in government services.

Representative democracy is at the heart of our political systems. Whether they are parliaments, congresses, or some other form of legislature, representative institutions such as these are created to serve the interests of citizens. Importantly, representation in democratic systems permits an orderly and fair (although imperfect) mediation of differing opinions and interests among citizens. Representative democratic institutions set out an alternative to dictatorships, monarchies, oligarchies, or any of the other systems we have covered in this book. Crucially, representative democracies ensure a level of political accountability. If a member of the legislature does not perform well, either as part of the government or as part of the opposition, his or her constituents can remove him or her from office at the next election.

The Judiciary

The rule of law in democracies is considered the bedrock of legitimacy. Citizens may be allowed to vote, but without recourse to law and the courts, their rights and liberties cannot be assured. The courts, legal codes, judges, and lawyers are all part of a fundamental aspect of modern democracies. And the judiciary—the name we give to the entire system—is an essential part of the separation of powers in any political system: the role of interpreting law must be kept separate from those who make the laws.

In a very broad sense, the judiciary performs three main functions: it rules on the constitutionality of public and private acts; it interprets laws; and it adjudicates disputes. Judiciaries are ordered in a hierarchical structure, usually with a supreme court at the top. Lower courts are made up of national and

The Canadian Press/Fred Chartrand

Canada's Supreme Court is the country's highest court, the final court of appeal, and the last legal resort for all litigants. The Supreme Court justices are seen here, with Chief Justice Beverley McLachlin in the centre of the front row.

regional institutions. In Canada, for instance, the Supreme Court represents the highest level of the judiciary, followed by the Federal Court and Tax Court, the Provincial and Territorial Courts of Appeal, the Federal Courts, and, finally, the Provincial and Territorial Courts (which include small claims, municipal, and criminal courts). Additionally, there are administrative tribunals in Canada to deal with various issues that arise from time to time.

In Canada, the powers of the judiciary are outlined in the constitution. Judges (or justices) in the Supreme Court, as well as superior, appellate (appeal court), criminal, and provincial and territorial judges, are appointed by the federal or provincial governments. Law in Canada is governed mostly by **common law**, which means that decisions are made on the basis of precedent, previous decisions, and case law. An exception to this rule is Quebec, which uses **civil law**, in which legislative bodies at the municipal and provincial levels enact laws through statutes, ordinances, and regulations. Later in this chapter, we will return to these two types of law.

CONSTITUTIONALITY RULING

Various levels of government will often refer legislation or intended legislation to the courts for an opinion as to whether it is within their jurisdiction. For example, before the Canadian constitution was **patriated** (brought to Canada) in 1982, the federal government asked the Supreme Court to determine the legality of its intended action.[2] And, as a result of the inclusion of the Charter of Rights and Freedoms in the constitution, many pieces of existing legislation have been referred to the courts in order to determine their constitutionality.

Thus, in the Canadian context, courts rule on whether a federal statute, provincial legislation, or a municipal bylaw is within the scope of the constitution. In those jurisdictions that have constitutional bills of rights, courts also have to rule on the content of individual rights, both in terms of the right itself and the extent of the duties that we all have regarding the rights of others. This is an important role for the judiciary, one that can often have widespread effects for the country as a whole. Decisions of the Supreme Court of Canada, for example, are *stare decisis*, which requires courts to follow legal precedents and, in the case of the Supreme Court, makes rulings binding for all lower courts.

JUDICIAL LEGAL INTERPRETATION

Statutes, common law, and other legal instruments are frequently unclear or have internal contradictions. In some political systems, even without recourse to legal

common law
legal system where decisions are made on the basis of precedent, case law, or previous decisions

civil law
legal system where legislative bodies enact laws through statutes, ordinances, and regulations

patriation
term used to describe the transfer of the constitution from the United Kingdom to Canada in 1982

Peter Hesse/CartoonStock

"I KNOW IT'S NOT CONSTITUTIONAL, BUT IT SURE WOULD BE FUN."

Fun or not, ruling on constitutionality is a vital role for the courts.

action, courts can be called upon to provide a binding interpretation. In other systems, they intervene only in the event of a dispute. In this latter scenario, legal interpretation is often shared with a variety of other structures (mostly bureaucracies), although court interpretations usually have higher legal and cultural status. One such case occurred in 1984, when the Supreme Court of Canada was asked to consider French language rights in Manitoba. At that time, many different authorities had various opinions on the legality of laws enacted only in English. The Supreme Court ruled that the Manitoba Act of 1870, as well as the Canadian constitution, required both languages to be used. Effectively, this meant that any laws not printed in French and English were not binding. However, the Court gave the province a five-year period to make necessary changes before the ruling came into effect.[3]

JUDICIAL DISPUTE ADJUDICATION

Conflict resolution through the courts is the most effective and most common means of dealing with disputes. Of course, there are governments that employ coercion or force to make citizens abide by the laws, but in liberal democracies the courts are there to provide a means of adjudication. In order to perform that function adequately, courts must be perceived as independent. To this effect, many political systems grant judges a degree of independence and security of tenure unparalleled by any other structure.

The appointment of judges is the most vulnerable point in this area. As we mentioned at the beginning of the chapter, judges who are elected (as is the case for certain courts in the United States) may be perceived as owing favours to their supporters and behave in such a way as to curry favour with the electorate. If, on the other hand, they are appointed, they can be viewed as tools of the governments or as being rewarded for political support. Neither of these views is necessarily wrong, as good arguments can be made for both, but it does highlight the sensitivity of judicial objectivity: no matter how they ascend to their positions, judges must be seen as fair.

Adjudication, then, is a crucial role for the court system. The entire range of legal disputes, from property cases to divorces and criminal charges, must have a form of adjudication that is seen as legitimate and effective.

The Bureaucracy

The bureaucracy is the part of government that most citizens interact with on a personal daily basis. Getting a driver's licence renewed, dealing with tax officials or customs and immigration officials at international borders, or ensuring that one's older relatives receive their pension will likely involve a level of bureaucracy. Thus, when people speak of dealing with the government, they are usually referring to some contact they have had with a public servant or bureaucrat. More often than not, these are seen as negative dealings, largely because we tend to recall unpleasant situations. But we shouldn't assume that bureaucrats just sit behind a wicket or answer a telephone inquiry (though the people who do are essential to the process). Indeed, there are multitudes of public servants carrying out important government work, including policy analysts, food safety inspectors, national and provincial museum employees, trade specialists, public safety commissioners, revenue officials, probation officers, auditors, legal clerks, and many others. If we think about the ways in which we encounter government, we cannot help but conclude that bureaucracies are an essential and even effective part of the system.

Nevertheless, Canadians are often frustrated by the seeming inflexibility and complexity of what they consider a simple procedure. This so-called red tape is a result of the fact that every public service activity is directed toward carrying out some specific law of the land. Hence, public servants assume a different kind of responsibility from most people offering services in society.

While many people in the private sector (such as clerks, farmers, labourers, or businesspeople) can use their discretion within the limits of their own or their company's policy without danger of violating a law in order to meet their customers' needs, public servants seldom have this ability. Further, bureaucrats also realize that they will suffer the consequences of stretching the rules because this part of the government is burdened by a monumental set of regulations that they must apply but had little input in formulating. The next time you feel unnecessarily delayed at a border crossing, think about the myriad responsibilities that border officials have. And think of what we expect of them: a safe and secure system that also operates efficiently. It's a tall order. That said, it is true that bureaucracies can be inefficient and even corrupt, especially in countries where accountability and democracy may not be held in high regard.

There is another, much smaller group of civil servants who are seldom seen or heard of but who wield enormous political power. These include the public servants who are in frequent contact with political leaders. They run the various government departments and have access to the political ministers responsible for the legislation affecting their areas. Although these individuals may have little latitude in actual decision-making (they are, after all, unelected officials), they can have tremendous influence with those who do. Thanks to their expertise and past experience, these senior government bureaucrats will often be called on by politicians needing assistance in directing

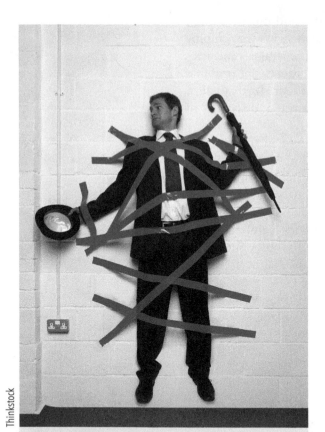

The term *red tape* originated with the English practice of binding official documents with red cloth bands. We now see it as a nuisance or unnecessary hindrance.

policy. How information flows in government and, importantly, how decisions are made about money will mean significant influence by certain members of the civil service. In Canada, the Privy Council Office (PCO) works as a hub of the civil service, providing a non-partisan link between the bureaucracy and the cabinet. The clerk of the Privy Council is considered the top civil servant in the Canadian government.

The size, structure, and operations of any governmental bureaucracy depend on the role that society gives to the state. In most Western democratic countries, the state has assumed responsibility for all sorts of social, medical, and educational programs. It has regulatory power over many spheres of economic activity, and this development has expanded the civil service to include experts in all areas of government involvement. In Canada, for example, there are well over half a million people who work directly for the federal government, people who are organized into departments, departmental corporations, agency corporations, proprietary corporations, and other agencies. Bureaucracies also exist in provincial/state and municipal governments. We can see, then, that government is also a major employer.

One of the questions often raised about the public sector is whether our public servants, particularly at the senior level, have the right to participate actively in partisan politics. Should any public official promote a party platform or candidate or run in an election? Since the public service is based on the merit system, those who carry out the policies of their political bosses must be neutral. While cabinets come and go and the political party in power switches according to the voters' will, the public servants' responsibility is to ensure that government services continue and to serve the party in power with equal loyalty no matter which one it is. This is easier said than done, especially at the higher levels where public servants give advice on policy content and implementation. This problem of neutrality is increased when one government remains in office for an extended period of time and public officials develop a personal relationship with politicians of one party.

There is a big difference between the bureaucracies of Canada and the United States. Whereas Canada's is permanent and (at least in theory) neutral, the American version changes after each election. US senior civil servants are brought in with the new administration and often follow the same political programs as the executive branch. This practice greatly weakens the role of the American bureaucracy as a moderating factor.

In both countries, the resilience of the civil service flows from its pivotal position in the system. There may be an occasional trade-off between the expertise we expect in bureaucracies and the sometimes exaggerated influence they may have in decision-making. In modern governments, the civil service houses and organizes the expertise required by the modern state. Because government ministers are generalists, they must rely on bureaucrats if they are to understand and resolve the complex problems they face. Legislatures and, in turn, political executives must continue to delegate decision-making power to civil servants and bureaucratic agencies. Civil servants are required to give meaning and purpose, through rulemaking, to the vaguely stated preferences of their political bosses. In short, the civil service does much more than implement policy passively. Permanent bureaucratic structures create an institutional culture and knowledge base that can only help the administration of government over time. Bureaucracies help make policy, shape the views of other politicians and citizens, and routinely enact decisions that profoundly influence citizens.

Presidential and Parliamentary Systems

Presidential and parliamentary systems are the two dominant political systems in the world today. The foundations for both are rooted in the history of the UK: the parliamentary system, as we've already seen, represents the Westminster model, while the presidential system is a result of the American Revolution (1775–83), a rebellion against parliamentary government. Although some totalitarian and authoritarian states have adopted some features of these systems (usually in an effort to lend some degree of legitimacy to their regime), both configurations of government, or hybrid combinations of the two, exist in liberal democracies.

The main feature separating the two systems relates to the manner in which power is granted to the levels of government—usually the executive, legislature, and judiciary but also at times the bureaucracy—and thereby prevented from misuse by one wing. The different methods of separating power in each system reflect an important feature of **political culture**: the prevailing attitudes about how connected (or disconnected) levels of government ought to be. A brief look at the American and Canadian examples illustrates this distinction.

The architects of the American system of government were concerned that arbitrarily giving some people power would lead to corruption. This feeling extended from the widespread belief in the United States that parliamentary government (and notably the example in the UK) created opportunities for unscrupulous government officials and politicians to manipulate other levels of government. Therefore, it was believed that some system of oversight was needed. But while some were concerned that power might lead to corruption, another prevailing view was that the strength of the nation would be diminished if a degree of control and authority were not given to some levels of government. There were a number of mechanisms put in place to try to overcome these two concerns, including the separation of powers.[4] Under this rule, the presidential system disallows anyone from holding office in more than one level of government and each level is given a review of proceedings at the other levels. For instance, the president cannot have a seat in Congress. Legislation passed in Congress must be approved by the executive—the president. However, if the president were to **veto** (the constitutional right to reject) the legislation, the matter might be returned to the Congress, where a two-thirds majority in both the House of Representatives and the Senate could overturn the veto. Similarly, the Congress has the right to reject bills proposed by the president,

political culture
set of attitudes, beliefs, and values that underpin any political system

veto
refusal to endorse, or the blocking of, a decision

approve or reject key cabinet appointments such as the Secretary of State, and even impeach the president. One can see that the American system emphasizes what is termed checks and balances, or the ability of one level of government to limit the independent actions of another.

In contrast, the parliamentary system places greater importance on representation, meaning that it is not limited by counterbalancing influences. This system relies on a **fusion of powers**, bringing together the responsibilities and rights of different levels of authority within government. In particular, the fusion of powers unites the capacity of the executive and legislative levels of government. For example, the Canadian prime minister must have a seat in Parliament. Members of cabinet and government must have seats as well, although there are some interesting variations (see Box 5.8). Advocates of this idea argue that it creates a more direct connection with citizens and an easier system of law-making. In *How Canadians Govern Themselves* (2010), considered by many as the keystone book for understanding Canadian politics, former

fusion of powers
combination of legislature and executive powers, though specific powers may be granted to each level

5.8 DOES A CABINET MINISTER HAVE TO BE ELECTED?

As Canadians steeped in the tradition of democratic governance, we might assume that all cabinet ministers are elected. After all, our fusion of powers means that these ministers must also be members of Parliament. But not all MPs are elected: senators are appointed and, at least technically, a cabinet minister doesn't have to be elected. Our political tradition does, however, require them to have a seat in Parliament. Thus, a prime minister may name someone to cabinet before he or she has a seat in Parliament (it is assumed that he or she would then seek one) or choose a senator for a cabinet position. Doing so is risky business–the prime minister may be criticized for overriding the principle of democratic representation–but it does happen. In 2006, Prime Minister Harper named Michael Fortier, a Quebec senator, minister of public works and government. With few Quebec Conservatives to call on, Harper chose Fortier to establish regional balance in cabinet. The appointment created a rather strange environment during question period when Fortier, who was not a member of the House of Commons, had his parliamentary secretary, James Moore (a member from British Columbia), answer questions.

Governments aren't the only ones who name people to cabinet from time to time. In 2007, former Ontario

premier Bob Rae was named to Liberal leader Stéphane Dion's shadow cabinet (the name given to a group of opposition members who concentrate on the actions of the government cabinet and voice an alternative to the government's policy) to be the opposition critic on foreign affairs. Until Rae was elected to the House of Commons, Bryon Wilfert, the associate foreign affairs critic, had to speak for Rae in the House. Coincidentally, Dion had experience in this regard. In 1996, then prime minister Jean Chrétien appointed Dion minister of intergovernmental affairs, even though Dion had no seat in either house. He was not able to speak or vote in the House of Commons until he won a seat the next year.

And then there are all those political actors who aren't part of government. Those elected under the banner of a competing party may find themselves in a legislature, congress, or parliament but not part of the governing authority of the political system. Rather, they are part of the opposition. This doesn't mean that their job is unimportant. On the contrary, a vital part of democracies is the existence of a vocal opposition constantly keeping the elected government in check. These different roles are all part of the democratic process.

political gridlock
lack of political progress because of entrenched differing of opinions

senator Eugene Forsey argues that parliamentary government avoids the kind of **political gridlock** that affects presidential systems because the different levels of government are required to work together in the legislature.[5]

Separation and fusion of powers represent different ideas of how democracy should best be implemented. Arguments can be made for either or even for a combination of both. But just try to convince a parliamentarian in Canada that they should adopt the American way or vice versa! Different political systems build a political culture that, over time, becomes a central aspect of society (see Chapter 8).

Government in Canada

We have touched on Canadian cases and examples throughout this chapter, but some further information is necessary if we are to understand our own political system and be able to compare it with others. In this final section of the chapter, then, we will consider the Canadian experience.

Canada is a constitutional democracy, and its institutions represent the division of powers within a modern federal democracy. Historically, Canada's chief constitutional document has been the Constitution Act of 1867, a legalistic document containing over 140 sections that outline the general rules by which the country's government is to be conducted. The preamble of the Constitution Act states that Canada is to have "a constitution similar to that of the United Kingdom." Because the British constitution is unwritten, Canada has inherited the British system of parliamentary government and the tradition of common law (with the previously noted exception of Quebec).

The Constitution Act, in addition to providing for the union of the colonies, had to encompass two contradictory constitutional principles: the evolutionary nature of British constitutionalism and the necessity of providing specific jurisdictional guidelines guaranteeing the protection of certain rights demanded by said colonies. The issue here concerned how to apply an existing constitutional system based on hundreds of years of collected history and political tradition to a newly minted system with its own unique features.

Thus, in accord with British tradition, three major branches of government were established: the executive, legislative, and judiciary. In order to take into account the consideration of local government, the constitution created a federal system and determined the distribution of legislative powers between the federal and provincial legislatures. This latter distribution of powers and the Charter of Rights and Freedoms (1982) are perhaps the most important elements of the Canadian constitution and are certainly the most controversial.

CANADIAN FEDERALISM

federalism
form of governance that divides powers between the central government and regional governments; often, particular roles and capacities are given to the regional governments

Federalism describes a manner of dividing and allocating power among different political authorities such as provinces and the federal government. (We will return to a more detailed discussion of federalism in Chapter 6.) It is also the most adequate description of the political structure in Canada. In 1867, the federal government was given what were considered the major powers, while the provinces were supposedly restricted in their authority to matters of local concern. Although we often hear of "Canadian Confederation," Canada was never a **confederal** state. Confederation refers to the union of unitary actors, where certain powers are gathered and given to a central authority while the pre-existing actors retain a large degree of independence in internal and external affairs. Many powers reside in the central government in Ottawa, and the provinces administer others. Given the range of powers that have been decentralized to the provinces, some prefer to use the term *quasi-federalism* to define Canada's structure.

confederalism
political system of divided powers where added power is given to the non-central governments and limited authority and power is conferred to the central government

The general division of powers between Ottawa and the provinces is set out in sections 91 and 92 of the Constitution Act. The Act gave the federal, or central, government the authority to "make laws for the peace, order and good government of Canada in relation to all matters not coming within the classes of subjects by this act assigned exclusively to the legislatures of the Provinces."[6] Here is where the commonly used phrase "peace, order, and good government" originated. Although it may not have the same ring as "life, liberty, and the pursuit of happiness," which appears in the US Declaration of Independence, it has come to summarize a great deal of Canadian political culture. However, as pointed out in the previous chapter, it is a residual clause that grants power not allocated elsewhere to the federal government, demonstrating again the tendency toward federalism.

The Constitution Act also included a list of specific powers intended to clarify those areas specifically within general jurisdiction. Among these comprehensive federal powers is authority over the public debt, Crown land, the raising of money by any mode or system of taxation, and the regulation of trade and commerce. By virtue of the reservation and disallowance provisions of the Act, the federal government can unilaterally invalidate any provincial law within a year of its passage. These conditions were first included in the constitution to permit the monarch to override decisions of parliament. Unused since 1943, they would certainly now be seen as an infringement on provincial affairs. Many want to remove the provisions, but they have remained.

The Constitution Act provides for no general power at the provincial level but specifies those areas exclusively within provincial jurisdiction. Among the most important areas are control over property and civil rights, the power of direct taxation, health care, and education—with certain qualifications. Section 95 of the Constitution Act gives the federal government and the provinces parallel jurisdiction over immigration and agriculture. A subsequent amendment has given the Canadian Parliament authority to enact laws in relation to old-age pensions.[7]

CANADIAN COURTS AND THE CONSTITUTION

One major aspect of change in Canadian federalism is the role for judicial interpretation of the constitution. As has been discussed earlier, both the central and provincial governments have the authority to enact laws within their respective domains; in so doing, either level of government may seek to amend the constitution.

In Canada, the judiciary is given the task of ensuring that legislation enacted at the provincial or federal level falls within the boundaries of the constitution. Following Confederation, the Judicial Committee of the British Privy Council (JCPC) was the final court of appeal for Canada. In 1949, it was replaced by the Supreme Court of Canada. Although bound by previous decisions in deciding cases, judicial interpretation has played an important role in shaping the direction of Canadian federalism.

The Constitution Act of 1982 is the other half of Canada's constitutional history. It signified full independence from the UK, created the Charter of Rights and Freedoms, included rights for Aboriginals, and established an amending formula for the constitution. The patriation of the Act met with some controversy regarding Quebec's refusal of support (see Chapter 4). Nevertheless, the Act is still considered binding throughout Canada.

With the passage of the 1982 Constitution Act, the role of the judiciary expanded immensely. Some critics of the new constitution claim that the Canadian Supreme Court will now resemble its American counterpart (but without the rights of review and confirmation of appointments currently enjoyed by the US Senate) and that this is a further erosion of the role of Parliament in the Canadian political system. Before the Constitution Act of 1982, the judiciary was called upon only to decide which level or levels of government had jurisdiction within a disputed area. The Charter of Rights and Freedoms, however, gave the judiciary new power.

THE CHARTER OF RIGHTS AND FREEDOMS AND INDIVIDUAL CITIZENS

The Charter of Rights and Freedoms has had broad implications for Canada's political system and has added an element of profound respect for basic civil liberties and human rights to our constitution. In effect, the Charter has extended the scope of the constitution from the macro level of the state and its institutions to the micro level of individual rights. This change had three significant ramifications for the political system. First, human rights issues achieved a new importance in Canadian politics, which reflects the focus on individual rights in the Charter. Second, the courts provided a new avenue of recourse for infringements on individual rights and freedoms. This is part of how the role of the courts has been extended since the patriation of the constitution. Third, provincial human rights codes and legislation pertaining to the individual moved into line with the federal Charter.

Some experts have argued that the inclusion of the Charter of Rights and Freedoms in our constitution has amounted to nothing less than a revolutionary change in our system of government. Of note here is the new role for the courts, which were given the authority to judge legislation outside the powers of both levels of government and thus much more policy-making power than they previously possessed. Others suggest that the Canadian judiciary has always had a fairly significant influence on policy, and the Charter only slightly expands this power, particularly with respect to questions of social justice and

5.9 THE CHARTER: INDIVIDUAL OR COLLECTIVE RIGHTS?

The Canadian Charter of Rights and Freedoms is no doubt considered a major part of the patriation of the Canadian constitution of 1982. Before the Charter, Canada had the 1960 Canadian Bill of Rights, but it had limited effect because it was not a constitutional document. The Charter changed that. At its core, it ensures the rights of individuals, something that was criticized by those who sought more attention to the rights of communities and the collective. Some wanted to see the Charter take on more of a "social charter" role, including welfare-type goods such as guarantees of housing, a minimum standard of living, and access to education. Given Canada's historical support for individual rights, such as those included in the United Nations Declaration of Human Rights, it is not surprising that the Charter would take the individual as its focus.

minority-language rights. Regardless, when the courts deem legislation unconstitutional because it violates the rights of individual citizens, the political consequences are immense: in some cases, either or both levels of government may be denied the right to legislate. Therefore, it is possible that policy-making authority could be shifted from other branches of government to the judiciary, in particular the Supreme Court.

CANADIAN LAW

As mentioned previously, there are two major legal systems in the world. The first has its roots in Roman law and is referred to as civil law. In a civil law country, the role of the legislature is emphasized over that of the courts. Statutes are assumed to constitute a complete, original statement of the social will of the community. Law, then, is derived from the actions of legislatures. The civil law system is found in continental European countries, especially those possessing a Roman heritage, as well as the province of Quebec. Much of civil law may be traced back to the Justinian Code, prepared for the Roman emperor Justinian in 533 CE. One of the better-known examples of civil codes is in France, prepared for the emperor Napoleon in 1804 and known as the *Code Napoléon*, or Napoleonic Code.

The other legal system was developed in England and is known as common law. Common law is defined in the authoritative *Black's Law Dictionary* as "the body of those principles and rules of action, relating to the government and security of persons and property, which derive their authority solely from usages and customs of immemorial antiquity, or from the judgments and decrees of the courts recognizing, affirming, and enforcing such usages and customs, and in this sense, particularly the ancient unwritten law of England." The UK, Canada (except Quebec), the United States, Australia, New Zealand, and many of the former British colonies adhere to this model of law. In practice, the two systems are no longer so distinct (or perhaps never were). Common law countries have endless statutory instruments, and civil law countries rely on precedents to some extent.

Among some of the important principles inherent in the Canadian legal system are that higher law takes precedence over inferior law, regardless of its origins from courts or legislatures, and that later laws replace earlier ones. Above all, Canada—like every political system claiming legitimacy—recognizes the principle of the rule of law. Simply stated, this idea means that people are to be governed according to a known set of rules that affect all members of a polity and are arrived at in a constitutional manner.[8]

Conclusion

This chapter has introduced you to the forms and composition of different branches in contemporary government. We have seen that, in many ways, the ideological roots of political systems influence their type of government and the scope of its powers. The relative importance granted to the executive, legislature, courts, and bureaucracies differs depending on prevailing philosophies and political culture. In recent years in Canada, we have seen the concentration of legislative and administrative power in both the executive and bureaucracy. In turn, the power of the legislative branch has decreased as policy-making has become more complex. Courts in turn have received new powers of interpretation under the Constitution Act, 1982. Understanding the individual roles these branches of government play, as well as their interrelationship, is essential.

The two political systems that influence us most are our own and the American variant. In a comparative context, we have analyzed the differences between the Canadian and American forms of government—parliamentary and presidential, respectively. Together, they represent the primary models of government employed by most states today. This chapter has also introduced you to the fundamentals of Canadian government, including its primary institutions, normative influences, and structure. The next chapter will take us a bit deeper into our study of different political systems. We will pick up on many of the themes of this chapter, particularly with regard to the division of power and authority among different actors.

Self-Assessment Questions

1. What are the four primary institutions in government? What are their individual responsibilities?
2. Why is it important to have separate branches of government?
3. What is meant by patriation of the constitution?
4. Why are bureaucrats unelected?
5. How is the principle of separation of powers applied differently in the presidential and parliamentary systems?
6. Why are constitutions of fundamental importance for liberal democracies?
7. How has the Charter of Rights and Freedoms placed new emphasis on the individual? How has it affected the role of the judiciary?
8. What is the difference between common and civil law?

Weblinks

Canada's Constitution
http://laws.justice.gc.ca/en/const/index.html

Canada's Court System
www.justice.gc.ca/eng/dept-min/pub/ccs-ajc

Governor General of Canada
www.gg.ca

Parliament of Canada
www.parl.gc.ca

Prime Minister of Canada
www.pm.gc.ca/eng/default.asp

United States Constitution
www.archives.gov/exhibits/charters/constitution.html

United States Courts
www.uscourts.gov

United States House of Representatives
www.house.gov

United States Senate
www.senate.gov

United States White House
www.whitehouse.gov

Further Reading

Bakvis, Herman, Gerald Baier, and Douglas M. Brown. *Contested Federalism: Certainty and Ambiguity in the Canadian Federation*. 3rd edn. Toronto: Oxford University Press, 2012.

Black, Henry Campbell. *Black's Law Dictionary*. 3rd edn. St. Paul, MN: West Publishing, 1933.

Brooks, Stephen. *Canadian Democracy: An Introduction*. 7th edn. Toronto: Oxford University Press, 2012.

Dawson, R. MacGregor, and W.F. Dawson. *Democratic Government in Canada*. 5th edn. Revised by Norman Ward. Toronto: University of Toronto Press, 1997.

Dyck, Rand. *Canadian Politics: Critical Approaches*. 6th edn. Toronto: Nelson, 2011.

Genovese, Michael A. *The Power of the American Presidency: 1789–2000*. New York: Oxford University Press, 2001.

Lowi, Theodore J., Benjamin Ginsberg, and Kenneth A. Shepsle. *American Government: Power and Purpose*. 9th edn. New York: W.W. Norton, 2006.

MacIvor, Heather. *Parameters of Power: Canada's Political Institutions*. 5th edn. Toronto: Nelson Education, 2010.

Welch, Susan, John Gruhl, Susan Rigdon, and Sue Thomas. *American Government*. 13th edn. Florence, KY: Wadsworth, 2012.

News Clips

Visit the companion website for *Politics: An Introduction*, 2nd edn, to access news clips related to the content of this chapter.

6 Political Systems

◄ One feature of Switzerland's unique political system is *Landsgemeinde*, an open-air meeting of the cantonal assembly. Currently practised in only two of the country's canons, this meeting includes public voting, as seen in this photo from an assembly in Glarus.

Photo: © Arno Balzarinil/EPA/Corbis

LEARNING OBJECTIVES

After reading this chapter, you will be able to

- differentiate between the unitary, federal, and confederal forms of government;

- identify the strengths and weaknesses of the unitary and federal systems of government;

- see the diversity that exists in real-world examples of both forms of government; and

- comprehend the nature of the Canadian federal system and the challenges it faces.

Introduction

As we have seen in earlier chapters, the state does not operate in the same way as a human individual does. For instance, Chapter 5 showed us that there are multiple fractures within the state, particularly between its executive, legislative, and judicial branches. In this chapter, we will see how the geographical distribution of power between a country's central and regional governments affects the nature of its political system.

A quick glance at most maps of Canada reveals that, in political terms, the country is not a single bloc but is divided into different geopolitical units (i.e. provinces and territories). These units maintain a specific relationship with each other and another with the national, or federal, government in Ottawa. Responsibilities, powers, and political and economic control are distributed between federal and provincial governments. At both levels, representatives are elected by the people. A similar situation exists in the United States, with the individual states bearing the responsibility for a wide range of issues and holding considerable political control and influence.

The United Kingdom represents another scenario. Even though there are geographical divisions similar to those in Canada (known as counties), it is quite clear that those units do not have nearly the same amount of power or control as Canada's provinces. In the UK, power, control, and responsibility are concentrated in London, where the national government has its home. In France, one of the world's most centralized and **unitary systems**, the national

unitary systems
political systems that concentrate political authority and powers within one central government, which is singularly responsible for both the domestic and foreign activities of the political unit

government in Paris dominates the political scene, while the *departements* retain limited scope for autonomous action.

The differences between these systems are best explained through a discussion of federal versus unitary political systems, two very different but equally important forms of organizing the nation-state in geopolitical terms. Both present certain assets and certain deficiencies, and good arguments can be made for each in terms of efficiency, stability, and representation. This chapter introduces you to these distinct ways of organizing the state and encourages you to consider their respective strengths and weaknesses, particularly in the Canadian context.

Indeed, it would be fair to say that understanding Canadian politics requires an understanding of the nature of federalism, particularly Canadian federalism. Many of the most pressing issues in present-day Canadian politics, government, society, and economics are directly affected by, or linked to, the particular brand of federalism practised in this country. As we will see in this chapter, Canadian federalism is unique, problematic, complex, and constantly changing. The fact that federalism is such a "living" issue in Canada also makes it a surprisingly exciting and dynamic area of study.

Distributing Power within the State: To Centralize or Share?

A key element for a clear understanding of the workings of different political systems is the actual physical or geographical distribution of authority. All political units, despite their ideological underpinning, must distribute the activities and functions of government within their territorial boundaries. The degree to which a political system parcels out political authority—or, conversely, keeps that authority in one place—is largely a result of history and societal demands.

The historical evolution of most countries in the international system, at least from the seventeenth century to the second half of the twentieth, resulted in the progressive concentration of power in central governments that were unwilling to share command with the geographic regions that made up their territory. By creating unitary states, political authority was not divided and control was easier. In fact, the concentration and **centralization** of political power was a central goal for most states. The need to consolidate internal control over territory led European monarchs to build institutions and systems of command that maximized their ability to dictate policy, to tax, and to mobilize the populations of their countries. Centralizing power had two goals: to defeat and suppress internal rivals to power and to strengthen the state vis-à-vis its neighbours.

centralization
concentration of power in a single body, usually the principal government

In other states, however, the only way to consolidate distinct geographic, ethnic, and cultural areas into one political body was through a form of power-sharing. By guaranteeing certain rights and areas of responsibility to the constituent parts, the central government could garner internal support for the broader project of state-building. This system, known as federalism, is used in

Canada and the United States. Both countries, formed out of various former British colonies, needed to bring diverse entities under one flag and singular political control. Power-sharing allowed them to achieve this goal and ensure a measure of unity that would otherwise have been impossible.

Some countries have gone even further in the sharing of power. Confederalism—in many ways the opposite of unitary governments—involves a group of regional or constituent governments giving some powers to a central government. Confederal systems, such as that created in the United States in its early years (1781–7), grant important powers to the constituent parts, which may be said to dominate the central government. The central government depends heavily on the regions for its authority and legitimacy and maintains only limited powers for itself. In short, in a confederal system, the central government has no final authority to override the regions' wishes or power. The **European Union (EU)**, with its concentration of limited authority in Brussels and retention of final political authority in the governments of the member states, is an example of a confederal arrangement.

Although Canada is often referred to as a confederation, it is not an example of this system. At the time of "confederation" (1867), the powers given to the provincial governments were vastly inferior to those of the central government in Ottawa. Canada was, as mentioned in previous chapters, something of a highly centralized quasi-federal state. It has further "federalized," but most final powers are still given to the central government. This chapter focuses on unitary versus federal systems, but the confederal model remains an interesting and important alternative that we will return to in the pages to come.

Elsewhere in this text, we have discussed the concept of sovereignty, the legitimate authority given to a government to rule a political unit. It is useful to

European Union (EU)
economic and political union of 27 European states

6.1 THE EUROPEAN UNION: A MODERN CONFEDERATION

In Chapter 9 we will learn more about the European Union (EU), but it is worthwhile to include it here as an example of a confederal structure. In this case, the confederation is made up of sovereign entities that have agreed to surrender certain elements of their authority to an overarching central government in Brussels. Since 1957, the process of European integration has involved two main processes. First, there has been the EU's "widening" to include new member states. Second, the EU has experienced a "deepening" process, whereby the member states have become increasingly integrated in political, economic, and social aspects. Both processes apply to the main topics of this chapter. By incorporating new states, the EU has seen a remarkable transfer of sovereignty from a large number of countries to its central decision-making structures. The deepening process has meant that these structures have grown in importance and power and now stand as real actors on the European and, indeed, global political stages.

But these processes have been tempered by the reluctance of states to surrender too much sovereignty. How much is too much is a tricky question, and the answer varies from country to country. However, the insistence of states to maintain their autonomy and not give absolute control to Brussels matches the features of a confederal structure.

think about sovereignty and where it is located when we compare unitary and federal systems. In unitary states, sovereignty is concentrated in the national government (although in some cases certain powers may be given to subnational authorities; this is referred to as **delegated authority**). In federal states, sovereignty is divided between the national government and the subnational governments (provinces, states, *länder*, zones, emirates, etc.). Of course, we must also recognize that the distribution of power within a country may change over time. If the central government wishes to consolidate its power relative to the regions, it may seek to centralize. However, if the regions successfully demand greater responsibilities and authority, there will be a process of **decentralization**.

Unitary Systems

Both unitary and federal systems are created and maintained largely as a result of the constitutional authority accorded to the geographical positions of power. The central government in a unitary system is singularly responsible for the activities of the political unit, both domestic and foreign. Put another way, unitary governments have a single, central authority that makes, interprets, and enforces laws and represents the political community abroad. Other levels of government, such as municipal, may exist, but they fall under the jurisdiction of the central unitary government.

An overwhelming majority of the states in the current international system, including Chile, Rwanda, Honduras and Ukraine (to name just a few), are unitary states. This strong presence is a reflection of many countries' desire to centralize power to overcome opposition, as well as a manifestation of the perceived need to increase efficiency and effectiveness in the decision-making process and implementation of policy. By centralizing power, national governments maintain closer control over the gamut of political activities and, in theory, are able to respond more quickly and on a national scale to specific challenges and problems. Proponents of unitary government argue that this system makes governance easier, eliminates prolonged national debates, and guarantees a more harmonized delivery of government services across the national territory.

This is not to say that the central authority in a unitary system will carry out each and every task related to government. In France, for example, certain powers are left to the *departements* (of which there are 90, grouped into 36 regions) and to the municipalities, which play an important role in daily life for a vast majority of French citizens. In Britain, some powers are left to the counties and towns and, at a lower level, to the villages (through the system of parish councils).

Political arrangements that give power to regional authorities but are not constitutionally or legally bound are referred to as **devolution**[1] systems. Within a devolved framework, regional governments exercise some jurisdiction, but

delegated authority
in a unitary system, the transfer of certain powers from the national government to subnational authorities

decentralization
process whereby power and authority is taken from the central government and conferred to non-central (e.g. state, regional, or provincial) governments

devolution
political system in which some authority is given to regional governments, but the power to oversee, dismiss, or entrench these authorities is still held by the central government

6.2   SCOTTISH INDEPENDENCE

The history of Scottish relations with its powerful neighbour England is a long and arduous one. Since the passing of the Acts of Union in 1707, the two countries have been formally merged. However, it is clear by looking at British history since that date that England has been the dominant partner in both political and economic terms. It is also obvious that Scotland, though closely related to England, has a distinct and vibrant social and political culture.

Since the mid-nineteenth century, there have been calls for a devolution of power from Great Britain to Scotland, and this sentiment has acquired momentum in the late twentieth and early twenty-first centuries. The Scottish National Party (SNP) was created in 1934 but acquired national importance when SNP members were elected to the British Parliament in the 1960s. A 1979 referendum came close to requiring the creation of a separate parliament, or assembly, for Scotland, but it was narrowly defeated due to low **voter turnout**. In 1997 the British Labour government held another referendum on the issue, which was overwhelmingly approved by Scottish voters. This outcome led to the creation of the Scottish Parliament in Edinburgh, which met for the first time in 1999. This parliament has control over all **non-reserved** and **non-excepted matters** (including health care and university costs) and has the authority to raise its own taxes. The SNP is the single largest party in the Parliament and its leader therefore serves as the first minister of Scotland. Scotland is also represented in the British Parliament by 59 MPs, who vote on all issues.

Inside the main court of the Scottish Parliamentary Buildings in Edinburgh. Scotland is currently involved in a changing relationship with the central government in Westminster.

Scotland's independence movement, however, has not stopped at obtaining a parliament. The SNP has issued a call for a 2014 referendum to seek Scottish liberation. Recent public opinion polls show that as much as 39 per cent of the population favours independence but that 50 per cent is opposed. It remains to be seen, and is of immense national importance in Britain, whether the SNP and the independence movement can mobilize its support to win the proposed vote.

voter turnout
number of voters who attend the polls on election day

non-reserved matters
powers that are given to a region and may not be recalled by the central government

non-excepted matters
powers that are held by the central government but may be transferred to a regional government at a later date

the power to oversee, dismiss, or entrench this clout remains with the central government. A state may choose to devolve power to its regions as a response to calls for greater autonomy or as a means of increasing the effectiveness of the policy process. The British government's 1997 decision to give limited authority to the Scottish and Welsh legislatures is an example of devolution. In this case, Britain responded to Scottish and Welsh citizens' calls for greater local control over policy and for a stronger cultural identity.

Once the process of devolution has begun, it may be difficult to halt. Citizens may be persuaded that a regional approach to power-sharing works in their interests, and they may begin to demand more decentralization. This appears to be the situation in Scotland, where a referendum for independence is scheduled for 2014 (see Box 6.2). Unitary governments often fear this phenomenon because it threatens their power base, as well as national unity.

However, in all cases of devolution, the national government has overriding authority and can therefore call back, or recentralize, powers if it so chooses. This change is possible because the powers of the regional or municipal bodies are not protected in the state's constitution or because the central government can easily override or change it. Recalling power has happened at various times throughout history, with the most recent example being London's direct rule of Northern Ireland from 1973 to 2007.

Many criticisms have been levelled at unitary forms of government over the years. One of the most common is that they are somehow less "democratic" than other forms because the central government does not respond to the wishes of different groups living in various regions but formulates national policies that may or may not reflect the wishes of people across the country. According to this argument, it is much easier for authoritarian governments to exist when power is centralized and concentrated in the hands of the national authority. Although it makes some sense in theory, the claim holds little weight in practice. Many of the world's most centralized systems of government, including the British and French models, are bastions of democracy and liberal political behaviour and thought. The extent to which a state is democratic is affected by a wide range of factors, and the level of centralization is only one of them.

Closely connected to the first critique is the idea that a centralized form of government cannot possibly be in touch with the needs of people across the national territory. This argument suggests that the closer consultation resulting from devolved or decentralized governments makes them much better informed about what is happening within the regions and better equipped to respond to challenges. Another criticism refutes the conclusion that a unitary government is more effective and efficient in implementing policies, arguing that it is less so because the central government is out of touch with local wants and needs and because there is a lack of strong local institutions.

The final set of criticisms concerns culture and diversity. A serious charge against unitary systems is that they do not reflect the cultural diversity present in most modern states and that they result in the hegemony of one culture over the others. Where one ethnic group dominates, a highly centralized government can be blamed for further restricting minority rights, especially if those minority ethnic groups are concentrated in specific geographical regions. This is a particularly grave issue in multicultural societies, although it applied to countries such as the UK and France even before the arrival of large numbers of immigrants. For years, the UK's central government was accused of favouring English (and in particular southern English) preferences and needs ahead of those from Scotland, Wales, or Northern Ireland. What's more, this dominance was blamed for a lack of understanding regarding the true nature of regional problems and for the rise in independence movements in Scotland and Wales. A similar situation has occurred between the Canadian federal government and Quebec.

Devolution of power is increasingly proposed as a solution to many of these problems of unitary government. Such devolution allows the central government to maintain control of the most important issues from a national perspective while letting the regions take more responsibility for the issues that mean the most to them on a daily basis. Still, even with devolution, the central government dominates all other jurisdictions within the national territory.

Federal Systems

A small number of states, including Canada, the United States, Germany, and Australia, are organized according to the federal model. At its core, federalism seeks to divide powers between the central and regional governments. Legal authority is given to the latter to act on behalf of citizens. Often, particular roles and capacities are also given to the regional governments, which work in conjunction with the central government. For instance, natural resource protection is a provincial responsibility in Canada, paid for in part from transfer payments from Ottawa.

Federal states are often marked by linguistic or cultural differences, and provincial or regional governments are frequently more sensitive to this fact. Further, different levels of government have different powers in both political and economic matters. Historically, many states evolved into federal systems as a response to the entire country's need for mutual defence and economic gain and for the maintenance of regional identities and interests. Canada is a perfect example of this evolution, as we will see later in the chapter.

A federal system of government is particularly appropriate for territorially large states. Dividing power between the central government and the regions is helpful in making the delivery of services more effective and in ensuring a greater sensitivity to local needs. Power is divided in such a way that each level of government, be it national, regional, or municipal (which answers to the regional level), maintains the final say over the areas under its control. These powers will be enshrined in a constitution, guaranteeing freedom from interference by other levels of government. This is not to say that all areas are controlled by only one level of government. Indeed, as is the case in Canada, co-operation and cost-sharing between different levels may be normal and necessary in some areas.

The division of powers between federal and regional levels differs from country to country. Generally, however, it is fair to say that the central government maintains control over national economic planning, trade and currency issues, and most functions relating to defence and foreign relations. Final say over issues of more local importance, such as health care, education, and social policy, is held at the provincial or state level. These levels may also hold power over questions of natural resource management or immigration (as we see in Canada).

The level of decentralization also varies between federal systems. We can think of two extremes: peripheralized, or decentralized, federalism, in which the regional governments dominate; and **centralized federalism**, in which the national government rules. In some systems, such as those found in Canada and Switzerland, the national government has given up important powers to the provinces or regions. In federal states such as Russia and Mexico, the culture of power centralization means that the national government retains overwhelming power.

It is important to remember that, in most cases, the decision to create a federal system did not come from the belief in some lofty idea of political justice but from political expediency. Distinct and diverse geographical units were induced to combine their forces and surrender part of their control in exchange for guarantees of protection and security from the new federal power. The advantages of economies of scale also played a role in many cases; by forming a single, larger economic entity, the regions were able to take advantage of synergies and access to markets and raw materials that would otherwise have been essentially foreign. Although the US began as a form of confederation, the founding colonies gradually accepted that the country's survival required a strong central government. Still, the individual states reluctantly gave up power to the federal government, transferring authority over military and defence, foreign policy and trade, and other areas of national interest while reserving control over a large number of issues. In fact, anything that wasn't specifically destined to be a federal power was explicitly reserved for the states. The Tenth Amendment of the US Constitution reads: "The powers not delegated to the

centralized federalism
process whereby federal government increases its power relative to that of the provinces

6.3 SWITZERLAND

Switzerland's particular brand of federalism is fascinating in many ways. The country's political system is unique in that it adopts direct democracy, which is the straight exercise of citizen voting on almost every major national issue. Through referenda, Swiss citizens can give their opinions and judgments on a wide range of policy matters on a regular basis. Further, Switzerland is the only country in the world to have an executive branch that is led by a collective presidency, the Swiss Federal Council, which consists of seven members nominated by the Swiss Federal Assembly.

But the federal-canton relationship is what is directly relevant for our purposes here. Founded as a country in the thirteenth century, Switzerland brought together a group of cantons, or regions, that reluctantly agreed to share power with a central authority. However, they agreed to do so only under the condition that the federal government was not given the ability to dominate them or limit their powers. As the country expanded and incorporated new areas, the configuration held together. The influence of a French invasion (1798) and a civil war (1847) pushed the cantons to integrate more fully and move from a confederation to a federation, giving increased powers to the central government. Even so, the guiding principle for the cantons has always been to surrender only as much autonomy as necessary and to maintain as much independence as possible.

Today the cantons maintain a high degree of freedom, governing issues as diverse as education, public health, citizenship, natural resources, policing, and cantonal taxes. This last area is important: by giving the cantons the ability to raise sufficient financial means, the constitution guarantees their autonomy from the central government and allows them to maintain the diversity of the country more easily.

6.4 THE UNITED STATES

The United States of America is a federal country that has seen an evolving dynamic relationship between the federal and state governments throughout its history. Arising out of a loose confederal structure of British colonies, the founding American states were anxious to not cede excessive power to the central government. This thinking drove them to insist on a formal division of powers between the levels of government in the Constitution and, even at the federal level, to protect their position by ensuring strong representation in the Senate (where each state has two senators). In the Constitution, the federal government is granted certain express powers, such as the right to declare war and to regulate trade between the states, but the spirit of this arrangement was to show that the states were ceding powers to the federal government rather than vice versa.

The theory of "dual federalism" holds that states and federal governments are co-owners of US sovereignty and that state consent is thus needed for all federal government actions not covered by the express powers. The states were also believed to retain all powers not explicitly granted to the federal government, but this idea was rapidly proven false. In fact, early debates between the federalist and anti-federalist parties showed that many in the United States believed that the states had given too much power to the central government and should try to take it back.

As time moved on, however, the US political system became more and more centralized, which became a contributing factor in the US Civil War (1861–5) as Southern confederate states attempted to break free of the national government's control. Of particular importance was the issue of an individual state's right to continue to allow slavery. Nonetheless, with the Northern victory, the federal government was further strengthened. And with an expansion of federal powers in the twentieth century due to increased taxation, increasing demand for government services, and the impact of the world wars, this level of government continues to dominate the US political scene.

United States by the Constitution, nor prohibited by it to the States, are reserved to the States respectively, or to the people."[2] Nor was this a one-time affair: the division of power between the US government and the states is frequently a matter of debate in contemporary American politics.

It is interesting that the particular division of powers embodied in a country's constitution at the time of its federal union will begin to assume a very different appearance as time passes and new political and economic realities emerge. What may have seemed unimportant areas of decision-making power at the time of union may in fact become hugely important, both in terms of their financial impact and their political significance. As we will see in the next section, education, health care, and natural resources seemed rather low-level issues at the time of Canadian Confederation. By the middle of the twentieth century, however, they had attained a much greater and more central role in the lives of Canadians.

According to federalism's proponents, one of the system's major advantages is that governments will be much more aware of citizens' needs and desires because of its proximity to those it seeks to rule and serve. It is also argued that the federal model upholds democratic institutions and practices much more effectively by giving the people another level at which to hold governments accountable. In reality, much of this ability depends upon the nature of the federal system. Whereas power is highly decentralized in Canada and the United States, it remains extremely concentrated at the centre in Russia, where democratic practice is questionable. Mexico offers an interesting example in this regard: even though there is a relatively extensive set of powers credited to the state governments, the federal government has maintained an overwhelming dominance over the regions. Despite becoming more democratic and ending one-party rule, Mexico continues to be a country in which power is highly centralized, largely because of the fiscal (taxing and spending) capacity of the central government (see Box 6.5).

One of the major criticisms of federalism is that it becomes difficult to maintain equality between the regions and, consequently, political stability when control of a country is divided in this way. By sharing power over important functions, it is hard to ensure equal provision of services (in both quantity and quality), levels of economic prosperity, and even public security across the national territory. In time these inequalities will lead to envy and discord if left unchecked and may push federal systems to fall apart. A number of federal systems have met such an end. The former Yugoslavia is a most unsettling example. Its constituent parts went to war with each other in the 1990s, after the federal union collapsed under the strains of ethnic tensions and inequalities. To avoid such an outcome, the conflictive forces created by imbalances within a diverse population need to be countered by the national government's coordination.

North American Free Trade Agreement (NAFTA) agreement in which Canada, the United States, and Mexico have opened their markets to each other

6.5 THE UNITED STATES OF MEXICO

Interestingly, all three member countries of the **North American Free Trade Agreement (NAFTA)**–Canada, the United States, and Mexico–are federal states. Yet each one is different, and Mexico stands out as the most centralized of the three. Mexico's full and proper name is Los Estados Unidos de Mexico, or the United States of Mexico, which gives a clue to the country's federal nature. Indeed, according to its constitution, the 31 states of Mexico have considerable powers and autonomy, and each state has its own constitution, legislative assembly, and elected governor. However, largely due to the political and economic history of the country, Mexico remains highly centralized, with overwhelming power being exercised by the federal government from the Federal District of Mexico City. The major cause of this centralization is that one political party, the Partido Revolucionario Institucional (PRI), stayed in power at the federal level for over 70 years

and dominated the country's politics, governing most of the states as well. By limiting the autonomy of the states and their powers of taxation, the federal government was able to control and coordinate almost all aspects of political life.

Since the 1990s, this situation has begun to change. As the dominance of the PRI weakened and was then lost, significant variation emerged across the country, with rival political parties ruling different states. Breaking from federal control, these states began to exercise more autonomy on a wide range of issues. Disparities in levels of economic growth have also played a role, with the richer northern states gaining greater autonomy due to their increased governmental incomes. However, the PRI returned to power in July 2012, leading many to believe that efforts to recentralize power in Mexico City will follow. For more on Mexico's politics, see Chapter 10.

In summary, it is difficult to say whether federal systems provide a better model than their more centralized, unitary counterparts. Much depends on the nature of federalism, its degree of decentralization, the political culture and institutions that guide it, and the homogeneity of the country concerned.

Canadian Federalism: An Evolving History

Before British North America became the country we now know as Canada, it was a grouping of different territorial units bearing diverse socioeconomic, geographical, and political aspects. Its origins owed perhaps more to international events than political or economic processes occurring within the region. The global struggle between Britain and France and the subsequent focus on dominating Europe's battlefields resulted in the French monarchy's failure to adequately supply its forces in North America. This abandonment opened a window of opportunity regarding the new country. The British had tried to assimilate the French-speaking and predominantly Catholic population of Quebec into British North American society after the victory of General Wolfe in Quebec in 1759, which had brought the entire region of North America under British rule. Certain success was achieved as French-speaking people in the region rapidly came to recognize British sovereignty and to see the importance of British protection if they were to avoid annexation by the United States.

Despite this process, significant differences remained between anglophone and francophone populations, and the latter worried about the suppression of their culture, language, and (especially) religion. The process of full integration began in 1841, with the uniting of Upper and Lower Canada (now Ontario and Quebec, respectively) into the Province of Canada. By bringing these two entities into a closer political union, institutions and processes of coordination began to emerge and would eventually lead to the creation of Canada as a modern country.

Nonetheless, the differences between Upper and Lower Canada actually grew after 1841, especially because of the rapid population growth in the former, bringing with it economic development and higher expectations. A more permanent and equal solution to the problem needed to be found. However, it is important to remember that, while they dominated the political scene in British North America in the nineteenth century, Upper and Lower Canada were not alone. The Maritime provinces were smaller, poorer entities looking for some way to make their economic futures more secure. And the vast expanse of land to the west and to the north of the Province of Canada represented an enormous opportunity if efforts could be coordinated successfully.

Just as important as the internal considerations for the future Canadian provinces was the concern with their mutual security. Throughout the nineteenth century, it became increasingly clear that the survival of British North America was far from assured. After the British defeat in the American Revolution, the United States posed an ever-present threat in terms of either

6.6   INDIA: CENTRALIZED GOVERNMENT IN THE WORLD'S LARGEST DEMOCRACY

As the world's second most populous country (with a population estimated at over 1.2 billion people) and the seventh largest country in the world measured in territorial extension, India presents a fascinating case study of federalism. It is the world's largest democracy and is highly diverse in ethnic, religious, linguistic, and economic terms. How then to maintain stability and unity in such a big and varied country? Part of the answer lies in the particular form of federalism operating in India. The country has traditionally experienced strong regional tendencies, both before independence and since, and its federal model was originally based on the Canadian experience. The federal government plays a strong centralized role in relation to the country's 28 states and 7 union territories, although the states still exercise significant autonomy (the union territories are governed directly by the federal government). Despite significant further centralization of power in the 1970s and 1980s—resulting from political emergencies and internal conflict—the states are important players in Indian politics.

Most importantly, the states are formed around linguistic and ethnic concerns. The reorganization of the Indian state in 1956 redrew political boundaries and formed the new states along mainly linguistic lines. This approach has helped the states to develop their own cultural identities and has promoted the diversity of India. In turn, it has helped to accommodate concerns about the central political authority dominating the regions while still allowing the former to act in the interests of national unity.

Figure 6.1   Federalism in India

invasion or annexation. Although the War of 1812 resulted in a more stable environment and a more institutionalized bilateral relationship between the US and Britain, two factors came into play as the century wore on. The first was that, like France before it, Britain shifted its focus, this time from the Americas to its new colonies in Africa and especially in India. Britain not only recognized the American Monroe Doctrine of 1823 (which excluded European intervention in the Western hemisphere), but it also signalled that its Canadian territories were far from a priority. By uniting into a closer political project, the Canadians could strengthen their defences against possible invasion.

The second factor was the American Civil War. As the American federal union was placed under increasing strain by the southern states' call for a freer relationship, Canadian elites saw the need for a more formal arrangement between the regions of British North America if they were to avoid the possibility of a civil war or a gradual deterioration of relations between them. Already by 1837, both Upper and Lower Canada had been subject to rebellions that had raised the spectre of deeper armed conflict.

What was needed on both fronts was a formal project of union that would bring economic, political, and military benefits while preserving the individual identities of the geopolitical units. It was this dilemma that faced the men who met in the 1860s to negotiate and design the political future of Canada. These individuals, later known as the Fathers of Confederation, included John A. Macdonald, who was to become the first prime minister of Canada. Macdonald, a lawyer, had been influenced in views of the country's future by his experiences during the 1837 rebellions, when he had given legal assistance to Americans who had participated in raids on Canadian territory. This work helped him to appreciate the vulnerability of Canada's geographical position and the need for stronger defences.

In 1864, Macdonald, the leader of the Conservative Party of Canada, joined George Brown (who led what was later to become the Liberal Party) and George-Étienne Cartier of the Parti Bleu from Lower Canada to form the Great Coalition. This alliance of the country's major political forces allowed for the relatively rapid negotiation of articles of confederation at three conferences—in Charlottetown (September 1864), Quebec City (October 1864), and London, England (1866). For reasons of self-interest, Upper and Lower Canada, New Brunswick, and Nova Scotia agreed to form a united country. Upper Canada supported the union because its leaders saw opportunities for economic growth and trade. Lower Canada joined because the union promised to protect its language and culture. New Brunswick and Nova Scotia saw the potential for benefits from the Province of Canada's wealth and for protection from foreign aggression (largely from the United States).

However, both Newfoundland and Prince Edward Island opposed confederation (there was also significant opposition within the Province of Canada, though it remained in the minority). Prince Edward Island decided against joining because its negotiators had been unable to win the desired concessions regarding political representation. Newfoundland presented a more intriguing case by choosing not to exchange its "responsible government" status (meaning that, although still dependent on Britain, it had acquired significant autonomy in policy-making) for what it saw as a junior partnership in the new confederation.

In 1867 the negotiated agreement was presented to the British Parliament in Westminster and the Constitution Act of 1867 (also known as the British North America, or BNA, Act) was passed, creating the Dominion of Canada. Upper and Lower Canada were split from each other and given their current names. Although Canada did not immediately become a fully independent country (its powers over foreign policy were limited until the 1931 Statute of Westminster), it began to adopt the shape and institutions that we recognize today. In terms of the relations between the provinces and the federal government in Ottawa, the arrangement that emerged from the Charlottetown and Quebec conferences was interesting when put in a historical perspective. Rather than giving the provinces a dominant position vis-à-vis the federal government, Ottawa held the strongest hand in terms of constitutionally mandated powers. This preference for centralized power reflected Canada's fear of repeating the American experience of civil war.

6.7   WHY OTTAWA?

The choice of Ottawa as Canada's national capital may seem strange to many, given that the city is neither a central location in terms of the country's geography nor an economic centre. Before Confederation, Ottawa was just a good-sized logging town on the border between Upper and Lower Canada. It held no special place in the political affairs of the nation. Why, then, was it chosen?

In fact, the decision was made by Britain's Queen Victoria. Although a number of apocryphal stories exist regarding her method of selection (i.e. sticking a pin in the map at random; having a penchant for art from the Ottawa area), the fact is that her advisors chose the city for a number of strategic reasons. Ottawa was relatively far removed from the border with the United States, making it easier to defend and protect in the event of an invasion from the south. This was a key consideration given the still-fresh memories of the War of 1812. By a similar logic, it was well defended by the surrounding forests and was adequately supplied with fresh drinking water that could not be tampered with by the Americans.

More importantly, the city reflected the traditional division of power between French- and English-speaking

The Parliament Buildings, Ottawa.

peoples in Canada and served as a reminder of the need to balance provincial interests. Located almost equidistant between Toronto and Quebec City and right on the border between Quebec and Ontario, Ottawa seemed an adequate choice in terms of helping to placate fears concerning the dominance of one group over the other.

Federal institutions played a key role in this centralization of power. By granting Ottawa the ability to affect the lives of citizens across the country, federal ministries strengthened the hand of the central government. The division of powers between Ottawa and the provinces was also an important factor in uniting the new country.

THE DIVISION OF POWERS

The Constitution Act of 1867 specified a number of areas of "sole jurisdiction," or exclusive responsibility, for the provinces of Canada. They included control over property and civil rights (meaning, in those days, relations between private citizens), prisons, hospitals and asylums, charities, municipal institutions, and education. Again, it is important to remember that these areas were deemed much less important in 1867 than they are today. Under section 92 of the Act, provinces were also granted **concurrent powers**[3] in agriculture and immigration. In other words, control is shared between provincial and federal levels of governments and both may enact laws in these areas. Immigration is an interesting case, in that Quebec is the only province that chooses to exert power in this matter, thereby exercising control over immigration into its territory.

Section 91 outlined the extent of the federal government's powers. The Peace, Order, and Good Government (POGG)[4] clause reserved all powers not specifically given to the provinces for the federal government. Section 91 goes on to list a number of issues that are to be treated exclusively by the federal government, including the military and defence, the regulation of trade and commerce, and fisheries (an important industry and source of revenue in nineteenth-century Canada). In addition, control of the postal service, census and statistics, navigation and shipping, Aboriginal peoples and reserve land, and criminal law was given to the federal government.

A crucial question of power concerned taxation and government income. Government services and activities are incredibly expensive and require significant income generation if they are to be effective. When the Articles of Confederation were negotiated, there was no income tax to boost government revenues. Taxes were applied instead to trade, luxury items, land, and housing. For their part, the provinces were limited to direct taxation in order to raise revenue for provincial policy activities. The meaning of this restriction has been a recurring question in the history of Canadian federalism and has been reviewed numerous times by the Canadian judiciary. Today, most provinces generate their income through personal and corporate taxes, sales tax, and licensing and royalties. The federal government, on the other hand, was granted broad taxing powers. According to section 91 of the Act, the federal government may raise revenues by any mode or system of taxation, including direct taxation (income or corporate taxes) and indirect taxation (duties and fees).

Most intriguingly, however, the Constitution Act also gave the federal government special methods for controlling the provinces and overriding their mandates. The first of these was the power of **reservation**,[5] which allowed the

concurrent powers
the sharing of control between provincial and federal levels of government

reservation
occurs when a lieutenant governor puts provincial legislation up for the federal cabinet's consideration

lieutenant governor of a province to propose provincial legislation to the federal cabinet, which could then approve or reject it. Secondly, any piece of provincial legislation could be rejected or vetoed by the federal cabinet through its power of **disallowance**.[6] This principle theoretically allowed the monarch, working through the governor general, to reject any law approved by the provincial

disallowance
occurs when provincial legislation is rejected or vetoed by the federal cabinet

TABLE 6.1 | FEDERAL vs PROVINCIAL POWERS

	Federal	Provincial	Shared
Legislative Control Over . . .	regulation of trade and commerce, postal service, census and statistics, the military, navigation and shipping, sea coast and inland fisheries, Indians and reserve land, and the criminal law, as well as international treaties, taxation (wide range: direct and indirect), unemployment insurance	hospitals, asylums, charities, municipal institutions, prisons, property and civil rights, education, taxation (limited, only direct)	agriculture and immigration, old-age pensions, amending the constitution if this change concerns one or more provinces, natural resources (although federal still has more power here), and direct taxation (through federal–provincial/territorial taxation agreements)
Intergovernmental Interaction	Department of Intergovernmental Affairs, First Ministers' Meetings	Department of Intergovernmental Affairs, First Ministers' Meetings, Council of the Federation. First created in 2003, the council is a provincial/territorial forum constituted by the premiers of each province and territory in Canada.	
Federal Control Over Provinces	*Reservation:* This allows the lieutenant governor of a province to reserve provincial legislation for the consideration of the federal cabinet. *Disallowance:* Even if the lieutenant governor granted assent to a piece of provincial legislation, the federal cabinet could subsequently disallow it through this power. *Declaratory power:* to place any local work or undertaking, which it deemed to be for the general advantage of Canada, under its control.		

declaratory power
a federal government's power to take control of any local project if it decides that doing so would be for the greater national good

legislatures if it were seen to go against the traditions of British law. Lastly, the federal government was given **declaratory power**[7] that could be used to take control of any local project if it decided that doing so would serve the greater national good. Convention now dictates that the federal government not use these powers—in fact, they have not been used since the 1870s—but in the early days of the federal system they served to emphasize the dominance of the central authority.

An important and frequent question in the study of Canadian federalism is why the Constitution Act came to be known as a confederation agreement and the founders of Canada as the Fathers of Confederation. The answer is that, in this case, the term *confederation* refers to the act of coming together to form a federal system rather than the confederal system itself. In this sense, the term is more abstract and indicates the process of creating a federation; "entering into confederation" meant joining a federal body. The founders of Canada never intended the country to be such a union. Indeed, the Canadian form of federalism that emerged after 1867 was much closer to the British unitary system of government than a confederal one. Nonetheless, it is true that Canada is one of the more decentralized federations.

THE EVOLUTION OF CANADIAN FEDERALISM

Throughout Canadian history, the balance of power between the federal and provincial governments has changed. Although the national authority has always maintained the upper hand, so to speak, there has been significant variation in the level of provincial autonomy. This independence is partly a result of the provinces becoming more involved in citizens' lives as the issues under provincial control grow more important. The provinces also have an increasing ability to raise revenue through direct taxation and, in recent times, indirect taxation as well. But it is also important to remember that the federal government has played a role in determining the level of freedom afforded to the provinces. During the Great Depression of the 1930s, for example, the provinces became increasingly dependent on the federal government for financing, which gave the central government more influence over them. The latter's "power of the purse" in this case involved financing social programs and welfare projects, traditionally areas of provincial control. During both world wars, the federal government exercised centralized federalism, again increasing its power relative to the provinces as it sought to unify the country and mobilize citizens for the war effort.[8]

co-operative federalism
co-operation and coordination of policy between the federal and provincial levels of government

At other times, a spirit of co-operation and coordination of policy has governed relations between the two levels of government. Such **co-operative federalism**[9] was particularly important in the postwar period as economic growth was accompanied by an expansion of the Canadian population and a sense that the federal bargain involved increasing benefits for both sides. Even in the areas of shared responsibility, relations between federal and provincial authorities were largely cordial and positive.

Since the 1960s, however, there has been a more conflictive relationship between the provinces and the federal government. This period has come to be known as **executive federalism**,[10] as the provinces have attempted (sometimes successfully) to achieve greater autonomy from Ottawa and the federal government has resisted or imposed a price on such freedom. For example, in the 1990s Ottawa reduced its own spending on social programs and thus forced the provinces to take on greater fiscal responsibility, such as increasing their levels of taxation, if they were not to go bankrupt.

The question of finance has always been central to Canadian federalism. As the demands for provincial services grew, especially with the improvement in health and education services in the early twentieth century, provinces found themselves without sufficient funds to provide for these increasingly expensive areas. To solve this problem, the federal government provided **conditional grants**[11] that gave the provinces the necessary funds but put controls and conditions on how they could be spent. Although the grants signified a considerable imposition by the federal government, the provincial authorities had little choice but to accept. The fiscal manifestation of the federal bargain continues to mark Canadian federalism to this day. The idea of conditional grants disappeared, but the basic problem of how to finance provincial programs remained.

To compound the problem, the provinces do not have equal capacities for raising revenue. Ontario, traditionally a rich province due to its industrial base and its strong services sector, has been seen as a "have" province throughout most of Canadian history, whereas the Maritime provinces have a long history of being poorer and therefore "have nots." (More recently, Ontario has struggled to maintain its status—and has even been a have not province—as a result of severe cuts to the manufacturing sector. Conversely, Newfoundland and Labrador has become a have province in recent years thanks to oil and gas revenue.) As we have discussed in previous chapters, particularly Chapter 4, the federal government has attempted to create a balance by transferring funds from the richer provinces to the poorer. This program of equalization payments[12] is highly contentious for the richer provinces, who complain that their economic prosperity is being drained away to parts of Canada that are either badly run in economic terms or simply economically unsustainable. Here we see the irony of equalization payments: whereas they were intended to bring the provinces into a more harmonious nation, they have also created divisions.

Financial transfers from the federal government have consistently come under scrutiny and revision. The Federal–Provincial Fiscal Arrangements and Established Programs Financing Act of 1977 (EPF) offered the provinces block grants (determined by per capita entitlements for each province) to finance education and health care with minimal interference from Ottawa. Financing was to come partly in the form of tax transfers, whereby the federal government reduced its tax take to allow the provinces to raise their taxes by the same amount, and partly in the form of cash grants. The EPF may have seemed positive for the provinces in that it gave them greater autonomy, but it also established their sole responsibility and therefore financial liability for these

executive federalism
a generally conflictive relationship between the provinces and the federal government, created when provinces try (often successfully) to achieve greater autonomy from the federal government, which resists such attempts

conditional grants
funds given to provincial authorities from the federal government, which assigns controls and conditions on how the monies may be spent

6.8 FISCAL FEDERALISM

As we have shown in this chapter, one of the fundamental questions related to federal political systems is that of revenue for the provinces or states. Unless significant flexibility is given to the provinces by the federal government in this area, they will either be limited in what functions they can carry out or depend on financial transfers from the central authority. In Canada, this issue has been one of contention since Confederation because the provinces have to fulfill their obligations in terms of providing services as well as maintain autonomy from the federal government.

In the period following the Second World War, the federal government established its dominance over the provinces by assuming all tax collection activities and then transferring money to the provinces through transfer payments. These funds came in the form of conditional grants to the provinces, in which the federal government could determine exactly how they should be spent. In the 1970s, as provincial influence and demands (inspired by Quebec) grew, the federal government agreed to **unconditional**

The issue of who gets what from the federal budget is a constant source of tension in Canadian politics.

grants, block payments that could be spent by the provinces in any way they saw fit. Under this rubric also came equalization payments.

unconditional grants payments from the federal government that may be spent by the provinces in any way they see fit

programs, which were rapidly becoming more and more expensive to uphold. What's more, the federal government was able to retain some degree of influence over the nature of health and education spending through legislative manoeuvring. Since 1977, this arrangement has been modified a number of times, with the provinces consistently complaining that the federal government is trying to push ever-greater financial burdens their way. For example, the federal government initially committed to raising the per capita entitlements in line with inflation but has failed to live up to that pledge.

Determining who has the power to tax and how it affects the economy and political life in Canada requires collaboration between the two levels of government. If both provincial and federal governments were to tax the same sector of the economy at high levels, economic growth and prosperity would be negatively affected. Further, if one level decides to raise taxes to increase government revenues at the same time that the other level cuts taxes in an effort to increase citizens' spending power, they would find themselves at cross-purposes. Just as important, the ability of some provinces, such as Alberta, to raise large amounts of public revenue through royalties and taxes on the natural resources sector creates a problem between the provinces, one caused by the envy of poorer entities and Albertans' reluctance to continue what they perceive as "bailing out" the rest of Canada.

Given that there needs to be ongoing consultation and coordination between the two levels, how do the provincial and federal governments interact? In addition to day-to-day informal contact and discussion between bureaucrats at provincial and federal levels, primary responsibility for organizing relations is assumed by the executive branches. Therefore, the federal/provincial/territorial First Ministers' Meetings (FMMs) have evolved to become the highest-profile means of contact. There is no regular schedule for the FMMs, and they heavily depend on the national political agenda. They have been more frequent when the federal system is under stress due to an economic crisis or the Quebec question (see the next section), such as during the 1970s and 1980s, but they have also been held to discuss specific policy issues, such as health care. Further, ministers' meetings have taken place when the respective ministers for a specific area (e.g. finance) from the federal, provincial, and territorial governments congregate to coordinate actions. In order to serve these interactions, the Canadian Intergovernmental Conference Secretariat (CICS) was created in 1973 as a permanent administrative support for intergovernmental co-operation and has served to significantly strengthen such collaboration in institutional terms. The CICS justifies its existence by arguing that, with Canada's federal structure, "there is a great need for governments to communicate, to consult each other, to harmonize their policies and programs, coordinate their activities, resolve conflicts, and, in some instances, develop policies jointly."[13]

In addition to the 10 provinces, of course, Canada also has 3 territories. Their position within the Canadian union is somewhat different, coming closer to a unitary system. Territories have no inherent, constitutionally designated jurisdictions but only what is given to them by the federal government; therefore, they are far less autonomous. (We discussed the territories in some detail in Chapter 4.) Whereas the provinces derive their power from the Canadian Constitution Act of 1867, the territories depend on the federal government for their powers. Nonetheless, each territory not only has significant devolved powers and its own legislative and executive branch of government, but it also participates in multilateral intergovernmental conferences alongside the provinces and the federal government. Each territory elects one MP and one senator to the federal legislature as well. Although these figures seem to indicate very little political representation at the national level, on a per capita basis the territories are better represented than any other part of Canada except Prince Edward Island.

The 1980s and 1990s were marked by a number of constitutional conferences in which the provinces attempted to achieve what they saw as a more equitable distribution of power between levels of government. The Constitution Act (1982), Meech Lake Accord (1987), and Charlottetown Accord (1992) sought to redefine the federal–provincial bargain. Increasingly, the provinces learned to coordinate their positions and now present a more unified front in negotiations with the federal government. This strategy has made it more difficult for the federal authorities to pressure the provinces into an agreement.

6.9 NATURAL RESOURCES

The provinces' control over their natural resources has always been a fundamental element in their portfolio of rights and responsibilities. In the early days of Confederation, the forests and wildlife of Canada presented significant economic opportunities in terms of timber and animal pelts, respectively. However, the true importance of this control would only become apparent in later years with the arrival of the oil industry in Alberta and other provinces.

Royalties and taxes on oil production have made Alberta the richest province in the country, while its importance in global oil and gas markets has made it an international power. As global oil prices soared in the first decade of the twenty-first century, Alberta received hundreds of thousands of new immigrants, people from abroad or other parts of Canada who were attracted by the employment opportunities connected with the oil and gas sector and especially by the very high wages. Although such dependence on oil and gas revenues means that Alberta's fortunes rise and fall with global prices in this area, the province has invested its new-found wealth in a wide range of social, business, and educational programs to diversify its economy and prepare for the future.

Canada Dept. of Mines and Resources / Library and Archives Canada / PA-021722

Natural resources have long been a source of wealth and economic development across Canada.

The Constitution Act of 1982 brought the provinces and federal government together to patriate the constitution. We have already discussed how this Act, signed by all provinces except Quebec, transferred control of the Canadian constitution from Britain to Ottawa and included the Canadian Charter of Rights and Freedoms. The previous chapters also explained the 7/50 formula, which dictates the rules for making further constitutional amendments and the relationship between the federal and provincial authorities (see, in particular, Box 4.6, p. 112). Quebec's refusal to assent to the patriation was seen as significantly weakening the legitimacy of the federal government and the Constitution

Act itself. Although the Supreme Court had previously ruled that no province had veto over the patriation process, the federal government and the other provinces believed that Quebec's agreement would greatly strengthen national unity. Therefore, in 1987, the Brian Mulroney Conservative government held the Meech Lake Conference to seek a way of placating Quebec and bringing it more firmly into the Canadian fold.

The Meech Lake Accord proposed five main points that would have reformed the constitution. First, it called on the provinces to accept that Quebec is a "distinct society" within Canada. Second, it proposed a constitutional veto for the provinces, greatly increasing their power within the federal–provincial bargain. Third, it granted increased powers to the provinces over immigration. Fourth, it promised to provide financial support to any province that sought to opt out of federal programs. Finally, it allowed for the provinces to have more say over the appointment of senators and Supreme Court justices.

The most controversial of these five proposals was, understandably, the first. Whereas the others would have resulted in a considerable transfer of power from the federal government to each of the provinces, the distinct society clause singled out Quebec for the possibility of special treatment. Initially, the provinces accepted the agreement. But before it could be ratified in each provincial parliament, a nationwide campaign led by Pierre Trudeau argued that the deal would severely weaken the nation and give Quebec special status. Faced with public opposition, the provinces reconvened to negotiate amendments to the original agreement but, despite unanimous assent by the premiers, ratification by the provincial parliaments proved a step too far. By the end of June 1990, the Meech Lake agreement was dead.

A further attempt to resolve the federal–provincial compact and the status of Quebec took place in 1992, with the negotiation of the Charlottetown Accord. This comprehensive agreement attempted to settle long-standing conflicts over the division of powers and to establish the basis for the idea of a Canadian identity (in what has come to be known as the Canada Clause) while still recognizing Quebec as a distinct society. Furthermore, the Charlottetown Accord would have abolished the anachronistic powers of reservation and disallowance. Despite gaining the support of all provincial and territorial premiers, as well as First Nations leaders, the Accord was defeated in a national referendum on 26 October 1992.

After three failed attempts to resolve the federal–provincial relationship in 10 years, Canada's political leaders decided to not risk any further political capital on the issue. Since 1992, there has been no serious national attempt to deal with the question of Quebec or with reforming federalism. To understand why these have been such thorny issues in Canadian politics, we must examine the question of Quebec nationalism and the challenge it poses to Canadian federalism.

QUEBEC AND CANADIAN FEDERALISM

No issue excites political sentiments in Canada more than the question of Quebec's proper place in the federal system. Should Quebec be treated the same as every other province in the country? Should it hold a special status?

Should it seek some form of new sovereignty-association with Canada or out-right independence? These are just some of the options that have emerged over the years as Quebec and the rest of Canada have struggled to accommodate the province in a way that satisfies both the requirements of Canadian federalism and the desire of the Québécois to protect and promote their identity.

The Quebec question has been a prominent one since the early years of the Canadian federal system. As we noted in Box 6.7, the choice of Ottawa as the capital of Canada had much to do with appeasing Quebec's fears of being dominated by English-speaking Canada. But the question of protecting the French language and Québécois culture goes far beyond the simple selection of the capital city. It is fair to say that the history of Canada is marked with numerous incidents and policies where both have appeared to be under threat, often through anti-French legislation passed by the federal and provincial governments. We could argue, therefore, that it is entirely understandable for Quebec nationalists to believe that their rights and aspirations for political self-determination would be better served either by independence or a new, less restricted relationship with Ottawa.

Although we can trace the ideological roots of Quebec nationalism and separatism back to the early days of British rule in Lower Canada, the modern separatist movement originated in the creation of the Parti Québécois (PQ) in 1968 and particularly in the leadership of René Lévesque, a highly charismatic and committed politician who led the party from its founding until 1985. Lévesque turned the PQ from a coalition of small parties and protest movements into the governing party of Quebec, serving as premier from 1976 to 1985.

sovereignty-association
arrangement by which a state or province acquires independence from the federal government but retains strong links to the country, generally in the form of economic policy

Lévesque's PQ government is remembered for a number of issues, most importantly the passing of Bill 101 (a highly controversial law promoting French as the dominant language of the province) and the May 1980 provincial referendum on the question of seeking a new **sovereignty-association** plan with the rest of Canada. In this plan, Quebec would have become a politically independent state but maintained a formal association with Canada. In other words, Quebec would have much more autonomy than before, but it would officially remain part of the country. This connection would be particularly important in economic affairs, as many in the separatist movement feared that Quebec would be economically isolated and disadvantaged by seeking independence. The PQ lost the referendum by 20 per cent of the vote. As a result, Lévesque had to adopt a more accommodating strategy regarding his relations with the federal government, which ultimately led members of his party to call for his resignation.

The PQ has since been led by other influential leaders, such as Jacques Parizeau and Lucien Bouchard, who have sought greater independence for the province. But there has yet to be a clear decision taken by the Quebec population in favour of changing the federalist deal. The closest that the separatist movement came was in 1995, when the Parizeau government held a referendum asking the following question: "Do you agree that Quebec should become sovereign after having made a formal offer to Canada for a new economic and political partnership within the scope of the bill respecting the future of Quebec and of the agreement signed on June 12, 1995?" The "No" side received 50.6 per cent of the vote while the "Yes" received 49.4 per cent; therefore, the proposal was narrowly defeated (some say because the question was confusing). With the French-speaking population of Quebec voting heavily in favour of the proposal and the English- and other-speaking (i.e. allophone) population voting overwhelmingly against, the issue seemed to be split along linguistic lines. This division continues to present a significant obstacle in Quebec, not only to the separatist movement but also (and more importantly) in terms of provincial unity.

Despite provincial referenda and federal–provincial conferences, a satisfactory solution to Quebec's place in Canada has not been found. One reason for this failure is that, although a majority of Québécois believe that the province and its citizens have a distinct identity, repeated opinion polls and plebiscites have shown that there is no clear majority in favour of any new federal arrangement. This situation has led to a recurring strain on Canadian federalism. The prospect that the second largest and one of the founding provinces might leave the Canadian union, dramatically altering the balance of economic and political power within the country and fundamentally changing its cultural identity, is almost unthinkable for many.

It is here, though, that federalism shows both its strengths and weaknesses. Because of the greater regional autonomy provided by Canada's federal structure, Quebec has been better able to develop its sense of a distinct identity by establishing language laws and government recruitment practices that have strengthened the place of francophones in the province and, indeed, in Canada as a whole. The provincial government, mainly under PQ rule, has also been a strong adversary of the federal government. The party has worked alongside the federal Bloc Québécois to demand more from the federal government. These factors have spurred the movement calling for more autonomy and maybe even independence. However, the inherent flexibility of federalism also allows for innovative approaches to dealing with the Quebec question without necessarily dissolving the Canadian union. It is quite conceivable that more power could be transferred to the provinces (all of them, not simply Quebec) without permanently damaging the existence of Canada as a unified country. Other states, such as Switzerland, have given increased powers to their regions while still maintaining national unity.

Today the separatist movement in Quebec is still alive and well, and a sizeable percentage of the population believes that Quebec should seek a new deal with Canada. In March 2012, one survey found that 44.5 per cent of Quebecers support separating from Canada if a constitutional deal satisfying the majority of the province's population cannot be reached. We must always take polling data with a pinch of salt and remember that such questions can be confusing or even misleading, but this result shows that there is still considerable discontent with federalism as it stands in Quebec.

Although Quebec's status is by far the most contentious question facing Canadian federalism, other regional challenges exist. The continued depressed economies of the Maritime provinces and the rise of the Western provinces have placed significant strains on Canadian unity. Left behind in economic terms in the twentieth and early twenty-first centuries, the Maritimes have called for greater investment from the federal government to raise living standards. On the other hand, Alberta's rising wealth and British Columbia's increasing influence have meant that these two provinces are more assertive in interprovincial and provincial–federal relations, challenging the traditional dominance of Ontario and Quebec. However these challenges are resolved, debates over federalism will continue to be a central feature of Canadian politics long into the future.

Conclusion

The political distribution of power within the national territory is one of the most important factors in determining the nature of the state. The choice between unitary and federal (or even confederal) systems will be based on a number of factors, including territorial extension, regional and cultural diversity, political traditions, and concerns of effectiveness and efficiency. Centralizing power in a unitary government has been the form adopted by a vast majority of countries in the world today as a way of overcoming social divisions and maximizing the state's capacity to implement policy on a national basis. The federal system, however, offers the alternative of providing closer contact between citizens and government, tailoring government policy more closely to regional needs, and encouraging diversity within the nation.

In Canada, the federal experiment has been successful for more than 140 years. Based on the need to unite diverse political entities for their mutual benefit and protection, federalism in Canada is a living system that is in constant flux. Quebec's place is clearly the most controversial and contested piece of the federal jigsaw puzzle, but so far the system has been flexible enough to accommodate the provinces' concerns, albeit in an imperfect way. Rest assured, federalism will be a major element for the duration of your study of Canadian politics.

Self-Assessment Questions

1. How do unitary, federal, and confederal states differ from each other?
2. Explain why some countries choose unitary systems and others choose federal.
3. Which do you think would work better in the Canadian context, the current quasi-federal structure or a looser confederation? Give reasons to support your answer.
4. What do the terms *reservation* and *disallowance* mean?
5. What is sovereignty-association?
6. How is Quebec's place in Canada's constitutional arrangement different from the other provinces?

Weblinks

Canadian Federalism
www.pco-bcp.gc.ca/aia/index.asp?lang=eng&page=federal

Equalization Program
www.fin.gc.ca/fedprov/eqp-eng.asp

Government of India
http://india.gov.in/

Health Canada
www.hc-sc.gc.ca

Powers of the National and Provincial Governments
www.pco-bcp.gc.ca/aia/index.asp?lang=eng&page=federal&sub=legis&doc=legis-eng.htm

Provinces and Territories of Canada
www.canada.gc.ca/othergov-autregouv/prov-eng.html

Further Reading

Bickerton, James. "Regionalism in Canada." In *Canadian Politics*, 3rd edn., edited by James P. Bickerton and Alain-G. Gagnon, 209–38. Peterborough, ON: Broadview Press, 1999.

Changfoot, Nadine, and Blair Cullen. "Why is Quebec Separatism off the Agenda? Reducing National Unity Crisis in the Neoliberal Era," *Canadian Journal of Political Science* 44 (2011): 769–87.

Filippov, Mikhail, Peter C. Ordeshook, and Olga Shvetsova. *Designing Federalism: A Theory of Self-Sustainable Federal Institutions*. Cambridge: Cambridge University Press, 2004.

Guy, James J. *People, Politics and Government: A Canadian Perspective*. 7th edn. Toronto: Prentice-Hall, 2010.

Howlett, Michael. "Federalism and Public Policy." In *Canadian Politics*, 3rd edn., edited by James P. Bickerton and Alain-G. Gagnon, 523–39. Peterborough, ON: Broadview Press, 1999.

Nye, Joseph S., Jr. *Understanding International Conflicts: An Introduction to Theory and History*. 6th edn. New York: Pearson Longman, 2007.

Potter, Jonathan. *Devolution and Globalisation: Implications for Local Decision-Makers*. Paris: OECD, 2001.

Robinson, Ian, and Richard Simeon. "The Dynamics of Canadian Federalism." In *Canadian Politics*, 3rd edn., edited by James P. Bickerton and Alain-G. Gagnon, 155–78. Peterborough, ON: Broadview Press, 1999.

News Clips

Visit the companion website for *Politics: An Introduction*, 2nd edn, to access news clips related to the content of this chapter.

7

Political Participation: Elections and Parties

◀ Barack Obama, the first African-American president of the
United States, speaks at a rally in Portland, Oregon, during
the 2008 presidential campaign. As the crowd at this event
suggests, voter turnout for the election was very high.

LEARNING OBJECTIVES

After reading this chapter, you will be able to

- understand the importance and significance of voting;
- distinguish between different forms of electoral systems;
- explain the importance and role of political parties;
- recognize the importance of campaign financing and the need for regulation;
- understand the pros and cons of the referendum as a democratic tool; and
- appreciate the role played by voting, elections, parties, and referenda in Canada.

Introduction

At local, national, and international levels, politics is one of the determining forces in our daily lives. However, it often seems to be an area that we have little power over, one that is directed by elites and by rich and powerful groups in society. Decision-making in the nation's capital, wars in foreign countries, and the process of integration in Europe are all outside of our control. In this way, we are not direct participants in politics—it is something that happens to us. But this viewpoint ignores a major part of the political environment that surrounds us. In reality, we are not truly removed from the "political" in our daily lives. We can all have an influence in the decision-making process and, in the best of cases, this involvement can serve to improve our lives.

The purpose of this and the next chapter is to introduce you to the various ways we become involved in the political process and to how this participation affects our lives and well-being and those of our communities. Politics is like any other form of socialization.[1] In fact, these two chapters are primarily about the political and social organizing of citizens. Participation in local, national, and global political processes is a product of the manner in which we are socialized.

The material introduced here builds on the ideological and institutional knowledge you have gained in the previous chapters. In many ways, participation is the most consequential aspect of political studies because it is only by understanding involvement in the political process that we can come to understand the larger issues of "who gets what, when, and how." This understanding also highlights some of the ways that you, as a student, citizen, and voter can get involved in politics: voting in elections, joining a political party, and making decisions. In many respects, this chapter deals with the issues that first come to mind when we think of politics and form a fundamental part of democracy.

Democracy and Voting

As you already know, democracy can take many forms and differs from country to country, as well as throughout history. However, at an abstract level we can differentiate between two basic types. **Direct democracy**,[2] as we will see later in this chapter, employs direct citizen involvement in the decision-making process through the referendum, whereby all eligible citizens express their opinions and preferences on policies. However, since it would be nearly impossible for every member of a society to be a direct part of the decision-making process all the time (a politician's occupation is, after all, a full-time job), most political systems use what is referred to as **indirect democracy**, or representative democracy,[3] in which citizens' opinions and preferences are defended and articulated by elected representatives. Indirect democracy, then, uses **elections**[4] to decide who will be given the authority to make decisions on behalf of the entire political grouping. Elections are the most direct forum for people in most countries and periods to influence the decisions made for society as a whole.

In modern liberal democracies such as Canada, voting in an election consists of eligible citizens selecting the candidate whom they want to represent them in government. Voters express their choice by casting a **ballot**, which traditionally is an official piece of paper (some countries, however, are beginning to use forms of electronic voting). Elections represent that aspect of the voter–government relationship that occurs at the federal, provincial, and municipal levels of democracy: the opportunity for individual citizens to choose politicians who best meet their interests and preferences. That said, electoral systems do not come without conditions. Every electoral system, whatever its composition, sets out formal restrictions on this choice, indicating who may vote and through what means.

Though considered generally open and liberal today, electoral systems were once highly restrictive. Most conspicuously, suffrage[5] was a more exclusive affair. Historical systems discriminated based on gender (usually only males were allowed to vote), age (often only certain age groups were given the right), economic status (requiring, for instance, individuals to be employed or own land or other valuable resources), or even literacy (thereby preventing those who were not educated from voting). These restrictions were slowly relaxed over time, but it was still impossible for women and some minorities to partake in the voting process until well into the twentieth century. In some countries, such as Saudi Arabia and Vatican City (a city-state), suffrage has still not been extended to these groups.

direct democracy
political system in which citizens are directly involved in the decision-making process

indirect democracy
political system of representation in which citizens elect a delegate to act on their behalf; also called representative democracy

election
a form of choosing political representatives whereby individual citizens cast their vote for their preferred candidate

ballot
card used to cast a vote; ballots are kept in a designated ballot box and counted by electoral officials

Canada's electoral system currently allows most people over the age of 18 to vote in elections. This rule raises the following question: What is it about an 18-year-old that makes them more deserving of the vote than a 17-year-old or, for that matter, a 7-year-old? Generally, states have decided to assign the voting age based upon the age of majority, when people are considered to be fully responsible adults. When democracies first extended the vote to the general public, the age of majority was set at 21, but it was reduced to 18 in most countries during the twentieth century. Reducing the voting age to 16 has recently been debated in some countries and was implemented in Austria in 2007. Significant regional support for reducing the age exists in Britain (particularly in Scotland, where it is likely that the minimum age for voting in the upcoming independence referendum will be set at 16); however, the national voting age remains at 18. Public debate regarding this topic also continues in Japan, where the voting age is set at 20.

On the other side of the coin, every country has restrictions governing who can legally run for election. While the rules about who can vote usually also apply in this matter, the laws surrounding election candidacy are often more stringent than those for voting. In some countries, membership in

7.1 WHO GETS TO VOTE?

In most democracies, it is assumed that all citizens vote in elections, with certain exceptions. For many years, prisoners in Canada were excluded from voting. Indeed, the Canada Elections Act of 2000 specifically prohibits them from taking part in the electoral process. However, in 2002 a case arguing that prisoners deserve equal treatment as Canadian citizens was brought before the Supreme Court. The court's decision in this landmark case, known as *Sauvé v. Canada*, declared that the Act violated the terms of the Canadian Charter of Rights and Freedoms and was therefore unconstitutional. Since 2002, all adult Canadians–including the mentally ill, who earned suffrage in 1988–have held the right to vote.

The question of age and maturity, however, is more controversial. In 2005, two young women from Alberta–Erin Fitzgerald and Christine Jairamsingh–tried to bring a case for allowing citizens under the age of 18 to vote before the Supreme Court. Noting that the Charter states that "every citizen of Canada has the right to vote in an election of members of the House of Commons or of a legislative assembly," Fitzgerald and Jairamsingh argued that such language

© Enigma / Alamy

Youth tend to be among the most politically active members of society. Should they be allowed the most basic political right–to vote?

should be interpreted to permit all Canadians, regardless of age, to vote. The court refused to hear the case, but this issue is sure to reappear.

political parties determines whether an individual is permitted to stand for election; if he or she is not a member of a party, he or she may not be allowed to run. In a high-profile case in Mexico in 2005, independent candidate, intellectual, and former foreign minister Jorge Castañeda was denied the right to run for the presidency because he lacked an official party affiliation. Since then, Mexico has changed its electoral laws to allow for "independent" candidates. Canada does not have party requirements, so **independents**[6] have always been able to run in elections.

Elections take place in **constituencies** (sometimes known as ridings), the geographical units into which voters are separated and within which candidates compete for votes. Most political systems try to create an equitable system of constituencies[7] to accurately match where the majority of the population lives, thereby giving more elected representatives to densely populated areas, such as cities, and fewer to sparsely populated regions, such as rural ridings. Electoral systems also establish rules regarding where voting occurs, who is given authority for **enumeration**[8] and ballot collection and counting, and how votes are actually converted into seats.

The process of enumeration can be highly sensitive in some countries, where politicians may manipulate constituency boundaries to affect electoral outcomes. Throughout history, political boundaries have been altered for political gain. In Britain **"rotten boroughs"**[9]—areas with very small populations and electorates but equal standing with normal-sized constituencies—existed. **"Pocket boroughs"**[10] tended to have very small electorates whose votes were in the pocket of (i.e. controlled by) the major local landowner. In Canada, rural ridings generally have smaller populations and thus smaller electorates than their urban counterparts, but Canadian electoral law allows for this difference.

In the United States, the process of altering election boundaries is known as **gerrymandering**[11] and is highly controversial. The practice seeks to form or divide groups of voters in order to maximize or reduce their power, depending on the situation. For example, dividing ethnic minorities into multiple voting districts can reduce their influence over electoral outcomes. Alternatively, grouping certain minorities who share certain political preferences might guarantee their dominance in the district or constituency. Canadian constituency boundaries have also been altered to affect election outcomes; however, the federal government's 1964 decision to entrust the drawing of these borders to Elections Canada, an autonomous agency, has largely solved the problem.

No doubt one of the most critical problems facing election systems today is **voter apathy**. This condition occurs when individuals simply decide not to vote or follow the election process because they believe, for whatever reason, that elections do not affect them or that their opinions have little influence over outcomes. In some countries, such as the United States, voter turnout is a major challenge; it is considered a "good" turnout if over half of registered eligible voters actually cast a ballot. In recent years, all major democracies have engaged in public awareness and education campaigns designed to increase participation, with a particular focus on young people. Programs such as Rock the Vote

political party
organization that seeks to gain and maintain political power

independents
electoral candidates who do not belong to a political party

constituencies
territorial or geographical localities represented by a politician chosen through the electoral process; also called ridings

enumeration
the process of determining the number of individuals eligible to vote in a constituency

rotten boroughs
in Britain, areas with very small populations and electorates that were given equal standing with normal-sized constituencies

pocket boroughs
in Britain, areas where very small electorates were in the pocket of (i.e. controlled by) the major local landowner

gerrymandering
controversial method of combining or dividing groups of voters in order to maximize or reduce their power

voter apathy
condition in which individuals do not vote or do not follow the election process because they believe that elections do not affect or influence them or that their vote has little influence over outcomes

7.2 GERRYMANDERING

THE GERRYMANDER.

The reshaping of electoral districts to guarantee election results is an old phenomenon.

The origins of the term *gerrymandering* trace back to 1812, when the governor of Massachusetts, Elbridge Gerry, signed into law a piece of legislation that reshaped electoral districts in such a way as to benefit his party in the next election. The *Boston Gazette* examined the new electoral boundaries and, noting that they resembled a mythical salamander or small dragon in form, combined the governor's name with the shape to produce the word *gerrymander*. The term has been in use ever since and continues to excite political controversy.

© Old Paper Studios / Alamy

have achieved some success in the United States and have been imitated around the world, but it is a constant struggle to maintain voter engagement.

It is easy to discard the role that casting a ballot[12] plays in our systems of government; the multitude of issues facing individual citizens in modern society often seems overwhelming, and the real role that we might play in the political process frequently seems small. Still, voting is an essential part of living in a

7.3 ROCK THE VOTE

Founded in 1990, Rock the Vote is an NGO dedicated to convincing young people of voting age to participate in elections. Started in Los Angeles, it has spread throughout the world and is active in many elections. The organization's mission is "to engage and build political power for young people in our country" (www.rockthevote.com/about/). Using music, new technologies, and mass media, Rock the Vote not only encourages voting among the young but also voter registration and ongoing participation in the important political debates of the day. Further, it has programs that engage high-school students in political issues to prepare them for their impending participation in elections.

7.4 THE SUFFRAGETTE MOVEMENT

Until the twentieth century, women in most parts of the world were prevented from voting. Even in the world's pre-eminent democracies, such as Canada and the UK, women were treated as second-class political citizens. However, as noted in Chapter 3, the rise of feminist thought in the nineteenth century and increasing demands for equal treatment led to the suffragette movement in Britain, Canada, and the United States. Led by such visionaries as Emmeline Pankhurst (Britain), Emily Howard Stowe (Canada), and Susan B. Anthony (United States), the movement used a program of civil disobedience, violent resistance, and hunger strikes to influence public and elite opinion. Though initially dismissed as dangerous revolutionaries, these pioneers were responsible for bringing full political participation to women in their countries and leading the movement for equal political rights across the world.

© The Print Collector / Alamy

Suffragette leader Emmeline Pankhurst was arrested by British police.

liberal democracy, one that millions of people struggled to obtain. Whether they were from oppressed minorities or lower socioeconomic classes, people throughout history have fought and risked injury, imprisonment, and even death to gain the right to vote. The suffragette movement, the anti-apartheid movement in South Africa, and democracy movements around the world battled for years (and continue to do so) to achieve what many of us take for granted. Therefore, it seems irresponsible not to exercise the right to a democratic voice.

Studies show that the tendency to vote and voting preference are highly determined by one's position in society, level of education, family background, and chosen profession. Those who belong to the upper echelons of society, are highly educated, and have a family background of political participation are much more likely to vote. This situation threatens to create an underclass of people who see little point in voting or other forms of political participation, which is clearly not healthy for democracy. To encourage voter participation, it is essential that society provide adequate and reliable information about the political parties and individual candidates standing for election. In recent years, this task has become easier thanks to the media and Internet. However, it has been argued that there is too much information available and that it confuses the public and increases voter apathy.

compulsory voting
system in which citizens
have a legal obligation to
vote in elections

What is certain is that voter turnout[13] across Western democracies has steadily dropped since the middle of the twentieth century. A number of countries have attempted to rectify this problem by implementing **compulsory voting**.[14] For example, citizens of voting age in Australia, Brazil, Peru, and Turkey have a legal obligation to vote in elections and may be fined or even imprisoned if they don't. Voters do not necessarily have to express a preference for one candidate or political party; they may spoil their ballot (by filling it in incorrectly) or indicate that they don't have a preference. It is argued that this system not only encourages greater citizen participation and awareness of political issues but also gives elected governments more legitimacy because they will represent a majority of voters. Arguments against compulsory voting state that voting is a right, not a duty, and it is therefore wrong to force unwilling citizens to vote. It is also claimed that doing so may actually make people resent the political process and see voting as an unwelcome obligation, thus damaging their commitment to democratic values.

At the other end of the scale, some have argued that voting should become a privilege rather than a right. According to this rather extreme position, potential voters should be tested on their knowledge of political parties, candidates, **election platforms**, and the basic workings of the political system before being allowed to vote. It is unlikely that any liberal democracy would ever implement such an approach because, by definition, it eliminates the right to vote, something that is an essential part of democratic systems.

election platforms
positions of political
parties or individuals
regarding issues and
political intentions

Types of Electoral Systems

Having established what voting is and how voters are organized into constituencies, we must examine the different types of electoral systems that exist in the world today. There are two basic forms that allow for the conversion of votes into legislative seats or, alternatively, the presidency. The **simple plurality**[15] system involves the election of the individual who obtains the greatest number of votes. This system is also called **first-past-the-post**[16], alluding to how a horse wins a race by being the first to pass the post. In this system, the winning candidate or party wins all the seats associated with a particular district or constituency; there is no reward for finishing second. It is quite possible that, in any given constituency, a candidate may lose by only one vote out of thousands and yet gain nothing from this result.

simple plurality
see first-past-the-post

first-past-the-post
electoral system in which
the winner receives the
most (but not necessarily
a majority of) votes; also
called simple plurality

Simple plurality is well-known for harming the chances of small political parties. Well-established parties that already have a strong voter base will be able to win seats and potentially form a government. But a party that garners, say, only 10 per cent of the vote is unlikely to win any constituency and will therefore find it difficult to raise its profile on the national stage. This system, then, tends to reinforce the position of the established parties and hinder the rise of new ones.

In general, the simple plurality system is also more likely to produce majority governments, in which one party gains more than 50 per cent (i.e. a majority) of the seats in the legislature. This result is commonly seen as beneficial to governance, as one party is able to control outcomes in the legislative branch. However, it is also quite common for a party to receive a majority of seats but less than 50 per cent of the overall vote. Such a situation raises questions as to the authority and legitimacy of the government, as well as the system. Those parties (and in turn their supporters) who garner large numbers of votes but not enough to control the legislature risk being excluded from the policy process.

Finally, a winning majority government might not receive any seats in certain regions, given the peculiarities of individual riding preferences. This outcome poses a challenge for governments because they may not have widespread support across the national territory but still attain a majority of seats in the parliament or congress. Questions about the nationwide legitimacy of a government and calls for greater consultation with the parties that dominate specific regions will inevitably follow.

In exceptional circumstances, as has been seen recently in Canada and in the United Kingdom, the result of a simple plurality system is the election of a **minority government**,[17] meaning that one party won more seats than the others but did not win 50 per cent or more seats. This party may not have the ability to govern on its own and will require the support of other parties in order to pass legislation. Such support can take the form of an official alliance, or coalition, or can be a less formal arrangement in which other parties agree to vote with the largest party on certain issues. This agreement can be tenuous and create a sense of uncertainty in policy-making.

Regardless of this possibility, the overall tendency of the first-past-the-post system to create majority governments is applauded in some quarters. Proponents argue that majority governments give more certainty, greater stability, and stronger direction to government without the need for constant negotiation and brokering that is common with minority governments. To summarize, we might say that the simple plurality system is highly efficient because it quickly and easily determines the winner in each constituency and at the national level. However, it suffers from the problem of leaving smaller parties underrepresented and minimally involved in the business of government. What's more, the system faces the problem of legitimacy because governments may not have majority support, either of the electorate or of all regions of the territory.

To overcome these problems, the simple plurality system can be supplemented with a second round of voting. This **two-round system**, or **run-off system**[18], involves the elimination of all but the two leading candidates after the first round of voting. In the next round, all voters get the chance to pick their preferred candidate from the reduced list. The process ensures that the winning candidate can claim that he or she has the support of the majority, thereby increasing the government's legitimacy. This system is employed in a number of countries, including France, Brazil, Ghana, and Indonesia.

The other basic category of electoral system is called **proportional representation (PR)**[19]. There are a number of different forms of PR used in the

minority government
government by the party that received the most, but not a majority of, votes in an election

two-round system
see run-off system

run-off system
a form of electoral system in which the two (or three) candidates receiving the most votes in the first round pass to a second round of voting to determine an outright winner; also called a two-round system

proportional representation (PR)
electoral system in which seats are designated according to the parties' popular vote; used in countries to institute proportions between votes allotted for all the parties

world, but each attempts to create a more direct link between the number of votes cast and the number of seats won for each party by designating seats according to the parties' popular vote. The first type, known as the **party list**[20] system, relies on multi-member constituencies where the political parties submit a list of candidates. Voters express their preference, and the parties are rewarded with a percentage of the seats available. In a four-member constituency, for example, a party receiving 100 per cent of the vote wins four seats, a party receiving 50 per cent two seats, and so on. There are two forms of the party list: a closed list (voters express their preference for the party) and an open list (voters indicate which candidates they prefer).

The second form of PR is called the **single transferable vote (STV)**[21] system, in which voters express their first and second choices for candidates. During the first count of the ballots, every candidate who receives sufficient votes will be elected. If all the seats are filled, the process stops. If seats are still available, the second choices of voters who picked the winning candidates are transferred and counted. In the unlikely event that all seats are not filled after the second count, the candidates with the least votes are eliminated and the second choices from those ballots are transferred.

Proportional representation provides a better assessment of the likes and dislikes of voters than simple plurality does. It also gives minor parties a better chance of being recognized. On the other hand, PR downgrades the relationship between constituents and their individual representatives because so much in the election rides on the weight and influence of the parties involved. This drawback is particularly true of the simple or national party list system, which does not directly link candidates to any constituency. In addition, some claim that there is also a lack of accountability for politicians appointed by this method, as their election does not depend on their success in delivering benefits for a local community but on serving the interests of the party.

The **additional member system**[22], which mixes the plurality system with elements of PR, attempts to eliminate this critique. In this form, the voters in each constituency elect a representative and also cast a vote for a political party. These second votes are counted at the national level, and additional seats in the parliament or congress are distributed among the parties according to the percentage of votes received. Supporters of this system argue that it combines the best of the simple plurality system with the benefits of PR. It maintains a link between representatives and their constituencies while allowing smaller parties to establish themselves and gain experience. The additional member system is used in Germany, the Republic of Ireland, and Mexico and in the regional parliaments of Scotland and Wales.

Despite its flaws, PR is often used as an example of what the Canadian electoral system might aspire to in an effort to overcome the problems associated with the simple plurality system. To date, however, there has not been a serious movement to bring about such a change, and initiatives to introduce it in Prince Edward Island and British Columbia have failed. A recent referendum in the UK, however, provides us with some interesting insights. British voters heavily

party list
voting system in which voters in multi-member constituencies choose from a list of candidates; parties are rewarded with a percentage of the seats available in each constituency

single transferable vote (STV)
voting system in which voters cast their ballot in multi-member constituencies, expressing their first and second choice for candidates; second choices may be transferred and counted if all seats are not filled in the first count

additional member system
mix of simple plurality and proportional representation voting; voters cast a vote for a representative and for a political party

rejected a proposal to shift from simple plurality to an STV system. The reasons for the rejection were numerous, but they focused on the cost of making the change, the possibility of favouring extremist parties, and concerns about upholding democratic traditions.

Political Parties

In daily life in Canada, we most closely connect the adjective *political* with the noun *parties*. In the media we see political parties as the most obvious manifestation of political processes and bargaining. What's more, we commonly give a negative connotation to political parties; they are often seen as manipulative, controlling, and sometimes disconnected from the real needs of the nation. But political parties are also a central element of the political identity of many Canadians. When we talk politics, we find it easy to use a form of linguistic shorthand that helps us and others to define our political positions, and we do so by referring to the party preferences we express at election time.

The need for organization has been a recurring theme throughout this book and is fundamental in politics. We have seen the organization of the state according to its different functions and to geography, as well as the organization of voting systems. Within the political system, the organization of individuals and their representatives according to their ideologies and preferences is also important. The most common form of organizing is through political parties.[23] Parties are first and foremost driven by the desire to control government through the election of their members. Although interest groups may be concerned with a particular issue or sector of a political system, the function of political parties is to present a clear perspective regarding the system's administration. In brief, political parties are organized groups that place members as candidates for election with the goal of governing the political system.

The rise of political parties was directly related to suffrage. As larger and larger groups of people were given the right to vote, there was a subsequent need to organize their interests in some institution. Parties thus arose as a result of society's need to represent the distinct views of the public interest. In some countries, parties were formed primarily around single issues, such as federalism (and anti-federalism) in the United States in the eighteenth and nineteenth centuries or, during the same period, questions of the monarchy and slavery in Britain.

For many voters, political parties seem to emerge only when there is an election. However, parties have a broader role in the political process. Aside from the capacity they have in society, they also have a direct role to play in the legislative setting. Parties allow for the grouping of elected members into coherent clusters and provide for governmental direction, as well as opposition in the legislature's daily activities.

Parties are created and operate on the basis of a set of ideologies,[24] or the underlying ideas for a political and economic system. Just like in the case of electoral systems, or as we will see regarding interest groups, political parties

one-party system
political system in which only one political party is allowed to form the government or compete in elections

competitive party system
liberal democratic electoral system in which political parties are permitted to compete with one another for the electorate's support

two-party system
competitive party system marked by two competing parties

multi-party system
competitive party system with more than two parties

cadre party
party created and directed by a small elite group; tends to control much power within legislatures

mass party
party organized in society at large rather than within government; has public influence through power of membership, not of a small minority elite

and their level of influence in society and government vary from country to country. In many states in the international system, for instance, only one political party is allowed to form the government. These are called **one-party systems**. Most of the communist systems in the Soviet era are representative of this form of government; current examples include China, Cuba, and North Korea. In liberal democracies, political parties are permitted to compete with one another for support from the electorate in what is referred to as **competitive party systems**[25]. There are a number of varieties within this system, such as those comprised of two competing parties (a **two-party system**)[26] or more than two (a **multi-party system**).[27]

However, these classifications tend to be alterable depending on the prevailing interests in society. The United States, for example, is often acknowledged as a two-party system, but the relative dominance of the traditional parties—the Republicans and the Democrats—was challenged by the upstart Reform Party (not to be confused with the Reform Party of Canada) in the 1990s. Similarly, the United Kingdom is often characterized as a two-party system dominated by the Labour and Conservative parties. Yet this portrayal ignores the role of many other groups, including the influential Scottish National Party and the Liberal Democratic Party. In the 2010 UK general election, the Liberal Democrats won sufficient seats to form a coalition government with the Conservatives. Although Prime Minister David Cameron is the leader of the latter, the former play a central role in the government.

In a similar vein, the role and influence of some parties in multi-party states is not always clear. Canada, for instance, has several significant political parties: Liberal, New Democratic (NDP), Green, Bloc Québécois (BQ), and Conservative. Yet only the Liberals and Conservatives (and its predecessor, the Progressive Conservative Party) have actually formed a federal government, although there were a few examples of "Unionist" governments made up of both parties. Does this mean, then, that the other parties are not as significant? Should the fact that the NDP has formed provincial governments but not a federal government give it a different level in the Canadian party system? In fact, developments in the Canadian political party system are really no different than in any other state. Political parties tend to rise and fall in their level of support among the public based on a variety of societal concerns and the major issues in the civic debate. This trend was proven in 2011, when the NDP eclipsed the Liberal Party and became the official opposition. Indeed, opinion polls in 2012 showed that the NDP had become the country's most popular party.

There are several types of political parties. **Cadre parties**[28] refer to those that are created and directed by a small elite group and that tend to control much power within legislatures. The history of cadre parties extends back to the initial process of suffrage, as powerful elites sought to protect their control over government from the influx of many more voters. By forming parties that they controlled, these elites offset the relative influence of huge masses of voters. **Mass parties**,[29] on the other hand, were formed partly to combat the power of cadre parties. Mass parties are organized in society at large, not within government. They exhibit a large public influence by placing a great degree of power in the hands of the membership rather than those of a small minority elite. **Umbrella**, or **catch-all, parties**,[30] which tend to cover a wide range of ideologies and beliefs in society, are formed and run with the idea of incorporating as many different groups in society as possible. Catch-all parties have been of particular importance in countries such as Mexico, where decades of single-party rule necessitated the absorption of many social and economic groups under the "umbrella" of the Partido Revolucionario Institucional (PRI). **Militia parties** are often found in military governments or communist systems. These party types have an extremely centralized leadership system and place extensive requirements on members. Militia parties are often led by martial leaders and found in one-party systems.

Political parties have many prominent functions in the political system. They play a **recruitment function**, in that they help to bring new voters into the political process. Because government members usually belong to parties that include private citizen participation, parties create a link between government and the people. Therefore, party leaders and government members will, at least in theory, be attentive to the concerns of their party colleagues. Parties also form a method of arranging and categorizing interests in society, as individuals that choose to join—or at least support—parties are essentially making a choice between different perspectives and policy proposals as well. Party support, then, gives us a sense of how the electorate feels about the role of government in society and the approach that administrations should take.

In a more functional way, parties are a basic way for private citizens, even if they do not support a party at large, to register their backing for individual potential representatives. Related to this role is parties' involvement in the instruction of future politicians and political actors. As institutions, parties embody established structures that might be used to train party workers and upcoming leaders. Once parties are elected to power, they are crucial in creating and upholding the direction, approach, and organization of government. In this way, parties determine not just the immediate bearing for an administration but also a "template" for future governments and supporters.

In many ways, parties are one of the central organizers in our political systems. Along with educating members, they also organize legislators within the parliament or congress, coordinating their positions, disciplining those who go against the party line, and negotiating with other political parties. These tasks are particularly important when the party in question is in opposition. In this situation, the party leaders will need to organize members effectively in their opposition to government initiatives and policies.

How can parties discipline their members? In several countries, parties employ a specific party member to enforce discipline. This person, known as the whip or chief whip, works to guarantee that all party members vote according to the preferences of the party, particularly on issues of central importance. In the UK, the term *whip* not only refers to the individual responsible for discipline but also describes the level of importance of particular votes in the House

umbrella party
see catch-all party

catch-all party
political party that covers a wide range of ideologies and beliefs in society, with the idea of incorporating as many different societal groups as possible; also called umbrella party

militia party
party system with a centralized leadership system; often having martial leadership and frequently found in one-party systems

recruitment function
political parties' efforts to help bring new voters into the political process

of Commons. A one-line whip indicates the party's preference in a non-binding way. A two-line whip indicates that members must attend the vote but are not required to vote one way or another. The strongest indication of party preferences is the three-line whip, which binds party members to attend the vote and to vote a certain way. A member who chooses to disobey a three-line whip can expect to be heavily sanctioned by the party. A particularly effective method of keeping members in check is threatening to expel non-conformist members or refusing to give them the party's endorsement in upcoming elections. When in government, parties may do the same thing, although a government's **patronage** powers will likely be a more effective tool.

Parties also help the democratic process by broadening consultation with society. By engaging in dialogue at the local level, issues important to the community stand a greater chance of finding their way into the halls of power. Over the years, parties have been responsible for pushing a wide array of issues onto the legislative agenda, from civil rights to environmental protection to immigration reform.

Registering voters is another crucial function performed by political parties in many countries. Clearly, it is in their interest to help as many potential supporters as possible to vote. Parties thus work hard, particularly close to election time, to facilitate voter registration. On the day of an election, parties also assist voters in getting to the polls, driving those who may not have their own transportation or who are unable to make it there on their own, and phoning registered voters to remind them of the importance of making their vote count.

As you may have guessed by now, today's political parties are highly organized, professionally run organizations. They have full-time staff, extensive databases, and widespread networks that can be called upon when necessary, especially during an election.

Election Campaigns

Different countries have different election cycles. In the United States, presidential elections happen every four years, on the first Tuesday of November. In Mexico, the presidential election occurs every six years (a period known as a *sexenio*), with elections occurring during the first week of July. In countries such as Canada and the UK, the maximum time between elections is five years, but a government may choose to call an election at any time during that period. This power gives the government a significant advantage because it can dramatically improve its chances of re-election by calling an election when it is enjoying high levels of public support. Using this strategy can backfire: if a government appears too arrogant and opportunistic, it may lose support.

Once an election has been scheduled, political parties play a central role in organizing campaigns and determining policy positions. Candidates need to be chosen by the parties, and this can occur in a number of ways. In some countries, a central party committee chooses candidates for specific constituencies. In others, such as the United States, potential candidates for

patronage
awarding of key government positions to favoured and loyal supporters

the presidency or Congress must compete against each other to win the party's official nomination. In the election campaign, conflict between the parties may get particularly intense. Throughout history, parties and candidates have used smear tactics[31] and negative campaigning[32] against each other. By highlighting mistakes, infringements of the rules, other negative issues, and in particular character flaws of the opposing candidate, one contender may hope to turn the electorate away from his or her opponent. We can observe the increasing use of negative and aggressive television and media advertising, or **attack ads**.[33] This tactic can be risky because the public often reacts badly to such negative tactics, particularly if the allegations are false. In some countries, such as Mexico, the use of negative campaigning is strictly regulated, which some see as a serious limitation on the democratic process and freedom of expression.

Another matter of concern in election campaigns is the public's awareness of the issues and the candidates' platforms. In an environment where candidates recognize that they will be given only sound bites in the media and where voters are inundated with information, it is difficult, if not impossible, to truly have a meaningful discourse about the issues or policies. As a result, the

attack ads
negative and aggressive advertising by one political party or organization against another

7.5 NEGATIVE CAMPAIGNING

Elections often bring out the uglier side of politics and politicians. In recent years, the use of negative campaigning and attack ads in Canada has become more common. In the 1993 federal election, the Progressive Conservative (PC) Party launched an advertising campaign that appeared to emphasize Liberal candidate Jean Chrétien's partial facial paralysis. The public reacted very negatively to this kind of tactic and the PCs lost votes. Thirteen years later, Liberal campaign ads suggested that PC leader Stephen Harper was an authoritarian who might impose martial law on Canada. Again, the tactic backfired and the Liberals suffered at the polls.

Negative campaigning is nothing new in politics. In the US presidential campaign of 1800, vice-president Thomas Jefferson's campaign insulted the opponent, President John Adams, by publicly saying that he had a "hideous hermaphroditical character, which has neither the force and firmness of a man, nor the gentleness and sensibility of a woman." Adams's campaign responded by calling the vice-president "a mean-spirited, low-lived fellow, the son of a half-breed Indian squaw, sired by a Virginia mulatto father." In this case, Jefferson's attacks proved effective and he narrowly won the election.

The Canadian Press/Adrian Wyld

In 1993, the Progressive Conservative Party used Liberal candidate Jean Chrétien's partial facial paralysis as a campaign strategy. The plan failed.

process of electioneering in modern society takes on a paradoxical dimension: candidates reduce what they say into digestible commentary and pursue marketing strategies to appeal to voters, while voters complain about not having the time to absorb what is being presented to them. Increasingly, elections become rather superficial contests that focus on personal qualities and presence rather than issues, platforms, and policies.

Finally, political parties play a key role in election campaigns by providing guidance. Well-established parties have an internal "machinery" (staff and organizational resources) that provides coherence to the campaign and helps the candidates transmit their message and receive support from the party rank and file. This infrastructure requires a substantial amount of money; therefore, parties must also raise funds.

Campaign Financing

How parties and candidates finance their bids for public office has recently become a particularly controversial part of the elections process. Candidates are spending more and more on their campaigns to meet the high costs of television, radio, and press advertising; extensive travel and appearances at high-profile events to ensure the widest possible media exposure; and the staff required to run an effective modern political campaign. In the case of the United States, the leading contenders for the presidency spend hundreds of millions of dollars (see Box 7.6). Although this figure is extreme, election campaigns have become exorbitantly expensive affairs across the world.

To raise the funds required for a competitive and hopefully successful campaign, parties and politicians need the help of both the party membership and the powerful and wealthy groups in society. Candidates seek contributions from a diverse array of sources, including individuals, groups, and corporations. It is

7.6 CAMPAIGN FINANCES AND THE 2008 AND 2012 US PRESIDENTIAL CAMPAIGNS

In recent years, there have been a growing number of questions raised by lawmakers and the public over the nature and implications of contributions to election campaigns. Nowhere has this been truer than in the United States, where the scale and intensity of election campaigns exceeds any other country. Since the 1996 presidential election campaign, in which the Democratic Party came under increasing scrutiny because of questionable fundraising methods (and sources of large contributions), the country has been engaged in an active debate about how to fund elections.

The sheer amount of money raised in the 2008 presidential campaign was astounding. The losing candidate, John McCain, raised over US$368 million and spent a total of $333 million. The winner, Barack Obama, raised over $745 million and spent $730 million. For the 2012 presidential campaign, the numbers were even higher. According to the Center for Responsive Politics, the Democrats and Republicans spent over $2.6 billion combined.[34] The enormity of this figure is evident when compared to the total spent by the 1976 presidential candidates: $66.9 million.

in this situation that private interests may seek to influence the political process through financial support. These contributions raise the spectre of wealthy groups or individuals buying political favours. Of course, such a trade-off is vigorously denied by both politicians and their donors, who argue that contributions merely reflect the latter's desire to see a candidate (re-)elected.

Because of this problem, many countries have passed legislation that limits the amount of a campaign contribution and demands transparency, along with accurate and detailed accounting of all donations and spending. For example, the limit for individual contributions to an American campaign is $117,000 every two years. In other countries, the state provides financing to political parties, relative to the number of candidates they intend to run and provided they achieve a certain minimum amount of the popular vote. Nonetheless, elections provide an opportune moment for private interest groups and corporations to buy the support of candidates. As long as an aspiring officeholder intends to seek re-election at some time in the future, he or she will be tempted to exchange political support for sizeable campaign contributions. Though this is hardly the rule in the political systems of most democratic states, it remains a serious concern. One way that some interest groups circumvent donation limits is to organize their own campaigns on behalf of a candidate (i.e. independent of the official campaign) by buying press space or media time in which they express their support. Some such television, radio, or newspaper ads do not even feature the name of the candidate in question but negatively influence the public against the opposing candidate(s). Because media exposure is often the most expensive element of an election campaign, doubts must also be raised about the legitimacy or ethical nature of such assistance.

An important distinction in the area of campaign contributions is that between "soft money" and "hard money." The first of these terms refers to funds given to the party as a general or non-specific contribution, whereas the second refers to monies donated to the party or candidate specifically for the purposes of an election campaign. This difference has come to be of particular importance in recent years in the United States. It has become clear that the line between the two types is frequently blurred, a problem that makes the issue of campaign financing even more complex.

Direct Democracy and the Referendum

To this point in the chapter, we have been learning about indirect democracy. There are times, however, when political systems call on the direct voice of the people to determine outcomes. Rather than let the institutions of politics (that is, parliament, political parties, and elected representatives) decide for the people, the people are asked to make a decision. It is in these situations that direct democracy occurs. Citizens of voting age are asked to express their opinions on a particular policy in an official vote, the results of which will determine whether that policy is adopted by the government. Such a vote is known as a referendum, or plebiscite.[35]

The best-known example of a country with frequent referenda is Switzerland. Swiss citizens are asked to vote on issues on a regular basis, and the outcome of these votes is then passed onto the states, or cantons. If a majority in favour of a measure is achieved in both the referendum and among the cantons, it becomes federal law. Referenda are also employed at other levels. In the EU, they have been used to determine individual state policy regarding further integration, as occurred in 1992 over the Maastricht Treaty and in 2005 over the creation of a European constitution. Within North America, California has seen a recent rise in the use of referenda. On issues from legalizing marijuana use to allowing gay marriage to curbing carbon emissions, Californian voters have had the chance (often at the same time as state-level elections) to determine the social and economic future of their state.

Directly involving citizens in the workings of the democratic system may seem like an admirable endeavour that strengthens democracy and encourages exactly the kind of participation that we've been reading about in this chapter. However, referenda can be controversial because they can be manipulated by politicians to help them reinforce their grip on power. Napoleon famously used plebiscites to cement his power in post-revolutionary France. In the contemporary world, the case of Venezuela stands out. Former president Hugo Chavez brought in a new constitution for the country—one that requires a referendum for any constitutional change or recall of elected officials—in 1999. Chavez's opponents argued that he used referendums to modify the constitution and overcome organized opposition by rival politicians and political parties. Chavez claimed that he was doing only what the sovereign people of Venezuela told him to.

Direct democracy will become more viable in the future as communications technologies make it more feasible for citizens to express their preferences instantaneously and in real time. We can all imagine a not-too-distant future in which every household is linked through the television, Internet, or games console to a central computer that registers citizen preferences on a wide range of everyday political issues. Whether citizens will become better educated, more informed, and less apathetic is another question.

Elections and Political Parties in Canada

We have already mentioned a number of important features about voting and elections in Canada. Almost every Canadian citizen over the age of 18 has the right to vote, and there is a maximum period of five years between federal elections. Canadian elections, which use the simple plurality system, are well organized and generally considered to be free and fair. Since the country's first general election in 1867, the Liberals and Conservatives have dominated Canadian politics, although other parties have achieved success at the provincial level or have made up the official opposition.

As in most countries, Canada also has rules about who may stand for elected office in the legislature. Candidates in federal elections must be eligible voters, which excludes non-citizens and people under the age of 18. Prisoners may not stand for office, and anyone who has been convicted of an election-related crime is barred from office for a number of years. Senators, provincial or territorial parliamentarians, judges, Crown (public) attorneys, and elections officers cannot hold these positions and serve as MPs in the House of Commons at the same time.

Canadian elections and political parties are involved in a process of ongoing development. For example, full suffrage was not achieved until the late twentieth century. Women in Quebec could not vote until 1940, and the federal government and some provinces excluded Aboriginal peoples and certain ethnic groups from voting until the early 1960s.

The situation of political parties also continues to evolve. In particular, the right side of the political spectrum has experienced considerable change in recent years. During the 1990s a new conservative political group, the Reform Party, grew in importance and split right-wing political support, helping the Liberal Party to maintain a dominant position. However, a merger between Reform's successor, the Canadian Alliance Party, and Progressive Conservatives produced the Conservative Party of Canada, enabling the new party to unite the right and win power in 2006. The leader of the Canadian Alliance, Stephen Harper, went on to become the leader of the Conservatives and Canada's first Conservative prime minister since Kim Campbell held the position in 1993.

Canada has also witnessed the emergence of parties with specific regional support. For instance, in the 1997 federal election, the Bloc Québécois dominated Quebec while Reform did the same in Alberta. Both parties received a majority of votes and seats, yet neither formed the federal government (the Liberals did). These two parties, then, have been referred to as regional parties[36] because of their strong provincial strength but weak national presence. For a period in the 1990s, the Bloc Québécois was the second largest party in the Canadian Parliament, creating the rather strange situation of the official opposition being a regional party that was seeking separation from the country.

Canada's system of election financing, embodied in the Election Expenses Act and the Canada Elections Act, provides state subsidies for candidates who achieve 10 per cent of votes and allows candidates to raise private funds, but it places limits on total spending and requires candidates to provide detailed accounts of all monies received and spent. These regulations were a response to parties' fundraising difficulties and to public outrage over scandals involving just the kind of influence buying discussed earlier in the chapter. In 2003, the limit for individual contributions to political parties and individual candidates at election time was set at $1100 annually (much less than the US limit mentioned earlier), and group and union donations are disallowed. Still, there is an active ongoing debate about how to ensure that wealthy groups and individuals do not circumvent these rules. Furthermore, the provinces set their own rules for provincial elections, the strictness of which varies widely.

In terms of direct democracy, the referendum has been used on a number of occasions in Canada but rarely at the federal level. The most famous Canadian referenda concern Quebec's future in the union and provide a good example of some of the problems associated with this device. In the 1980 referendum, the question posed to the Québécois asked if they wanted to negotiate a relationship of sovereignty-association with the rest of Canada. Sixty per cent of the population did not, but by offering the citizens of Quebec a question with a simple "yes"/"no" answer, the referendum did not allow for different or intermediate points of view to be expressed. What's more, the wording of the question maximized the potential for a "yes" vote. A similar situation occurred in the referendum of 1995 (see pp. 174–75). The outcome left almost half of the Quebec population unhappy, further prolonging the uncertainty about the province's future.

Structuring neutral questions on a referendum—that is, posing a question in such a way that it does not unduly influence the result—is an ongoing challenge for direct democracy in Canada and the rest of the world. Another problem is voter fatigue. We might welcome the fact that government is consulting us more broadly and directly, but many of us do not want to make regular political decisions beyond choosing our representatives. Indeed, many would argue that decision-making is precisely why we pay professional politicians to represent us.

Conclusion

This chapter has introduced you to some of the most important issues surrounding formal political participation. Voting was presented as a fundamental element of any democracy and the primary form of political participation available to the average citizen. In indirect democracies, this participation takes the form of electing representatives to act on behalf of citizens' interests. An alternative form of involvement, direct democracy, uses the referendum to allow citizens to influence policy. We also looked at political parties as one method of aggregating individual interests and concerns into large public forums. While political parties are primarily created in order to seek political power, they also serve multiple functions in society and in the political system, organizing diverse actors into recognizable groups and helping to engage citizens in the political process.

Self-Assessment Questions

1. Would you lower the voting age in Canada? Why or why not?
2. What are the advantages and disadvantages to making voting compulsory in Canada?
3. Should people be tested on their political knowledge before being allowed to vote? Give reasons to support your answer.
4. Why is it important to regulate campaign financing?
5. Is direct democracy a good alternative to Canada's representative democracy? Why or why not?

Weblinks

Bloc Québécois
www.blocquebecois.org

Canada's Members of Parliament
http://webinfo.parl.gc.ca/MembersOfParliament/MainMPsCompleteList.aspx?TimePeriod=
Current&Language=E

Conservative Party
www.conservative.ca

Elections Canada
www.elections.ca/home.asp

Green Party
www.greenparty.ca

Liberal Party
www.liberal.ca

New Democratic Party
www.ndp.ca

Rock the Vote
www.rockthevote.com

Further Reading

Farrell, David M. *Electoral Systems: A Comparative Introduction*. Houndmills, UK: Palgrave, 2011.

Gunther, Richard, José Ramón Montero, and Juan J. Linz, eds. *Political Parties: Old Concepts and New Challenges*. Oxford: Oxford University Press, 2002.

Kitshelt, Herbert, and Steven I. Wilkinson, eds. *Patrons, Clients, and Policies: Patterns of Democratic Accountability and Political Competition*. Cambridge: Cambridge University Press, 2007.

Norris, Pippa. *Electoral Engineering: Voting Rules and Political Behavior*. Cambridge: Cambridge University Press, 2004.

Reilly, Ben, and Andrew Reynolds. *Electoral Systems and Conflict in Divided Societies*. Washington, DC: National Academy Press, 1999.

Schaffer, Frederic Charles. *The Hidden Costs of Clean Election Reform*. Ithaca, NY: Cornell University Press, 2008.

Stoker, Gerry. *Why Politics Matters: Making Democracy Work*. Houndmills, UK: Palgrave Macmillan, 2006.

Taagapera, Rein, and Mathew Soberg Shugart. *Seats and Votes: The Effects and Determinants of Electoral Systems*. New Haven, CT: Yale University Press, 1989.

News Clips

Visit the companion website for *Politics: An Introduction*, 2nd edn, to access news clips related to the content of this chapter.

STEWARDSHIP
NOT
OWNERSHIP!

DECOLONIZE
NOW!

8 Political Socialization and Culture

◀ Citizens in Vancouver protest the proposed Enbridge
Northern Gateway pipeline project. Such protests, and their
depictions in the media, are agents of political socialization.

Photo: © Andy Clark/Reuters/Corbis

Introduction

In this chapter, we will examine the less traditional forms of political activity, including some that have become very important and highly controversial in recent times. We will introduce you to multiple forms of political expression and show you that you do not have to wait for an election or referendum to "become political" or join a political party to gain a political identity. In many ways, we are all socialized into becoming different types of political animals throughout our lives. What's more, you will see how unelected groups and actors in society have extensive influence over the political process.

Political Culture

As we now know, each citizen exists within a particular society and political system. We have the opportunity to contribute to the political process through political parties, elections, and referendums. But we exist as political beings and participate in politics in a host of other, less formal and less conventional ways. As we saw in Chapter 1, politics surrounds us and many of our actions take on a political significance when viewed in that context. By forming interest and protest groups, choosing one source of political information over another, organizing politically themed discussion groups on the Internet, refusing to buy certain products because of how they are manufactured, or simply engaging in debate and dialogue over political issues, we take part in this broader political reality. That is why we need to look beyond the more limited boundaries of formal political action and involvement to understand how societies and individual citizens can and do play an important role in politics.

Though we may not be fully aware of it, there is a set of attitudes, beliefs, and values that underpins any political system. These foundations may come in a variety of forms, be they religious, cultural, linguistic, or class-based, but they all contribute to our general outlook regarding our political system and our relations with each other and the rest of the world. Collectively referred to as our political culture,[1] these attitudes, beliefs, and values are an integral part of the political socialization process that we will describe in this chapter. Think about the rights and freedoms that are constitutionally guaranteed as part of your citizenship. These liberties allow you to form groups with others, express your views without persecution, pursue your own religious beliefs, and have an open and free system of information and communication. In many ways, we take these rights for granted. Now imagine life in an authoritarian state, where these rights and freedoms are denied you. The political culture of an authoritarian state will differ from your own, largely because of the type of system in which it exists. What's more, it will impact not only your behaviour but also the way you think and express yourself.

Political culture is an important element of our community, tradition, and identity as citizens. In other words, it is a fundamental part of our society, one that evolves over time. However, at any given moment, it helps to determine the scope of viable political options, influences political processes and public policy, and shapes political views and opinions. Providing an exhaustive list of the attitudes, beliefs, and values that make up Canadian political culture would be difficult. But most of us would be able to identify some of them.

Political culture is also activated by and influences political activities. For instance, the relative freedom of the media, the role of interest groups and political action committees, the impact of parties, the collective bargaining among unions and corporations, and the relationship between constituents and elected officials are all profoundly affected by the prevailing political culture in a political system. Just as different political systems exist—whether they are liberal democracies or authoritarian states, presidential or parliamentary systems, federations or unitary countries—so does the distinctive political culture in every country affect the desires and hopes for its citizens.[2] The North American Free Trade Agreement (NAFTA), Quebec's future in the federation, the legalization of narcotics, and Aboriginal rights and land agreements are examples of contentious areas of public policy in Canada. But most issues of governmental policy in Canada are less combative because the country's prevailing political culture concedes to the legitimate role of the federal government in decision- and policy-making.

It is vital to recognize that the political culture of the country or province we live in has a profound impact on how we participate. Although we have the opportunity to help define the future of our political culture, most of us find that our political views and modes of participation are more shaped by that culture than vice versa.

In addition, political culture is part of what makes politics different across countries and regions. Canadian political culture is markedly different from that in the United States, which is dramatically different from the Mexican variety. One of the clear differences between these cultures lies in the search for political consensus. In Canada, that process involves a to-and-fro between government and opposition, while the two main parties in the United States tend to reach a compromise after a highly adversarial process, both between the parties and between the executive and legislative branches. Mexico has a long-standing tradition of building consensus before embarking on any major policy initiative. At the same time, these three countries increasingly share certain elements of political culture. As they all become more and more integrated into global political society, values such as transparency, accountability, democratic practices, and minority rights have become entrenched across the continent.

In the 1960s, political scientists Gabriel Almond and Sidney Verba proposed three distinct categories of political culture. The first, which they named parochial, refers to a political culture in which citizens feel that they are removed from and have little influence over the central decision-making processes of the country. Part of a parochial political culture is a lack of interest in politics for the simple reason that citizens are uninformed of the procedures and feel that there is little chance of shaping outcomes. In the second category, subject political culture, citizens are subjected to the decisions of central government without much consultation, involvement in the decision-making process, or chance of influencing results. Here citizens may be informed, but they do not play an active role in politics on a regular basis. The last category is participant political culture and is one in which citizens play an active role in the political process, influencing outcomes on a daily basis and engaging in a constant dynamic relationship with political authorities. Each of these categories is, of course, a simplified version of reality, but they are useful in analyzing political systems around the world. Nonetheless, they will never be able to give us a detailed, complex understanding of the particular political culture of any country, which instead requires in-depth examination and description.

Political culture matters because it forms a central part of the political environment within which citizens and political authorities at all levels behave and participate in politics. As such, it provides us with both incentives and disincentives for distinct forms of behaviour. However, political culture is open to change, as we can observe by the rise of such political values as democracy, tolerance, and respect for minorities over the past hundred years.

The nature of political organization and the type of political rule, as well as other factors such as geographical region, history, culture, language, religion, and relations with neighbours, will all deeply affect the political culture of a nation and state. One of the most important factors leading to a political

8.1 THE SYMBOLS OF CANADA AS A FORM OF POLITICAL SOCIALIZATION

The use of symbols to create and nurture loyalty, social cohesion, and obedience is nothing new. Monarchs, religious organizations, and the state have used such symbols to create a sense of identity among their subjects, members, and citizens for centuries. This practice is often so subtle that it is unnoticeable. Singing the national anthem, using the flag, and wearing a national emblem on articles of clothing are all ways in which we are indoctrinated into the national identity.

You have probably been exposed to Canadian national political symbols since your birth or arrival in this country. The ubiquitous nature of these symbols and their effective use by both government and business mean that we are constantly being reminded, consciously or not, of our membership in this particular political community.

Like those of every country, the symbols of Canada are unique. One such emblem is the country's flag. For many years, the Canadian red ensign (a red flag with the Union Jack and the Canadian royal coat of arms) had been used. The search for an official Canadian flag began in 1925 but was then abandoned for decades. After a fervent national debate, the red-and-white design with a maple leaf was chosen in 1964 and officially inaugurated as the national flag on 15 February 1965. Red and white reflected the official colours of Canada (in use since Victorian times but officially proclaimed in 1921); the maple leaf had been a symbol of Canada since the 1700s, was used as such by the Canadian Armed Forces for many years, and had been worn by Canadian athletes since 1904.

The beaver was chosen as an official emblem when it was recognized as "a symbol of the sovereignty of Canada" in an Act of Parliament that received royal assent on 24 March 1975. The beaver may be thought of as a strange choice; other nations choose lions, eagles, or dragons to represent their sovereignty. But the beaver is once again uniquely Canadian. It reflects the importance of the fur trade in the country's early

One of several national symbols in Canada, the beaver serves to highlight elements of Canadian identity.

economic development and, in recent years, has come to be regarded as bearing Canadian attributes: it is modest, ingenious, hardworking, persevering, and constructive.

A non-visual symbol of importance is the national anthem. Written in the nineteenth century in French, the lyrics reflect the idea of Canada as a nation "strong and free." It generates feelings of belonging ("our home and native land," "true patriot love") and of defence ("we stand on guard for thee"). These lyrics, however, have experienced various incarnations, with the current version being approved by Parliament and accepted as the national anthem in 1972.

The use of these and other symbols in official ceremonies, at sporting events, and in particular in schools is part of the political socialization process that permeates Canadian society and that, for the large part, goes unnoticed and unquestioned by citizens.

culture is how socialization binds and informs citizens. Socialization is never the same for every citizen—there are too many variables involved—but there are often some constants that affect us all. With this in mind, let's turn our attention to how we become accustomed to our political systems: the process of political socialization.

Political Socialization

Political socialization is the process through which individuals are educated and assimilated into the political culture of a community. This can happen in both formal and informal ways. The lessons, values, and symbols that exist in any given country's education system are part of the formal method. By singing the national anthem, pledging allegiance to the flag, or learning a particular version of the nation's history, children are socialized into the national political culture. If you attended elementary and high school in Canada, recall how often you were exposed to the Canadian flag, the national anthem, and lessons extolling the achievements of great historical figures (e.g. Samuel de Champlain, Wilfrid Laurier, John A. Macdonald, or Nellie McClung) and you can begin to see education's importance in this process. When we remember that provincial education ministries generally set the school curriculum, we can also see how political authorities can exercise influence over the socialization process and how doing so allows for diversity and differentiation of political cultures. In countries with a nationwide curriculum, such as Britain, there is the potential for a more harmonized political socialization of young people at the national level. Even though education is not federally controlled by the government in Canada, the national anthem is played every day in many of the country's elementary schools and students are required to show this state symbol the appropriate respect.

The influence of the classroom remains crucial at the post-secondary level, but we also see the central role played by student organizations, peer groups, and activism. Almost every university and college campus in the world offers abundant opportunities for political participation, learning, and socialization. Traditionally, university campuses have been centres for protest and dissidence, although this has recently been less and less the case in countries such as Canada. Regardless of whether you are politically active at your university or college, you will be aware that political culture is distinctly more prevalent there than at, for example, your high school.

But socialization goes far beyond the classroom and the formal educational system. In fact, the primary agent of political socialization is the family. The information that we receive from our parents, their views, and the level of political debate in the home are all fundamental factors in shaping our attitudes toward politics. Although it is natural for children to reject their parents' opinions, studies have shown that there is a considerable degree of continuity from one generation to the next, not just in voting preferences but also in a wider range of basic values that will affect political beliefs and actions throughout an individual's life.[3] In many cases, the broader ethnic group into which we were born and socialized will also play a role. For immigrant families, the ties to their country of origin will likely have an impact in determining both their identity and political views. Moral and ethical values will greatly influence your political attitudes, as well as basic life lessons concerning work, religion, sports, and charitable activities. Ask yourself how much your family and ethnic background has shaped your own political views.

8.2 QUEBEC'S STUDENT PROTESTS

As you are probably all too aware, the cost of university tuition has been rising across Canada in recent years, resulting in complaints from students and parents alike that higher education may be moving beyond their means. Tuition rates are not the same across the country; therefore, increases have affected some provinces more than others. Quebec presents an intriguing case. Historically, the province has had the lowest tuition in Canada. Tuition fees were frozen at $540 per student per year between 1968 and 1990, a direct result of social protests in the late sixties. In 1994, Quebec fees rose to $1668 but were again frozen until 2007. By comparison, tuition in Nova Scotia was $1941 in 1990 and rose to $6571 by 2007, becoming the third highest in the country (after Ontario and New Brunswick).

In November 2011, the Quebec government responded to rising costs and budget shortfalls by announcing that tuition fees would increase by $254 annually for seven years. After years of resisting large tuition fee increases, Quebec's student movement organized a walkout in February 2012. Over the next few months the "strike" gathered strength and numbers, with sit-ins and violent protests taking place on university campuses and on the streets of Quebec cities and preventing a large number of students from attending classes. The protests split public opinion between those who advocated open access to higher education and those who felt that, because the fees were still lower than those in other provinces, Quebec students had little to complain about.

In May 2012, the National Assembly of Quebec passed emergency legislation, commonly known as Bill 78, that suspended the academic year and placed severe restrictions on student protests. A particularly controversial provision of the law states that police have to be given eight hours' notice before large demonstrations may proceed. Commonly seen as restricting political rights, Bill 78 helped to galvanize public support for the student movement.

Demonstrators march through Ottawa in support of the Quebec student protests.

Paul McKinnon/iStockphoto

This issue presents us with a classic dilemma for governments. University education is expensive and, even with the higher fees, Quebec's students would pay only a fraction of what their classes cost the Quebec and Canadian taxpayer (Quebec is a net recipient of transfer payments). At the same time, having a well-educated population is important in the maintenance of a growing and competitive economy. What's more, universities provide a nurturing environment for young people before they enter the workforce (which they would otherwise enter at a much younger age) and serve as the centres of much innovation and research. How much should the taxpayer be willing to subsidize this education in order to receive the social and economic benefits of university education? What should governments do to streamline their finances, improve fiscal responsibility, and make education more efficient? On a different level, how tolerant should we be of social protest, even if it severely disrupts social or educational services and infringes on the rights of others?

The importance of socioeconomic status must also be taken into account. A person's belief system and values will be fundamentally influenced by the economic and social opportunities available to him or her. To give a simplistic example, someone in a high tax bracket is less likely to be in favour of a progressive taxation system that requires the rich to pay more income tax than people who make less money.

It is also common for people to adopt political views that are similar to those of their peers, a process that is easy to understand when we consider how much time we spend with people of analogous income levels and backgrounds. Think about your own political views and how they have been shaped by, or been reactions to, the views of your friends.

A further influence on political socialization comes from one's geographical region. The predominant political views of the local society will play an important role in determining what an individual comes to believe. The importance of community versus the individual, traditional versus modern values, and identity will all be significant factors. In Canada, the regional component of political socialization is blatant. A less interventionist political culture exists in provinces such as Alberta than it does in provinces such as Saskatchewan. We cannot understand political socialization in Quebec without the elements of language and identity. In the north of Canada and particularly in the territories, Aboriginal cultures and values play a role in the process.

Religion is another factor that should not be ignored. Although it is increasingly common for religion to play a less prominent role in Canadian society, it is still one of the most important forces in politics around the world. Religion and politics are inseparable in many parts of the United States, although there is a constitutionally mandated separation between church and state. In some parts of Africa and the Middle East, Islam is an integral part of political culture and plays a role in defining laws and framing debates.

One of the most important agents of political socialization today, however, and one that we will explore more thoroughly later in this chapter, is the media.[4] By controlling and shaping the flow of information received by citizens, media outlets (i.e. newspapers, radio stations, television channels, and websites) are increasingly determining factors in the process of shaping viewpoints. The media is a particularly important agent of socialization because it affects the political attitudes and beliefs of individuals of all ages. Especially in their formative years, people are susceptible to the media fashioning their basic opinions toward politics. Subsequently, the state can play a role in this process through state-controlled media outlets, such as public television and radio, and through government ministry websites that regulate the flow of information.

Public Opinion

Political participation can also come in the form of expressing an opinion in public discourse, which allows citizens to proclaim their views regarding government activities in a sanctioned manner.[5] Public opinion is measured by **opinion polls**,[6] which find patterns among the public's outlook on certain issues.[7] These polls have acquired importance in recent decades, especially in the run-up to elections and in the formation of public policy. Polling firms such as Gallup, Zogby, Ipsos, and MORI have played a key role in measuring public sentiment during election campaigns, gauging public support for incumbent

opinion poll
investigation of public opinion conducted by interviewing a sample of citizens

8.3 MEXICO'S ELECTION AND THE CONTROVERSIAL ROLE OF POLLSTERS

Polling firms are considered more or less reliable metres of public opinion in Canada. Though they may not always get their electoral predictions right, they provide us with a measure of the public's political preferences at a specific conjuncture. As we noted in this chapter, politicians are increasingly interested in opinion polls and pay great heed to what polling firms tell them about the popularity of their policies.

In the 2012 Mexican elections, however, polling firms became controversial when they hugely underestimated the popularity of the left-wing candidate, Andrés Manuel López Obrador (AMLO), in their surveys. Most pollsters placed his popularity at around 26 per cent in the week before the election, but he received more than 31 per cent of the votes on election day. This result led some critics to claim that the polling firms were biased against AMLO and even to suggest that their undervaluation of his popularity helped the winning candidate, Enrique Peña Nieto, by convincing some left-wing supporters that voting for AMLO would be a wasted effort.

Though there is no evidence to support this claim, the pollsters' failure was remarkable and raises questions about their methodology. Were the sample sizes (the number of potential voters consulted each time) too small? Were the samples not sufficiently diverse in terms of geography, age, or socioeconomic level? The country's polling firms are currently trying to address these issues in the hope of providing a more accurate reading of the Mexican political pulse in the future.

politicians and their opposing candidates. Such polling helps to keep track of the popularity of candidates and the impact of policies and public statements. But it has also become controversial because there appears to be a permanent election campaign underway in some countries, with polling firms testing the public's opinion of candidates on a near-constant basis.

Questions have also arisen over the capacity for opinion polls to influence election outcomes. Some countries have prohibited holding election-related opinion polls in the days leading up to a major election. The fear is that the public will be influenced by the polls' results, with some deciding not to vote because one party is dramatically out-polling its rivals and the election therefore seems to be a foregone conclusion.[8] Others may decide to change their vote, given the apparent dominance of one party or candidate over the others.

Governments have increasingly turned to polls to measure the impact of proposed policies on public opinion. This habit has been questioned for its ability to push governments toward populism, designing policies not for their effectiveness or efficiency but for their popularity. Populism threatens to change the role of government from providing for the population's needs to one catering to its whims and desires. This approach becomes a particularly sensitive issue in the months leading up to an election, with the government holding back potentially unpopular policies (such as raising taxes or cutting public services) to increase its support.

Our opinions often might seem so straightforward and accepted that we do not even recognize them as opinions. For instance, our attitudes toward our system of tolerance, economic openness, and free expression may simply be

perceived as accepted attitudes regarding our relations with our government, but they are actually part of the opinion we hold about our entire political system. Our opinions, then, might be quite fixed, depending on the issues involved. But they can also be more flexible, depending on our age, location, economic status, or education level. For example, someone who has recently lost his or her job will no doubt form a very different opinion regarding job creation, benefits, and unemployment benefits than when he or she was employed. Or someone who has just been the victim of a robbery or assault is more likely to support stricter sentences for criminals.

The strength of our views also influences public opinion. As we've pointed out, religion is a key component of political socialization and religious beliefs are a strong indicator of public opinion; this is one reason why pollsters and public opinion firms ask respondents to indicate their religion as a means of identifying the views held. Attitudes regarding issues such as abortion and church schools, therefore, are heavily influenced by the relative strength of the individual's religious beliefs. Other issues, such as public works projects and the creation of national parks, may not be as affected by the intense opinion that influences other matters.

There are many political scientists who devote their professional lives to the study of public opinion, and these people provide a good example of the crossover between the world of academia and the real world of politics. Experts in public opinion use their skills and experience to analyze the results of polls and interpret their results, not only to the broader public through the media but also to governments, businesses, and political parties. The demand for such analysis is partly responsible for the recent dramatic growth in this area of the discipline, particularly in the United States.

The Media and Politics

Perhaps the most pervasive element of information in our modern society is the media. When the United States and its allies invaded Iraq in early 2003, military forces embedded journalists from television, radio, and newspapers among the troops. The world was able to follow the conflict on a seemingly first-hand basis and was continuously informed of its progress and setbacks. This example shows both the importance of the media as a source of information and an agent in the process of political socialization, but it also demonstrates how the media can become an unwilling government servant, a channel for the official dissemination of political messages. The US military's and other authorities' control of information flows during the Iraq War highlighted many of the challenges of maintaining a free and open media in the modern world.

fourth estate
the media; the other estates are the clergy, nobles, and commoners

The importance of the press and the media has been recognized since at least the early nineteenth century. Quoting statesman and philosopher Edmund Burke, Thomas Carlyle commented on the importance of the **fourth estate**, arguing that it matched, if not surpassed, the significance of the other three (clergy, nobles, and commoners, respectively). Ideally, the fourth estate acts as another check on the power of government, as a watchdog that ensures that public authorities do not go beyond their mandates or abuse their position of power.[9]

The media has also become the most organized form of information in our society. Twenty-four-hour news channels, international correspondents, and a seemingly endless barrage of newscasts, print media, and Internet dispatches afford ordinary citizens a view of the world that was simply not available to previous generations. In particular, the popularity of social media such as Facebook, YouTube, and Twitter has assured the rapid and global dissemination of information and opinion in a matter of seconds. Consequently, we sometimes feel as though we are overwhelmed and confused about which news source we should turn to for honest reporting.

We must be careful about the reliability and bias of our news sources. News reporting, like any other form of information outlet, is a competitive environment. It is expensive for media organizations to keep correspondents around the world and to employ technicians and other professionals to produce and transmit the broadcasts. News reporting requires advertising revenue,

8.4　*CITIZEN KANE*

In 1941, the actor Orson Welles directed, produced, and starred in an epic film documenting the life of Charles Foster Kane, a fictional newspaper and media magnate who became a multi-millionaire and had a profound impact on American life. The film was a thinly veiled study and critique of newspaper and media magnate William Randolph Hearst, who dominated the US newspaper business throughout the mid-twentieth century. Despite receiving critical acclaim (it is often referred to as the greatest movie ever made), the film almost did not see the light of day. Hearst was so outraged by his depiction that he offered the film studio, RKO Pictures, US$800,000 to burn every copy they had made. When RKO refused, Hearst prohibited all his media outlets from even mentioning the film, which contributed to disappointing box office revenues. However, in the long run, Hearst and Kane have become inextricably linked and the film stands as a fascinating treatment of media control.

In the 1941 film *Citizen Kane*, Orson Welles portrays Charles Foster Kane, a newspaper magnate who attempts a foray into politics.

which operates in a very aggressive market. In order to lure these funds from advertisers, news organizations must constantly be aware of how many viewers, listeners, or readers they attract. The result is that newscasts are often not as informative or inclusive as they might be.

To entice and captivate an audience, news organizations "package" their news much like a network television program. Some stories, particularly those that are deemed tedious, are given rather short shrift while even the most riveting issues of the day are bundled into a summary piece with titles, graphics, and main players. It is intriguing that the broadsheet newspaper, such as *The New York Times*, *The Times* (London), or *The Globe and Mail*, is becoming an endangered species. There is now less public demand for in-depth print analysis of the daily news.

The media is a two-way street. Just as with opinion polls, political decision-makers take note of what is being reported in order to recognize and anticipate citizen concerns. Thus, the trepidation regarding opinion polls can also be applied here: if policy-makers are primarily worried about the media impact of a particular decision, efficiency will be less important. What's more, by making decisions

8.5 *ALÓ, PRESIDENTE*: HUGO CHAVEZ AND THE CONTROL OF VENEZUELAN TELEVISION

In Venezuela, control of the country's media outlets has been a highly controversial issue for a number of years. After winning the presidency in 1999, Hugo Chavez steadily increased his control of newspapers and television stations, refused to renew licences for stations that offered open support for the opposition, and launched his own pan-American TV channel, Telesur.

But Chavez exerted a more direct influence on Venezuela's television audience through his weekly show, *Aló, Presidente*, on which he answered telephone calls from viewers, highlighted his administration's achievements, and made public statements against his enemies, both national and foreign. One of the more remarkable aspects of the show was that the president often had cabinet members with him. If a viewer called in to complain about, say, a failure in the electricity supply, Chavez dispatched his energy minister to solve the problem then and there. On the 2 March 2008 episode, Chavez ordered a general to send 10 battalions to the border with Colombia after the country had launched a military campaign inside neighbouring Ecuador's territory. The troops were not deployed, but the announcement caused international concern.

Aló, Presidente was also notable for its lack of a formal structure. The show was different every time it was broadcast,

Hugo Chavez salutes journalists in Caracas, Venezuela.

and each episode ended when Chavez ran out of things to say, usually after a few hours (the record was eight). Chavez, who died on 5 March 2013, was criticized by his opponents for his show's populist tendencies. Its viewership dropped precipitously in the later years of his presidency, and many doubted its political impact.

about what gets the most attention, news organizations affect the course of public debate and participation in society.[10] We citizens, after all, can respond only to what we hear or see. This reality gives the media enormous influence.

For these reasons, questions of the media's autonomy acquire a special significance. We must ask which media outlets are owned by the government, which are controlled by the government (due to the exercise of political influence), and which are dependent on the government for information flows. A media that can keep political power in check must be independent from government control, have independent sources of information, and have competent, experienced, and capable journalists who can both conduct investigative reporting and provide insightful commentary on major news stories.

But a strong, independent, and competent media is not enough. Throughout history, private control of most countries' media outlets has been held in very few hands. This concentration of ownership is also evident in today's major news sources. Perhaps the best modern example is Rupert Murdoch and his control of News Corporation, a multimedia conglomerate that controls newspapers, radio, and television stations across the globe (see Box 8.6). These news

8.6 RUPERT MURDOCH AND NEWS CORPORATION

A media conglomerate with interests in the broadcasting, newspaper, publishing, Internet, and entertainment industries, News Corporation began with a single newspaper (*The News*) in Adelaide, Australia, and the vision of one man, Rupert Murdoch. Since the 1950s, Murdoch has expanded his activities and interests to the UK, United States, and around the globe, as well as into new areas and technologies. A quick survey of News Corporation's current global reach and concentration of ownership is astounding. Of particular importance is the firm's control over news sources and the editorial line exercised over the selection and presentation of news stories. Most famously, News Corporation owns Fox Broadcasting Company and Fox News, which has come to be vilified in many circles as providing a strongly biased, right-wing slant on news around the world, particularly in its preference for US Republican policies.

In 2012, Murdoch and News Corporation came under fire for using overly aggressive tactics in newsgathering, including illegal phone tapping. The scandal hit the UK media hard, and Murdoch was forced to resign from the boards of a number of his newspapers. The vociferous public and governmental reaction to this scandal points to the highly controversial nature of media control.

Rupert Murdoch's News Corporation is one of the world's most powerful media entities.

© Idealink Photography / Alamy

But News Corporation is just one example of this impressive concentration of ownership in the media. News and information are fed to us from a very limited number of sources, which raises questions about the independence and reliability of the news we receive and the political power wielded by the owners.

outlets offer a particular perspective on world events, which is known as the **editorial line**. In Canada, right-wing political groups and parties have often accused the media of having a left-wing or Liberal bias.

editorial line
particular perspective on world events offered by news outlets

Civil Society and Non-Governmental Organizations

In recent years, academics and policy-makers have paid considerable attention to the growing role of private citizen groups in day-to-day politics. The increasingly high profile of NGOs such as Greenpeace, Amnesty International, Transparency International, and Médecins Sans Frontières (Doctors Without Borders) in issues of international importance, as well as the rising prominence of a host of smaller organizations at the national and local levels, has revealed a broader reality of political life and intercourse than we had considered in earlier times.[11] Civil society organizations, and NGOs in particular, stand as intermediaries between governments and private citizens. Generally issue-specific, they represent diverse groups of individuals and seek to organize them in such a way as to maximize their impact on the policy process and in the execution of non-governmental activities.[12]

Civil society is a term used in academic and policy circles to refer to the actions and organization of private citizens around shared goals, interests, and values. It is incredibly diverse and embraces sports, politics, hobbies, belief systems, community groups, development, labour movements, self-help groups, and business associations. Essentially, any group that is not a part of the state's apparatus or that operates without interest in gaining political office can be included in the definition of civil society. However, in political studies, we generally think of civil society organizations in terms of NGOs. These most commonly tend to be oriented toward advocacy, political pressure, and economic and social development.

We find civil society organizations everywhere in modern society, whether it is in the area of environmental protection, the promotion of human or civil rights, or the defence of traditional or modern lifestyles. NGOs provide an opportunity for many citizens who are disillusioned with traditional politics to get involved, express their views, and participate in the public sphere. In recent years in Canada, NGOs have been particularly active in the areas of human rights, drug policy, and climate change.

It would be easy to suppose that NGOs and civil society in general are a relatively modern political phenomenon. However, in many Western societies, NGOs have been active in the public sphere for hundreds of years (thousands if we include faith-based organizations), although they were not recognized by that name. Think of the importance of trade unions in redefining labour relations and winning important victories for workers' rights since the nineteenth century or of women's organizations that have struggled for over a century to win the vote, civil rights, and gender equality in the workplace.

8.7 CIVIL SOCIETY AND GLOBALIZATION

In recent years, one of the most vocal, high-profile, and best-organized civil society movements has been the anti-globalization movement. Now a regular feature at all major international summit meetings between government ministers or leaders, the movement originated in Berlin in 1988 with demonstrations against the International Monetary Fund (IMF) and World Bank at their annual meeting. The anti-globalization movement has since grown in size and activity, incorporating protests, hunger strikes, and e-mail and Internet campaigns. Although the movement includes several different groups and organizations, an umbrella network known as Peoples' Global Action has recently been used to bring together diverse causes.

The anti-globalization movement focuses its efforts against the manifestations of global capitalism, that is, against organizations such as the World Trade Organization (WTO), IMF, World Bank, the Group of 8 (G8), and MNCs. One company that has been a particular target over the years—through the bombing and vandalizing of restaurants—is McDonald's Corporation.

However, despite its high media profile, anti-globalization has achieved very little. It has failed to derail any major conference or halt the spread of global capitalism or the signing of international free trade agreements. A more serious charge against the movement is that it is amorphous,

Roy Peterson/Simon Fraser Library

Many civil society organizations have been criticized for their undemocratic and unrepresentative nature.

undemocratic, and ultimately unaccountable to the society it claims to represent. This criticism can be laid at the feet of civil society organizations more broadly, and it becomes more important as they play a larger role in the policy process.

The Participation of Private Actors in the Decision-Making Process

Understanding the interaction between political authority and societal actors in policy formation is vitally important in obtaining a comprehensive grasp on the dynamics of political participation and the policy process itself. Governments clearly need the involvement of non-state actors, such as interest groups, businesses, and labour unions, if they are to make policies that are not only politically acceptable to key groups but also functionally viable.

In contemporary political systems in Europe and North America, governments and bureaucracies do not simply formulate their policies in a vacuum. Instead there is often an intense system of consultation and collaboration with the nation's important economic interests and actors. Governments rely on the expertise of private actors in a multitude of areas so that policies can be designed and implemented to be more efficient and more broadly accepted. Such consultation takes place in all levels of government; in Canada and most countries, it is most clearly seen in industry consultations regarding economic policy. In the banking sector, for example, banks are closely consulted before any new regulations affecting their activities are applied. In the area of safety and public health standards, the government will consult with a host of private-sector actors from industry, academia, branches of government, and civil society organizations.

There is a danger, however, that the government will depend too much on the opinions of one group over another, which is especially problematic if regulatory policy is too heavily influenced by private business and if the industry concerned attempts to skew regulation so that it increases profitability yet sacrifices other goods such as safety, soundness, or public welfare. In areas such as finance or high-technology, there is often a serious inequality in the level of expertise between policy-makers and industry representatives. This variation can make it extremely difficult for governments to design efficient policies without the help of the actors they seek to regulate. In this case, concerns can be raised about the independence of government policy-makers and the effectiveness of economic policy. In the aftermath of the 2008–9 global financial crisis, evidence has emerged that the close relationship between bankers and regulatory authorities meant that preventive action wasn't taken.

These concerns are particularly important in the area of environmental regulation, where large corporations such as oil companies can afford to hire expensive lawyers and teams of scientists to "prove" that their economic activities will have only a minimal impact on the environment. Because governments rely on information in the policy process and because specialized information is expensive, such large corporations have an advantage over environmental protection groups in their influence over government.

The issue of expertise in the policy-making process is even greater in developing countries. Governments in this part of the world are especially handicapped in their ability to negotiate with corporations because of the extra financial constraints they face. Large multinational corporations (MNCs) in particular are able to dominate negotiations over investment and regulation because they can utilize both the best personnel from that particular country and recruit expert personnel from all over the world.

We have already seen that some political systems encourage more citizen participation than others, and the same is true of business involvement. In the 1980s, Jeffry Frieden produced a groundbreaking study of the Latin American debt crisis and studied how Argentina, Brazil, Chile, Mexico, and Venezuela reacted to that common challenge. Using what he called a "modern political economy" approach, he argued that the way in which each state allowed private actors into the policy process was a crucial element in explaining its response to the crisis. Frieden found considerable variance across the five states, not just in the amount of access but also in the organization of that access. Such examinations remain an integral part of political economy to this day.

Policy Communities

As should now be clear, politics and policy-making involve a variety of actors, both within and outside government. If we are to fully understand how policy is made, particularly in the economic realm, we have to identify the group(s) of actors that participate in the process. In *Policy Communities and Public Policy in Canada* (1990), William Coleman and Grace Skogstad employ the concept of a **policy community** to understand the making of policy. A policy community is a collection of actors who have a direct or indirect interest in a certain issue. These actors will have different levels of influence over the policy process, but they each play a significant role even if they do not directly pressure policy-makers.

This concept is useful because it allows us to identify key actors in politics and encourages us to include individuals and groups that we would normally overlook. For example, the non-governmental groups involved in the formation of government policy concerning climate change would include scientists, industry representatives, and NGOs such as Greenpeace and the David Suzuki Foundation. There is, of course, no natural limit to the size of a policy community or to the kind of actors that get involved. Policy communities are of particular importance in open political systems, but we can also use the idea to examine closed or authoritarian systems. Policy communities will exist even within a military dictatorship, as the armed forces governing the country consult with industry and other elites to smooth the business of government.

policy community
collection of actors who have a direct or indirect interest in an issue

Interest Groups

Although civil society and NGOs cover a huge area of non-state-based political activity in modern society, they do not embrace everything. We must also be aware of the role played by **interest groups**, or **pressure groups**.[13] Increasingly in our society, interest groups have affected decision-making and the approach taken by government. In many ways, interest groups are similar in their effect to political parties; however, the former is not concerned with controlling who runs for election. Their primary focus is on influencing the decision-making process, not through direct means (as politicians may use) but by convincing politicians and government officials to adopt their preferred policies. Therefore, interest groups are an integral part of the political community of policy-makers.

Interest groups seek to either alter or maintain the government's approach without taking a formal role in elections or seeking an official capacity in government. Just as political parties differ from country to country, interest groups have varying degrees of importance depending on the country in which they exist. In countries such as Japan, government leaders do not usually give interest groups a substantial role in decision-making. Though there may be some attention paid to the groups' concerns, the more traditional form of government in that country—which places greater importance on the customary

interest groups
groups in a political system that seek to either alter or maintain the approach of government without taking a formal role in elections or seeking an official capacity in government

pressure groups
see interest groups

political action committees (PACs) conglomerations of several interest groups with the purpose of influencing the decision-making process more effectively

associational interest groups interest groups closely related to particular political objectives

non-associational interest groups interest groups not closely related to or not connected with particular political objectives

anomic interest groups ad hoc interest groups that do not have a standard organized composition; formed to deal with short-term issues

lobbying method by which business/interest groups apply direct pressure to the executive, legislative, and bureaucratic parts of government

and formal delineation of authority in society—limits the influence that these groups might have. For the Japanese decision-making process, greater attention and value is placed on the opinions and interests of formal corporate and business interests than on interest groups (see Chapter 9). On the other hand, various other countries, such as the United States, place such high relevance on the role of interest groups that there are laws regulating their formal part in government–societal relations.

There are a number of different types of interest groups. **Political action committees** are conglomerations of several groups that have combined their resources to influence the decision-making process more effectively.[14] **Associational interest groups** are closely related to particular political objectives, but **non-associational interest groups** are not connected to such goals. Ad hoc interest groups are called **anomic interest groups** and do not have a standard organized composition. Instead, they are formed to deal with short-term issues and concerns.[15]

Interest groups attempt to convey their point of view primarily through **lobbying**, which refers to those activities—petitions, meetings, hearings, demonstrations, etc.—that groups use to get their perspectives across to political decision-makers. Interest groups often hire professional lobbyists whose job it is to carry on these activities on behalf of the group. The next section discusses lobbying and its important function in articulating citizen views.

There are competing opinions regarding the presence and role of interest groups in liberal democracies. Keep in mind that interest groups are not inclusive; that is, they do not represent the views of all or even a majority of citizens. They bring attention to concerns that some sectors of the public find important. This purpose tends to draw criticism from those who see interest groups as the voice of the elite rather than the representative of a broad segment of society. Not all groups are capable of forming organized groups and/or hiring lobbyists to try to alter the approach of government. This perspective argues that interest groups corrupt the true purpose of democracy, which is to represent and account for the views of all.[16]

Yet others consider interest groups to be an integral part of democratic society. They argue that there are not enough formal avenues for individual citizens to vocalize their concerns or views in the governmental process. Voting is a relatively infrequent event and does not allow citizens to do anything more than simply choose a representative. And joining a political party may not be sufficient for some people. According to this view, then, interest groups allow for a more informal role in the approach of government. Those who see interest groups as a positive force in society argue that true democracy is pluralist, meaning that it involves a number of groups and addresses multiple concerns.[17]

Whereas it might be true that interest groups are created to deal with the particular concerns of members of the group, we should recognize that they play a bigger purpose in society. Interest groups are a basic means of tying the function of government to that of society's groups. In this way, interest groups are a bond between the formal and informal segments of our society that influence the approach of our political systems. Interest groups provide a feedback loop for government, funnelling information back to their members and the public at large.[18] Given their level of expertise, these groups also provide essential information to decision-makers. Interest groups can be particularly important for members of the public service, who are responsible for accounting for the public's views and providing all necessary information to decision-makers in the legislature and the executive. Again, the notion of policy communities is important here: supplying information and input to the policy process can result in more access to policy-makers.

When we stop to consider the real impact that interest groups have on the political process, substantial contrasts to voting behaviour and political party involvement emerge. Unlike the immediate consequence that voting or parties demonstrate in the political domain, interest group influence is not as easy to measure. There are, after all, many different interest groups competing for attention and influence, and the opinions that they put forward may be changed substantially by the time governments set out to make decisions. However, there are some factors that help define the relative success and sway that these groups have. First, if the opinion of the group tends to match that of the government of the day somehow, the group's importance will rise. Second, interest groups will have more influence if there is no real contending perspective. Finally, the level of stability and availability of resources of the group is important. Groups that have experienced lobbyists, plentiful resources, and an organized structure are more likely to have the ear of government at any level.

In sum, interest groups are one of the most important means of real influence that citizen groups have in the governmental process. Interest groups are becoming increasingly influential in democratic societies, largely as a result of their level of organization and the considerable expertise and substance that they bring to the process.

Lobbying

One of the most important ways in which business/interest groups interact with the policy process is through lobbying, which applies direct pressure to the executive, legislative, and bureaucratic branches of government. The roots of the word *lobbying* are disputed. Some claim that it derives from the hallway of the British House of Commons, where constituents could meet with their representatives and demand their support for legislation. Others have suggested that it came into use in the early nineteenth century and referred to the lobby of either the New York State Capitol building or the Willard Hotel in Washington, DC, both places where private citizens and interest groups could directly pressure legislators. Whatever the word's origins, lobbying has become an integral part of modern politics in democratic and even non-democratic systems.

Lobbying can be an activity in which the interested party, either an individual or a group, directly meets with those involved in the policy process and

attempts to secure the support of these individuals. Increasingly, however, individuals or groups contract a professional lobbyist who understands the political process and has contacts within it to represent them. Lobbyists often prefer to call themselves public relations experts, lawyers (if they have a law degree), communications specialists, or consultants.

Lobbying has a mixed reputation. It can be seen as a vital part of the policy process, ensuring that diverse views are represented and that relevant information is taken into account in decision-making. However, lobbying can be viewed as an example of some groups having undue influence at the expense of others, where well-organized, often wealthy or economically powerful groups buy the endorsement of important members of the policy process.

A key word here is *expense*. Lobbying is not a cheap business, and groups may pay upwards of tens of thousands of dollars to engage the services of a professional lobbyist for one issue. Some large corporations keep a lobbying firm on contract full-time so that their interests are continually represented in the political process, an enterprise that can cost hundreds of thousands or millions of dollars annually. Because this expense puts lobbying beyond the reach of most individuals and groups, we have to ask if lobbying is truly compatible with the pursuit of democracy in modern political systems. Does lobbying allow certain groups to have a disproportionately high level of influence over the political process? Or is it simply the best way for decision-makers to consider the views of interested parties?

We must also ask whether political favours are being bought in exchange for material rewards, either financial or in kind. If so, lobbying certainly crosses the line between acceptable and unacceptable behaviour. But what about the personal relationships formed between lobbyists and government members? Do they contravene the principles of democracy? Can lobbying be seen as a mere extension of corporate hospitality activities, where one corporation courts another with perks (e.g. tickets to sporting or cultural events) in an attempt to secure a business contract? Or do we have to draw a distinction between the world of business and the world of politics?

Interest groups are not the only organizations to hire lobbyists. Governments employ them when authorities at one level seek to influence policies at another, such as when municipal or provincial governments try to affect federal policy. Perhaps a more important use of lobbyists and consulting firms is their being contracted to represent a national government's interests in another country. Usually, this situation occurs when foreign governments seek to influence policy in the United States, but the phenomenon exists around the world, with foreign governments taking advantage of local expertise to lobby the national government. A very important example of such lobbying took place in the early 1990s, when the Mexican government employed Washington-based lobbyists to secure congressional approval of the North American Free Trade Agreement (NAFTA) and thus counter the anti-free-trade forces in Washington led by presidential candidate Ross Perot. In the 2012 Mexican election, the winning candidate, Enrique Peña Nieto, employed a consulting firm to represent and improve Mexico's image in the international arena.

8.8 CLIMATE CHANGE AND PUBLIC RELATIONS: THE CASES OF WIND AND "CLEAN COAL"

As evidence of the human causes of climate change mounts, states, societies, and businesses search for new ways to produce energy. Clean, green, and renewable sources such as wind or hydroelectric power are one obvious option, but some of the more traditional sources of energy are trying to reinvent themselves, both in the technological sense and in terms of their public image. In the United States, this effort has taken on a very public dimension with press and television media spots outlining the advantages of "clean coal" over other sources. The photograph in this box was to be seen across the Washington, DC area in the summer and fall of 2009, as the coal industry attempted to convince US government officials and members of Congress that coal was the best option available. The campaign has also used websites such as www.cleancoalusa.org to stress the benefits of the fuel and potential of clean coal technology.

Opponents of clean coal have employed different media outlets to get their point across. A famous television spot put forward by The Reality Coalition–which includes the Alliance for Climate Protection, Sierra Club, National Wildlife Federation, Natural Resources Defense Council, and League of Conservation Voters–and efforts by other environmental organizations have tried to counter the coal industry's public relations campaign.

© Braden Gunem / Alamy

The debate between traditional and green sources of energy involves intense public relations campaigns.

The relationship between lobbying and governments raises the issue of the "revolving door" between the two domains. Insiders are in great demand with professional lobbying, consulting, or public relations firms because their influence is an invaluable addition to the struggle to be heard in the policy process. Conversely, governments (and certainly political parties) can gain from the expertise of individuals who have experience in public relations and communications. Doubts can be raised about the benefits of such a revolving door, however. Is inside knowledge of government business a commodity that should be traded like any other form of specialized knowledge? Or is it different because it confers such an advantage on those who can pay for it?

Corporatism

A significant challenge for capitalist countries over the past hundred years or so has been to avoid direct clashes between what may be seen as, and sometimes are, opposing interests. For what makes sense to the owners and controllers of industry may be anathema to those who work in their factories and corporations. The idea of price controls and the minimum wage, for example, will be more popular with the representatives of labour than with producers and employers. Increasing the maximum number of working hours per week, on the other hand, may be favoured by industry but vigorously opposed by labour unions. Such controversial policies provide ample opportunity for conflict, economic disruption, strikes, or even private industry's departure to countries with a more favourable business climate. It may be preferable, therefore, for government policy to minimize the level of conflict between opposing interests.

In several countries of 1970s Northern Europe and Scandinavia, an alliance developed among government, business, and labour that came to be known as **corporatism**. This approach to governance entails close co-operation and coordination between these three organizations in the expectation that such activity will bring more stability to the political economy and produce a larger degree of consensus, making economic and social policies more acceptable to important constituencies in society.

One of the most powerful arguments in favour of corporatism is that it will include and benefit a broader section of society than more traditional systems, in which elites tend to dominate the policy process. However, that same criticism can be levelled against corporatism because selected business and labour agencies are chosen to represent the views and interests of their wider communities. There is a tendency for business representatives to favour big business in the demands they place on government, whereas labour delegates tend to support the larger, more powerful unions. Perhaps more worrying is the accusation that business and labour representatives "climb into bed" with each other and the government and are liable to compromise the interests of those they represent. Of equal concern is the issue of corruption, the danger that the leaders of business and labour will seek individual rather than collective gains, thus sacrificing the interests of their members in return for personal reward.[19]

In the 1980s and 1990s, the corporatist approach to economic and political management fell into disrepute in some European countries, particularly in Great Britain. This change was largely a response to the feeling that organized labour had gained too much power and was jeopardizing the long-term economic interests of the nation. However, as we will see in Chapter 9, quasi-corporatist arrangements still exist in Japan and other Asian countries. Indeed, such close co-operation among government, labour, and business has been seen by many as one of the fundamental reasons for Asian economic success since the 1950s.

Canadian Political Culture and Socialization

Canada has a political culture that, broadly speaking, reflects many of the features of European culture. Our political culture is founded on the rule of law, which gives certainty and predictability to processes and to individuals. Democratic processes and institutions are seen as fundamental, not only in the national Parliament and federal elections but also at the provincial and local levels. The existence of elections bodies at both federal and provincial governments and the emphasis given to democracy in all levels of education highlights this significance. Along with

---

corporatism
approach to governance that entails close co-operation and coordination among government, business, and labour in the expectation that such activity will bring more stability to politics

accountability, the concept of transparency in political, legal, and administrative processes has become an important feature in recent years. These elements are evident in the increasing scrutiny of government activities and accounts, as well as the media's role in providing citizens with access to reliable information.

Canada can also be said to prefer gradual, peaceful, somewhat evolutionary change over the sudden, violent, revolutionary sort. This inclination can be seen throughout Canadian history, from its emergence as a post-colonial dominion to its gradual assertion of full sovereignty and its piecemeal redistribution of political power among the provinces and regions.

But beyond these elements of political culture, Canada exhibits a well-estab-lished connection to the ideals of negotiation and compromise, with a strong tendency toward respecting minority views. This feature is closely tied to the modern values of tolerance and respect for diversity (both in terms of culture and opinion). The contemporary manifestation of these values lies in the idea of multiculturalism, but they have been part of Canadian political history for a long time and have been reinforced by the Westminster parliamentary model.

The Canadian Charter of Rights and Freedoms is an essential element in identifying individual rights and liberties in the Canadian context. At various points in this book, we have referred to the Charter and how it has been used to question, correct, or overturn government policy. It continues to define much about political culture and is closely connected to debates concerning such issues as rights for minority groups.

Perhaps above all else, we can say that "peace, order, and good govern-ment" (POGG) sum up the heart of Canadian political culture. POGG continues to define the core values of Canadian politics in the twenty-first century. It is surprising how a phrase first used in the 1867 Constitution Act is still relevant and how often it is quoted in political dialogue and debate.

The process of socialization in Canada is similar to that in many modern liberal democracies. The teaching of basic elements of civic culture and his-tory in elementary and secondary schools, the government's use of the mass media to emphasize the importance of core values, and the process by which new immigrants are asked to take courses acquainting them with the nation's history, culture, and society are all examples of how socialization occurs on a daily basis. But the media, civil society, and (occasionally) business also play a role in the development and reinforcement of those core values and identity. Increasingly, we can also see cross-pollination between Canadian political cul-ture and the cultures of other countries. American culture is clearly influential, but we may also point to the origins of large immigrant populations.

Another matter to consider is the emergence of certain global features of political culture. With the ubiquity of the Internet and with global communi-cations strategies by NGOs, many ideas that began in one part of the world are spreading internationally. Notions of transparency and accountability, which are currently seen as essential components of well-functioning democracies, were still considered exotic concepts only a few decades ago.

All these factors lead us to recognize that Canada's political culture and mode of political socialization is distinctive yet far from being static. The country's economic, political, and social openness contribute to this evolutionary understanding of political culture, and we can even argue that this same openness is now a fundamental part of the process of socialization. The influence of migrant populations, the increasing willingness of Canadians to travel (for vacation, business, student exchange programs, etc.), and the impact of social media and new technologies make political culture a much harder concept to define than in earlier periods of Canadian history.

Conclusion

This chapter has introduced you to the diverse forms of politics outside of the formal electoral and political party processes. It also established political socialization as a forerunner to any kind of political involvement. We are all socialized in a particular political culture that embodies certain values and ideals about politics. Our attitudes and disposition to the world of politics is shaped by the socialization process of our society, by the exposure to family, community, institutions, government, and more and more by the media. This process is far from neutral and reflects the distribution of power within society and the political and economic systems.

This chapter also presented you with the concepts of civil society, interest groups, policy communities, and corporatism as diverse methods of aggregating individual interests and concerns into large public forums. You should now be aware of the multiple forms of participation that are available to you as a citizen and the ways in which you can become involved. It is up to you to decide if, when, and how you engage in this dynamic world.

Self-Assessment Questions

1. What are the defining features of Canadian political culture?
2. Where do you get most of your political information? Why do you choose and trust these sources?
3. Find out who owns your local newspapers. Are they part of a national news chain? What is the perspective of these papers?
4. What are policy communities? Why are they important?
5. What is the difference between an NGO and an interest group?
6. What are the basic features of corporatism?

Weblinks

Anthems and Symbols (Canada)
www.pch.gc.ca/eng/1266258105305/1266214672512

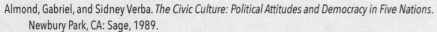

Cultural Diversity and Rights
www.pch.gc.ca/eng/1266246238320/1266202785200

Free Press
www.freepress.net

Lobbying Database (United States)
www.opensecrets.org/lobbyists

Office of the Commissioner of Lobbying of Canada
www.ocl-cal.gc.ca/eic/site/lobbyist-lobbyiste1.nsf/eng/home

Further Reading

Almond, Gabriel, and Sidney Verba. *The Civic Culture: Political Attitudes and Democracy in Five Nations*. Newbury Park, CA: Sage, 1989.

Althaus, Scott L. *Collective Preferences in Democratic Politics: Opinion Surveys and the Will of the People*. Cambridge: Cambridge University Press, 2003.

Asher, Herbert B. *Polling and the Public: What Every Citizen Should Know*. 2nd edn. Washington, DC: Congressional Quarterly Press, 1992.

Berger, Suzanne, ed. *Organizing Interests in Western Europe: Pluralism, Corporatism, and the Transformation of Politics*. Cambridge: Cambridge University Press, 1981.

Coleman, William D., and Grace Skogstad. *Policy Communities and Public Policy in Canada*. Toronto: Copp Clark Pitman, 1990.

Dahl, Robert. *Polyarchy: Participation and Opposition*. New Haven, CT: Yale University Press, 1971.

Frieden, Jeffry A. *Debt, Development and Democracy: Modern Political Economy and Latin America 1965–1985*. Princeton, NJ: Princeton University Press, 1991.

Gamson, William, and David Meyer. "Framing Political Opportunity." In *Comparative Perspectives on Social Movements: Political Opportunities, Mobilizing Structures, and Cultural Framings*, 3rd edn., edited by Doug McAdam, John D. McCarthy, and Mayer N. Zald, 275–90. Cambridge: Cambridge University Press, 1996.

Inoguchi, Takashi, Edward Newman, and John Keane, eds. *The Changing Nature of Democracy*. Tokyo: United Nations University Press, 1998.

Linz, Juan J. "Totalitarian and Authoritarian Regimes." In *Handbook of Political Science*, edited by Fred I. Greenstein and Nelson W. Polsby, 175–411. New York: Addison-Wesley, 1975.

Middlebrook, Kevin. *Dilemmas of Political Change in Mexico*. San Diego: Center for U.S.-Mexican Studies, UCSD, 2004.

Milner, Helen V. *Interests, Institutions, and Information: Domestic Politics and International Relations*. Princeton, NJ: Princeton University Press, 1997.

Mingst, Karen A. *Essentials of International Relations*. 3rd edn. New York: W.W. Norton, 2004.

Norris, Pippa. *Electoral Engineering: Voting Rules and Political Behavior*. Cambridge: Cambridge University Press, 2004.

Olson, Mancur. *The Logic of Collective Action: Public Goods and the Theory of Groups*. Cambridge, MA: Harvard University Press, 1971.

News Clips

Visit the companion website for *Politics: An Introduction*, 2nd edn, to access news clips related to the content of this chapter.

9 Politics in Developed States

◄ Russian President Vladimir Putin and Japanese Prime Minister Shinzō Abe meet in Moscow in April 2013. Their visit aimed to break years of stalemate regarding a territorial dispute dating from World War II.

Photo: Kirill Kudryavtsev/AFP/Getty Images

LEARNING OBJECTIVES

After reading this chapter, you will be able to

- understand the comparative method in political studies;

- appreciate the important links between politics and the economy in development and between domestic economy and foreign economic policy;

- recognize some of the most important issues facing developed nations;

- identify how we apply political concepts to specific countries; and

- compare and contrast the political economies of Canada, the United States, Japan, and the EU.

Introduction

We have made several references to "developed" and "developing" countries in this textbook. As you might appreciate, no two countries are exactly the same or even necessarily close to the same; therefore, the way we categorize countries is important. For instance, we could divide the world along political lines, distinguishing among democratic, communist, autocratic, military-led, or monarchical states. Or we might look at the economies of different countries. But in what manner? Should we look at simple gross domestic product (GDP) or citizens' purchasing power based on the strength of domestic currencies and markets? On the other hand, we could turn to social issues such as literacy, women's rights, or access to medical care and education. Simply put, there is a wide variety of criteria we can choose from to classify countries. This endeavour is tricky, however, because the range of possibilities makes it almost impossible to find any common ground among them. Yet we continue to sort countries in an effort to make sense of their differences.

Previous chapters have introduced you to several important aspects of contemporary political studies, governance, political ideas, and political involvement. By now you should feel fairly comfortable with most of the major political concepts and the way political scientists use them. This chapter and the next will introduce you to the practice of comparative politics, which comprises an entire subdiscipline of political studies. In fact, comparative analysis is one of the most important activities in the field and, as you will recall from Chapter 1, a main endeavour of this book.

We begin this chapter with an overview of the methods of comparative politics. Then we present some of the major themes and issues facing the politics of advanced industrialized states, or the **developed world**, and consider the differences between these countries and those of the **developing world** (which we will return to in Chapter 10). This section will provide a political-historical overview of developments during the postwar era, a time that was crucial to the growth of institutions and regulations governing global politics and the global economy, most of which are still in place today. Finally, we will use the comparative method to apply the concepts and ideas we have already discussed to case studies on Canada, the United States, Japan, and the European Union (EU). Interestingly, industrialized nations have areas of mutual concern and interests yet remain a diverse lot. Each of these states has had a unique experience of political and economic development.

Comparative Politics

Even the most passing glance at global politics today shows us that change and upheaval are defining aspects of our modern world. The Arab Spring, briefly discussed in Chapter 4, presents an excellent example of rapid transformation in parts of the world previously defined by relative continuity. But the process of democratic revolution has been different in each affected country. Why is this the case? Can't we simply apply past practice to other situations and expect the same results?

The answer, of course, is no. If anything, the swift change in global affairs forces us to examine the differences among nation-states more closely. We've already looked at the nature of politics and its relationship to important concepts such as power, legitimacy, and authority. Comparative politics, or the comparative approach, assesses similarities and differences among countries regarding types of governance or political leadership based on a number of criteria, including time period, system type, or geographical region.

The comparative method—or really methods, since there are several—displays a fascinating array of approaches and ideas about politics. Recall the discussion of inductive and deductive reasoning in Chapter 3. Comparative analysis uses both. We can study a particular case (e.g. social democracy in France, social benefit distribution in Canada) and use it to develop a general theory about political behaviour. On the other hand, comparative analysis can start with a general hypothesis and then examine case studies. For instance, we might begin with the idea that social democratic states are more likely to seek the redistribution of social benefits than conservative ones are. Looking at case studies will help provide evidence for our hypothesis.[1]

Comparison helps us put our analysis in relative terms. Let's take defence spending as an example. Canada allocates 1.5 per cent of its national budget

developed world
industrialized nations that are part of a structurally integrated system of global capitalism; includes the countries of Western Europe and North America, Japan, Australia, and New Zealand; also known as developed countries (DCs), industrialized world, the North, and the First World

developing world
nations that are less developed than the industrialized countries and that are not part of a structurally integrated system of global capitalism

to this area. Is that a lot or a little? Compared with Saudi Arabia, which spends over 11 per cent, it seems paltry but not when put against Iceland's 0.1 per cent. Hence, the relative aspect is always significant.

What other details emerge from comparing these three countries? They are in different geographical areas and have different topographies. Iceland is an island; Saudi Arabia is situated in a conflict-riddled part of the world and shares borders with other states. But both must deal with a severe climate and natural conditions (tundra and desert, respectively) and both have valuable natural resources. Canada has few neighbours and a close defence relationship with strong allies. Yet it also has resources and a challenging climate. These characteristics only scratch the surface of why each country spends what it does on defence, but it shows why a relative comparison is a good place to start.

Comparative politics can involve any country or region. Forms of political organization, the nature of state power, types of political systems, ethnicity, culture, political economy, and citizen participation are some of the themes that comparative analysts use in their work. Comparing different or similar political systems, systems over time, and the changing nature of governance form some of the various methods in comparative politics. The objective is to strip down assumptions that we may have about certain countries and system types and to avoid bias in our research. "The more you know about others, the more you learn about yourself" may be a good maxim for comparative politics, since we hope that the process will teach us as much about the unique nature of our own system as it does about others.

What Are Developed States?

Electoral systems, government types, ideologies, and citizen rights and participation are only some of the major topics we've dealt with in our introduction to politics. Perhaps the greatest factor relating to politics, however, is economics. Certainly, the story of the developed world is as economic as it is political. But attention to the political economy (the interrelationship of politics and economics) of advanced nations is still a relatively recent phenomenon in political studies.

As recently as the early twentieth century, the physical security of states was the predominant area of interest for analysts of state affairs. Indeed, it was not until the middle of the century that the economic welfare of states became a major arena of critical examination in political studies. The rise of the welfare state was undoubtedly the single most important development in industrialized states after the end of World War II. Simply put, governments began spending vast sums on improving the standard of living. As a result of growing trade and investment, international economic interaction among states became the norm in the international system, largely because of the development of national economies and the expansion of economic freedoms for individuals

9.1 WHAT IS "DEVELOPMENT"?

Categorizing political systems and states is not always a simple endeavour, as countries often defy our attempts to label and position them. For instance, the "developed world" as a designation has changed over time and the criteria used to define the category has expanded. Starting with economic indicators, the most highly developed countries are those that, according to the World Bank, have a per capita income of over US$12,000. Western European countries, the United States, Canada, Australia, Japan, and Israel are included. But others, such as South Africa, Turkey, or French Guiana may also be included because they have high incomes as well. Social conditions, political freedoms, or legal and human rights should also be considered when seeking a true idea of development.

The map in this box shows how the UN divides countries. It combines several sets of data, ranging from the economy to education, social issues, and health, to form its Human Development Index (HDI). HDI is certainly a better way of dividing the world than other methods, but every country presents its own case of development.

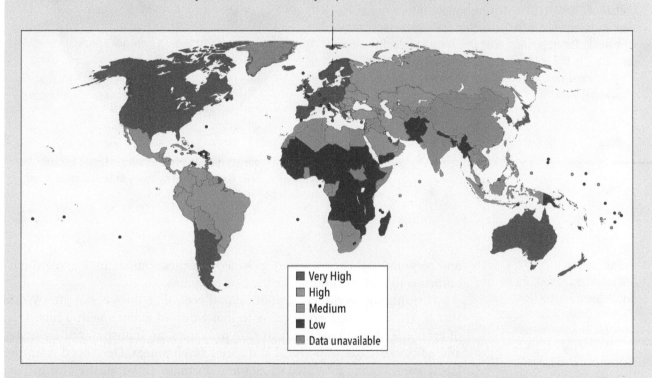

Legend:
- ■ Very High
- ■ High
- ■ Medium
- ■ Low
- ■ Data unavailable

Figure 9.1 The developed world is often referred to as the North, but this map shows that such designations can be arbitrary.

Based on data from United Nations Development Program, *Human Development Report 2011* (New York: UNDP, 2011), Table 1, p. 127. http://hdr.undp.org/en/media/HDR_2011_EN_Complete.pdf.

9.2 POLITICAL ECONOMY

Before the modern term *economics* became popular, political economy was used to describe the study of commerce, production, and labour in a political system. Writing in the late 1600s, Sir William Petty was among the first to advocate a laissez-faire approach to government. Other early political economists, including Adam Smith and David Ricardo, took up this perspective. Karl Marx and others, however, had competing views about the proper relationship between governments and markets.

Political economy examines the links between human behaviour and decision-making and the institutions of economic governance. It assumes that one cannot separate the two fields. Today, political economy takes an interdisciplinary approach to the political–economic relationship. Its offshoot, international political economy, looks at this relationship at the global level.

Hulton Archive/Getty Images

Although theorists such as Adam Smith are better known, Sir William Petty is considered by many to be the architect of modern political economic thought.

North
industrialized nations, including Western Europe, North America, Japan, Australia, and New Zealand, that are part of a structurally integrated system of global capitalism

post-industrial
developed economies that maintain a high-technology, or high-value, economy

Third World
largely Cold War categorization of less developed nations that are not part of a structurally integrated system of global capitalism

and corporations. The increased revenue from these transactions allowed governments to find the funding for the new programs.

Dividing the world along political and economic lines began after World War II. The developed world refers to that group of nations with a high level of economic development, a high GDP per capita, an industrialized economy, and advanced stages of political and social development. Developed countries (DCs) are sometimes referred to as the industrialized world, the **North**, First World, or **post-industrial**. They are separate from the communist countries of the Second World and the developing nations of the **Third World**.

A Brief Postwar History of the Developed World

Before the end of World War II, it seemed that the dominant form of state interaction was war and conflict among political actors. The lack of routine economic relations among political actors had a direct effect on the physical

9.3   ONE WORLD?

The term *Third World* is dated. First used in the immediate postwar years, it referred to a group of developing states that were not aligned to either the Western or the communist world. As this period drew on, however, the term came to describe a very large and diverse group of nations. Countries such as South Korea and Singapore, quite developed in their own right, were labelled alongside other more challenged nations such as Ghana and Bangladesh. To confuse matters further, once the former countries of the Soviet Union and its allies converted to democracy and economic free markets in the 1990s, the term *Second World* largely disappeared, yet the *Third World* did not. There are no apt descriptions for such a wide array of countries; however, like so many other concepts in political studies, the term *Third World* has taken on a short-form meaning for a very complicated issue.

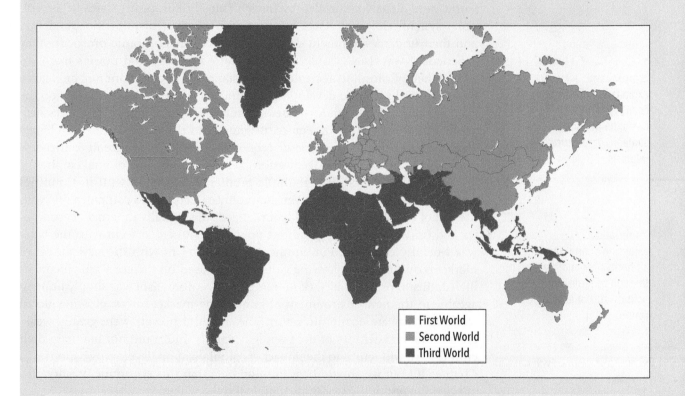

First World
Second World
Third World

Figure 9.2   In the post–World War II years, the world was starkly and simplistically divided.

Based on: www.nationsonline.org/bilder/third_world_map.jpg

interwar period
the years between the two world wars (i.e. 1919–39)

autarky
condition of complete self-sufficiency and isolation from the rest of the system

colonialism
exploitation of a weaker country(ies) by a stronger one(s) for political, strategic, or resource interests

imperialism
extension of one country's authority over another through conquest or political and/or economic control

well-being of states and their governments. In the **interwar period**, a state of **autarky** (non-interaction and isolation among states) was the defining feature of political relations.

Making matters worse was the fact that the state of general non-interaction in the economic sphere—combined with a confusing and ever-changing array of rules implemented by different governments at different times—was not limited to the largely (or seemingly) benign realm of economics. In fact, this autarkic system was a major contributor to the more widespread dynamic of suspicion and distrust that existed among states in the international system. Further, a lack of coordinated economic relations was one of the major contributing factors leading to World War II. Increased economic competition led to economic conflict, which contributed to the downward spiral into violence.

Coupled with this situation, many states in the developing parts of the world were directly controlled by foreign (mostly European) states in the colonial system. Colonial states were stripped of most of their independence, and their underdevelopment deepened as whatever economic prosperity they experienced was usually only to the benefit of the imperial powers that controlled them. **Colonialism** created circumstances of severe economic imbalance between developed and developing countries, but it also created strains on the imperial power. By the mid-twentieth century, European imperial countries such as the UK, Portugal, Spain, France, Belgium, and the Netherlands were barely able to sustain their own domestic economies (thanks in large part to two devastating wars and the Great Depression), let alone maintain colonial empires.

Colonialism, then, had multiple problems associated with it. Countries under colonial rule were not given autonomy or a chance to compete fairly with the rest of the world. The world had changed substantially in terms of economics and **imperialism**, and the direct political control that went with the latter was woefully outdated. Put another way, it didn't fit with the new model of market economics and growing global trade. Based on the economic theory of mercantilism, or nationalist economic control, colonialism was simply unmanageable in the new environment of burgeoning market forces, growing global trade, and private economic actors. The imperial powers were greatly weakened in the first decades of the twentieth century and could not maintain their empires. We will return to the impact of colonialism on developing countries in Chapter 10, but we should bear in mind here that this economic practice also affected the rest of the world, including developed countries.

At the close of World War II, state leaders sought a mechanism to avoid another autarky. The resulting agreements (and there were many, dealing with a variety of spheres that ranged from finance and banking to development and reconstruction, from international loans and currency stability to trade) were first and foremost an effort to sidestep the conditions that the leaders agreed had caused the war. Trade and economic growth, it was thought, would lead to peace.

Not everyone was on the same level, however. The development of advanced industrialized economies after the end of World War II occurred in a variety of forms. Some nations, including Canada and the United States, were largely protected from the war's direct damage, such as the sheer devastation experienced in Europe and Asia. They were therefore able to establish a foothold in the world economy and in all spheres very quickly. For example, at the end of the war the United States alone was responsible for over half of all global production.[2] Although this number may seem astounding, it is not altogether surprising given the level of reconstruction that was required in Europe and Asia. Moreover, the United States did not have to rebuild its industries and infrastructure the way that European countries did and, as a result, enjoyed a high level of immediate economic strength. This amount of relative productive output declined as economies in Asia and Europe began to rebuild and re-establish their pre-war capabilities. Nonetheless, the United States maintained the world's largest productive output, and it remains the world's largest economy today. Despite this difference between countries, a system was needed to avoid another disastrous war. New ideas emerged for a truly revolutionary structure of global trade and economic relations. And this structure entwined security and prosperity.

Post-Industrialization and Political Authority

Security has always been the central objective of any political unit throughout history because a community that is not secure cannot seek a better way of life. As we learned in Chapter 4, states may pursue goals that benefit the welfare of constituents only after security is achieved. Programs that we have come to expect in our day-to-day lives, such as employment benefits, health care, and government funding for social policies, cannot be pursued unless a government can first secure the state against internal insecurity or possible attack by foreign parties.

It is important to keep in mind that the growth of the modern social welfare state is a relatively new development. In fact, if we were to study the major policy questions facing nations before World War II, we would find that issues pertaining to physical security, concerns of alliances and possible conflict with foreign parties, and internal stability would fill the daily docket of governmental mandates in advanced industrial nations.

The growth of a modern global economy and the postwar creation of institutions and organizations designed to help govern peaceful economic relations (as per the **Bretton Woods Agreement**; see Box 9.4) allowed states to concentrate not only on the security of their people and territory but also on the benefits that might be allocated to citizens and improve their way of life. As we will see in Chapter 13, Bretton Woods set out a series of new institutions that governed global monetary and financial relations. Harmony on these matters, while it lasted, allowed capitalist states to integrate their economies and better contribute to their welfare goals. Economic co-operation was key.

This is not to suggest that governments suddenly became altruistic for no cause: there was a perception that supplying these programs and benefits would

Bretton Woods Agreement
postwar system of fixed exchange rates and heavy controls on private banks and other financial institutions, thereby limiting their roles in international finance

9.4 BRETTON WOODS AND POLITICAL ORDER

The United Nations Monetary and Financial Conference (named Bretton Woods, after its location in the New Hampshire town) was held in July 1944. Forty-four nations were represented at the conference, invited by US President Franklin Roosevelt to discuss the future of the international economic order. Institutions that still exist today, such as the International Monetary Fund and the World Bank, were conceived at these meetings. The International Trade Organization failed, but the General Agreement on Tariffs and Trade and, later, the World Trade Organization managed to fulfill most of the participants' trade-related goals. Bretton Woods was instrumental to the postwar order because it saw the creation of a foreign exchange market system (which linked different currencies to one another), a system of financial lending and assistance, and US leadership for the new global order.

AP Photo/Abe Fox/CP

The UN Monetary and Financial Conference at Bretton Woods, New Hampshire, in 1944 charted a new structure for the global economy. Some aspects are still in place today.

improve the governments' general ambitions in an environment of increasing economic mutual dependence and openness. In the immediate postwar years, national governments were also concerned about political survival in light of the pressures of millions of soldiers returning from service and the costs of rebuilding conflict-torn societies. Creating a welfare state was understood to be in the best interest of national governments. Industrialization facilitated the allocation of social benefits in advanced states, leading to the globalized economy we experience today.

Case Studies

This final section turns its attention to the political economies of four states: Canada, the United States, Japan, and the EU (which is composed of other states). As we've established in other parts of this book, Canada and the United States are closely entwined. Their governments share similar objectives, but the economy is the most significant element of their political relationship. Japan and the EU, however, represent distinctive examples of alternative paths for political and economic development. Japan took a focused approach to international trade and commercial relations, while the EU saw strength in **regional integration**.

regional integration
economic or political integration in a defined territorial area

Although both Japan and the EU relied on external assistance after World War II, the former had a more dependent relationship with the United States. Because of specific circumstances that constrained the activities and development of Japan's politics and economy, its shift from a country decimated by war to a global economic powerhouse is particularly striking. Japan represents a different mode of capitalist development and maintains a rather individual democratic experience, leading to a very separate level of growth and prosperity in the international system. Today it offers its citizens one of the highest standards of living in the world and has tremendous influence in international relations.

The EU is undoubtedly the best current example of political and economic regionalism. Following World War II, Europe saw a formal union that combined the strengths of each nation as an option for peace and prosperity. Regionalism is quite widespread globally, with countries recognizing a common benefit in binding together on economic, political, or other issues. While the early days of the EU didn't involve as many states or issues as today, over time the union developed into the most advanced and sometimes controversial example of regionalism.

CANADA

Although many of the characteristics of Canada's political system have been discussed in earlier chapters, we will review them here for comparison purposes (we'll do the same in the section on the United States). Canada is a federal parliamentary democracy with divided responsibilities: some powers are given to the 10 provinces and 3 territories, and others are held by the federal government in Ottawa.[3] Canada's basic law is its constitution. Ultimate power and authority resided in the UK until 1931, when the passing of the Statute of Westminster in the British Parliament officially granted Canada autonomy. Still, any changes to the Canadian constitution had to be approved by Britain until the patriation of the constitution in 1982 gave Canada full decision-making authority.[4]

The British monarch, represented by the governor general, remains the official head of state in Canada. Though there is no set term for the governor general, it is usually five years; he or she is appointed by the monarch on the recommendation of the prime minster. The head of government is the prime minister, who is leader of the dominant party in Parliament and is responsible for creating and leading the federal cabinet. Parliament is split into two houses: the Senate, whose 105 members are appointed by the governor general on the advice of the prime minister; and the House of Commons, which has 308 members elected by a representative-by-population allocation grounded on a popular vote system in the constituencies. The number of House seats will increase to 338 with the 2015 general election as a result of the Fair Representation Act, or Bill C-20.

Senators, who represent provinces rather than smaller constituencies, have to meet certain criteria to qualify for the position. The Canadian Constitution Act of 1867 sets out these conditions, so some of the details appear rather dated. One must be at least 30 years old and own property valued at $4000 or more (equivalent to approximately $70,000 today). Senators are appointed for life but serve only until they are 75 years old. Legislative bills may originate in the Senate (unless they are "money bills" that require appropriating funds), but usually the Senate is used to review legislation coming from the House of Commons. Although it has the power to veto a bill, it rarely does. Changes and suggestions, however, are often made and quite frequently adopted.

Most legislation in Canada originates in the House of Commons, where its members represent individual ridings from across the country. The number of members of Parliament (MPs; Senators are MPs as well) in the House changes depending on results from each census, which is conducted every 10 years. Although ridings are now added based on population, unique assessments of representation done at the time of Confederation mean that some small provinces, such as Prince Edward Island, have a disproportionately high number of MPs for their population.

In recent years, Canada has dealt with the phenomenon of minority governments, in which the governing party (the one that received the most seats in Parliament) does not have a majority. Both the Liberals and the Conservatives have had minority governments in the past decade, partly because of the number of parties competing for votes but also because of shifting allegiances among Canadians. For instance, the New Democratic Party (NDP), once considered a third option in Canadian party politics, received official opposition status in the 2011 election. The NDP was able to attract many socially democratic supporters in Quebec, leaving the BQ with only four seats.

Canada is best described as a liberal plural state with a diversity of interests that reflect its regional, cultural, and socially plural population, as well as

Jack Layton, shown here at a 2011 event, revolutionized social democratic support in Canada by leading the NDP to official opposition status in the general election. Soon after, however, Layton was forced to step down from his role as opposition leader due to illness. He died in August 2011.

© The Toronto Star/ZUMAPRESS.com / Alamy

its linguistic duality (English and French). Canada's parliamentary democracy places a great deal of concentration of power over political and economic affairs at the executive level. The prime minister is responsible for powers of appointment in the Canadian government. Cabinet ministers, also appointed by the prime minister, have the most real power over the state, with support bureaucracies responsible for goal articulation and the implementation of policy.

Canada is a resource-rich country with abundant geographical space, as well as access to the high seas. These geopolitical attributes give the nation a comparative advantage in global relations, thanks to both access to needed resources and the infrastructure to trade them with the outside world. Consequently, Canada has maintained trade and military alliances with the United States and the countries of the Americas, Europe, and the Asia Pacific rim. Economically, Canada is part of the **North Atlantic triangle**, along with the United States and the European Union—so named because these three partners represent the most significant and strategic modes of interaction for each other.

Canada's economy is diversified, benefitting from not only import–export trade with its partners but also high-technology trade, **foreign direct investment** (both by Canadians abroad and from foreigners in Canada), and membership in crucial economic organizations. Two-thirds of Canada's GDP comes from its foreign trade, which means that its overall economic health greatly depends on a favourable international trade and commercial environment. In other words, Canada's economy is highly interdependent with the world's and requires consistent relations with its partners to maintain its welfare state programs and quality of life.

Canadian power and influence in domestic and foreign political relations is largely a function of its influence among and with greater powers as well as its emphasis on group membership. On the first point, Canada is most commonly considered a **middle power** because of its influence and close relations with the United States; unlike other comparable powers such as Australia or the Netherlands, Canada has an inordinately close and strategic relationship with the world's only superpower. The two countries share similar cultural values, democratic principles, and an adherence to market capitalism. Much of Canadian politics and economics is driven by this relationship, which has necessarily led Canada to coalesce many of its policies with its southern partner. However, despite what we might commonly think of as its reliance on the United States for its economic vitality, Canada is neither a satellite nor a dependent state. In fact, it retains a great deal of autonomy in its policy-making and is often at odds with the United States on key issues, such as west-coast fishing, economic relations with Cuba, and the war in Iraq. Canada's middle-power status, then, is not just a measurement of power but represents Canadian attributes in policy-making, as well as its style and history of domestic and foreign relations.

On the second point—group membership—Canada is a world leader in its emphasis on the importance of **international organizations (IOs)** and institutions in helping to guide political and economic relations. Canada is a member of many diverse organizations that include cultural and linguistic groups such

North Atlantic triangle
geographic region of Canada, the United States, and the EU; most significant and strategic modes of interaction for each other; historically, the relationship between Canada, the United States, and the United Kingdom

foreign direct investment (FDI)
investment in real foreign assets, such as domestic structures, equipment, and organizations

middle power
country that does not have great power or superpower status but has significant influence in international relations

international organizations (IOs)
international groupings, governmental or non-governmental, with activities in several states

as *La Francophonie*; economic associations such as the North American Free Trade Agreement (NAFTA), the Asia–Pacific Economic Cooperation (APEC), the Organisation for Economic Co-operation and Development (OECD), and its constituent body, the Development Assistance Committee (DAC); political organizations such as the United Nations (UN) and its component bodies, the Organization of American States (OAS) and the Organization for Security and Co-operation in Europe (OSCE); strategic alliances such as the North Atlantic Treaty Organization (NATO), and the North American Aerospace Defense Command (NORAD) partnership with the United States. Canada does not join and stay with these organizations lightly. There is a much higher purpose for membership in such groups. Though respected in the international community, Canada, as a middle power, is simply unable to create or alter the rules and regulations that pertain to nation-states and their interaction. Institutional membership, however, allows Canada a degree of independence in its policy-making since it is able to assert its views and opinions in groups and often affect the international agenda and decision-making of other states. This capacity has real repercussions for Canada's international relations.

THE UNITED STATES

Countries are usually created out of a cause, or a motivation: revolutions, a new ideology, or the recognition of a distinct people are examples. Certainly, the motivation behind the creation of the United States was independence from Britain, which was manifested in the Declaration of Independence in 1776; the resulting revolutionary war fought between the two; and official independence, formalized in 1783. The United States became one of the first new republics in the late eighteenth century, with political authority through the people with representative government. For the next century or so, the United States continued as a federal union of quasi-sovereign states and a useful collective authority. That changed in 1861 with the American Civil War, when 11 Confederate States of America (Southern slave-owning states) broke away from the Union to try to form a separate country. This war, which lasted until 1865, became the new defining period in US politics, and the outcome was a new attention to unity and indivisibility. Despite lingering animosities that would run well into the twentieth century, the United States became, once and for all, a unified nation.

In comparison with the rest of the world, the United States is the fourth largest country with the third largest population. Native Americans first settled in the United States more than 12,000 years ago. Today, fewer than 2 per cent of Americans are Native Americans or Hawaiians. Europeans arrived in the fifteenth century, but large-scale European immigration took place in the mid-1800s, followed by waves from Asia and Eastern Europe later in that century and further Asian and Latin American immigration in the twentieth century.

The United States is a democratic federal constitutional republic, meaning that its political system is democratically governed, with ultimate authority in its central government and political powers that are divided among its 50 states,

9.5   SLAVERY AND THE AMERICAN CIVIL WAR

The American Civil War is just one example of a civil war, in which citizens of a state battle with each other over the political authority of the government or to change the government. There may be outside influences, but the war's main players are citizens of the same state. The American Civil War is undoubtedly the most famous, partly because of its ferociousness (with over 620,000 dead, it had the highest casualty rate of any American war) but also because of its lasting effects on one of the nineteenth century's most influential countries.

Although there were other contributing factors to the war, such as immigration, religion, and the economy, the largest issue by far was slavery in the Southern states. Abraham Lincoln stated in 1858 that he was committed to the extinction of slavery, and his election to the presidency two years later convinced many observers that war was imminent, particularly after South Carolina seceded from the Union. Ten other Southern states eventually declared their independence from the north in a new Confederate States of America.

The American Civil War left a lasting sense of division between north and south that still resonates to some degree. Yet it also firmly established the principle of US freedom and rights, granted to all slaves in Lincoln's 1862 Emancipation Proclamation. US historians suggest that the horrible experience of the Civil War forged a new direction for the country and a clearer sense of unity and common purpose.

© Lebrecht Music and Arts Photo Library / Alamy

After four years of conflict, the Confederate Army surrendered to the Union side in April 1865. In this image, Confederate Commander Robert E. Lee (left) officially offers his surrender to Union Commander Ulysses S. Grant at Appomattox, VA.

a single district (District of Columbia, or DC), and the federal government located in that district's capital (Washington). Modern federalism, in fact, owes much to the United States. When the country was formed, several of the states did not want to see such a concentration of powers in Washington. But the counterargument was that reasonable government would need a strong central authority. The compromise—a balance between ensuring existing powers of the states and granting some oversight to the central government—was the federal system: a separation of powers that was constitutionally defined. This division of authority is the single most important defining aspect of American politics.

The American political system is unlike the British parliamentary model. It represents one of two major examples of revolutionary republicanism (France is the other one). Breaking from the Westminster parliamentary tradition,

Norman Jung/CartoonStock

"I PREFER TO CALL IT THE SYSTEM OF CHECKS AND BALANCES IN ACTION, SENATOR, NOT GRIDLOCK."

American politics ensures that different levels can oversee the actions of each other. For some, this is an important democratic principle; for others, it merely slows–or stops–the political process.

Electoral College
in the United States, officials chosen from each state who directly elect the president and vice-president; the number of officials in each state is based on population

American politics was based on a definite separation of powers among the levels of government, with a firm role to be played regarding the review of each other's actions—the checks and balances of the American system, in contrast with Canada. The American executive consists of the cabinet and the president. The president leads the executive and is also both head of government and head of state. The legislative branch of government is bicameral, with an elected upper house (Senate, with 100 members who serve a six-year term) and lower house (House of Representatives, with 435 members who serve a two-year term).

The US Constitution, which entered into force in 1789, is the world's oldest written constitution (refer back to Chapter 4 for more information about written constitutions). It has been altered 27 times, most recently in 1992. The US Bill of Rights, which is similar to the Canadian Charter of Rights and Freedoms, is laid out in the first 10 amendments to the Constitution. These amendments explain the basic individual and collective rights of all US citizens.

The American system relies on the input and involvement of all citizens in a form of indirect democracy, which denotes the representation of citizen views by elected officials. As a federal democracy, the United States divides decision-making and authority among different layers of power—national, state, and municipal. American politics separates executive (or presidential) power from that of the legislature (the bicameral Congress) and the judiciary (the courts). And then there is the bureaucracy, which (as in most countries) could be referred to as the fourth level of government, given its important role in the definition of policy-making and implementation.

As a presidential democracy, the US leader is chosen in a separate vote on election day. The president and vice-president are formally elected by the **Electoral College**, a system outlined in the American Constitution and made up of a group of 538 officials from each state (distributed based on population) who are voted for by the electorate. These officials act on behalf of US voters and, although they may legally vote for anyone in the presidential race, in practice they pledge their ballots for their state's choice. To win the election, a candidate must gain a majority of these college votes. The president is elected to a four-year term and may hold office for only two terms.

The American judicial system still retains vestiges of the British legal system but with a strong tradition of judicial review of legislative acts, which gives ultimate power of interpretation to the courts. Supreme and federal court judges are appointed by the president and approved by the Senate, while citizens elect

EDGAR ARGO

"DOES THE ELECTORAL COLLEGE HAVE A FOOTBALL TEAM?"

Edgar Argo/CartoonStock

Unlike other colleges, the electoral college is a group of people whose shared duty is to formally elect the US president and vice-president.

lower court judges. Supreme Court judges are responsible for ensuring that no government legislation violates the US Constitution, and they have the right to override both the Congress and the president.

It may seem odd for such a large political system, but just two major political parties have dominated American politics since the US Civil War (but see Box 9.6.) The Democrats have traditionally occupied the more "left-leaning" side of American politics, with the Republicans on the "right" of the political spectrum. In the real world, the two parties are actually rather close—at least compared with more radical political movements—in terms of most of their platforms, ideology, and political practice. Other political parties exist and some have had influence, but these two have controlled most of American politics in the modern era.

In terms of political culture, US politics reflects a lot of what Canadians might recognize: freedoms (religion, speech), democratic values, the essential equality of citizens, and respect for authority. Traditionally, the United States has been thought of as a melting pot of immigrant cultures that blends all into something new and different: Americans. But the United States is actually a very diverse country. Like other multicultural nations, pockets of different traditions, languages, and cultures dominate different areas. For instance, Hispanics now represent more than 15 per cent of the total US population. The old idea of being "an American" has given way to a more diverse notion of nationality.

American economics provides a prime example of liberalism and market freedom but with government regulation. The United States is commonly seen as the "home of capitalism," a place where the market reigns supreme. But the

9.6　"THIRD" PARTIES IN US POLITICS

The domination of the Democratic and Republican parties has always been challenged by others, but they usually don't receive much support. That changed in 1992 when Texas businessman H. Ross Perot ran for the presidency against incumbent Republican George H.W. Bush and Democrat Bill Clinton. Clinton won the election with 43 per cent of the vote, but Perot took 19 per cent, a startling percentage. After the election, Perot formed the Reform Party (no connection to the Canadian party of the same name) and ran again in 1996, receiving 8 per cent of the vote.

In the 2000 election, Ralph Nader received thousands of votes from environmental supporters. Critics argued that he "spoiled" the election for Democrat Al Gore, who also ran on an environmental platform. Gore lost the Electoral College vote to George W. Bush by 537 ballots in Florida. Nader received over 97,000 votes in that state, leading some to suggest that even a few hundred of his supporters might have made the difference for Gore had they switched allegiances. Since that election, no third party has had such an influence. However, factions of the big parties, such as the right-wing Tea Party and left-leaning Occupy movements, illustrate that the dominant parties have lost some of their former broad base of support.

© Visions of America, LLC / Alamy

© Reuters/CORBIS

Ross Perot, seen here in California in 1992, almost single-handedly made third parties relevant in the United States in the 1990s.

Ralph Nader, shown here in Arkansas in 2000, led the Green Party in that year's US general election.

US economy became the world's largest thanks to a combination of private initiative and effective government management by agencies at the federal and state levels. Today the US economy is the world's largest by far, with a GDP of over US$15 trillion. The EU's is larger, but it is not a lone state. As single countries, China and Japan are rivals for second place, with GDPs of $5.8 trillion and $5.4 trillion, respectively. While the United States doesn't have the same predominant role it played in the years following World War II (more on this in Chapter 13), it is still the most important economy in the world, with its dollar as the basic global currency unit and a concentration of a large number of global manufacturers and financial institutions.

US auto manufacturers were hit particularly hard by the economic downturn in 2008. The US government approved $25 billion in funds to save Chrysler and General Motors (a GM assembly plant is pictured here) from shutting down completely.

In addition to regulating and managing the economy, the US government is also a consumer of enormous dimensions. Each year the US federal budget involves over US$1.5 trillion in spending. This gives the government immense influence over the economy and raises the possibility for lobbying and pressure over the awarding of government contracts. It also gives the government the option of providing a large stimulus to the economy, if it should choose to. For instance, in 2008 and 2009, the US government spent almost $800 billion in an effort to stimulate the domestic economy. Called the American Recovery and Reinvestment Act, the incentives, relief funds, and investments were made in the areas of health care, education, tax benefits, infrastructure, and energy technologies.

The United States spends more than any other nation on research and development (R&D), and one element of its global dominance has been the spread of American multinational corporations (MNCs) throughout the world (see Chapter 13 for more details). Through this global corporate reach, American brands and companies have become much more than just products and services. Indeed, American products have a cultural impact as well: McDonald's, Nike, IBM, General Motors, and Citibank—just to name a few— have enormous visibility far beyond American shores. The broader impact of American culture, including music, film, and literature, is arguably more widespread than any other. For better or for worse, this extends American culture to a wider global market. A trip to any major city throughout the world quickly reveals the influence of American products and culture.

From an economic standpoint, the American capitalist economy means that the production and distribution of goods and services in the American system relies on private profit-making and capital. There is no doubt that the most significant actor in the modern global economy is the American one, both for its leadership role and top economic position. Of all the economies in the international system, the United States is most intertwined with the rest; however, due to its vast size and internal consumption, it is less dependent on the world economy than other countries.

The United States took on the role of undisputed leader in the international system in terms of both military and economic power at the close of World War II. At that time a series of international institutions, organizations, and regimes was created to guide decisions made by states. The idea here was not so much to strip countries of their sovereign power but to give international institutions an important role in providing a peaceful way to alleviate potential conflict. Importantly, the new international system of institutions needed a leader to uphold the structure and to provide a military and economic guarantee. That leader was the United States.

It was significant that the United States was chosen for this role. Most of the former international leaders—the colonizing powers of Europe such as the UK, France, Belgium, and Germany—were simply so weakened at the end of the war that they were unable to uphold their position in the global order. And, while it might seem clear to us that the United States would lead the new system, this decision met with some resistance. As part of what became known as the **transatlantic bargain**, the former great European powers ceded to American leadership in exchange for the United States agreeing to uphold the economic and military stability of the Western world. The United States thereby retained the position of **hegemon**, or principal power among states.

But by the 1970s, the American political economy, as well as its position in the international system, looked very different than it had in previous decades. The country was in an economic downturn, and a global economic **recession** made matters worse. It took a decade before the US economy rebounded, and the 1980s **neo-conservative** movement under President Ronald Reagan featured a reduced governmental role in the economy and far greater emphasis on private capitalism.

During the next decade, some economists thought that the dominance of the US economy was eroding. Other countries, such as Germany, Japan, and (later) China, posed real challenges, and the United States found itself overextended and greatly in debt. Renewed strength in the US economy righted much of the imbalance felt in Washington, but there was no doubt that other actors (such as the aforementioned countries or global corporations and institutions) were playing a much more significant role than in the past. Even though the United States is unquestionably the most powerful economy in the world today, its relative position is very different than it was after World War II. It now shares a great deal of global decision-making and is no longer considered the undisputed leader it once was.

The United States has also undergone significant challenges in the twenty-first century. First, the 2001 terrorist attacks left many feeling vulnerable and uncertain. The policies of the Bush administration changed substantially on

transatlantic bargain
postwar arrangement whereby former great powers of Europe conceded to American leadership in exchange for the latter supporting European economic and military stability

hegemon
one country with inordinate capability to uphold and protect the global system

recession
decline in economic productivity or affluence; specifically, a decline in GDP for two or more consecutive fiscal quarters

neo-conservative
advocate of the return to conservative values or policies

11 September of that year, as this relatively new government waged a "war on terrorism" that framed much of US domestic and international policy for the rest of the decade. A war unlike any other, it brought allies closer to the United States, then quickly repelled them. Political challenges in the new century became multifaceted: managing an economy under siege, building public confidence and security, and—most importantly—fighting two wars concurrently (in Afghanistan and Iraq). The end of hostilities in Iraq and the withdrawal of troops in Afghanistan did not halt the long-term cost incurred by the wars or the ongoing restructuring process in those two countries. The United States, then, bears the costs of maintaining a role as a global power.

Thanks to these costs and an economic downturn, the financial stability of the 1990s gave way to government deficits and growing debt. The balance of trade with other countries became more negative, with the country importing more goods than it exported, and the dollar fluctuated with a shifting economy. By 2009, the new Obama presidency was in the throes of the country's worst recession in 80 years and, as we previously mentioned, spent billions on bailouts and stimulus packages to revive—or at least save—an economy in peril.

Nevertheless, the United States is one of the very few states in today's international system that can lay claim to a global sphere of influence. Despite severe challenges, the basis of the US economy will ensure its impact in the world for many years to come. The rest of the world is reliant on the United States for a huge percentage of global production, innovation, and finance. However, this influence extends beyond the economy: it remains an exemplar of democracy and political freedoms, its culture is widely accepted around the world, and it continues to be a global leader in international relations.

JAPAN

Japan is a constitutional monarchy with a bicameral legislature. The emperor—who serves as the monarch and head of state—has had a largely symbolic role since the modern Japanese constitution was implemented in 1947. Although this role is not unlike the Canadian governor general, the Japanese emperor maintains a high degree of reverence as a link to a time when the emperor was considered a deity on earth. The Diet, or Japanese Parliament, is divided into the upper House of Councillors and the lower House of Representatives. Though the Japanese political system is multi-party, the Liberal Democratic Party (LDP) has largely dominated domestic politics since 1955.

The Japanese prime minister is appointed by the emperor, much like Canada's governor general is selected by the British monarch. As in Canada, the prime minister is the leader of the party with the most seats in the Diet and is head of government. He or she names officials to the executive cabinet, which is responsible to the Diet in the same way that the Canadian cabinet holds ministerial responsibility.

Another area of similarity between Japanese and Canadian politics is found in their respective judicial systems. Both are based on appointments, which

Diet
Japanese Parliament

9.7 *GYOKUON-HŌSŌ*: NO LONGER A LIVING GOD

On 15 August 1945, Japan's Emperor Hirohito delivered a speech that was significant in many ways. First, he announced that Japan had accepted the Potsdam Agreement, which spelled out the country's unconditional surrender in World War II. Japan's military, economic, and political independence was effectively over, and the years ahead affected its future in dramatic ways. Second, the address marked the first time that Japanese citizens heard their emperor's voice. The emperor was considered a "living god" and did not interact with everyday people. This tradition made the address significant in another way: Hirohito, or the Showa Emperor, renounced his divinity and declared himself to be human. Some Japanese did not know how to respond to these events and some Japanese soldiers tried to take control of the government, ignoring Hirohito's demand that everyone accept his statement. The address was known as *Gyokuon-hōsō*, or "jewel voice broadcast," referring to the voice of the emperor.

© Pictorial Press Ltd / Alamy

Emperor Hirohito (1901–89), pictured here during World War II.

lends a level of independence. The Supreme Court tops the hierarchy of courts in Japan, and the country's constitution, like Canada's, includes a Bill of Rights for its citizens.

Japan presents a fascinating example of a country that emerged from relative isolationism to become a global economic powerhouse in the postwar era. A formal imperial power, Japan is currently one of the most important countries in the world, with one of the biggest economies, close relations with the United States, and major significance in global politics.

With one of the oldest and most sophisticated political and economic histories among the advanced industrialized nations, Japan took its first steps to nationhood in the fifth and sixth centuries. The belief system of this early civilization served as the foundation for Shinto, or "the way of the gods," which is Japan's traditional religion. Shinto emphasizes the need for humans to live in harmony with nature and the environment.

In this early period, its political system was highly centralized, but over time political leadership weakened and power was decentralized. Decentralization led to a more **feudal system** that borrowed heavily from the experience in China and prospered for centuries. While regional aristocrats were given some authority for their lands, the imperial court at Kyoto was still generally

feudal system
political or social system based on the relationship between landholders and those with permission to use and live on the property in exchange for fees, political loyalties, or other commitments

recognized as the governing authority for judging land claims and awarding government positions. By the mid-twelfth century, the central authority, even as limited as it was, was called into question. Wars became the common way of settling various disputes between groups of nobles.

National unity was finally restored in the late sixteenth century. The peace that came with it fostered change, growth, and the mobilization of the Japanese economy. European states saw Japan as a strategic trade link to the rest of Asia and forged deeper relations. Toward the end of the eighteenth century, for instance, both the Russians and the British tried to increase their economic interactions with the Japanese. However, Japan remained highly isolationist and resisted these attempts, as well as those of the Americans, to coax them into a trade deal. This refusal was largely successful, at least until the mid-nineteenth century.

In July 1853, an American fleet under Commodore Matthew C. Perry entered Tokyo Bay. Perry demanded that Japan open itself to trade with the Americans. Faced with the threat of war, Japan had few alternatives but to agree. Subsequently, two small ports were opened to US ships and an American consulate was

Commodore Matthew C. Perry's "black ship" arrives in Japan in 1853.

© Glasshouse Images / Alamy

put in place. Other treaties were soon reached with the UK, Russia, France, and the Netherlands. Political changes to the legislature, a modern cabinet system, and a civil service system all followed (the latter two have remained largely unchanged since their establishment). A new Japanese constitution was drafted, reinforcing the sovereign authority of the emperor.

Previously isolated for hundreds of years, the Japanese came to be a strongly unified people. This sense of nationalism contributed to the creation of the Japanese Empire throughout the 1880s and 1890s, with control over Taiwan and the Korean Peninsula. Victory in the Russo-Japanese War (1904–5) gave Japan control of the Liaotung Peninsula and Manchuria. Japan declared war on Germany in 1914 and seized control over German colonies in the East.

During the interwar period, Japan began to distance itself from the West, falling back into isolationism. Later, Japanese militarism began with the swift and total conquest of Manchuria in 1931. Japanese policy rapidly shifted from isolationism to expansionism on the Asian continent. This period of heightened nationalism and colonialism, which continued into World War II, formed the basis for much of the other Asian states' mistrust and animosity toward Japan, feelings that remain even today.

Japan was devastated at the end of World War II. In addition to being attacked by atomic bombs at Hiroshima and Nagasaki, the country's economic infrastructure was decimated by the war's demands. Between 1945 and 1952,

Yoshida Doctrine
postwar Japanese political and economic policy intended to establish a more non-interventionist role in international affairs, support the United States as hegemon in the global system, deepen links with the Americans, and focus on the domestic economy of Japan as a means of reassembling power and influence; named after Japan's postwar prime minister, Shigeru Yoshida

the Americans occupied Japan and played a significant role in rebuilding the country, both economically and politically. Concepts such as nationalism became taboo, and the Japanese not only had little interest in rebuilding their military but were also prevented from doing so by limits written into their new constitution. Instead, Japanese and American energies were focused on the redevelopment of the economic and civil infrastructure of the country.

The postwar years represent the most remarkable period in modern Japanese economic history. The country's government began a strategic effort to rebuild its domestic economy and industry and to engage in sectors of the international economy that would aid in its reconstruction efforts. The broad policy implemented and followed by the Japanese during this time was a combination of three basic elements: establish an essentially non-interventionist role in international affairs; support the United States as the hegemon in the global system and strengthen links with the Americans; and focus on the domestic economy as a means of reassembling power and influence. This approach came to be known as the **Yoshida Doctrine** and was a largely successful policy of domestic attention and international interaction.

Perhaps the most significant medium for this development was the creation of the federal Ministry of International Trade and Industry (MITI), now known as the Ministry of Economy, Trade, and Industry (METI). This ministry was, and still is, in charge of orchestrating domestic economic ventures and targeting within the international environment. MITI was responsible for the strategic marketing of Japanese technology and consumer electronics worldwide. Partly because of the country's corporatist model of government, which allows for the integration of business interests, unions, and government officials in decision-making, MITI was very successful in both identifying emerging consumer and corporate markets in the industrialized world and in distributing its goods globally.

From this brief (and incomplete) history, we can see how Japan's domestic politics and global position underwent severe alterations in the past few hundred years, most notably in the latter half of the twentieth century. From regional great power to defeated nation to global economic presence, the country and its power and influence shifted drastically in a short period of time.

Japan's emergence in the latter half of the twentieth century as a major economy gave it a clear economic, if not political, leadership role in the North Pacific. Japan is in the centre of one of the most volatile and robust parts of the world (see Figure 9.1). It is surrounded by potentially belligerent countries, such as North Korea and China. North Korea frequently makes bellicose

Shigeru Yoshida, Japan's prime minister from 1946 to 1947 and 1948 to 1954, established the Yoshida Doctrine, the basis of Japan's economic relationship with the United States.

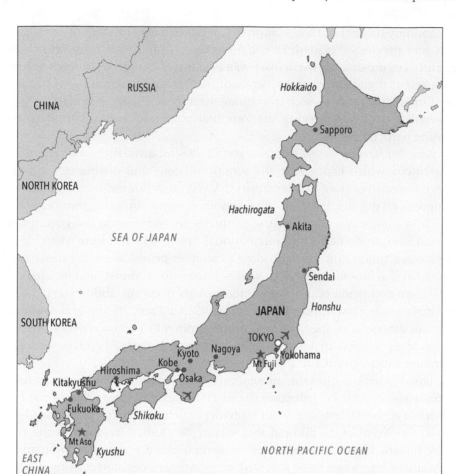

Figure 9.3   Japan and Its Neighbours

Based on: www.wordtravels.com/Travelguide/Countries/Japan/Map

comments about impending conflict with Japan; the former's political instability, coupled with efforts to develop nuclear weapons, only further complicates
prospects for peace. Russia's uncertain democratic development and China's
balancing act between totalitarianism and capitalism make Japan's bilateral relations complex and sensitive. Other countries in Japan's larger geopolitical area,
such as India and Pakistan, also present a source of insecurity. Having fought
wars with most of the region's major players, Japan's present and future depends
on close trade and commercial relations. The country's size (it is slightly smaller
than California) and lack of arable land also make trade a necessity.

The reasons for Japanese success in the postwar and post–Cold War eras are
numerous, but there are several that are particularly irrefutable. Japan re-built

its economy on the solid foundations of an industrialized system of production that had previously existed. In other words, it didn't start from scratch but extended its pre-existing strengths. Japan's careful planning contributed to long-term regional and international strength. Rather than attempting to immerse itself in existing sectors—such as primary resources or heavy manufacturing—it targeted future and **emerging markets** that were not already saturated with existing participants.

Another factor was self-imposed regulations on areas such as international investment, which kept credit and wealth at home and discouraged the foreign ownership of domestic enterprises. A very high domestic savings rate was achieved, giving the Japanese economy impressive financial resources with which to manoeuvre. Later, as the country's economy grew, the government relaxed laws on domestic and international investment at a time when investment opportunities increased, leading to another period of growth in Japanese multinational interests abroad, as well as international investment in Japan.

Japan also made critical assessments of its domestic abilities and needs. For instance, it must import most of its domestic food, energy, and resources. Strategic assessments, then, allowed the government to set objectives in regards to goods and services that had to be imported versus those in great supply, such as manufactured goods and high technology.

Japan benefited from the international liberalization of markets, openness in trade and commerce, reduction in **tariffs**, and careful integration of national modes of economic interaction and interdependence. Japan's position of global economic preeminence allowed it to ensure that others adhered to the rules while it gained from the system and its own politics. Corporatism in Japan not only allows businesses to be involved in government decision-making but also aids the government through the direct input in and observation of private economic players. This exchange results in a more efficient relationship and a legitimate way for the Japanese government to take certain advantages of the global economic order.

Finally, Japan's success is a result of its distinctive political history, culture, and domestic economy. Japan reaps the benefits of international openness, institutions, and world markets yet does not position itself on the import side to the same degree that other trading nations do, or must. Though a strong international player, Japan has often been criticized as being a protectionist state that would always seek to uphold its domestic interests over the health of the international economy. Further to this idea is the Japanese tradition of *keiretsu*, which is the vertical integration of large industrial groups that permits like-minded entities to bind together to influence the policy process.

In the 1990s, though, the Japanese government was faced with a problem. A deep financial crisis struck the country in the early part of the decade, breaking several banks that had earlier ranked among the largest in the world. This banking crisis was matched by a crash in the real estate market, which had become hugely inflated in the 1980s. For the first time since World War II, the Japanese economy began to shrink as corporations and individuals faced bankruptcy. For

emerging markets
poorer economies with potential for future growth

tariff
duty placed on a particular categorization of imported or exported goods or services

keiretsu
a business group or set of companies found in Japan that work together in decision-making and production to provide increased benefits for all

many Japanese people, this disaster (which became known as the Lost Decade) challenged their assumptions concerning their nation's economic dominance and efficiency. Political instability followed and, for the first time in decades, the LDP lost power, albeit temporarily. Because Japan was the world's second largest economy, its situation exacerbated a deep economic crisis in Asia (in Thailand, Indonesia, and South Korea in particular) as the Japanese market for Asian exports shrank. This crisis underscored Japan's importance in the international economy. It recovered some strength only to decline again, along with other industrialized nations, in the early 2000s. After a decade of slow recuperation, the Japanese economy once more slumped dramatically at the onset of the 2008–9 global recession.

More so than many other industrialized nations, Japan suffered from high public debt. Only Zimbabwe, with its severe and unique debt problems, had a higher debt-to-GDP level in the world. Japan also suffered from shrinking trade, declining production, and reduced investment. The nuclear disaster at Fukushima Daiichi in March 2011 compounded Japan's economic woes. Politically, the Japanese government was criticized for its handling of the crisis, first suggesting that the disaster was not as severe as it actually was and then mishandling the relief efforts and economic compensation. Eventually, Prime Minister Naoto Kan stepped down in the midst of political turmoil, ceding power to Yoshihiko Noda.

Japan is a remarkable example of how an ancient system of politics can be significantly altered to fit another era. Of course, the post–World War II experience in Japan could only have happened with the specific circumstances stemming from the war and its outcome. The urgent need to revamp a political and economic system in that country, coupled with its close relationship with the United States, allowed Japan to take advantage of strategic changes in the global system and quickly become a major force in the new wave of

9.8 JAPAN'S INFLUENCE ON BUSINESS-GOVERNMENT RELATIONS IN ASIA

In many Asian countries, the relationship between business and government is a very close one, with a high level of interaction between the state and large corporations. The goal of this co-operation is to produce both economic stability and higher levels of international competitiveness. In South Korea, such a relationship existed and appeared to work very well until the financial and economic crisis of 1997–8. The largest industrial and business conglomerates, families of corporations known as *chaebol*, worked closely with the government in the formation of domestic economic, trade, and investment policies. Many analysts saw this practice as one of the great advantages of countries such as South Korea because it allowed states to harness the power of the national government to assist in the development of competitive industries and ensure the collaboration of big business in achieving the goals of the government, both domestic and international.

When the deep financial and economic crisis of 1997 hit South Korea, these long-standing assumptions were rapidly reconsidered. It emerged that the relationship between government and big business had been, perhaps, too close.

globalization. It would be difficult, if not impossible, to completely replicate Japan's experience because it presents a unique and circumstantial case. However, Japan is currently affected by chronic political problems and economic stagnation.

THE EUROPEAN UNION

Europe is much more than geography; its long history has given it a cultural and political identity as well. While the idea of "Europe" is ambiguous, to say the least, the modern conception of the region can be found in the revival of classical learning during the Renaissance. In this context, Europe was perceived as the geographical and cultural heir to the Roman Empire, but it did not symbolize a single political domain. Even its current boundaries do not rest on any clear-cut geographical divide. The Ural Mountains were once designated as the eastern boundary of Europe, but this frontier has expanded since the end of the Cold War and the demise of the Soviet Union. For instance, Russia is now more "European" than it was during the latter half of the twentieth century.

It is also impossible to define Europe or Europeans in culturally or ethnically homogeneous terms. In many countries, immigration from the West Indies, Africa, and Asia has produced an ethnic mix more diverse than at any time since the decline and collapse of the Roman Empire. By the same token, emigration from Europe since the fifteenth century has spread various European identities across the globe.

The European movement appeared in the interwar period. After World War II, British Prime Minister Winston Churchill spoke of a "kind of United States of Europe" to create unity and avoid another continental war. As time went on, political actors used the European movement to deal with the reconstruction of Europe for largely the same purposes that Churchill envisioned: peace and prosperity in the region.

David Mitrany proposed the theory of **functionalism** to describe this movement.[5] He argued that countries could not respond to the problems associated with modern economies on their own; a collective approach was necessary to provide a full range of social and welfare services. These needs would be accomplished by functionally specific international organizations (hence the term *functionalism*) that would be independent of governments, or enjoy a great deal of functional autonomy. The final goal was peaceful economic development. This **institutionalism** is, in essence, the basis of the EU system.

Much of the political impetus for European integration emerged before World War II ended, when countries began considering ways to handle the ongoing conflicts of the major powers. Increasingly, the idea of a unified Europe found widespread popular support among diverse political perspectives. Importantly, the influence and policies of the United States were crucial: this country saw European co-operation as solving the problem of European security and reviving the European and international economies. It also offered a way to avoid a future war and further US involvement.

functionalism
collective approach to provide a full range of social and welfare services through functionally specific international organizations

institutionalism
belief in utility of institutions to provide collective goods

Treaty of Paris
European treaty of April 1951 that created the European Coal and Steel Community (ECSC)

Like the postwar rebuilding scenario in Japan, European countries developed their new economic systems on the pre-existing industrial base. Germany is notable here because, as the war's aggressor, it had the most to lose in those precarious first years. But with careful economic planning and close political relations with the rest of Europe and the United States, Germany avoided the plight that it faced after World War I (i.e. acute economic depression and limited relations with its neighbours) and rapidly became Europe's leading economic actor.

Behind European integration is the idea that intergovernmental institutions could facilitate greater co-operation among countries and hence less chance of future conflict. The European Union (EU) is one such organization. Other regional bodies, such as NAFTA and APEC, exist, but none have the same level of integration combined with such an evolution of politics, economics, and institutional structures. Importantly, the EU is not a government but an international organization that consists of sovereign states.

This institutional system was formed in April 1951, when the **Treaty of Paris** created the **European Coal and Steel Community** (ECSC) among the original six signatories (Belgium, the Netherlands, Luxembourg, France, West Germany, and Italy). The ECSC, which began operating in July 1952, established a **common market** in coal, coke, iron, steel, and scrap (at this time, the coal and steel industry was still regarded as the foundation of an industrial economy). The unique feature of the ECSC was the degree of **supranational** authority that it gave to its main institutions. Later, in 1958, these six countries created the **European Economic Community** (EEC) and the **European Atomic Energy Community** (EURATOM) with the **Treaties of Rome**. The former established free trade in both industrial and agricultural products, set out prospects for a complete common market among the signatories, and created a **common agricultural policy** (CAP), which provided economic benefits to agriculture in all countries in order to allow stable pricing and profits for agricultural producers. In 1993, the organization was renamed the European Union to reflect the growing integration of its economies and the increasing importance of regional institutions.

As soon as the ECSC was introduced, talk began about expanding the group from the original six. There have been seven expansions to the organization since 1951, bringing the current total membership to 27 countries (see the map in Box 9.9). Most importantly, these processes confirmed the importance of internal trade and political relations over those with non-EU members. In addition, successive enlargement and integration among EU members forced the outside world to adjust their own policies. As the EU grew, so did our ideas about economic integration. For instance, one of the strongest reasons for NAFTA was its response to deepening trade relations in Europe. Expansion has not been a smooth process, however, and changes have often been prompted by outside events such as new applications for membership, changes in the policies of major outside powers such as the United States, the collapse of communism in Europe, the reunification of Germany, and the economic and political development of former communist countries.

European Coal and Steel Community (ECSC)
first institutional version of European integration; formed in 1951 by Belgium, the Netherlands, Luxembourg, France, West Germany, and Italy

common market
an economic arrangement among states intended to eliminate barriers that inhibit the movement of factors of production–labour, capital, and technology– among its members

supranational
international organization or union in which decision-making is shared by all members

European Economic Community (EEC)
formed in 1958, second institutional version of European integration; involved Belgium, the Netherlands, Luxembourg, France, West Germany, and Italy

European Atomic Energy Community (EURATOM)
community created to govern atomic energy in Europe, entered into force in 1958

Treaties of Rome
European treaty of 1958 that created the European Economic Community (EEC) and the European Atomic Energy Community (EURATOM)

common agricultural policy (CAP)
European Union program that provides economic benefits to agriculture in all countries in order to allow stable pricing and profits for the industry

9.9   WILL TURKEY JOIN THE EU?

Joining the EU is no easy task, but Turkey has had a rougher time than many other applicants, even though it has done everything it should to be favourably considered. An "associate member" since 1963, Turkey formally applied to join in 1987, when the EU was still the European Community.

Turkey (represented here by its flag–a white crescent moon and star on a red background) continues to seek membership in the EU (represented by the circle of gold stars on a blue background). Its application was first recognized in 1999, and it has been suggested that it will be at least 2013 before its membership could be complete. This situation has caused great debate about the extent of the organization's expansion and what really constitutes "Europe."

A largely Islamic country, Turkey is a secular state and a close ally of the United States. It is also a member of the OECD, NATO, the Council of Europe, and the Western European Union. Critics of Turkey's possible membership say that the country hasn't done enough on human rights and democracy. While supporters see Turkey offering an important link to the Islamic world as well as Asia (since Turkey straddles the easternmost parts of the European continent), former French president Nicolas Sarkozy remarked that Turkey "has no place inside the European Union."[1] When he was president of the Convention on the Future of Europe, Valéry Giscard d'Estaing stated that allowing Turkey to join "would be the end of Europe."[2] Austria and France have both indicated that they would not support

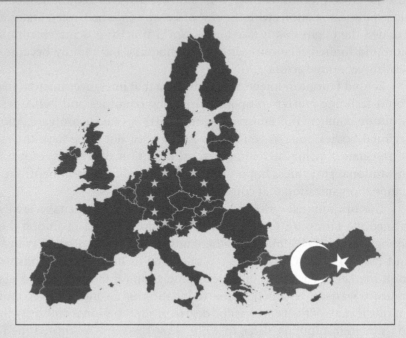

Figure 9.4   The EU and Turkey

Turkey's membership. Since accession to the EU requires the unanimous support of all member states, it is difficult to envision a smooth path for Turkey's European aspirations.

Notes

1. "France Snubs Turkey on EU Talks," BBC News, last updated 25 June 2007, http://news.bbc.co.uk/2/hi/europe/6238526.stm.
2. "Turkey Entry 'Would Destroy EU,'" BBC News, last updated 8 Nov. 2002, http://news.bbc.co.uk/2/hi/europe/2420697.stm.

European Parliament
parliamentary assembly
for the EU

There are six main institutions in the EU: the European Parliament; European Council; European Commission; Court of Justice; Court of Auditors; and the European Central Bank. Although the Treaties of Rome established the Parliamentary Assembly, it was only in 1987 that the title was legally recognized. Members of the **European Parliament** (MEPs) are elected directly by citizens of EU member states and are chosen on the basis of multinational

Figure 9.5   The EU Institutions

Like any governmental organization, the many institutions of the EU are interrelated. Each carries out its own specific task, such as legislation, policy-making, and judicial interpretation.

party affiliations rather than nationality. Rules for these elections, which are held every five years, are determined by the individual states. The European Parliament consists of 754 members; representation roughly reflects differences in the size of members' populations, although the smaller countries are over-represented on a proportional basis. The Parliament is located in two places: Strasbourg, France, and Brussels, Belgium. The Parliament's general secretariat (its administrative offices) is in Luxembourg.

The Parliament has three main roles. First, it shares legislative power with the Council of Ministers. Second, it is responsible for democratic supervision over all EU institutions, particularly the commission. Third, the Parliament has authority (again with the council) over the EU's budget and the power to adopt or reject it. Like legislatures in national governments, this "power of the purse" gives the Parliament influence and control. However, neither the commission nor the Council of Ministers can be considered responsible to Parliament in the sense of the Westminster model. A bigger problem facing the European Parliament is the lack of public interest in the body, with voter apathy being a significant factor in elections.

The **Council of the European Union** is an important decision-making institution of the EU. Its membership is made up of ministers from the EU national governments and is based on areas of concern, such as health, indus-try, transportation, or social affairs. The most important part of this body is the **European Council** (the two councils are not the same), comprising the heads of state and government and the president of the **European Commission**. The European Council is responsible for setting up and overseeing the broad

Council of the European Union
main decision-making institution of the EU, made up of ministers from the EU national governments

European Council
a body of the European Union; part of the Council of the European Union and composed of the heads of state and government and the president of the European Commission

European Commission
body responsible for implementing activities mandated by the European Parliament and Council

9.10 WHY BRUSSELS?

The real influence brokers in the EU are the large economic and military powers of the UK, France, and Germany. One might expect, then, that the EU's "home" would be in the capital city of one of those countries. However, you would have to go to Brussels, Belgium, to visit most of its institutions. Part of the European Parliament, the Council of the European Union, the European Commission, and the European Council are all located in Brussels, the Belgian capital. Although other cities, including Strasbourg, France, and the country of Luxembourg have seen European institutions set up, Brussels pushed hard to be seen as the location for Europe's new structures. This location was considered the best compromise: Brussels is not only a modern city close to most major capitals, but it also has space for institutional growth, a thriving urban centre, good relations with member states, and no ulterior motives. This is a good example of the advantage of being small and being on good terms with others. As the EU has expanded, so has the impact on Brussels, where a third of its citizens are non-Belgians. About 100,000 people in the city work for the EU or EU-related businesses, and billions of euros flow into the local economy every year.

© Piotr P. Gorecki / Alamy

Some of the EU member states' flags fly outside the European Parliament buildings in Brussels, Belgium.

agenda of the council as a whole. All 27 member states are represented at council meetings, but the particular ministerial representation depends on the topic under discussion. Major issues, including common foreign and security policy, taxation, and asylum and immigration, normally require unanimity. Other issues (usually procedural decisions) are decided by a simple majority or by "weighted" majority voting, which ensures that the five largest member states cannot outvote the seven smallest. The bigger the country's population, the more votes it has. But the number is not strictly proportional: it is adjusted in favour of smaller states.

The European Commission is responsible for implementing activities mandated by the European Parliament and the European Council. For example, it ensures that treaty provisions and EU rules are implemented and observed. The 27 commissioners are nominated by national governments and appointed by unanimity for a renewable term of five years. They are to act independently of national governments and to further the interests of the EU as a whole. The commission functions as the initiator of policy proposals and the executive arm of the EU, rather like the Canadian cabinet. One of its most important functions is to negotiate, on the EU's behalf, economic agreements with non-members, either bilaterally or in multinational bodies such as the World Trade Organization (WTO). The European Commission is served by an international secretariat, located mostly in Brussels (some parts are in Luxembourg). The secretariat employs over 25,000 people, many of whom are translators—there are 23 official languages in the EU—as well as others used in meetings and deliberations.

Comprising 27 judges (one judge per country), the **Court of Justice** makes certain that EU legislation, which is also known as "community law," is evenly and fairly interpreted and applied in all member states. The court has the power to settle legal disputes between member states, EU institutions, businesses, and individuals. It also adjudicates, at the request of a national court, on the interpretation or validity of points of EU law. At the request of an EU institution, member state, or individual citizen, the court can declare void any legal instruments adopted by national governments, the commission, or Council of Ministers that are incompatible with EU law.

Based in Luxembourg, the **Court of Auditors** comprises 27 members (one from each country) appointed for six-year terms. It functions as the financial watchdog of the EU. The court reports annually on the implementation of the budget and examines whether revenues and expenditures have been handled in a lawful and proper manner. The court may also issue special reports on specific questions and deliver opinions at the request of other EU institutions. In co-operation with national audit authorities, it can carry out investigations in individual member states. (Canada's auditor general performs similar functions.)

The **European Central Bank (ECB)** was set up in 1998 to prepare the EU for its new single currency, the euro. Since the euro came into circulation on 1 January 2002, the ECB has been responsible for framing and implementing the EU's economic and monetary policy. The 17 members of the EU "euro area" or "Eurozone" (i.e. states using the euro; see p. 260) and their central banks, together with the ECB, make up what is called the Eurosystem. Located in Frankfurt, Germany, the ECB works with the European System of Central Banks (ESCB), which covers all the EU countries, including those that have not

Court of Justice
EU court; responsible for ensuring that EU legislation is evenly and fairly interpreted in all member states; can also settle legal disputes between EU entities and declare certain legal instruments as incompatible with EU law

Court of Auditors
a body of the European Union that provides financial oversight on budget, revenues, and expenditures

European Central Bank (ECB)
independent central bank of the EU that implements economic and monetary policy

adopted the euro. The ECB is independent, meaning that neither the member states nor EU institutions can try to influence it or the national central banks. To maintain the euro's stability, the ECB is tasked with managing price stability in the EU and safeguarding the euro's purchasing power. It does so by controlling money supply (monetary policy) and monitoring price trends in the euro area.

Other important institutional agencies of the EU include the European Economic and Social Committee (EESC), an advisory body designed to give various economic and social interest groups an influence on EU policy; the Committee of the Regions, an advisory body composed of representatives from Europe's regional and local authorities ensuring that such identities and prerogatives are respected; and the European Ombudsman, who deals with complaints from citizens concerning maladministration by an EU institution.

The complicated politics and interrelationships between the various institutions of the EU operate on transnational, transgovernmental, and international levels. Moreover, the decision-making process involves a whole network of transactions and official contacts that cut across lines of national jurisdiction. In EU law, the principle of **subsidiarity** defines the division of powers. Decisions, it is thought, should be made as "closely" to the citizen as possible, meaning that member states will have authority on matters where they would best act alone, and the EU will regulate in areas where a common approach would be preferable.

Two major developments affecting the EU over the last 20 years bear mention. First, a common market was created with the ratification of the **Single European Act** in 1987. This Act removed **non-tariff barriers** (**NTBs**) to the free movement of goods, services, capital, and labour in 1993. Examples of such barriers include national preferences in government purchases, different national safety standards and product specifications, different criteria for professional qualifications, and exchange controls. In the years since, the EU has established itself as the most ambitious example of an existing multinational common market.

The second event was the establishment of the Economic and Monetary Union (EMU) in 1999 and the previously mentioned introduction of the euro. A common currency was discussed as early as 1969, but didn't get much attention until the creation of the European Monetary System (EMS), which fixed exchange rates among members, in 1979. Seventeen states joined the EMU: Austria, Belgium, Cyprus, Estonia, Finland, France, Germany, Greece, Ireland, Italy, Luxembourg, Malta, the Netherlands, Portugal, Slovakia, Slovenia, and Spain. Their currencies were removed from circulation and replaced by the euro. A few states joined after 1999: Greece (2001), Slovenia (2007), Malta and Cyprus (2008), and Estonia (2011).

The Eurozone was severely challenged in 2010 as a result of the global economic crisis that began two years earlier. After more than a decade of relative success, the Eurozone was threatened by its own diversity. Some countries, such as Germany and France, were relatively protected by their careful economic

subsidiarity
principle of law in the EU dictating division of powers; states that decisions should be made at the lowest governmental level whenever possible

Single European Act
European removal of non-tariff barriers, allowing the free movement of goods, services, capital, and labour; ratified in 1987

non-tariff barriers (NTBs)
national content requirements on certain products or quotas on their import

planning, solid systems of social welfare, and strength in production. Others, including Greece, Portugal, Ireland, and Spain, were more seriously affected and were unable to manage their balance of payments and budgetary commitments. Crippling national debts led these countries to seek a financial stability package from other Eurozone members. Despite the funds made available— over 750 billion euro—many countries saw their credit rating drop drastically. Many economists speculated that it would cause the Eurozone to break up, but EU members (particularly France and Germany) have stated that they would not allow this to occur.

Throughout the process of EU integration, politics has been the driving force. Not only is it about the politics of who gets what, when, and where at both the national and subnational levels but also about the contemporary role of nation-states, the redefinition of what Europe is, and the future for the region. How the EU operates is driven by the vital interests of these historical nation-states. Today, it may be said that it is not so much the survival of the members that is at issue but their role in a highly interdependent Europe and the terms of their co-operation.

Conclusion

The years following World War II brought significant challenges to developed countries. The reconstruction effort required much of their resources, and the growing integration of their economies took on a whole new approach with the rapid enlargement of the welfare state. This new interdependent relationship between a country's economy and political structure became more outward-looking as nations increasingly relied on one another for trade and commerce. Economic stability and growth is a key element of a modern state's political stability and reputation internationally. Therefore, countries focused more on the welfare goals of their citizens as the need to concentrate entirely on military and defensive security became less important than in the past.

As we will see in the following chapter, developing states have their own set of concerns, which are often quite different from those of the developed world. Yet one of the main themes that binds both types of nations is their focus on growth and change in an increasingly competitive environment.

Self-Assessment Questions

1. How did countries alter their view of security and economics after World War II? How was this change affected by the welfare state?
2. Describe how Canada's political and economic system is so intricately tied to that of the United States.
3. American hegemony has changed a great deal since the end of World War II. Are there real challengers to US power on the horizon? Give reasons to support your answer.
4. What was the Japanese MITI miracle, and how did it relate to the Yoshida Doctrine?
5. The EU offers a distinctive mode of developing political and economic systems in a very competitive global environment. What are the main institutions of the EU? How do they interrelate, and how do they limit the sovereignty of its member states?

Weblinks

CBC News In Depth: September 11
www.cbc.ca/news/background/sep11/

Europa: European Union Online
http://europa.eu/index_en.htm

Japanese Government Links
http://web-japan.org/links/government/index.html

Further Reading

Caramani, Daniele, ed. *Comparative Politics*. 2nd edn. Oxford: Oxford University Press, 2011.
Clemens, Walter C., Jr. *America and the World, 1898–2025: Achievements, Failures, Alternative Futures*. Houndmills, UK: Palgrave Macmillan, 2000.
Hayes, Louis D. *Introduction to Japanese Politics*. 5th edn. Armonk, NY: M.E. Sharpe, 2004.
Mintz, Eric, Livianna Tossutti, and Christopher Dunn. *Democracy, Diversity, and Good Government*. Toronto: Pearson, 2011.
O'Brien, Robert, and Marc Williams. *Global Political Economy*. 3rd edn. New York: Palgrave Macmillan, 2010.
O'Connor, Karen, and Larry J. Sabato. *American Government: Continuity and Change*. 11th edn. New York: Longman, 2011.
Yeşilada, Birol A., and David M. Wood. *The Emerging European Union*. 5th edn. New York: Longman, 2010.

News Clips

Visit the companion website for *Politics: An Introduction*, 2nd edn, to access news clips related to the content of this chapter.

10

Politics in Developing States

LEARNING OBJECTIVES

After reading this chapter, you will be able to

● define the terms *development* and *developing*;

● assess the importance of democratization;

● identify the link between political and economic development; and

● compare and contrast the political and economic challenges currently facing developing countries.

Introduction

Developing countries face many of the same problems as those nations we consider to be developed. Issues of justice, equality, economic growth and stability, and inflation all feature in the political debates and conflicts of states in Latin America, Africa, Asia, and Eastern Europe. Governments, citizens, and corporations in developing countries, however, confront a wide range of challenges that the nations of Western Europe, Scandinavia, North America, and Japan have already overcome or that are unique to political and economic development in the early twenty-first century. These problems include overpopulation, disease control, capital flight, environmental degradation, democratization, public order, and the creation of a viable infrastructure.

In this chapter, we will examine the political and economic systems of **less developed countries** (LDCs), particularly those of China, Mexico, India, and Mali. These countries face many challenges, some of which they have in common.[1] Each has taken a markedly different development path that has presented them with obstacles large and small, short- and long-term, national and international. At the beginning of the twenty-first century, such problems pose a strong challenge to the stability and well-being of the world's developing countries, but they also provide the student of political economy with a myriad of interesting research cases. As we will see, the dual challenges of political and economic development are linked. Many developing countries face a difficult situation in which they must stabilize their economies—an often painful

less developed countries (LDCs) countries that may be characterized by low levels of per capita income, high inflation and debt, large trade deficits, low levels of socioeconomic development, a lack of industrialization, or undeveloped financial or legal systems

process for ordinary people in economic terms—while they try to consolidate democratic practices and the legitimacy of their regimes.

A word should be said about the terminology used in this chapter. The poorer countries in the international system have been referred to in a number of ways. During the Cold War, they were known by some as the Third World (after the First World of Western industrialized states and the Second World of the communist bloc). Others (quite inaccurately in geographic terms) divided the world into North (the wealthy countries) and **South** (the poorer states). Today's financial analysts and economists talk of "emerging markets," poorer economies with potential for future growth. This chapter, however, prefers to use the terms *LDCs* and *developing countries*.

South
categorization of less developed nations that are not part of a structurally integrated system of global capitalism

Political and Social Development

For many years, development was seen in a purely economic sense, implying growth and industrialization of the economy and little else. Scholars have gradually come to see the problems of development in a multi-dimensional manner and have accepted that progress must be understood in various ways and that truly developed societies must provide more than just economic benefits for their members. For example, citizens should be involved in the decisions that affect their futures, through group representation, direct democracy, or perhaps decentralization of power. The governing of society should be less arbitrary and more rules-oriented, guaranteeing due process of law and security of person. Of course, economic growth should be a priority, but it has become obvious to us that the issue is far more complex. Questions of distribution, stability, and the compatibility between growth and environmental protection are fundamental in building a sustainable development path.

Although there are a large number of LDCs that are young states, many having been created since the end of World War II and the retreat of colonialism (see p. 234), some have been in existence for hundreds or, in the case of China, thousands of years. They often share a lack of developed political institutions and well-established civil societies. What their societies seek in their development paths are essentially the political values (justice, order, freedom, etc.) described in Chapter 2. One of the most common values sought by developing country governments is legitimacy. In some cases, their short history as independent states makes it difficult for governments to achieve true validity in the eyes of the people. In others, it is not the brevity but the turbulence of their history that makes legitimacy an elusive goal.

Democracy, the issue that has come to dominate discussions of political development in recent decades, is one way to achieve legitimacy in the eyes of both national and international societies. Since the end of the Cold War, democratization has been seen by both national and international authorities and organizations as a priority for developing countries, a political liberalization to go hand in hand with the progressive (and in some cases rather rapid)

10.1 THE HUMAN DEVELOPMENT INDEX

Instead of focusing exclusively on the size of a nation's economy, or even on the size of the economy per person, the UN decided to employ a broader indicator of national development that considers a wide range of relevant factors. The Human Development Index (HDI) uses a combined measurement of income, life expectancy, and literacy to determine the level of individual development granted by national economies. These factors are chosen because they increase an individual's freedom to direct and control his or her own life. The index gives a rating to each country; the closer that number is to one, the higher its level of development. Countries such as Norway, Australia, and the Netherlands frequently appear at the top of this list with ratings above 0.95, but most of the world's LDCs don't fare as well. Countries such as China feature in the middle of the list (0.77), but Niger comes in at number 186 overall, with an HDI rating of only 0.34. It is noteworthy that all but one of the bottom 20 countries on the list are African states.

TABLE 10.1 | HUMAN DEVELOPMENT INDEX 2011: TOP 20 NATIONS VS. BOTTOM 20

Top 20 Countries (High Human Development)	Bottom 20 Countries (Low Human Development)
1. Norway	168. Gambia
2. Australia	169. Zambia
3. The Netherlands	170. Côte d'Ivoire
4. The United States	171. Malawi
5. New Zealand	172. Afghanistan
6. Canada	173. Zimbabwe
7. Ireland	174. Ethiopia
8. Liechtenstein	175. Mali
9. Germany	176. Guinea-Bissau
10. Sweden	177. Eritrea
11. Switzerland	178. Guinea
12. Japan	179. Central African Republic
13. Hong Kong	180. Sierra Leone
14. Iceland	181. Burkina Faso
15. Republic of Korea	182. Liberia
16. Denmark	183. Chad
17. Israel	184. Mozambique
18. Belgium	185. Burundi
19. Austria	186. Niger
20. France	187. Congo (Democratic Republic of the)

Source: UNDP (United Nations Development Programme). 2011. *Human Development Report 2011: Sustainability and Equity: A Better Future for All.* http://hdr.undp.org/en/reports/global/hdr2011/.

liberalization of their economies. By including all adult citizens in the electoral process and allowing voters to choose their government rather than having it imposed upon them, a democratic political system helps to guarantee its own survival. As we will see in this chapter's examination of specific countries, however, democratization is a complex and controversial issue. Democracy is difficult to institute in society, as the process in Western Europe between the eighteenth and twentieth centuries demonstrated. It requires the overthrow of established power elites and the creation of strong institutions that guarantee democratic representation. At a fundamental level, it requires the presence of a liberal ideology that will drive individuals and groups to fight for democracy.

It should not be thought that democracy acts as a cure-all for the political challenges faced by developing countries. Democracy cannot, for example, on its own rectify deep social divisions or guarantee justice. It cannot eliminate the use of violence as a means of exercising power or the political advantages conferred by wealth. Democracy does not imply stability or even security and is not necessarily the best-suited system for all societies. Most of human political history has been undemocratic (and even anti-democratic). The norm throughout history has been repression of the many by the few, of might equalling right. Even those societies (tribal or otherwise) that have been egalitarian in nature have been based on the group or family rather than the individual. Many societies today still hold the group in higher regard than the individual and may thus not be ideally suited for democracy as practised by European and North American states.

On the other hand, liberal democracy appeals to us for the reasons we saw earlier in this book. Morally, it makes sense to us as North Americans to accord every individual member of our society the same right to decide his or her political future. A commitment to democratic values means seeking peaceful resolutions to conflict before resorting to violence. Democracy, when applied in its Western form, means including groups and minorities, a quality that leads to a higher probability of stability and sense of community. Just as important, the history of many developing countries demonstrates that non-democratic regimes find that they are sooner or later unable to hold on to power, even if they are not then replaced by democratic regimes.[2]

As we saw in Chapter 9, democracy works in developed countries such as Canada, the United States, and Japan and in Europe because of the political institutions that enforce and implement its principles. Institutions such as a competitive party system, parliaments or congresses in which elected representatives may not only voice the concerns of the electorate but also influence the policy process, and electoral commissions that ensure that elections meet universally accepted rules and regulations all encourage the use of democratic and non-violent means of resolving political conflicts. As we will see in the case of Mexico, free and fair elections require an independent federal elections commission as well as the involvement of observers from other countries and from international organizations. If democracy is going to work and become embedded in a country's political culture, it is crucial that the electoral system function effectively. This means choosing a system that adequately represents the views and interests of significant minority groups and parties while ensuring stability and a government's ability to both pass and implement legislation.

A free and independent media establishment is one of the private institutions that are desirable for democracy to function effectively, yet in most LDCs it has remained an elusive goal. Some governments control television, radio, and newspapers with little viable competition, whereas others enforce severe reporting restrictions and censorship regulations that allow them to control the flow of information. China is a good example of this practice. Not only does the Chinese government control the flow of information, but it also censors the arts to prevent criticism of its own activities and has been active in prohibiting Internet access (see Box 10.2). For many developing countries, there is still a shortage of access to reliable information and independent evaluation of the government and political system. However, as technology has become cheaper and access to televisions, computers, and mobile devices more common, there has been a positive effect on both the spread and consolidation of democracy.[3]

Not all political institutions are concerned with democracy, though they can help to consolidate its place in society. The structure of political parties greatly influences the ability of the state to formulate and implement policy.[4] Some other institutions help governments to rule. A well-run, professional, and independent bureaucracy will grant the government the expertise it needs to govern a country efficiently.

A reliable, predictable, egalitarian, and transparent legal system is essential to achieve legal justice, ensure equal and predictable treatment for a country's citizens, and help resolve private conflicts peacefully. Attaining justice is a vital element of political and social development because without it the government will face constant opposition from those treated unfairly by the system. Increasingly, the search for justice in LDCs is focused on respect for human rights as understood by international society. A high level of human rights abuses is a strong signal that a country is socially and politically underdeveloped, although

10.2   THE BEIJING OLYMPICS AND INTERNET CENSORSHIP

In 2008, the eyes of the world fell on Beijing as it hosted the summer Olympic Games. This was an opportunity for China to show the world how far it had come in terms of economic, political, and social development over the past 30 years. The infrastructure, planning, and the Games themselves were a huge success, generating enormous global television audiences. However, it became clear early on that the Chinese government was censoring journalists' access to the Internet in the official media centre. The government had promised "complete freedom to report" in its Olympic bid, but journalists found that they were unable to access websites related to human rights issues, Chinese politics, or Tibet. Despite international outcry at the censorship and some slight changes in the level of control, journalists were never able to attain complete, unrestricted access during the Games.

developed countries also commit such offences from time to time and, in some Asian countries, human rights are seen as a Western idea imposed on their culture. Three of the countries studied in depth in this chapter (China, Mexico, and Mali) have consistently been under international scrutiny for their human rights records in recent years, although each has used different methods to deal with this situation.

A country's legal system is also an important weapon in the fight against corruption. This particular problem has become high profile in recent years as international aid agencies have linked their programs to efforts to reduce the influence of corruption in developing countries. There is an important connection between anti-corruption policies and democracy: a system's benefits cannot be universally shared and enjoyed if they are reserved for those with economic, social, or political influence. The legal system must be seen to apply equally to all if all are to respect that system. Likewise, the government and the bureaucracy won't be seen as legitimate if people don't have free and equal access to them.[5]

Restraining the non-legitimate use of violence is a further political challenge for developing countries. Around the world, national governments fail to control all their territory or face significant challenges from guerrilla groups or from organized crime. In Africa, Asia, and Latin America, such groups threaten not just the sovereignty of states but also their survival in their present forms. The existence of rival military factions in a country may signify military weakness on the part of the government, but (more important) it denotes a lack of universal legitimacy. The same can be said of governments who fail to keep public order in their cities and towns. When there is rioting and widespread disrespect for the rule of law, governments must take measures (through either reform or suppression tactics) to ensure that the social and political systems survive.

A perennial issue for many LDCs has been the military's role in politics. Where it has not been placed under strict civilian control in a state's constitution, and thus restricted to a legitimate and restrained role in national affairs, the military tends to intervene in political life, especially during times of political, social, and economic crisis. Most such interventions claim to be in the broader national interest, and military leaders often argue that such actions are necessary to restore the right conditions for a successful democracy. Many military coups are carried out on the principle that military rule will be temporary; yet most have retained control over politics much longer than they first promised.

Another concern involving the issue of force is territorial integrity. Although almost all developed countries have held their present geographic boundaries for extended periods of time, many developing countries are involved in border disputes and conflicts with neighbouring states. It was 1998 before Peru and Ecuador settled their border dispute, which began in 1941 with a war over the regions of El Oro and Loja.[6] India and Pakistan continue to come to blows periodically regarding the region of Kashmir, over which they both claim sovereignty. Such conflicts are partially the result of the complex and often messy

10.3 COLOMBIA: THE WAR ON DRUGS AND THE FARC

Colombia is a developing South American country that faces a host of challenges relating to economic and political development. However, Colombia has become synonymous over the past decade with the twin problems of drug trafficking and armed insurgency, both of which seriously test the state's integrity and the prospects for sustained development. Fundamental to understanding the problems of development in Colombia are the high levels of inequality that have marked the country's history.

The last decade of the twentieth century saw a progressive deterioration of government control of large areas of Colombian territory because drug cartels and rebel groups attacked government forces and corrupted government officials. However, in 2002 Álvaro Uribe came to power and immediately launched an all-out offensive against left-wing rebels, in particular the Fuerzas Armadas Revolucionarias de Colombia (FARC), and against the drug lords. The Uribe government used a multi-pronged attack involving intelligence, military action, and international co-operation to achieve significant successes against both the drug cartels and the FARC, securing the release of long-term hostage Ingrid Betancourt. With considerable military assistance from the United States through Plan Colombia—an anti-drug initiative from the Bush administration—the government has beaten

Ingrid Betancourt (centre right) was released from captivity during a crackdown by Colombian President Álvaro Uribe.

back guerrilla groups. Though armed rebel groups remain active throughout the country, the FARC has been vanquished from most urban areas and appears to be on the verge of collapse. The war on drugs continues, but the Uribe government's determined approach seems to have turned the tide for the Colombian state.

situations left behind by withdrawing colonial powers. In colonial Africa, for example, borders were drawn without significant references to tribal or ethnic distribution, resulting in a number of prolonged conflicts. The war in Biafra, Nigeria, from 1967 to 1970, the war between Eritrea and Ethiopia, and the conflict between Somalia and Somaliland all stand out as legacies of colonialism.

Frequently, however, territorial disputes also arise when national leaders seek to consolidate their domestic power and influence by unifying the electorate and important domestic constituencies behind a national cause involving conflict with a neighbouring state. As long as a nation's territorial boundaries are disputed, there will probably be an enhanced role for the military in that country's political life. What's more, it is likely that a developing country will be forced to divert valuable resources from other more deserving and productive purposes.

One such productive purpose, which has unfortunately remained a secondary goal in a large number of LDCs, is public education. The majority of

10.4 AIDS AND THE DEVELOPING WORLD

Due to the effect of weak education and health systems, the countries of the developing world have been harder hit by the global AIDS crisis than their developed counterparts have. Infection rates are higher, treatment is relatively more expensive and largely unavailable, and social stigma and prejudices regarding the disease are more widespread.

The continent that continues to be hardest hit by the spread of the virus is Africa. The infection rate is rising daily in Africa, and there seems to be little that health authorities, both national and from international organizations such as the World Health Organization (WHO), can do to stop it from spreading. Part of the problem stems from a lack of education, part from cultural values preventing the use of condoms, and part from economic realities. In Africa, many men are forced to travel far from their homes to find work, spending months away from their families. While separated from their wives, many of these migrant workers will have (usually unprotected) sex with local prostitutes. Because so many men have sexual relations with the same prostitutes, the rate of infection is very high. These men then go back to their wives, to whom they pass on the disease.

In recent years, some progress has been made in tackling the problem of treatment as developing countries such as Brazil, South Africa, and India have broken international patents on medicines to produce cheaper, generic versions of the drugs. This improvement has helped treat those already infected, although the infection rate is still frighteningly high.

TABLE 10.2 | THE PROBLEM OF AIDS: ADULTS AND CHILDREN LIVING WITH HIV (2010)

Global	33,300,000
Sub-Saharan Africa	22,500,000
East Asia	740,000
Oceania	57,000
South and South East Asia	4,100,000
Eastern Europe and Central Asia	1,400,000
Western and Central Europe	820,000
North Africa and the Middle East	460,000
North America	1,500,000
Caribbean	240,000
Central and South America	1,400,000

Source: UNAIDS Report on the Global AIDS epidemic 2010 (available at http://www.unaids.org/globalreport/Global_report.htm)

developing countries have failed to develop effective systems regarding this area, which hinders not only economic development but also the development of mature political and social institutions. The problems of instituting a comprehensive system of public education are enormous; not the least of them is the fact that, in most LDCs, child labour is very common and indeed necessary for many families if they are to generate sufficient income.

Another vital social issue is health care. Modern health care systems are incredibly expensive to run, absorbing more than 10 per cent of the GDP of countries such as Canada. LDCs, which have much smaller economies and tax bases but generally much larger populations, are in no position to provide comprehensive health care at the level found in the developed world. Thus

10.5   EDUCATION, GENDER, AND THE OPORTUNIDADES PROGRAM

A major challenge facing most developing countries is education. Throughout the developing world, children drop out of education at an early age, leaving them ill-equipped to deal with the challenges of the modern world. The problem is particularly marked for girls. Parents often keep their daughters at home to help with household chores or to work in the fields because they believe that education is wasted on women.

In 2002, the Mexican government initiated Oportunidades (Opportunities), a new social program aimed at getting more children to stay in school, at least through secondary school. By paying mothers a bonus depending on the age of the child and his or her attendance record, the program has been highly successful in boosting school attendance. An interesting, though controversial, aspect of the program is that mothers receive more money from the state if their daughters continue to attend school than if their sons do. This incentive has helped to increase female school attendance drastically. Serious questions remain, however, over the quality of the education received and whether the program is making a real difference in women's lives.

the majority of LDC citizens face a life plagued by the worry of ill-health and disease, which in turn has an enormous cost for the economy.[7] To compound the problem, sexually transmitted diseases such as AIDS and insect- and water-borne diseases such as malaria and cholera are much more common in the developing world. For some countries in Africa, AIDS has become a threat not just to individuals and families but also to the strength of nations as a whole.

Questions of gender have also risen in importance recently. Whereas women in the developed world made many important strides toward gender equality in political, social, and economic spheres in the twentieth century, women in most LDCs continue to face a far more difficult future than men do. Women earn much less than men for similar work (which remains the case in most developed countries as well), and many are denied reliable access to the vote, health care, and education.

Economic Development

The previous section outlined several challenges for LDC governments; however, the biggest one is economic development. This area is a highly contentious issue, both in the real world and in academic studies, and no sure path to economic development has been found. While some LDCs, particularly the **newly industrializing countries (NICs)** of Asia, experienced high levels of growth from the 1960s to the late 1990s, developing countries in other parts of the world were unable to replicate this outcome.[8] Since the 1980s, the dominant philosophy of economic growth has been liberal, but its results are as yet uncertain. Debates continue to rage in most developing countries about the wisdom and benefits of free markets and open economies. The future of economic

newly industrializing countries (NICs)
countries benefiting from external trade relationships, growing export markets, and burgeoning industrial development

development still seems to lie in liberal models, but questions continue to be raised about their sustainability (see p. 81).

Although economic growth is an important factor, it is not enough to secure development. A number of other conditions must be met if economic growth is to have a positive impact on living standards. For example, the economy should grow at a rate higher than that of the population. If the population grows faster than the economy, the benefits received by individuals will gradually decline. Further, benefits and costs of economic development should be equitably distributed among society's members if widespread support for the development program is to remain.

Just as important for a country's long-term economic development is the concept of sustainability. *Sustainable development* is a term that came into widespread use in the 1990s and marked an entirely new approach to the development dilemma. Sustainable development recognizes that many models of economic growth result in severe environmental degradation and the use of non-renewable resources. Although such models may initially succeed, they are unsustainable in the longer term. Sustainable development seeks a model of economic growth that does not rely on non-renewable resources and does not destroy the environment in which human beings have to live. Essentially, it is a development path that does not compromise the ability of future generations to meet their own development goals. This is, of course, a very simple and logical calculation, at least in theory. Its application has proven much more complex because strategies based on this concept have tended to be more expensive than others and have been slow to produce tangible gains.

Economic development has to be sustainable in other ways. It must not produce cycles of boom and bust, phases that have afflicted many developing countries over the years. Economic growth should ideally be more steady and progressive, producing smaller gains in the short term but greater benefits in the medium and long terms. The chosen path of economic growth should also be politically sustainable, which generally means ensuring that the benefits of

10.6 THE BRUNDTLAND COMMISSION REPORT AND SUSTAINABLE DEVELOPMENT

In 1987, the World Commission on Environment and Development (the Brundtland Commission) issued its report, *Our Common Future*. This report prescribed a development path for LDCs that did not "compromise the capacity of future generations to satisfy their own needs" and outlined the concept of sustainable development. Though this proposal seems uncontroversial, many developing country governments have seen it otherwise. They have argued that the notion of sustainable development is another way that the wealthy countries have tried to pass the costs for environmental protection onto the poor while those same wealthy countries long ago destroyed their own forests and have pumped billions of tons of pollutants into the earth, oceans, and atmosphere.

Kuznets effect
economic formula that
demonstrates that, as
a country develops
economically, income
distribution will become
more unequal before it
becomes more equal;
named after Simon
Kuznets, the Russian-
American economist who
formulated this concept

economic growth are widely dispersed and that the population experiences an improvement in its standard of living. Connected to this issue is the commonly observed **Kuznets effect**. This economic formula demonstrates that, as a country develops economically, income distribution will become more unequal before it becomes more equal. In the short to medium term, then, developing countries are likely to experience a widening gap between rich and poor. This situation has been one of the main criticisms of Mexico's liberal model of economic development. As the country becomes more democratic, the divergence becomes a greater problem for the government. India is also experiencing a large income gap between rich and poor as growth increases. China faces a similar problem that may become a political one as the gap between rural and urban populations widens.

Since the mid-twentieth century, the developing world has attempted both integration with and isolation from the wealthy countries and the international system. Purely national development proved too slow and inefficient for most LDCs in the postwar period, which was one of the factors that propelled them to attempt liberalization and the opening of their economies in the 1980s. However, the international financial and economic crises that hit many LDCs in the second half of the 1990s caused a re-evaluation of openness and, particularly in some parts of South America, governments and societies have turned away from liberalism to more socialist economic models.

The Link between Political and Economic Development

One of the most perplexing and challenging aspects of development studies is the analysis of the connection between political and economic development. The argument that sustainable economic growth and stability cannot be achieved without stable democratic institutions is often made. Almost as frequently, we hear that workable democracy cannot be achieved without first obtaining high rates of economic growth.[9] Certainly, the connection has often been made between economic liberalization and democratization, particularly in the aftermath of the end of the Cold War and the dual transitions in Eastern Europe.

Yet the relationship between these two spheres remains elusive. There does appear to be a connection between economic development and progress on the one hand and more stable democratic institutions on the other. In countries where socioeconomic inequality reaches high levels, democracy is often under threat. But some analysts have claimed that undemocratic regimes may actually be better suited to the business of reforming and modernizing an LDC economy, often citing Chile's experience under General Augusto Pinochet or, as we will see in this chapter, China's since the late 1970s. The argument here is that economic liberalization and reform incur high levels of social and political costs and that an autocratic or authoritarian regime is better equipped to deal with the resulting pressures than other systems are. These two examples, however, do not seem to be representative. A more thorough examination of LDCs demonstrates that democracy actually contributes to stability, and stability to the prospects for economic growth.

Population Growth

A perennial challenge for most developing countries is the size of their populations and, more important, the rate of population growth. LDCs with an annual growth rate of 2 per cent experience a doubling of their populations every 30 to 35 years. (If the rate is closer to 3.5 per cent, the population will double every 25 years.) This increase can put immense strains on the economic system. New jobs, new housing, and education must be provided for all these new people.

One of the costs of population growth comes in the form of government services. Providing health care and public utilities (e.g. potable water, electricity) for a rapidly expanding population is enormously costly. Such populations also lead to massive human migrations, both within and outside a country. As can be seen in the case of Mexico, high levels of migration lead to strains on government services and on US–Mexico relations.

Controlling a nation's population might avoid such problems, but the issue is a highly contentious one. The use of contraceptives is still limited in many countries (particularly in Africa and Latin America) for cultural and religious reasons, and overcoming these obstacles has proven incredibly difficult. China, as we will see, achieved considerable success in limiting population growth in the latter part of the twentieth century, but only through policies that were repressive and highly intrusive into the private lives of its citizens.

10.7 THE POLITICS OF POPULATION: NIGERIA

The ever present tensions between the regions and ethnic groups of Nigeria have made the question of regional population size a perennial issue of debate. In 1962, the government conducted a census to determine the correct distribution of political power and financial resources. The census became a heavily contested matter and the importance invested in it was reflected in its results and the reaction to them. First, the census showed that the southern part of the country had grown rapidly in size, to the point where it surpassed the historically more populous northern part. Second, it quickly became clear that the figures for the eastern region were inflated. In response, the north announced that it had overlooked eight million people in its region, a number sufficient to restore its numerical superiority.

When the census effort was repeated a year later, the outcome was even more ridiculous. The results showed that the population had increased by over 80 per cent in the last 10 years but still with a northern majority. Despite this incredible outcome, the north's political forces managed to secure official acceptance of the census, thus guaranteeing them higher levels of support from the federal government.

Furthermore, population growth can eventually become a strength.[10] China's enormous population will constitute the world's largest national market at some point in the first half of the twenty-first century, giving the country increased economic influence in the international system. India's population is growing even more rapidly than China's, and its recent burst of economic growth has turned it into a force with which to be reckoned.

The Role of International Organizations

The international aspect of development has become more and more important to LDCs in recent years. The World Bank and the IMF have been the most prominent organizations in this regard. Though the latter is not officially a development organization, its financial facilities are used almost exclusively by LDCs. The lending activities of these two organizations have been essential in rescuing developing countries in Asia, Africa, and Latin America from economic and financial crises.

A strong and credible criticism of international development organizations in recent history has been that they try to impose neo-liberal, free-market policies upon LDC governments. In many of the developing world's crises during the past 30 years, we have seen the IMF and the World Bank behaving in this way, even when a country is not prepared for the high levels of competition that ensue.

China: The Politics of an Emerging Global Power

With approximately 1.3 billion inhabitants, China is the world's most populous country. It will also, at some point in the twenty-first century, have the world's largest economy. China is a nuclear power and occupies one of the five permanent seats on the United Nations Security Council. In international summits such as the G20, China is seen as one of the essential participants, alongside the United States and the EU. Over the past 35 years, China has achieved very high and sustained rates of economic growth. It has managed to pull hundreds of millions of its citizens out of poverty and has provided a strong stimulus for economic growth at the global level.

Yet for all of these qualities, China still faces some serious and deep-rooted problems. A large percentage of its citizens remain in poverty. China's political system continues to be highly undemocratic, and there are few signs of it changing in the near future. Health care and environmental protection are still woefully underdeveloped, and there are significant ethnic and regional tensions across the country.

This section studies the politics of China and addresses the major challenges lying ahead for the Chinese people and their government. It shows us a country that is indelibly marked by its history and one in which economic reform has not been accompanied by real political change.

CHINA'S POLITICAL SYSTEM

The People's Republic of China (PRC) is a single-party socialist republic in which power rests with the president, the **Chinese Communist Party (CCP)**, the Central People's Government (the federal government), and provincial and local governments. Although power is highly centralized at the federal level, there is significant autonomy for provincial governments in the area of economic policy, which has increased steadily since the 1980s.

The CCP and government are intimately entwined, with the head or general secretary of the party generally serving as president (the head of state) as well. The position is currently held by Xi Jinping. The president officially shares power with the National People's Congress (NPC) and the State Council, both of which are dominated by the party. The NPC has the power to elect and to change the president. However, in many ways it is the office of the general secretary of the party that is the centre of political power in China and the Politburo, or more specifically the Standing Committee of the Politburo (the elite steering committee of the CCP), that serves as the president's cabinet and decides on all major policy issues.

Although the country is a single-party state, eight other parties exist. However, they lack independence, accept the leadership of the CCP, and serve to legitimize its activities. In the absence of competitive parties, elections mean very little in China, although there have been experiments in recent years with open elections at the local level.

CHINESE HISTORY: THE HERITAGE OF IMPERIALISM AND REVOLUTION

Long before the countries of Western Europe had organized themselves into coherent nation-states that we would recognize today, the Chinese empire had united a huge territory and many disparate peoples under one system of government, using the strong arm of military force to bring them peace, prosperity, and innovation. During the more than 2,000 years of imperial rule, China developed a mode of government that was highly authoritarian, would use violence to suppress dissent, and stressed the value of the group over that of the individual. This governmental and cultural tradition continues to exert a strong influence on modern China, though in the early twenty-first century the pervasive values of Western culture are knocking hard at China's door.

The end of China's imperial history came with an armed uprising in 1911–12. This conflict ushered in a long period of civil war in which regional warlords struggled for supremacy and two parties, the Nationalist Kuomintang Party (KMT) and the CCP, struggled for control of the country's government.[11] During a brief alliance in the late 1920s, the KMT turned on the CCP and slaughtered hundreds of thousands of its supporters. After that, the latter party split into two competing factions. The more successful of these was led by Mao Zedong (sometimes written as Mao Tse Tung and also known as Chairman

Chinese Communist Party (CCP) governing political party in China, founded in 1921 as part of the revolutionary movement; committed to Marxist revolution

Mao); it turned away from the traditional socialist focus on the working class and toward the rural peasant class, a group that made up over 85 per cent of the Chinese population. Mao created the People's Liberation Army (PLA), a guerrilla army made up of poorly equipped peasants that was at first unable to withstand the KMT's professionally trained soldiers but which eventually became the country's dominant military force.[12]

Before and during World War II, China was occupied by Japanese forces, and this invasion of Chinese sovereignty discredited the KMT in the eyes of the Chinese people. With the close of the war, the civil conflict resumed and, this time, the PLA defeated the nationalist forces. By 1949, the KMT and its supporters withdrew to the nearby island of Taiwan (creating the Republic of China) while the PRC, led by Mao, was born on the mainland. Communist ideology governed policy in the PRC, with Mao developing his own branch, one based on constant vigilance against the forces of capitalism and the bourgeois. In practice, Mao's version of communism resulted in a turbulent and bloody period in the country's post-revolution history.

China's economy grew rapidly from 1949 to 1976, an achievement brought about by a series of policies in which the government played a central role. From 1949 to 1958, the government used Soviet-style policies of industrialization that had been employed in Stalinist Russia but which were ultimately unsuited to China's mostly agrarian economy. Over the next four years, Mao instituted the **Great Leap Forward**, a program of economic policies designed to revolutionize rural production by replacing private ownership of land with communes in which all agricultural production was to be sold to the state.[13] The chaos that ensued from this program resulted in the loss of, in some estimates, 25 million lives from starvation and malnutrition.

As horrific as these figures are, they represent only one of the more unpleasant features of Mao's rule over China. Until his death in 1976, Mao and his followers used terror tactics to maintain control and to weed out dissident factions. Most infamous was his Cultural Revolution, in which Mao oversaw the creation of Red Guard units throughout the country, units that were aimed at eliminating any subversive bourgeois or capitalist elements in Chinese society. Families were split apart as children were encouraged to give evidence against their parents. During this program of repression, between 3 and 20 million people were killed.

THE ORIGINS OF MODERN CHINA

Politics as they transpire in China can only be understood if one understands the internal struggles and processes within the CCP. Even before Mao Zedong's death, Chinese political and economic development was determined and shaped by divisions such as the struggle between the Red faction, a radical Marxist group led by Mao, and the Expert faction, a more pragmatic grouping led by Chinese President Liu Shaoqi and the future leader of China, Deng Xiaoping. Though the Red faction was victorious in this struggle and Mao

Great Leap Forward
Chinese program of economic policies designed to revolutionize rural production by replacing private ownership of land with communes in which all agricultural production was to be sold to the state

imprisoned or executed many of the leading members of the Expert faction, the ideas of the latter group would come to dominate Chinese development by the late twentieth century.

Mao's passing was marked by a leadership struggle within the CCP. His widow and three of his most radical supporters, known collectively as the Gang of Four, were held as scapegoats and blamed for the horrors of the later years of Maoist rule. Hua Guofeng, Mao's immediate successor, had the Gang of Four arrested. Deng Xiaoping soon replaced Hua, and much of the old CCP cadre was weeded out.[14] Maoist policies and ideology were officially discredited, and the modernization of China began apace.

Yet the internal divisions within the CCP did not end there. Chinese development since the early 1980s has been defined by the struggle within the communist party between those, such as Deng, who favour a rapid transition toward a market-oriented economy and those who prefer a slow and gradual movement in the same direction. A radical return to communist production has long since ceased to be a viable alternative for the party and China, and adherents of such Maoist policies have no voice in the politics of modern China.

Today's CCP has over 50 million members and reaches every level of Chinese society. It is organized hierarchically from the national level—with the

10.8 THE TIANANMEN SQUARE MASSACRE

The economic boom that China experienced since Deng Xiaoping began his program of economic reforms brought not only increased wealth but also new political problems. These problems involved calls for democratization and greater choice in the political arena, as well as complaints brought on by a growing income gap between rich and poor and between rural and urban populations. The result of this growing discontent was a mass protest in Beijing's Tiananmen Square in the summer of 1989. For several weeks, protesters occupied the square, demanding that the Chinese political system be opened up. Coming as it did at the same time as the end of the Cold War, many Western observers predicted that this protest would mark the beginning of a similar political transition in China.

The reality, as it turned out, was quite the opposite. On 4 June, Chinese tanks rolled into the square, destroying protesters' barricades and killing several hundred people. International condemnation of the massacre was immediate, yet the Chinese government neither expressed remorse nor gave any sign of reforming the nation's political system.

One of the most memorable photos in history: a lone protester stands in front of Chinese tanks during the Tiananmen Square demonstrations.

AP Photo/Jef Widener/CP

Politburo and Standing Committee, which determine major policy directions and make important day-to-day decisions, situated at the top—down through provincial and local levels. Though the NPC officially serves as the highest authority in the CCP, it plays a relatively minor role in legitimizing rather than directing government policy, and the only other body at the national level that performs an important function is the Central Committee, which serves as a representative body for CCP members and votes on major policies. However, the NPC has at times played a role in displaying popular discontent with government policies, as happened in the debate over the Three Gorges Dam in 1992, which took place shortly after the Tiananmen Square massacre. The government is not directly accountable to the NPC, but the latter elects the Central Committee, and the government will face pressure from that body to respond to discontent manifested in the Congress.

This last example points to an often neglected fact of Chinese politics, namely, that pluralism exists in the system but in a very different form than in democratic systems in Canada and other advanced capitalist nations. Though the most important officials in the CCP do not depend on popular re-election for their mandates, they must always be mindful of their power bases in other areas, such as the military and main sections of the communist party. In her 1994 study of the liberalization of the Chinese economy, *How China Opened Its Door*, Susan Shirk[15] demonstrated this point by examining how economic reform depended upon support from within the government and party structure, as well as upon China's quite decentralized federal structure, for its success. Shirk found that the role of internal party support for economic reforms was of particular significance during times of political instability and especially during leadership struggles. As we learn more about the internal workings of the CCP, we should expect that this way of explaining Chinese politics will take on increasing importance.

CHINESE ECONOMIC REFORM

We tend to think that the emergence of a market-oriented economy in China began in the 1990s, with the end of the Cold War. In fact, the process began long before the fall of the Soviet Union was ever envisaged. The reform of the centrally planned Maoist economy of the 1970s began in earnest almost as soon as Mao died. Deng Xiaoping, who had proposed economic reform in the 1960s and been imprisoned for his audacity, led a steady process of introducing market-oriented practices to economic management.[16] From the late 1970s onward, the Chinese government began decentralizing production and economic decision-making, giving more power to the provinces, which served as an incentive for them to increase productivity. A further step was the institution of rural enterprise reform in 1979, when the system of collectives was gradually replaced with a system giving responsibility to household farms. These households were entitled to keep the profits they received from their agricultural production. Though they still had to sell their required quota to the state, they were allowed to sell any surplus goods at free-market prices. This incentive appears to have worked well, as productivity increased rapidly in the early 1980s.

Following on from rural reform, the Chinese government focused on expanding the non-state sector and increasing inter-firm competition in the economy. This program resulted in large increases in private sector employment and in productivity and competitiveness. Throughout the later 1980s and the 1990s, there were further market reforms and the gradual opening up of China's economy to foreign trade and investment with the implementation of the **Open Door Policy** and the creation of **special economic zones (SEZs)**.[17] By the end of the century, China was experiencing the highest levels of foreign investment in the world and was seeking membership in the World Trade Organization, the global trading regime.

The Chinese government, however, maintains active involvement in the economy. In addition to its role as economic planner and manager, the government also acts as banker and entrepreneur, continuing to control many state-owned industries. Large-scale privatization of Chinese industry had still not occurred by the end of the 1990s, but mergers and joint ventures with foreign MNCs had dramatically changed the shape of the Chinese economic landscape.

China has also been highly successful in controlling one of the most important areas of growth for most LDCs, that of the population. By limiting its citizens to one child per couple, the government has been able to contain population expansion to within reasonable limits. The methods used by the government, however, go against most Western conceptions of the right to privacy and freedom of choice. The government has severely limited the individual rights of many Chinese men and women, and this may be unsustainable in the future. On the positive side, real income growth throughout history has resulted in lower reproduction rates; therefore, this problem may in time solve itself.

The results of China's economic reforms are that the country has consistently experienced the highest rates of economic growth in the world, surpassing even the Asian Tigers (Hong Kong, Singapore, South Korea, and Taiwan) with annual rates of growth around 10 per cent. China's economic strength and sound management ensured that the country weathered the Asian economic crisis that began in 1997 without having to devalue its currency or deal with high levels of capital flight.

At the time of writing, China is experiencing an economic slowdown, with growth rates dropping from 8.1 per cent to 7.6 per cent a year. Although this figure may sound like an impressive growth rate by Canadian standards, it is dangerously low in relation to China's trajectory over the past 30 years and threatens the delicate balance by which Chinese citizens accept one-party rule in exchange for high rates of growth. Restarting growth as the Chinese economy matures is just one of the many challenges faced by Xi Jinping and his successors.

FUTURE CHALLENGES FOR CHINA

In the twenty-first century, China's prospects may at first look promising, but the country faces many challenges in both the political and economic spheres.

Open Door Policy
approach taken by the Chinese government, starting in the late 1970s, to introduce the Chinese economy (and by extension political system) to the Western world

special economic zones (SEZs)
regions in China with different economic regulatory controls and more independence meant to spur economic growth

Human rights continue to be a problem for the government, which encounters significant international opposition to its policies concerning political prisoners, labour camps, and freedom of expression. An increasingly wealthy middle class will likely demand greater freedom of choice in the political sphere. The political protests that culminated in the Tiananmen Square crackdown are also likely to resurface, and the government will once again have to choose between tolerance and repression. A policy of tolerance would be more popular with foreign governments and human rights groups, but it may encourage further questioning of the Chinese political system as a whole and thereby threaten the CCP's hold over the country.

China's economic challenges are also still considerable. The reform of the Chinese economy must be seen as a work in progress that must continue to bring tangible benefits to key constituencies if it is to remain sustainable. The government needs to increase agricultural prices and public investment in agriculture if production levels are to rebound to the levels they reached in the 1990s. Rural poverty also remains a problem, and the government should not forget Mao's lesson that the key to Chinese political power lies with the peasantry. The government must also continue to modernize the country's infrastructure, building roads, bridges, and electrical networks to support a modern economy. However, all these projects cost huge amounts of money. The government will be forced to find additional sources of revenue by reforming the nation's tax system, a move that could prove highly unpopular.

China will also have to handle other growing pains. As some regions grow faster than others, political tensions will emerge and calls for redistribution will either have to be ignored, thus further aggravating these tensions, or placated, risking the alienation of wealthy provinces. Ethnic problems have already reared

10.9 TAIWAN

The exile of Kuomintang forces from mainland China in 1949 led to the birth of a new state in the international system, Taiwan (also called Chinese Taipei). The United States and its allies immediately recognized Taiwan as the legitimate government of the whole of China, denying recognition of Mao's communist regime. Since then, the mainland Chinese government has campaigned successfully to have itself recognized as the legitimate voice of the Chinese people. However, it has also campaigned continuously to limit the recognition of Taiwan by other states in the international system and has used the threat of force to attempt to destabilize and weaken the strength of the government in Taipei. In recent years, these threats reached new heights, with the Beijing government firing missiles toward the island. This action brought an immediate response from the US government, which has committed itself to the defence of Taiwan.

Taiwan is more than just a cause of tension in the China Sea. Since 1949, it has become a highly successful economy, industrializing at a rapid rate and dramatically raising its people's standard of living. However, it has done so with the help of an authoritarian political system that has consistently limited political freedoms. Ironically, the Chinese government has looked to Taiwan as an example of how to implement a capitalist economic system without democratization.

their head in the western provinces, particularly in those with large Muslim populations. The government will either have to provide sufficient economic benefits to these people or use the PLA to suppress rebellion. Lastly, China has to face the responsibilities of becoming a regional and global power and decide if its future lies in encouraging regional co-operation or trying to dominate the weaker countries on its borders. It must decide what to do with Taiwan and how to define its relationship with the United States, which continues to be the most important force in the Pacific. The relationship with the US has become particularly complex in recent years as China has become the largest holder of US dollars in its national reserves, amounting to over $1.3 trillion, mostly in the form of US government debt. It is the largest holder of US national debt (8 per cent of the total in 2011), which gives it a privileged position. But it also exposes China to the dangers of devaluation of the dollar, meaning that its reserves and debt holdings would be worth less as time goes by. How China restructures its economic and political relations with the US is one of the key questions facing the world in the twenty-first century.

Mexico: The Challenges of Democratization

Perhaps more than any other developing country, Mexico highlights both the problematic link between political and economic development and the divorce between the theory and practice of political economy. As discussed in Chapter 6, Mexico is a democracy in which one party dominated for decades before fully competitive elections allowed for a transition to an alternative party in 2000. After 12 years of that party's rule, Mexicans decided, in July 2012, to return the former governing party to power. Mexico has a presidential system, but in recent years the Mexican Congress has taken on a more active role in government and policy-making. Mexico is a NIC and an emerging market, yet every time it appears to be getting close to achieving its goal of developed country status, it seems to fall into economic crisis and has to begin the long climb back. Mexico is a country that, it is claimed, has the highest number of billionaires per capita but has regions where more than 50 per cent of its people live in extreme poverty.

HISTORY

Mexico was one of the first areas of the New World colonized by the Spanish in the fifteenth and sixteenth centuries, and the chaos of conquest was followed by an equally turbulent birth and adolescence as a nation. Mexico's early history saw the assimilation of indigenous and imperialist cultures, with much intermarrying between Spanish and native peoples. This is not to say that indigenous peoples fared better than their counterparts in Canada and the United States; disease, war, and episodes of genocide all took their toll on the country. Unlike these two nations, however, Mexico was an incredibly rich colony for many years, promising unimaginable reserves of gold and silver to the conquering nation. As has seemed to happen throughout Mexican history, this wealth failed to produce lasting benefits for the country or its people.

Mexico's history as an independent country began in 1821 with the end of the war of independence against Spain. Disorder and deep political instability followed, with a succession of weak presidencies. A disastrous war against the United States in 1848 and the secession of the state of Texas left Mexico with only half of its original territory, and the country found itself in an impoverished and uncertain situation. The solution to a part of these problems was found in the autocratic, authoritarian rule of Porfirio Díaz, who became president of Mexico in 1876. Though he was highly successful in stabilizing the country and attracting foreign investment into Mexico, Díaz headed a gravely repressive regime, which was arbitrary in its rule and severely limited individual rights.

In 1910, several groups rose up in revolution against his regime. Most notable among them was the band led by Emiliano Zapata, a peasant of both indigenous and Spanish heritage who sought to defend farmers and native rights against the central government. The revolution proved a long and bloody affair that resulted in the creation of the Partido Revolucionario Institucional (PRI; Institutional Revolutionary Party). This party ruled Mexico for more than 70 years and, like the Díaz regime, provided considerable stability to Mexico. Unfortunately, it also possessed some less desirable features, such as repressing political opposition, having an authoritarian style of governance, and limiting the freedom of the media.

MEXICO'S POLITICAL SYSTEM

Mexico has a highly democratic and inclusive political system that closely mirrors that of the United States, at least in theory. The Mexican constitution sets up a federal system in which the powers of the president are balanced and checked by those of the Congress. Individual states (of which there are 32, including the Distrito Federal, or Federal District of Mexico City) are given considerable powers. Each state has its own elected state legislature and governor (the Distrito Federal has its own head of government, one of the most influential positions in the Mexican political system). In reality, however, the country's political system has been highly centralized since the revolution. The federal government controls most spending (over 80 per cent), with state and municipal governments (*municipios*) sharing the rest. To make matters worse, *municipios* depend on the upper levels of government for over 80 per cent of their income, having very few independent sources on which to draw. However, in recent years state governments have grown in power as financial resources have been transferred from the federal level to the governors of the states with little or no requirements regarding transparency or accountability.

This centralization in taxation and government spending has been compounded by the fact that many of Mexico's states are desperately poor, whereas others (particularly in the north) have income levels close to those of some developed countries. The divergence in wealth and influence means that there is little unity among the states.[18]

The dominance of the PRI meant that the governing party was able to limit the independence of the states through patronage. Since 2000 and the Partido Acción Nacional's (PAN; National Action Party) coming to power, this kind of control has been weakened and the governors have begun to play an important role, not only at the state level but also to once again be considered key national political actors.

THE MEXICAN PRESIDENCY

The Mexican presidency has traditionally been the focal point of power in the system. As chief executive and head of state, the president is given wide-ranging powers under the constitution, which creates the potential for presidential dominance of the other branches of government. In the past, the president has traditionally been responsible for almost all the important legislative initiatives that are passed into law by Congress. Thanks to the PRI's long-running supremacy of both the presidency and Congress, legislation initiated in Los Pinos (the Mexican equivalent of the White House) rapidly became law. Until the 1980s, many Mexican presidents used this power to alter the constitution; however, the PRI has since been unable to obtain the two-thirds majority needed to effect a constitutional amendment because of increased electoral competition.

The president in Mexico is popularly elected but limited to one six-year term (*sexenio*). This limitation was created as a response to Diaz's dictatorship. After the PRI's dominance, the PAN won the 2000 election and Vicente Fox became president. Six years later, the PAN again won the presidency, with Felipe Calderón forming a government; however, the presidential election was incredibly close, with the candidate from the Partido de la Revolucíon Democrática (PRD), Andrés Manuel López Obrador, losing by only a few thousand votes.

In July 2012, Mexicans voted again in presidential elections. The PRI, after 12 years out of power, won the election under the leadership of Enrique Peña Nieto. Although many in Mexico and abroad fear that PRI's return to government will mean a return to authoritarianism, it is unlikely that this is possible given that, in the past two decades, Mexico's political and democratic institutions have matured greatly. What we have now is the very real probability of the presidency alternating between different parties, thus strengthening Mexican democracy.

THE MEXICAN CONGRESS

Like the US Congress, Mexico's is divided into lower and upper chambers, the Chamber of Deputies and Senate, respectively. Unlike the United States model, there was traditionally very little division and conflict between the legislative and executive branches of government in Mexico because of the PRI's control of both branches. However, this changed when the party lost its majority in Congress in 1997, and **political cohabitation** between the Congress and

political cohabitation
political co-operation among parties without forming a coalition

presidency has become a reality. This has made policy-making much more complicated in Mexico, with the opposition parties often blocking legislation to score political points over the ruling party. Both Fox and Calderón suffered from this political gridlock, and it has held back many important initiatives in the areas of labour policy, energy, and political reform. Adopting a long-term perspective, we may see that this practice is part of the process of a maturing democracy that will probably lead to a stronger democratic system.

In 2012, the PRI became the largest party in Congress once again but failed to achieve a majority in either house. As a result, Peña Nieto will suffer from problems similar to those faced by Fox and Calderón. However, because the PRI is very close to a majority, he will likely be able to convince enough deputies and senators from the opposition parties to give him the majority he needs. It will be much more difficult for him to gain the two-thirds majority required for constitutional change, however, which will complicate some of his plans for energy and other structural reforms that the economy desperately needs.

ELECTIONS IN MEXICO

Elections in Mexico are often marked by intrigue and controversy. For example, in 1988, with one-third of the votes counted in the presidential election, the FDN (Frente Democrático Nacional) coalition presidential candidate, Cuauhtémoc Cárdenas, held a clear lead over PRI candidate Carlos Salinas de Gortari. At that point, the computers tallying the votes lost power.[19] When power was restored, Salinas had gained the lead and went on to win the election by a very small margin. Though the PRI denied tampering with the election and post-election opinion polls suggested that Salinas would probably have secured victory regardless, the election highlighted the very real problem of electoral fraud in Mexican politics. Since then, the Federal Electoral Institute (Instituto Federal Electoral, or IFE) has greatly improved its elections monitoring, thanks in no small part to support from international and foreign national agencies, both governmental and non-governmental. The IFE was recognized throughout Mexico as being an honest guarantor of free and fair elections. In fact, it was so successful that it became an important international actor, participating in elections monitoring in other countries around the world. The role of the IFE is crucial in Mexico because its work is the only way that elections have come to be seen as legitimate.

However, in the 2006 presidential election, the IFE's reputation came under attack. With widespread reports of electoral fraud, errors in vote counting, and missing ballot boxes, the result hung in the balance

© Peter Jordan / Alamy

Carlos Salinas won the Mexican presidency in 1988 under suspicious circumstances.

10.10 MEXICO'S STUDENT MOVEMENT, MEDIA BIAS, AND THE 2012 ELECTIONS

As the Mexican presidential election campaign of 2012 entered its closing stages, a new issue emerged that was to galvanize the political attitudes and participation of university students across the country. On 11 May, PRI candidate Enrique Peña Nieto appeared at the Iberoamericana University in Mexico City. Unlike the vast majority of his previous speaking engagements, this event was not smooth or expertly handled. His speech was greeted with boos and abuse from the students, who were protesting police brutality in the state of Mexico in 2006, when Peña Nieto had been governor there. Unable to get the students' co-operation, the PRI candidate left the stage and withdrew from the university.

In an effort to control what looked like a public relations disaster, the party campaign team claimed that many in the audience were not students but protesters that had been brought in by one of Peña Nieto's left-wing rivals. This claim was repeated by the country's two leading television stations, Televisa and TV Azteca, both of which had been accused of bias toward the PRI and Peña Nieto.

Within a matter of days, the Iberoamericana students had made a YouTube video in which 131 registered students showed their student cards and testified that they had been present at the event. This video generated a nationwide interuniversity movement of students against media bias that rapidly turned into an anti-Peña Nieto and anti-PRI movement. Named Yo Soy 132 (I Am 132) to show solidarity with the 131 students in the video, this group captured the attention of students and university authorities in both public and private institutes of higher education and produced repeated marches against both the PRI and the TV stations. The movement was able to generate this support and activism with the help of Facebook and Twitter, bringing tens of thousands of students to the streets of major Mexican cities.

Although Yo Soy 132 could not change the outcome of the election, it highlighted an exciting element of Mexico's democracy. Student political activism has been important across the world for decades and played a major role in civil unrest in Mexico in the 1960s. In 2012, however, the students showed their ability to use social media to generate massive support and to coordinate protests and marches across the country.

for months before Calderón was finally declared the unequivocal winner. In the meantime, the IFE was accused of hiding evidence, covering up illegal practices by the major political parties, allowing the government to use the advertising of public programs as a thin cover for electioneering, and generally failing to guarantee free and fair elections. Subsequently, the governing council of the IFE was changed and a new group of councillors took over.

The 2012 election was largely clean in terms of activity at the ballot box, but defeated PRD candidate Obrador accused the PRI of essentially buying votes by giving out gifts, cash, and store discount cards to potential voters. The results of an investigation by the Mexican electoral authorities will influence the behaviour of all parties in future elections, although it will not change the outcome of this one.

THE MEXICAN ECONOMY

In terms of natural endowments, Mexico is one of the world's richest lands. The country has vast oil and gas reserves, huge forests, access to ocean resources on

both the Atlantic and Pacific sides, and tourism opportunities that would make any country jealous. Yet because of mismanagement, exploitation, and corruption, Mexico has been unable to take full advantage of these resources.

In the twentieth century, national economic development was driven by the state for long periods. Between the revolution and the 1980s, Mexico underwent a period of rapid industrialization that gave its citizens hope that they would one day join the ranks of the First World. The Mexican government acted not only as economic planner and manager but also as owner and director of many of Mexico's most important industries, most significantly and symbolically of Petróleos Mexicanos (PEMEX), the nation's oil company. The nationalization of such industries during the middle of the century went along with a large degree of state intervention in the economy as a whole, regulating both wages and prices. In this period, Mexico experienced high levels of growth, particularly as a result of the policy of stabilized development in the 1960s.

In the next decade, however, economic development became much more complex in Mexico, despite the discovery of huge oil reserves in the Gulf of Mexico in 1976. The governments of Luis Echeverría (1970–6) and José López Portillo (1976–82) dramatically increased government spending and borrowing, mostly from foreign banks. This money was not spent wisely, however, and was used up in unproductive projects and public-sector wages. With the onset of the Latin American debt crisis in the mid-1980s, the billions of dollars owed by Mexico created a national financial and economic crisis, which required the intervention of the IMF and World Bank to stabilize and later resolve (see Chapter 13). For Mexico, as for much of Latin America and the developing world, the 1980s was a lost decade, where very little positive economic growth was seen, living standards and real wages declined, and the enthusiasm and optimism of earlier decades evaporated.

ECONOMIC LIBERALIZATION AND OPENNESS

Beginning in 1982 with the Miguel de la Madrid *sexenio*, Mexico gradually opened and liberalized its economy, allowing foreign competition into the country and slowly removing the state from direct involvement in the economy. A key factor in this liberalization was the IMF's demand that the Mexican government improve the efficiency of its economy through structural adjustment policies. From a largely closed and state-run economy, Mexico has transformed itself into an open and relatively dynamic one. The role of the private sector has increased; foreign investment, both **portfolio investment** (short-term capital that can easily move into and out of a national economy) and foreign direct investment (FDI), have grown dramatically; and Mexico has become an active proponent of free trade. On this last point, Mexico became the first developing country in the world to join a free trade association with developed countries when it signed the NAFTA in 1992. Studies seem to indicate that this agreement has benefited Mexico, guaranteeing the country access to the markets of Canada but, much more important, the United States.[20]

portfolio investment
acquisition of shares (stocks) in a corporate actor for the purpose of profit; does not imply ownership

The NAFTA was a significant event for Mexico because it signalled once again that the country was close to First World status. President Salinas, who pushed for Mexican membership in this organization and signed the treaty, was determined to bring Mexico into a true partnership with the US, and the NAFTA marked the high point of that effort. Mexican hopes, however, were dashed at the end of 1994, when Mexico went into deep economic and financial crisis less than 12 months after the agreement came into force. Fortunately, this situation took much less time to stabilize and resolve than the debt crisis of the 1980s, but its effects on the general population were just as keenly felt.

Since that crisis, which again required IMF loans to resolve, Mexico has continued with its liberal economic policies, examining privatization of many national industries (including PEMEX) and signing a series of free trade treaties. However, despite some important advances in terms of poverty reduction, Mexico's economy faces major challenges in the years to come. It has been overtaken by other LDCs, such as Brazil, India, and China, in terms of competitiveness and growth levels. Although Mexico has maintained financial and economic stability, it must grow faster and achieve better income distribution if the aspirations of its people are to be met.

ORGANIZED CRIME, DRUGS, AND PUBLIC SECURITY

For many years, drug trafficking organizations (DTOs) have used Mexican territory as a route to move drugs from South American countries such as Colombia to the United States. Until the 1990s, Mexican DTOs merely moved the product for their counterparts from the south, but Mexican drug cartels then started to become drug producers and distributors. For decades, Mexican presidents have tolerated the presence of DTOs in the country and have struck an implicit bargain with them that, as long as they do not disrupt public security, the government would leave them alone.

This arrangement changed in 2006, after Calderón became president. Recognizing that large areas of the country had slipped beyond the federal government's control and that drug lords were bribing or threatening public officials to the point where they effectively controlled these authorities, the Calderón administration—with significant help from the United States—began a full-scale war on drugs, with the military being used to patrol city streets in the north of the country and to conduct campaigns against the drug cartels.

With this approach, Mexicans have increasingly felt that they live in a permanent state of siege, and the rising rate of kidnapping and violence in both cities and rural areas is alarming. Since 2006, more than 60,000 people have died in the drug conflict. Mexican citizens, though generally in agreement with the Calderón government's goal of reducing DTO influence, have tired of the violence. This attitude was reflected in their decision to elect Peña Nieto in July 2012, and he has promised to continue the fight against organized crime by employing a 40,000 strong paramilitary force rather than the army. The outcome of this shift in tactics remains to be seen.

THE FUTURE OF MEXICO

Mexico's democracy has matured greatly since the electoral shenanigans of 1988. Twelve years of PAN party rule, reform of electoral institutions, and an acceptance of the normality of a return to PRI government suggest that the political system continues to evolve in a positive direction. Democratization and economic liberalization are beginning to bring perceptible benefits to Mexicans, and the country appears to be handling the transition to a multi-party electoral system well, without sacrificing too much of its stability.

However, major problems such as political and economic corruption, economic mismanagement, human rights abuses, and the political bias of the media endure. The violence that plagues the country threatens not only human life but also economic prosperity as it deters FDI. Mexico is also now one of the most dangerous countries in the world to be a journalist, with killings of reporters rising to record levels in the last six years.

Despite these challenges, Mexico is a major international player and an important North American partner to Canada and the United States through the NAFTA. It is predicted that it will become one of the world's 10 largest economies in the next 20 years if the government can enact the needed reforms. Mexico's young democracy and economic prosperity may not yet be totally secure, but they are showing many signs of evolution and strength, and the country will continue to be an important case for students of politics and development.

India: Politics and Development in the World's Largest Democracy

A country with 1.2 billion people, an ancient civilization, ethnic and religious diversity, extreme poverty, and one of the world's most dynamic economies, India has thrust itself onto the world stage in the past decade. It provides us with a fascinating example of how democracy and development affect one another and of how rising prosperity is often matched by growing inequality.

Throughout its modern history, India has been afflicted by political violence, both between ethnic and religious groups and directed at federal and local governments. In some ways, this conflict is the result of its colonial history and the rather arbitrary way in which its borders were drawn up when it became an independent nation. In others, it is a direct result of the failure of successive Indian governments to overcome the challenges of diversity and economic development.

HISTORY

Throughout its history, India has been host to a multitude of religions, ethnicities, and societies. Indian civilization can be traced back to the third millennium BCE in the Indus Valley. It was also around this time that Hinduism, still India's dominant religion, emerged (its earliest texts were written between 1700 and 1100 BCE). For centuries, the geographical space that we consider India has been fought over and disputed by tribes and empires of many nations, leading to multiple reformulations of its shape and structure. The most important of these changes occurred in the nineteenth century, when the British Empire formalized authority over the subcontinent. The British East India Company had previously exercised almost complete control over Indian territory under a mandate from the British government. Upon taking control of India, the British Raj began as a period of Indian history that lasted until India finally won independence in 1947.

During this period, India developed some of the features of an independent country and individual "princely states" retained significant autonomy as long as they recognized British sovereignty, but the country as a whole remained firmly under the control of the government in London. The country received high levels of investment, the structure of modern government, and the building of infrastructure such as railways that dramatically changed communications. At the same time, however, citizen rights were repressed and recurring famine and widespread poverty continued to be serious problems.

After the participation of over one million Indian soldiers under British control in World War I, the Indian independence movement—headed by the Indian National Congress party (INC, whose leader was Jawaharlal Nehru) and by Mohandas Gandhi, also known as the Mahatma, who created a nation-wide non-violent resistance movement—rapidly expanded, led by the INC. Gradually, the British recognized that Indian independence was not only inevitable but also desirable. However, an actual break from the British came only after further Indian involvement in World War II and decades of protest and repression.

The move to independence resulted in the creation of two new states, India and Pakistan. The Muslim League, a political party based on Islam and led by Muhammad Ali Jinnah, called for the creation of a separate, Muslim state during the independence process, a demand to which the British acquiesced over the protests of many in the INC, including Gandhi. The partition of India into two countries (Pakistan was later split into Pakistan and Bangladesh) was a chaotic and turbulent process, with 12.5 million people forced to move, either Hindus from Pakistan into India or Muslims from India into Pakistan. In the process, as many as one million people lost their lives as a result of violence between religious and ethnic groups and because the newly formed governments were unprepared to deal with such massive refugee flows. Today, Pakistan is still a predominantly Muslim state (around 98 per cent of its population), and India is 80 per cent Hindu but with significant Muslim, Sikh, and Christian minorities.

INDIA'S POLITICAL SYSTEM

Upon gaining independence, India became a dominion for three years and began work on its constitution, which was completed in 1950 and established the country as a sovereign, secular, democratic, and parliamentary republic. As one of the first former colonies to win independence in the postwar era, India set an important precedent in creating a constitution that protected individual rights and established limits for the national government. The structure of the Indian system is federal in nature, with 28 states and 7 union territories (5 of which are ruled directly by the federal government).

At the federal level, India has a parliamentary system based on the Westminster model. The head of state in India is an elected president, who is given significant powers by the constitution (he or she is the head of the armed forces and has the power to pardon individuals) but in reality depends on the Council of Ministers, headed by the prime minister. The prime minister is by convention the head of the largest party in the lower house of Parliament. The legislative branch is made up of two houses: the Rajya Sabha (Council of States) is the upper chamber and the Lok Sabha (House of the People) is the lower. Members of the Rajya Sabha are elected for six-year terms by state-level legislatures. The Lok Sabha responds more directly to India's population, with its 545 members being elected via popular vote.

Throughout India's history as an independent nation, two parties or coalitions of parties have dominated: the INC, the party of Nehru, Indira Gandhi and her son, Rajiv; and the Bharatiya Janata Party (BJP), which has briefly replaced it at various times as the party of government. The country is currently ruled by the United Progressive Alliance (UPA), a coalition formed around the INC, with Manmohan Singh serving his second term as prime minister.

INDIAN DEVELOPMENT

Immediately after winning independence, India faced enormous developmental challenges, including extreme poverty, poor infrastructure, a weak manufacturing sector and an undeveloped financial system. In response, the country adopted a socialist development model that focused on central economic planning by the federal government. This approach required the creation of an enormous bureaucracy at the federal level as prices, wages, and production targets were set and then monitored. Major industries were nationalized and high tariffs were applied to imported goods. India's economy was based largely on agricultural production but, despite the successes of the Green Revolution in helping to solve the problem of recurring famine, this model failed to generate sufficiently high levels of growth to lift the population out of poverty.

In 1991, the government abruptly changed course and implemented a liberal economic program that eliminated much of the red tape and bureaucracy, opened up markets, removed restrictions on investment, and sold off state-run enterprises. This proved to be a hugely beneficial move, as India's economic growth rapidly accelerated from this point on. For example, the country has developed a strong manufacturing sector and has specialized in textiles, the services economy, and the pharmaceutical industry. It has grown to become the eleventh largest economy in the world and will likely become the third largest by the middle of the century. This growth has drastically altered India's place on the global stage, and the country is now recognized as one of the most important economies in the world.

But this rising wealth has not solved the country's myriad developmental problems. Hundreds of millions of Indian citizens still live in atrocious economic conditions (similar to the Chinese situation), there are important ethnic and religious conflicts in many parts of the country (religious-based terrorism has proved a constant threat over the past 30 years), and security relations with neighbouring Pakistan are frequently tense. As the economy has expanded, inequality among the population has worsened. By 2011, the top 10 per cent of the population was earning 12 times as much as the bottom 10 per cent, double the rate of the 1990s.[21]

India is the second most populous country in the world. Its vast population is part of the country's economic strength and one of its most challenging aspects. Poor families find themselves in a situation where they would rather not have a daughter because they would have to pay a dowry when she marries. As in China, the preference for boys has encouraged selective abortions and even the killing of newborn baby girls. This terrible situation has attracted international attention in recent years, but the miserable conditions in which so many Indians live make it an intractable problem.

Another enduring problem in Indian society is the caste system, a complex social class system based on birth and ancestry. Caste exists in other countries around the world, but it has been a defining factor of Indian society. Depending on which caste you are born into, there will be certain careers that you should practise and others which you are prevented from entering. Five main castes exist: the Brahman, or priestly class; the Kshatriyas, or warriors; Vaishyas, or traders; Shudras, or workmen; and the Panchama, or untouchables. The lowest level of the caste system, the Panchama, are subject to widespread systemic prejudice and have traditionally been forced into the lowest paying jobs, which the other castes would not consider. In recent years, the Indian government has taken steps to try to overcome discrimination against the untouchables and several members of that caste have risen to high rank in politics and the economy, but it continues to be one of India's less attractive aspects.

THE FUTURE OF INDIA

India's booming population (which will surpass China's in the near future), its immense size and diversity, and (most important) the growing inequality that comes with rapid economic growth will produce strains that test the strength of its political and economic systems. The ancient roots of Indian society have been a source of strength and unity in the past, but this new phase of rapid growth, which brings with it changing aspirations for the population, and new values associated with the capitalist economic model will undoubtedly create a clash between the country's traditional and modern elements. As India becomes ever more integrated into the global society of states, foreign monitoring of and interference in questions of human rights, gender equality, and social policies will necessarily become more common. These changes will test India's religious and social institutions but will also strengthen the more progressive elements in its society.

India will also have to decide how to manage its international affairs. As a regional great power, it faces challenges not only from neighbouring Pakistan but also from China, which is a neighbour across the Himalayas and a rival for influence in Asia and the Indian Ocean. These two emerging giants will have to find a way to co-exist peacefully for the good of the region and the world.

Mali

In January 2013, the North African country of Mali burst onto the world's headlines when French troops were sent to push back Islamist rebel groups from their attacks against the Malian government in the northern provinces of Tombouctou, Gao, and Kidal. A conflict that had seemed to be a minor civil war when it broke out the year before suddenly assumed global dimensions as other governments in the developed world, including those of the United States and Canada, offered support to France and the national government based in the Malian capital, Bamako. This turmoil stands in stark contrast to the country's situation in the early 1990s, when it was widely considered to be one of the most stable African democracies. Mali's recent history highlights many of the challenges faced by developing countries in Africa, including the legacy of colonialism.

THE HISTORY OF MALI: FROM EMPIRE TO INDEPENDENCE

A thousand years ago, what is now the country of Mali formed part of the Ghanaian Empire, a loosely defined territorial and political unit that extended throughout much of West Africa. In the fourteenth century, that realm was replaced by the Mali Empire (which gives the country its modern name), stretching from the Atlantic in the west to the city of Tomboctou (Timbuktu) in the east. The might of the Mali army allowed the empire to establish itself as the most effective military force in the region.

The Mali Empire became a focus for regional and international trade and contained centres of learning and religion. The control of trans-Saharan trade during that period was crucial in building the power of Mali, and gold, salt, copper, and slaves became the economic basis of power and prosperity for the rulers, enabling them to dominate neighbouring peoples. Also important to the economic elites was the Niger River, as it became a means of controlling trade from east to west. Along with prosperity came a cultural influence and an emphasis on learning that spread the use of the Malian language and laws throughout the region. The Mali Empire adopted a decentralized structure that gave significant autonomy to local rulers but maintained a flow of tribute to the centre. This approach helped the empire to last longer than any similarly sized empire in Africa, before or since.

Ultimately, however, the Mali Empire was overturned by the Songhai, one of the cultures it had previously subjected to imperial rule. The Songhai people, based in what is modern-day Nigeria, rose to prominence in West Africa by challenging the rule of the Mali elites, who had become embroiled in an internal conflict that severely weakened their power. Again, the Songhai sought to control the lucrative trans-Saharan trade routes. But their rule was ended by an invasion from Morocco, and the arrival of European trading ships to the African coast in the sixteenth century destroyed the economic power basis of the traditional elites in West Africa as commodities could now leave the region to the west rather than moving northward across the desert.

A combination of slavery, drought, famine, and recurring conflict left Mali as a weakened region until the late nineteenth century when, as part of the "race for Africa," the French subsumed the country into the colonial dominion of French Sudan. French colonial rule in Mali followed many of the common features of European empires: often brutal treatment of the local peoples, including slavery; the drawing of arbitrary boundaries that made little ethnic or economic sense; and a dislocation of the local economy by forcing people to engage in cash cropping and industrial scale commodities production. Slavery was never comprehensively abolished in Mali and remains a problem to this day.

Between 1959 and 1960, however, an independence movement achieved rapid success. This movement won freedom from French colonial rule in June 1960 and became established as the Republic of Mali on 22 September of the same year. The new government was socialist in orientation and allied itself with the Soviet bloc, nationalizing natural resource industries and engaging in a program of economic modernization. However, despite the government's efforts to raise economic growth, poverty remained a serious problem for the country and led to high levels of social discontent.

A coup in 1968 led to military rule, which transitioned to one-party rule in 1974 under the Democratic Union of the Malian People (UDPM) party and its leader, Moussa Traoré. This authoritarian political system was based on often brutal repression of opposition movements and on the suppression of social protest. Continued economic stagnation and the implementation of austerity measures after a loan from the IMF kept Mali's people mired in poverty. Combined with the pro-democracy movements sweeping Africa in the 1980s, this situation contributed to increasing calls from the Malian population for a democratic transition.

In 1991, after months of anti-government protests, the head of Traoré's personal guard, Amadou Toumani Touré, led a military overthrow of the government, arresting the president and setting the stage for a transition to democratic government. Competitive elections were held a year later, and Alpha Oumar Konaré, the candidate of the Alliance for Democracy in Mali (Alliance pour la Démocratie au Mali, or ADEMA), was elected president.

In the two decades following the 1992 elections, Mali was hailed internationally as a model for African democracies, with peaceful transitions between parties. Economically, however, not much changed. The Malian people still experienced extreme levels of poverty, high fertility and infant mortality rates, and a fragile relationship with representative government and peace.

THE PEOPLE OF MALI

Mali is a good example of a multi-ethnic state, being comprised of diverse linguistic and cultural groups. The Bambara is by far the largest group in the country and the Bambara language is spoken by approximately half of the population, but eight other major ethnic groups (Soninké, Khassonké, Malinké,

10.11 CANADA AND MALI

For over 50 years, Canada has been actively engaged in aid activities in Mali, financing poverty reduction projects, health programs, and public policy support through the Canadian International Development Agency (CIDA, which is now part of the newly restructured Department of Foreign Affairs, Trade and Development). In 2009, CIDA had identified 20 "countries of focus"—including Mali—to which 80 per cent of the agency's resources would be devoted. Although the Canadian government suspended its aid payments to Mali after the coup d'etat in 2012, it continued to deliver development assistance through NGOs and multilateral channels.

When the international intervention in Mali (known as Operation Serval) began in January 2013, the French government requested that Canada provide heavy lift capacity for transporting troops, equipment, and military transports. In response, the Canadian government committed a transport plane (a Royal Canadian Air Force CC-177 Globemaster III, sometimes called the C-17) and 40 Royal Canadian Air Force personnel. In the first month of the operation, the Canadian plane conducted 27 flights, moving more than 765,000 kilograms of personnel and equipment around the African country.

The Harper government had earlier announced that it would not undertake any direct military mission in Mali. Furthermore, it has not committed to playing a direct role in any future peacekeeping mission, which the Canadian press saw as further evidence of the decline in Canada's

The Canadian Press/Richard Lam

An official guides a C-17 Globemaster III into position. Canada contributed one of its large C-17 military cargo planes to deliver supplies to Bamaka after a request from France.

capacity and willingness to engage in international military operations. Despite Canada's proud history of participating in peacekeeping missions, by January of 2013 the country ranked 56th out of 114 countries in terms of contributions to peacekeeping operations.[1]

Note

1. Lee Berthiaume, "Canada Can Help Bring Stability to Mali, UN Official Says," 18 March 2013, http://o.canada.com/2013/03/18/canada-can-help-bring-peace-and-stability-to-mali-un-official-says/.

Fula, Voltaic, Songhai, Tuareg, and Moor) are represented throughout Mali's territory. Around 90 per cent of the population is Muslim.

Since 1960, the population of Mali has grown from around 4 million to 15.5 million people, thanks largely to a high fertility rate (the world's second highest at 6.4 children per female).[22] As a result, the country's population is very young, with almost 50 per cent of its people below the age of 15. Poor medical conditions and a high incidence of violent conflict mean that life expectancy is low, at approximately 53 years (compared with Canada's life expectancy of 80.8 years). Mali also has one of the world's worst infant mortality rates, with 106 deaths per 1,000 live births in 2007.

Poor health care and violence, however, are just two of the causes of Mali's low life expectancy. With a largely rural base, Mali's people continue to be among the world's poorest. The country ranked 175 out of 187 countries on the UNDP's 2011 Human Development Index, and it is estimated that half of the population lives on under $1.25 a day. Recurring food shortages and food crises make life persistently precarious for many. To make matters even worse, there are possibly as many as 200,000 people living as slaves in Mali.

THE POLITICAL SYSTEM

Modern Mali was set up by the negotiations between political parties in 1991, and the constitution of 1992 created a presidential representative democratic republic in which executive power is exercised by the government, legislative power by the National Assembly, and there is an independent judiciary.

The president of Mali is a powerful figure, acting as head of state and commander-in-chief of the armed forces. The president personally appoints the prime minister, who is the head of government. The former is elected for a five-year term and can serve a maximum of two terms. After the experiences of colonialism and military dictatorship, this limit is of crucial importance in the country.

The legislative branch consists of the National Assembly, in which 160 representatives are elected directly for five-year terms. The Assembly votes on legislation that has been proposed by its own members and by the government. A multi-party system encourages negotiation between the eight main parties. According to the constitution, parties cannot be organized based on ethnic, religious, regional, or gender lines. This rule is especially important given the traditional divisions and conflicts between the different ethnic groups in Mali.

From 1992 to 2012, Mali experienced a period of relative stability. However, the early years of democracy were hardly problem-free. In 1997, for example, the two main opposition parties boycotted the presidential elections in protest over Konaré's decision to annul the legislative elections that year. The turnout was below 30 per cent in the presidential election, and Konaré received 84 per cent of the votes. This situation made the elections of 2002 particularly sensitive, with Konaré unable to stand again due to constitutional term limits and the leader of the 1991 coup, Touré, running as an independent candidate. Touré won the presidency with over 64 per cent of the vote and was re-elected in 2007 with even greater support. The peaceful electoral transition from one president to another suggested to the world that Mali was maturing as a democracy.

However, violence in the northern provinces of Mali continued to be a serious problem. Since the early 1990s, the Tuareg ethnic group had challenged the dominance of both the Bambara and the central government, inciting armed resistance to rule from the capital. Uniting with other rebel groups, the Tuareg-dominated Mouvement National pour la Libération de l'Azawad (MNLA) called for the northern provinces to unite as an independent entity, known as Azawad. After the re-election of President Touré in 2007, the levels of violence increased, and in January 2012 open conflict enveloped the northern provinces. In March, only a month before the presidential election, Touré was removed by the military due to his incompetent handling of the crisis. The political chaos in the capital meant that the national government could not mount an effective campaign in the north. Throughout the rest of the year, rebel groups took control of key cities, declaring independence for the Azawad region in April.

In the capital, Mali's constitutional court called on Dioncounda Traoré to assume the presidency on an interim status, with Cheick Modibo Diarra appointed as interim prime minister. The military made it clear that the coup was intended as a temporary interruption of civilian rule and that democracy would return to Mali as soon as possible. However, in December, the military forced Diarra to resign, claiming that he had been trying to block the transition back to democratic rule.

In January 2013, the government of Mali called for international assistance to retake northern cities from Islamist forces, who had by now installed Islamic law (sharia) across the region. The government of François Hollande authorized the French military to assist the Malian government, and in a matter of weeks the combined French/Malian forces had re-established control of the north. In the process, however, food supplies were interrupted and international aid agencies suspended their work, creating an intense humanitarian crisis for the region's already vulnerable population.

THE FUTURE OF MALI

Mali has shown considerable promise in recent years, mostly in terms of its ability to sustain 20 years of democratic rule. Despite recent problems, Mali could benefit further from Africa's recent revival, driven in part by an increased global demand for its commodities, the use of new technologies, and extended periods of peace. These benefits could easily spread to the country, bringing down birth rates, aiding economic innovation, and increasing prosperity.

However, Mali remains a dangerous and difficult place to live. The economy—based on raw materials and agriculture—is highly vulnerable to variations in global prices as demand for its exports rises and falls. Extreme poverty is a challenge that successive governments, both authoritarian and democratic, have failed to overcome. Political instability is unlikely to subside in the short term as regional and ethnic divisions continue to define national politics. What's more, the country's recent pattern of reverting to authoritarian rule suggests that it will be difficult to establish a democratic system based on the division of powers and checks on the presidency. Lastly, the need for outside intervention to regain control of the northern provinces tells us that the central government lacks the necessary coercive power to establish full sovereign authority over its territory. Like those of many other African countries, Mali's is a fragile political and economic system and is unlikely to solve its problems in the short to medium term.

Conclusion

This chapter has introduced you to some of the myriad challenges that face developing countries in this century. China, Mexico, India, and Mali have some elements of these challenges in common, such as the need to secure the support of key constituencies for economic reform; however, these countries are at different stages of development in widely divergent social, political, geographical, and economic settings. Part of the challenge for each nation, as for all LDCs, is to find its place in an increasingly interdependent world and to seek out co-operative modes of development that harness the economic power of the developed states. LDCs can accomplish this goal only by understanding the nature of the international system.

Self-Assessment Questions

1. Why are there rich and poor countries in the world?
2. How important is democracy to political stability, and why?
3. Why have some LDCs been able to achieve sustainable growth while others have failed?
4. What is the link between political and economic development?
5. What should international organizations and foreign governments do to encourage democracy and respect for human rights?
6. Is equality or growth more important for developing countries? What are the tensions between the two?

Weblinks

Global Issues: Debt and Development
www.globalissues.org/issue/28/third-world-debt-undermines-development

Global Issues: Poverty
www.globalissues.org/issue/2/causes-of-poverty

Human Rights Watch
www.hrw.org

Transparency International
www.transparency.org

UN Conference on Trade and Development (UNCTAD)
www.unctad.org

UNDP Human Development Index (HDI)
http://hdr.undp.org/en/statistics/

World Bank
www.worldbank.org

Further Reading

Balaam, David N., and Michael Veseth. *Introduction to International Political Economy.* Upper Saddle River, NJ: Prentice Hall, 2001.

Cohn, Theodore H. *Global Political Economy: Theory and Practice.* 4th edn. New York: Pearson Longman, 2008.

Dominguez, Jorge, and Michael Shifter. *Constructing Democratic Governance in Latin America.* Baltimore: Johns Hopkins University Press, 2003.

Eisenstadt, Todd A. *Courting Democracy in Mexico: Party Strategies and Electoral Institutions.* Cambridge: Cambridge University Press, 2004.

Heywood, Andrew. *Political Ideas and Concepts: An Introduction.* New York: St. Martin's Press, 1994.

Lipset, Seymour M., and Stein Rokkan. "Cleavage Structures, Party Systems, and Voter Alignments." In *The West European Party System*, edited by Peter Miar, 91–138. Oxford: Oxford University Press, 1990.

Lustig, Nora. *Mexico: The Remaking of an Economy.* Washington, DC: The Brookings Institution, 1992.

Miar, Peter, ed. *The West European Party System.* Oxford: Oxford University Press, 1990.

Middlebrook, Kevin. *Dilemmas of Political Change in Mexico.* San Diego: San Diego Center for US–Mexican Studies, USCD, 2004.

Mingst, Karen A. *Essentials of International Relations.* 3rd edn. New York: W.W. Norton, 2004.

Norris, Pippa. *Electoral Engineering: Voting Rules and Political Behavior.* Cambridge: Cambridge University Press, 2004.

Rueschemeyer, Dietrich. *Capitalist Development and Democracy.* Chicago: Chicago University Press, 1992.

Smith, Brian C. *Good Governance and Development.* Houndmills, UK: Palgrave Macmillan, 2007.

Shambaugh, David. *China's Communist Party: Atrophy and Adaptation.* Berkeley: University of California Press, 2008.

News Clips

Visit the companion website for *Politics: An Introduction*, 2nd edn, to access news clips related to the content of this chapter.

11

International Politics and Foreign Policy

◄ UN delegates converse following a report from the organization's Independent International Commission of Inquiry on Syria in June 2013. The UN provides a platform for political discussion at an international level.

Photo: Fabrice Coffrini/AFP/Getty Images

After reading this chapter, you will be able to

- see the unavoidable connections between domestic and international politics;

- discuss some basic concepts in international politics, including the nation-state, power, the international system, foreign policy, and interdependence;

- distinguish among the actors involved in and the various approaches to international politics;

- explain the context of globalization in contemporary global politics; and

- recognize the role of foreign policy and decision-making in states' international relations.

Introduction

Covering such topics as war and conflict, diplomacy, the environment, development, and economics, international politics is one of the more prominent subfields of political studies. In many ways, the characteristics of international politics are quite similar to those of domestic politics. As in domestic politics, actors in international politics compete in a structured environment for limited resources. This means that substantial inequity often exists in the world, with people in some countries enjoying an advantageous way of life while others live in misery. Both types of politics also involve several different types of actors (military, economic, cultural, large and organized, small and diffuse, and so on) that have to relate mutually to one another. These differences often lead to outright competition. Another factor contributing to the fundamental inequity that pervades the international system is the very clear separation between those who have power and those who do not. Finally, just as in domestic politics, our main focus in analyzing international politics is to understand the allocation of public goods and benefits within the system and to explain the relationship among the main actors.

Although we need to recognize that domestic and international politics are intertwined, we must examine the two levels separately. International politics introduces a new set of concepts and ideas that, while related to our basic notion of politics and political life, force us to stretch the boundaries of relations to a global scale. In the real world of current politics, it is often impossible to make this separation, as events at home have a direct effect on the global

11.1   DOMESTIC AND INTERNATIONAL POLITICS: THE ELIÁN GONZÁLEZ AFFAIR

When revolutionary leader Fidel Castro overthrew the government of General Fulgencio Batista in Cuba in 1959, US–Cuban relations changed radically and immediately. Thousands of Cubans fled their country after the revolution and came to be known as the Golden Exiles, thanks largely to tales of prosperity in their new home. Attempts to escape to the United States resulted in the unofficial "wet feet/dry feet" policy of the American authorities: Cubans caught on the seas (wet feet) were sent back to Cuba, while those found on land (dry feet) could stay and claim refugee status.

Forty years after the revolution, the plight of a five-year-old Cuban boy in Miami, Florida, would highlight the peculiar quandary faced by Cubans trying to make it to the United States. In late 1999, Elián González and his mother were part of a group trying to reach Florida's shores. His mother and most of the other group members drowned during the journey, but Elián and the other survivors were rescued by fishermen. Elián was turned over to a relative in Miami, but his father, who was in Cuba, claimed that he wanted him back. US authorities were left with a conundrum: send the boy back to his father or allow him to stay with relatives. Advocates for both sides of the argument made impassioned pleas as expatriate Cuban groups made their arguments and the old rivalries between the two nations were rekindled.

In April 2000, US Attorney General Janet Reno finally decided to send Elián back, but his Miami relatives threatened to use force to protect him. Heavily armed border

AP Photo/Alan Diaz/CP

The excessive force used to remove Elián Gonzalez from the United States created great controversy among the Cuban community in south Florida.

patrol agents broke into the house where Elián was being kept and forcibly removed him, leading to anger in Miami's Cuban community, riots, and charges of excessive force. Interestingly, Elián joined the Cuban Youth Communist Party and enrolled in military school when he was a teenager.

This case represents a good example of domestic and international politics intersecting. Different communities in two countries advocated widely different courses of action. A little boy's predicament captured the attention of people around the world, and two governments–diametrically opposed in so many ways–were forced to seek some compromise.

environment and vice versa. But in our analysis of politics, we have to make decisions about the nature of our study: What will we study? What are the limits of our inquiry? How can we compensate for the inherent limitations we face because of these decisions?

This chapter will discuss some of the primary areas of interest for international politics and foreign policy specialists. To that end, it will cover the nature of the nation-state in international affairs, the intricacies of the international system, different actors in international politics, globalization, some of the approaches used, and diplomacy. The intention here is to familiarize you with some of the main concepts, structures, and issues facing those who study international politics today.

International Politics, International Relations, Foreign Policy, and the State

Just as politics affects our everyday lives, sometimes in ways that we do not necessarily notice, international politics influences many of our daily activities. Topics trending on Twitter, blogs, news feeds, and newscasts let us see, often in immediate and vivid detail, the surprising closeness of our global community. Election and war coverage, sporting events, entertainment, and even local weather broadcasts are available to us on demand. Streaming information over the Internet—from around the block or from the other side of the world—is made instantaneously available to us.

11.2 THE TWITTER EFFECT: ELECTIONS IN IRAN

Iran has a very young demographic, with over half of its population between the ages of 14 and 30. Its political leaders, however, tend to be much older. A major study by the RAND Corporation in 2008 accurately concluded that this imbalance would lead to political, ethnic, religious, and economic vulnerabilities and inevitable "popular dissatisfaction with the current system."[1] The 2009 election was seen by progressive Iranians as an opportunity to change the seeming belligerence of President Mahmoud Ahmadinejad's government. Ahmadinejad is a polarizing figure whose rhetoric concerning the destruction of Israel and the "deviant" religions of Christianity and Judaism, along with charges of corrupt political behaviour, contribute to the global condemnation of Iranian domestic and foreign policy. The country's attempt to illicitly develop nuclear weapons added to international criticism, not to mention anxiety over its objectives. However, the voting in this election was regarded as being severely rigged, with charges of manipulation and voter intimidation. Iranians, who are used to election fraud, were astounded at the level of deception. Despite a huge voter turnout, results were announced just two hours after the polls closed, a virtual impossibility. Ahmadinejad was declared the winner and citizens took to the streets in protest.

Although news coverage of these demonstrations was limited due to a government crackdown, individuals began reporting the events via social network updates, blogs, and (especially) tweets. Many major news outlets also used this

Thousands of Iranians gather in Tehran in 2009 to protest the election results.

information as a major source for their stories. As a result of this reliance on social media, the protests were termed the Twitter Revolution. Similar protests during the Arab Spring were also detailed in tweets. While the "revolution" may not have brought about a change in government in Iran, it certainly made clear the growing role for social media in news-gathering and reporting.

Note

1. Keith Crane, Rollie Lal, and Jeffrey Martini, *Iran's Political, Demographic, and Economic Vulnerabilities* (Santa Monica, CA: RAND Corporation, 2008), xvii.

It is often said that we live in a **global village**, where events happening on one side of the world have instant repercussions on the other. To a degree, this is true: for example, the collapse of stock trading in another part of the world or the death of a prominent public figure will surely have an effect—sometimes quite a dramatic one—on our more localized way of life. But we should be wary of phrases such as "the global village" because we are also constantly reminded of the ways in which we are divided from the rest of the world, even as we become more connected to it. That is to say, identifying with a larger community also means separating from others. This situation is most evident in the "us versus them" mentality, such as economic protectionism (see Chapter 13) or—more seriously—ethnic cleansing, that frames so much of the world affairs that we witness on a daily basis.

This is one of the greatest paradoxes of studying international politics: the world is increasingly disparate yet somehow joined. Even as we learn more about relatively unknown parts of the world or of different cultures and peoples, modern international politics is also still very much about identifying oneself and one's community, often at the expense of others. There can be no doubt, however, that we are more aware of politics around the world today than

global village
term used to describe the "shrinking" of the world, largely due to modern communications, into a more interconnected place where all people have a closer relationship and more frequent contact

11.3 CLICHÉ ALERT! THE "GLOBAL VILLAGE"

Like any other field, political studies is often the quarry of clichés. A prime example is the term *global village*. Although this term is currently used to describe our contemporary age of globalization, it was coined by Canadian communications theorist Marshall McLuhan to describe the growth of technology and an envisioned world where information was universal and instant.

Problems arise when we think about both words in the term. There's nothing truly "global" about today's modern communications, economy, or politics. Select parts of the world, mostly the developed countries, benefit intensely while the advantages of the rest of the world, particularly the developing states, are nowhere near the same level. Furthermore, decision-making, economic growth, and communications are more regionally located than global. The word *village* implies a small community of individuals who live in close proximity and are social and familiar with one another. The World Wide Web, global organizations, and broader education may make us more knowledgeable about the rest of the world and even a little more

Marshall McLuhan, pictured here in 1963, was a Canadian philosopher and media theorist whose ideas greatly influenced communications analysis.

Erik Christensen/*The Globe and Mail*/CP

sensitive to other ways of action and thinking, but we live in an environment far apart from anything that resembles a village.

previous generations. And that is one reason why international politics is such a popular field of political studies.

International politics is often referred to as international relations (IR) and those that study this topic as international relations specialists. In broad terms, international relations can include almost any aspect of interactions at the international level. In this sense, the 2012 Olympic Games, the Toronto International Film Festival, or travel tours arranged in one country and held in another are as much about international relations as are the G8 meetings, NATO's talks with Russia, or international trade agreements such as NAFTA. However, it would be impossible to study everything about all types of relations in the international community. The task would be overwhelming and provide very little understanding of the broader political relationship among countries. International politics highlights the decidedly political nature of relations at the international level. Although the two terms are usually used interchangeably, there is a clear difference between them.

foreign policy
foreign diplomatic relations and policies of a country beyond its borders

Another term used in this area of political studies is **foreign policy**, the legislated, or legalistic, relations of a state in the international system. Whereas international politics is about the mutual relationship of two or more actors at the international level, foreign policy is essentially about the manner in which individual states present themselves to the international community. In other words, the latter term refers to the guidelines that govern state relations beyond national borders, or the relationship between a state and its external environment.

Given its influence and power in the world, it is not surprising that the state is the most important actor in international politics. Remember that states are considered sovereign; therefore, no other international actor (not even the UN) can override their rights of self-determination and authority within their territory. The modern notion of the sovereign state follows the collapse of medieval universalism. Under the Holy Roman Empire, Europe shared a religion, a culture, a written language, and, to a certain extent, political institutions. The religious and political reforms of the sixteenth century shattered this cohesion and created a political vacuum that allowed for the development of modern sovereign nation-states. Ideas challenging the previous notion that all states held similar views or aspirations were born. Various political writers, including Hugo Grotius in The Netherlands, Emerich de Vattel in Switzerland, Niccolò Machiavelli in Italy, and Jean Bodin in France, wrote famous works on aspects of emerging states' power and legitimacy. By the time France's Montesquieu wrote, in *The Spirit of the Laws* (1748), that government should be adaptable to the needs and circumstances of its citizens, the concept of sovereignty was well accepted in law and in practice.[1]

Rex May/CartoonStock

"My foreign policy isn't working — write me up another one."

Though many political leaders might wish that foreign policy could be made so easily, it's a complicated process involving the political, legislative, and judicial bodies of a country's government.

Montesquieu's monumental work not only made the case for change in government (as opposed to a fixed system that is unbending to the changing will of the people), but it also detailed the various roles and authority that different government institutions should have.

Sovereignty as we know it today emerged with the Peace of Westphalia in 1648, whose Osnabrück and Münster treaties ended the Thirty Years' War and the Eighty Years' War, respectively. The states involved in the peace process were located in modern-day Germany, Sweden, France, Spain, and the

11.4 PATRIOTISM OR NATIONALISM?

Patriotism and *nationalism*, although related terms, are all too often used interchangeably. The former means "love of country," while the latter is an ideology that revolves around ideas of nationhood, or the identity one feels for a larger community of individuals. While patriotism is necessarily limited to the country in question (think of the statement "I am Canadian"), nationalism is much broader because it can be based on—but not necessarily reducible to—religion, race, culture, ethnicity, language, or even a form of government. When this identity becomes a movement to create a separate political unit, nationalism is born.

Most often, nationalism is peaceful. For instance, nationalist movements in Czechoslovakia at the end of the Cold War led peacefully to the new countries of the Czech Republic and Slovakia. In Scotland and Wales, such actions have produced only heated political debate and constitutional reform. This is not to say that the demands of these nationalist groupings have been satisfied, but the pattern has been one of non-violent resolution of conflict rather than more extreme measures. Some other examples, however, have been anything but peaceful. Many of the conflicts that have dominated world headlines involved disputes and fighting between different ethnic groups, such as those in Bosnia-Herzegovina, Rwanda, Burundi, East Timor, and Kosovo. Such conflicts led Harvard professor Samuel Huntington to argue that the twenty-first century would be dominated by what he called "the clash of civilizations."

There are potentially thousands, if not tens of thousands, of ethnicities in the world. If each were allowed to form its own political unit, the system of states that we

What does it mean to be Canadian?

Comstock/Thinkstock

currently know would be turned upside down—imagine a system made up of thousands of micro-states. The consequences for the stability of the international system and for the institutions that we have recently turned to for stability and economic and political benefits are immense. How could co-operation be organized among such a huge number of tiny states? More importantly, how could these states effectively provide for the economic and social well-being of their citizens? Would they be politically stable?

Netherlands, but none were modern states. At that time, there was an odd assortment of political units and authorities, including imperial states, countries, city-states, and principalities, with no real sense of commonality. After Westphalia, governments became the ultimate authority within their borders, other states recognized their legitimacy, and external actors were not to interfere in the activities of internal politics elsewhere. Territorial integrity is still the benchmark of the Westphalian system, which typifies the current global order.

In its modern sense, sovereignty means a monopoly of power over territory, people, and resources. The state (often in co-operation or conflict with other states) creates a boundary consisting of legal elements that prevent (within certain limitations) external interference and reinforce internal solidarity. Boundaries define the territorial extent of the jurisdiction of sovereign political-administrative units and are therefore legitimized by law and/or informal principles agreed upon by the area's people. Because borders retain their significance only if citizens see them as valuable, it is to the state's advantage to influence public opinion to coincide with its objectives. By emphasizing patriotism and similarities within the state and by exaggerating the linguistic and cultural differences of outsiders, the state reinforces national territorial boundaries.

Some states used other methods, such as force, to assert and maintain their authority. As you may recall from Chapter 4, authoritarian states preserve their power through the direct use of threats and fear among citizens and groups. Totalitarian states also seek a fundamental reordering of societal values and belief systems to match the wishes of the rulers.

The idea of using the state as the central unit of analysis is not without its challengers. Following World War II, and particularly with the emergence of the UN and a greater internationalization of economic activities, many scholars and politicians proclaimed that the nation-state would be replaced. Fervent state nationalism was, after all, considered responsible for the horrors of the two world wars. In reality, however, the prediction that the state would disappear has been proved wrong. At the end of World War II, the UN had 51 member states; it now has 193. Four centuries after Westphalia, the study of international politics still involves a complicated set of interrelated relations and actors, with a wide variety of goals sought by states and levels of interaction.

The International System

African Union
international organization
founded to promote
co-operation among the
independent nations
of Africa

In simple terms, an international system may be any grouping of two or more states that have organized and regular relations with one another. In this sense, the members of NAFTA—Canada, the United States, and Mexico—form an international system, as do the respective member states of the EU, the *Francophonie*, NATO, and the **African Union (AU)**. The term *international system* is most commonly used to refer to the entire globe, encompassing every state in the world, which is how we will use the term for most of this chapter. However, this definition is not the only one and might not be entirely accurate for every context.

An international system's framework is one of the most important determinants affecting how a state achieves its goals. Actors in the international system (predominantly states but also including such players as multinational corporations and international organizations) are distinguished and divided on the basis of their **relative power**, or the way that their capabilities may be compared to those of another. For instance, states with a powerful military may have far more influence and effect in the international system than those states whose power is based on limited physical resources because military power may enable a state to achieve long-term objectives more easily. Conversely, physical resources may be seen as being more crucial at different times. Whether waging war or mining minerals, a state's capability and relationship with others will vary.

Although all actors are part of the international system (and also of **subsystemic** groupings, such as NAFTA), we are still primarily members of individual political states rather than of the world community. Here again, sovereignty, patriotism, and nationalism are all part of why the state is still so important. State decision-making structures and processes have become more developed, and few political actors are willing to cede authority or legitimacy to global institutions and organizations, even major bodies such as the UN, out of concern that doing so would diminish the role of the state and the concept of state sovereignty.

Some regional subsystems such as the EU, NAFTA, and APEC are representative of a growing tendency to work as a body of political entities—all the while retaining individual sovereign power—in order to achieve certain economic goals. This preference shows that the international system may involve different states, but it is certainly not global. While international systems exist (e.g. the global natural environment, the global economy), smaller organized bodies that are international in nature but involve a limited number of specific actors are far more common.

Actors in World Politics

Though we deal primarily with nation-states in international relations, there can be no doubt that other **units of analysis** on the world stage are also important. We might consider some actors as being more prominent than others, but it is nonetheless essential to have a grasp of the competing influences.

Let's begin with the state. As mentioned above, sovereignty is one of the more consequential concepts in international relations because sovereign states are given certain rights and responsibilities that others do not have. For instance, only nation-states are permitted to enter into formal legal treaties or to wage wars with other states. These privileges date back to the creation of the first political systems hundreds of years ago. States are still the most important actors in the international system because of **structural anarchy**, which simply means that there is no political authority greater than the sovereign state in international affairs. States exist in this condition of anarchy when there is no

relative power
method of distinguishing the comparable strength of a political unit by contrasting it with another

subsystemic
international groupings or relations among states that do not include all actors

units of analysis
entities studied in politics; the "what" or "whom" as the basis of analysis

structural anarchy
in international relations, the assumption that no higher authority exists above the nation-state

"world government" (not even the UN) and they are ultimately responsible for their own behaviour within their borders.

international governmental organizations (IGOs) institutions formed by three or more countries with a common economic, social, cultural, or political purpose

Other actors, such as the UN, are **international governmental organizations (IGOs)**. These actors are larger conglomerates of nation-states that have grouped together for a common purpose. For instance, the UN was formed in 1945 to deal with problems that simply could not be dealt with by individual states—for example, international insecurity, global indebtedness, world hunger, and underdevelopment. NATO, a military alliance, was formed in 1949 by states in North America and Western Europe and has since expanded dramatically. Members of these IGOs do not give up their sovereignty, but they do agree to work with other states to reach common positions on these and other issues. Significantly, they agree to abide by the decisions of the organization, which means that, in exchange for group attention to common problems, the individual member states sometimes surrender part of their autonomy and freedom of action for the common good.

Non-state actors sometimes form international institutions. NGOs such as the Red Cross, Doctors Without Borders, or Amnesty International are groupings of like-minded organizations that all seek to work together on problems of a common nature but without the direct input of governments in the decision-making process. NGOs often have to work with governments, such as in the distribution of aid, but the latter are not part of the organization. Increasingly, NGOs are becoming more of a presence in international affairs as a result of the growing nature of world problems that cannot be dealt with by states alone.

Aside from these two examples, which are both international organizations (IOs), another type of non-governmental actor is the multinational corporation (MNC), which has activities in at least two countries. MNCs are unlike both IOs and states in that their constituency (that is, whom they must answer to) is made up of shareholders or board members. Like any other corporation, MNCs are international corporations that seek to make a profit in the globalized economy. MNCs are now one of the world's most important actors because there are so many. The number is constantly growing, but there are currently over 850,000 "home" offices and affiliates worldwide, according to the United Nations Conference on Trade

iStockphoto/Thinkstock

Headquartered in New York City, the United Nations is an IGO dedicated to building global peace, economic and social progress, and human rights.

11.5 NATO

The North Atlantic Treaty Organization (NATO), founded in 1949, united the countries of Western Europe and North America in the common struggle against communism and the Soviet Union. For 50 years, NATO stood face to face with the Warsaw Pact, its Eastern bloc counterpart, and defined security relations between Western nations. With the end of the Cold War in the late 1980s, several analysts predicted that NATO would be dissolved since its raison d'être had disappeared. The countries of Western Europe and North America, it was argued, would not be willing to pay the costs of a security organization that had become an anachronism.

Instead of becoming part of history, however, NATO grew in size and membership. In 1993, the organization invited Eastern European states of the former Warsaw Pact to join the Partnership for Peace (PFP), an initiative designed to increase co-operation in political and military affairs throughout Europe, to augment stability, and to remove threats to peace. Six years later, NATO welcomed the Czech Republic, Hungary, and Poland into the alliance. Further expansion in 2004 and 2009 brought NATO's membership to 28 nations.

NATO continues to act as a collective defence organization, meaning that states agree to mutually defend all members from external attack. Still the world's largest and most important security organization, NATO's role has moved beyond the North Atlantic in recent decades. Starting in the 1990s, it was involved in enforcing UN arms embargoes in the former Yugoslavia, which included military airstrikes against Serbian forces. NATO was also involved in radar

The official flag of NATO, adopted in 1953, symbolizes the unity of its member states.

Thinkstock

aircraft missions as part of the Gulf War in 2003 and took part in numerous humanitarian missions. But its mission in Afghanistan, beginning in 2003, has been its most significant of all. That conflict involved almost 130,000 troops from over 50 countries, including non-NATO partners.

and Development. However, many of these are quite small, relatively speaking. The large MNCs are far more powerful than nation-states, and not just developing states. Exxon Mobil and General Motors, for instance, had larger yearly sales than the entire **gross national product (GNP)** of countries such as Finland and Hong Kong. This economic clout clearly shows the importance of these corporations, especially when they invest in foreign economies or negotiate with weaker states regarding access to local markets. We will return to the impact of MNCs on international relations in Chapter 13.

gross national product (GNP)
total value of goods and services produced in a country in one year plus the total of net income earned abroad

11.6 HUMAN MIGRATION

One of the challenges for states in the twenty-first century is handling the threat of mass human migration. The movement of huge numbers of people has been a threat to national governments for hundreds of years, as these new arrivals absorb precious resources and contribute to political and economic instability. With the end of the Cold War and the resulting instability, Western European governments were forced to deal with the prospect of mass migrations of people from the former Eastern bloc searching for a better life. The civil violence and genocide in Rwanda that started in 1994 led to almost 2.5 million people fleeing to other countries, including Uganda, Burundi, Tanzania, and (then) Zaire. In 1999, hundreds of thousands of Kosovars sought shelter and refuge from the violence in their country by migrating to Albania, which cost the nation hundreds of millions of dollars that it could ill afford. Closer to home, human migration finds one of its starkest examples at the US–Mexico border. In the states of California and Texas in particular, this border has been crossed by millions of undocumented Mexicans and Central Americans who seek employment and prosperity in "El Norte." As a result, signs such as the one in this box are common near the border and serve to warn drivers that people may run across busy highways in their attempts to elude officials.

This situation has drawn a vehement response from many US citizens in the southern states, who argue that illegal immigrants take jobs from Americans and drain the social security and health systems. By way of response,

James Steidl/iStockphoto

Signs such as this one, which warns motorists that illegal migrants might be present on highways, are quite common along the US–Mexican border.

the US government has erected high walls and fences and established border patrols to keep illegal aliens from entering US territory. However, the activities of the so-called coyotes, individuals who organize the illegal transport of immigrants into the United States, continue to evade these restrictions. The coyotes, who charge thousands of dollars for their services, also routinely abuse, rob, and maltreat their human cargoes.

Finally, we cannot forget the importance of people and groups. Think, for example, of the influence of notable and well-known individuals such as the pope, the Dalai Lama, Bono, or Steve Jobs. These people can often change the mindsets of millions of people, or even whole countries, based on the roles they play internationally or the causes they support. Groups of people, often short-lived or unorganized, regularly have an effect as well. Student protest groups in China, the Occupy movement, or agricultural workers in Europe may form for only a brief period of time, but in that time they may affect the way we view the world.

11.7 THE OCCUPY MOVEMENT

A phenomenon in global protest, the Occupy movement began relatively innocuously in September 2011, when the Canadian-based anti-consumer *Adbusters* magazine proposed that people draw attention to social and economic inequality by physically occupying the area around New York's famed financial district. Eventually setting up tent villages in major cities around the world, advocates adopted the slogan "We are the 99%," referring to the huge amount of wealth controlled by the richest 1 per cent of people. Criticized for not having a central theme, or even any agreed-upon alternative, Occupiers nonetheless felt that their movement identified a variety of issues, including economic disparity, unemployment, globalization, corporate greed, military spending, and social inequality. While some, including some Occupiers, felt this was a new "revolution" in socioeconomic protest, others pointed convincingly to previous eras of social and global protest: the suffragette movement, civil rights demands, and–most recently–the anti-globalization movement of the late 1990s.

Anti-globalization, which faded with post-9/11 anti-terrorist legislation and shifting attention to other issues, was quite similar to the Occupy movement, as it also spread around the globe and was similarly criticized for having no central objective or leadership. Unlike these protests, which

Though the Occupy movement started in New York City, it quickly spread around the world. This photo shows protesters in Amsterdam.

frequently used violence, the Occupy movement expressed its concerns in a generally peaceful manner. Nonetheless, the sheer extent of the Occupy movement, involving worldwide events, widespread use of social networking, and massive media coverage, illustrates the enduring power of people-based protests, even if the precise goals of such demonstrations are not immediately apparent to observers.

Before his death in 2011, Steve Jobs not only changed the way we think about computers but also music (iPod, iTunes), movies (Pixar), communications (iPhone), retail (Apple Store), and publishing (iBooks).

Globalization

We hear about globalization daily, but few of us really understand what the term means or how it can have different meanings to different people. In their book *Whose World Order? Uneven Globalization and the End of the Cold War*, Hans-Henrik Holm and Georg Sørenson define globalization as "the intensification of economic, political, social, and cultural relations across borders."[2] This is a good basic definition, but it doesn't really inform us about the broad nature or the development of globalization.

Globalization began after World War II, an important watershed in international politics. The end of the war signalled the end of an era (i.e. the age of empire and European domination) and brought about the leadership of the United States and the rise of international institutions to help regulate an increasingly complex international system. It also initiated a wider understanding of the type of relations considered to be important, moving from the almost singular attention to security to a wider definition of social and economic considerations.

Globalization has many attributes, but we will begin with **economic globalization**. The postwar era brought about major shifts in world economics, both in trade and monetary relations. The level of world trade had been gradually rising for several centuries, but it greatly accelerated after the war. In addition to non-political technological and economic factors, trade was encouraged by the belief that trade barriers had contributed to the economic collapse that preceded and (some argued) helped cause World War II. As a result, and in their own interest, many countries agreed to remove tariffs and other trade restrictions. The result was the creation of the General Agreement on Tariffs and Trade (GATT) and, later, the World Trade Organization (WTO), which absorbed the GATT together with other institutional arrangements. One outcome of this greater trade was increasing economic interdependence. Today, the economies of almost all countries rely on foreign markets and sources of supply.

Monetary relations were also considerably revamped at the end of the war, primarily at Bretton Woods (see Chapter 9). The resulting monetary arrangements, known as the Bretton Woods system, were based on the gold standard and the strength of the American dollar. This system lasted until the early 1970s, when a number of factors, including the weakening of the dollar and the US government's unwillingness to sell gold at a **fixed** (and no longer realistic) rate, brought the world to a new **floating** system; that is, currencies are exchanged on the basis of supply and demand. The Bretton Woods structure also included the IMF, which was designed to help stabilize currency exchange rates by loaning countries money to meet international currency demands, thereby keeping supply and demand stable.

The GATT and the IMF were two of the major institutions created in the immediate postwar era. (The other was the International Bank for Reconstruction and Development [IBRD], or World Bank.) These institutions will receive more attention in Chapter 13. Institutionalization was an important development in

fixed exchange rate system
system in which states agree upon set values for their currencies in terms of other national currencies

floating exchange rate system
system in which the market decides the relative values of national monies

the new era. Nation-states agreed to permit co-operative governance of different aspects of the global economy such as trade, finance, and banking because the alternative—conflict—was so troubling. These states had already seen two wars, and the possibility of another was real.

The drive to create institutions in the immediate postwar period was also largely in recognition of the causes of World War II. In 1944, world leaders were concerned that the lack of regulation, integration, and normalcy of economic and political relations during the 1930s had led some states, such as Germany and Italy, to react to what they viewed as a system balanced against them. Those who met at Bretton Woods felt that a new system of **multilateralism** (involving many states in a co-operative manner) was necessary to normalize a very fractious state of affairs. This regulation was achieved through a systemic development of international organizations, institutions, and forums for deliberation that, it was hoped, would ameliorate any future conflict. In many ways, this new institutionalism was one of the main forces behind the emerging process of globalization.

Globalization is also seen in sociological and cultural terms. In this sense, the term refers to the emergence of a sense of global society and norms. The former means that individuals across the globe are increasingly associating with both their local or national societies and billions of other people around the world. To say that one was a "citizen of the world" used to be considered strange, but it has become more accepted, at least to the degree that our everyday lives are certainly more affected by world activities than in the past. The UN, in fact,

multilateralism
integration or coordination of policies or decision-making by three or more nation states

11.8 CULTURAL SENSITIVITY: TORRES STRAIT ISLANDERS AND *AUSTRALIA*

The film *Australia* (2008), starring Nicole Kidman and Hugh Jackman, addresses the treatment of Australia's Aboriginal peoples and includes many actors of Aboriginal descent. Non-Australian viewers might be a bit surprised to read the statement that appears before the titles: "Aboriginal and Torres Strait Islander people should be aware that this film may contain images of people who have since passed away and may cause sadness or distress." This statement is very similar to ones on Australian websites, books, and television programs with Aboriginal persons or characters. Australian Aboriginal and Torres Strait Islanders have deep cultural sensitivies regarding the dead. In fact, the film itself deals with the matter of "not speaking the name" of persons who have passed away. That a major Hollywood film addressed such traditions provides an interesting case of cultural globalization.

© Suzanne Long / Alamy

The Torres Strait Islands are located between Australia and Papua New Guinea.

presents an annual award to an individual who has made a difference globally: past recipients include Bill Clinton, Angelina Jolie, and Nicole Kidman.

The emergence of global norms and cultural standards is underway, as communications become easier and faster and people around the world exchange opinions and experiences. The international consensus over human rights that came about at the end of World War II was a major step forward in this area. But we would be mistaken to believe that our greater connectedness means that we all see things the same way or share the same global culture.

political globalization
political processes that span national borders and frequently circumvent them entirely

The political element is the last, and most controversial, of these facets of globalization. **Political globalization** refers to the emergence of political processes that span national borders and frequently circumvent them entirely. These processes do not merely concern international relations and diplomacy, which have been a part of our political reality for hundreds of years. Rather, political globalization implies that the influences on policy-making at both national and international levels derive from many different sources and involve actors with a global reach. One example has been the creation of NGOs that are represented in many different countries, such as Greenpeace and Amnesty International. Another example is the global movement for democracy that spread throughout the developing world in the 1990s. Political globalization ties national governments together through common pressures.

We can easily see how the end of World War II affected the international system and the ensuing globalization. There can be no doubt that the very functions and purpose of state relations radically altered after the war. However, perhaps the most important element of the postwar period was the emerging conflict between the United States and the Soviet Union. Known as the Cold War, this hostility created a strategic arrangement of states in the international system that existed from 1945 to 1991.

Although the United States and the Soviet Union were united during World War II in their attempts to stop German imperialism under Hitler, they did not view the world in the same manner or have the same attitudes about its direction. Soon after the war ended, both sides began to pursue independent goals for the international system. On the one hand, the United States and its allies sought an international environment marked by economic opportunity, political freedom, and international liberalism. On the other hand, the Soviet Union envisioned a world united in socialism, with centralized and controlled economies that would seek to redistribute wealth in a more equitable manner. These antithetical approaches influenced all aspects of international politics during the postwar period. The possession of nuclear weapons by both sides and the subsequent ability to destroy the world exacerbated the situation and added to the sense of fear and distrust (Chapter 12 will delve deeper into the problems with weapons and war.)

During this time, all aspects of international life—strategic, economic, cultural, and political—were deeply affected by the ideological divisions between the United States and the Soviet Union. Some aspects of global relations were touched more than others, such as states' manner of seeking military security through the forging of tight alliances with more powerful states. Even seem-ingly innocuous events such as the Olympic Games were victim to the Cold War animosity; in 1980 the United States and most of its allies boycotted the Moscow Summer Games, a decision mimicked by the Soviets four years later, when the Olympics were held in Los Angeles.

The Cold War had a number of different phases. Immediately following World War II, tensions between the two sides brought about what has sometimes been referred to as the long decade of the 1950s, marked by the first detonation of a Soviet nuclear device in 1949 and the corresponding American doctrine to contain Soviet expansionism. The signing of the Limited Test Ban Treaty in 1963 was considered by many to be the first real recognition by both sides that nuclear weapons escalation was out of control. The 1970s were branded the decade of **détente**, as both countries sought a degree of **rapprochement**.

However, the election of Ronald Reagan in 1980 and his emphasis on a military build-up as a response to the perception of a Soviet threat ushered in what was called the second Cold War. Actually a continuation of the existing war, this phase featured a return to colder, more remote relations and a corres-ponding renewed fear of nuclear war. Finally, the election of Mikhail Gorbachev as general secretary of the Communist Party of the Soviet Union in 1985, along with his program of restructuring Soviet politics and economics, brought about the beginning of the Cold War's end. The Soviet Union collapsed six years later. On Christmas Day 1991, the Soviet flag was removed from the Kremlin in Moscow and replaced with the flag of Russia.

détente
warming of relations

rapprochement
reconciliation

11.9 THE END OF THE SOVIET UNION

Alain-Pierre Hovasse/AFP/Getty Images

On 25 December 1991, Soviet leader Mikhail Gorbachev announced on television that the Soviet Union would offi-cially end at the stroke of midnight on New Year's Eve with the removal of the Soviet flag from the Kremlin buildings. However, unbeknownst to him, workers actually replaced the flag with the Russian one as soon as his address was finished.

The Soviet and Russian flags fly over the Kremlin buildings in Moscow in 1991.

Despite the changes to the international system after the end of the Cold War, a constant and basic world reality is that the substantial majority of people and countries are poor. To briefly recap the details given in Chapter 10, the vast majority of developing countries (known as the South) are situated either near or below the equator. In contrast, world wealth is concentrated in a few industrialized countries that lie in the northern hemisphere (the North). Although the absolute economic and related social conditions of the South are improving slightly, the gap between the North and the least developed countries in the South is widening at an alarming rate. Other countries in regions such as Asia and Latin America have had stronger levels of development and have therefore been more fortunate. But for the majority of countries in the developing world, the prosperity gap is a major obstacle. Since the 1970s, the less developed countries (LDCs) have demanded a fundamental restructuring of the distribution of wealth and the end of trade and monetary policies that favour the North. The North's response has been limited to date, and the question of Third World development and North–South relations will remain a perplexing and contentious aspect of international relations for years to come.

Compounding this increasing variance in economic opportunity is the more recent rise of the so-called newly industrializing countries (NICs). Whereas we once had a fairly simple model of relative wealth in the international system—basically the highly industrialized OECD member states and their partners versus the rest of the world—the current relationship is far more complicated. The past two decades have witnessed the rise of new, stronger economies, sometimes from states that were once considered Third World. As a result of strategically positioning themselves in the international economic environment and liberalizing their economies, states such as China, Mexico, Malaysia, Singapore, Taiwan, Hong Kong, Thailand, Brazil, and Argentina can no longer be considered LDCs. In addition, the very uneven progression of economies in the former Soviet bloc (the countries of Eastern and Central Europe) has left us with a number of different levels of economic and political development today.

Globalization affects us all (some more than others), but the distribution of costs and benefits is far from equal. Individuals in some areas of the globe, in particular in the advanced capitalist democracies of North America, Western Europe, and Japan, are highly integrated into the process of globalization, taking advantage of advanced technologies and communications to maintain contact with the rest of the world. This integration is even more apparent in a world marked by a global system that includes the Internet, social networking, and modern communications (e-mail, texting). However, developing countries (and especially their rural regions) seem relatively unaffected by advances in telecommunications and the growth of the Internet. The daily lives of citizens in these parts of the world are nonetheless affected by economic globalization, as the value of the goods they produce and consume and the value of their national currencies, and thus their personal wealth, shift according to the activities of global markets.

Though certainly not exhaustive, the preceding discussion gives us some insights into the nature of change in the international system. Indeed, one of the constant features of any international system is the transformation and variance of relations among the primary units of analysis. Politics is naturally a dynamic force in social life, and this dynamism is perhaps most evident in the international system. The fundamental alteration of the international system after the Cold War illustrates this tendency and the role of globalization in such changes.

Competing Approaches to International Politics

In this chapter we will study the numerous theoretical orientations to the study of world politics and the variations within them. The main ones, however, can be roughly divided into three basic groups: realism, liberalism, and Marxism. There are no neat lines separating these approaches from each other. In fact, many scholars and political leaders will use more than one, depending on the political or analytical needs of the situation. For the purpose of discussion and analysis, we will look at each one in turn.

POWER POLITICS: THE REALIST APPROACH

More than any other approach, realism assumes that states are driven by a desire for economic or military power. Distrust and self-interest mean that co-operation is unlikely and that the international system is marked by a constant power struggle. There are many examples of historical works depicting the emphasis on power in state relations. Over two thousand years ago, Kautilya, adviser to the first Maurya emperor, Chandragupta of India, wrote, "The possession of power . . . in a greater degree makes a king superior to another; in a lesser degree, inferior; and in an equal degree, equal."[3] This view has continued to dominate the thinking of most decision-makers involved in international affairs.

During most of the post-World War II period and until 1970, realist theory was also the main theme of academic international relations theory. Probably the most influential realist theorist of the twentieth century was Hans Morgenthau, who defined politics as a "struggle for power." His *Politics Among Nations*, published in 1948, argued that human nature and societies are imperfect.[4] Therefore, conflict is an inherent danger. Given that reality, Morgenthau claimed that decision-makers should structure their policies and define national interest in terms of power. They should follow policies designed to maximize their power and should avoid policies that overstep the limits of their powers. Realists believe that political leaders can avoid war by not pursuing goals that they do not have the power to achieve. It is thus necessary to understand the goals and power of opponents so as to avoid underestimating their abilities or threatening their vital interests.

Realism envisions the state as the key variable in the study of international politics. Other actors, such as international institutions or corporations, may become involved, but realists believe that the state will always wield the most power. Politics, for realists, is a struggle for limited resources in a competitive and non-cooperative environment. In this vision, the stronger states will likely determine the nature and rules of the international system. This idea has also existed for a long time. The ancient Greek rhetoric and philosophy teacher Thrasymachus famously argued in Plato's *Republic* that justice was the "advantage of the stronger."[5]

Realism became the basic theoretical approach to international relations after World War II as politicians and academics came to advocate a relatively pragmatic approach to world politics, sometimes called **realpolitik**. This orientation argues that countries should practise politics on the basis of power rather than morality. In the postwar period, this view was largely about balance of power politics, where states strive to achieve a power equilibrium in order to prevent any other country or coalition of countries from dominating the system. A country can achieve this goal through a variety of methods, including building up its own strength, allying with others, or dividing its opponents.

Morgenthau's ideas were popular, given his emphasis on a practical approach to the limits of power and the inherent nature of competition in the world. Other thinkers presented Morgenthau's arguments in a more modern context, taking into account the conditions of the postwar order. Most famous among these thinkers is Kenneth Waltz, whose *Theory of International Politics* became a mainstay in international relations theory almost as soon as it was published in 1979.[6] Waltz took a structural approach to international relations, arguing that the core ordering principle in the international system is anarchy, in which no authority above the state can override sovereignty. Waltz thought that, while each state is effectively trying to do the same as others (i.e. gain power), all are constrained by the structure of the system, which limits the choices of individual states. This situation is ultimately more important than the moral choices (or lack of them) that actors may have. Waltz was one of the new realists, leading to a school of thought known as **neorealism**, or structural realism, as Waltz would have it.

While realism allows that co-operation is possible, it is not always likely, given the level of suspicion and inherent struggles in the world. For realists, this is a never-ending situation: when one state achieves some degree of security, it comes only at the expense of another's, resulting in what realists call the **security dilemma**. The upshot is a generally self-centred and competitive world.

PROCESS AND CO-OPERATION: THE LIBERAL APPROACH

Many scholars and policy-makers reject the idea that international affairs should or must be played according to the dictates of power politics. They suggest that the real world of politics demonstrates that co-operation is inevitable because participants—states and otherwise—inevitably come to recognize that the **zero-sum game** of the realists' world is self-defeating and misdirected. Instead, liberalism suggests that the way the international system really works

realpolitik
pragmatic approach to world politics; idea that countries should practise balance-of-power politics and strive to achieve an equilibrium of power in the world to prevent any other country or coalition of countries from dominating the system

neorealism
"new" realism approach that views international relations from a systemic approach where states are constrained by the international structure; also called structural realism

security dilemma
conception in world politics that states are both protected and threatened by the existence of other states

zero-sum game
political or economic situation in which whatever is gained by one side is lost by the other, resulting in a net change of zero

shows us that politics may take place in a co-operative manner, though not without competition.

Liberals have been criticized for being too idealistic in their approach. In fact, early liberals such as Woodrow Wilson, US president from 1913 to 1921, were sometimes called idealists because of their positive view of a world united in its cause for human rights and progress. With the growth of institutions to facilitate co-operative behaviour, liberals took a less idealistic perspective. Though they maintained that benefits would come from co-operation, institutions were seen as a way to better "enforce" agreements. Liberals viewed the success of institutions as evidence that the world could see **positive sum** gains,

positive sum
relationship between two or more entities that yields benefits for all participants

11.10   WOODROW WILSON AND THE FAILURE OF THE LEAGUE OF NATIONS

Woodrow Wilson was president of the United States during a very important time in his country's history. In office during World War I, he brought the country into the war and steered the nation to a more assertive and active role in international relations. He tried to remain neutral, but the United States was ultimately drawn into the war as German aggression became increasingly impossible to ignore. As the war came to a close in 1918, Wilson (a Democrat) described the American role as being one in pursuit of progressive, rights-based principles of democracy, open trade, and diplomacy. His "Fourteen Points," a speech he made to the US Congress that same year, advocated democracy, free access to the seas, free trade, rights to citizens of colonized nations, and a series of independent rights to specific countries affected by the war. Although many other states did not agree with all Wilson's arguments, the Fourteen Points became the basis of the Treaty of Versailles, which set out the conditions of peace between Germany and the allied powers, and a new international organization called the League of Nations.

The league was created to provide a peaceful forum for its members, opportunities for free trade and diplomacy, and the basis for collective security (i.e. members would be protected against possible attack by others thanks to their alliance with the league). Although it reflected much of Wilson's points, the United States never joined. Like any international treaty, the league could be considered binding only when a nation's legislature passed it. The Republicans, especially Henry Cabot Lodge, refused to lend their support,

The "Big Four" meet in Versailles, France, in 1919. From the left are Britain's David Lloyd George, Italy's Vittorio Emanuele Orlando, France's Georges Benjamin Clemenceau, and the United States' Woodrow Wilson.

arguing that the league would oblige the United States to support situations it could not or would not want to uphold, including intervening if another member were attacked. As a result, the league never gained its intended legitimacy or effect. It was unable to stop the Japanese invasion of Manchuria, the rearmament of Germany under Adolf Hitler in the 1930s, or Germany's belligerent policies in Europe. At the end of World War II, the league split up and was replaced by the United Nations.

HEY — **THIS** GUY SAYS WE CAN SKIP CAPITALISM AND GO STRAIGHT TO STATE SOCIALISM!

LENIN

B.100

Lenin reinterpreted some of the original ideas of earlier Marxist theory. For instance, he did not feel that states had to pass through a capitalist phase before embarking on a socialist path.

liberal institutionalism
international relations theory that suggests that international institutions make co-operation more likely and advantageous

as nations can benefit from collective action in a way that would be impossible were they to act alone.

The liberal approach differs from realism in a number of ways. First, liberals do not believe that acquiring, preserving, or applying power is the essence of international relations. Instead, they argue that foreign policy should be formulated according to more collaborative and ethical standards. Second, the liberal approach also dismisses the charge by some realists that pursuing ethical policy works against the national interest. In fact, liberals suggest that ethical policy may be in the national interest of states. Third, the liberal approach believes that the world must seek a new system of order; it argues that it is imperative to find new paths to co-operate. Finally, in contrast to realists, liberals are prone to think that humans and countries are capable of achieving more co-operative, less conflicting relations.

This co-operation, according to the liberals, is illustrated in the rise of institutions in global political and economic affairs. Institutionalism therefore became a central part of liberal theory. Now a prominent part of liberal international relations, **liberal institutionalism** encapsulates these ideas about co-operative behaviour. Liberal institutionalists, such as Stephen Krasner, argue that the real world of collaborative interaction that is so evident in the many institutions that states join and work within shows the strength of liberal thought and the weakness of theories such as realism.[7] Krasner pioneered research on regimes, suggesting that these forms of institutionalism create ways to distribute authority and control in international politics but also give states incentives to work together. Today, we see examples of regime behaviour in trade agreements, financial regulations, economic zones, and even military alliances.

REJECTING REALISM: THE MARXIST APPROACH

In contrast to the other two perspectives, the Marxist approach advocates a completely separate form of political interaction on the world stage. Marxists suggest that realism is behind the current world situation rather than the conditions of the world driving the theory of realism. In effect, they argue that the "orthodoxy" that led to the dominance of realism also established the conditions of inequity and poverty worldwide. The Marxist approach primarily concentrates not on the political nature of the state but on the economic nature of the process of interaction. That is to say, Marxists suggest that a more equitable distribution of ownership and goods would create an international political system of greater fairness and security.

Marxists see socialism as one stage of a process leading to a desired objective: communism. The pure communist ideals espoused by Marx at the end of the nineteenth century envisioned the end of the nation-state, which he saw as an instrument of the oppressors against the oppressed.[8] The state, then, did not have a long-term role to play in Marx's vision. In the 1920s, Soviet leader Vladimir Lenin considered the nature of the international system from a Marxist approach, actually employing the state in a critical perspective that denied its viability as a unit. Nonetheless, Lenin saw the imperialist tendencies of industrialized economies as the highest stage of capitalism and the most severe dimension of a fundamentally unequal system.[9]

Political scientists and politicians who operate from the Marxist perspective believe that economic forces and conditions play a primary role in international relations. Some analysts in this general group study political structure and process from the perspective of the control and distribution of economic forces. For them, the economic base (the modes of production) determines the **superstructure** (the political, legal, cultural, and religious justifications, structures, and practices) that corresponds to a given economic system. They contend that a historically inevitable series of economic pressures and counter pressures (**dialectical materialism**) will, and should, lead to the destruction of capitalism and the triumph of communism.

Perception and Politics

As much as international relations is based on actual experiences and events at the global level, world politics is nonetheless often based on perception rather than reality. Political developments are often creations of the public and/or the people involved. Whether events are noticed and what they mean depend on the observers' situations and the language that reflects and interprets those situations. A global economic or military problem, a political enemy, or a leader is both an entity and a signifier (that is, it conveys meaning) with a range of connotations that vary in ways we can at least partly understand. For example, in 1938, British Prime Minister Neville Chamberlain spoke of "peace for our time" after meeting with German leader Adolf Hitler and signing the Munich Agreement. Despite Chamberlain's claims, that agreement permitted Germany to annex the Sudetenland (a region of Czechoslovakia) in exchange for Germany's agreement not to move further. Germany broke this deal and invaded the rest of Czechoslovakia, which eventually led to World War II. Critics called the Munich Agreement "appeasement" and suggested that Chamberlain should have been stronger in his opposition to Hitler's aggressive expansion. But Chamberlain's perception was that Hitler would be satisfied with the Sudetenland and war would be avoided. International politics is thus more than a matter of objective facts. It is a study of subjective judgments based on images of oneself and other international actors.

Although the study of international politics is largely analytical, behaviouralism (see Chapter 1) was also employed in this area. This "scientific school" of political studies is interested in recurring patterns and causal relations of

superstructure
political, legal, cultural, and religious justifications, structures, and practices

dialectical materialism
Marxist notion that material forces affect politics through social and economic change

international behaviour. Behaviouralists often use quantitative methods to form and prove hypotheses that will explain why certain events have occurred and under what circumstances they might occur again. They also often use cross-cultural analyses to test whether similar or divergent causal patterns occur between different political systems as well as over time.

Like realists, behaviouralists have little interest in advocating fundamental changes in the world system. Where they differ is that realists accept "what is" and often advocate that politicians should also accept and operate within the world of power politics. Behaviouralists are more disinterested in the good or ill of world politics. They tend to operate from a value-free posture, only describing what is and why and trying to predict what will be. This approach has been the source of some criticism from those who contend that the problems and stakes of the world are too great to be studied dispassionately.

Diplomacy and Foreign Policy

Whether we know it or not, we often think about foreign policy when we consider international relations. The US invasion of Iraq in 2003, for instance, had massive implications for international relations. States all over the world were forced to condemn or support the conflict, and the war affected global terrorism as well as the international political economy. But the invasion was also a foreign policy decision: US President George W. Bush considered his options and ultimately decided that the best alternative was to invade, and the US Congress authorized his choice in October 2002.

Foreign policies are the ways in which states seek to interact with each other in the international system. The word *policy* is meaningful here because it indicates that such matters are legislated and authoritative. States do not simply "do" foreign policy. There is an effective and understood process behind how it is made and how it is undertaken. The diplomatic element is crucial as well. **Diplomacy** refers to proper international negotiation and discussions that take place on an official—and sometimes unofficial—level among states. Depending on the level of seriousness surrounding the issue (e.g. war, the economy, culture), different actors will be involved in the process. And the process itself will be vastly different depending on the issue at hand.

Thinking about foreign policy helps our understanding of the international system more generally, as much of what is done in the system involves states acting beyond their borders. Foreign policy varies, depending on the state in question and the circumstances of the policy. Therefore, we should spend a bit of time reflecting on the forces behind creating foreign policy. To truly explain and understand the structure of relations among states, it is necessary to understand the political nature within states. Reviewing all nation-states and their particular political nature is beyond the scope of this book; however, there are some commonalities in the making of foreign policy.

diplomacy
international negotiation and discussions that take place on an official–and sometimes unofficial–level between and among states

11.11 DIPLOMACY GOES AWRY: APRIL GLASPIE AND SADDAM HUSSEIN

Sometimes even the most experienced diplomats fail to make their point clear. There are usually opportunities to correct the problem; however, in rare cases, a misguided phrase or misinterpreted action can lead to bigger problems. In August 1990, Iraq invaded Kuwait in what was almost unanimously considered an aggressive use of force. Leading up to the invasion, there were signs that all was not well on the border between the two countries. Iraq had built up huge numbers of troops at the border and had previously complained that Kuwait was not only slant-drilling for oil into Iraqi oil fields but also demanding that Iraq repay money it had been given to help fight its 1980–8 war with Iran. Tensions were high, and no one could be sure that Iraq's Saddam Hussein, an unpredictable leader at the best of times, would not use his military against Kuwait.

As the American ambassador to Iraq, April Glaspie was instructed to meet with Hussein to discuss the military buildup. In her meeting, she pressed Hussein to explain why he had his military at the border and expressed concern on behalf of the United States. She also told him, "We have no opinion on the Arab–Arab conflicts, like your border disagreement with Kuwait." This statement, which she later argued was merely meant to convey the importance of Iraq settling its dispute with Kuwait through diplomacy and without the involvement of other countries (including the United States), was interpreted by Hussein as a signal that the Americans would not intervene and would likely only make a statement against the use of force. Some analysts think that if Glaspie had been clearer about the US response, Iraq would not have invaded Kuwait. But the United States hadn't really considered its response beyond wanting to avoid war.

This low-resolution photo is the only known image of Ambassador April Glaspie's (left) fateful meeting with Iraqi leader Saddam Hussein (translator Sadoun al-Zubaydi is in the middle). The meeting was not meant to create the controversy it did.

Hussein ordered the invasion on 2 August 1990, which led to Operation Desert Storm, the international alliance against Iraq, in 1991. Glaspie was widely blamed for not being clearer in her remarks to Hussein. But she did urge him to find a peaceful way of solving the impasse. Defending her words as obvious to anyone, including Hussein, she later remarked, "We foolishly did not realize he was stupid." Hussein was deposed in 2003 during a subsequent invasion by the United States and was executed after a trial by the Supreme Iraqi National Tribunal.

The state's actions in making foreign policy are determined by several factors other than international law. Some of the more important are power, domestic capabilities, tradition, ideology, and perceptions of the national interest. These factors, admittedly, are rather imprecise. National interest, for example, can mean whatever the person using the term wants it to mean, whether it is military gains, economic relations, or reputation. In any case, these factors are informed to some degree by the following characteristics.

GEOGRAPHY

A nation's size and location in the world is always part of the power equation. For example, Canada's position as the second largest country in the world and its shared border with the United States mean that our resources and friendly relations will be of constant interest to our neighbour. Likewise, the location and economic strength of Germany in the middle of Europe means that it will remain a significant player in the EU and in the politics of Europe more generally. But geography has its limitations. Unlike other attributes contributing to foreign policy-making, there is little a country can do about its geography. Canada's relatively low level of defence spending, for instance, is in part due to its location. Were Canada to be situated in the Indian subcontinent, its military expenditures undoubtedly would be far higher.

There are other geographic issues affecting foreign policy. Whether a country is landlocked or a maritime state, its terrain, or its habitability is as much a factor in its interests as relations with allies or economic strength. The resources a country may have—closely related to geography—constitute a category of its own.

NATURAL RESOURCES

A country's natural resources play an important part in establishing the power of a state. Some countries are close to being self-sufficient in terms of critical resources. For example, South Africa is almost completely self-sufficient in food production. The United States and Canada also have vast resources, though they choose to import some for economic reasons. Still others have to rely on imports in such critical areas as energy and food. Some countries, such as Japan and Korea, are able to offset relative shortages of natural resources by basing their economy on high technology, which is made possible by an extremely skilled labour force and elevated levels of foreign trade. Other countries, particularly underdeveloped ones, are under constant pressure to share or sell their resources at artificially low prices in order to receive other benefits.

Increasingly, countries are now concerned with access to resources rather than outright ownership of them. In a highly interdependent world, it is simply unnecessary for countries to have direct control over all the resources they need for their citizens. Access—through trade—provides a more efficient way of realizing their resource objectives. Despite all the attention paid to technological development in the modern economy (which is obviously very important), natural resources will always be essential. Countries will not be able to sustain their way of life without food, water, minerals, primary resources, and raw materials. But states in possession of these assets will have greater flexibility with their foreign policy objectives.

POPULATION

Population is a major factor in determining a state's political, economic, and military power. A very small population (particularly in relation to the physical size of the country) will prevent a state from being very powerful unless the country occupies a strategic location and has other capabilities that offset its small population. On the other hand, a very large population that lacks an industrial base and suffers from food shortages will also lack the means required to exert power in the international world. Where that population lives (i.e. population density) will also affect a country's foreign policy decisions. For instance, population growth in China and India, two countries with more than 1 billion citizens each, greatly affects these countries' domestic and foreign policies and also places strain on their development objectives.

Canada's population density provides an interesting example. It is widely known that, in large part due to the fierce climate, most Canadians live in

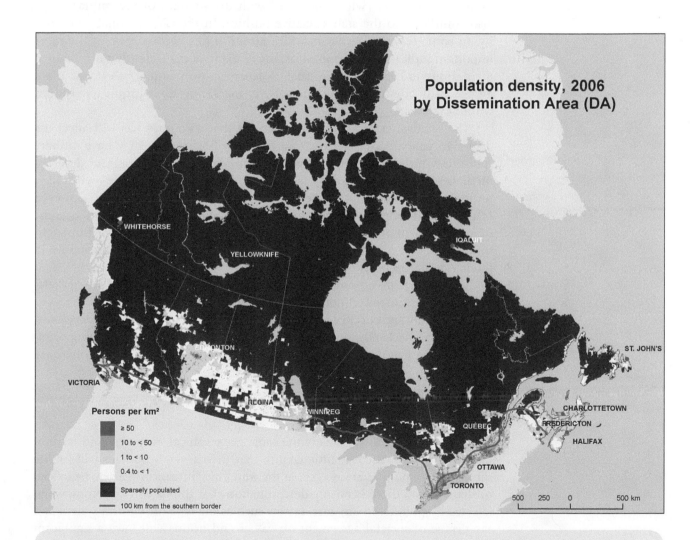

Figure 11.1 Canada's Population Density

Canada's Population Density. Most Canadians live just a short drive from the US border.

the southern portion of the country. But it is perhaps less known that, as we mentioned in an earlier chapter, nearly 80 per cent of Canadians live within 160 kilometres (100 miles) of the US border.[10] This fact is not surprising once we take into account the close economic relationship between the two countries, as well as the natural connection that occurred as both nations gained independence from Britain and established their own distinctive yet interrelated political systems.

TECHNOLOGICAL DEVELOPMENT

The level of technological development in general and in the specific area of military technology (when combined with the strength of the military) will also contribute to the state's relative position in the international community. In some respects, technological innovation has become one of the most important indicators of economic strength; many of the states that have shown their ability to compete today, such as Japan, Taiwan, and South Korea, place a great deal of emphasis on strategically marketing their productive output within the world.

The relative technological development that a country has will affect the degree to which it can alter its foreign policy. Technology may have military spin-offs, which will provide a level of security from attack. Economic development is greatly influenced by technology; more advanced states will enjoy technological levels that provide a better way of life for their citizens. However, countries that suffer from low levels of technological development will become more dependent on others for their security and economic welfare. Ultimately, technology can go a long way in providing independence and autonomy in foreign policy decision-making.

For this reason, a primary goal of many developing countries' foreign relations is to guarantee technology transfer, whereby they are given access to—or appropriate by legal or other means—technologies being used in the developed world. Since the 1960s, this objective has been a priority for developing countries. As Chapter 10 showed in greater detail, countries such as China have recently been particularly successful in this regard.

INTERNAL POLITICAL STRUCTURES AND PROCESSES

Even if two states have virtually the same geographical, resource, and technological attributes, there is little chance that their foreign policies will be the same because politics always gets in the way. This "intrusion" can be beneficial or detrimental; there is no pre-determination that things will go wrong when affected by politics. In any case, factors such as the type of political system and the degree of societal agreement on values and norms will have a significant effect on the outcome of foreign policy.

Take the case of Canada and the United States as an example. In many ways, these two countries share a great deal regarding their foreign policy decisions, which follow some of the same general principles: democracy, multilateral behaviour, and open economic markets. But the individual political system of each nation makes the decision-making process much different. The fusion of executive and legislative authority in Canada means that the creation of foreign policy follows a different sequence than in the US model, which features a more directed and concentrated separation of powers. That's not to suggest that either model is necessarily better or that one gives less attention to a particular level of government but that the systems reflect distinctive histories, political development, and tradition.

Such questions as the nature of groups participating in the decision-making processes, the maintenance of the political system's functions, and the extent of support for the system will all shape the state's behaviour in the international arena. History, prevailing political ideologies, and dominant perceptions of national interest will also be contributing factors. The experience of some state relations has made historical friends or enemies. For example, the history of hostility between China and Japan still creates difficulties for these two countries, even though they trade freely with one another. Some countries have a long history of being "world powers" (e.g. France and the UK), whereas other states are relative newcomers to the international stage. Prevailing ideologies both from the outside and inside also give direction to foreign policy. As we have seen in earlier chapters, there are various pressures and influences in the political planning of any state; this extends to the decision-making process and, in turn, foreign policy.

Finally, each and every state has some notion of what is in its best interest. Such notions transcend ideologies, elite behaviour, and any other considerations because they are embedded in that particular polity's way of life. The items discussed in this section are some of the main determinants of foreign policy that operate independently of any particular decision or program. While these factors do not determine every policy outcome, they are always a part of the decision-making process.

Canada and the World

For the most part, the issues regarding Canada's position in international relations can be placed into three categories: the economy, relations with the United States, and multilateralism. Security, sufficiency, and prestige for Canada come with a certain standard of life: a positive and robust economy. Canada's GDP of approximately US$1.7 trillion ranks eleventh among the world's economies. However, the country has a small domestic market—under 25 million consumers from a total population of just over 34 million. Simply put, Canada produces more than its domestic market can buy. Therefore, it must export its excess goods and services. Over 45 per cent of Canada's total GDP comes from its export markets. (Almost 80 per cent of those exports are sent to the United States.[11]) Like most other major economies in the world, Canada is sensitive to the global trade economy, but its potential vulnerability is higher than other industrialized nations because of its dependence on global trade markets.

Given the amount of trade that Canada has with the United States, one can easily see how much the former depends on its relations with the latter. According to the Canadian Department of Foreign Affairs, Trade and Development (DFATD), Canada–US cross-border trade is almost CA$1.4 million every minute of every day. Add to this the over 200 million people who cross the border yearly and it is clear that this relatively fluid boundary is a strategic one for Canada.[12] Since the signing of the Canada–US Free Trade Agreement in 1988, followed by NAFTA's taking effect in 1994, trade between the two countries has grown every year.

Canada's relationship with the United States is a broad one. They share membership in NATO and NORAD, defence agreements that require each country to aid the other in case of an attack. Canada's role in the war in Afghanistan, discussed in greater detail in Chapter 12, is the result of NATO invoking Article 5 of its Charter, which states that an attack against one (in this case 9/11) is an attack against all. Though Canada's military is small by relative comparison, its main thrust is the defence of North America, pursued jointly with the United States. More generally, Canada shares a cultural relationship with the United States. Though many Canadians would strongly defend their individuality, there is no doubt that many aspects of Canada's culture, including fashion, music, entertainment, art, and sport, are closely interrelated with that of the United States. The result is an inescapable tie between the two countries on deep-seated issues of values, mores, and society.

Multilateralism has been another important part of Canada's international relations. Historically, Canada's foreign policy has always focused on international co-operation and organization as a means to achieve objectives. In the postwar era, institution building was strongly supported by Canada. It reflected the nation's evolving internationalism, which became an effective basis for enhancing its global influence. Collaboration, co-operation, and compromise through multilateral bodies such as the UN and NATO bore clear results over what surely would have been a greatly diminished role had Canada been forced to act alone.

Canadian multilateralism following World War II, which emphasized co-operative policies over individual goals, led to the conventional opinion of Canada as "helpful fixer."[13] The country's tradition of multilateral behaviour expanded to include all aspects of its foreign policy, including military, cultural, political, and economic affairs. Given Canada's power relative to larger states such as the UK and the United States, multilateralism certainly was its best option for pursuing national and international interests.[14] In the Canadian experience, emphasis on multilateralism, in concert with its middle-power status, permits Canada to have its objectives achieved in the international system, even without being a "great" power.

The conventional view of Canada's international relations is in part due to Canadians' own view of their place in the world. Peyton Lyon and Brian Tomlin have explored the conceptions and attitudes that surround Canadian roles in world politics. These authors suggest that the terms *mediator*, *middle power*, *community-builder*, *peacekeeper*, and *bridge* characterize Canadians' self-perception of their influence in the international system.[15] To some extent, non-Canadians abroad also believe that these characteristics are descriptive of Canada. Many Canadians have heard about Americans travelling with a maple leaf stitched onto their luggage, a move that will open doors that might otherwise be shut to them. It would be a mistake, however, for Canada to become complacent about its place in the world. Positive reputations come from positive accomplishments, and reputations may be lost if those achievements are not forthcoming.

Conclusion

Today's international relations take place in a frenzied and dangerous environment. Economic downturns, ethnic strife, terrorism and wars, environmental challenges, and persistent underdevelopment would lead anyone to conclude that the current state of world politics is far from ideal. Instead of nations and peoples living together in harmony, the world is divided. The daily global drama has a cast of national and international actors at odds with one another, forever calculating what is good for them and then defining those ends in terms of universal justice and the common good.

In this chapter, we have examined the formation and development of the modern international political system. Filling the gap created by the breakdown of the Holy Roman Empire, dominant states within Europe developed a body of conventions and laws under the new Westphalian model by which to conduct interstate affairs. The prominence and legitimacy of the nation-state are important features of the modern international world. Coupled with the sovereignty of the nation-state is the importance of ideological, religious, and environmental concerns. These issues confound the ability of the state to bring about solutions independently of each other and lead to the creation of international organizations through which international co-operation can be achieved.

Although there are always examples showing a lack of co-operation and understanding between states, there is also evidence that increasing demands for international peace, a solution to the arms race, and a consideration of global pollution are resulting in new avenues of collaboration between states. The following two chapters will deal with two more areas of conflict and co-operation: international security and economics.

Self-Assessment Questions

1. How might we distinguish among international politics, international relations, and foreign policy? In what ways do they overlap?
2. Why is the concept of state sovereignty held so strongly in the international system?
3. Does globalization create benefits or challenges for nation-states today? Why or why not?
4. How did the Cold War era shape and influence international politics?
5. What are the primary approaches to understanding international politics, and how do they differ? What is the role for the state in each of these approaches?
6. What are the prospects for growing regionalism in the international system? Discuss whether state actors have anything to fear in this regard.

Weblinks

African Union
www.africa-union.org

Amnesty International
www.amnesty.org

Asia-Pacific Economic Cooperation
www.apec.org

Doctors Without Borders
www.doctorswithoutborders.org or www.msf.ca

European Union
http://europa.eu/

Group of Eight
www.g8.utoronto.ca

International Monetary Fund
www.imf.org

La Francophonie
www.francophonie.org

North American Aerospace Defense Command
www.norad.mil

North American Free Trade Agreement Secretariat
www.nafta-sec-alena.org

North Atlantic Treaty Organization
www.nato.int

Organisation for Economic Co-operation and Development
www.oecd.org

Red Cross
www.redcross.ca

United Nations
www.un.org

World Bank
www.worldbank.org

World Trade Organization
www.wto.org

Further Reading

Art, Robert J., and Robert Jervis. *International Politics: Enduring Concepts and Contemporary Issues*. 10th edn. Toronto: Longman, 2011.

Dougherty, James E., and Robert L. Pfaltzgraff, Jr. *Contending Theories of International Relations: A Comprehensive Survey*. 5th edn. Toronto: Pearson Education, 2001.

Dunne, Tim, Milja Kurki, and Steve Smith. *International Relations Theories: Discipline and Diversity*. Oxford: Oxford University Press, 2010.

Knight, W. Andy, and Tom Keating. *Global Politics*. Toronto: Oxford University Press, 2010.

Mingst, Karen A. *Essentials of International Relations*. 5th edn. New York: W.W. Norton, 2010.

News Clips

Visit the companion website for *Politics: An Introduction*, 2nd edn, to access news clips related to the content of this chapter.

12 International Security

◀ An Afghan National Police officer mans a checkpoint on the outskirts of Maidan Shahr in Wardak province. In most of the country, the National Police and army now provide security without assistance from international troops.

Photo: AP Photo/Anja Niedringhaus/CP

LEARNING OBJECTIVES

After reading this chapter, you will be able to

- understand the nature of security and insecurity in international relations;

- appreciate the history of war among states and the way war has changed;

- understand enduring and emerging security dilemmas such as international terrorism and humanitarian intervention;

- discuss methods to reduce conflict, especially through peacekeeping; and

- explain the particular challenge that Canada faces regarding the future of its military involvement.

Introduction

When people think of world politics, they often imagine scenes of war and conflict. After all, media reports tend to reflect the darker side of global affairs. Many notable observers share this more negative view. No less than Winston Churchill, who was British prime minister during World War II, wrote in 1932: "The story of the human race is War. Except for brief and precarious interludes, there has never been peace in the world."[1] Others support Churchill's opinion that the human race has always been prone to conflict. Gwynne Dyer, a Canadian historian and columnist, wrote:

> It can never be proven, but it is a safe assumption that the first time
> five thousand male human beings were ever gathered together in one
> place, they belonged to an army. That event probably occurred around
> 7000 BC—give or take a thousand years—and it is an equally safe bet
> that the first truly large-scale slaughter of people in human history
> happened very soon afterward.[2]

We can be certain of one thing: Dyer was correct that it would be impossible to prove his argument. On the other hand, it is difficult to imagine what other purpose would bring those 5,000 males together.

This view of humankind might appear rather bleak, but it is quite realistic given our history. Many long debates have taken place regarding the nature of human conflict and whether it is a natural or learned characteristic. We certainly will not solve that controversy in this chapter—nor will we attempt to—but security in political studies is undoubtedly an important concern, whether it's a matter of domestic or international politics. In fact, we suggest that it is the most fundamental concern for political communities.

This chapter considers security in international relations. From a historical perspective, this topic has always been a primary concern for states, from ancient wars of empire to modern fears of terrorism. The methods of human brutality may have changed (although in many respects they have not), but the security of the state is still a priority. As a result, it is not surprising that wars and conflict receive so much attention in international relations. Conflict is dramatic and stimulates our thinking, reactions, suspicions, and vigilance. It is not necessarily beneficial, although some good can come from certain forms and instances of conflict, but it captures our attention. Major news headlines usually are reserved for bad news, and wars tend to

This cave painting found in France shows prehistoric peoples at war. Can you think of another reason for so many men to be gathered in one place?

fall into that category. Drama and uncertainty sells because we all—individuals and communities—worry for our own security. In that light, humans have not changed much over time.

Insecurity in the world is no doubt commonplace in our international system, and for many states it is a way of life. Nevertheless, most state activities are actually aimed at preserving or improving the conditions of their citizens and aiding peace among nations. Most of what states do does not fall in the category of front-page news. In fact, in contrast to the excitement of these events, the day-to-day operations of states are rather mundane: trade, diplomacy, and routine relations with other states, for example. Yet these regularized activities are, in some ways, an ongoing effort to mitigate conflict in the international system.

Security and Insecurity

Security exists when there is a relatively low probability of threat or damage to citizens, government, territory, resources, wealth, and even values such as culture or identity.[3] As discussed previously, conflict comes about when there are disputes concerning these areas, particularly when groups of people are involved. And war can take place when these groups resort to the use of armed hostilities. Security can never be completely assured for any state in the world, even the most powerful (consider, for example, the insecurity felt in the United States after 9/11, in London after the bombings of 7 July 2005, or in Boston after the April 15, 2013 bombings). Individuals and even states can feel insecure due to real threats and violence or an

The London Underground and transit buses were targeted in a coordinated attack on 7 July 2005.

© Trinity Mirror / Mirrorpix / Alamy

geopolitics
association between a state's political relationships and its geographical location

imagined threat felt in the international system. Whether a nation is under direct attack from another or merely feels that its values and culture are threatened by the influence of another, insecurity may indeed be present.

A state's security was once almost completely based on its location and its proximity to potential allies and enemies. States in Western Europe, for instance, were constantly balancing the power of other alliances in an effort to keep one side from becoming strong enough to threaten another with force. This relationship between political interactions and a state's geographical location is known as **geopolitics**. Access to resources, beneficial or detrimental relations with neighbours, physical strength, population, and natural attributes all fall into the considerations of geopolitics. Although security is thought of differently today, geopolitics is still relevant. Think of the geographical position that Canada occupies in the world. It is close to the United States, a superpower and Canada's closest ally, is separated physically from some of the most dangerous regions in the world by oceans and the Arctic, and benefits from one of the best standards of living thanks to its peaceful system of politics, large resource base, and educated citizens. If Canada were in the Asian subcontinent or the Middle East, its relative security would undoubtedly be challenged by unstable regional politics, concerns over access to resources, and uncertainty about potential threats from neighbours. It would certainly be a very different environment for Canadians.

Geopolitics is also important because it allows states to achieve certain goals without necessarily having to possess the features required for those objectives. Some states, such as Japan, are unable to produce or obtain what is required for their very existence. However, in the modern world, such states only have to have access to them. This access is possible through trade and alliances with other states.

International security is in fact about the conditions caused by insecurity because states in the international system are fundamentally concerned about their own self-preservation. A state is insecure if it is unable to provide for itself as a government or for its citizens. Without security, any other goal of the state—such as economic prosperity and a better life for its people—would be impossible.

Insecurity can arise from a variety of causes. In simple terms, it involves threats to a physical place, person, or group or to important values felt by the community. Alternatively, these threats might emerge as pressures placed on individual or collective material welfare. That is to say, prosperity may be threatened due to conflict. Although the roots of these conflicts clearly cover a wide spectrum of threats, all of them can ultimately lead to more serious conflict or even war. Finally, threats may be directed at one's identity.

Threats also come in a variety of forms. Military threats involve physical harm. Economic threats relate to material welfare. Political threats deal with governance, control, and instability. Cultural threats are those directed at our values and way of life. Environmental threats affect the conditions that sustain our communities. Interestingly, some have suggested that only environmental security has the potential to affect us all. Whereas politics, economics, and culture come in various forms, the environment is one aspect that is truly "universal." While certain parts of the world may be more vulnerable than

12.1 HUMAN SECURITY

Human security emerged in the 1990s as an alternative to traditional "statist" security. At that time, prominent non-governmental groups such as the International Campaign to Ban Landmines (ICBL) and academics such as Edward Newman and Ken Booth began looking at approaches that focused on the security of the person rather than the state.[1] Human security entails protection from threats that accompany aspects of non-territorial insecurity, such as environmental scarcity, human rights violations, genocide, and mass migration. The concept's assumption that an individual's protection comes from both the safeguarding of the state and access to well-being and a better quality of life created a fair amount of controversy in international security studies. Human security is often considered problematic because it is more difficult to assess personal security than, say, an attack by one state on another. For instance, people disagree about whether someone without access to, say, social infrastructure or health care would be considered "insecure."

The notion of security has been contested for a very long time. We can define it in terms of military protection, meaning the defence of citizens, territory, and resources by military means. We can also think of it in political terms, such as the protection of government organizations and political ideology. Alternatively, economic security might be considered as the maintenance of citizen welfare and access to finance and markets. Societal security refers to the preservation of culture, social order, and communal identity. Environmental security signifies the conservation of natural ecosystems. All of these forms impact the individual in some way. Therefore,

Greg Gorman

US peace activist Jody Williams won the 1997 Nobel Peace Prize for her work with the ICBL.

we might say that any form of security can be connected to human security.

Note

1. For more on the development of the human security concept, see George A. MacLean, "Human Security and the Globalization of International Security," *Whitehead Journal of Diplomacy and International Relations* 7 (Winter/Spring, 2006/07): 89–99.

others—such as the Maldives, where rising sea levels could completely submerse the island if climate change continues at its current pace—all countries feel the effect of environmental changes. Flooding, weather patterns, deforestation, desertification, and dozens of other environmental effects have led to varying states of insecurity. As we will discuss later, the environment is an important part of the "human security" viewpoint.

It is evident, then, that security and conflict are complex dynamics involving much more than simply declaring war or using armed force against another actor. Given the wide variety of sources, it is not surprising that conflict has always been present in international relations. Part of the reason for the rising frequency of conflict is **international anarchy**, a condition in international relations that has been around for hundreds of years. The term *anarchy* tends to bring about images of chaos and destruction, a lawless environment of all against all, but this is not what we mean here. The term literally means "absence of hierarchy"; however,

international anarchy
condition where there is no "world government"; the sovereign nation-state is the highest authority in the international system

12.2 "ANARCHY IN THE UK"

In 1975, the Sex Pistols exploded on the British music scene with a style that reflected disenfranchised youth living in the midst of an economic recession and chronic unemployment. Considered front men for the country's burgeoning punk movement, the Sex Pistols and their song "Anarchy in the UK," from their 1977 album *Never Mind the Bollocks, Here's the Sex Pistols*, galvanized a counterculture and shocked the elites.

The song's aggressive lyrics (e.g. "Get pissed, destroy") and pessimistic take on British society conveyed both a hopeful and hopeless meaning: to the punk movement, the song typified its sense of disengagement and provided a vehicle for their collective anger and calls for change; for "conventional" society, the song was a threat and a challenge to social norms. The use of the term *anarchy* gave the song several connotations. It was anti-establishment and anti-Monarchy, contained violent social commentary, and acted as a siren call for many similar bands in the UK and abroad. Lead singer John Lydon (aka Johnny Rotten) later said that the song showed what energy he gained from living in poverty and that he used the word *anarchist* because it rhymes with *Antichrist*, which he sings at the beginning of the song.

"Anarchy in the UK" speaks of the "coming" state of anarchy as an alternative to the broken social order at that time in England. It advocated the collapse of the

"Anarchy in the UK" was released to coincide with Queen Elizabeth II's silver jubilee celebration.

political system through anarchism, reflecting the classic philosophical roots of political anarchism, which promotes the sanctity of individuals as self-determining and purposeful decision-makers. The song also inspired a number of punk acts to think about political criticism in their lyrics and, arguably, spawned a movement that is still alive today.

in international relations, *anarchy* is a fairly simple principle that refers to "no world government," or that the authority of nation-states is the most important power in the world. With an anarchical international system, state security is left to the individual ability of states and their relations with others in the system.

The issue of anarchy at the international level is fundamental to our studies of the international system. It not only allows states to be the ultimate authority in international relations, which means that citizens have an identifiable institution (that is, the state or government) that they can look to for protection, representation, and guidance, but it also creates the security dilemma for states (see Chapter 11). Put in most basic terms, all states are potentially insecure because the very attempt by one to make itself secure makes others less secure. The underlying assumption is that not all states can be secure, given the limited resources and competing interests that exist. Even if states don't actively seek out conflict with others, the security dilemma suggests that conflict will ultimately arise. The reason is that, while one state maintains a military to protect itself, the presence of this force could create tensions and insecurity for another state, since the latter might see the military presence as a potential threat.

How do states respond to this dilemma? The most common method is through defence spending. Every state will have its own defence spending policies based on assessments of risk and capability. (Although some countries, such as Costa Rica, have no military at all.) According to the Stockholm International Peace Research Institute (SIPRI), one of the most respected authorities on the topic, global spending on defence is over US$1.7 trillion dollars, or about 2.5 per cent of GDP worldwide. Some countries spend far more than others: the United States, with a defence budget of over US$700 billion, accounts for more than 40 per cent of the global total, which translates to more than the next 32 countries combined.[4] But when we place the total amount spent in the context of how wealthy countries are, the relative standings change. As mentioned in an earlier chapter, defence spending in the United States totals 4.7 per cent of the country's GDP. Several countries spend more as a percentage of their GDP. Saudi Arabia spends more of its GDP than any other country, totalling over 11 per cent. Like many issues in politics, defence budgets can be seen in different ways.

Security in the twenty-first century is a complicated and multifaceted dynamic. It is affected by modern technology and globalization but is still driven by the same geopolitical tendencies that have accompanied international relations for centuries. Unfortunately, the most violent form of conflict—war—is as much with us today as it ever was.

War in International Relations

International security is about much more than war. With human society comes conflict. Generations of social scientists have debated the issue, but we still cannot know for certain if conflict is innate in humans simply because it is impossible to study humans away from civilization. All human groups form some type of civilization and all civilizations deal with conflict in one way or another; hence our conclusion that conflict emerges from society. Conflict may be rooted in problems over territory, access to resources, religion, culture and ethnicity, family or tribal relations, alliances we have formed, or economic prosperity. It may come as the consequence of one, or any grouping, of these causes. It is used as a means of achieving goals and solving problems in society. Conflict may not seem like an optimal method, but it's always been an option and is often very effective.

Conflict can come in many forms. Loosely defined as the opposition of incompatible wishes or needs of a person or group of persons,[5] conflict does not necessarily mean outright war.[6] To begin, we need to be clear that the terms do not mean the same thing, though they are intricately related. Whereas conflict can mean disagreements, debates, threats, and all sorts of other differences of opinion, war is a more serious consequence of conflict. There may be conflict without war but not the other way around. Since war is always an option, citizens and leaders are concerned about conflict getting out of control.

Even the most stable and secure governments must still deal with conflict. States use foreign and defence policies to form responses to potential conflict in the world—and war must be considered "policy." Military theorist Carl von Clausewitz is famously known for writing that "war is the continuation of politics by other means."[7] Clausewitz felt that war must be seen as a legitimate tool for states to respond to insecurity in the international system. This means, then, that war must have rules and must be waged according to them.

Regrettably, history is full of examples of how frequently states are prepared to use this method negatively. There are several ways in which power is used in a "negative manner" in international politics. For example, states use their power, in particular military power, to coerce others to do as they wish. They protect their sovereignty by threatening to use military force in protection of physical territory. Demands against other states are frequently made with the stated or understood threat of military intervention in the case of non-compliance. States also threaten or use trade embargoes and physical blockades to influence the behaviour of other states. Finally, states use purely military force in order to accomplish their goals.

However, there is another dimension to the use of state power as it pertains to conflict management and resolution. States often use their powers of influence, gained through respect and authority in the international system, to avoid conflict. Powerful states will often send representatives to negotiate with other states as a means of obtaining settlement. In addition, states sometimes use the threat of their power to persuade other states from taking actions that may be deemed detrimental to the international system.

Canadians might find it difficult to legitimize the use of war as a means of policy. Indeed, there has been a long-standing discussion in Canada about whether the country is a war-fighting or peacekeeping nation.[8] The reality is somewhere in between. Moreover, some would reason that warfare should be an obsolete policy since far better courses of action are available to governments. But for better or worse (largely worse), war is still with us and we must still strive to understand it.

12.3 JUST WARS

War may be among the most brutal of human actions, but that is not to say that it doesn't fall within some legal guidelines. Civilizations have always figured out new and innovative ways to attack and fight others; however, efforts to stem the activities of war have also existed. The Law of Armed Conflict (LOAC), which is actually a collection of many laws, is meant to protect innocents–those caught in the crossfire, either literally or figuratively–in the waging of war. *Jus in bello*, or laws in war, outline acceptable practices, as well as violations (including war crimes). The Geneva Conventions, for instance, are treaties governing standards of international law in warfare. Sovereign states agree to recognize these conventions as binding with regard to proper and acceptable actions of states engaged in war.

Another set of international law deals with the acceptable justifications for war. *Jus ad bellum*, or laws of war, stipulate the acceptable use of force. A broader philosophical strain underpins this idea: just war doctrine. Stemming from teachings of the Catholic Church and Roman philosophy, just war theory considers the conditions necessary to make war acceptable. There are several different interpretations of just war theory, with many requirements. Six, however, stand out as consistent in most interpretations. First, there must be satisfactory conditions for waging war; just cause, for example, might emerge when lives may be saved only through the use of force. The "right intention" for war, then, must be to right a wrong. Second, these just wars must be separated from those fought for aggression. Third, the war should address comparative justice; that is, it must address a significant suffering felt by one side, meaning that one side should have suffered more than the other. This greater suffering would suggest a "right" by one side to use war to defend itself or its interests. For instance, were Country A to use state-sponsored terrorism to attack innocents in Country B, the latter might invoke comparative justice as a means of legitimizing the use of force and killing. Fourth,

In his *Summa Theologica* (an overview of Christian theological teachings), St. Thomas Aquinas (pictured here) built on ideas of St. Augustine of Hippo and others toward an understanding of what might be considered "just" in war.

© World History Archive / Alamy

wars must be waged by legitimate authorities, who must use acceptable and lawful agents, such as militaries–not, say, terrorist organizations. Fifth, the war may not be futile but must have a sense that it can be won. Finally, it should be fought with proportional methods, meaning that the use of overwhelming force such as nuclear weapons would be considered only if these means were employed by the other side.

Whereas the winning country once simply dictated the aftermath of a war, laws of war have more recently included *jus post bellum*, or the conditions regarding termination and follow-up. These terms are considered necessary for providing a peaceful and fair termination to war, including treaties, just treatment of combatants, provisions against unjust gains by the winning side, and avoidance of vengeance.

There is great debate about whether humans are more "war-like" today than in the past. Comparisons of historical studies and contemporary instances of war are controversial for a number of reasons. Our recorded account of war today is far more detailed and accurate than in the past. Also, there are now many more states in the world today; consequently, we should expect the number of conflicts to rise. Different interpretations of the term *war* have existed throughout the ages: for example, religious wars, civil wars, ethnic wars, guerrilla wars, and world wars.

Despite these difficulties, many analysts have attempted to number conflicts in the past as compared to the current number. Although the totals tend to vary, it's generally accepted that the past 3200 years have seen more than 3,000 violent conflicts.[9] Many research studies, from the SIPRI and the Correlates of War Project, have shown that the relative instance of war has increased since the end of World War II. Although these numbers may not hold up to scientific precision, they do provide a basic benchmark for the instances of war in different periods. Many of these wars lasted more than one year, and many involved several countries at the same time. Some battles are so contentious that even analysts cannot always agree whether they count as wars. The point here is not the actual numbers but that violent conflict is increasing in the modern world.

Perhaps more noteworthy is where violent conflict occurs. Since World War II, most wars in the world have taken place in the developing world—in South and Southeast Asia, Central and South America, Africa, the Middle East, and Eastern Europe. (A quick glance at Figure 12.1 confirms that violent conflict is more common in these parts of the world.) These days, conventional wars

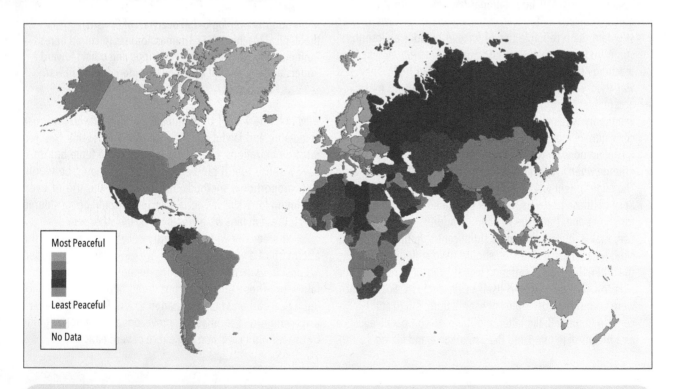

Most Peaceful

Least Peaceful

No Data

Figure 12.1 Global Peace Index 2012

The GPI ranks countries of the world based on their relative levels of insecurity and security.

Based on: Global Peace Index 2012 Interactive Map

taking place in Western Europe or North America are unheard of, although countries in these regions have participated in wars waged elsewhere. We can conclude from this situation that the more advanced and developed a region, the less likely that violent conflict will occur there.

Further, the reasons that states go to war with each other tell us a lot about the use of conflict today. Although we live in an age of technology and globalization, wars are still fought for most of the same reasons as they were in the past: to create a state, settle disputes over territory or ideological differences, defend oneself or an ally, maintain a governmental regime, or protect an ideology. This similarity, along with the fact that so much of the violence in the current international system is reminiscent of past violence, tells us that international security remains a vital part of the study of international relations. As the saying goes, the more things change, the more they stay the same.

12.4   "VIDEO GAME" WAR, 1991

The First Gulf War (1990–1) was a war like no other. Seen instantly by millions of viewers around the world, images of precision-guided munitions and missiles (PGMs) and so-called smart bombs were carried by every major media outlet. The strange and eerily surreal video of tracer fire and bombs exploding over Baghdad on that first night of the war made viewers feel at once involved and detached from the conflict. Commentators almost immediately began likening the footage to a video game, in which the player (or, in this case, the viewer) has an isolated and often unemotional relationship to the images on the screen. Viewers watched the war but had no connection to it: they didn't see the death and destruction caused by the bombs and explosions, and the whole event had a sanitized quality. This situation wasn't a great surprise, as the Vietnam War had taught the US military some hard lessons about giving journalists unfettered access. At that time, uncensored pictures of the killing and devastation led many Americans to reject the war.

In 1991, technology had given the United States and its allies a huge advantage by allowing it to present a false image of the conflict as a tidy war with few casualties, at least for the alliance. However, the reference to video games soon became a form of criticism of the war and our impressions of it. More extreme references, such as "war porn," were used to describe the constant depiction of a war on the other side of the world, far from immediate effect on our lives. In 2003,

REUTERS/Patrick De Noirmont

For many, the television images of Bagdad being bombed in 1991 created the impression of "virtual," or simulated, conflict.

with the Second Gulf War in Iraq, pundits resurrected the video game metaphor. This time, however, there was a larger sense of reality. Secretary of State Colin Powell cautioned Americans: "Remember, this is a real war—not a video game."[1]

Note

1. Mia Consalvo, "It's No Videogame: News Commentary and the Second Gulf War," paper delivered at the Digital Games Research Association Conference, Utrecht, the Netherlands, November 2003.

Terrorism

The terrorist attacks on New York City, Washington, DC, and Shanksville, PA, on 11 September 2001 were not the first case of international terrorism. But the sheer magnitude of the attacks, combined with the fact that the target was the most powerful country in the world, caused our collective understanding of international insecurity to focus on the problems of terrorism and the very real threat that it poses to anyone, anywhere, and at any time.

The attacks on the United States were the most severe acts of terrorism in history. Close to 3,000 people were killed, billions of dollars in costs were immediately incurred, and the more long-term effects included a US–led intervention in Afghanistan in 2001 (which led to the NATO alliance conflict in that country) and renewed conflict in Iraq from 2003–11. The attacks also had "spin-off" results that negatively affected international economic markets, tourism and travel, and relations among allies in Europe and North America and raised serious questions about the future of international relations and American leadership in the world system. So many aspects of our lives, from the most banal (removing your shoes and checking the size of your toothpaste tube at airport security) to the more solemn (hearing of another Canadian soldier being killed by a roadside bomb in Afghanistan) were direct consequences of 9/11.

What made these terrorist attacks an essential matter in terms of international relations was that they were staged by illegitimate actors in the international system, caused such massive unrest, and completely altered the focus of US foreign policy, thereby affecting the entire global system. Prior to 9/11, President George W. Bush faced an economic downturn, and citizens

Both towers of the World Trade Center burn after being struck by commandeered passenger jets on 11 September 2001. The 9/11 attacks still have a far-reaching effect on American foreign and domestic policies.

Andrew Slayman/Artful Media LLC / Alamy

wondered what his presidency (then only months old) would mean for the country. All that changed in a matter of hours on that Tuesday morning. The United States had been hit directly on its own soil, and our approach to terrorism (studying it, responding to it) would never be the same.

Unlike conventional threats or attacks made by states against each other, terrorism has a different set of causes, motivations, and targets. Terrorism is more than simple criminal behaviour; it is a strategy of violence designed to bring about political change by instilling fear in the public at large.[10] The target is not necessarily a government, but citizens. The causes of terrorism are also multifaceted. Political, cultural, religious, social, and economic causes—and sometimes several of these at the same time—can lead to terrorist attacks.

Terrorism is based on the idea that the kind of change desired can be achieved only with violence. Psychological studies inform us that terrorists are motivated to commit violence because they believe that they cannot bring about change using the conventional or accepted modes offered in society. In other words, they view violence as their only option. Terrorists also believe that there is a real lack of political opportunity for them in existing political structures. They deem these structures to be illegitimate (just as we believe that terrorism is illegitimate) and are disillusioned with the prospects for the change they desire. Those political structures cannot be changed to suit the terrorist, so they must be destroyed. Such individuals usually project their attitudes onto others who feel the same way, thus creating terrorist groups.

Disgruntled groups often choose terrorism because it is difficult for governments to predict when a terrorist act will take place. Also, the modes of terrorist actions are usually relatively inexpensive. For example, some of the 9/11 terrorists used knives and box cutters as weapons. Considering this example, we see that it is extremely difficult for governments to respond to, let alone prevent, terrorist acts effectively.

Making matters even more complicated is that many states in the international system—states that are recognized as legitimate by others—support terrorist actions. This sponsorship is often used because it is thought that terrorism could achieve objectives where conventional military forces would not be practical or effective. States such as Libya, North Korea, Afghanistan, Sudan, Syria, and Lebanon have all been labelled "sponsoring" states at some time.

Terrorism will remain a particularly difficult problem for international security because it is a unique example of a threat in the international system. Responding to terrorism is made more difficult because, if we simply treat it as a crime, we underestimate its political nature. Reacting to terrorism under the conventions of warfare is also likely to be unsuccessful because doing so might give the terrorist actions legitimacy in the eyes of their supporters or other observers. Moreover, putting policies in place to dissuade terrorism often comes at the cost of civil liberties (such as the US Patriot Act, which expanded the ability of American policing and legal authorities to prosecute suspected terrorists). For instance, concerns about terrorist activities might lead overzealous authorities to disallow legitimate political protests.

12.5 AL-QAEDA

Al-Qaeda ("the base") represents a particularly nefarious example of current globalization. Rather like a corporation or an international organization, al-Qaeda has taken advantage of modern communications, transportation, finance, and technology to establish a truly twenty-first-century version of an ancient means of political violence. But unlike these other types of institutions, al-Qaeda is a terrorist group dedicated to eliminating any foreign influence in the Muslim world and creating a new Islamic political system. In many ways, al-Qaeda is no different from other terrorist organizations: it seeks political change, uses violence, and targets innocent citizens in its ruthless attempts to alter the political system in which it exists. Formed in 1988, al-Qaeda rose from the ashes of the mujahedeen movement in Afghanistan, a group that fought the Soviet occupying forces and was initially backed by the United States. The mujahedeen went on to establish several different groups, with Osama bin Laden leading the newly formed al-Qaeda. Aside from its most notorious 9/11 attacks (and an earlier, lesser-known attack on the World Trade Center in 1993), the group is also responsible for terrorist strikes in Turkey, Tanzania, Kenya, and Yemen.

As part of the Gulf War, Operations Desert Shield and Storm saw thousands of American troops stationed in Saudi Arabia, considered sacred due to its Muslim holy sites such as Mecca and Medina. In 1996, bin Laden issued a fatwa against the United States, effectively declaring war. Bombings in Khobar, Saudi Arabia, then against the *USS Cole* off the coast of Yemen and at US embassies in Tanzania and Kenya, signalled the seriousness of al-Qaeda's fatwa. Bin Laden was killed in May 2011 by US Navy SEALs special forces during a raid of his compound in Abbottabad, Pakistan. The group lives on, however, under the new leadership of Ayman al-Zawahiri, bin Laden's former deputy.

Although the 9/11 attacks were the organization's master stroke, its key to success lies in its organization. A multifaceted structure, al-Qaeda contains a military wing, an internal financial system, a political and legal division, and even a public relations and media section. A truly "global" organization, al-Qaeda has operations in dozens of countries and–regrettably–shows how global organization can be used for reprehensible purposes.

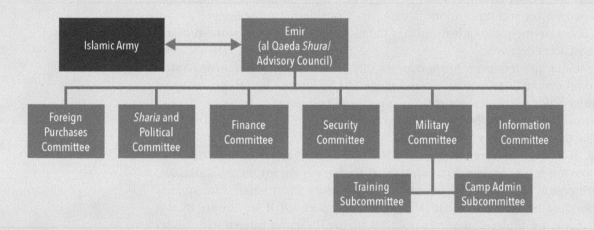

Figure 12.2 Al-Qaeda's Organizational Structure

Al-Qaeda's organizational structure is not unlike other forms of globalized groups, such as businesses or inter-governmental organizations.

Based on: www.globalsecurity.org/military/world/para/images/al-qaida-structure.jpg

Deterring terrorism, therefore, is easier said than done. Unlike other forms of insecurity in the international system, terrorism is particularly problematic. Simply understanding the causes of terrorism requires a full-bore overview of almost every aspect of international relations that could possibly explain why some individuals and groups feel severely ostracized or unable to accept what the rest of society—or even the world—feels is legitimate. There will always be those who feel marginalized, but that does not necessarily mean they will become terrorists. Furthermore, trying to establish "root causes" of terrorism often leads to simplistic answers about why terrorists choose their approach in the first place. Unfortunately, terrorism will remain an option for those who feel that violence is the only way to create change. Thus, governments will continue to be challenged to respond to terrorist actions and to try to protect their citizens from terrorism.

Humanitarian Interventionism

It is easy to see how countries intervene in the affairs of others. Indeed, we've already discussed many aspects of intervention in this book without even mentioning the term outright. The nature of competing ideas, the need for trade and commerce, cultural relations, and global media all inevitably lead to some degree of intervention by someone or other. After all, just getting involved with the affairs of another can be seen as intervention, even if it takes a mild form. Intervention can be much more serious, however.

In international relations, states are constantly intervening in the politics of others; it's really a natural part of the daily interaction among various global actors. But humanitarian intervention is of a different sort. Reflecting its name, this type involves the actions of one or many on behalf of those unable to care for themselves. Humanitarian intervention, which is very controversial, involves interference in a sovereign state's affairs with the intention of reducing the suffering felt by its people.

Intervention can be justified for a variety of reasons, some more compelling than others. It is hard to find true examples of altruism in international relations, as interventions tend to occur when and where states seek to make some gains. Many, for instance, defended the Age of Empire as a necessary means of civilizing parts of the world that were considered barbarous. Nineteenth-century philosopher John Stuart Mill, for one, argued that it was the right and responsibility of civilized states to intervene in the interests of international morality.[11] While in the modern era it is much harder to make the case that one group may be considered more "civilized" than another, the basis for humanitarian interventionism is based on many of Mill's ideas. The basic theory is still in place: one group (a government, ethnicity, or community) is considered unable to provide the basic humanitarian needs for its citizens or, worse, is actively depriving its citizens of these needs.

12.6   INTERVENTION FAILURE: RWANDA

One of the worst examples of humanitarian crisis began with a plane crash in April 1994. Rwandan President Juvénal Habyarimana and Burundi President Cyprien Ntaryamira were killed instantly when their plane went down under suspicious circumstances (it is known that the plane was shot down but not by whom). At that time, the UN had a military force in Rwanda, the United Nations Assistance Mission for Rwanda, to police the ceasefire ending the Rwandan civil war. Canadian Lieutenant General Roméo Dallaire was in charge of this mission and sought to protect Rwandan Prime Minister Agathe Uwilingiyimana, who was constitutionally next in line of authority. However, she and her 10 Belgian UN guards were killed, along with others who supported the peace agreement. Almost immediately, ethnic Tutsis were sought out and murdered by Hutu militia groups, which aimed to eliminate the Tutsis in Rwanda. Stories of extreme brutality emerged over the coming months as between 800,000 and 1,000,000 Rwandans were killed. It is estimated that about 90 per cent of these victims were Tutsis.

The UN troops were not allowed to intervene unless given express authority to do so by the organization's headquarters in New York. Evidence of genocide was considered necessary before this approval would be given. The UN was fearful of creating a negative reaction and being drawn into a protracted civil conflict without the resources or support to respond effectively. Despite the pleas of General Dallaire and others, the UN command refused to allow the peacekeepers to use force. Dallaire's peacekeepers were ordered to concentrate on removing foreigners and officials from Rwanda; meanwhile, thousands of Rwandans were slaughtered in many mass killings.

Although he was ordered otherwise, Dallaire set up "safe areas," where over 20,000 people were protected by the small military force that the UN kept in the country. Still, many more died in what is now considered an avoidable human catastrophe. Former US president Bill Clinton later stated that the US and the UN community should have heeded Dallaire's warnings. Many agreed that even a small military force would have avoided the largest share of the

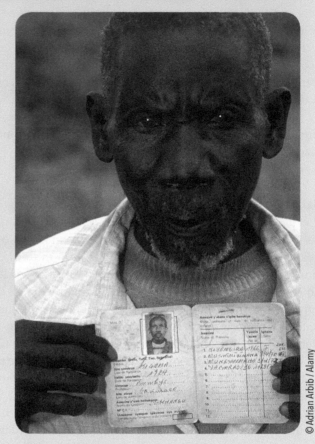

© Adrian Arbib / Alamy

From 1933, Rwanda citizens were required to carry identification that indicated their ethnicity. Those IDs were used to determine who was killed in the 1994 genocide. This man holds his ID card, which shows that he is Twa.

mass murders. The Rwandan genocide led to a disaster hardly rivalled in modern history—in a few months perhaps a million dead, hundreds of thousands displaced, a failed state, and the exposed weakness of an institution (the UN) that was created in part to avoid this sort of situation. Rwanda and humanitarian intervention will always be linked due to this horrible example of the consequences of apathy.

The end of World War II and the public and official acknowledgement of the genocide committed in the Holocaust galvanized views regarding the necessity for collective action against any future atrocities. During the Holocaust, more than six million Jews and millions of other peoples, including homosexuals, those with disabilities, and ethnic groups such as Roma and Poles, were systematically exterminated by Adolf Hitler's Nazi regime. Though the full extent of these horrors wasn't revealed until after the war, the collective guilt and shame felt by Allied countries for not doing all they could to stop the killings led them to a new consideration regarding humanitarian intervention—the need to intervene to protect the unprotected.

Of course, to intervene in every case of human suffering would be practically impossible. Supporters and detractors interpret humanitarian intervention differently, but it can be said that the idea assumes a moral responsibility to stop the killing of people, even in foreign countries. Perhaps the best recent attempt to codify humanitarian intervention is the International Commission on Intervention and State Sovereignty, established by the Canadian government in 2000 to examine and promote the concept and offer clear options for the international community. The commission's 2001 report, *The Responsibility to Protect (R2P)*, captured the emerging theory that the global community must try to stop known incidents of killings and major human rights abuses. In 2005, the UN adopted the principle, and its Security Council passed a resolution affirming its backing of R2P the following year. These actions had wide implications for state sovereignty as we know it. While the UN Charter upholds the principle that no actor should have control over governments, it also supports the preservation of the individual. Consequently, the UN is in many ways caught between these objectives.

The R2P doctrine has emerged as more than just words in recent years. For instance, in 2011, the UN Security Council passed a resolution requiring that the Libyan government protect its citizens. (Russia and China, two permanent members of the council, abstained from the vote.) However, atrocities continued, government forces killed citizens, and the Libyan regime under Muammar Gaddafi remained defiant of the UN ultimatum. Later, NATO-led airstrikes against Libyan government forces resulted in the fall of the Gaddafi government. Although not everyone agreed with this use of military force, it was defined as a case of R2P in action.

Critics of humanitarian interventionism argue that identifying a legitimate case requires some subjective consideration. What might those considerations be? Regardless of how rigorous the process, can we be certain that people's true interests will be upheld and that state governments will not act in their own self-interest? Will intervention simply be another, more modern, case of imperialism, in which the rich industrialized nations decide to intervene because poorer countries are thought to be ungovernable? Were this to be the case, Mill's thoughts on intervention might be as vital today as they were in the nineteenth century.

Defenders of humanitarian intervention feel that intervention is possible, and even desirable, under strictly defined conditions and in the interests of people, not governments. Major developments such as R2P help to redefine our thinking about when we must intervene in the affairs of others. Examples such as the Holocaust and the Rwandan genocide remind us that the sanctity of the sovereign state is not infallible and that we have a collective responsibility to humanity, regardless of our national identity. The 2011 Libyan military intervention and other such events show how R2P may become the benchmark for the future.

Peacekeeping, Conflict Management, and Resolution

Managing conflict in a globalized world is a more complicated matter than it was in the past. More states and issues, coupled with major advances in military weaponry, make conflict management an immediate concern for all states. Management and resolution can come in a variety of forms. In fact, war is a form of resolution: there's a conflict between two parties, a war occurs, one side wins, and the conflict is resolved. However, even the most cursory examination of this process shows real problems. One side will likely not be satisfied with the "resolution," the other side may take advantage of its victory to punish its enemy, and in all likelihood the conflict will one day emerge again.

Other management tools are needed in modern international relations. Diplomacy (see Chapter 11), **negotiation**, **mediation**, and **arbitration** are less likely to cause adverse effects for any side and more likely to offer the hope of peaceful resolution. Negotiation involves bargaining and discussion to resolve a conflict. Much of foreign policy diplomacy falls within negotiation, as the participants position themselves and their objectives, knowing that they will likely have to relent on at least some of their goals. When negotiation is unsuccessful, mediation is often employed. Parties are not usually bound to the results of this process; therefore, mediators must balance the various points of view and compose a scenario where all may be satisfied, even if none receive what they initially anticipated. Since parties will often be completely displeased with a suggested resolution, mediation will sometimes fail. In these cases, arbitration takes mediation to a higher level, often requiring that parties adhere to the recommendation. However, these "binding" results are very hard to enforce because comparable institutions, such as courts in international relations or international law, do not have the same level of enforceability.

Peacekeeping is less common than these three methods, but it is perhaps the best example of conflict management in the modern age. This approach presents a unique way to use military force, namely, to enforce a ceasefire rather than to resist attack or attack others. Peacekeeping involves sending lightly armed soldiers to zones before or after outright hostilities have broken out. Its intention is to provide a forceful peace until a long-term resolution can be arranged. In recent years, this purpose has broadened to include more robust activities such as peace enforcement, or peacebuilding.

It has often been suggested that peacekeeping is a Canadian invention because Lester B. Pearson, a former external affairs minister and later prime

negotiation
bargaining process in which the parties involved try to resolve a dispute in a mutually satisfactory manner

mediation
voluntary process using an impartial party to resolve a dispute

arbitration
authoritative dispute resolution made by an impartial person and agreed upon by all parties involved

peacekeeping
placing of military and civilian personnel in a conflict area as an attempt to stop or contain hostilities or supervise the carrying out of a peace agreement

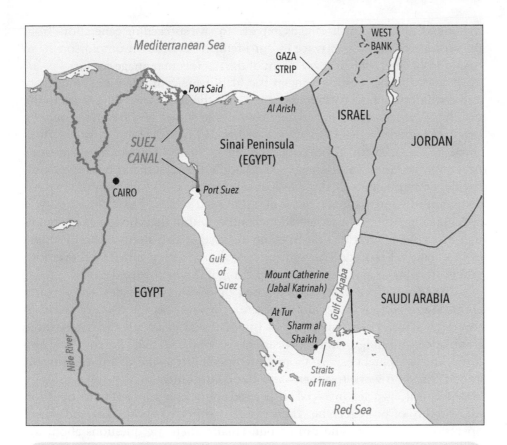

Figure 12.3   Suez Canal region

minister of Canada, proposed the first real peacekeeping mission in 1956. (Prior to this time, there were missions sponsored by the UN in Greece, India, Pakistan, and the Middle East [after the Arab–Israeli War], where the United Nations Security Council sent observers to try to maintain peace amongst adversaries.) The issue was a conflict in the Suez Canal region. The canal connects the Mediterranean and Red Seas and is required by treaty to be open to all ships.[12] However, Egyptian President Gamal Nasser nationalized the canal in 1956, leading France, the UK, and Israel to begin plans to attack Egypt in retaliation. Pearson suggested that the UN send an "emergency force" to maintain a truce while a political solution was sought. The United Nations Emergency Force (UNEF) was a success and ushered in a new, strong mandate for the UN.

The UN is an excellent example of an institution created to deal with conflict management. The UN has many roles—political forum, conflict mediator, security organization, and economic development institution. However, the primary objective of the UN is evident in the first line of its charter (which is rather like its "constitution," with which all members must agree before becoming members). The opening line reads in part: "to save succeeding generations from the scourge of war, which twice in our lifetime has brought untold sorrow to mankind." Clearly, the primary intent of the UN was to manage conflict.

The UN defines peacekeeping as the "deployment of international military and civilian personnel to a conflict area, with the consent of the parties to the conflict, in order to: stop or contain hostilities or supervise the carrying out of a peace agreement." Since 1948, there have been 67 peacekeeping missions sponsored by the UN, with 17 ongoing missions in 2012.[13] Most of these missions have been in Africa, Latin America, the Middle East, Southeast Asia, the North Pacific, Eastern Europe, and the Indian subcontinent—the areas most prone to conflict in the international system. Even though relatively safe countries such as Canada are not as concerned about conflict within their borders, they maintain an active interest in peacekeeping because of the interdependent nature of international security. That is, insecurity in one region might spill over into others, drawing in nations that otherwise might not be involved.

Criticisms of peacekeeping are based on a variety of issues. Some worry about the role of an international organization such as the UN in a world of sovereign states. Others suggest that international peacekeeping has become overloaded, meaning that the UN cannot respond effectively to emerging security threats. Apprehensions about "interoperability"—the ability of different armed forces to work together—and the communications between military and political agencies involved in peacekeeping also lead some to question the viability of peacekeeping. There are also concerns about how and where operations are defined and carried out. Finally, there are questions about the continued support of peacekeeping from great power nations such as the US, the UK, and China.

Despite these problems, peacekeeping remains one of the most positive contributions to international stability in the last century. As other organizations, such as NATO and the African Union (AU), take on international peacekeeping as part of their mandate, there will inevitably be disputes between these agencies and the UN. In the next section, we'll look more closely at one operation that included peacekeeping and a lot more—NATO's mission in Afghanistan.

Peacekeeping's useful contribution to the cause of international peace and security assures its continued and robust role in the future. In large part this is because peacekeeping has been shown to be a significant part of conflict management and resolution.[14] It stands out as an example of conflict management because it is so noticeable; military force rarely avoids attention. And in cases where conflict has escalated to hostility, peacekeeping is very effective.

Canada in Afghanistan

In response to 9/11, the United States and its allies invaded Afghanistan. Al-Qaeda, the terrorist organization responsible for the attacks, had its headquarters in the country and was given sanctuary by the Taliban-controlled government. At that time, the Taliban was not recognized as a legitimate government; only Pakistan, Saudi Arabia, and the United Arab Emirates gave it diplomatic recognition. Both the United Nations Security Council and NATO sanctioned this invasion. The International Security Assistance Force (ISAF) was created by the UN in late 2001 to oversee military operations. ISAF first concentrated on establishing peace and security in Kabul while military forces from some countries, notably the United States and the UK, continued a separate military operation called Operation Enduring Freedom (OEF) in other parts of the country. In 2003, NATO took control of ISAF and slowly began to expand its geographical reach to include the rest of Afghanistan.

The international alliance of states involved in this invasion included Canada. A month after 9/11, Operation Apollo, a naval mission involving the HMCS *Charlottetown*, HMCS *Iroquois*, and HMCS *Preserver*, was sent to the Arabian Gulf. Later, in November, members of Canada's elite military commando unit, the Joint Task Force 2 (JTF2), were part of international operations against Taliban and al-Qaeda fighters. In February 2002, Canadian soldiers from the Princess Patricia's Canadian Light Infantry (PPCLI) landed in Afghanistan and set up base at Camp Julien, on the outskirts of Kabul, the capital city. By 2004, the Canadian contingent stood at just over 2,000 personnel, one of the largest national groups in the country.

Until 2005, the Canadian mission was almost entirely at Camp Julien, where the situation was much calmer than in the rest of the country. Canada's mission in Kabul was part of the ISAF mandate there and part of its being a

George MacLean

Camp Julien, named after decorated Korean War soldier Private George P. Julien, is seen here from the windows of the destroyed Darul Aman ("abode of peace") Palace outside of Kabul. Tajbeg Palace is seen in the distance.

member of the Kabul Multinational Brigade (KMNB). From 2003 to 2005, Canada's Operation Athena aided the reconstruction effort by providing local peacekeeping, military patrols, and civilian assistance in the city and the region.

Canada's role in Afghanistan began to change markedly in 2005. In August, the Canadian government shut down its mission in Kabul and moved to the much more dangerous Kandahar region to take control of the Kandahar Provincial Reconstruction Team (KPRT) and the KMNB there. Building on the multifaceted approach it had adopted in Kabul, Canada's work included aid and assistance, political relations, policing, training, and military operations. But it was the military operations that garnered the most criticism.

Until Canada moved to the southern part of Afghanistan, casualties in the contingent had remained relatively low. In the mostly safer areas of Kabul, Canadian military deaths remained in the single digits. While commentators, politicians, and the public in Canada scrutinized these deaths, they were primarily considered a tragic necessity of being in a war zone. However, in the unstable Kandahar region, where the Taliban had its centre of power during its rule and where hundreds of fighters had fled due to the war in the rest of the country, the Canadians had a harder fight to wage. Operation Archer, the name given to Canada's Kandahar mission, involved far more conventional battle operations with Taliban insurgents. The death toll quickly rose and with it new criticism and public outcry over the methods of the mission. For many, Canada's image as a peacekeeping country (which has always been questioned by those familiar with Canada's actual war history) did not fit with this new and robust military role.

The Canadian mission in Afghanistan was complicated. Canada came to the aid of its military ally, the United States, but in a mission authorized by the UN and NATO. As part of NATO, Canada is required to assist when another member is attacked. Moreover, Canada's involvement in Afghanistan was not only military. In fact, much of the development and assistance work undertaken by Canadian agencies—including NGOs, the RCMP, DFATD (which also includes the former Canadian International Development Agency), and the Canadian Forces—was ignored in media reports while the more sensationalistic stories about military deaths caused by roadside bombs and suicide bombers received more attention.

Canada removed its military forces from Kandahar in 2011 and placed 950 personnel in Kabul as part of a training mission for Afghan forces. Afghanistan receives the second-largest amount of Canadian foreign aid annually (after Haiti). Although trade between the two countries is still quite small, prospects for more Canadian investment in natural resource development (mostly mining) in Afghanistan appear positive.

The Afghan mission is an excellent example of the changing nature of international security today. A terrorist organization sheltered by a reclusive illegitimate regime struck a devastating blow against the most powerful nation on earth, changing the course of history and the focus of international relations.

But the response to that event—which is still ongoing—is perhaps more significant: the success or failure of the mission in Afghanistan will speak volumes about the ability of rich nations to develop and facilitate change in the most underdeveloped and forgotten parts of the world. The mission is multifaceted by design and by necessity; a military undertaking alone would not solve the problem and would certainly only usher in more instability after the battles were fought. If it is successful, the development side of the mission could provide a template for other countries facing similar dire circumstances.

In a relatively short time, much has changed regarding Canada's security role. Previously renowned for its peacekeeping contributions, primarily in the UN, Canada's focus shifted to a more forceful projection of its military following the 9/11 attacks. Aiding the NATO alliance in Afghanistan brought Canada distinction for its leadership and sacrifice. More recently, the shift from war-fighting to stabilization in Afghanistan meant that Canada's security interests altered again. Discussions took place regarding the next steps for the Canadian military. The Canadian government pledged to purchase new equipment for its forces (notably new ships and fighter aircraft), but security isn't just about armed forces.

Intervention and conflict is expensive, results in casualties, and can often lead to change in foreign policy more generally. Some Canadians (such as writer and broadcaster Noah Richler) have argued that the decade in Afghanistan changed citizens' real view of their own history. This view tends to be nuanced in politics, alliance behaviour, power, ideology, and history, just to name a few. What is your view of Canada's security interests?

Conclusion

International security is a wide-ranging and important part of international relations and political studies. War and conflict have always been a part of human interaction, and the history of human relations shows the various ways in which we inflict increasing levels of suffering and fear on one another. In an anarchical international system, arms races, weapons of mass destruction, and the use of force will continue to be used by nation-states as a means of attaining goals. Perhaps more optimistically, we might look to developments in peacekeeping and human security as more constructive ways to view and utilize armed force in international relations.

We have seen how international security often means that states will disagree or come into conflict with one another over a variety of reasons. But a simple "all against all" view of the world is counterbalanced by a co-operative aspect to security. Conflict management requires co-operative behaviour, and modern conflict avoidance means working with others to achieve stability and peace. One aspect of political studies that requires collaboration is the international political economy, the subject of the next chapter.

Self-Assessment Questions

1. How do geopolitics and international anarchy affect a country's relative security?
2. How does the security dilemma potentially make all states in the world less secure?
3. Can you have war without conflict? Conflict without war? Give reasons to support your answer.
4. What was the connection between terrorism and Canada's involvement in Afghanistan?
5. How does humanitarian interventionism include the responsibilities of states?
6. How is peacekeeping a form of conflict management?
7. Should Canada become involved in international conflicts under any circumstances? Why or why not?

Weblinks

BBC News: Rwanda: How the Genocide Happened
www.bbc.co.uk/news/world-africa-13431486

CBC News: Canada's Military Mission in Afghanistan
www.cbc.ca/canada/story/2009/02/10/f-afghanistan.html

Correlates of War
www.correlatesofwar.org

Human Security Network
www.austria.org/humansecurity-network

International Security Assistance Force
www.nato.int/ISAF

Stockholm International Peace Research Institute (SIPRI)
www.sipri.org

United Nations Department of Peacekeeping Operations
www.un.org/en/peacekeeping/

Further Reading

Alexander, Chris. *The Long Way Back: Afghanistan's Quest for Peace*. Toronto: HarperCollins, 2011.

Baylis, John, James J. Wirtz, and Colin S. Gray. *Strategy in the Contemporary World: An Introduction to Strategic Studies*. 3rd edn. Oxford: Oxford University Press, 2010.

Collins, Alan. *Contemporary Security Studies*. 2nd edn. Oxford: Oxford University Press, 2010.

Nacos, Brigitte L. *Terrorism and Counterterrorism: Understanding Threats and Responses in the Post-9/11 World*. 4th edn. Toronto: Prentice Hall, 2012.

Strachan, Hew, and Andreas Herberg-Rothe. *Clausewitz in the Twenty-First Century*. New York: Oxford University Press, 2007.

News Clips

Visit the companion website for *Politics: An Introduction*, 2nd edn, to access news clips related to the content of this chapter.

13

International Political Economy

LEARNING OBJECTIVES

After reading this chapter, you will be able to

- discuss the major tenets of the most important theories and perspectives of international political economy;

- describe the growth of economic interdependence between states;

- explain the link between wealth and power in the international system;

- understand the development of international trade, production, and finance since the nineteenth century; and

- comprehend the importance of international economic organizations.

Introduction

The economy always seems to be in trouble. Whether it's at the local, national, or international level, economic affairs present a constant conundrum: when things are good, it's bad for some; when things are bad, there appears to be no bright side at all. Economic problems are nothing new and won't go away any time soon. Since 2008, the rich countries of the world have been afflicted by a series of financial and economic crises that have produced massive unemployment, huge losses in wealth, and the need for intense international co-operation. In 2011–12, the situation in Europe was particularly bad. For a region of the world that has been blessed with stable and prosperous nations for decades, this situation was especially worrisome.

At the risk of oversimplifying a complicated circumstance, the European crisis was caused by the very thing that was credited for its stability and prosperity: economic integration. As explained in Chapter 9, Europe is a regional economy with highly developed institutions and regulations. Partly due to the global downturn that began in 2008, European countries experienced economic problems, including banking instability, trade disruptions, and a currency crisis. Some countries in the EU (such as Greece, Ireland, Spain, and Portugal) had a harder time reconciling their balance of payments and their budgets. As the crisis deepened, other EU members came to the financial aid of their partners, but debts continued to rise in the most affected countries. Other countries,

The economic crisis in Europe left many wondering if it would bring about the end of the euro, the common currency used by 17 of the 27 EU nations.

Hemera/Thinkstock

including Canada and the United States, were asked for assistance, and international organizations such as the IMF were brought in as well.

The fact that the EU is made up of 27 countries makes integration difficult at best. At its worst (as we witnessed in 2011–12), it could spell disaster for economic co-operation and integration. The crisis is an excellent—albeit unfortunate—example of the modern global economy. As we will see in this chapter, state economies today are mutually dependent. You will also be introduced to the international political economy (IPE), an area of study that has grown remarkably in the past 40 years. IPE became a subdiscipline of political science and international relations in the 1970s and has since produced many of the most important insights in advancing our understanding of the international system, of the dynamic relationship between politics and economics, and indeed of politics itself. IPE covers a vast area of political and economic activity and clearly demonstrates the intimate connection between national and international processes. As the recent European crises demonstrate, this connection can virulently affect partners and those in close connection.

What Is IPE?

IPE studies the interaction between politics and economics, between states and markets, in the international system. This does not mean that other levels of analysis are ignored. On the contrary, IPE explicitly recognizes that domestic and international actors and processes continuously interact. The most obvious example of this relationship is the making of foreign economic policy.[1]

IPE examines how the activities and distribution of power between states and other political authorities affect the international economic system; it also looks at the impact of state activities and power on international economic processes and actors. In this way, it studies the interaction between the distribution of power and wealth, as well as the intimate connection between economic and political power.[2] Throughout history, states have depended upon their economic capabilities to develop power and influence in other forms. For example, in the fourteenth and fifteenth centuries the Spanish Crown relied upon the supply of gold and silver from its New World colonies to underwrite its military prowess. In the nineteenth century, the UK built its primacy on its industrial leadership and dominance of international trade. And the American global predominance at the beginning of the twenty-first century was dependent on the continuing strength of its domestic economy.

The scope of IPE is broad: IPE scholars study trade, finance, environment, gender, and energy policy, to name just a few areas of focus. What's more, IPE encompasses the activities of many different actors, both state and non-state. The work of the IMF, the World Bank, and the World Health Organization fit equally well into the scope of IPE, as do the operations of Walmart, Exxon/Mobil, Toyota, and other major multinational firms. Of particular importance and interest is the study of the interaction between different kinds of actors and the balance of economic power between them. In international financial affairs since 1945, for example, there has been a fundamental shift in power and influence away from states and toward private financial actors, such as banks and securities firms. Such changing relations and their impact on the shape of the international economic system are a primary concern of IPE.

The Perspectives of IPE

Three major perspectives dominate the discipline of international political economy: liberalism, Marxism, and nationalism.[3] The liberal perspective on IPE is guided by the central concerns of liberal ideology, both political and economic. In terms of IPE, liberalism refers to the free functioning of markets, increased individual freedom, and progress in the form of increased wealth. Liberalism is also concerned with the issue of international co-operation between states, particularly but not exclusively, in the area of trade. It is through co-operation that states can reduce the distorting effects of tariffs, as well as form institutions that in turn create rules for international economic interaction, and can rescue the international economic system in times of trouble, such as the role of the EU's central bank and the IMF during the 2011–12 financial crisis. The focus of the liberal perspective, however, is mainly aimed at removing the state from the economic sphere as much as possible, thereby increasing the market's role in issues of distribution, competition, and pricing.

Marxists have quite a different outlook on the international system. They view the international capitalist economy as a tool of oppression whereby the controllers of capital exploit the labouring classes. This perspective is extended to states: for Marxists, wealthy, powerful states exploit their poorer, weaker counterparts. As we saw in Chapter 10, LDCs face many development challenges, but Marxists see the structure of the international system as a major hurdle of true development. The major concerns of Marxist international political economists, therefore, are to analyze the unequal conditions of the international economy and to study the exploitation of certain groups by others. It is important to remember that, for most Marxists, analysis of the international system's exploitative nature goes hand-in-hand with a commitment to change it.

Finally, nationalists see the international economy as an arena in which states are involved in a constant battle for, at the least, survival and, at the most, supremacy. International economic relations, therefore, are viewed in a competitive light, with states striving to surpass each other not only in their levels of productivity, growth, and power but also in the benefits that each gains from economic intercourse. Nationalists call for an expanded role for the state so that it can manage its external economic relations to the best advantage. Mercantilism is the best example of a nationalistic approach to IPE, for it sees the state directing its foreign trade according to the principle of state power maximization. A good historical example of economic nationalism at work is Nazi Germany in the 1930s. Under Adolf Hitler and his finance minister, Hjalmar Schacht, the German government increased the state's power by manipulating trade and financial relations with other states.

These three perspectives, each useful in its own way, allow us to view the international economic system from different points of view. As we will see, the history of IPE in this century alone is a mixture of growth, liberalization, state control, and exploitation of the weak by the powerful. The competing perspectives on IPE, therefore, should not be seen as mutually exclusive. We should instead use them to ask interesting and important questions about the international economic system, questions such as the following:

- What are the most important actors in the international economic system?
- Who gains from an economic relationship, and how much?
- Who pays the costs of an economic process?
- How are bargains struck between important actors?
- What are the conditions of co-operation?
- Is the state's role in the economy increasing or decreasing?

Economic Interdependence

Much of this chapter's discussion of the international economy's development is the story of growing interdependence between states.[4] The term *interdependence* refers to the mutual but not necessarily equal dependence between states. It can take an economic, political, environmental, or security form, but it always implies that actions and policies taken in one national political or economic system will affect other states in the international system.

An excellent example of interdependence can be found in the relationship between the United States and Canada. These two states have maintained peaceful relations since 1812, and their economies have become highly interconnected. It is natural to think of Canada as being dependent upon the United States because it is clearly the less powerful of the two. But it would also be fair to say that the United States is dependent upon the Canadian economy for a large part of its well-being. We must remember that the US–Canada trading relationship is the largest bilateral association in the world, that many thousands of citizens from both countries live and work in the other, that production processes extend from north to south just as much as they do from east to west, that millions of jobs depend on this production, and that the environmental effects of economic activities in each country affect the other.

Interdependence, however, does not merely take the bilateral form that we see in the US–Canada relationship. It also applies to the interactions within and between regions and between groups of states. As will be discussed later in this chapter, the international financial system, perhaps more than any other area of the global economy, has tied national economic systems together through flows of capital and currency trading.

International Economic Co-Operation

The state of the current global economy reflects developments that started almost seven decades ago. After World War II, unprecedented levels of economic co-operation occurred among the great powers. Growth in international trade and finance, coupled with the emergence of new technologies and new markets in developing countries, pushed the industrialized states toward ever higher levels of interdependence. It would be easy to think that this growth was a natural phenomenon. Yet states and other forms of political authority played a central role in increasing global economic interaction.[5] Politics, in other words, deeply affected postwar interdependence just as much as the development of technology and economic progress did.

International organizations (IOs) and institutions were essential to the growth of interdependence. To manage interdependence, and in many cases to propel it, the powerful states of the international economy created IOs and international institutions that facilitated the signing of multilateral agreements. Organizations such as the IMF, World Bank, the General Agreement on Tariffs and Trade (GATT), and the World Trade Organization (WTO) were all designed to increase levels of co-operation between states and thus maximize the beneficial effects of interdependence and minimize the probability of conflict.[6]

But why are such institutions so important to international economic co-operation? Could states not just sign bilateral agreements and manage the international economy without the help of IOs? Maybe, but history has shown

13.1 INTERNATIONAL ECONOMIC ORGANIZATIONS AND THEIR FUNCTIONS

- International Monetary Fund (IMF): international monetary co-operation, provides balance of payments stability, financial aid, and technical aid
- World Bank: lends money to developing countries for (usually long-term) development projects
- Bank for International Settlements (BIS): also known as the central bankers' bank, arranges loans for central banks and encourages central bank co-operation

- International Labour Organization (ILO): created in 1919, strives to improve working conditions around the world by setting minimum standards, providing technical assistance, and promoting the development of labour unions
- World Trade Organization (WTO): created in 1995, promotes free trade of goods and services between nations

that co-operation is more likely and more productive when IOs are used to promote it. IOs perform many functions that contribute to the efficiency and probability of co-operation, such as providing a forum for negotiation and setting out definite rules and processes that make negotiation and the resulting deals more predictable and reliable. These organizations also tie states into longer-term patterns of co-operation, which means that each individual state is less likely to cheat on a deal (because it would miss out on the potential benefits of such arrangements in the future). IOs can help to monitor and verify the implementation of international agreements, which helps to reassure negotiating parties that deals will be respected. These tasks apply not only to the international economy but also to other areas of interstate interaction. Nevertheless, they have proven particularly important in the management of the international economy since 1945.

The World Trading System

Enter any grocery, department, or hardware store and you will find the shelves stocked with goods from all over the world. The average consumer can now eat mangoes in any season (providing he or she is willing to pay for them) and choose from an array of home electronics assembled in other countries. By the beginning of the twenty-first century, international trade had brought an unprecedented level of consumer choice to our society.[7] Trade, however, does not have merely economic effects. It can be a source of cultural contact between peoples and is often responsible for the transmission of new ideas and technologies. Trading routes have linked distant peoples throughout history. The ancient Phoenicians brought goods from the eastern Mediterranean to the shores of the British Isles, thus connecting their respective peoples through trade. African peoples who would never see each other's homelands were connected by trade routes that stretched for hundreds, even thousands, of kilometres.

trade protection
tendency of countries
to safeguard their own
economic sectors or
industries using tariffs,
quotas, or other forms
of trade and investment
legislation

International trade is often credited with creating employment, increasing consumer choice, introducing new ideas and cultural ideals, and contributing to economic efficiency.[8] Indeed, there is a lot of evidence to support each of these claims. But international trade is not an issue on which everyone agrees, and historically it has been a divisive issue in both national and international politics. Just as trade creates employment, it has been known to destroy jobs in uncompetitive economies and industries, either in terms of their pricing or their quality. When such economies and industries are exposed to open international competition, they simply cannot maintain profitability and may be forced to cut production and lay off workers to survive. At times such as these, workers and producers alike call for **trade protection** from the government, seeking subsidies to supplement their income, protective tariffs to reduce the price advantage of foreign goods, or other non-tariff barriers (NTBs) such as import licensing or quality controls.[9]

Equally controversial is the cultural aspect of international trade. As previously mentioned, its proponents argue that trade introduces new ideas and norms to closed societies, thus contributing to mutual understanding between states and peoples.[10] However, trade can also be accused of contributing to the spread of dominant cultures at the expense of traditional values and norms. The spread of American products throughout the world, for example, has not been value-free. All one has to do is look at a cereal box to realize that US culture is transmitted by the most unobtrusive means. Furthermore, trade does not refer merely to manufactured goods or foodstuffs. Books, films, music, and technology (e.g. computers and software) are also included within the sphere of international trade. Faced with the overwhelming choice presented by goods from the industrialized states, traditional cultures and economic models become unattractive, particularly to young people. The ideals of consumer choice and freedom to choose one's own career are persuasive concepts in traditional societies.

THE GROWTH OF TRADE SINCE 1846

High levels of growth in international trade have usually followed periods of rapid economic development. Although current international trade, with its rapid transportation of goods from one side of the world to the other and its extremely low levels of government involvement and taxation, is a very recent development, the modern concept of this form of trading began to take shape in the nineteenth century. When it did, its development depended heavily on three factors: ideology, domestic political decisions, and the exercise of state power in the international system. Ideology concerned the growing acceptance of Adam Smith's revolutionary ideas concerning free trade, published in *The Wealth of Nations* (1776). Prior to this work, mercantilism had been the dominant approach to international trade. Smith's argument was that free trade brought benefits in terms of efficiency, cost, and the division of labour.[11] Domestic politics related to the effects of industrialization. As the UK went through the Industrial Revolution and its economy became the most developed in the world, British producers needed to secure cheap supplies of food for their workers so that they could keep wages low. Pressure from these British industrialists caused the government to liberalize its food policy in 1846 by repealing the **Corn Laws**, a set of laws regulating the trade in grains and providing agricultural subsidies. This action led to the liberalization of Britain's agricultural trade, which in turn set the stage for the country opening its borders to all kinds of products from producers throughout the world.

Other nations reciprocated, though not to the same degree, and the overall result was a dramatic growth in the level of world trade, particularly among the European countries and their present and former colonies in Africa, India, and the Americas. Even when other states did not completely open their economies to trade, Britain still allowed their goods to enter with low tariffs. Britain was able to do so because its economy had become much larger than other states' and thus the relative costs of such a policy were low. In order to maintain international trading routes, however, mere openness was not enough. The British navy, at the time by far the largest in the world, used its predominance to keep sea routes open so that goods could travel unimpeded from one part of the world to the next. The transportation of goods was also greatly helped by British (and to a lesser degree German) investment in railway systems around the world.

The growth in international trade that went along with British economic and naval predominance continued until the early years of the twentieth century. With World War I and the destruction that it wrought on European economies, trade would not regain its previous levels until long after World War II. One of the lessons of this period was that trade and peace were inextricably linked. Clearly, it was very difficult for trade to flourish in a world where political and military relations between the great powers were unstable. However, some liberal theorists have also argued that high levels of trade between states help maintain peace.[12] The logic here is that, if they depend on each other for their economic well-being, states would be unwilling to go to war because they would be sacrificing the benefits of trade. Others have argued that the historical example of World War I proves that even states with high levels of trade between them (such as Britain and Germany at the end of the nineteenth century) will go to war with each other if they are rivals for military, economic, and cultural dominance.

In 1846, UK Prime Minister Sir Robert Peel's retracting of the Corn Laws alienated farmers but ushered in the first major era of free trade in modern history.

Corn Laws
set of laws regulating the British grain trade; the abolition of these laws in 1846 opened up British agricultural trade

THE GATT

The end of World War II saw the emergence of the United States as an economic and military superpower. From this position of dominance, it decided to shape the international economic system through the creation of institutions and organizations aimed at international economic management. In the area of trade, the institution that emerged (in 1947) was the GATT.[13]

Though originally intended only as a temporary arrangement, the GATT became the world's permanent trade regime when the Havana Charter, a treaty aimed at creating an international trade organization (ITO), failed to be approved by the US Congress. The GATT was designed to promote several values (still held today) considered to be central by the United States and its allies:

- **multilateralism**: decisions would be taken in consultation with all members and in their interests;
- **reciprocity**: the liberalization of trade would be beneficial for all parties concerned;
- **non-discrimination**: no members could be excluded from the benefits that one member state extended to another; and
- free trade: efficiency, prosperity, and peace would be promoted.

The GATT proved incredibly successful in opening up international trade among the developed countries and, in particular, in reducing tariffs between them. However, the GATT system did not benefit all states in the international system equally. The communist bloc countries were excluded due to the political tensions of the Cold War, but so were many developing countries whose industrial sectors were not sufficiently competitive to benefit from free trade. A large number of LDCs chose to stay outside of the GATT—at least until the second half of the 1980s—rather than accept its principles, opting instead for policies of protectionism and state control of industries to aid rapid growth.

One of the major reasons why LDCs delayed joining the GATT system was that its achievements in liberalizing trade were limited in one very important way. Until the late 1960s, the system focused on manufactured goods and neglected agricultural trade and commodities, traditionally two of the most difficult areas to liberalize. Agriculture and raw materials were also areas in which many LDCs had a comparative advantage; thus, it could be said that the GATT's operations were biased in favour of the developed states. This partiality reflected the dominance of the rich countries in the organization and their concern about improving the competitiveness of their main industries.

In response to these inadequacies of the GATT system, the developing states attempted to set up a rival organization for international trade in the 1960s. Under the auspices of the United Nations, the Conference on Trade and Development (UNCTAD) was created in 1964.[14] As its name suggests, the UNCTAD attempted to link the issues of trade and economic development directly, speaking to many of the developing states' concerns about agriculture and

reciprocity
complimentary or mutual behaviour among two or more actors; view that liberalization of trade would be beneficial for all parties concerned if co-operative policies were pursued

non-discrimination
principle that no member of an organization should be excluded from the benefits that one member state extends to another

commodities. Though the creation of the committee was a great achievement, the developed states refused to allow it to replace the GATT but decided to placate LDCs by making small changes to the system.

Despite the deep economic recessions that hit the industrialized states in the 1970s, early 1980s, and late 2000s, international trade continued to grow rapidly throughout this entire period, slowing its rate of growth in the late 1990s only because of the financial and economic crises that hit Asia, Russia, and Brazil. Indeed, the growth in world trade has consistently outpaced the growth in the global economy as a whole, and it continues to provide employment in many parts of the world.

THE WTO

The GATT was largely responsible for much of the growth of international trade from 1947 to 1995. During the **Uruguay Round** of GATT negotiations, which began in 1986, the world's most important trading nations agreed to overhaul the trading system and create a permanent international organization—the WTO—that would be much more ambitious than the GATT was ever intended to be.[15] In 1995, the GATT was made part of this new IO.[16] The institution was not discarded but became part of a more formal international organization. The WTO has a legal status matching that of the other major international economic organizations, such as the IMF and World Bank, and places trade at the top of the international economic agenda, alongside monetary and financial affairs.

The WTO is one of today's most important international organizations. It deals with all aspects of trade, from manufactured goods to commodities, environmental elements of trade to intellectual property, and agriculture to trade and development. One of the key achievements of the WTO has been to institute a system of **dispute resolution**, by which trading disagreements between member states can be resolved by an impartial tribunal, thus (theoretically at least) preventing such disputes from becoming too political or controversial.

Despite these achievements, the WTO has not been a success. In 2001, a new round of negotiations, aimed at expanding international trade and tackling some of the major concerns of the developing countries, began in Doha, Qatar. Known as the Doha Development Round, the talks immediately hit an obstacle as Europe and the United States failed to agree on reducing their agricultural subsidies, one of the most intractable issues in the organization since the 1960s.

At the 2003 WTO ministerial conference in Cancun, Mexico, the G20, a new group that would further complicate international trade negotiations, emerged. Led by five important LDCs (China, India, Brazil, Mexico, and South Africa), the G20 has successfully operated as a bloc in WTO negotiations to prevent any agreement that goes against their interests. The issue of agricultural subsidies was the touchstone for the group. Subsidies on agricultural production in developed states damage the competitiveness of developing countries' agricultural producers, preventing them from growing and thereby holding back development. The G20 has therefore refused to allow the Doha Round to progress unless

Uruguay Round
longest round of GATT negotiations (1986-94), eventually leading to the establishment of the World Trade Organization

dispute resolution
process by which trading disagreements between member states can be resolved by an impartial tribunal, thus preventing such disputes from becoming too political or controversial

the issue is resolved in a satisfactory way. Doha has yet to be completed, and analysts fear that it is unsalvageable. Negotiations broke down several times, most notably in 2008, at the beginning of the last major global recession. If an agreement is not reached, it would be the first time since the creation of GATT that a round of trade negotiations failed completely, raising further questions about the resilience of the international trading system. Yet over 10 years after Doha began, talks continued on major issues, including agricultural subsidies, intellectual property, the environment, and broadening trade.

Since 2008, the situation has worsened as the United States and Europe have little enthusiasm for further trade liberalization in the aftermath of the financial and economic crises. Given this gridlock in the WTO, the organization presently faces an uncertain future. While many of its day-to-day mechanisms (such as the General Council and the Dispute Settlement Body) continue to function, it seems unlikely that significant progress will be achieved in the near future.

PRESENT AND FUTURE CHALLENGES FOR TRADE

Trade continues to be one of the most controversial areas of IPE. As we have seen in the case of the G20, many LDC states continue to see the trading system's structure as a reflection of developed states' power and success and are pressing within the WTO for greater concessions that would spur growth in their economies. The link between trade and environmental issues remains a vital area for research and political action. But the biggest challenges for the future of the international trading system lie in the classic question of the struggle for power.

The first of these concerns the growing regionalism that has become a feature of the world economy since the 1980s. The emergence of regional free trade blocs, most importantly in Europe and North America, provides the world's largest economies with an alternative to international trade. As a result, they have a fallback option in the event that the WTO fails to maintain the current healthy state of global trade, which in turn offers a test of their commitment to maintaining that system. The countries of the EU and NAFTA have shown a distinct tendency over the last decade to trade more and more within their respective blocs, a trend that some see as threatening international trade. These fears may be exaggerated. Both intra- and interregional trade is growing, but the former is doing so at a faster rate (see the section on economic regionalism).

The second challenge lies in the conflict between these two regions. It is important to remember that the European and North American (and in particular US) conceptions of economic liberalism are far from identical. Europeans have traditionally seen a more expanded state role in the economy and are more comfortable with free trade taking a back seat to political and social concerns. Generally, the United States has pushed for a reduced role for government, even if its government is a larger entity than those of European states. While Canada may be seen as being between Europe and the United States, liberalism here is more moderate than in Europe. The 1999 disputes between the United States

13.2 THE US–EU BANANA DISPUTE

Though the United States and European Union are highly interdependent, their relations are not trouble-free. In 1975, the EU (then known as the European Community) set up the Lomé Convention with certain African, Caribbean, and Pacific (ACP) states. This arrangement gave these nations access to the European marketplace at preferential tariff levels as a means of aiding LDCs in their economic development.

Bananas were one commodity included under the convention. In 1999, the United States accused the EU of distorting the international trade in bananas by giving the European market preferential access to banana producers from select developing countries. The US argued that this practice was contrary to the rules and principles of free trade protected by the WTO, which enforces the principle of non-discrimination between members. The US brought the matter before the WTO's Dispute Settlement Body, which judged against the EU. The organization was forced to dismantle its system of preferential access and grant the same privileges to all outside banana producers or to none.

Why did the United States force this issue? The government stated that its goal was to promote and protect the principle of free trade in the world economy. A closer examination, however, suggests that the government was promoting the interests of American corporations that produced bananas in areas outside of the Lomé Convention, countries such as Mexico and Brazil. These corporations wanted the same access to European markets as those producers based in the ACP states, who were largely of European origin. This series of events showed once again that the link between states and markets, public and private actors, remains a major force in shaping international trade.

and EU over hormones in beef and the international banana trade are but two examples of clashes between these two economic giants.

The third issue is the rise of China, India, Mexico, and Brazil as major economies and trading nations. In 2011, China replaced Germany as the world's largest exporting nation, and its power in international negotiations has led many analysts to see it, alongside the United States, as the essential partner in any international trade agreement. As these four countries continue to grow in power and influence and try to establish their place in the WTO (while the United States and Europe attempt to maintain their leadership), we are likely to see increased tension and rivalry in trade.

The International System of Money and Finance

While the international trade system is responsible for moving goods and services around the global economy, the **international financial and monetary system** is responsible for ensuring that money flows to those areas of the global economy where it is needed.[17] It can be compared to the root system of a plant: just as the roots invisibly provide minerals, nutrition, and moisture to a plant, so the financial system provides currency and credit to the international economy. Without a reliable and steady supply of loans and investment, the international economy would soon wither and die.

international financial and monetary system set of rules, institutions, and agreements governing the flow of money in the international system; the relative values of currencies and the settling of accounts

13.3 THE BRICs AND BRICSAM

In 2003, the investment firm Goldman Sachs published *Dreaming with BRICS: The Path to 2050*, a report that identified four rapidly growing developing country economies–Brazil, Russia, India, and China, collectively known as BRICs–as having enormous potential for economic growth in the future and for redistribution of power in the international economy. Between them, these four countries currently account for over 40 per cent of the world's population and promise much higher growth rates than developed countries' economies. Goldman Sachs predicted that, by 2050, these four economies combined would be larger than today's leaders, with China being the world's largest and India, Brazil, and Russia in third, fourth, and sixth places, respectively.

Political scientists and IPE scholars have begun to refer to the BRICSAM countries (comprising the BRICs, South Africa, the Association of Southeast Asian Nations (ASEAN) countries, and Mexico) because of their growing political and economic weight in the system. The G5 countries (Brazil, China, India, South Africa, and Mexico) have already been included in a number of G8 summits as important representatives of the developing world, and we should expect their influence to grow in the near future.

International finance is nothing new. In the fifteenth and sixteenth centuries, Italian banks lent huge sums of money to European monarchs for the purposes of exploration, personal enrichment, and war. The City of London emerged as the dominant financial centre of the nineteenth century, channelling funds to traders, investors, and governments throughout the world. Money and finance have always been central to the development of the international economy, and the health and stability of the two systems have always been intertwined.

WHAT IS THE INTERNATIONAL MONETARY SYSTEM?

For international economic interaction to be feasible and efficient, it is necessary to have either a global currency (that is, one form of money acceptable in every

Sterling silver coins such as this one were once used as a standard of exchange for British currency. The "pound sterling" gets its name from this accounting system.

© Money & Coins @ Ian Sanders / Alamy

national economic system) or internationally agreed-upon rules dictating the relative values of national currencies. In former times, gold performed the function of a global medium of exchange, being acceptable to individuals and governments all over the world. In modern times, two alternative systems have emerged, a fixed exchange rate and a floating exchange rate. Debates continue over which system provides more stability and efficiency to the international economy.

WHAT IS THE INTERNATIONAL FINANCIAL SYSTEM?

Very closely connected to the monetary system is the international financial system, the means by which capital and funds are moved from one national economy to another. The financial system is made up of the financial

13.4   THE GREAT CRASH OF 1929

The 2008 global financial crisis surprised many who believed that financial crises happened in developing countries such as Mexico, Brazil, or Turkey. However, financial crisis has in fact been much more common in the developed world and has a long history going back to at least the nineteenth century.

The most famous crisis occurred in 1929 in the United States. New York had by then replaced London as the world's most important financial centre and was closely linked to the international economy through a system of loans and credits. The financial markets in New York, however, were prone to what analysts have variously called manias, euphoria, or irrational exuberance, meaning that money would pour into the market periodically according to the latest trend in investment. When attitudes and perceptions changed, money would be rapidly withdrawn from the markets, causing panics and crashes.

This turbulence was seen repeatedly throughout the 1920s, famously with the case of Florida real estate in the mid-1920s. The biggest crash came in 1929, when an inflated stock market began to slip, setting off a panic that ruined thousands of stockbrokers and bankrupted hundreds of thousands of investors. The stories of this period are now classic—brokers and investors leaping from the upper floors of office blocks rather than face bankruptcy, individuals selling assets worth thousands of dollars (such as cars) for only a hundred dollars to try to get enough cash to settle their debts.

Crowds gather in 1931 to withdraw their savings (a "run" on the bank) as the American Union Bank fails—one of over 9,000 US banking institutions to collapse during the Depression.

But the effects of the 1929 crash were not just felt by individuals involved in the market. It caused a massive contraction of credit as banks called in loans, shrinking the economy and forcing many firms to either lay off workers or close down completely. Internationally, it interrupted the flow of capital from New York to debtor countries, causing economic and financial crises there. What followed was the Great Depression in the United States, and the world economy began a slippery slide toward economic conflict and then war.

transactions between states, international financial institutions such as the IMF and World Bank, banks, and other private financial institutions, corporations, and individuals. Throughout history, the level of political control over the international financial system has varied from almost complete control in the 1940s and 1950s to the dominance by private financial actors at the beginning of the twenty-first century. The international financial system is fundamental to the international economy because, without it, surplus capital in one part of the globe could not be assigned to those parts where it can be put to good and profitable use. A badly functioning financial system compromises economic efficiency; more important, however, it also restrains economic development.

THE BRETTON WOODS SYSTEM

We have already mentioned Bretton Woods in Chapters 9 and 11. The economic planners who attended this conference, particularly those from the United States and the UK, were determined to avoid the mistakes of the interwar years, which saw high levels of economic nationalism and competition between states and eventually led to World War II. Foremost in their minds was the promotion of free trade and prevention of another financial depression. This group believed that the solution was to create a system of fixed exchange rates and put heavy controls on private banks and other financial institutions so that their role in international finance would be limited. In the place of private banks, the American and British representatives established the IMF and the International Bank for Reconstruction and Development (World Bank). As we've seen, the IMF was designed to oversee the international monetary system, enforce a regime of fixed exchange rates, and lend money to states experiencing balance of payments difficulties. The World Bank was created to provide funding for the reconstruction of Europe after the destruction of World War II and for programs of economic development in the Third World.

This set-up left very little space for private institutions. In the years following 1945, private finance remained largely national while international finance was dominated by the IMF and World Bank, the **Marshall Plan**—a massive US government loan program to help the devastated countries of Western Europe—and, later, government-to-government loans in the form of **bilateral aid**.[18] This system of fixed exchange rates and public international finance lasted for 25 years, bringing both stability and unprecedented levels of global economic growth. During this period, the flow of finance obeyed distinctly political purposes, with inter-state loans being used to strengthen friendly regimes and to buy the support of governments in the Cold War struggle.

In August 1971, however, this situation changed. The US government of Richard Nixon made a unilateral decision that the Bretton Woods system no longer served the interests of the United States, and it abandoned fixed exchange rates. Despite months of negotiations, a rules-based alternative could not be found. From 1973 onwards, the world's major currencies have been

Marshall Plan
US government loan program designed to help the devastated countries of Western Europe after World War II

bilateral aid
military or development assistance given by one country to another

floating; that is, their values have been decided by the activities of global currency markets. This new arrangement is sometimes referred to as a **non-system** because clearly defined rules determining relative currency values are absent.[19] The transition represented political authorities abdicating power over one of the most important areas of economic management and can be seen as part of a wider trend toward less state control over the economy.

Even before the system of fixed exchange rates was dropped, private finance was beginning to break free from the controls instituted at Bretton Woods. European banks succeeded in evading national regulatory control by lending money in currencies other than those used in the national economy. Such practices gave private banks the freedom to engage in international lending without the interference of national governments (see Box 8.7, p. 215). Private banks, in particular those of the United States, had gradually expanded their operations outside of national markets in response to the growth of MNCs and their need for capital. These two developments propelled the growth of private international finance and helped to create our current system.

Another factor in the globalization of finance was technological advances, especially in the area of communications. The development of satellite communications and computer technology allowed the transmission of information and funds from one side of the world to another at the touch of a

non-system

system of international money and finance that replaced the Bretton Woods system; so called because it lacked explicit rules

13.5 THE EUROMARKETS

In the 1950s, the Soviet government faced a problem. It needed to maintain US dollar reserves in banks outside the Soviet Union for buying exports, commodities in particular. However, to place the money in US banks would risk the US government freezing the funds and thus cutting the Soviet state off from its deposits. Instead of risking this eventuality, the Soviet government persuaded a French bank to provide an account. The bank's cable address was EUROBANK and thus Eurodollars and the Euromarkets were born. (A Eurodollar is simply a dollar held in a bank account outside of the United States.) The process can be copied with other national currencies to produce Europounds, Eurofrancs, Euroyen, etc. The bank does not have to be in Europe for the currency to become a Euro currency.

The advantage for banks in providing such accounts was that they could evade the guidelines of national authorities that chose to regulate only transactions conducted in the home country's national currency. This meant that huge amounts of capital were released from the control and supervision of national regulators and were free to flow around the world as the bankers saw fit.

Euromarkets continue, but they have become much more complex. It is possible to not only set up a bank account in a currency other than that of the country where the bank operates but also borrow money and conduct bond releases, swaps, and options in Euro currencies. This growth in the complexity and size of international finance contributed greatly to the process of deregulation that took place in the 1980s and 1990s and, some claim, to the growing instability of global finance. By deregulating and speeding up international finance in this way, the stability of the international financial system has increasingly come under threat. The ability to move billions of dollars from one national economy to another very rapidly has contributed to a number of the deep financial crises witnessed at the end of the twentieth and beginning of the twenty-first centuries.

button. Capital could be transferred instantaneously, and banks and investors could seize opportunities whenever, and wherever, they occurred.

It was not only technology and the drive for profits that caused the internationalization of finance. States also played a central role. Particularly in the 1980s and 1990s, Western governments began to eliminate regulations restricting foreign competition in national financial markets, as well as those limiting the activities of banks and other financial actors. This deregulation of finance was undertaken because it matched both the liberal ideology and the economic goals of leading states such as Britain and the United States. By the late twentieth century, national financial centres such as London, New York, and Tokyo were actively competing among themselves for the business of finance. One advantage that a financial centre could offer was that its level of restrictions was lower than that of its competitors.[20]

THE LATIN AMERICAN DEBT CRISIS

After the end of the Bretton Woods system and the relaxation of many national restrictions on foreign lending, banks in the advanced industrialized economies (especially in the United States) began looking to developing economies as an outlet for the capital that had been deposited with them. Developing countries offered potentially very high profits for the banks, as they were rapidly industrializing and were willing to pay higher interest rates than borrowers in developed markets.

However, the area of the globe that benefited most from this trend in the 1970s was Latin America. Those countries that exported oil, such as Mexico, were prime candidates for loans as the price of oil soared during the OPEC crisis. The flow of loans to Latin America in this decade and the early 1980s was truly immense, reaching between US$150 and $200 billion by 1983. This amount would not necessarily have become a problem if the money had been invested wisely by the recipient governments and corporations. Instead, much of it was wasted in the form of economically non-viable projects and corruption. In addition, Latin American states' economic growth slowed at the end of the 1970s because of a number of factors (including declining commodity prices), and thus their ability to meet debt interest payments was reduced. The only way these economies were able to continue making debt payments was by accepting more money from the financial institutions to which they were already heavily indebted.

debt crisis
situation in which a country is unable to meet its international debt obligations; sometimes used to refer to the Latin American situation in the 1980s

The combination of these elements brought about a situation in which several Latin American states found themselves unable to make their debt payments. In 1982, the Mexican government announced that it would not be able to make the interest payments on its debt, and the **debt crisis** began. Brazil followed suit in 1986. These defaults led to a crisis of confidence on the part of the banks, which then refused to lend any further money to economies in the region. This abrupt cut-off meant that other Latin American countries could not meet their own debt obligations, thus deepening the crisis.[21]

13.6 FOREIGN AID AND TIED AID

In the post–World War II period, the advanced industrialized states began a system of bilateral aid, lending money to developing states in the form of economic or military assistance. This system replaced the private flows of capital that had been a feature of the nineteenth century and interwar years. Foreign aid became a crucial source of income for many states, and there were calls for aid to be increased throughout the 1960s, 1970s, and 1980s.

But foreign aid is not simply the transfer of money from one national government to another. It can take various forms, such as material (food, grain, emergency supplies, or military equipment), loans at preferential rates, or sometimes grants. Often, aid comes with a commitment on the part of the recipient to fulfill some responsibility to the donor state.

During the Cold War, this commitment was usually to support the foreign policy goals of either the Soviet Union or United States, thus involving the LDCs in the ideological conflict.

Aid has also been "tied" in other ways. Frequently, loans given to LDCs by a developed state can be used only to purchase goods from producers in that state. In doing so, the lending government stimulates its own economy by lending money to the LDC and makes interest on its loan. Another example is the donation of some form of high-technology machinery to a developing country. Though the machinery is given free of charge, maintaining the equipment will require both expertise and parts from the donor state. Aid can therefore actually become a drain on the recipient state's economic resources.

Finding a solution to this crisis took many years. The IMF acted as a coordinating agency, bringing together both creditors and debtors, but was unable to come up with anything more than stop-gap measures between 1982 and 1989. During this period, many years of economic growth were lost and investor confidence in the region was put on hold. In 1989, a debt reduction plan proposed by US Treasury Secretary Nicholas Brady offered a lasting solution.

INTERNATIONAL FINANCE AND THE LATE 1990s CRISIS

With the ending of the Latin American debt crisis, a different era in international finance began. This was to be a period in which banks faced stiff competition from other kinds of financial institutions (such as mutual fund companies, in which thousands of individuals pool their investments and the company invests the total amount) and international capital became much more mobile. The increased size and mobility of international capital proved to be both a blessing and a curse for the system. On the positive side, it enabled huge sums of capital to move rapidly around the globe to take advantage of investment opportunities. On the negative side, however, this increased mobility meant that billions of dollars could be withdrawn from a national economy in a matter of hours.

Such was the case in Mexico in December 1994. Following a political crisis and rapidly worsening economic situation, the Mexican government devalued the national currency (the peso), causing both Mexican and foreign investors to pull their money out of the country. These events precipitated a deep economic crisis in the country, one that took several years to resolve. Michel Camdessus, a former managing director of the IMF, called the Mexican crisis the "first financial crisis of the twenty-first century" because it involved millions of investors and enormous and immediate capital flight, unlike the preceding Latin American debt crisis.[22]

The Mexican crisis was followed three years later by similar crises in a number of Asian economies. Beginning in Thailand in July 1997, the crisis spread throughout the region, a phenomenon that had deep effects not only on the area but also on the world economy as a whole. In addition to Thailand, countries such as Indonesia and South Korea, long considered economic powerhouses, were reduced to petitioning the IMF for loans to allow them to restructure their economies. In 1998, Russia, Brazil, and Argentina suffered economic and financial crises. It was not until 2003 that these crises stopped appearing in the developing world.

THE GLOBAL FINANCIAL CRISIS, 2008

Deregulation in the United States in the early 2000s led to the most serious financial crisis since the 1929 stock market crash. This time, the crisis began in US real estate markets. Because of a shortage of qualified buyers, regulations had been eased to let more people get approved for home loans even though they didn't meet normal eligibility requirements (this type of borrower and loan are both known as subprime). Standards were reduced and risky mortgages were approved. As the economy declined, subprime buyers eventually couldn't make their mortgage payments, resulting in defaults and widespread foreclosures.

The US subprime housing crisis spread to Britain and other developed countries throughout the world. Banks found themselves unable to absorb the wave of loan defaults from individual customers who had borrowed more than they were capable of repaying.[23] The crisis spread rapidly across the world's financial systems and brought about a deep economic recession that came close to the levels of the Great Depression.

liquidity
rate at which assets may be converted to cash

Solving the crisis required a massive injection of **liquidity** from the world's leading central banks, emergency loans to the banks, and international coordination of economic and financial policy among the world's leading powers. Even so, the recession caused the loss of hundreds of thousands of jobs in countries such as the United States and negative global economic growth for the first time since 1945. Growth remained negative in 2009 but made a slow recovery in 2010. The crisis caused analysts and policy-makers to rethink their commitment to liberal, free market policies and ideas, and governments increasingly turned to regulation of financial markets and capitalism in general.

Despite some positive developments in 2010, the crisis remained in other aspects, including unemployment, national debt issues, and reduced investment. For some countries, such as those in Europe, the effects of the 2008 crisis led to serious repercussions. In the case of the EU, real questions were raised about the effectiveness of regionally integrated zones.

13.7 THE G8 AND MULTILATERAL LEADERSHIP

We often hear talk of "leaders" and the exercise of "leadership" in the international economy, but few of us question what that leadership is or why it is necessary. By leadership in the international economy, we are generally referring to actions by one or a group of states that deliver some good to the system that would not otherwise be provided. In recent years, we have come to think of leadership as offering effective responses to problems or crises facing the international economy, such as the financial crises that struck Asia and Brazil in the late 1990s. Such responses may take the form of providing financial assistance to economies in crisis, formulating new rules for international finance or opening up a domestic market to absorb exports from distressed economies.

For most of the post–World War II period, we have become accustomed to thinking of the United States as the only leader of the capitalist world. Indeed, from 1945 to the 1960s, the US was able to manage and guide the Western system with little help from its allies. However, beginning in the mid-1960s, the United States was forced to seek the help of Europe and Japan in stabilizing the system through the coordination of economic policies. This necessity became even more pressing in the aftermath of the end of Bretton Woods, the oil crises of the 1970s, and the ensuing turbulence in the world economy. In November 1975, the United States and five other major economic powers (France, Britain, Germany, Japan, and Italy) came together in Rambouillet, France, to discuss the major political and economic challenges facing their countries. In 1976, in San Juan, Puerto Rico, these six states were joined by Canada to form the Group of Seven (G7).

Since 1976, the G7 has become one of the most important organs of world economic management, coordinating macroeconomic policies and national positions in fora such as the IMF. In the mid-1980s, the G7 played a central role in attempting to restore stability to international currency markets through coordinated central bank interventions, but the importance of the grouping would grow in the 1990s. The G7's response to the financial crises that struck Mexico, Asia, Russia, and Brazil determined the longevity of these crises and the future shape of the international financial system. Though the reform of that system is far from complete, all important decisions concerning its future must first be approved by the G7.

In 1998, the seven members were joined by Russia to form the G8, and by 2006 an active debate began over whether the membership of this elite group needed to be expanded again to include the rising developing countries of the G5.

Economic Regionalism

There can be little doubt that national economies have become more and more interdependent and that trade, production, and investment have greatly advanced from their predominantly national basis since 1945. But the globalizing trend has been matched in recent years by another tendency toward economic development based on geographic regions, or economic regionalism. We have already discussed the concerns over the regionalization of trade, but the same trend can be observed in finance and production as well.

In Europe, Asia, and North America, investment flows and production patterns have become based more and more on the region. This development has taken place for several reasons. In Europe and North America, the logic has been to take advantage of existing free trade arrangements and to produce goods within these regional markets. Another rationale has been to make the most of lower wages in other economies in the region. This method has been a driving force behind the regionalization of investment and production in Asia, Latin America, and North America. Since 2010, negotiations have been underway for the Trans-Pacific Partnership (TPP), a proposed free trade agreement that would include Australia, Brunei, Chile, Canada, Malaysia, Mexico, New Zealand, Peru, Singapore, the United States, and Vietnam (Japan is also interested in joining the process.) Canada announced in the summer of 2012 that it would seek membership in this initiative, and it is now thought that the TPP offers an opportunity to further North American integration by focusing on issues that are not included in NAFTA and providing an interesting cross-regional approach to the challenges of economic interdependence.

Liberal economists predict that the regionalization process will lead to the economic enrichment of participating members, particularly the poorer

13.8 GENDER AND THE *MAQUILAS*

In the last quarter of the twentieth century, a number of LDC states allowed the creation of what came to be known as *maquiladora* ("assembly") zones, or *maquilas*, in their countries. These zones hold a special status because they allow foreign corporations to come in, produce goods, and then export them back to their home country duty-free. *Maquilas* became an important source of employment and income to LDC economies and further increased the level of interdependence between developed and developing economies.

These zones provide employment and wages that are generally higher than those available locally; however, they are a mixed blessing. Many companies operating in *maquilas* tend to hire women to work in the assembly plants, on the justification that female labour is better suited to the task involved and is generally cheaper than its male equivalent. This situation is problematic, but women in the *maquilas* face a range of other challenges.

Sexual harassment is one. Local governments tend to leave foreign producers alone when they operate in these zones, and so regulation and enforcement is often weak. Men, some of whom are foreign, generally dominate management positions. There have been many documented cases of managers sexually harassing or even raping female employees. A second area of rights abuse has been

© Annie Griffiths Belt/Corbis

Mexico's assembly plants are famous for their hiring of women and the bad conditions under which they have to work.

compulsory pregnancy testing. Despite the fact that such testing is illegal according to Mexican law, a woman must take a pregnancy test before she is hired and periodically during her employment. If she is pregnant, she will not be hired or, if already employed, will be fired. The *maquilas* pose a challenge for state policy-makers, women's rights groups, and gender analysts, and they raise the issue of gender relations within the new international production structure.

countries. Within NAFTA, for example, Mexico has benefited from very high levels of foreign direct investment, a phenomenon that stems from the combination of its access to the US market and its comparatively low wage levels. This situation should lead, in the long term, to a more highly developed Mexican economy and, it is hoped, a higher standard of living for Mexicans. Within TPP, developed countries such as Australia, Japan, Canada, and the United States are working with developing countries such as Chile, Peru, and Vietnam to establish beneficial trading relations for all.

Less orthodox analysts of regionalization, however, claim that the trend toward economic regionalism is resulting in the exploitation of poor nations' cheap labour and natural resources. Consequently, these nations will keep their inferior position in relation to the economies of the advanced industrialized states.

Oil and Oil Prices

One area of international production that remains central to the world economy is that of oil.[24] Because so much of our means of production, transportation, and energy generation depend directly or indirectly on petroleum products, oil continues to affect the health of the entire international economy. For many years, the international oil industry was dominated by the **Seven Sisters**, that is, the seven largest oil companies in the world (Esso, Royal Dutch Shell, British Petroleum, Mobil, Chevron, Gulf, and Texaco). Since the early twentieth century, this group had controlled oil supplies and prices, manipulating the market to their advantage. However, in 1960 five of the world's most important oil-producing states—Iran, Iraq, Kuwait, Saudi Arabia, and Venezuela—formed OPEC, an organization designed to strengthen the hand of the oil producers and to bolster the international price of oil and thus their revenues.

Seven Sisters group of major oil companies in the mid-twentieth century: Esso, Shell, British Petroleum, Mobil, Chevron, Gulf, and Texaco

A dramatic change occurred in 1973, when OPEC and the major oil companies failed to come to a lasting agreement on the price of oil and the fourth Arab–Israeli war began, driving up the market price. The oil-producing states soon realized that they possessed the power to control the supply and thus the price of oil in the world marketplace, a power that had once belonged exclusively to the Seven Sisters. The price rose from US$2.48/barrel at the end of 1972 to US$11.65/barrel a year later. For the next five years, OPEC would manipulate the supply and price of oil, consistently raising the latter. The net result was a massive transfer of capital from the oil-importing states to the OPEC countries.

A second major price rise took place in 1979 and 1980. With the joint developments of the Iranian Revolution and the onset of the Iran–Iraq War, the supply of oil was threatened because these two states were responsible for 10 per cent of the global oil supply. This shock to the international oil market forced prices as high as US$41/barrel, bringing still further transfers of wealth from the industrialized states to OPEC.

The effects on the international political economy should not be underestimated. States that had previously played only a secondary role in global politics became major players. Saudi Arabia, in particular, became a state of primary importance because it was the central country in OPEC. The dramatically higher oil prices contributed to the growing problem of inflation in the advanced industrialized states as prices for almost all goods were pushed higher. Capital transfers from the advanced industrialized states to OPEC members resulted in an enormous inflow of funds into the international financial system. This influx occurred because many OPEC states were earning more from oil than they could possibly spend on economic development and infrastructure and thus deposited the surplus into international banks. Much of this money was funnelled to other developing states and contributed to the debt crisis in the 1980s.

Oil prices fell and remained very low between the early 1980s and the late 1990s, dropping as low as $10 a barrel in 1998 (around $16 in current value). But high prices returned by 2007 as rising demand outpaced supply. This high demand was driven largely by economic growth in China and other developing countries, forcing the price of oil up to $150 a barrel in 2008. That same year also saw a collapse in prices when the global recession slashed demand for energy. Prices hit a low of $35 in December of that year, but production and transportation costs kept the "price at the pump" higher. As the economy recovered, so did oil prices, which topped $100 in 2011–12 once again before new supplies in the United States pushed the price back down to $85.[25]

13.9   BRAZIL AND RENEWABLE ENERGY

In the 1970s, Brazil faced a serious challenge to its economic development, as it was entirely dependent on oil imports during the OPEC price hike. In order to reduce oil imports, the country's government began to subsidize the production of sugar cane–based ethanol, to be blended with gasoline for use in automobiles and trucks. This program greatly benefited the country's sugar farmers and helped to develop the world's leading ethanol industry. Although the problem seemed to be only a national one at the time, the world looked to the Brazilian model when oil prices again reached record levels in 2007 and 2008 and climate change became a growing concern.

Brazil now exports ethanol, although the world's largest ethanol consumer is currently the United States, which restricts imports of Brazilian ethanol to protect its own corn-based ethanol industry. In the years to come, ethanol and the renewable energy sector in general promises to be a major source of growth and income and is one of the multiple reasons why Brazil promises such high levels of economic development.

Brazil has invested massive amounts of money in the development of sugar cane-based ethanol, creating new technologies that have made the fuel competitive with gasoline. This photo shows an ethanol plant in the Brazilian state of Pernambuco.

If we've learned anything from oil prices over the past few decades, it's that there is no certainty in the field. Predicting oil prices is both a science and an art that requires economic analysis, a clear sense of global politics and security, and perhaps a measure of clairvoyance as well. Nonetheless, as economic growth recovers and demand continues in the years to come, we should expect high oil prices to remain in the future.

An issue that may affect long-term oil prices concerns the possibility of alternative sources of energy. Indeed, one of the effects of high oil prices has been a new enthusiasm for renewable energy sources, such as wind, solar, and biofuels (ethanol, biodiesel, etc.). With high oil prices, these alternative sources of energy became economically viable. Given the finite supply of oil and the very real impact of oil use on climate change, renewable and clean energy sources are vital if sustainable development is to become possible on a global scale. The advances that take place in this area over the next few years will be pivotal in determining the fate of the global economy and the planet.

One of the most exciting developments in recent years has been the discovery of vast, untapped reserves of natural gas in underground rock formations across the world. Known as shale gas, these reserves hold the prospect of providing massive new, relatively clean energy supplies. Natural gas produces less than 50 per cent of the greenhouse gases that are produced by coal or oil and is highly cost efficient due to the quantities that have been discovered. But shale gas is controversial because its extraction requires huge amounts of water and chemicals to be pumped into the earth (in a process commonly called fracking). Many environmental organizations claim that this process runs the risk of contaminating groundwater. At the present time, both Canada and the United States have moved toward large-scale production of shale gas, whereas France, for example, has banned its extraction.

However, as an essential "input" for global economic production and development, oil remains the single most important—and strategic—commodity in the world. Yet much has changed on the oil landscape, including where it is used most, the way it is priced, and who controls it. The Seven Sisters were exclusively Western, based in the United States, the United Kingdom, and the Netherlands, with branch plants around the world. Today the world's largest petroleum companies in order of size of oil reserves are Saudi Arabian Oil Company; National Iranian Oil Company; Qatar General Petroleum Corporation; Iraq National Oil Company; Petróleos de Venezuela S.A.; Abu Dhabi National Oil Company; and Kuwait Petroleum Corporation. ExxonMobil, the biggest Western oil company, is a distant seventeenth.

Multinational Corporations

Oil companies are certainly some of the biggest economic actors in the world today. ExxonMobil may be the seventeenth largest oil company based on reserves, but in revenue it is the largest company in the world, with earnings of almost half a trillion dollars a year. According to the IMF, these revenues are more than the GDPs of countries such as Denmark, Argentina, Austria, or Taiwan.[26] Walmart, one of the top three companies in the world in terms of revenue, is also the world's largest private employer. Numbers are one thing, but the economic and political clout of corporations must also be taken into account.

Throughout most of human history, production has been organized on a local basis, with small cottage industries predominating. This situation began to change in the seventeenth and eighteenth centuries, when the Industrial Revolution created large firms producing for national (and to a lesser extent international) markets. At the same time, improvements in communications and transportation created the right conditions for the national integration of production processes.[27]

The nineteenth century saw the internationalization of trade but not of production. Although raw materials were transported across great distances to be used in national production processes, production itself remained rooted at the nation-state level. It was only in the second half of the twentieth century that production took on an international dimension. With the expansion of US firms into Europe and then Asia, these processes began to be integrated, in turn drawing together national economies. Indeed, it was the spread of US MNCs that began a practice that has led to the globalized production we see today.[28]

In 1945, the United States dominated world production. With the economies of Europe and Japan in ruins, the United States was the only large economic system producing the goods necessary for postwar rebuilding and economic recovery. As such, US producers found themselves in the enviable position of facing minimal competition from firms in other states. Not only did this allow them to make huge profits in the early postwar years, but it also encouraged a process by which US corporations invested directly in European and Asian economies, setting up productive capacities there rather than merely exporting from their US base. Helping this internationalization was the strength of the US dollar, which was also in great demand by European and Asian nations. US firms were thus able to invest in foreign economies very cheaply.

As US firms set up production facilities in various countries around the world, their production became multinational and the era of the MNC was born. The main advantage of multinational production is economies of scale, whereby mass production can be organized for huge numbers of consumers spread across many different nations. The post–World War II period saw a dramatic rise in this kind of production. By the 1960s, US MNCs had been joined by European and Japanese competitors and, later, by MNCs from developing states (such as CEMEX, a Mexican building materials and cement producer).

By the next decade, some academics and policy-makers had begun to ask serious questions about the power and influence of MNCs, particularly with reference to their relations with LDC governments. Raymond Vernon even wrote of states facing a situation that could best be described as "sovereignty at bay," where governments were increasingly challenged by large MNCs.[29] The reasoning behind this claim was simple: throughout the postwar period, MNCs had grown in size to the extent that their economic and technical resources matched or even dwarfed those available to many LDC governments. What's more, with developing states desperate for foreign investment, MNCs found themselves in a strong bargaining position. To make matters worse, even if a state secured investment from a foreign MNC, the corporation could always withdraw or divest from that country if the level of rewards became unsatisfactory.

Such power enabled MNCs to negotiate preferential conditions for their investments, securing tax breaks and cheap access to labour and raw materials. More sinister, however, was the suggestion that MNCs were engaging in political activities within their host states, activities designed to manipulate the democratic process so that firms' political and economic preferences were promoted. A famous example of such interference concerned the US telecommunications corporation ITT. In Chile in the 1970s, the firm conspired to bring down a Marxist government that threatened its interests.[30]

Honda's Odyssey minivan first appeared as the Isuzu Oasis in 1995. Sales success in North America led to rebranding and, later, production in Ontario, the United States, and China. Today, with manufacturing concentrated in Alabama, the Odyssey is considered the fourth most "American" car on the market, with over 80 per cent of its parts made in the United States.

Other concerns about the influence of MNCs related to their close relationship with their home governments. Though there is little evidence to support it, the accusation has been made that MNCs sometimes act as their respective government's agents in foreign countries. Through espionage, political activities, or economic dependence, MNCs have the potential to advance the interests of their home country at the expense of the host.

The internationalization of production has not only seen firms producing goods in many different geographical locations. The actual process of production has also become global. Automobiles, televisions, computers, and a host of other products are not made in a single country but assembled from parts manufactured in many different ones. Honda, for example, has integrated its vehicle production process on both a regional and worldwide basis. The significance of integrated production processes is immense; it means the transmission of corporate management strategies and technologies and a connection between workers and consumers across the globe.

Conclusion

The current international political economy is almost unrecognizable from the system that was created at the end of World War II. The role of private actors has increased dramatically, and the level of interaction between states has reached levels unseen since before World War I. Trade and financial flows continue to

grow, both within and between regions, and advances in the fields of communications and transportation have made the world seem much smaller than it
once did.

Yet many of the fundamentals of IPE remain the same. State power still
matters and the powerful continue to shape the international economic system. Efficiency and competitiveness remain primary goals of states as they seek
to retain an edge over their rivals (and friends). Many of the questions that
haunted the beginning of the postwar international economy have returned.
How much freedom should states grant to private finance? What should be
done to assist the poorer nations of the world? What is the role of the state in
economic management?

The international economy remains in a state of constant flux. Our study
of it reveals a great deal about the nature of political economy and the interaction among politics, economics, states, and markets. The development of the
international economy in the early years of this century will bring new forces
and substantial transformations to the fore, many unforeseen. We can hope
to understand the political economy of our own nation only if we take into
account the system of which it is a part.

Self-Assessment Questions

1. What is the role of negotiation and co-operation in the international economy?
2. What have been the major forces behind the growth in international trade since 1945?
3. What is the balance between political authorities and market actors in the world economy today?
4. Why does the international financial system tend toward crisis?
5. What do you see as the future of the international energy system? Will gas and oil remain the major source of energy for the global economy, or is it feasible to move to "greener" options? Give reasons to support your answers.

Weblinks

Bank for International Settlements
www.bis.org

International Monetary Fund
www.imf.org

Multinational Monitor
www.multinationalmonitor.org

World Trade Organization
www.wto.org

Further Reading

Balaam, David N., and Bradford Dillman. *Introduction to International Political Economy*. 5th edn. Upper Saddle River, NJ: Prentice Hall, 2011.

Cohn, Theodore H. *Global Political Economy: Theory and Practice*. 6th edn. New York: Pearson Longman, 2011.

Haslam, Paul, and Jessica Schafer. *Introduction to International Development: Approaches, Actors, and Issues*. 2nd edn. Toronto: Oxford University Press, 2012.

Hülsemeyer, Axel. *International Political Economy: A Reader*. Toronto: Oxford University Press, 2010.

Keohane, Robert O., and Joseph Nye. *Power and Interdependence: World Politics in Transition*. 2nd edn. Cambridge: HarperCollins, 1989.

Santiso, Javier, and Jeff Dayton-Johnson. *The Oxford Handbook of Latin American Political Economy*. New York: Oxford University Press, 2012.

Yergin, Daniel, and Joseph Stainslaw. *The Commanding Heights: The Battle for the World Economy*. New York: Simon & Schuster, 2002.

News Clips

Visit the companion website for *Politics: An Introduction*, 2nd edn, to access news clips related to the content of this chapter.

14 Conclusion

◄ A Yemeni resident cycles past a sign that reads "Freedom is made by the people." The 2011 Yemeni Revolution and uprisings in Tunisia, Egypt, and Libya became known as the Arab Spring and, to many, were a symbol of freedom, hope, and political possibility.

Photo: Reuters/Mohamed al-Sayaghi

After reading this chapter, you will be able to

- review the major themes of the text;
- relate significant concepts and theories to contemporary political activity;
- demonstrate how we've introduced the major subfields of political studies; and
- provide a "road map" for future studies in politics.

Introduction

Unless you like to read the end of a book first (and spoil the development of the plot), we can presume that you've read at least most of this book. Indeed, you've likely read it all during your introductory course and are probably comfortable with most of the material. Most introductory texts don't include a conclusion but simply end with the final chapter, usually one dealing with politics on a global scale. There are reasonable arguments for not having a conclusion— devotees of art films sometimes might make the case for a "non-resolution" to the plot, thereby allowing the viewer to construct his or her own ending and leaving the future for characters and plots open or up for personal interpretation. We aren't suggesting that others see the end of a text as interpretative; instead, we feel it's necessary to take the time to consider what we've dealt with, how we can use this information, and where we can go from here. After all, your involvement with politics doesn't end with this text or this course. While you could try to avoid politics by not taking further courses, the "political" in your life is permanent, as we've suggested throughout this book. And now that you understand the nature of politics, it's not likely that you'll want to just leave that part of your life on the sidelines. This final chapter will give us that opportunity to take stock and look ahead.

What Have We Learned?

At the very beginning of this text, we discussed our tendency to become cynical about politics. It's an understandable reaction. Even the most fleeting read of newscasts or feeds shows ample reason to be skeptical of any good that might come from politics. It isn't surprising, then, that even the word *political* becomes a disparaging reference: "That committee has become so *political*" or "I don't want to get involved because the others are *playing politics*." In this sense, the word gets reduced to a very simplistic meaning. Politics becomes a "power grab" or a contest of rigid views rather than a process of deciding how our communities and systems can be improved or how we can make a positive difference in the lives of others. On the other hand, it's as easy to be as overly optimistic about politics as it is to be pessimistic. Some undergraduate students feel that they will "change the world" (or at least their world) with a little political studies under their belts. And certainly there have been many who have had an enormous effect.

One of the biggest problems in our world is apathy, a common condition of modern life. We hope that you are now of the mind that even the smallest contribution can make a positive effect. Aside from acting malevolently, which few actually do, the worst thing we can do in our lives is to be indifferent. That

I JUST CAN'T DO IT....
THE SCRIPT SAYS ENTER STAGE LEFT
AND I'M A CONSERVATIVE

Lindsay Foyle/Cartoon Stock

Some people deal with their politics intensely.

14.1 FROM "ME TO WE": MARC AND CRAIG KIELBURGER

Any time you hear that one person can't make a difference or that children have no effect on the world around them, think of the Kielburger brothers. Marc and Craig Kielburger established Free The Children in 1995, when they were only 17 and 12, respectively. This charitable organization was created to draw attention to the plight of child workers the world over by financing education for children and young adults.

Free The Children began after Craig read a newspaper report about a child who was murdered for defending the rights of child workers in Pakistan. Shocked to hear that people his age were being persecuted for demanding their basic rights rather than going to school and enjoying childhood, Craig, Marc, and their friends began fundraising and raising awareness about child labour. They managed to get the attention of then prime minister Jean Chrétien, who was travelling to Asia to bolster Canadian trade with the region. Starting a dialogue with the Canadian government brought more attention to the Kielburgers' cause. Using money primarily raised among and by children, the organization took on development projects across Asia and Africa to improve education and social conditions for children.

In addition to Marc's earning degrees in international relations from Harvard and law from Oxford and Craig's obtaining one in peace and conflict studies from the University of Toronto, followed by an executive MBA from York, the brothers haven't stopped their work. Still involved with Free The Children, they have also started the national Me to We movement, aimed at improving social and

The Canadian Press Images/Dominic Chan

Craig (left) and Marc Kielburger on stage at the 2012 We Day, an annual youth empowerment event and initiative of Free The Children, held at the Air Canada Centre in Toronto.

environmental conditions through awareness, volunteerism, and fundraising. The two have authored books, produced television specials, and worked with media and political leaders to aid their cause. They've been honoured many times over the years, receiving honorary degrees from universities, the Order of Canada, and many other prestigious awards.

Not all of us can dedicate our lives to changing the world. However, we are all capable of effecting change. Our impact can and should be felt beyond our own lives, but it doesn't have to be worldwide.

is tantamount to ignoring our real responsibility as citizens, which is to be engaged in our communities. After all, if we don't act, who will act for us?

We've spent a great deal of time in this book considering what ought to be a natural conclusion: we are inextricably connected with our social environment. This connection includes the smallest details, such as the seemingly insignificant decision to rezone a neighbourhood in another part of town, far from where we live. But this change could affect us in several ways. What if that rezoning created a precedent that permitted a commercial development in the park across your street? What if your quiet street became a four-lane boulevard? Would it be too late to get involved then?

14.2 COWS OR CLIMATE?

The Amazon rainforest, which is mostly in Brazil but also includes parts of Peru, Venezuela, Colombia, and five other countries, is a massive ecosystem. It is the largest rainforest in the world, with over 5.5 million square kilometres of rainforest in its full 7-million-square-kilometre area. A delicate system, it is home to millions of species of insects and thousands of different plants and animals. Some of the rainforest, it is felt, may never have been explored by humans.

The rainforest is also a bionetwork under siege. Over a half million square kilometres have been forested, mostly for the growing global demand for Brazilian beef.[1] In fact, deforestation in Brazil's rainforest is more the result of the need for grazing land than of the logging industry. Exports of Brazilian beef have increased massively in recent years, and the number of cattle in that country doubled in the 1990s alone.

To say that beef is the core reason for the clearing of the Amazon rainforest would not be entirely correct. The sensitive nature of the rainforest's soil, which is used for soybean cultivation, is also a contributing factor. Unlike other parts of the world, the rainforest cannot be constantly reused for agriculture. After a short time, the soil is rendered useless for further planting. Logging and agriculture have both led to there being more roads built, more towns erected, and more human interference in the area. At the current rate of development, it's expected that the rainforest will have

Beef production in the Amazon region has added pressure to the area's natural ecosystem.

been reduced to about half its original size by 2020. Brazil and other countries in the region, however, claim that the rainforest needs to develop. Finding a way to allow for sustainable development of the Amazon rainforest is one of the most serious environmental and economic issues we face today.

Note

1. Fred Pearce, "Brazil's Beef Trade Wrecks Rainforest," *New Scientist* 2442 (10 Apr. 2004).

To take this matter a few steps farther, more serious issues such as poverty in sub-Saharan Africa or the razing of the Brazilian rainforest may also seem disconnected from our lives. Yet both may be more like a municipal rezoning than we first think. Poverty leads to chronic underdevelopment, civil conflict, mass migration, disease, and animosities that extend far beyond borders. The rainforests provide the largest amount of oxygen in the Western hemisphere. These are not peripheral matters. Just as we may someday feel the effect of a decision in another neighbourhood, poverty in Africa and environmental degradation of the rainforests could ultimately affect us in Canada.

We are indeed members of a global community. Although that statement may seem meaningless because of its overuse and commercialization (think of the numerous advertisements you've seen that use our "global identity" to sell a product), it's still the truth. We are political citizens of a particular country and live in specific provinces, cities, or towns. While our primary allegiances and actions will likely affect our own local and national communities first, they will also have an impact, intended or not, on the global scene.

Drawing conclusions about human nature was not a goal of this book, but we did make the point that humans are both co-operative and competitive in their efforts to govern themselves. The very nature of politics is to strike a balance between these tendencies, as good can come from both. Balance is not always possible, so conflict emerges over the best options. The common good, however, is often overlooked. Competitiveness is sometimes used as an excuse for some countries doing better or having more than others. The "good" in this sense is not shared: the few with tremendous wealth or the countries that enjoy peace are not necessarily seeking ways to apportion their gains with others. And that is precisely where governance, or more precisely government, comes in: governments distribute benefits. Co-operative behaviour may or may not be the core of our nature, but it can become a routine part of our lives when we see the rewards.

We considered this situation in the context of public goods in society—those things that are provided for us, usually by government, and are supposed to be available for all. In reality, public goods aren't so universally obtainable. The simple fact is that some will always have more than others, whether it is money, power, security, freedom, rights, or influence. A common theme that has appeared in this book is the fundamental inequity of modern life. To be sure, life has never been equal for all—far from it—but it is nevertheless troubling that we continue to exist in a global system where a lot of attention is paid to the imbalance of public goods but there's never enough done to rectify the situation. It leaves one wondering whether we, as a collective, are truly interested in making the necessary changes to provide for global equality.

Cast your memory back to the earliest parts of your course, when we explained several concepts (some new, some familiar). At this point, it should be obvious that we need to understand the terminology before we can really get into any topic. It's a bit like getting to know the characters before settling into a book or a movie. Concepts aren't exactly the characters of this book, but we can agree that, like any character, there are multiple angles we can use to describe or use them. For example, it's unlikely that the person who sits next to you in class has exactly the same view of, say, power than you do. You may agree on certain aspects, such as the use of power or the resources needed to carry out power, but no doubt you'll have diverging opinions on its utility or importance for politics. That's a good thing: we don't expect students to read this textbook and have the same views. Our goal has been to introduce and explain concepts for you to consider.

Some of these concepts are very broad, and you were probably familiar with them at the outset. Power and order, for instance, are concepts that even people not majoring in political studies should be able to discuss. Others, such as the state or the nation, may elicit more confusion. Most people see these concepts as interchangeable. You now know that they aren't, even if you accept that they're regularly used as synonyms. Still others, such as legitimacy or anarchy, would cause most individuals to stop and think about them before responding. They are more specific concepts, used in a special way by political scientists.

Then there are the concepts that move us from the "hard ground" of definitions and argued positions to "softer ground" of interpretation and analysis. Values and justice, for instance, would give any of us pause were we asked to describe them in short form. They require more thought, more elucidation, and greater context. They aren't necessarily more important, but interpretation is always more difficult than description.

All of these concepts, and the many others that we covered in Chapter 2, were used repeatedly in this text. Your course instructor also used them widely in lectures and seminars. Like any field, political studies uses a specialized language that must first be understood (or, at the very least, recognized) before moving ahead. You are now conversant in this language.

Most readers of this text will have some confidence in their knowledge about basic Canadian politics. We've used Canada as a foundation for this text because we believe that it's essential to know your own system before studying others. Canadians ought to have a basic understanding of their political structures, and Canadian political scientists should begin by analyzing their governments and politics. To that end, we've tried to refer to the Canadian context as much as possible, but we've also looked at other countries—including the United States, EU members, Japan, Brazil, India, China, Mali, and Mexico—in detail. Some, such as the UK, the US, and Mexico, have appeared more than others. Again, given our concentration on Canada, it's logical to look carefully at those countries with which we have an especially close relationship. In so doing, we've considered politics in a broadly comparative context but also provided some perspective on Canadian interests at home and abroad.

The external environment constantly affects Canadian politics. Therefore, our introduction must include the world beyond our borders and look at other countries, international relations, foreign policy, international security, and international political economy. Moreover, countries such as Canada continually operate in a global environment. Our changing role in Afghanistan, our free trade in North America, our part in international culture, and even our notion of citizenship in Canada are all affected by the essential role we play in global affairs and the immediate impact felt by events in other areas. A citizen of Canada is also a member of a much larger community of nations, a relationship that this text has explored in detail.

Regardless of the country in question, some topics are essential. Our overviews of governments, participation, and political systems, for instance, showed the similarities and differences among various countries. Concepts such as sovereignty may apply to all states globally, but forms of political systems or modes of citizen participation vary widely. These sections provided some context for concepts in action, but they were also necessary for the following chapters that featured comparative country studies.

One enduring issue for all realms of political studies has been the various levels of political action that occur simultaneously. Individuals, non-state actors, states, international organizations and corporations, and global players may compete with or assist each other. Importantly, as we've learned, these actors perform their duties at the same time. For instance, an international financial transaction may involve an individual trader, a banking institution, government policy, international financial institutions, and global trading regulations. Another example is a political leader deciding whether to intervene militarily in another country. He or she must consider the opinions of global institutions such as the UN, other nation-states' actions, and the viewpoints of domestic actors such as individuals, pressure groups, and political parties.

We can't possibly ascertain what's happening at all levels at a certain period—there's just not the time or the capacity to do so. Instead, we make crucial decisions about what and whom to study. These choices involve the levels of analysis, where evaluations are made about the most significant actors to scrutinize and why. Choosing what to analyze isn't the same as the levels of interaction, where we make connections between various actors. In short, we can't know it all, so we must perfect our ability to settle on what is most important—that's why choosing a level of analysis becomes crucial. The ability to measure and select the most significant factors in a political event is an important skill that all political scientists must master. Knowing what to study and what to leave aside makes our job easier and more relevant.

This textbook has also examined various approaches to political studies, including analytical, behavioural, post-behavioural, political economy, realist, liberal, socialist, feminist, and conservative. It's safe to say that, at times, this textbook has employed some of these perspectives. For instance, the political approach was used in the chapters on politics and economics, and the empirical examples such as country studies certainly employed some degree of the analytic approach. But we've tried to avoid the potential pitfalls of using a dominant approach at the expense of others. Instead, we've attempted to introduce the discipline of political studies in a comprehensive manner. There will be plenty of opportunities for you in future courses to consider the pros and cons of using a particular methodological or theoretical framework.

Despite the fact that this course is an introductory one, teaching this material can be challenging for many instructors. None of us is an expert in all these different fields, and each of us has specific areas of specialty. It's tempting, then, to concentrate on what one knows best. Both of the authors of this book, for instance, are international relations specialists. But we have other areas of interest (domestic politics, theory, comparative studies) that reflect our primary concentration. You have also likely been more interested in certain topics covered in this text and course than in others. That's natural and expected. Regardless of where we are in our studies, from an introductory student to a senior professor, our interests will bend and change over time. But we'll find those fields that intrigue us most.

To that end, we've tried to introduce all the major areas of political studies in a balanced way. Canadian politics, comparative studies, theory, international relations—all of these overlap in many ways and each has its own subfields.

If you choose to continue studying politics, you'll likely have to make choices about courses and fields that are most intriguing to you. We hope that this book has helped you make those decisions. With this in mind, let us turn our attention to your future as a politics student.

Where Do We Go from Here?

With one course in political studies completed, what should you take next? This introductory class has prepared you for any of the major subfields—Canadian politics, comparative politics, international relations, political theory, or public administration. Some of these will be more interesting to you than others, but keep in mind that a broad base in politics will help you down the road if you continue with this discipline. You may discover, for instance, that you really need that political theory background when, years later, a professor asks you to assist in classroom instruction or research in your undergraduate, or maybe graduate, degree.

If you decide to major in political studies, the program guidelines at your university or college would be the logical place to start. However, most departments require second-year students to take a series of courses that introduce them to the subdisciplines of the field. This is your chance to concentrate on those areas that really piqued your interest in this course.

A common question posed by students, particularly in the early stages of their studies, is "What kind of job will I get with this degree/diploma?" You've no doubt thought about it, too. It would be odd, in fact, for anyone to enter a post-secondary program without thinking about his or her future prospects. This thinking is further complicated by pressure from family members who want to know what you'll "do with your life" and the common wisdom that suggests a BA or social science diploma will not properly prepare you for any career.

As in politics, it's easy to succumb to cynical thinking about undergraduate studies, especially when the economy slumps. Pursuing a degree or diploma is a big decision because it involves years of your life, thousands of dollars, and choices that will affect your future. At this point, you might have chosen a program or be taking courses on a selective basis. In either case, you've taken this course for one reason or another. We can presume that this decision had something to do with your interest in politics. That means

STATE UNIVERSITY

"I'm majoring in political science and minoring in ballet — I want to be a spin doctor."

Rex May/CartoonStock

You might be surprised at what you can do with your political studies degree!

something: you know what you want to study and where your interests and abilities lie. Therefore, whatever choices you've already made cannot be wrong because you're following your interests. You may discover, however, that politics is not your passion. But that's not a failure—it's part of your exploration of post-secondary studies.

It's certainly true that politics is not a trade such as plumbing or drywall installation. Nor is it exactly the same as fields such as medicine or commerce. All of these areas, however, involve specialized knowledge. Politics is part of the social sciences, one of the two major wings of most arts faculties (the other is the humanities). Studying politics hones the analytical mind. It trains us to utilize frameworks such as theories and methodologies and to explore new directions. Politics does not always fit an existing structure; therefore, we become expert problem solvers and our critical capacity is always part of our analysis. We know that events don't always meet an existing category or outline. Part of our ability is to find the dissimilar, identify the new, and frame the innovative in a way that allows other researchers to use our findings in their work. This practice is part of what we call the **heuristic method**. We have called on past research in our study of introductory politics; you may someday find a new direction that will assist others in their analyses.

Your first step should be to ignore the cynical opinions. Those who tell you that you'll never get a job with a BA, for example, are wrong. Those who tell you that you'll never make a decent living are wrong. But the emphasis on jobs distorts the real issue. Political studies graduates haven't trained for jobs but prepared for careers. They often go on to study at the master's level or pursue fields such as law, commerce, the public service, or journalism. A BA on its own may not be what earns you the career of your choice, but it's hard to imagine obtaining that career without one. It is possible, of course, to enter law school or journalism with no undergraduate degree. But these are exceptions. Most lawyers or journalists, for example, will tell you that their choice of undergraduate specialty made them a far better professional. The BA gives you a field of emphasis, a speciality based on knowledge and study. On that score, a degree in politics can be far more adaptable than many others. For example, if the foreign service interests you, your background in politics will serve you in a greater fashion than a degree in another social science or humanities field.

Just to give you an idea of what we've been talking about, here is a brief list of the jobs that some of our former undergraduate students have gone on to do:

- senator
- member of Parliament
- diplomat
- intelligence and security specialist
- government analyst
- financial analyst
- stock trader

heuristic method
process of laying out experience as a way to assist future research

- international textile importer
- oil trader
- sustainable development expert
- consultant
- industrial espionage specialist
- professor of international relations
- migrant worker rights advocate
- public service worker
- UN worker
- business owner
- lawyer
- journalist

For those of you who are still unconvinced or looking for hard evidence that a BA is a good idea, consider this. A *Globe and Mail* article highlighted a study that followed the career direction of hundreds of arts, science, and applied science (engineering) graduates in Ontario. This study showed that arts graduates earned as much as their pure science colleagues when they were hired. As time went on, those arts graduates rose higher in their institutions and had higher incomes than pure science and applied science graduates.[1]

Talk to your family about your choices. Get information from friends and peers who have taken similar programs, whether they've graduated yet or not. And most important, discuss your future with your professors. Use those instructors who are more open to your ideas or whom you just "click" with better as a resource. Talk about your aspirations, ask questions about your courses and your program, and compare what they all have to say. No one will tell you exactly what you ought to do; that's up to you. But you'll get to that point much more quickly with the help and advice of others.

Conclusion

At the outset of Chapter 1, we welcomed you to the study of politics. That chapter promised that this text would introduce you to the widest array of topics and issues that we could accommodate in a comprehensive first-year volume. If this book has been a success, it has made you think about issues that you hadn't before, challenged your opinions on things you thought you knew and understood, and no doubt left you in complete disagreement at other times.

Furthermore, it should have stimulated a deeper fascination with politics. Satisfying this interest will take time, much more time than your course could provide. Both of us still feel moved in different directions by our research and teaching, and we hope that continues as long as we remain political scientists. The dynamism of politics is what brought us in and keeps us here. We hope that you feel the same way. Welcome.

Self-Assessment Questions

1. What is the difference between an explanation of an idea and an interpretation of one?
2. What are some of the main concepts that have reappeared throughout this book?
3. What is the difference between theory and methodology?
4. What are the main subdisciplines in political studies? How do they overlap?

Weblinks

Canadian Political Science Association: Careers
www.cpsa-acsp.ca/guides.shtml

Careers in Political Science
www.sfu.ca/politics/department/careers.html

Careers in the Social Sciences
www.ssc.uwo.ca/careers/resources/workOpportunities.asp

Political Science Majors: Careers
http://navigator.wlu.ca/career/student/planning/discipline/political-science.htm

Further Reading

Brooks, Stephen. *Canadian Democracy: An Introduction*. 7th edn. Toronto: Oxford University Press, 2012.
Inwood, Gregory J. *Understanding Canadian Public Administration*. 4th edn. Toronto: Pearson Education Canada, 2012.
Jackson, Robert, and Georg Sørensen. *Introduction to International Relations: Theories and Approaches*. 4th edn. New York: Oxford University Press, 2010.
Kesselman, Mark, Joel Krieger, and William A. Joseph. *Introduction to Comparative Politics*. 6th edn. Toronto: Nelson Canada, 2013.
Veltman, Andrea, ed. *Social and Political Philosophy: Classic and Contemporary Readings*. Toronto: Oxford University Press, 2008.

News Clips

Visit the companion website for *Politics: An Introduction*, 2nd edn, to access news clips related to the content of this chapter.

Notes

CHAPTER 1

1. See Jennifer MacMillan, "Bono and Bob Geldof Take the Reins," *The Globe and Mail*, 10 May 2010, www.theglobeandmail.com/news/world/g8-g20/africa/bono-and-bob-geldof-take-the-reins/article1561664/.
2. Although there are different names for the study of politics, we have chosen to use *political studies* throughout this book because it accurately reflects a broad perspective of the discipline.
3. Thomas Hobbes, *Leviathan, Or, the Matter, Forme and Power of a Commonwealth Ecclesiasticall and Civil*, ed. Michael Oakeshott (New York: Collier Books, 1962).
4. Harold Lasswell, *Politics: Who Gets What, When, How* (New York: Meridian Books, 1958).
5. Aristotle, *Politics*, trans. T.A. Sinclair (Harmondsworth, UK: Penguin, 1986), 7.
6. For a classic analysis of the comparative method, see Adam Przeworski and Henry Teune, *The Logic of Comparative Social Inquiry* (New York: Wiley, 1970).
7. For more on comparative politics, see Gabriel A. Almond, G. Bingham J. Powell Jr, Russell J. Dalton, and Kaare Strøm, *Comparative Politics Today: A World View*, 9th edn (Toronto: Longman, 2008).
8. Isaac Asimov, *Asimov on Science Fiction* (New York: Doubleday, 1981), ix.
9. Laozi, *Tao Te Ching* (Harmondsworth, UK: Penguin, 1963/1976).
10. Kenneth McRoberts, "The Future of the Nation-State and Quebec–Canada Relations," in *The Fate of the Nation State*, ed. Michel Seymour (Montreal and Kingston: McGill-Queen's University Press, 2004), 390.

CHAPTER 2

1. Andrew Heywood, *Political Ideas and Concepts: An Introduction* (New York: St. Martin's Press, 1994), 4.
2. Ibid., 56–7.
3. Richard Gunther, José Ramón Montero, and Juan Linz, eds, *Political Parties: Old Concepts and New Challenges* (Oxford: Oxford University Press, 2002), 43.
4. Michael E. Morrell, "Deliberation, Democratic Decision-Making and Internal Political Efficacy," *Political Behavior* 27, 1 (2005): 51.
5. Michael Kenny, *The Politics of Identity: Liberal Political Theory and the Dilemmas of Difference* (Cambridge: Polity Press, 2004), 1–7.
6. Heywood, *Political Ideas and Concepts*, 116–17.
7. Robert Putnam, *Bowling Alone: The Collapse and Revival of American Community* (New York: Simon and Schuster, 2000), 67–8.
8. Samuel P. Huntington, *Political Order in Changing Societies* (New Haven, CT: Yale University Press, 1968), 3–4.
9. Max Weber, "The Profession and Vocation of Politics," in *Weber: Political Writings*, ed. and trans. Peter Lassman and Ronald Speirs (Cambridge: Cambridge University Press, 1895/1994).
10. Karen A. Mingst, *Essentials of International Relations*, 3rd edn (New York: W.W. Norton, 2004), 83–4.
11. Robert O. Keohane and Joseph S. Nye, *Power and Interdependence: World Politics in Transition*, 2nd edn (Cambridge: HarperCollins, 1989), 11–19.
12. Steven Lukes, *Power: A Radical View* (Houndmills, UK: Palgrave Macmillan, in association with British Sociological Association, 2005), 9–10.
13. Susan Strange, *States and Markets* (New York: Basil Blackwell, 1988).
14. William J. Lahneman, "Changing Power Cycles and Foreign Policy Role-Power Realignments: Asia, Europe, and North America," *International Political Science Review* 24, 1 (2003): 106–8.
15. Jason A. MacDonald, "Agency Design and Postlegislative Influence over the Bureaucracy," *Political Research Quarterly* 60, 4 (2007): 683.
16. Huntington, *Political Order*, 74–5.
17. Heywood, *Political Ideas and Concepts*, 89–90.
18. Stanley A. Renshon, "Political Leadership as Social Capital: Governing in a Divided National Culture," *Political Psychology* 21, 1 (2000): 200.
19. Anthony Oberschall, "Opportunities and Framing in the Eastern European Revolts of 1989," in *Comparative Perspectives on Social Movements: Political Opportunities, Mobilizing Structures, and Cultural Framings*, 3rd edn, ed. Doug McAdam, John D. McCarthy, and Mayer N. Zald (Cambridge: Cambridge University Press, 1996), 97–9.
20. Ronald Inglehart, *Human Values and Social Change: Findings from the Values Surveys* (Leiden, The Netherlands, and Boston: Brill, 2003), 5–7.

21. Heywood, *Political Ideas and Concepts*, 266–90.
22. Daniel Horowitz, "Rethinking Betty Friedan and *The Feminine Mystique*: Labor Union Radicalism and Feminism in Cold War America," *American Quarterly* 48, 1 (1996): 2.
23. Claus Offe, "Fifty Years after the 'Great Transformation': Reflections on Social Order and Political Agency," in *The Changing Nature of Democracy*, ed. Takashi Inoguchi, Edward Newman, and John Keane (Tokyo: United Nations University Press, 1998), 39–46.
24. Dennis R. Hoover, Michael D. Martinez, Samuel H. Reimer, and Kenneth D. Wald, "Evangelicalism Meets the Continental Divide: Moral and Economic Conservatism in the United States and Canada," *Political Research Quarterly* 55, 2 (2002): 356.
25. David Miller, *Liberty* (New York: Oxford University Press, 1991), 6.
26. Judith N. Shklar, *Political Thought and Political Thinkers*, ed. Stanley Hoffmann (Chicago: University of Chicago Press, 1998), 95.
27. Eric Nelson, "Liberty: One Concept Too Many?" *Political Theory* 33, 1 (2005): 60.
28. Heywood, *Political Ideas and Concepts*, 198.
29. Ibid., 152.
30. Ibid., 138.
31. Jean Blondel, "Democracy and Constitutionalism," in *The Changing Nature of Democracy*, ed. Takashi Inoguchi, Edward Newman, and John Keane (Tokyo: United Nations University Press, 1998), 82.

CHAPTER 3

1. Judith N. Shklar, *Political Thought and Political Thinkers*, ed. Stanley Hoffmann (Chicago: University of Chicago Press, 1998), 161–73.
2. Theodore H. Cohn, *Global Political Economy: Theory and Practice*, 4th edn (New York: Pearson Longman, 2008), 108.
3. Karen A. Mingst, *Essentials of International Relations*, 3rd edn (New York: W.W. Norton, 2004), 320.
4. Stephen C. McCaffrey, *Understanding International Law* (Newark: LexisNexis, 2006), 155.
5. Shklar, *Political Thought*, 10.
6. Pablo Beramendi and Christopher J. Anderson, *Democracy, Inequality, and Representation: A Comparative Perspective* (New York: Russell Sage Foundation, 2008), 39.
7. Mingst, *Essentials of International Relations*, 40.
8. David N. Balaam and Michael Veseth, *Introduction to International Political Economy* (Upper Saddle River, NJ: Prentice Hall, 2001), 14.
9. Andrew Heywood, *Political Ideas and Concepts: An Introduction* (New York: St. Martin's Press, 1994), 9–10.
10. These movements are named after the philosophers and theorists Robert Owen, Henri de Saint-Simon, and Charles Fourier.
11. Anthony Giddens, *The Global Third Way Debate* (Cambridge: Polity Press, 2001), 23.
12. Christopher M. Federico and Jim Sidanius, "Sophistication and the Antecedents of Whites' Racial Policy Attitudes: Racism, Ideology, and Affirmative Action in America," *Public Opinion Quarterly* 66, 2 (2002): 152.
13. Joel S. Migdal, *State in Society: Studying How States and Societies Transform and Constitute One Another* (Cambridge: Cambridge University Press, 2001), 30.
14. Cohn, *Global Political Economy*, 99–100.
15. Joan E. Spero and Jeffrey A. Hart, *The Politics of International Economic Relations*, 6th edn (Belmont, CA: Wadsworth Thomson, 2003), 2.
16. Heywood, *Political Ideas and Concepts*, 57–60.
17. Henk Dekker, Darina Malová, and Sander Hoogendoorn, "Nationalism and Its Explanations," *Political Psychology* 24, 2 (2003): 347.
18. Sanford Lakoff, "Tocqueville, Burke, and the Origins of Liberal Conservatism," *Review of Politics* 60, 3 (1998): 447.
19. Sonia E. Alvarez, "Latin American Feminisms 'Go Global': Trends of the 1990s and Challenges for the New Millennium," in *Cultures of Politics/Politics of Cultures: Re-visioning Latin American Social Movements*, ed. Sonia E. Alvarez, Evelina Dagnino, and Arturo Escobar (Boulder, CO: Westview Press, 1998), 295.
20. Hanspeter Kriesi, "The Organizational Structure of New Social Movements in a Political Context," in *Comparative Perspectives on Social Movements: Political Opportunities, Mobilizing Structures, and Cultural Framings*, ed. Doug McAdam, John D. McCarthy, and Mayer N. Zald (Cambridge: Cambridge University Press, 1996), 168.
21. Rajeev Patel and Philip McMichael, "Third Worldism and the Lineages of Global Fascism: The Regrouping of the Global South in the Neoliberal Era," *Third World Quarterly* 25, 1 (2004): 233.
22. Alan Carter, "Analytical Anarchism: Some Conceptual Foundations," *Political Theory* 28, 2 (2000): 231.
23. Pippa Norris, *Electoral Engineering: Voting Rules and Political Behavior* (Cambridge: Cambridge University Press, 2004), 62.
24. See Michel Albert, *Capitalism Against Capitalism* (London: Whurr, 1993).
25. Cohn, *Global Political Economy*, 99–100.

CHAPTER 4

1. For more information on the Canadian budget, see www.budget.gc.ca.
2. US budget information is available at www.gpo.gov/fdsys/browse/collectionGPO.action?collectionCode=BUDGET.
3. Carl Bernstein, *A Woman in Charge: The Life of Hillary Rodham Clinton* (New York: Knopf, 2007).
4. Obama's health care act is available at www.gpo.gov/fdsys/pkg/PLAW-111publ148/pdf/PLAW-111publ148.pdf.
5. Adam Smith, *An Inquiry into the Nature and Causes of the Wealth of Nations*, 5th edn, ed. Edwin Cannan (London: Methuen, 1904).

6. See Anthony Giddens, *The Third Way and Its Critics* (Cambridge: Polity Press, 2000).
7. Plato, *The Republic*, trans. G.M.A. Grube, rev. C.D.C. Reeve (Indianapolis: Hackett, 1992).
8. Aristotle, *Politics*, trans. Benjamin Jowett (North Chelmsford, MA: Courier Dover Publications, 2000).

CHAPTER 5

1. David Beetham presents an excellent study of this in *The Legitimation of Power* (New York: Palgrave Macmillan, 1991).
2. *Patriation* is a term invented largely to describe the process of bringing the constitution to Canada. To "repatriate" means to bring something back to its home country. The Canadian constitution, however, never resided in Canada; *patriation* in this case refers to the constitution's move from London to Ottawa.
3. Supreme Court of Canada, *Reference re Manitoba Language Rights*, [1985] 1 S.C.R. 721.
4. An excellent source for the mechanism of the US government is Susan Welch, John Gruhl, Michael Steinman, John Comer, and Susan Rigdon, *American Government*, 10th edn (Florence, KY: Wadsworth, 2005).
5. Eugene Forsey, *How Canadians Govern Themselves*, 7th edn (Ottawa: Library of Parliament, 2010).
6. Canada, Constitution Acts, 1867 to 1982. For a good overview of peace, order, and good government, see Peter J.T. O'Hearn, *Peace, Order and Good Government: A New Constitution for Canada* (Toronto: Macmillan, 1964).
7. R. MacGregor Dawson and W.F. Dawson, *Democratic Government in Canada*, 5th edn, rev. Norman Ward (Toronto: University of Toronto Press, 1997), 90.
8. See Philip Sworden, *An Introduction to Canadian Law*, 2nd edn (Toronto: Emond Montgomery, 2006).

CHAPTER 6

1. Jonathan Potter, *Devolution and Globalisation: Implications for Local Decision-Makers* (Paris: OECD, 2001), 16.
2. See www.archives.gov/exhibits/charters/bill_of_rights_transcript.html.
3. Mikhail Filippov, Peter C. Ordeshook, and Olga Shvetsova, *Designing Federalism: A Theory of Self-Sustainable Federal Institutions* (Cambridge: Cambridge University Press, 2004), 232.
4. Hamish Telford, "The Federal Spending Power in Canada: Nation-Building or Nation-Destroying?" *Publius: The Journal of Federalism* 33, 1 (2003): 28.
5. Kenneth McRoberts, "Canada and the Multinational State," *Canadian Journal of Political Science* 34, 4 (2001): 702.
6. Paul Romney, "Provincial Equality, Special Status and the Compact Theory of Canadian Confederation," *Canadian Journal of Political Science* 32, 1 (1999): 31.
7. Michael Howlett, "Federalism and Public Policy," in *Canadian Politics*, 3rd edn, ed. James P. Bickerton and

Alain-G. Gagnon (Peterborough, ON: Broadview Press, 1999), 532.
8. Ian Robinson and Richard Simeon, "The Dynamics of Canadian Federalism," in *Canadian Politics*, 3rd edn, ed. James P. Bickerton and Alain-G. Gagnon (Peterborough, ON: Broadview Press, 1999), 250–1.
9. Joseph F. Zimmerman, "National-State Relations: Cooperative Federalism in the Twentieth Century," *Publius: The Journal of Federalism* 31, 2 (2001): 18–20.
10. David Cameron and Richard Simeon, "Intergovernmental Relations in Canada: The Emergence of Collaborative Federalism," *Publius: The Journal of Federalism* 32, 2: 49.
11. Telford, "Federal Spending Power in Canada," 24–5.
12. James P. Bickerton, "Regionalism in Canada," in *Canadian Politics*, 3rd edn, ed. James P. Bickerton and Alain-G. Gagnon (Peterborough, ON: Broadview Press, 1999), 223.
13. www.scics.gc.ca/english/view.asp?x=177.

CHAPTER 7

1. Michael Zürn and Jeffrey T. Checkel, "Getting Socialized to Build Bridges: Constructivism and Rationalism, Europe and the Nation-State," *International Organization* 59, 4 (2005): 1045.
2. Donald P. Haider-Markel, Alana Querze, and Kara Lindaman, "Lose, Win, or Draw?: A Reexamination of Direct Democracy and Minority Rights," *Political Research Quarterly* 60, 2 (2007): 304.
3. Pippa Norris, *Electoral Engineering: Voting Rules and Political Behavior* (Cambridge: Cambridge University Press, 2004), 4.
4. Stephen C. Craig, Michael D. Martinez, Jason Gainous, and James G. Kane, "Winners, Losers, and Election Context: Voter Responses to the 2000 Presidential Election," *Political Research Quarterly* 59, 4 (2006): 579.
5. Gerry Stoker, *Why Politics Matters: Making Democracy Work* (Houndmills, UK: Palgrave Macmillan, 2006), 20.
6. Robert G. Moser, "Independents and Party Formation: Elite Partisanship as an Intervening Variable in Russian Politics," *Comparative Politics* 31, 2 (1999): 154.
7. Joseph A. Aistrup, "Constituency Diversity and Party Competition: A County and State Level Analysis," *Political Research Quarterly* 57, 2 (2004): 267.
8. I. MacAllister, R.J. Johnston, C.J. Pattie, H. Tunstall, D.F.L. Dorling, and D.J. Rossiter, "Class Dealignment and the Neighbourhood Effect: Miller Revisited," *British Journal of Political Science* 31, 1 (2001): 45.
9. Gary W. Cox and Scott Morgenstern, "Latin America's Reactive Assemblies and Proactive Presidents," *Comparative Politics* 31, 2 (2001): 186.
10. Richard Gunther, José Ramón Montero, and Juan J. Linz, eds, *Political Parties: Old Concepts and New Challenges* (Oxford: Oxford University Press, 2002), 116.
11. Frederic Charles Schaffer, *The Hidden Costs of Clean Election Reform* (Ithaca, NY: Cornell University Press, 2008), 152.

12. Yves Schemeil, "Democracy before Democracy?" *International Political Science Review* 21, 2 (2000): 111.

13. David M. Farrell, *Electoral Systems: A Comparative Introduction* (Houndmills, UK: Palgrave, 2001), 201–4.

14. Norris, *Electoral Engineering*, 168.

15. Farrell, *Electoral Systems*, 170.

16. Ben Reilly and Andrew Reynolds, *Electoral Systems and Conflict in Divided Societies* (Washington, DC: National Academy Press, 1999), 19.

17. Norris, *Electoral Engineering*, 224.

18. Reilly and Reynolds, *Electoral Systems and Conflict*, 19.

19. Ibid., 21.

20. Ibid., 22.

21. Ibid.

22. Rein Taagepera and Matthew Soberg Shugart, *Seats and Votes: The Effects and Determinants of Electoral Systems* (New Haven, CT: Yale University Press, 1989), 26.

23. Adam Przeworski, Susan C. Stokes, and Bernard Manin, eds, *Democracy, Accountability, and Representation* (Cambridge: Cambridge University Press, 1999), 151.

24. Stoker, *Why Politics Matters*, 66–7.

25. Herbert Kitschelt and Steven I. Wilkinson, eds, *Patrons, Clients, and Policies: Patterns of Democratic Accountability and Political Competition* (Cambridge: Cambridge University Press, 2007), 28–30.

26. Gunther et al., *Political Parties*, 293.

27. Ibid.

28. Ibid., 140–5.

29. Ibid., 116–20.

30. Ibid., 120–2.

31. Lee Sigelman and Mark Kugler, "Why Is Research on the Effects of Negative Campaigning So Inconclusive? Understanding Citizens' Perceptions of Negativity," *Journal of Politics* 65, 1 (2003): 144.

32. Kim Fridkin Kahn and Patrick J. Kenney, "Do Negative Campaigns Mobilize or Suppress Turnout? Clarifying the Relationship between Negativity and Participation," *American Political Science Review* 93, 4 (1999): 879.

33. John G. Geer and James H. Geer, "Remembering Attack Ads: An Experimental Investigation of Radio," *Political Behavior* 25, 1 (2003): 70.

34. www.opensecrets.org

35. Stoker, *Why Politics Matters*, 189–90.

36. R. Kent Weaver, "Electoral Rules and Electoral Reform in Canada," in *Mixed Member Electoral Systems: The Best of Both Worlds?*, ed. Matthew Soberg Shugart and Martin P. Wattenberg (New York: Oxford University Press, 2001), 551–4.

CHAPTER 8

1. Gabriel Almond and Sidney Verba, *The Civic Culture: Political Attitudes and Democracy in Five Nations* (Newbury Park, CA: Sage, 1989), 7.

2. Juan J. Linz, "Totalitarian and Authoritarian Regimes," in *Handbook of Political Science*, ed. Fred I. Greenstein and Nelson W. Polsby (New York: Addison-Wesley, 1975), 270.

3. Jennifer Glass, Vern L. Bengtson, and Charlotte Chorn Dunham, "Attitude Similarity in Three-Generation Families: Socialization, Status Inheritance, or Reciprocal Influence?" *American Sociological Review* 51, 5 (1986): 685–98.

4. William Gamson and David Meyer, "Framing Political Opportunity," in *Comparative Perspectives on Social Movements: Political Opportunities, Mobilizing Structures, and Cultural Framings*, ed. Doug McAdam, John D. McCarthy, and Mayer N. Zald, 3rd edn (Cambridge: Cambridge University Press, 1996), 287–8.

5. Scott L. Althaus, *Collective Preferences in Democratic Politics: Opinion Surveys and the Will of the People* (Cambridge: Cambridge University Press, 2003), 289–96.

6. Ibid., 4–10.

7. Herbert B. Asher, *Polling and the Public: What Every Citizen Should Know*, 2nd edn (Washington, DC: Congressional Quarterly Press, 1992), 152.

8. Ibid., 96.

9. Chappell Lawson, "Building the Fourth Estate: Media Opening and Democratization in Mexico," in *Dilemmas of Political Change in Mexico*, ed. Kevin J. Middlebrook (San Diego: Center for U.S.–Mexican Studies, UCSD, 2004), 57.

10. Gamson and Meyer, "Framing Political Opportunity," 287.

11. Karen A. Mingst, *Essentials of International Relations*, 3rd edn (New York: W.W. Norton, 2004), 40.

12. Juan J. Linz and Alfred Stepan, "Toward Consolidated Democracies," in *The Changing Nature of Democracy*, ed. Takashi Inoguchi, Edward Newman, and John Keane (Tokyo: United Nations University Press, 1998), 64.

13. Robert Dahl, *Polyarchy: Participation and Opposition* (New Haven, CT: Yale University Press, 1971), 200.

14. Pippa Norris, *Electoral Engineering: Voting Rules and Political Behavior* (Cambridge: Cambridge University Press, 2004), 143.

15. Suzanne Berger, ed., *Organizing Interests in Western Europe: Pluralism, Corporatism, and the Transformation of Politics* (Cambridge: Cambridge University Press, 1981), 312.

16. Mancur Olson, *The Logic of Collective Action: Public Goods and the Theory of Groups* (Cambridge, MA: Harvard University Press, 1971), 12.

17. Dahl, *Polyarchy: Participation and Opposition*, 191–2.

18. Éric Montpetit and William D. Coleman, "Policy Communities and Policy Divergence in Canada: Agro-Environmental Policy Development in Quebec and Ontario," *Canadian Journal of Political Science* 32, 4 (1999): 695.

19. Philippe C. Schmitter, "Still the Century of Corporatism?" in *Review of Politics* 36, 1 (1974): 4.

CHAPTER 9

1. Patrick H. O'Neil provides an excellent introduction to comparative politics in his *Essentials of Comparative Politics*, 3rd edn (New York: Norton, 2010).

2. Geir Lundestad, *East, West, North, South: Major Developments in International Politics Since 1945*, 5th edn (London: Sage, 2004), 1.

3. Earlier in this book, we examined the distinctive nature of Canada's federal character, which many refer to as quasi-federalism. See K.C. Wheare, *Federal Government*, 4th edn (Oxford: Oxford University Press, 1967).

4. For more on the Canadian constitution, see David Milne, *The Canadian Constitution: From Patriation to Meech Lake* (Toronto: J. Lorimer, 1989).

5. David Mitrany, *The Functional Theory of Politics* (New York: St. Martin's Press, 1975).

CHAPTER 10

1. David N. Balaam and Michael Veseth, *Introduction to International Political Economy* (Upper Saddle River, NJ: Prentice Hall, 2001), 321.

2. Dietrich Rueschemeyer, Evelyne Huber Stephens, and John D. Stephens, *Capitalist Development and Democracy* (Chicago: University of Chicago Press, 1992), 10.

3. Brian C. Smith, *Good Governance and Development* (Houndmills, UK: Palgrave Macmillan, 2007), 1–3.

4. Seymour M. Lipset and Stein Rokkan, "Cleavage Structures, Party Systems, and Voter Alignments," in *The West European Party System*, ed. Peter Miar (Oxford: Oxford University Press, 1990), 120.

5. Brian C. Smith, *Understanding Third World Politics: Theories of Political Change and Development*, 2nd edn (Bloomington: Indiana University Press, 2003), 164–7.

6. Mark W. Zacher, "The Territorial Integrity Norm: International Boundaries and the Use of Force," *International Organization* 55, 2 (2001): 229.

7. T.W. Croghan, A. Beatty, and A. Ron, "Routes to Better Health for Children in Four Developing Countries," *The Milbank Quarterly* 84, 2 (2006): 345.

8. Theodore H. Cohn, *Global Political Economy: Theory and Practice*, 4th edn (New York: Pearson Longman, 2008), 325–6.

9. Rueschemeyer et al., *Capitalist Development*, 60.

10. David Shambaugh, *China's Communist Party: Atrophy and Adaptation* (Berkeley: University of California Press, 2008), 7.

11. Ibid., 40.

12. Smith, *Understanding Third World Politics*, 12.

13. Daniel Yergin and Joseph Stanislaw, *The Commanding Heights: The Battle for the World Economy*, rev. and updated edn (New York: Simon & Schuster, 2002), 185–7.

14. Shambaugh, *China's Communist Party*, 42–5.

15. Susan L. Shirk, *How China Opened Its Door: The Political Success of the PRC's Foreign Trade and Investment Reforms* (Washington, DC: The Brookings Institution, 1994).

16. Takatoshi Ito and Anne O. Krueger, *Growth Theories in Light of the East Asian Experience* (Chicago: University of Chicago Press, 1995), 73–94.

17. For more about China's Open Door Policy, see Ito and Krueger, *Growth Theories*. For the SEZs, see Mary E. Gallagher, "'Reform and Openness': Why China's Economic Reforms Have Delayed Democracy," *World Politics* 54, 3 (2002): 345.

18. Alberto Díaz Cayeros, "Decentralization, Democratization and Federalism in Mexico," in *Dilemmas of Political Change in Mexico*, ed. Kevin J. Middlebrook (San Diego: Center for U.S.–Mexican Studies, UCSD, 2004), 57.

19. Denise Dresser, "From PRI Predominance to Divided Democracy," in *Constructing Democratic Governance in Latin America*, ed. Jorge Domínguez and Michael Shifter (Baltimore: Johns Hopkins University Press, 2003), 67.

20. Nora Lustig, *Mexico: The Remaking of an Economy* (Washington, DC: The Brookings Institution, 1992), 79.

21. "India's Income Inequality Has Doubled in 20 Years," *The Times of India*, 7 Dec. 2011, http://timesofindia.india times.com/india/Indias-income-inequality-has-doubled-in-20-years/articleshow/11012855.cms.

22. United Nations Department of Economic and Social Affairs, Population Division Population Estimates and Projections Section, "Mali," http://esa.un.org/unpd/wpp/country-profiles/country-profiles_1.htm.

CHAPTER 11

1. Charles de Secondat, Baron de Montesquieu, *The Spirit of Laws* (Amherst, NY: Prometheus Books, 2002).

2. Hans-Henrik Holm and Georg Sørenson, *Whose World Order?: Uneven Globalization and the End of the Cold War* (Boulder, CO: Westview Press, 1995).

3. Jayantanuja Bandyopadhyaya and Rikhi Jaipal, *A General Theory of International Relations: Origins, Growth and Potential for World Peace* (Mumbai: Allied Publishers, 1993), 138.

4. Hans Morgenthau, *Politics Among Nations: The Struggle for Power and Peace* (New York: Alfred A. Knopf, 1948).

5. Plato, *The Republic Of Plato*, trans. F.M. Cornford (New York: Oxford University Press, 1945), 14.

6. Kenneth N. Waltz, *Theory of International Politics* (New York: McGraw-Hill, 1979).

7. Stephen D. Krasner, ed., *International Regimes* (Ithaca, NY: Cornell University Press, 1983).

8. Karl Marx and Friedrich Engels, *Manifesto of the Communist Party* (New York: Cosimo, 2006).

9. Vladimir Ilyich Lenin, *Imperialism, the Highest Stage of Capitalism* (Moscow: Progress Publishers, 1963).

10. "Canada." http://travel.nationalgeographic.com/places/countries/country_canada.html.

11. Data taken from CIA World Factbook, 2009, and Statistics Canada 2008.

12. "By the Numbers: The Canada/U.S. border" (CBC News, 30 July 2004).

13. See Alvin Finkel, *Our Lives: Canada After 1945* (Toronto: J. Lorimer, 1997), 120; John Herd Thompson and Stephen J. Randall, *Canada and the United States: Ambivalent Allies*, 3rd edn (Athens: University of Georgia Press, 2002), 248; "The Helpful Fixer: International Relations of Canada," *Canada and the World Backgrounder* (September 1999).

14. Tom Keating, *Canada and World Order: The Multilateralist Tradition in Canadian Foreign Policy*, 2nd edn (Toronto: Oxford University Press, 2002), 16.

15. Peyton V. Lyon and Brian W. Tomlin, *Canada as an International Actor* (Toronto: Macmillan, 1979).

CHAPTER 12

1. Winston S. Churchill, *Amid These Storms: Thoughts and Adventures* (New York: Charles Scribner's Sons, 1932), 245.
2. Gwynne Dyer, *War: The New Edition* (Toronto: Random House, 2004), 11.
3. Stephanie Lawson has a good discussion of security and insecurity in her book *International Relations* (Hoboken, NJ: Wiley-Blackwell, 2003).
4. See SIPRI, "Recent Trends in Military Expenditure" (2012), available at www.sipri.org/research/armaments/milex/resultoutput/trends.
5. For an excellent discussion of what conflict is, see Sandra Cheldelin, Daniel Druckman, and Larissa A. Fast, eds, *Conflict: From Analysis To Intervention* (New York: Continuum International Publishing Group, 2003), especially Part I.
6. One source for more ideas about the concept of war is Edward N. Zalta, ed., *Stanford Encyclopedia of Philosophy* (Stanford, CA: Center for the Study of Language and Information, 2000/rev. edn 2005).
7. There are many translations of this famous line. Though this is the common version, there are others. For example, "war is merely the continuation of policy by other means" is given in Carl von Clausewitz, *On War*, trans. Michael Howard and Peter Paret (Oxford: Oxford University Press, 2007), 28.
8. Canadian author Noah Richler tackles this debate in *What We Talk About When We Talk About War* (Fredericton: Gooselane, 2012).
9. George C. Kohn, *Dictionary of Wars*, 3rd edn (New York: Facts On File, 2006).
10. There are many definitions of the term *terrorism*. The one used here is a combination of two separate interpretations made by Walter Reich and Brian Jenkins. Their definitions, and others, are found in Gus Martin, *Understanding Terrorism: Challenges, Perspectives, and Issues* (Thousand Oaks, CA: Sage Publications, 2006).
11. John Stuart Mill, "A Few Words On Non-Intervention," *Fraser's Magazine* (1859). Reprinted in *Foreign Policy Perspectives* 8 (1987): 2–6.
12. For more on the Suez Canal and its treaties, see J.F. McClure, Jr, "The Law of International Waterways: An Approach to a Suez Canal Solution," *University of Pennsylvania Law Review* 105, 5 (Mar. 1957): 714–44.
13. See www.un.org/en/peacekeeping/.
14. Michael J. Butler explores peacekeeping as one of five major approaches to conflict management. The others are peace enforcement and support operations, negotiation and bargaining, mediation, and adjudication. See *International Conflict Management* (New York: Routledge, 2009).

CHAPTER 13

1. David N. Balaam and Michael Veseth, *Introduction to International Political Economy* (Upper Saddle River, NJ: Prentice Hall, 2001), 3.

2. Peter Hall, "The Role of Interests, Institutions, and Ideas in the Comparative Political Economy of the Industrialized Nations," in *Comparative Politics: Rationality, Culture and Structure*, ed. Mark I. Lichbach and Alan S. Zuckerman (New York: Cambridge University Press, 1997), 185.
3. Theodore H. Cohn, *Global Political Economy: Theory and Practice*, 4th edn (New York: Pearson Longman, 2008), 11.
4. Robert O. Keohane and Joseph S. Nye, *Power and Interdependence: World Politics in Transition*, 2nd edn (Cambridge: HarperCollins, 1989), 8–11.
5. Milan Svolik, "Lies, Defection, and the Pattern of International Cooperation," *American Journal of Political Science* 50, 4 (2006): 911.
6. Karen A. Mingst, *Essentials of International Relations*, 3rd edn (New York: W.W. Norton, 2004), 256–62.
7. Cohn, *Global Political Economy*, 208.
8. Joan E. Spero and Jeffrey A. Hart, *The Politics of International Economic Relations*, 6th edn (Belmont, CA: Wadsworth Thomson, 2003), 113.
9. Ibid., 6.
10. Judith Goldstein, "Ideas, Institutions, and American Trade Policy," in *The State and American Foreign Economic Policy*, ed. G. John Ikenberry, Michael Mastanduno, and David A. Lake (Ithaca, NY: Cornell University Press, 1993), 187, 197.
11. Patrick J. McDonald, "Peace Through Trade or Free Trade?" *Journal of Conflict Resolution* 48, 4 (2004): 549.
12. Adam Przeworski and Fernando Limongi, "Political Regimes and Economic Growth," *Journal of Economic Perspectives* 7, 3 (1993): 62.
13. Mingst, *Essentials of International Relations*, 262–4.
14. Spero and Hart, *Politics of International Economic Relations*, 140.
15. Mingst, *Essentials of International Relations*, 262–4.
16. Spero and Hart, *Politics of International Economic Relations*, 6.
17. Cohn, *Global Political Economy*, 208.
18. Ibid., 22.
19. Spero and Hart, *Politics of International Economic Relations*, 20–4.
20. Balaam and Veseth, *Introduction to International Political Economy*, 62–3.
21. Kenneth M. Roberts, "Neoliberalism and the Transformation of Populism in Latin America: The Peruvian Case," *World Politics* 48, 1 (1995): 82–116.
22. Joan M. Nelson, "The Politics of Economic Adjustment in Developing Nations," in *Economic Crisis and Policy Choice: The Politics of Adjustment in the Third World* (Princeton, NJ: Princeton University Press, 1990), 32.
23. Bank for International Settlements, "The Global Financial Crisis," in *BIS Annual Report 2008/09* (Basel, Switzerland: Bank for International Settlements, 2009). www.bis.org/publ/arpdf/ar2009e2.htm.
24. Roger Stern, "Oil Market Power and United States National Security," *Proceedings of the National Academy of Sciences of the United States of America* 103, 5 (2006): 1650.

25. All prices noted from New York Mercantile Exchange, http://nyse.nyx.com.

26. International Monetary Fund, "Report for Selected Countries and Subjects," World Economic Outlook Database, www.imf.org/external/pubs/ft/weo/2012/02/weodata/index.aspx.

27. Balaam and Veseth, *Introduction to International Political Economy*, 211.

28. Daniel Yergin and Joseph Stainslaw, *The Commanding Heights: The Battle for the World Economy*, rev. and updated edn (New York: Simon & Schuster, 2002), 406–8.

29. Raymond Vernon, "Big Business and National Governments: Reshaping the Compact in a Globalizing Economy," *Journal of International Business Studies* 32, 3 (2001): 516.

30. Cohn, *Global Political Economy*, 307–8.

CHAPTER 14

1. George Fallis, "More Than a Pretty Degree: Never Underestimate the Practical Value of the Liberal Arts," *Globe and Mail*, 10 February 1999; see also Jennifer Lewington, "Arts Background No Handicap in Quest for Jobs," *Globe and Mail*, 26 October 1998.

Glossary

additional member system mix of simple plurality and proportional representation voting; voters cast a vote for a representative and for a political party

African Union international organization founded to promote co-operation among the independent nations of Africa

agency individual or group action in a social context

analytical approach perspective that views politics as an empirical discipline rather than a science; argues that politics cannot be broken down into parts but must be seen comprehensively

anomic interest groups ad hoc interest groups that do not have a standard organized composition; formed to deal with short-term issues

arbitration authoritative dispute resolution made by an impartial person and agreed upon by all parties involved

aristocracy political system ruled by a hierarchical elite

associational interest groups interest groups closely related to particular political objectives

attack ads negative and aggressive advertising by one political party or organization against another

autarky condition of complete self-sufficiency and isolation from the rest of the system

authoritarianism political system requiring absolute obedience to a constituted authority

authority power or right to force obedience

balance of power situation in international politics in which states strive to achieve equilibrium of power in the world in order to prevent any other country or coalition of countries from dominating the system

ballot card used to cast a vote; ballots are kept in a designated ballot box and counted by electoral officials

behaviouralism perspective that concentrates on the "tangible" aspects of political life rather than values; objective was to establish a discipline that was "scientific" and objective

bicameral legislative or parliamentary body with two assemblies

bilateral aid military or development assistance given by one country to another

body politic entirety of a political community

bourgeois according to socialists such as Marx, the property-owning class that exploits the working class (proletariat)

Bretton Woods Agreement postwar system of fixed exchange rates and heavy controls on private banks and other financial institutions, thereby limiting their roles in international finance

bureaucracy division of government responsible for carrying out public policy and staffed by public employees

cadre party party created and directed by a small elite group; tends to control much power within legislatures

caliphate government inspired by Islam that rules over its subjects using Islamic law

capitalism economic system in which production and distribution of goods rely on private capital and investment

catch-all party political party that covers a wide range of ideologies and beliefs in society, with the idea of incorporating as many different societal groups as possible; also called umbrella party

caucus group of elected representatives, usually based on party membership but which may also be grouped by race, gender, geographic representation, etc.

centralization concentration of power in a single body, usually the principal government

centralized federalism process whereby federal government increases its power relative to that of the provinces

checks and balances system of inspection and evaluation of different levels and branches of governments by others

Chinese Communist Party (CCP) governing political party in China, founded in 1921 as part of the revolutionary movement; committed to Marxist revolution

citizenship status granted to people that comes with responsibilities and duties as well as rights

civil law legal system where legislative bodies enact laws through statutes, ordinances, and regulations

Cold War period of rhetorical, non-violent hostility; most often used as a reference to the period of 1945–91 and the relationship between the United States and the Soviet Union

colonialism exploitation of a weaker country(ies) by a stronger one(s) for political, strategic, or resource interests

common agricultural policy (CAP) European Union program that provides economic benefits to agriculture in all countries in order to allow stable pricing and profits for the industry

common law legal system where decisions are made on the basis of precedent, case law, or previous decisions

common market an economic arrangement among states intended to eliminate barriers that inhibit the movement of factors of production—labour, capital, and technology—among its members

communism political theory, based on the writings of Marx and Engels, that espouses class conflict to form a system where all property is publicly owned and each citizen works to his or her own best ability and is compensated equitably

community social, political, cultural, and economic ties that bind individuals to one another

comparative approach method of political analysis that compares different systems of political authority based on system type, time period, or form of leadership

competitive party system liberal democratic electoral system in which political parties are permitted to compete with one another for the electorate's support

compulsory voting system in which citizens have a legal obligation to vote in elections

concept general idea emerging from events or instances

concurrent powers the sharing of control between provincial and federal levels of government

conditional grants funds given to provincial authorities from the federal government, which assigns controls and conditions on how the monies may be spent

confederalism political system of divided powers where added power is given to the non-central governments and limited authority and power is conferred to the central government

conflict differences in preferred outcomes among social groups

conflict resolution process in domestic or international affairs that attempts to reconcile antagonism (either existing or potential) through the use of mediation and negotiation

Confucianism philosophy and political thought of Confucius that stresses social harmony, obedience, and morality

constituencies territorial or geographical localities represented by a politician chosen through the electoral process; also called ridings

constitution the basic law of a country, upon which all other laws are based

constitutionality being in accordance with a constitution

co-operative federalism co-operation and coordination of policy between the federal and provincial levels of government

Corn Laws set of laws regulating the British grain trade; the abolition of these laws in 1846 opened up British agricultural trade

corporatism approach to governance that entails close co-operation and coordination among government, business, and labour in the expectation that such activity will bring more stability to politics

Council of the European Union main decision-making institution of the EU, made up of ministers from the EU national governments

Court of Auditors a body of the European Union that provides financial oversight on budget, revenues, and expenditures

Court of Justice EU court; responsible for ensuring that EU legislation is evenly and fairly interpreted in all member states; can also settle legal disputes between EU entities and declare certain legal instruments as incompatible with EU law

cronyism in politics, the practice of choosing or preferring friends or associates for positions of authority

debt crisis situation in which a country is unable to meet its international debt obligations; sometimes used to refer to the Latin American situation in the 1980s

decentralization process whereby power and authority is taken from the central government and conferred to non-central (e.g. state, regional, or provincial) governments

decision-making mechanism or pattern of relations involving different levels of government in which determinations and judgments regarding the governance of the political system are made (sometimes referred to as the black box)

declaratory power a federal government's power to take control of any local project if it decides that doing so would be for the greater national good

delegated authority in a unitary system, the transfer of certain powers from the national government to subnational authorities

democracy political system based on the principle that governance requires the assent of all citizens through participation in the electoral process, articulation of views, and direct or indirect representation in governing institutions

deregulation removal of government controls in an economic sector

despot political leader who rules with absolute power and authority

détente warming of relations

developed world industrialized nations that are part of a structurally integrated system of global capitalism; includes the countries of Western Europe and North America, Japan, Australia, and New Zealand; also known as developed countries (DCs), industrialized world, the North, and the First World

developing world nations that are less developed than the industrialized countries and that are not part of a structurally integrated system of global capitalism

devolution political system in which some authority is given to regional governments, but the power to oversee, dismiss, or entrench these authorities is still held by the central government

dialectical materialism Marxist notion that material forces affect politics through social and economic change

dialectics in Marxism, points where ideas and processes throughout history come up against each other and form a new reality

Diet Japanese Parliament

diplomacy international negotiation and discussions that take place on an official—and sometimes unofficial—level between and among states

direct democracy political system in which citizens are directly involved in the decision-making process

disallowance occurs when provincial legislation is rejected or vetoed by the federal cabinet

dispute resolution process by which trading disagreements between member states can be resolved by an impartial tribunal, thus preventing such disputes from becoming too political or controversial

duties related to rights; responsibilities to protect rights

economic justice redistribution of economic resources from certain groups in society to others

editorial line particular perspective on world events offered by news outlets

election a form of choosing political representatives whereby individual citizens cast their vote for their preferred candidate

election platforms positions of political parties or individuals regarding issues and political intentions

Electoral College in the United States, officials chosen from each state who directly elect the president and vice-president; the number of officials in each state is based on population

electorate people in a political system with the right to vote in elections; enfranchised citizens

emerging markets poorer economies with potential for future growth

empirical analysis based not on concepts and theory but on what can be observed or experimented upon

enumeration the process of determining the number of individuals eligible to vote in a constituency

equality parity in a political system

ethnic and religious conflict war or opposition among different racial, linguistic, or religious groups

ethnocentrism belief that one's culture or group is superior to others or that other cultures or groups must be examined in relation to one's own

European Atomic Energy Community (EURATOM) community created to govern atomic energy in Europe, entered into force in 1958

European Central Bank (ECB) independent central bank of the EU that implements economic and monetary policy

European Coal and Steel Community (ECSC) first institutional version of European integration; formed in 1951 by Belgium, the Netherlands, Luxembourg, France, West Germany, and Italy

European Commission body responsible for implementing activities mandated by the European Parliament and Council

European Council a body of the European Union; part of the Council of the European Union and comprised of the heads of state and government and the president of the European Commission

European Economic Community (EEC) formed in 1958, second institutional version of European integration; involved Belgium, the Netherlands, Luxembourg, France, West Germany, and Italy

European Parliament parliamentary assembly for the EU

European Union (EU) economic and political union of 27 European states

executive usually the top level of government or the leader; maintains leadership of the entire political system and often reflects the leadership and preoccupations of the dominant political party

executive federalism a generally conflictive relationship between the provinces and the federal government, created when provinces try (often successfully) to achieve greater autonomy from the federal government, which resists such attempts

federalism form of governance that divides powers between the central government and regional governments; often, particular roles and capacities are given to the regional governments

feudal system political or social system based on the relationship between landholders and those with permission to use and live on the property in exchange for fees, political loyalties, or other commitments

first-past-the-post electoral system in which the winner receives the most (but not necessarily a majority of) votes; also called simple plurality

fixed exchange rate system system in which states agree upon set values for their currencies in terms of other national currencies

floating exchange rate system system in which the market decides the relative values of national monies

foreign direct investment (FDI) investment in real foreign assets, such as domestic structures, equipment, and organizations

foreign policy foreign diplomatic relations and policies of a country beyond its borders

fourth estate the media; the other estates are the clergy, nobles, and commoners

freedom ability to act without constraint

functionalism collective approach to provide a full range of social and welfare services through functionally specific international organizations

fusion of powers combination of legislature and executive powers, though specific powers may be granted to each level

general will will of the community as a whole

genocide deliberate and systematic killing of a group based on their ethnicity, nationality, culture, or race

geopolitics association between a state's political relationships and its geographical location

gerrymandering controversial method of combining or dividing groups of voters in order to maximize or reduce their power

globalization intensification of economic, political, social, and cultural relations across borders

global village term used to describe the "shrinking" of the world, largely due to modern communications, into a more interconnected place where all people have a closer relationship and more frequent contact

government the institutions and people responsible for carrying out the affairs and administration of a political system

Great Leap Forward Chinese program of economic policies designed to revolutionize rural production by replacing private ownership of land with communes in which all agricultural production was to be sold to the state

gross domestic product (GDP) total value of goods and services produced in a country in one year

gross national product (GNP) total value of goods and services produced in a country in one year plus the total of net income earned abroad

hegemon one country with inordinate capability to uphold and protect the global system

heuristic method process of laying out experience as a way to assist future research

identity a person's understanding and expression of their individuality or group membership

ideology set or system of ideas that form the basis of a political or economic system and provide guidance and direction for political leadership

imperialism extension of one country's authority over another through conquest or political and/or economic control

independents electoral candidates who do not belong to a political party

indirect democracy political system of representation in which citizens elect a delegate to act on their behalf; also called representative democracy

influence the ability to change behaviour in others without exerting direct power over them

insecurity threat of danger or injury

institutionalism belief in utility of institutions to provide collective goods

institutions groupings that have developed to attend to particular societal needs

interest groups groups in a political system that seek to either alter or maintain the approach of government without taking a formal role in elections or seeking an official capacity in government

international anarchy condition where there is no "world government"; the sovereign nation-state is the highest authority in the international system

international financial and monetary system set of rules, institutions, and agreements governing the flow of money in the international system; the relative values of currencies and the settling of accounts

international governmental organizations (IGOs) institutions formed by three or more countries with a common economic, social, cultural, or political purpose

international organizations (IOs) an international grouping, governmental or non-governmental, with activities in several states

international politics the study of foreign policy and relations among states and other actors at the international level; also called international relations

international system system of two or more actors that interact regularly in the global arena, using established processes in given issue areas

interwar period the years between the two world wars (i.e. 1919–39)

invisible hand Adam Smith's notion that economic forces left on their own would lead to maximum efficiency and economic growth over time as they engage in competition against each other; benefits to society as a whole exist without political interference

Islamic fundamentalism religious movements advocating a return to the fundamentals of Islamic religious texts

jihad moral struggle or struggle for righteousness; form of holy war

judicial review power of a country's courts to interpret its constitution, varying from the ability to resolve disputes between levels of government in federal systems to the ability to annul legislative and executive actions outright

judiciary judicial (courts) level of governance

junta military government, usually a dictatorship

justice state of affairs involving the maintenance of what is right and fair within a society

keiretsu a business group or set of companies found in Japan that work together in decision-making and production to provide increased benefits for all

Kuznets effect economic formula that demonstrates that, as a country develops economically, income distribution will become more unequal before it becomes more equal; named after Simon Kuznets, the Russian-American economist who formulated this concept

laissez-faire "to let be"; economic theory that suggests that a reduction in political control will benefit the economic system

laws rules imposed on society by the governing authority

leadership group of individuals that lead society

legislation laws enacted by a governing authority

legislative referring to the body of a political system with the responsibility to make laws; known as the legislature

legitimacy what is lawful, proper, and conforms to the standards of a political system

legitimation providing legitimacy, or legal force or status, to political decisions; in accordance with established or accepted patterns and standards

lesbian, gay, bisexual, and transgender (LGBT) movement movement recognizing diversity in sexual and gender identities

less developed countries (LDCs) countries that may be characterized by low levels of per capita income, high inflation and debt, large trade deficits, low levels of socioeconomic

development, a lack of industrialization, or undeveloped financial or legal systems

levels of analysis approach to political studies that suggests that accurate analysis must be inclusive of international, domestic, and individual arenas of interaction

liberal democracy political system based on freedom and the principle that governance requires the assent of all citizens through participation in the electoral process, articulation of views, and direct or indirect representation in governing institutions

liberal institutionalism international relations theory that suggests that international institutions make co-operation more likely and advantageous

liberalism view of politics that favours liberty, free trade, and moderate social and political change

libertarianism ideology based on a limited government role and freedom of speech, action, and thought

liberty freedom from despotic control

licence unlimited freedom to do as one pleases

liquidity rate at which assets may be converted to cash

lobbying method by which business/interest groups apply direct pressure to the executive, legislative, and bureaucratic parts of government

Marshall Plan US government loan program designed to help the devastated countries of Western Europe after World War II

mass party party organized in society at large rather than within government; has public influence through power of membership, not of a small minority elite

materialist in Marxism, understanding the physical and economic basis for society

mediation voluntary process using an impartial party to resolve a dispute

member of Parliament (MP) representative of voters in a parliamentary system

middle power country that does not have great power or superpower status but has significant influence in international relations

militia party party system with a centralized leadership system; often having martial leadership and frequently found in one-party systems

ministerial responsibility principle in parliamentary systems that requires members of the political executive, both individually and as a group, to remain accountable to the legislature

minority government government by the party that received the most, but not a majority of, votes in an election

monarchy form of government by a single ruler who holds at least nominally absolute power

most different systems method of comparative analysis that examines political systems that share no (or few) common features yet have a similar outcome or phenomena

most similar systems method of comparative analysis that examines political systems that have many common features in an effort to identify different variables

multiculturalism peaceful coexistence of several racial, cultural, or ethnic identities in one nation

multilateralism integration or coordination of policies or decision-making by three or more nation states

multinational corporations (MNCs) corporate bodies that operate in more than one country

multi-party system competitive party system with more than two parties

nation group of persons who share an identity that is based on, but not limited to, shared ethnic, religious, cultural, or linguistic qualities

nation-state autonomous political unit of people who share a predominant common culture, language, ethnicity, or history

negative liberty areas of activity in which governments do not interfere and an individual is free to choose

negotiation bargaining process in which the parties involved try to resolve a dispute in a mutually satisfactory manner

neo-conservative advocate of the return to conservative values or policies

neorealism "new" realism approach that views international relations from a systemic approach where states are constrained by the international structure; also called structural realism

nepotism in politics, the practice of choosing or preferring relatives for positions of authority

newly industrializing countries (NICs) countries benefiting from external trade relationships, growing export markets, and burgeoning industrial development

non-associational interest groups interest groups not closely related to or not connected with particular political objectives

non-discrimination principle that no member of an organization should be excluded from the benefits that one member state extends to another

non-excepted matters powers that are held by the central government but may be transferred to a regional government at a later date

non-governmental organization (NGO) non-profit group organized on a local, national, or international level

non-reserved matters powers that are given to a region and may not be recalled by the central government

non-system system of international money and finance that replaced the Bretton Woods system; so called because it lacked explicit rules

non-tariff barriers (NTBs) national content requirements on certain products or quotas on their import

North industrialized nations, including Western Europe, North America, Japan, Australia, and New Zealand, that are part of a structurally integrated system of global capitalism

North American Free Trade Agreement (NAFTA) agreement in which Canada, the United States, and Mexico have opened their markets to each other

North Atlantic triangle geographic region of Canada, the United States, and the EU; most significant and strategic modes of interaction for each other; historically, the relationship between Canada, the United States, and the United Kingdom

one-party system political system in which only one political party is allowed to form the government or compete in elections

Open Door Policy approach taken by the Chinese government, starting in the late 1970s, to introduce the Chinese economy (and by extension political system) to the Western world

opinion poll investigation of public opinion conducted by interviewing a sample of citizens

opposition one or more parties that are not part of government but form a check on the ruling power of the elected party

order condition in which both units and interaction within a political system are marked by regularity and stability with the imposition of accepted and enforced rules, structures, and practices

organizations structured relations existing within a political community that are established to distribute both the responsibilities and the privileges that arise from formal association with others

particular will will of the individual, as expressed by Rousseau

party list voting system in which voters in multi-member constituencies choose from a list of candidates; parties are rewarded with a percentage of the seats available in each constituency

patriation term used to describe the transfer of the constitution from the United Kingdom to Canada in 1982

patronage awarding of key government positions to favoured and loyal supporters

peacekeeping placing of military and civilian personnel in a conflict area as an attempt to stop or contain hostilities or supervise the carrying out of a peace agreement

philosophy study of questions about existence, knowledge, ethics, justice, and morality based on logical reasoning rather than empirical methods

pluralism society in which several disparate groups (minority and majority) maintain their interests and a number of concerns and traditions persist

pocket boroughs in Britain, areas where very small electorates were in the pocket of (i.e. controlled by) the major local landowner

policy law or principle of performance adopted by a government

policy community collection of actors who have a direct or indirect interest in an issue

political action committees (PACs) conglomerations of several interest groups with the purpose of influencing the decision-making process more effectively

political cohabitation political co-operation among parties without forming a coalition

political culture set of attitudes, beliefs, and values that underpin any political system

political economy approach that views political and economic spheres as harmonious and mutually dependent perceptions of the world; relationship between people, government, and the economy

political globalization political processes that span national borders and frequently circumvent them entirely

political gridlock lack of political progress because of entrenched differing of opinions

political party organization that seeks to gain and maintain political power

political realism approach to politics that emphasizes power and interests over ideas or social constructions

political studies formal study of politics within and among nations

portfolio investment acquisition of shares (stocks) in a corporate actor for the purpose of profit; does not imply ownership

positive liberty freedom to achieve one's full potential

positive sum relationship between two or more entities that yields benefits for all participants

post-behaviouralism approach that attempted to reconcile the problems of behaviouralism by allowing for values and ideology in its analysis

post-industrial developed economies that maintain a high-technology, or high-value, economy

power ability to achieve goals in a political system and to have others do as you wish them to

pressure groups see **interest groups**

progress advancement in society toward a better and improved state of affairs; an integral element of liberal political theory

propaganda spreading of information, true or otherwise, for the purpose of aiding a cause or making an audience react in a certain way

proportional representation (PR) electoral system in which seats are designated according to the parties' popular vote; used in countries to institute proportions between votes allotted for all the parties

protectionism tendency of countries to safeguard their own economic sectors or industries through tariffs, quotas, or other forms of trade and investment legislation

public goods resources that are present in a political system whose use by one individual should not affect use by others

question period time allotted in the House of Commons for MPs to ask questions of the prime minister or cabinet ministers

rapprochement reconciliation

realpolitik pragmatic approach to world politics; idea that countries should practise balance-of-power politics and strive to achieve an equilibrium of power in the world to prevent any other country or coalition of countries from dominating the system

recession decline in economic productivity or affluence; specifically, a decline in GDP for two or more consecutive fiscal quarters

reciprocity complimentary or mutual behaviour among two or more actors; view that liberalization of trade would be beneficial for all parties concerned if co-operative policies were pursued

recruitment function political parties' efforts to help bring new voters into the political process

regional integration economic or political integration in a defined territorial area

relative power method of distinguishing the comparable strength of a political unit by contrasting it with another

representation the act of standing for the views of others; election of a representative to symbolize the collective view of all constituents

representative democracy political system in which voters elect others to act on their behalf; also called indirect democracy

republicanism political idea that gives supreme power to the people or elected representatives of the people

reservation occurs when a lieutenant governor puts provincial legislation up for the federal cabinet's consideration

rights socially acceptable, morally correct, and just privileges granted to members of a political community

rotten boroughs in Britain, areas with very small populations and electorates that were given equal standing with normal-sized constituencies

run-off system a form of electoral system in which the two (or three) candidates receiving the most votes in the first round pass to a second round of voting to determine an outright winner; also called a two-round system

security freedom from danger or injury

security dilemma conception in world politics that states are both protected and threatened by the existence of other states

self-determination ability to act in free choice without external compulsion

separation of powers division of powers among several government institutions (e.g. legislature, executive) to avoid concentration of authority

Seven Sisters group of major oil companies in the mid-twentieth century: Esso, Shell, British Petroleum, Mobil, Chevron, Gulf, and Texaco

sharia law sacred law of Islam

simple plurality see **first-past-the-post**

Single European Act European removal of non-tariff barriers, allowing the free movement of goods, services, capital, and labour; ratified in 1987

single transferable vote (STV) voting system in which voters cast their ballot in multi-member constituencies, expressing their first and second choice for candidates; second choices may be transferred and counted if all seats are not filled in the first count

social constructivism sociological and political meta-theory that explains the interactions between individual agents, their social groupings, and their environment

socialization process whereby individuals act in a social manner; creation of social and political authority and rules to regulate behaviour and thus permit operation of social units

social justice equitable distribution of goods and values in society

social order recognized structure of power, responsibility, and liberty

social sciences scientific study of human society and social relationships

South categorization of less developed nations that are not part of a structurally integrated system of global capitalism

sovereignty recognition by other political authorities that a government is legitimate and rightful for a political community

sovereignty-association arrangement by which a state or province acquires independence from the federal government but retains strong links to the country, generally in the form of economic policy

special economic zones (SEZs) regions in China with different economic regulatory controls and more independence meant to spur economic growth

state recognized political unit, considered to be sovereign, with a defined territory and people and a central government responsible for administration

structural anarchy in international relations, the assumption that no higher authority exists above the nation-state

structural-functionalism approach that focuses on the role of political structures and their functions in society

subjective reality perspective of reality that is influenced by our personal experiences and bias

subsidiarity principle of law in the EU dictating division of powers; states that decisions should be made at the lowest governmental level whenever possible

subsidies payments made by governments to compensate businesses for inefficiencies and lack of competitiveness

subsystemic international groupings or relations among states that do not include all actors

suffrage granting of the right to vote

superstructure political, legal, cultural, and religious justifications, structures, and practices

supranational international organization or union in which decision-making is shared by all members

sustainable development model of economic growth that seeks to use renewable resources so as not to destroy the environment in which human beings have to live

system group of individual entities or actors that interact with each other to form an integrated whole

systems theory approach that views politics as a system of interaction, binding political structures such as government to individual action; argues that politics is a dynamic process of information flows and responses that encompasses political institutions, groups, and individuals

tariff duty placed on a particular categorization of imported or exported goods or services

terrorism strategy of violence designed to bring about political change by instilling fear in the public at large

theocracy political system ruled by religious leaders

Third World largely Cold War categorization of less developed nations that are not part of a structurally integrated system of global capitalism

toleration acceptance or protection of individuals, groups, and types of behaviour that may be disapproved of by the majority in society

totalitarianism authoritarian political system that not only controls most social interaction but is also marked by a government's desire to force its objectives and values on citizens in an unlimited manner

trade protection tendency of countries to safeguard their own economic sectors or industries using tariffs, quotas, or other forms of trade and investment legislation

traditional approach method in politics drawing heavily on fields of law, philosophy, and history and relying on subjective evaluation of the observer; also called the analytical approach

transatlantic bargain postwar arrangement whereby former great powers of Europe conceded to American leadership in exchange for the latter supporting European economic and military stability

transitional government political system in which the move from authoritarianism to liberal democracy results in elements of both, with a gradual change to democracy

Treaties of Rome European treaty of 1958 that created the European Economic Community (EEC) and the European Atomic Energy Community (EURATOM)

Treaty of Paris European treaty of April 1951 that created the European Coal and Steel Community (ECSC)

two-party system competitive party system marked by two competing parties

two-round system see run-off system

tyranny government by a single ruler who often exercises arbitrary power for his or her own benefit rather than that of the community

umbrella party see catch-all party

unconditional grants payments from the federal government that may be spent by the provinces in any way they see fit

unicameral legislative or parliamentary body with one assembly

unitary systems political systems that concentrate political authority and powers within one central government, which is singularly responsible for both the domestic and foreign activities of the political unit

units of analysis entities studied in politics; the "what" or "whom" as the basis of analysis

Uruguay Round longest round of GATT negotiations (1986–94), eventually leading to the establishment of the World Trade Organization

utilitarianism branch of political thought that states that the worth of a particular action is determined by its contribution to overall utility, meaning the balance of happiness and unhappiness in society

Utopian idealized place or system, an ideally perfect society; individual or approach aspiring to impractical perfection

values principles, standards; what an individual or community esteems as meaningful

veto refusal to endorse, or the blocking of, a decision

voter apathy condition in which individuals do not vote or do not follow the election process because they believe that elections do not affect or influence them or that their vote has little influence over outcomes

voter turnout number of voters who attend the polls on election day

war use of armed forces in conflict with an enemy

welfare legislation or social action taken to provide citizens with physical, financial, health, or other assistance

Yoshida Doctrine postwar Japanese political and economic policy intended to establish a more non-interventionist role in international affairs, support the United States as hegemon in the global system, deepen links with the Americans, and focus on the domestic economy of Japan as a means of reassembling power and influence; named after Japan's postwar prime minister, Shigeru Yoshida

zero-sum game political or economic situation in which whatever is gained by one side is lost by the other, resulting in a net change of zero

Index

parochial political culture, 204
Parti Bleu, 164
participant political culture, 204
participation: and liberal democracy, 113; political, 20, 179–99, 397–8; voter, 183–6
Parti Québécois, 174
particular will, 66
Partido Acción Nacional (PAN), 287, 292
Partido de la Revolucíon Democrática (PRD), 287
Partido Revolucionario Institucional (PRI), 161, 191, 286, 287, 288, 289, 292
partisanship: and bureaucracy, 141; and executive branch, 130
Partnership for Peace (PFP), 315
party list system, 188
Patient Protection and Affordable Care Act, 104
patriation, 138, 172–3
Patriot Act, 34, 351
patriotism: v. nationalism, 311
patronage, 192
"peace, order, and good government," 110, 145, 166, 223
peacekeeping, 298, 356–8, 362; and Canada, 360, 361; in Rwanda, 354; UN definition of, 358
Peace of Westphalia, 99–101, 120, 311–12
Pearson, Lester B., 356–7
peers: political socialization and, 208
Peña, Enrique Nieto, 209, 220, 287, 288, 289, 291
People's Liberation Army (PLA), 280
Peoples' Global Action, 215
Perot, Ross, 220, 244
Petróleos Mexicanos (PEMEX), 290, 291
Petty, William, 232
philosophy, 55; political, 54, 55–7
Pinochet, Augusto, 276
platforms, political, 186, 193–4
Plato, 11, 30, 55, 57; and community, 47; and duties, 44; and equality, 40; and Republic, 56, 109, 324
plebiscites, 195–6
pluralism, 113; in China, 282
plurality, simple, 186–7
"pocket boroughs," 183
policy, 39; common agricultural (CAP), 255; and ideas, 86–7; and political culture, 203, 204; and private actors, 215–19; war as, 346; see also foreign policy
policy communities, 217, 219
Politburo, 282
political action, 33–9
political action committees, 218

political cohabitation, 287–8
political culture, 142, 201–5; categories of, 204; in Canada, 204, 222–4; in US, 243
political economy, 15–16, 71, 216, 232; see also international political economy
political gridlock, 144
political organization: concepts in, 29–33
political parties, 189–92; in Canada, 190, 196–8; and candidates, 183; and elections, 192–4; and electoral system, 186, 187, 188; and executive branch, 130; functions of, 191–2; regional, 197; single, 289; small, 186, 187; third, 244; types of, 190–1; umbrella, 191; in US, 243, 244
political philosophy, 54, 55–7
political science, 15
political studies, 7–8, 403–5; careers in, 7, 25, 404–5, 406; departments of, 12, 13
political systems, 151–77; and foreign policy, 332–3; and ideology, 107–9
political theory: and ideology, 63
political thought, 53–89; history of, 57–62
politics: approaches to, 11–17; and daily life, 17–18; definition of, 8–11; domestic, 20–2; and economics, 367–8; identity, 49; and power, 5–7; study of, 3–25, 403–5; see also international politics
polity, 29
population: in Canada, 331–2; in China, 277–8, 283; and foreign policy and, 330–2; in India, 295; in LDCs, 275, 277–8; in Mali, 298–9; in Mexico, 277
populism, 36, 209
portfolio investment, 290
positive sum, 325–6
post-behaviouralism, 14
post-industrial world, 232, 235–6
Potsdam Agreement, 248
Powell, Colin, 349
power: abuse of, 34; active, 34; and authority, 36–8; balance of, 92–3; concurrent, 166; declaratory, 168; definition of, 35; "faces of," 34–5; federalism and, 144–5, 158–62, 166–8; fusion of, 143–4; hard/soft, 35; ideological, 34; and international politics, 323–4; and judiciary, 138; and legislative branch, 132–4; and legitimacy, 37–8; and Machiavelli, 59; middle, 35, 239–40; military, 346; in parliamentary and presidential

systems, 142–4; and political action, 33–9; and politicians, 125; and politics, 5–7, 9; "of the purse," 168; recalling, 157; relational, 35; relative, 313; "separation of," 34, 142–4; static, 34; structural, 35; and unitary and federal systems, 153–77; and wealth, 368
precedents, legal, 138
presidential system, 129, 142–4, 242; Mexican, 287
pressure groups: see interest groups
prime minister: in Canada, 117–18, 130, 149, 237, 239; in Japan, 247
Prince Edward Island, 188; and confederation, 164–5
Princess Patricia's Canadian Light Infantry, 359
prisoners: and voting, 182, 196–7
Privy Council Office (PCO), 141
production: internationalization of, 390; and regionalism, 385–7
program development: as government activity, 102, 103–4
progress, 42–3; and liberalism, 64
Progressive Conservative Party, 77, 190, 197, 193
propaganda, 81–2
proportional representation (PR), 187–9
prorogation, 117
protectionism, 18
protest: anti-globalization, 215; in Iran, 308; in Russia, 92; student, 207, 289
Proudhon, Pierre-Joseph, 83
provinces, 177; autonomy of, 168; federal control of, 166–7; and federalism, 102, 118, 133, 144–5, 151, 154, 162–76; "have" and "have not," 169; Western, 176; see also specific provinces
public goods, 9–10; and government, 101, 102
public opinion, 208–10
public service: see bureaucracy
punk movement, 344
Pythagoras, 55

al-Qaeda, 85, 352, 358
quasi-confederation, 145
"quasi-federal system," 118, 154
Quebec: and constitution, 112, 146; and federalism, 166, 172–6; law in, 138, 147; as nation, 32; referenda in, 197–8; student protest in, 207; women's vote in, 46, 197
Quebec Act, 111
question period, 129, 130, 135
Qutb, Sayyid, 85